COMPUTATIONAL AND NUMERICAL SIMULATIONS

Edited by **Jan Awrejcewicz**

Computational and Numerical Simulations
http://dx.doi.org/10.5772/57035
Edited by Jan Awrejcewicz

CBS, Edition 2016

Contributors

Alexander Ivanovich Kartushinsky, Sergey Abramov, Victoriya Abramova, Vladimir Lukin, Benoit Vozel, Kacem Chehdi, Jaakko Astola, Karen Egiazarian, Mario Sporcic, Matija Landekic, Magdi Shoucri, Bedros Afeyan, Jiann-Ming Wu, Jung-Chao Ban, Chun-Chang Wu, Flavius Dan Surianu, Beatriz Rosa Mancinelli, Fernando Minotti, Leandro Prevosto, Héctor J. Kelly, Yio Rudi, Medhat Hussainov, Igor Shcheglov, Sergei Tisler, Igor Krupenski, David Stock, Jean-Luc Autran, Daniela Munteanu, Takaaki Uda, Zhong-Xin Li, Ke-Li Gao, Yu Yin, Dong Ge, Cui-Xia Zhang, R. C. Mehta, Lyudmila Ryabicheva, Dmytro Usatyuk, Hao Lu, Tomasz Jan Kopecki, Luiz Martins-Filho, Adrielle Santana, Ricardo Duarte, Gilberto Arantes Jr., Gilles Gasiot, Philippe Roche, Christopher Hyde, Wei Sun, Thomas Hyde, Mohammed Saber, Adib Becker, Rosa Munoz-Luna, Antonio Jurado-Navas, Lidia Taillefer de Haya, Jan Awrejcewicz

Published by InTech

Janeza Trdine 9, 51000 Rijeka, Croatia

Publishing Process Manager Iva Lipovic

Technical Editor InTech DTP team

Cover InTech Design team

Additional hard copies can be obtained from orders@intechopen.com

Computational and Numerical Simulations, Edited by Jan Awrejcewicz

p. cm.

ISBN 978-953-51-1220-4

Contents

Preface

The proposed book contains a lot of recent research devoted to computational and numerical simulations. It presents both new theories and their applications, showing bridge between theoretical investigations and possibility to apply them by engineers of different branches of science.

Chapter 1 by Awrejcewicz et al. describes possibility of application of the Lyapunov exponents and wavelets in studies of plates and shells. It focuses on characterization of their regular and chaotic dynamics, using different methods including Finite Element Method, Bubnov-Galerkin Method, Poincarè maps, power spectra or phase portraits.

In chapter 2, Kartushinsky et al. present effect of the pipe diameter at a constant Reynolds number in the particulate turbulent flow by focusing on the external effect of the flow configuration instead of internal effect with variation of the parameters of the flow.

In chapter 3, Kartushinsky et al. extend their investigation of Reynolds stress turbulence model (RSTM) by numerical simulations of the channel particulate flow with rough walls and initial level of turbulence. RSTM model was applied and investigated for different cases, for both horizontal and vertical flows, with channel cross-sections of rectangular and square, also for channels with smooth and rough walls and with obstacle in form of the vertical grid of different mesh size.

Validation of the most frequently used plasma cutting torch models is presented by Mancinelli et al. in chapter 4. They describe plasma torch model with physical details, model assumption, governing equations, and the boundary conditions are verified by confrontation with temperature and velocity values.

In chapter 5, wall pressure fluctuations m oscillations over the hemisphere-cylinder and unsteady flow characteristics of over blunt bodies at high speed are analyzed. As an example Mehta used the bulbous payload shroud of a typical satellite launch vehicle and the conical spoke attached forward to the facing blunt body. Determined was also the influence of different technical parameters on the overall characteristics of the flow.

Ryabicheva and Usatyuk in chapter 6 approach the problem of quality improvement of automotive parts applying theoretical analysis in form of computer modeling to the stress-strain state, temperature field and density distribution during radial-direct extrusion of porous powder billets.

In chapter 7, Kopecki presents results of experiments concerning post-critical behavior of thin-walled load-bearing structures. It is focused on number of variants of thin-walled cylindrical shell structures utilized commonly in aircraft design. Changes in post-buckling deformation of fuselage skin segments in aircraft structures were observed.

Martins-Filho et al. (chapter 8) discuss possibility of using co-simulation approaches, such as Processor–In-The-Loop and Hardware-In-The-Loop, for development of applications for embedded systems and for designing of controllers to be performed by dedicate processors. The chapter is focused on example of a module function for the attitude control to be performed by an embedded digital processor, but finds also application on design of artificial satellite embedded systems.

In chapter 9 Hyde et al. deal with approach of modeling creep crack growth using finite element modeling. Obtained theoretical results are compared with corresponding experimental data. Multiple specimen geometries are tested for validation, in terms of crack growth and final crack length.

Lu in chapter 10 describes summary of recent efforts in research on improvement of subgrid-scale parameterization, that aim at the increase of large-edgy simulation reliability in studies of turbulent flow and of atmospheric boundary layer.

Munteanu and Autran investigate in chapter 11 the possibility of application of 3-D numerical simulation for determination of sensitivity to heavy-ion irradiation of junctionless double-gate in metal-oxide-semiconductor field effect transistor (MOSFET). Obtained results are confirmed by already published experimental and simulation data.

In chapter 12, relativistic Vlasov-Maxwell Code is applied by Shoucri and Afeyan for stimulated Raman scattering. They report results concerning Raman forward scatter in plasmas and their ability to excite kinetic electrostatic electron nonlinear waves .

Wu et al. in chapter 13 describe application of synchronous computations of recurrent multilayer perceptrons for tracking mean field dynamics. By means of numerical studies, it is proved that proposed approach can be successfully applied for translation of mean field equations of solving the graph bisection problem.

Abramov et al. describe in chapter 14 methods for blind estimation if speckle variance in SAR images. They present results of simulations of noise characteristics, then compare them with real-life data. They consider applicability of the blind estimation of noise characteristics method and compare it with other mapping methods.

In chapter 15, Munoz-Luna et al. discuss development of the frequency domain, concentrating mostly on algorithm which obtains the first two formants of a vowel segment. Those two formants correspond to mouth opening and tongue position and are crucial for non-native speakers oral training as they provide necessary information for proficient pronunciation.

Surianu presents in chapter 16 experimental and numerical simulations of the validation of the mathematical models of the effects of electromagnetic interferences into overheated power lines with double circuit. This research can become useful tool for the professionals in electric power system and for increasing safety of high voltage maintenance workers.

Chapter 17 by Autran and Munteanu is devoted to the development of a numerical simulation code that can be applied for computation of the soft-error of floating-gate flash memories. Computational modeling and Monte Carlo simulations are validated by comparison with experimental data.

Li et al. present in chapter 18 application of Fourier transform for development of mathematical model for the lightening response of a grounding system buried in multilayered Earth. This novel method can be applied for high accuracy computation of the lightening currents flowing in the grounding system of a high voltage. It has been validated through numerical simulations and experimental results from literature.

Chapter 19 by Uda et al. is devoted to predictions of development of sand spits and cuspate forelands with rhythmic shapes and their deformation by means of the numerical modeling. Investigated is the influence of the construction of costal structures effect on the shape of sand spits.

Sporcic and Landekic present in chapter 20 the results of the investigation of efficiency of forest management in Croatia. They constructed nonparametric model for business performance evaluation and compared its results with real-life data.

I would like to thank all book contributors for their patience and improvement of their chapters. In addition, it is my great pleasure to thank Ms. Iva Lipović for her professional support during the book preparation.

Jan Awrejcewicz
Department of Automation, Biomechanics and Mechatronics,
Lodz University of Technology, Lodz, Poland

Department of Vehicles, Warsaw University of Technology
Warsaw, Poland

Chapter 1

Application of the Lyapunov Exponents and Wavelets to Study and Control of Plates and Shells

J. Awrejcewicz, V.A. Krysko, I.V. Papkova,
T.V. Yakovleva, N.A. Zagniboroda, M.V. Zhigalov,
A.V. Krysko, V. Dobriyan, E.Yu. Krylova and
S.A. Mitskevich

Additional information is available at the end of the chapter

http://dx.doi.org/10.5772/57452

1. Introduction

We study regular and chaotic vibrations of continuous mechanical systems using the following structural members: plates, flexible shells and cylindrical panels. They are often used in various measurement devices, and numerous ship and planes constructions. Owing to a high development of technology and due to industrial requirements, in many cases the mentioned structural members are subjected to action of high intensity loads being spatially and time dependent. The structural member exhibit either regular or chaotic dynamics, and hence an important question arises: How to predict safe and dangerous regimes of behavior of the studied mechanical objects?

In order to solve the mentioned problems, the investigations are carried out using the achievements of the qualitative analysis of differential equations and non-linear dynamics. Namely, we analyze time histories (signals), phase and modal portraits, Poincaré sections, autocorrelation functions, Lyapunov exponents, Fourier and wavelet spectra. Charts of vibration regimes versus the load excitation amplitude and frequency are constructed, which allow to control the vibration character of plates and shells.

Usually the data provided by numerical experiments are presented in time domain. In other words, we take time as an independent co-ordinate, and amplitude as a dependent co-ordinate, and the studied signal as analyzed through its amplitude-time representation. However, in order to understand deeply non-linear continuous systems subjected to various types of load actions and in order to fully understand the occurring dynamics, we have to apply the information hidden in the spectral signal characteristics. The Fourier transformation has been applied for a long time. However, it has been demonstrated recently that the Fourier analysis (FFT) is reliable only for the study of frequency components of stationary processes, i.e. the processes which through the whole period of investigation keep constant frequency components in time. It happens that in particular the dynamics of continuous mechanical systems may exhibit quite complicated output, and their frequency characteristics may change strongly in time. This is why in spite of the standard Fourier approach the wavelet analysis is applied allowing us to detect and understand many interesting non-linear phenomena of the mentioned mechanical systems.

Chaotic dynamics of structural members has been investigated by many researchers [1-10]. In this work we propose a novel approach to study non-linear vibrations of a plate based on the neural network approach and we analyze dynamics of flexible shells with constant stiffness and density subjected to harmonic load action. In the latter case mathematical model is built on the Kirchhoff-Love hypothesis and taking into account non-linear relation between deformation and displacement in the von Kármán form. This approach yields a system of non-linear PDEs regarding the deflection function and stresses (Airy's function) as well as the system of equations regarding displacements [11]. We use further FDM with approximation $O(h^2)$ and BGM in higher approximations, which allows to study the system with infinite numbers of degrees of freedom without any truncation of the obtained system of ODEs, which is solved via the fourth-order Runge-Kutta method.

2. Lyapunov exponents computation via neural networks an the generalized Benettin's algorithm

We illustrate and demonstrate the efficiency of the neural network approach to study a flexible plate with an infinite length. The governing equations are within the Kirchhoff hypothesis and they have the following non-dimensional form [11]:

$$\begin{gathered}\frac{\partial^2 u}{\partial x^2} + L_3(w,w) - \frac{\partial^2 u}{\partial t^2} = 0,\\ \frac{1}{\lambda^2}\left\{-\frac{1}{12}\frac{\partial^4 w}{\partial x^4} + L_1(u,w) + L_2(w,w)\right\} + q - \frac{\partial^2 w}{\partial t^2} - \varepsilon\frac{\partial w}{\partial t} = 0,\end{gathered} \tag{1}$$

where $L_1(u, w)$, $L_2(w, w)$, $L_3(w, w)$ – non-linear operators; $w(x, t)$– plate element bending in normal direction; $u(x, t)$– plate element longitudinal displacement; ε– dissipation coefficient; E– Young modulus; h – height of the transversal panel cross section; γ– specific plate material gravity; g –Earth acceleration; t – time; $q = q_0\sin(\omega_p t)$– external load.

The non-dimensional parameters are as follows:

$$\lambda = \frac{a}{h}, \quad \overline{w} = \frac{w}{h}, \quad \overline{u} = \frac{ua}{h^2}, \quad \overline{x} = \frac{x}{a}, \quad \overline{t} = \frac{t}{\tau},$$
$$\tau = \frac{a}{p}, \quad p = \sqrt{\frac{Eg}{\gamma}}, \quad \overline{\varepsilon} = \frac{a}{p}, \quad \overline{q} = \frac{qa^4}{h^4 E}, \tag{2}$$

and bars over the non-dimensional quantities have been already omitted in equations (1).

We demonstrate how to determine four first Lyapunov exponents applying pinned boundary conditions:

$$w(0,t) = w(1,t) = u(0,t) = u(1,t) = w_{xx}^{//}(0,t) = w_{xx}^{//}(1,t) = 0, \tag{3}$$

and the following initial conditions

$$w(x,0) = \dot{w}(x,0) = u(x,0) = \dot{u}(x,0). \tag{4}$$

The boundary value problem (1), (3), (4) is reduced to the Cauchy problem via FDM (Finite Difference Method) of the second order accuracy. The obtained ODEs are solved by the Runge-Kutta method of the fourth and sixth orders. Validity and reliability of the obtained numerical results are confirmed by the FEM results (Finite Element Method). The initial problem of infinite dimension is substituted by that of finite dimension via partition of the interval $x \in [0, 1]$ into 120 parts.

One of the ways to compute the spectrum of Lyapunov exponents is the neural network approach based on the generalized Benettin algorithm. It includes the following successive steps: 1. Choice of the appropriate time delay via tests; 2. Computation of an embedding space dimension; 3. Reconstruction of pseudo-phase trajectories using the method of time delays; 4. Neural network approximation; 5. Teaching of neural networks to compute successive iteration vectors; 6. Computation of the spectrum through the generalized Benettin algorithm with the help of the neural networks approach.

We apply the neural network with the following properties: It is an analog network regarding the input data (information is delivered through real numbers); It is self-organized with respect to its teaching aspects (output space of solutions is defined only through the input data); It belongs to the neural networks of straight signal distributions (all neural network couplings come from the input neurons and go to the output neurons); the neural network possesses dynamic couplings (control and improvement of synaptic couplings is carried out during the neural network self-teaching process $\left(\frac{dW}{dt} \neq 0\right)$, where W stands for the net weight coefficients). Let point x_0 belong to attractor A of a dynamical system. The trajectory of evolution of point is called the unperturbed trajectory. We choose the positive quantity ε essentially less than the attractor dimension. Next, we choose an arbitrary (perturbed) point in a way to satisfy the relation Then, we monitor the evolution of chosen and in time interval T, and the corresponding new points obtained after that time interval are denoted as and respectively. Vector is called the perturbation vector. We are ready to estimate λ:

$$\tilde{\lambda}_1 = \frac{1}{T}\ln\frac{\|\Delta x_1\|}{\varepsilon}. \tag{5}$$

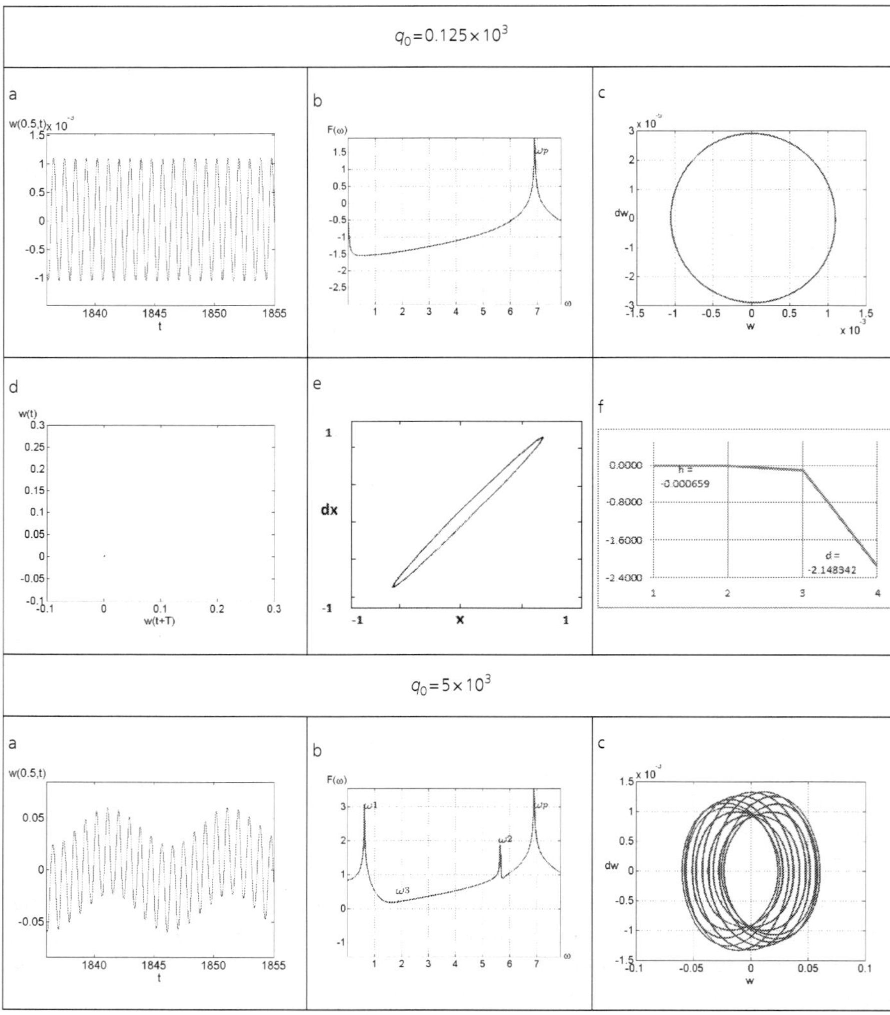

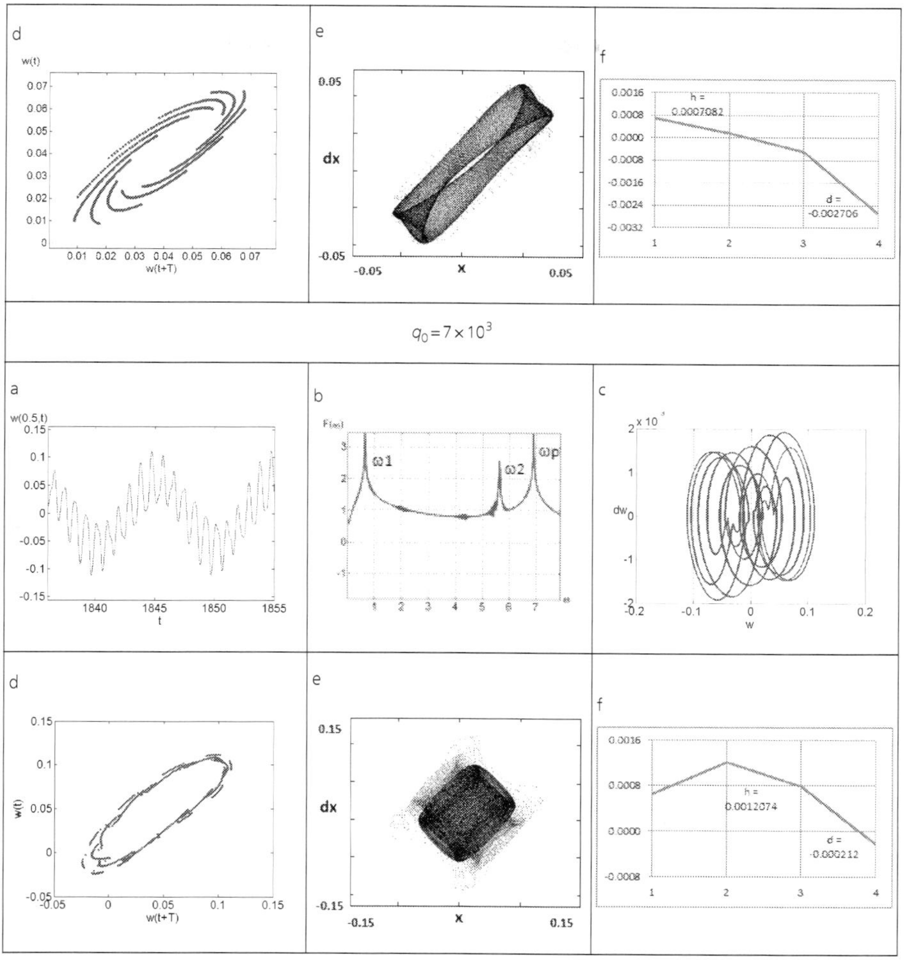

Table 1. Plate output characteristics

Time interval T is chosen in a way to keep the perturbation amplitude less than the linear dimensions of the space non-homogeneity as well as less than the attractor dimension. We consider the unit normalized perturbation vector and the corresponding new perturbation point $\tilde{x}_1^{/} = x_1 + \Delta x_1^{/}$. We extend the so far described approach by using points and $\tilde{x}_1$ instead of x_0 and respectively. We repeat the described procedure M times, and we may estimate λ as an average arithmetic quantity $\bar{\lambda}_i$ of those obtained on each computation step. The proposed approach has been tested using the standard classical examples including that of the Henon map [12], the Lorenz system [13] and the logistic map.

We consider vibrations of our mechanical object with the following fixed parameters: $\lambda=50$, $\varepsilon=1$, $\omega_p=7$, $q=q_0\sin(\omega_p t)$, and for the following amplitudes of the harmonic excitation: $q_0=0$, $125\cdot10^3$;$5\cdot10^3$; $7\cdot10^3$. In order to study chaotic dynamics of flexible plates we need to monitor and analyze the following output characteristics: time histories (a), phase (c) and modal portraits; phase portraits yielded by the neural networks approach (d); Fourier power spectra (b); wavelet spectra, Poincaré sections (e); spectra of Lyapunov exponents, where d stands for the fractional part of dimension and h is the Kolmogorov-Sinai entropy (f); auto-correlation functions (some of them are reported in Table 1). Analysis of the obtained results implies that for $q_0=0$, $125\cdot10^3$; periodic vibrations appear, whereas for $5\cdot10^3$ chaos is exhibited, and for $7\cdot10^3$ the hyper-chaotic vibrations occur.

3. Wavelets approach to study plate dynamics

One of the first important tasks to be solved is associated with the choice of a suitable wavelet, which fits well with the stated problem. In order to solve this query we have studied the non-stationary signal (Table 2) obtained via the numerical experiment as an output of the mathematical model of the rectangular flexible isotropic plate subjected to the periodic shear load acting in the shell volume unit. The mathematical model is as follows [11]:

$$\begin{aligned}&\frac{1}{12(1-\mu^2)}\left(\nabla_\lambda^4 w\right)-L(w,F)+\frac{\partial^2 w}{\partial t^2}+\varepsilon\frac{\partial w}{\partial t}-q(x_1,x_2,t)+2S\frac{\partial^2 w}{\partial x_1\partial x_2}=0,\\&\nabla_\lambda^4 F+\frac{1}{2}L(w,w)=0,\end{aligned}\tag{6}$$

where: $\nabla_\lambda{}^4=\frac{1}{\lambda^2}\frac{\partial^4}{\partial x_1{}^4}+\lambda^2\frac{\partial^4}{\partial x_2{}^4}+2\frac{\partial^4}{\partial x_1{}^2\partial x_2{}^2}$,

$L\ (w,\ F)=\frac{\partial^2 w}{\partial x_1{}^2}\frac{\partial^2 F}{\partial x_2{}^2}+\frac{\partial^2 w}{\partial x_2{}^2}\frac{\partial^2 F}{\partial x_1{}^2}-2\frac{\partial^2 w}{\partial x_1\partial x_2}\frac{\partial^2 F}{\partial x_1\partial x_2}$ – the known non-linear operator, whereas w and F stand for the plate deflection and Airy's function, respectively.

System (3.1) is reduced to the non-dimensional form using the following non-dimensional parameters: $\lambda=a/b$, $x_1=a\bar{x}_1$, $x_2=b\bar{x}_2$ – non-dimensional parameters regarding x_1 and x_2, respectively; $w=2h\bar{w}$– deflection; $F=E(2h)^3\bar{F}$– Airy's function; $t=t_0\bar{t}$– time; $q=\frac{E(2h)^4}{a^2b^2}\bar{q}$– external load; $\varepsilon=(2h)\bar{\varepsilon}$– damping coefficient of the surrounding medium, $S=\frac{E(2h)^3}{ab}\bar{S}$– external shear load. In the equations bars have already been omitted over the non-dimensional quantities. The following notation is introduced: a, b– plate dimensions regarding x_1 and x_2, respectively; μ– Poisson's coefficient. Zero value initial conditions and the following boundary value conditions are attached to system (2.6):

$$\begin{aligned} &w=0, \quad \frac{\partial^2 w}{\partial x_1^2}=0, \quad F=0, \quad \frac{\partial^2 F}{\partial x_1^2}=0 \quad \text{for} \quad x_1=0;1; \\ &w=0, \quad \frac{\partial^2 w}{\partial x_2^2}=0, \quad F=0, \quad \frac{\partial^2 F}{\partial x_2^2}=0 \quad \text{for} \quad x_2=0;1. \end{aligned} \tag{7}$$

The external harmonic shear load has the form $S = s_0 \sin\omega_p t$. PDEs governing dynamics of our investigated plate are reduced to the ODEs via the FDM (Finite Difference Method) with the approximation $O(h^2)$ regarding spatial co-ordinates. Next, ODEs are solved via the fourth-order Runge-Kutta method, and additionally on each of the iterations a large system of linear algebraic equations should be solved with respect to the stress (Airy's) function. Time integration step has been chosen using the Runge rule. The partition number of spatial co-ordinates is n=14 while applying FDM. Validity and reliability of the obtained results regarding the number of partitions has been discussed by Awrejcewicz et al. [14].

The term $2S\frac{\partial^2 w}{\partial x_1 \partial x_2}$ introduced in the governing equations exhibits the action of shear stresses located in shell middle plane and it essentially influences non-linear dynamics of the investigated shell. The numerical simulation indicates that the output signal (shell vibrations) may change in time repeatedly. We apply this signal to choose a methodology suitable for the investigation of non-stationary processes, and in addition, we illustrate advantages and disadvantages of the standard Fourier approach versus the wavelet transform procedure. The studied signal has been obtained analyzing the system with the following fixed parameters: s_0=8.4 and ω_p=26. We show that frequency characteristics taken in different time intervals essentially differ from each other. It should be emphasized that the system stability loss occurs not only via the change of chosen control parameters but also keeps all of them fixed owing to the system time evolution. In the first time interval $t \in [50;56]$ the shell exhibits two frequency quasi-periodic vibrations. Instead of the vanished excitation frequency, two independent frequencies have appeared. A further long time evolution of chaotic vibrations with the exhibition of a few dependent frequencies is observed. In the Fourier spectrum the excitation frequency is not visible. The last studied time interval corresponds to harmonic vibrations, which is also in agreement with the Fourier power spectrum.

We constructed wavelet spectra regarding the mentioned signal. We applied the following wavelets: Haar, Shannon-Kotelnikov, Meyer, Daubechies wavelets from db2 up to db 16, Coiflets and symlet wavelets, as well as the Morlet and Gauss (real and imaginary) wavelets, on the basis of the derivatives from 2 to 16. Haar and Shannon-Kotelnikov wavelets are not suitable for the analysis of shell structures. The first one is badly localized regarding frequency, whereas the second one, contrary to the previous wavelets, is badly localized in time. On the other hand, the analysis regarding the Doubechies wavelets, as well as symlet and Coiflets wavelets implies an increase of the frequency resolution assuming that the filter properties are increased. Neglecting differences regarding the wavelet forms and the associated filters, the wavelet spectra obtained through the Dobechies wavelets as well as symlet and Coiflets wavelets are practically identical. However, their localization with respect to frequency is not suitable for the analysis of continuous systems dynamics. In the case of the Gauss functions, an increase of their derivative order implies an increase of the frequency resolution.

Fourier spectrum ($50<t<56$) of quasi-periodic vibrations	Fourier spectrum ($130<t<225$) of chaotic vibrations	Fourier spectrum ($230<t<286$) of periodic vibrations
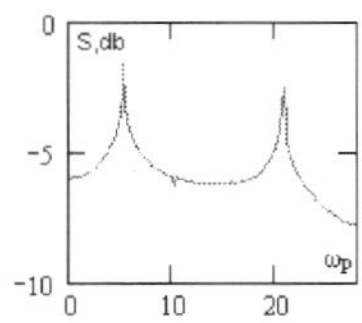	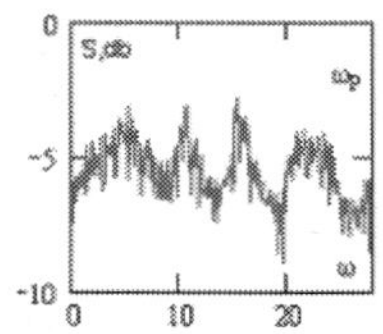	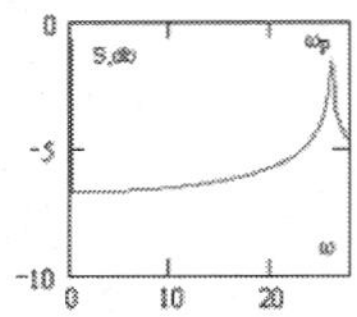
Signal		
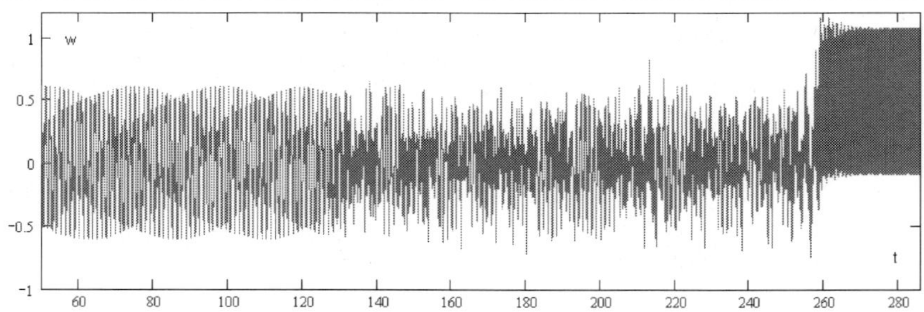		

Table 2. Fourier spectra and a signal

Table 3 gives results associated with the application of different wavelets (Meyer, Morlet, complex Morlet, real and complex Gauss with 16 derivative order, Daubechies) to analyze non-linear shell vibrations. One may conclude from Table 3 that the localization regarding frequency increases with an increase of the number of the wavelet zero moments.

4. Equations governing dynamics of flexible elastic shells

In a frame of non-linear classical theory we study a shell with constant stiffness and density and harmonic load $q = q_0 \sin(\omega_p t)$, where q_0 - amplitude of excitation, ω_p- frequency of excitation. In the rectangular co-ordinates the 3D space is:

$\Omega = \{x_1, x_2, x_3 \mid (x_1, x_2) \in [0;a] \times [0;b],\ x_3 \in [-h/2; h/2]\},\ 0 \le t < \infty.$

Wavelet spectrum: Meyer	Wavelet spectrum: Daubechies 16	Wavelet spectrum: complex Morlet
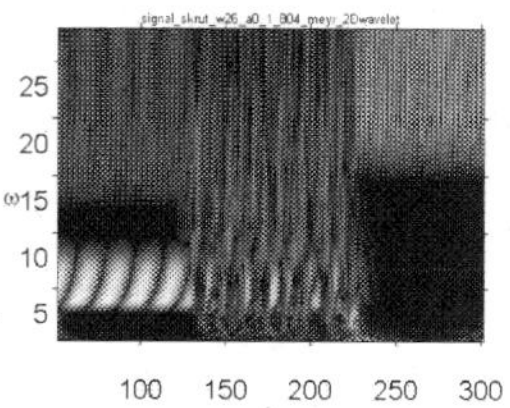	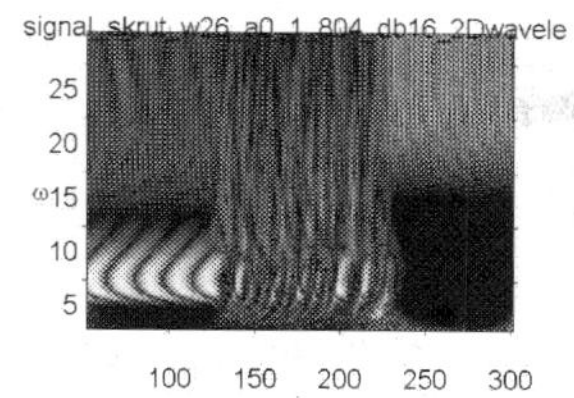	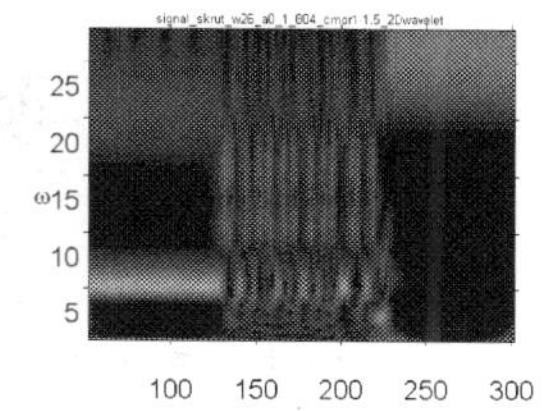
Wavelet spectrum: Morlet	Wavelet spectrum: Gauss 16	Wavelet spectrum Gauss: 16 complex
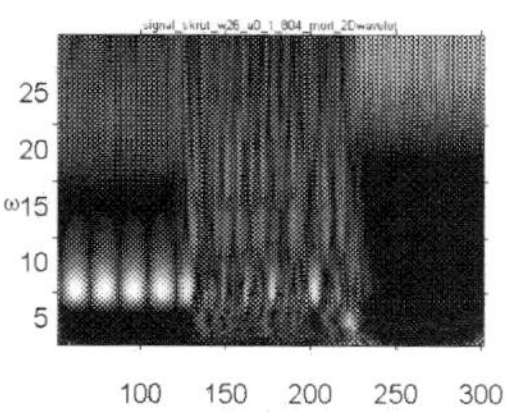	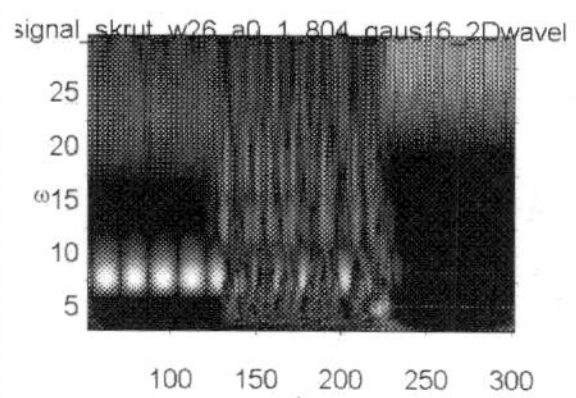	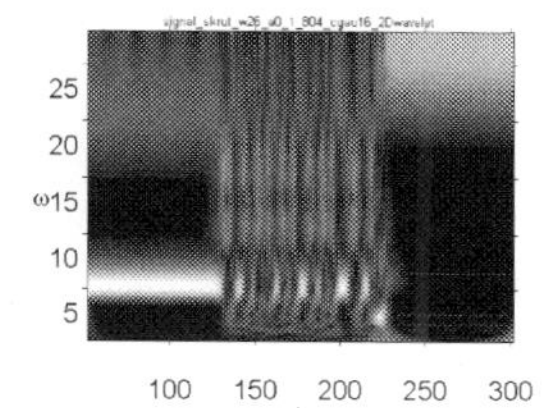

Table 3. Wavelets spectra

The governing non-dimensional equations are given in the hybrid form:

$$\begin{aligned}
&\frac{1}{12(1-\mu^2)}\left(\nabla_\lambda{}^4 w\right) - k_{x_2}\frac{\partial^2 F}{\partial x_1{}^2} - k_{x_1}\frac{\partial^2 F}{\partial x_2{}^2} - L(w,F) + \frac{\partial^2 w}{\partial t^2} + \varepsilon\frac{\partial w}{\partial t} - q(x_1,x_2,t) = 0,\\
&\nabla_\lambda{}^4 F + k_{x_2}\frac{\partial^2 w}{\partial x_1{}^2} + k_{x_1}\frac{\partial^2 w}{\partial x_2{}^2} + \frac{1}{2}L(w,w) = 0,
\end{aligned} \tag{8}$$

whereas equations regarding displacements follow

$$\begin{aligned}
&\frac{\partial^2 u}{\partial x_1^2} + \frac{1-\mu}{2}\frac{\partial^2 u}{\partial x_2^2} + \frac{1+\mu}{2}\frac{\partial^2 v}{\partial x_1 \partial x_2} + \frac{\partial w}{\partial x_1}\frac{\partial^2 w}{\partial x_1^2} - \left(k_{x_1} + \mu k_{x_2}\right)\frac{\partial w}{\partial x_1} + \frac{1+\mu}{2}\frac{\partial w}{\partial x_2}\frac{\partial^2 w}{\partial x_1 \partial x_2} + \frac{1-\mu}{2}\frac{\partial w}{\partial x_1}\frac{\partial^2 w}{\partial x_1^2} - \frac{\partial^2 u}{\partial t^2} = 0,\\
&\frac{1+\mu}{2}\frac{\partial^2 u}{\partial x_1 \partial x_2} + \frac{\partial^2 v}{\partial x_2^2} + \frac{1-\mu}{2}\frac{\partial^2 v}{\partial x_1^2} - \left(\mu k_{x_1} + k_{x_2}\right)\frac{\partial w}{\partial x_2} + \frac{\partial w}{\partial x_2}\frac{\partial^2 w}{\partial x_2^2} + \frac{1+\mu}{2}\frac{\partial w}{\partial x_1}\frac{\partial^2 w}{\partial x_1 \partial x_2} + \frac{1-\mu}{2}\frac{\partial w}{\partial x_2}\frac{\partial^2 w}{\partial x_1^2} + \frac{\partial^2 v}{\partial t^2} = 0,\\
&\frac{1}{\lambda^2}\Bigg[\nabla^4 w - \left(k_x + \mu k_{x_2}\right)\frac{\partial u}{\partial x_1} - \left(\mu k_{x_1} + k_{x_2}\right)\frac{\partial v}{\partial x_2} + \left(k_{x_1}^2 + k_y^2 + 2\mu k_{x_1} k_{x_2}\right) w - \frac{k_{x_1} + \mu k_{x_2}}{2}\left(\frac{\partial w}{\partial x_1}\right)^2 -\\
&\qquad - \frac{k_{x_2} + \mu k_{x_1}}{2}\left(\frac{\partial w}{\partial x_2}\right)^2 - \frac{\partial}{\partial x_1}\left\{\frac{\partial w}{\partial x_1}\left[\frac{\partial u}{\partial x_1} + \mu\frac{\partial v}{\partial x_2}\right] + \frac{1-\mu}{2}\frac{\partial w}{\partial x_2}\left(\frac{\partial u}{\partial x_2} + \frac{\partial v}{\partial x_1}\right)\right\} -\\
&\qquad - \frac{\partial}{\partial x_2}\left\{\frac{\partial w}{\partial x_2}\left[\frac{\partial v}{\partial x_2} + \mu\frac{\partial u}{\partial x_1}\right] + \frac{1-\mu}{2}\frac{\partial w}{\partial x_1}\left(\frac{\partial u}{\partial x_2} + \frac{\partial v}{\partial x_1}\right)\right\}\Bigg] - q + \varepsilon_1\frac{\partial w}{\partial t} + \frac{\partial^2 w}{\partial t^2} = 0,
\end{aligned} \tag{9}$$

where: $\nabla_\lambda^4 = \frac{1}{\lambda^2}\frac{\partial^4}{\partial x_1^4} + \lambda^2 \frac{\partial^4}{\partial x_2^4} + 2\frac{\partial^4}{\partial x_1^2 \partial x_2^2}$,

$L(w, F) = \frac{\partial^2 w}{\partial x_1^2}\frac{\partial^2 F}{\partial x_2^2} + \frac{\partial^2 w}{\partial x_2^2}\frac{\partial^2 F}{\partial x_1^2} - 2\frac{\partial^2 w}{\partial x_1 \partial x_2}\frac{\partial^2 F}{\partial x_1 \partial x_2}$ – known non-linear operator, $w(x_1, x_2, t)$– element normal; $u(x_1, x_2, t)$, $v(x_1, x_2, t)$– element displacement regarding x_1 and x_2, respectively; $F(x_1, x_2, t)$- stress function; ε – dissipation coefficient; E– Young modulus; h – height of the transversal panel cross section; γ– specific unit gravity of the shell material; g– Earth acceleration; t– time; $q = q_0 \sin(\omega t)$ – external load.

The following non-dimensional parameters are introduced:

$$\begin{gathered}\lambda = \frac{a}{h}, \quad \lambda_1 = \frac{a}{b}, \quad \bar{w} = \frac{w}{h}, \quad \bar{u} = \frac{ua}{h^2}, \quad \bar{v} = \frac{va}{h^2}, \quad \bar{x}_1 = \frac{x_1}{a}, \quad \bar{x}_2 = \frac{x_2}{b}, \quad \bar{t} = \frac{t}{\tau}, \quad \tau = \frac{a}{c}, \\ c = \sqrt{\frac{Eg}{\gamma}}, \quad \bar{\varepsilon} = \frac{a}{c}, \quad \bar{q} = \frac{qa^4}{h^4 E}, \quad \overline{k_{x_1}} = \frac{k_{x_1} a}{\lambda}, \quad \overline{k_{x_2}} = \frac{k_{x_2} b}{\lambda}, \quad \bar{F} = \frac{F}{Eh^3}.\end{gathered} \tag{10}$$

System of differential equations (4.1)-(4.2) should be supplemented by boundary and initial conditions (see [11]. Since we cannot solve the stated problems analytically, we reduce the problem to ODEs and solve it numerically by the fourth-order Runge-Kutta method (see [15] for more details).

As the first example, we consider a spherical rectangular shell governed by equations (4.1) and with the following homogeneous conditions:

$$w|_\Gamma = 0; \quad M_n|_\Gamma = 0; \quad N_n|_\Gamma = 0; \quad \varepsilon_n|_\Gamma = 0 \ \text{ for } \ x_1 = 0;1, \quad x_2 = 0;1, \tag{11}$$

which can be recast to the form

$$w = 0; \quad \frac{\partial^2 w}{\partial x_1^2} = 0; \quad F = 0; \quad \frac{\partial^2 F}{\partial x_1^2} = 0; \quad w = 0; \quad \frac{\partial^2 w}{\partial x_2^2} = 0; \quad F = 0; \quad \frac{\partial^2 F}{\partial x_2^2} = 0 \tag{12}$$

and the following initial conditions

$$w(x_1, x_2)|_{t=0} = 0, \qquad \frac{\partial w}{\partial t} = 0. \tag{13}$$

Geometric parameters of the shell curvature $k_{x_1} = k_{x_2} = 24$, $\lambda = 1$, and the damping coefficient $\varepsilon = 1$. We apply the BGM in Vlasov's form, and the we are looping for the functions w and F, satisfying (4.5), in the following form

$$w = \sum_{i=1}^{N} \sum_{j=1}^{N} A_{ij}(t) \sin(i\pi x_1) \sin(j\pi x_2), \qquad F = \sum_{i=1}^{N} \sum_{j=1}^{N} B_{ij}(t) \sin(i\pi x_1) \sin(j\pi x_2). \tag{14}$$

5. Numerical analysis of shells non-linear dynamics

In what follows we investigate vibrations of flexible shells via the BGM versus the partition number N in periodic (Fig. 1) and chaotic (Fig. 2) zones. We consider the point $A(q_0, \omega_p) = A(5;25) \in \{q_0, \omega_p\}$ marked on the type vibration chart (Fig. 3), which belongs to harmonic vibrations zone. For all N harmonic (one frequency) vibrations are observed. Increase of the approximations number $N = 11$, 13, 15 implies the full coincidence regarding both frequency and amplitude. Further, we study the BGM convergence in a chaotic zone (Fig. 2). We analyze the point $B(q_0, \omega_p) = B(180;38) \in \{q_0, \omega_p\}$ on the chart (Fig. 3). Although we cannot achieve the signal convergence as it occurred in the previous case, but we get the convergence in average sense through Fourier integrals of power spectra.

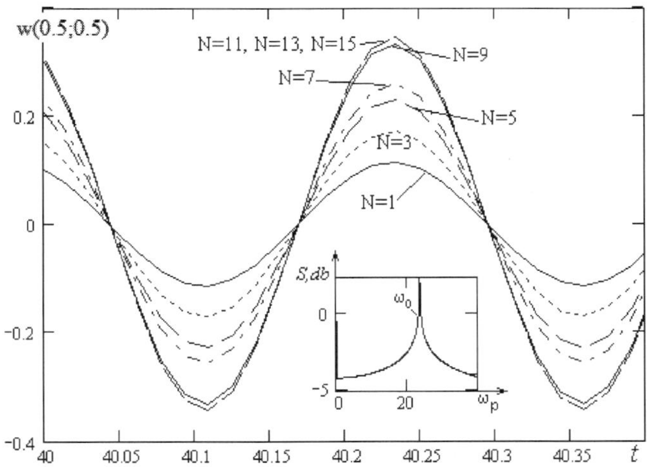

Figure 1. Time histories ($w(0.5, 0.5, t)$) and power spectrum for different approximations of the Bubnov-Galerkin method for $t \in [40; 40.4]$.

We investigate further the convergence of the FDM versus a number of partitions of the mesh $m \times n$ for a flexible rectangular shell taking into account the same parameters. We consider first the shell center motion in an harmonic zone (Fig. 4). Let us fix the point

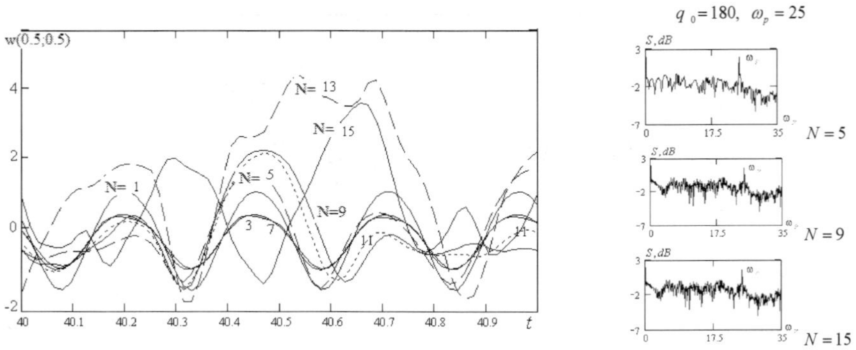

Figure 2. Time histories ($w(0.5, 0.5, t)$) and power spectrum for different approximations of the Bubnov-Galerkin method for $t \in [40; 41]$.

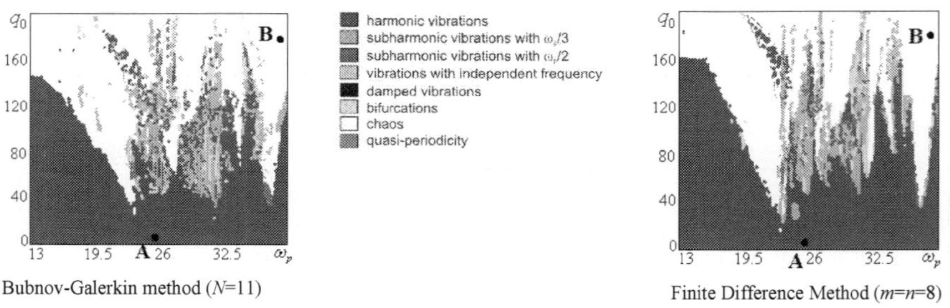

Figure 3. Vibration charts in the control parameters plane $\{q_0, \omega_p\}$.

$A(q_0, \omega_p) = A(5;25) \in \{q_0, \omega_p\}$ on the vibration chart. Three curves are reported in Fig. 4 for $n=m=8;\ 16;\ 32$. For all partition points $n=m=8;\ 16;\ 32$ harmonic vibrations are observed. On the other hand for given $n=m$ time histories differ from each other (see Fig. 5), but their convergence regarding the Fourier power spectra are evident ($n=m=16;\ 32$).

We now compare the results obtained through two qualitatively different approaches, i.e. FDM and BGM. The convergence of those two methods is numerically confirmed with respect to time histories and Fourier power spectra for small amplitude of excitation. Although in the case of chaotic vibrations the convergence regarding time series is not achieved, but it is achieved with respect to integral Fourier characteristics.

In what follows we address the problem of vibration chart identification versus a step of variation of the control parameters q_0 and ω_p. We consider the vibration charts for five applied resolutions given in Table 4: a – resolution 50×50, b -100×100, c –200×200, d –300×300, e - 400×400.

http://dx.doi.org/10.5772/57452

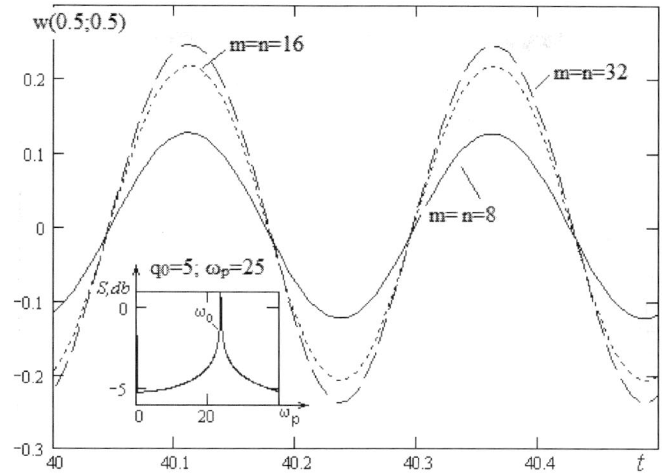

Figure 4. Deflections ($w(0.5, 0.5, t)$) and power spectra for different partitions $m=n=8; 16; 32$ in a periodic zone for $t \in [40; 40.5]$.

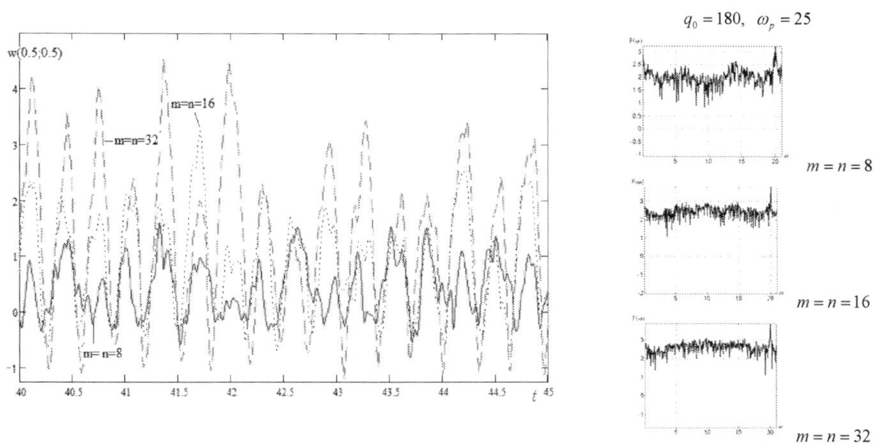

Figure 5. Dependence ($w(0.5, 0.5, t)$) and power spectra for different partition $m=n=8; 16; 32$ in a chaotic zone for $t \in [40; 45]$.

Increase of the resolution implies the results improvement. Results obtained for the cases 1d and 1e coincide in full. In Figure 3 vibration charts for the rectangular spherical shell, which have been obtained using the BGM for N = 11, as well as the FDM for partition number 8x8 and accuracy $O(h^2)$ regarding the spatial coordinate are shown. In both cases the initial

50×50	100×100	200×200
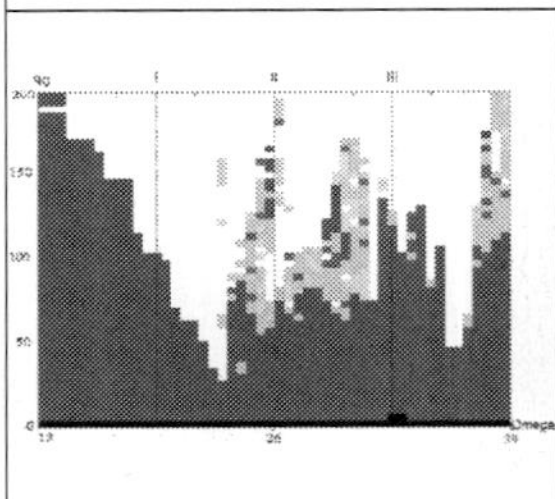	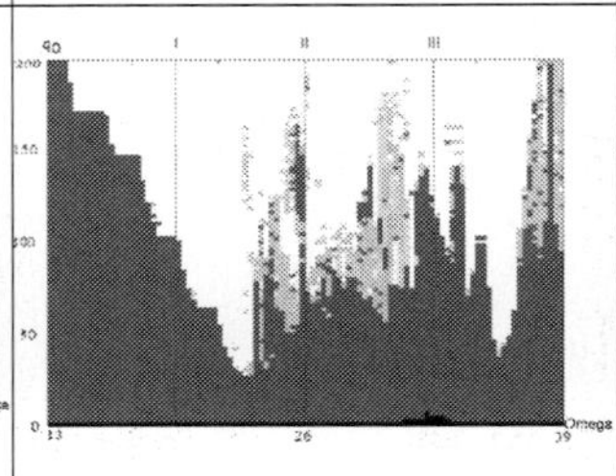	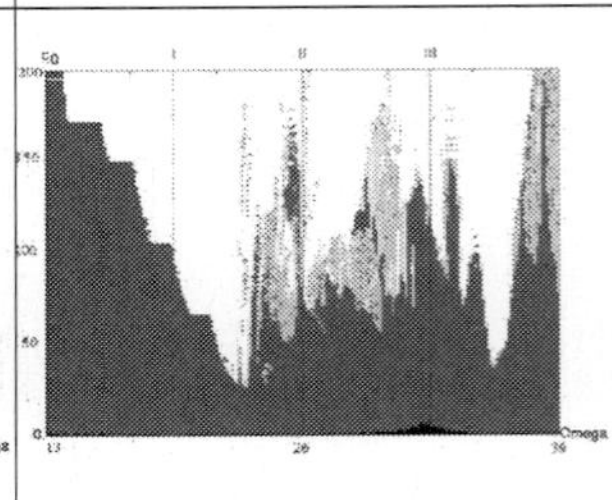
300×300	400×400	
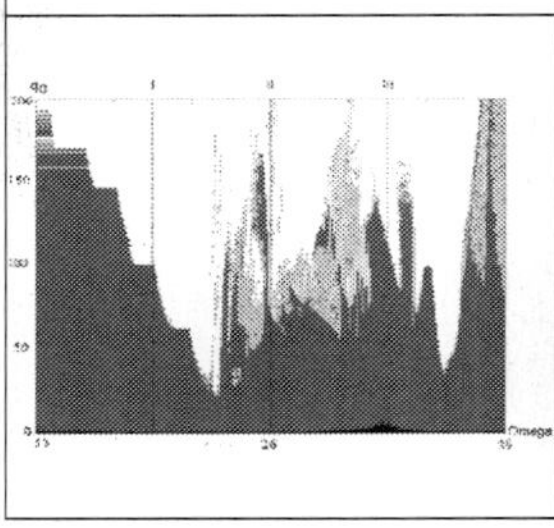	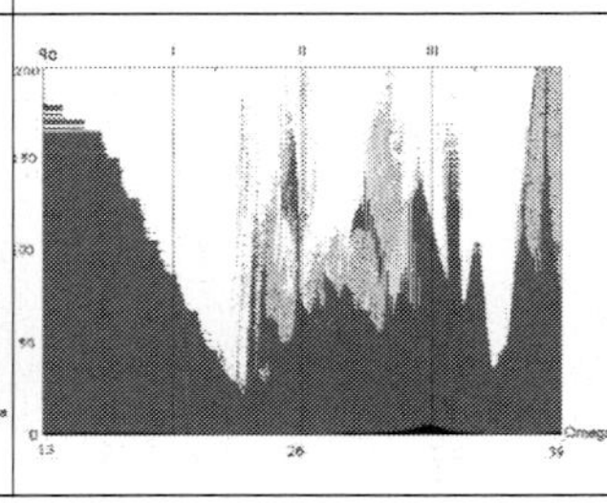	harmonic vibrations subharmonic vibrations with $\omega_p/3$ subharmonic vibrations with $\omega_p/2$ vibrations with independent frequency damped vibrations bifurcations chaos quasi-periodicity

Table 4. Charts of shell vibrations in the $\{q_0, \omega_p\}$ plane.

problem is solved via the fourth order Runge-Kutta method. It should be emphasized that in order to remove potential errors in the obtained results and in order to confirm its reliability and validity, one needs to apply different numerical approaches while studying non-linear dynamics of 2D mechanical objects. The obtained vibration charts allow controlling the vibration regimes and a transition form dangerous zones to those of the required/engineering acceptable zones. One may observe that both charts obtained via the qualitatively different approaches are close to each other. For small values of the load ($q_0 \leq 30$) the system exhibits periodic vibrations. Increase of the excitation amplitude implies occurrence of chaotic dynamics. There are also zones of the Hopf bifurcations and two-frequency quasi-periodic orbits. However, both charts exhibit a qualitative difference in the resonance zone ($\omega_p = \omega_0$), i.e. errors introduced by numerical techniques increase in the resonance conditions. However, increase of of the partition number of the applied mesh as well as increase of the applied terms of the series for the case of BGM again yields the reliable and validated results, although with a higher costs of time computation.

Approximation of $N=15$ for the BGM and of $n=m=16$for the FDM are most suitable to keep the validated results as well as economically reasonable computation time. Computational time of the BGM is lower than that of the FDM, since in the latter case we need to solve a system of algebraic equations (for $n=m=8$ we have 64 equations, for $n=m=16$-256 equations, $n=m=32$-1024 equations), which requires additional computational time.

Therefore, in the case of our 2D mechanical object we have achieved only the integral convergence regarding the Fourier spectrum, and hence one my study a 1D problem.

The second computational example deals with the infinite cylindrical panel harmonically and transversally loaded. In this case equations (4.2) yield

$$\begin{gathered}\frac{\partial^2 u}{\partial x_1{}^2} - k_{x_1}\frac{\partial w}{\partial x_1} + L_3(w,w) - \frac{\partial u^2}{\partial t^2} = 0,\\ \frac{1}{\lambda^2}\left\{-\frac{1}{12}\frac{\partial^4 w}{\partial x_1{}^4} + k_{x_1}\left[\frac{\partial u}{\partial x_1} - k_{x_1} w - \frac{1}{2}\left(\frac{\partial w}{\partial x_1}\right)^2 - w\frac{\partial^2 w}{\partial x_1{}^2}\right] + L_1(u,w) + L_2(w,w)\right\} + q - \frac{\partial^2 w}{\partial t^2} - \varepsilon\frac{\partial w}{\partial t} = 0.\end{gathered} \tag{15}$$

with the following boundary

$$w(0,t) = w(1,t) = u(0,t) = u(1,t) = w''_{x_1 x_1}(0,t) = w''_{x_1 x_1}(1,t) = 0, \tag{16}$$

and initial conditions

$$w(x_1,0) = \dot{w}(x_1,0) = u(x_1,0) = \dot{u}(x_1,0) = 0. \tag{17}$$

	50×50	100×100	200×200	300×300
$n=16$	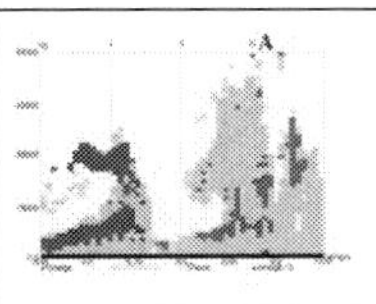	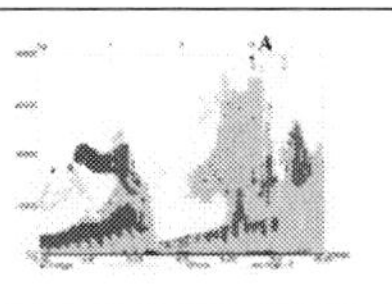	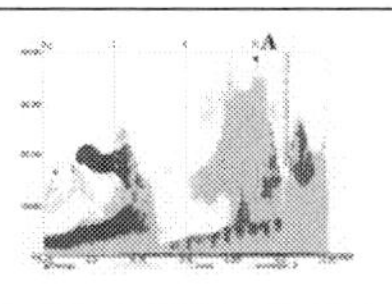	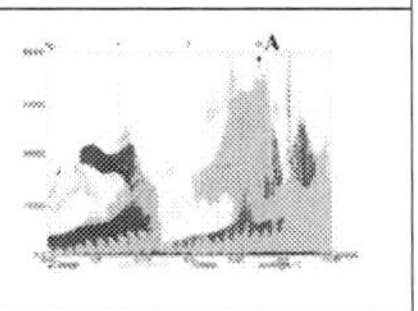
$n=32$	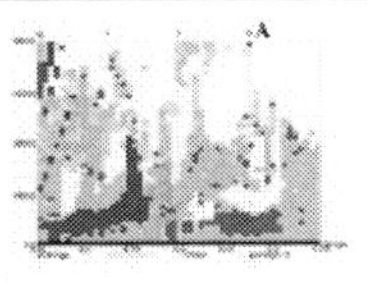		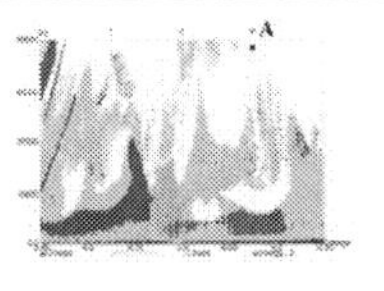	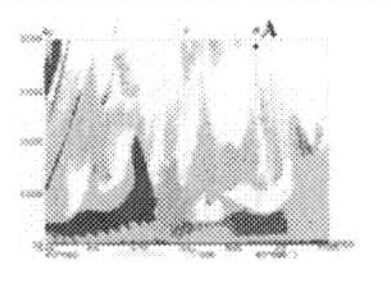
$n=40$	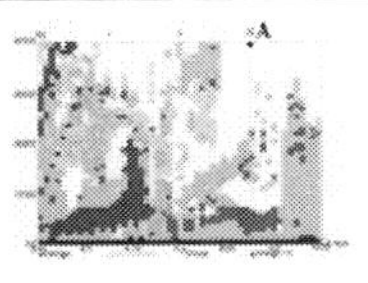	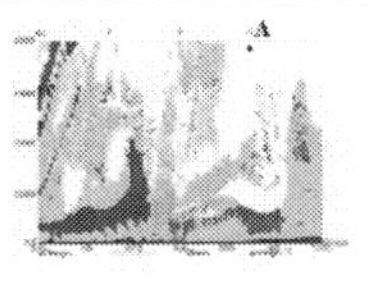		

Table 5. Vibration charts $\{q_0, \omega_p\}$ for different n and different resolutions

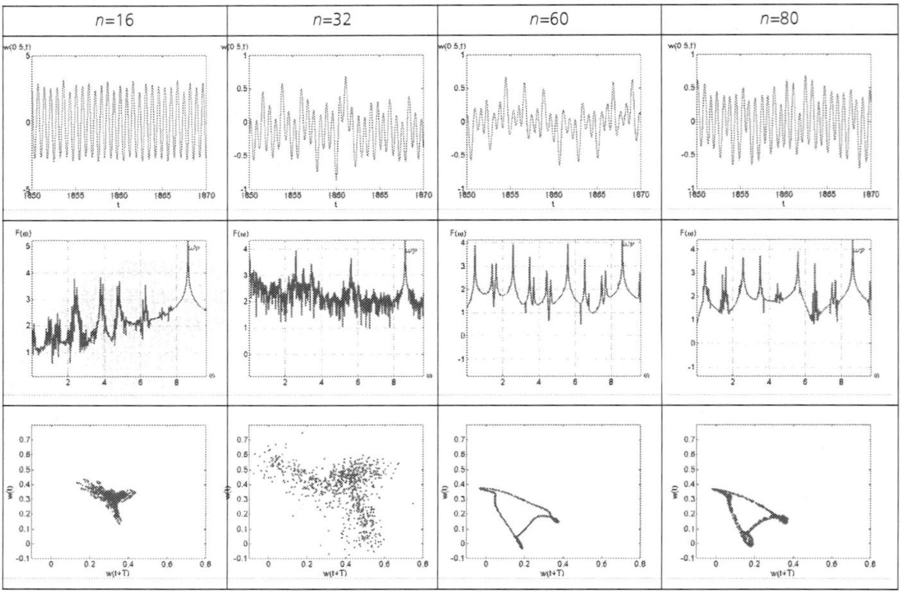

Table 6. Time histories ($w(0.5, t)$), Fourier spectra, and Poincaré maps for different panel partitions.

Observe that neither the input governing equations (5.1) nor more complex system of equations (4.2) cannot be solved analytically. The results obtained through FDM have been compared with the results obtained FEM (Finite Element Method) in the Bubnov-Galerkin form. The following characteristics are applied: time history ($w(0.5, t)$), power spectrum and the Morlet wavelets. Charts of the vibration regimes present all peculiarities and a general picture of the studied non-linear process within the investigated intervals of the control parameters. However, one would expect an optimal choice of the applied nodes (n) of the mesh, as well a number of partition of the excitation frequency (ω_p) and the excitation amplitude (q_0). In Table 5 charts of the vibration regimes on the control parameters plane $\{\omega_p, q_0\}$ and the interval partition regarding $x_1 \in [0;1]$, including the applied color notation is presented for $\{\omega_p, q_0\} = 50 \times 50;\ 100 \times 100;\ 200 \times 200;\ 300 \times 300$, and the interval $x_1 \in [0;1]$ is divided into 16, 32 and 40 parts.

We have already mentioned that a crucial role in analysis plays the time of computation to get time histories and carry out their analysis. Taking into account the reported results we conclude that the most optimal chart resolution is that of 200×200; 300×300.

It should be noted that the constructed charts on a basis of only power spectra are not sufficient to decide about the results convergence versus the partition number (n) regarding the spatial coordinate. In order to get the validated results we apply the following fixed parameters (boundary conditions (5.2) and initial conditions (5.3)):

$\varepsilon=1;\lambda=\frac{a}{h}=50;\omega_p=8,\ 625;q_0=59000;k_{x_1}=0.$

For the given parameters the system is in a chaotic regime, what is approved by the reported charts (Table 5, point A). In what follows we analyze the obtained signal versus number of partition of the spatial coordinate. Namely, we construct the power spectra and Poincaré maps (Table 6) for n=16, 32, 40.

Comparison of the amplitudes of the analyzed time histories allows to conclude that the convergence is achieved for. Now, taking into account the Poincaré maps we that for $n \geq 60$ a chaotic strange attractor appears, which has not been detected for a smaller number of applied partitions. The Fourier power spectrum exhibits a remarkable localization of dominating frequencies including the excitation frequency for different introduced partitions, but the convergence is not achieved.

Therefore, taking into account the mentioned remarks, the following parameters have been applied through computations:

- PDEs are solved via FEM;
- Charts resolution -200×200;
- Number of partitions regarding the spatial coordinate $-n=80$.

In the chapter part devoted to study non-linear vibrations of shells, we have chosen suitable charts resolutions and partition numbers to follow various scenarios of transitions form regular to chaotic dynamics and to optimal reduction of the computational time simultaneously keeping the reliable and validated results.

6. Concluding remarks

In the chapter part devoted to plate analysis we have shown that the obtained validated spectra of the Lyapunov exponents allow for the estimation of Kaplan-Yorke dimension, Sinai-Kolmogorov entropy, and velocity of the phase space compression. Furthermore, we have illustrated that the complex Morlet and Gauss wavelets have better localization with respect to frequency, in comparison to their real analogues, but time localization is better for the real wavelets. Therefore, one may either apply real or complex Morlet and Gauss (order bigger than 16) wavelets while studying plates/shells dynamics.

Acknowledgements

This work has been supported by the grant RFFI No 12-01-31204, and the National Science Centre of Poland under the grant MAESTRO 2, No. 2012/04/A/ST8/00738, for years 2013-2016.

Author details

J. Awrejcewicz[1*], V.A. Krysko[2], I.V. Papkova[2], T.V. Yakovleva[2], N.A. Zagniboroda[2], M.V. Zhigalov[2], A.V. Krysko[3], V. Dobriyan[2], E.Yu. Krylova[2] and S.A. Mitskevich[2]

*Address all correspondence to: awrejcew@p.lodz.pl

1 Department of Automation, Biomechanics and Mechatronics, Lodz University of Technology, 90-924 Lodz, 1/15 Stefanowski St. and Department of Vehicles, Warsaw University of Technology, Warsaw, Poland

2 Saratov State Technical University, Department of Mathematics and Modeling, Saratov, Russia

3 Saratov State Technical University, Applied Mathematics and Systems Analysis, Saratov, Russia

References

[1] Chin C.M., Nayfeh A.H. (1996) Bifurcation and Chaos in Externally Excited Circular Cylindrical Shells. Journal of Applied Mechanics 63: 565–574.

[2] Min Sup Hur, Hae June Lee, Jae Koo Lee (1998) Parametrization of Nonlinear and Chaotic Oscillations in Driven Beam-Plasma Diodes. Physical Review E 58(1): 936-941.

[3] Chen L.Q., Zhang N.H., Zu J.W. (2003) The Regular and Chaotic Vibrations of an Axially Moving Viscoelastic String Based on 4-order Galerkin truncation. Journal of Sound and Vibratins 261:764–73.

[4] Awrejcewicz J., Krysko V.A. (2003) Nonclassical Thermoelastic Problems in Nonlinear Dynamics of Shells. Berlin: Springer. 427p.

[5] Yang X.D., Chen L.Q. (2005) Bifurcation and Chaos of an Axially Accelerating Viscoelastic Beam. Chaos, Solitons and Fractals 23:249–258.

[6] Samoylenko S.B., Lee W.K. (2007) Global Bifurcations and Chaos in a Harmonically Excited and Undamped Circular Plate. Nonlinear Dynamics 47: 405–419.

[7] Awrejcewicz J., Krysko V.A. (2008) Chaos in Structural Mechanics. Berlin: Springer. 434p.

[8] Touzé C., Thomas O., Amabili M. (2010) Transition to Chaotic Vibrations for Harmonically Forced Perfect and Imperfect Circular Plates. International Journal of Non-Linear Mechanics 46(1): 234-270.

http://dx.doi.org/10.5772/57452

[9] Yong-Gang Wang, Hui-Fang Song, Dan Li, Jing Wang (2010) Bifurcations and Chaos in a Periodic Time-Varying Temperature-Excited Bimetallic Shallow Shell of Revolution. Archive of Applied Mechanics 80: 815–828.

[10] Yu-Gao Huangfu, Fang-Qi Chen (2013) Single-Pulse Chaotic Dynamics of Functionally Graded Materials Plate. Acta Mechanica Sinica 29(4): 593–601.

[11] Volmir A.S. (1972) Nonlinear Dynamics of Plates and Shells. Moscow: Nauka, in Russian.

[12] Henon M. (1976) A Two-Dimensional Mapping with a Strange Attractor. Communications in Mathematical Physics 50(1): 69–77.

[13] Lorenz E.N. (1963) Deterministic Non-Periodic Flow. Journal of the Atmospheric Sciences 20(2): 130–141.

[14] Awrejcewicz J., Krylova E.Y., Papkova I.V., Krysko V.A. (2012) Wavelet-Based Analysis of the Regular and Chaotic Dynamics of Rectangular Flexible Plates Subjected to Shear-Harmonic Loading. Shock and Vibration 19: 979-994.

[15] Krys'ko V.A., Narkaitis G.G., Awrejcewicz J. (2006) Nonlinear Vibration and Characteristics of Flexible Plate-Strips with Non-Symmetric Boundary Conditions. Communications in Nonlinear Science and Numerical Simulation 11(1): 95–124.

Chapter 2

RANS Numerical Simulation of Turbulent Particulate Pipe Flow for Fixed Reynolds Number

Alexander Kartushinsky, Ylo Rudi, Igor Shcheglov, Sergei Tisler and Igor Krupenski

Additional information is available at the end of the chapter

http://dx.doi.org/10.5772/57216

1. Introduction

Particulate flows in pipes have numerous engineering applications ranging from pneumatic conveying systems to coal gasifiers and chemical reactor design and are one of the most thoroughly investigated subjects in the area of multiphase flows. These flows are very complex and influenced by various physical phenomena, such as particle-turbulence and particle-particle interactions, deposition, by gravitational and viscous drag forces, particle rotation, and lift force.

Numerous theoretical and experimental researches, e.g., [1-20], studied various aspects of the behavior of gas and solid particles in particulate pipe flows.

The present study focuses on the effect of variation of the pipe diameter for a constant Reynolds number applied to vertical particulate turbulent pipe flows. The numerical investigation discussed here examined in detail the effects of direct and indirect particle-turbulence interaction (no-coupling and coupling) and gravity for various flow mass loadings of 250, 500 and 700 μm coal particles. Additionally, the viscous drag force and the Magnus and Saffman lift forces are also taken into account. The behavior of the particulate phase was under consideration, both for the fine particles being liable to the turbulent fluctuations of gas and the larger particles, which have the lesser response to the flow turbulence.

The presented numerical model makes use of the two-fluid model, e.g., [21-25], and the Reynolds-averaged Navier-Stokes (RANS) approach [18, 19] applied to gas and solid particles.

Within the frame of the two-fluid model, the gas and the particles are considered as two coexisting phases that span the entire flow domain [18, 19]. Therefore, in order to describe the flow of the particulate phase within the two-fluid model, the presented model implements the RANS approach. This approach is the most general and frequently used in modeling, its closure equations have been verified by numerous experiments, and the boundary conditions are easy to determine. The given modeling employs the model [14], which is the most relevant to account for mechanisms of a turbulence modulation caused by particles, since it includes both the turbulence enhancement and its attenuation by particles. The inter-particle collisions is another mechanism accounting for capture properties of turbulent particulate pipe flows, which has been modeled, e.g., in [16]. These two models enables comprehensive mathematical simulation of the two-phase upward pipe flow.

The presented model allows covering 100 and more calibers of a pipe flow. This is the main advantage over the numerical models based, for example, on direct numerical simulation (DNS) codes, (e.g., [26]), that handle usually with a short pipe length up to 10-20 calibers with imposing the upper limit for the flow Reynolds number.

The utilized two-fluid model with adoption of original collisional closure model [16] together with the applied numerical method has been verified and validated in our previous researches [18, 19] by comparison of numerical results with the experimental data [6]. In the given study, the effect of variation of the pipe diameter (or transport velocity) at a constant Reynolds number is numerically investigated in the particulate turbulent flow. This is a step forward for analyzing the external effect, namely, the flow configuration rather the internal effect with variation of the parameters of the flow.

2. Governing equations and numerical method

The sketch of the computational flow domain is shown in Fig. 1, where $\bar{u}$ is the gas average velocity, F_G is gravity, F_D is the aerodynamic drag force, F_{LR} is the lift force that arises from particle rotation (the Magnus lift force), ω_s is the angular velocity of a particle.

It is assumed that the particulate phase is polydispersed and composed of several known mass fractions. These fractions can be of single material density and characterized by equivalent particle diameter of the fraction δ. According to [16], in the given formulation of the governing equations that follows, three solid fractions are assumed to be present. It is assumed that the aerodynamic forces, such as the drag, lift forces and gravity, act on all the particulate fractions.

2.1. Governing equations for the 2D RANS model

The model is based on the time averaged Navier-Stokes equations (RANS method), without any simplifications, such as the boundary layer simplifications. The vertical pipe flows are 2D unless the study of rotating flows.

A short presentation of the governing equations written for the axisymmetric channel case is as follows:

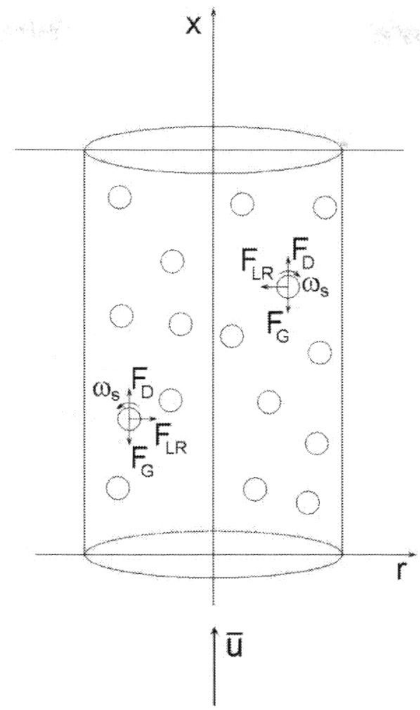

Figure 1. Upward turbulent particulate flow in a pipe.

continuity equation for the gas phase:

$$\frac{\partial u}{\partial x}+\frac{\partial (rv)}{r\partial r}=0, \tag{1}$$

where u and v are the longitudinal and radial velocity components of the gas phase.

longitudinal linear momentum equation for the gas phase:

$$\frac{\partial}{\partial x}\left(u^2-\tilde{v}_t\frac{\partial u}{\partial x}\right)+\frac{\partial}{r\partial r}r\left(uv-\tilde{v}_t\frac{\partial u}{\partial r}\right)=-\frac{\partial p}{\rho\partial x}+\frac{\partial}{\partial x}\tilde{v}_t\frac{\partial u}{\partial x}+\frac{\partial}{r\partial r}r\tilde{v}_t\frac{\partial v}{\partial x}-\alpha\left(\frac{u_r}{\tau'}+C_M\Omega v_r\right), \tag{2}$$

where $\tilde{v}_t = v_t + v$ is effective viscosity, which is the sum of turbulent and laminar viscosities, while v_t is calculated following the Boussinesq eddy-viscosity concept; p is pressure; α is the mass concentration of particles; $u_r = u - u_s$ and $v_r = v - v_s$ are the relative velocities of particles along the longitudinal and radial directions, respectively. Here $\tau^{'}=\tau/C^{'}_{D}$ is the particle response time that specifies the drag, defined by the expression $C^{'}_{D}=1+0.15\mathrm{Re}_s^{0.687}$ for the non-Stokesian regime [27]. The particle Reynolds number and Stokesian particle response time are defined as $\mathrm{Re}_s=\delta\,|\vec{V}_r|/\nu=\delta\sqrt{u_r^2+v_r^2}/\nu$ and $\tau=\rho_p\delta^2/(18\rho\nu)$, respectively. $\Omega=\omega_s-0.5(\partial v/\partial x-\partial u/\partial r)$ is the angular velocity slip, with ω_s being the angular velocity of the given particle fraction. The coefficient of the Magnus lift force C_M is calculated according to Crowe et al. (1998); ρ and ρ_p are the physical densities of air and the particle material, respectively.

radial linear momentum equation for the gas phase:

$$\frac{\partial}{\partial x}\left(uv-\tilde{\nu}_t\frac{\partial v}{\partial x}\right)+\frac{\partial}{r\partial r}r\left(v^2-\tilde{\nu}_t\frac{\partial v}{\partial r}\right)=-\frac{\partial p}{\rho\partial r}+\frac{\partial}{\partial x}\tilde{\nu}_t\frac{\partial u}{\partial r}+ \\ +\frac{\partial}{r\partial r}r\tilde{\nu}_t\frac{\partial v}{\partial r}-\frac{2\tilde{\nu}_t v}{r^2}-\alpha\left(\frac{v_r}{\tau'}-(C_M\Omega+F_s)u_r\right). \tag{3}$$

F_s is the coefficient for the Saffman lift force, which is due to the local shear of the flow; it is given for finite values of the particle Reynolds numbers by the correction [28].

turbulence kinetic energy equation for the gas phase:

$$\frac{\partial}{\partial x}\left(uk-\tilde{\nu}_t\frac{\partial k}{\partial x}\right)+\frac{\partial}{r\partial r}r\left(vk-\tilde{\nu}_t\frac{\partial k}{\partial r}\right)= \\ =2\nu_t\left\{\left(\frac{\partial u}{\partial x}\right)^2+\left(\frac{\partial rv}{r\partial r}\right)^2+\frac{1}{2}\left(\frac{\partial u}{\partial r}+\frac{\partial v}{\partial x}\right)^2\right\}+\frac{\alpha}{\tau}\left(u_r^2+v_r^2+k_s\right)-\varepsilon_h, \tag{4}$$

where k and k_s are the turbulence kinetic energy of the gas- and particulate phases, respectively. The hybrid dissipation rate ε_h is calculated for the two-phase flow via hybrid turbulence length scale defined as harmonic average of the integral length scale of single-phase flow and inter-particle spacing [14].

continuity equation for the particulate phase:

$$\frac{\partial}{\partial x}\left(\alpha\tilde{u}_s\right)+\frac{\partial}{r\partial r}r\left(\alpha\tilde{v}_s\right)=0, \tag{5}$$

where $\tilde{u}_s$ and $\tilde{v}_s$ are the longitudinal and radial components of the drift particle velocity of the given fraction, given by expressions $\tilde{u}_s=u_s-(D_t+D_c^x)\partial\ln\alpha/\partial x$, $\tilde{v}_s=v_s-(D_t+D_c^r)\partial\ln\alpha/\partial r$. Here D_t is the coefficient of turbulent diffusion of particles, which is calculated by the model

[29]. The pseudoviscosity diffusion coefficients along x and r directions $D_c^{x,r}$ stem from the particle collisions [16].

momentum equation in the longitudinal direction for the particulate phase:

$$\frac{\partial}{\partial x}\left(\alpha u_s \tilde{u}_s\right)+\frac{\partial}{r\partial r}\left(r\alpha u_s \tilde{v}_s\right)=-\frac{\partial}{\partial x}\left(\alpha \overline{u_s'^2}\right)-\frac{\partial}{r\partial r}\left(r\alpha \overline{u_s' v_s'}\right)+\alpha\left[\frac{u_r}{\tau'}+C_M \Omega v_r-g\left(1-\frac{\rho}{\rho_p}\right)\right], \tag{6}$$

where g is the gravitational acceleration.

momentum equation in the radial direction for the particulate phase:

$$\frac{\partial}{\partial x}\left(\alpha v_s \tilde{u}_s\right)+\frac{\partial}{r\partial r}\left(r\alpha v_s \tilde{v}_s\right)=-\frac{\partial}{\partial x}\left(\alpha \overline{u_s' v_s'}\right)-\frac{\partial}{r\partial r}\left(r\alpha \overline{v_s'^2}\right)+\alpha\left[\frac{v_r}{\tau'}-\left(C_M \Omega+F_s\right)u_r\right], \tag{7}$$

where $\overline{u'^2_s}, \overline{u'_s v'_s}, \overline{v'^2_s}$ are the velocity correlations due to particle collisions and induce momentum swap in the longitudinal and radial motions of the given fraction [16].

angular momentum equation in the longitudinal direction for the particulate phase:

$$\frac{\partial}{\partial x}\left(\alpha \omega_s \tilde{u}_s\right)+\frac{\partial}{r\partial r}\left(r\alpha \omega_s \tilde{v}_s\right)=-\frac{\partial}{\partial x}\left(\alpha \overline{u_s' \omega_s'}\right)-\frac{\partial}{r\partial r}\left(r\alpha \overline{v_s' \omega_s'}\right)-\alpha C_\omega \frac{\Omega}{\tau}, \tag{8}$$

where $\overline{u'_s \omega'_s}$ and $\overline{v'_s \omega'_s}$ are the linear-angular velocity correlations of particles due to inter-particle collisions calculated according to [16].

2.2. Boundary conditions for the RANS model

As inlet boundary conditions, it is assumed that particles enter the previously computed, fully developed flow domain of the single-phase flow, having the initial longitudinal velocity determined by the lag coefficient. The equilibrium outlet boundary conditions were set at the exit cross-section $x=100D$, i.e. the non-gradient derivatives from all velocities of all phases, turbulence kinetic energy and mass concentration over longitudinal coordinate were written according to [19]. Since the particulate flow in the vertical pipe is considered as axisymmetrical, the non-gradient boundary conditions were set at the pipe axis for the longitudinal velocity components of gas and particles, the turbulent energy and particle mass concentration. The boundary conditions were set zero at the pipe axis for the radial velocities of both phases and the particle angular velocity. The concept of "wall functions" [30] has been applied to set the boundary conditions at the wall. While applying the balance of the production and dissipation rate of kinetic energy "near the wall" with using the eddy-viscosity concept [31], it can link the friction velocity v_* and shear stress τ_w through the turbulence kinetic energy as

$v_*^2 = \tau_w / \rho = c_\mu^{0.5} k$. The computations near the wall were carried out at the half-width of the control volume off the wall. Then, for the longitudinal velocity of the gas phase and for the turbulence energy computed by means of its production P_k, the following boundary conditions are as follows:

$$\begin{cases} u = \sqrt{\dfrac{\tau_w}{\rho}} \dfrac{1}{æ} \ln(y^+) + C = v_* \dfrac{1}{æ} \ln\left(E \dfrac{y}{\nu} v_*\right) & 11.6 \le y^+ < 500 \\ u = \dfrac{v_*^2 y}{\nu} & y^+ < 11.6 \end{cases}, \quad (9)$$

$$P_k = \frac{2\tau_w^2}{æ \rho c_\mu^{0.25} k^{0.5} y}, \quad (10)$$

where empirical constant $æ = 0.41$; $y = \Delta / 2$ (Δ is the width of the control volume).

The wall boundary conditions for the particulate phase have taken into account the particle's velocity lag determined through particles-wall interaction [19].

2.3. Numerical method

The control volume method was applied to solve mass and momentum equations of both phases by using the implicit lower and upper matrix decomposition method with flux-blending differed-correction and upwind-differencing schemes [31]. Calculations were performed in dimensional form for all flow regimes. The number of the control volumes was varied from 280000 to 1120000, corresponding to the increase in the pipe diameter from D=30.5 mm to D=61 mm, and their size remained constant across the pipe flow.

3. Numerical results

The numerical results presented in the figures have been obtained at a distance of x / D=100 from the pipe entrance. At this distance it was reasonable to stipulate that the steady flow conditions have been reached and there was no influence of the entrance conditions. The results presented here are mainly dimensionless, but some of them are given in dimensional form. 250-, 500 and 750 μm coal particles (physical density $\rho_p = 1600$ kg/m^3) were used in investigations. The flow mass loading was $m^* = 1$ and 10 kg dust/kg air. The applied particles were light enough to respond to turbulent fluctuations of gas.

The Reynolds number Re was assigned as the constant through all calculations and set equal to 4.4×10^4. The pipe diameter D was 30.5, 45.75 and 61 mm for the gas average velocities $\bar{u} = 21.6$, 14.6 and 10.8 m/s, respectively. The average longitudinal velocity and turbulence energy radial distributions calculated for these three regimes are shown in Figures 2 and 3.

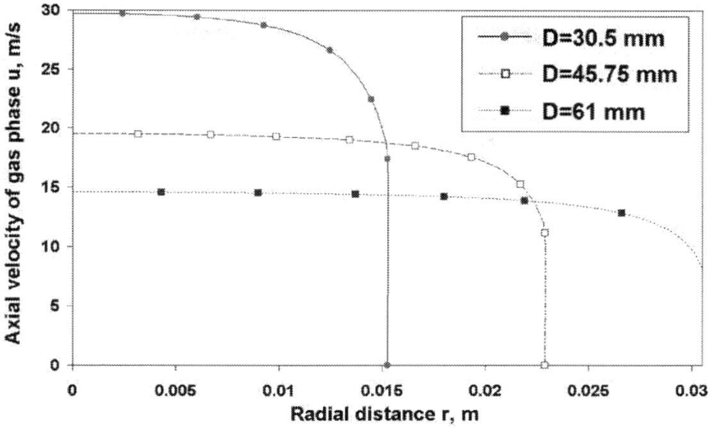

Figure 2. Profiles of the longitudinal gas velocity in the pipes D=30.5, 45.75 and 61 mm, Re=4.4×10^4.

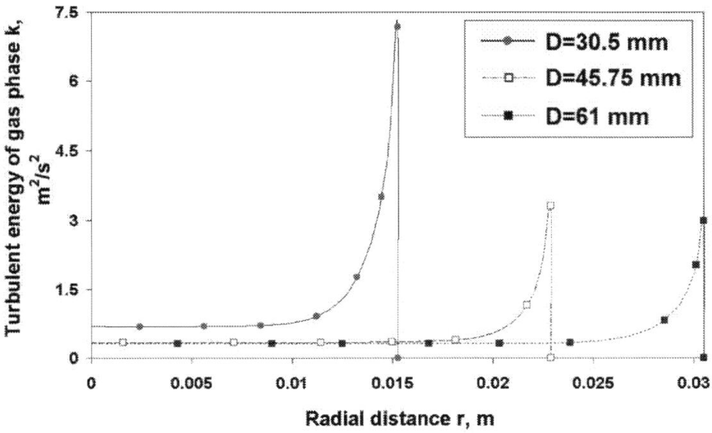

Figure 3. Profiles of the turbulence energy of gas in the pipes D=30.5, 45.75 and 61 mm, Re=4.4×10^4.

The profiles of particles velocity u_s normalized to the longitudinal gas velocity, which was taken place at the pipe axis, and the particles mass concentration α normalized to its magnitude obtained at the pipe axis, are shown in Figure 4 for 250 μm particles at the mass loading of $m^* = 1$. The turbulence modulation TM determined as $TM = (k / k_0 - 1) \times 100\%$, where k and k_0 are the turbulence energy of the gas phase for the particulate flow conditions and the gas flow

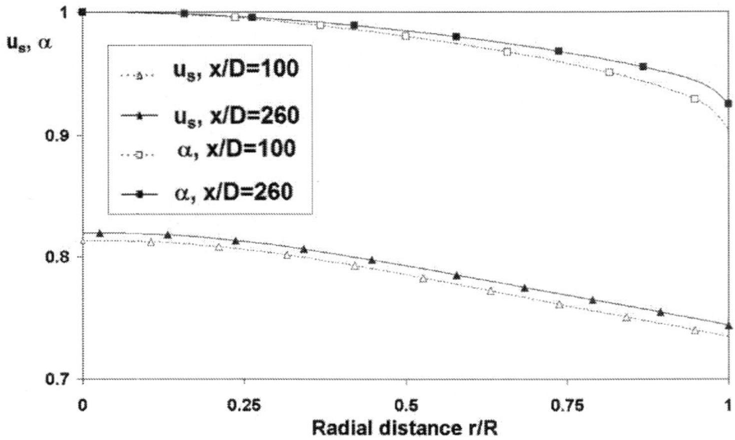

Figure 4. Profiles of the normalized longitudinal velocity of particulate phase and particle mass concentration of 250 μm coal particles in various c-oss-sections x / D, $m^* = 1$, D=30.5 mm,Re=4.4×10^4.

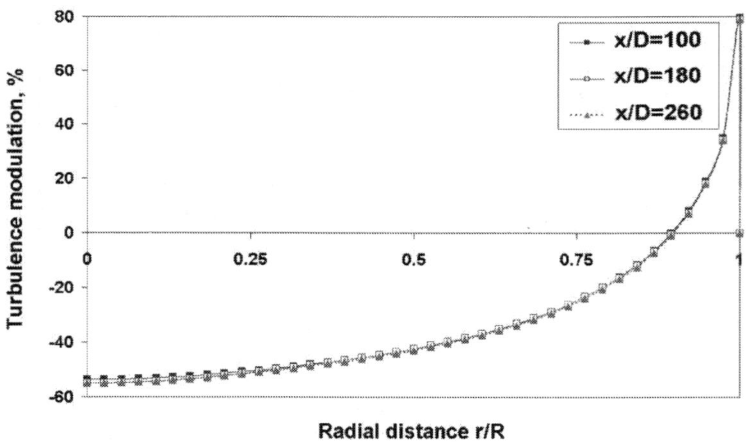

Figure 5. Profiles of the turbulence modulation by 250 μm coal particles in various cross-sections x / D, $m^* = 1$, D =30.5 mm, Re=4.4×10^4.

unladen with particles, respectively, is presented in Figure 5 for various exit cross-sections x / D=100, 180 and 260. Based on the results shown in Figures 4 and 5, one can conclude that for the saving of computation time, the exit cross-section x / D=100 can be considered as the steady-state two-phase pipe flow section.

The following figures show the influence of various force factors on cross-sectional distributions of the velocity lag, particle mass concentration and turbulence modulation originated from the particles. Separately, there were analyzed the effect of the direct (turbulence) and indirect particle-turbulence interaction (no-coupling and coupling) and the inter-particle collisions.

The analysis of behavior of the normalized longitudinal velocity lag is shown in Figure 6 for various force factors for the 250 μm coal particles at $m^* = 1$. Here and below the longitudinal velocity lag is presented as the ratio of the longitudinal velocity slip between the gas and particulate phases to the terminal velocity of particles $(u - u_s)/v_t$, where v_t is the particle terminal velocity. One can see that larger particles have less magnitude of axial velocity lag then those of small particles with noticeable velocity difference. It looks like unexpected result, however, formation of velocity lag is multifold process.

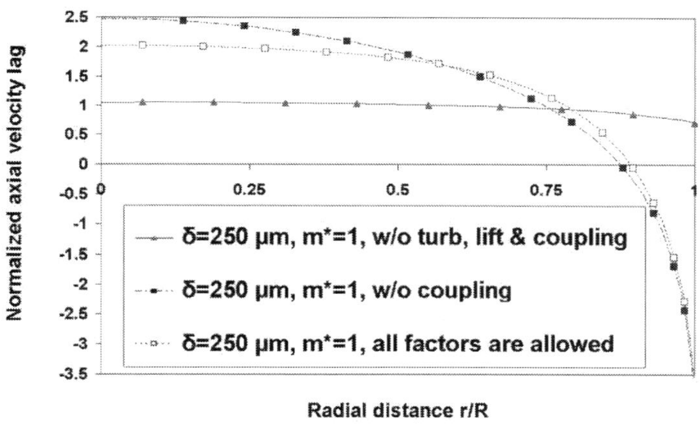

Figure 6. Profiles of the normalized longitudinal velocity lag for 250 μm coal particles obtained for various flow conditions, $m^* = 1$, D=45.75 mm, Re=4.4×10^4.

If the motion of particles is exposed only by the viscous and gravitation forces (without the direct effect of turbulence, lift forces and coupling), the velocity lag between two phases approaches to the particles terminal velocity occurring in the steady-state flow domain, i.e. the ratio u_r / v_t converges to unity (the curve marked by triangles, Figure 6). However, as the numerical simulation shows, if the motion of particles is exposed by various force factors, then the normalized longitudinal velocity lag increases above the particles terminal velocity.

On the face of it, the increase in the particle size should result in increase of absolute value of the velocity lag occurring for the given pipe diameter. However, the more detailed analysis shows that increase of the particles size results in reduce of the normalized longitudinal

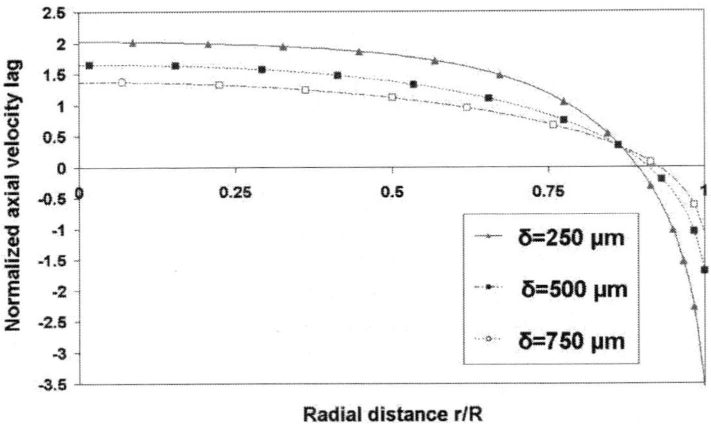

Figure 7. Profiles of the normalized longitudinal velocity lag for 250, 500 and 750 μm coal particles, $m^* = 1$, D=45.75 mm, Re$=4.4 \times 10^4$.

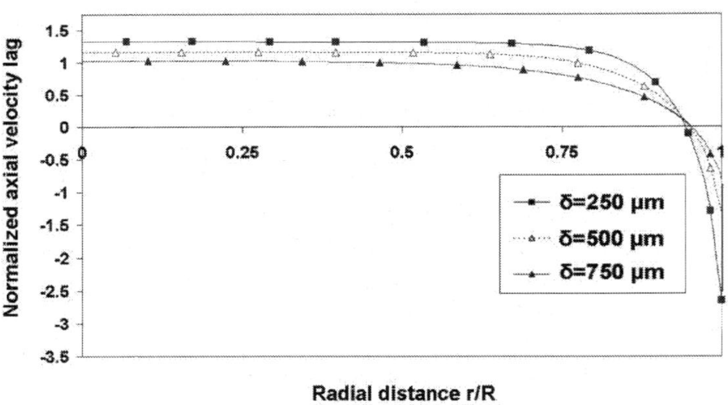

Figure 8. Effect of mass loading on longitudinal velocity lag, $m^* = 10$; the flow conditions are the same as in Figure 7.

velocity lag (Figures 7 and 8). This effect is more pronounced with increase of the flow mass loading (cf. Figures 7 and 8).

Diminishing of the normalized longitudinal velocity lag observed for relatively dense flow at $m^* = 10$ (s. Figure 8) clearly depicts the tendency of the turbulence attenuation by particles, or, in other words, decrease of direct effect of turbulence on the particles motion.

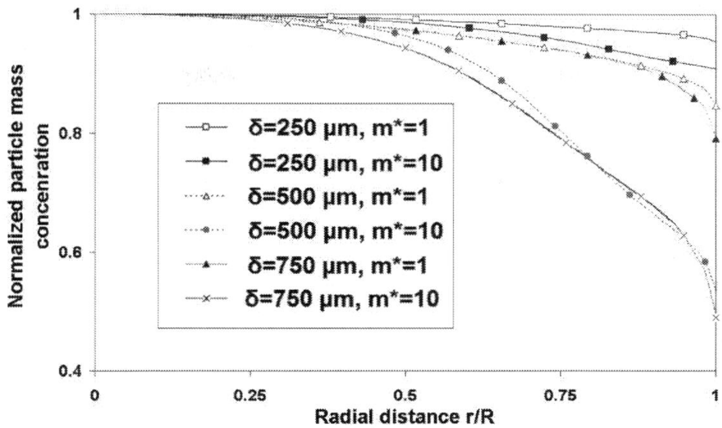

Figure 9. Profiles of the mass concentration of 250, 500 and 750 μm coal particles, $m^* = 1$ and 10, D=45.75 mm, Re=4.4×10^4.

In order to trace the effects of the particles size and mass loading on the turbulence modulation let us first examine the distribution of the particle mass concentration presented in Figure 9. As one can see, the growth of the particle size and flow mass loading makes profiles steeper [16, 32] with more pronounced tendency with respect of the particle size variation. The smaller particles are easier spread out of the pipe flow domain due to the higher value of turbulent diffusion coefficient, and the growth of the mass loading diminishes turbulence and its diffusion aligning process.

Figures 10 and 11 explicitly address to the coupling effect, which was observed for two flow mass loadings $m^* = 1$ (Figure 10) and $m^* = 10$ (Figure 11) for 250, 500 and 750 μm coal particles. Obviously, the higher mass loading leads to the higher rate of the turbulence modulation, i.e. if there was turbulence attenuation occurred for the given particle size, then this process was intensified for the higher mass loading (cf. the corresponding curves plotted for the same particle sizes in Figures 10 and 11).

The next series of plots (Figures 12–18) show the effect of the pipe diameter for the constant Reynolds number on distribution of the normalized velocity lag, the particle mass concentration and the turbulence modulation.

Figures 12, 13 and 14 show the profiles of the normalized longitudinal velocity lag obtained for various pipe diameters for 250, 500 and 750 μm coal particles. One can see that decrease of the pipe diameter results in the higher velocity lag and, as a result, in the stronger particles involvement into the turbulent motion. This fact is proved by the data of Figures 2 and 3 showing that the smaller pipe diameter corresponds to the higher level of the turbulence energy, and, sequentially to the higher rate of the particles involvement by the gas flow.

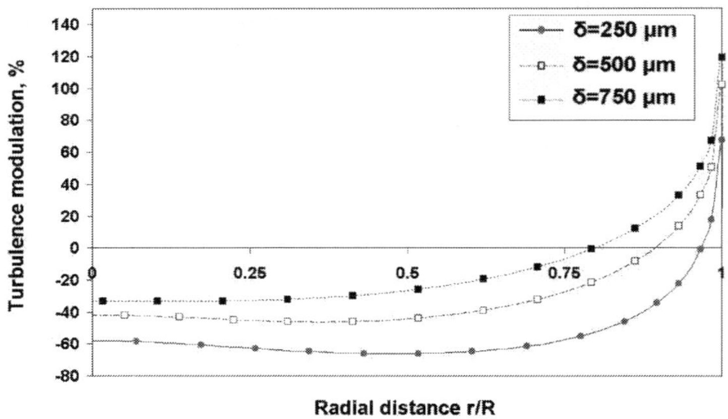

Figure 10. Profiles of the turbulence modulation by 250, 500 and 750 μm coal particles, $m^* = 1$, D=45.75 mm, Re=4.4×10^4.

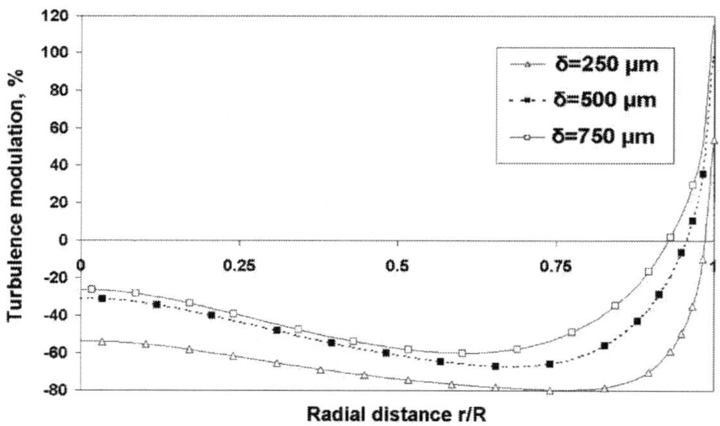

Figure 11. Effect of the mass loading on the turbulence modulation by 250, 500 and 750 μm coal particles, $m^* = 10$, D=45.75 mm, Re=4.4×10^4.

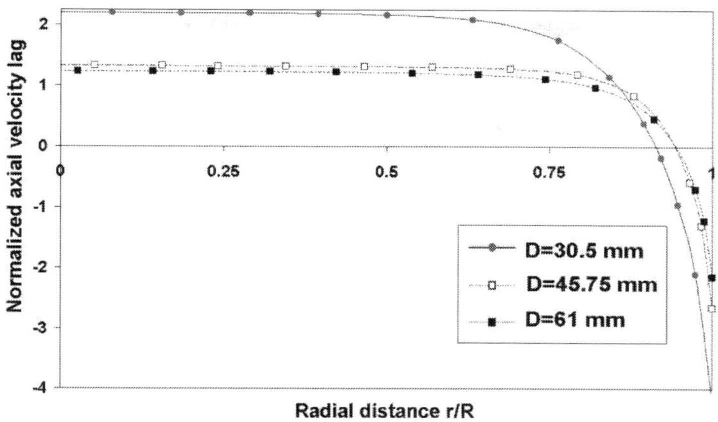

Figure 12. Profiles of the normalized longitudinal velocity lag for 250 μm coal particles in the pipes D=30.5, 45.75 and 61 mm, $m^*=10$, Re=4.4×10^4.

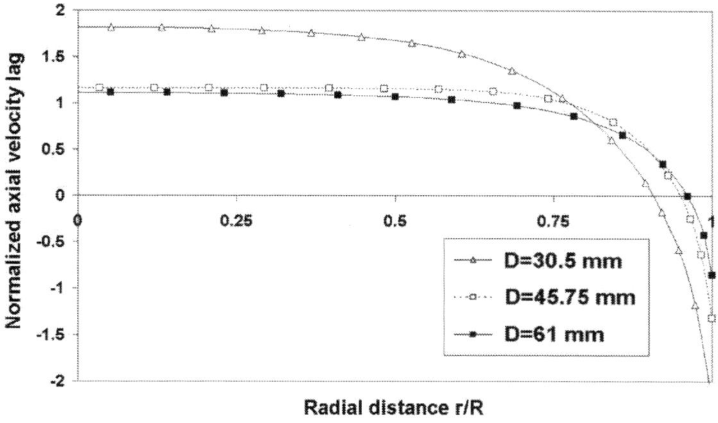

Figure 13. Profiles of the normalized longitudinal velocity lag for 500 μm coal particles in the pipes D=30.5, 45.75 and 61 mm, $m^*=10$, Re=4.4×10^4.

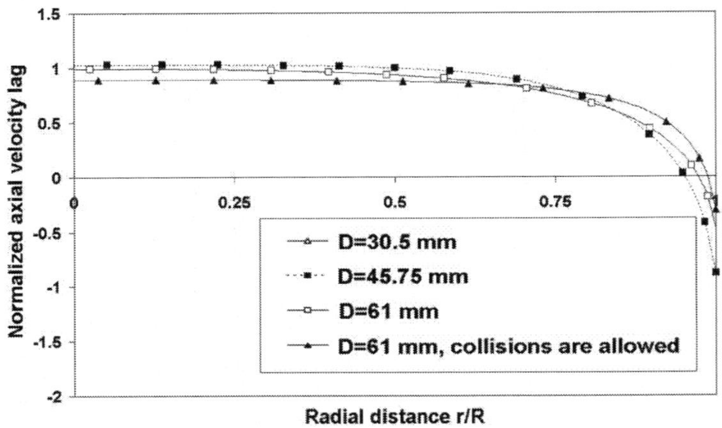

Figure 14. Profiles of the normalized longitudinal velocity lag for 750 μm coal particles in the pipes D=30.5, 45.75 and 61 mm, $m^* = 10$, Re=4.4×10^4.

The effect of the particles collisions that may occur at the higher mass loading of $m^* = 10$ (s. Figure 14) brings this process to slow down the particles motion. Therefore, the particles collisions result in the decrease of the normalized velocity slip as compared with the case of no collisions (cf. Figures 12, 13 and 14).

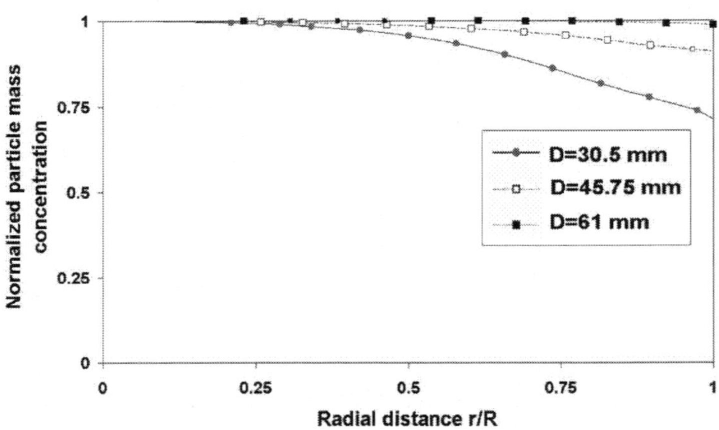

Figure 15. Profiles of the normalized mass concentration for 250 μm coal particles in the pipes D=30.5, 45.75 and 61 mm, $m^* = 10$, Re=4.4×10^4.

One can see that the effect of the pipe diameter has the same tendency as the effect of the particle size, i.e. the increase of the pipe diameter acts like the decrease of the particle size, straightening the profiles of the particle mass concentration (Figures 15 and 16). An accounting of the inter-particle collision effect intensifies the particle dispersion (s. Figure 16).

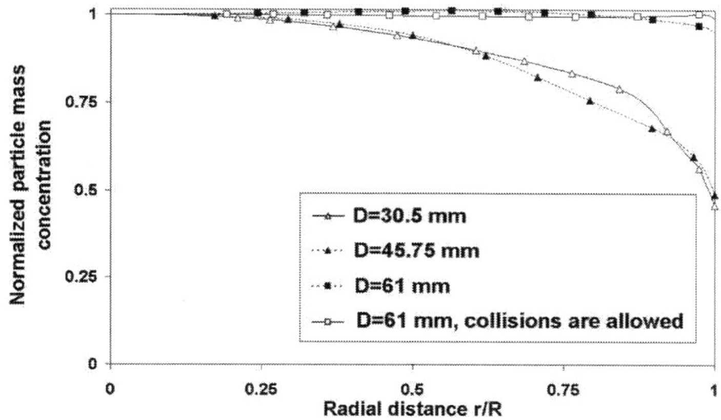

Figure 16. Profile of the normalized mass concentration for 750 μm coal particles in the pipes D=30.5, 45.75 and 61 mm, $m^* = 10$, Re=4.4×10^4.

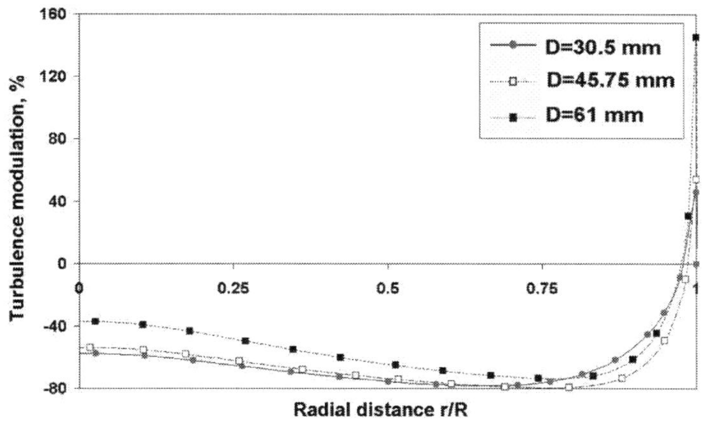

Figure 17. Profiles of the turbulence modulation for 250 μm coal particles in the pipes D=30.5, 45.75 and 61 mm, $m^* = 10$, Re=4.4×10^4.

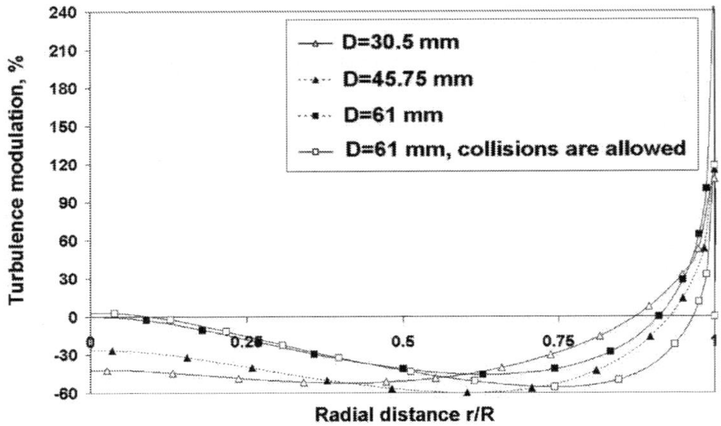

Figure 18. Profiles of the turbulence modulation for 750 μm coal particles in the pipes D=30.5, 45.75 and 61 mm, $m^*=10$, Re=4.4×10^4.

The turbulence modulation is shown in Figures 17 and 18 for the considered particles sizes in two marginal cases: δ=250 and 750 μm. It is evident that the increase of the particle size leads to decrease of the attenuation rate of turbulence. The effect of the inter-particle collisions (Figure 18) results in the enhancement of turbulence by particles in vicinity of the flow axis and its damping, that occurs in the region locating between the flow axis and the pipe wall.

4. Conclusions

2D RANS numerical method fitted with the appropriate closure equations was applied for the computational investigation of the upward turbulent particulate pipe flow at the distance of 100 calibers from the pipe entrance. The axial velocity lag, turbulent kinetic energy of gas and particles mass concentration, effected by the gravity, viscous drag, the particle-turbulence, particle-particle, particle-wall interactions as well as the Saffman and Magnus lift forces, were examined for various particle sizes and flow mass loadings at the same flow Reynolds number.

The obtained numerical results allow to draw the following conclusions pertaining to behavior of solid particles under the conditions of the upward turbulent pipe flow:

1. It is obvious that if the motion of particles is exposed only by the viscous and gravitational forces (without the direct effect of turbulence, lift forces and coupling), the absolute magnitude of the axial velocity lag approaches to the particles terminal velocity. However, simultaneous accounting of all force factors, effecting on the fine particles, results in substantial exceeding of their axial velocity lag as compared with their terminal velocity, that is due to intensification of influence of turbulence on a motion of the fine particles.

2. It was revealed that the effect of the particles size appears as follows:

- the increase of the particles size results in reducing of the relative axial velocity lag. The absolute magnitude of the velocity lag approaches to the particles terminal velocity;
- the fine particles spread more uniformly in the cross-section of the pipe as against the coarse ones, due to their higher coefficient of turbulent diffusion;
- enlargement of the particles size gives the lower rate of the turbulence attenuation.

3. The given investigation shows that the effect of the flow mass loading acts in the following way:

- the increase of the flow mass loading causes the diminution of the relative velocity lag, and this is more pronounced for the fine particles. The same tendency also takes place when considering the inter-particle collisions for the large flow loading;
- the increase of the flow loading results in the turbulence attenuation that is followed by the non-uniform cross-sectional distributions of the particles mass concentration, while the accounting of the inter-particle collisions causes the opposite trend, i.e. their flattening.

4. The effect of the pipe diameter acts in the way that its increase: a) gives rise to decrease of the relative velocity lag, b) results in flattening of the cross-sectional distributions of the particles mass concentration and c) induces the decrease of the turbulence attenuation rate.

Acknowledgements

The work was done within the frame of the target financing under the Project SF0140070s08 (Estonia) and supported by the ETF grant Project ETF9343 (Estonia). The authors are grateful for the technical support of Computational Biology Initiative High Performance Computing Center of University of Texas at San Antonio (USA) and Texas Advanced Computing Center in Austin (USA). This study is related to the activity of the European network action COST MP1106 "Smart and green interfaces - from single bubbles and drops to industrial, environmental and biomedical applications".

Author details

Alexander Kartushinsky*, Ylo Rudi, Igor Shcheglov, Sergei Tisler and Igor Krupenski

*Address all correspondence to: aleksander.kartusinski@ttu.ee

Research Laboratory of Multiphase Media Physics, Faculty of Science, Tallinn University of Technology, Tallinn, Estonia

References

[1] Pfeffer R., Rosetti S., Licklein S. Analysis and Correlation of Heat Transfer Coefficient and Heat Transfer Data for Dilute Gas-Solid Suspensions. NASA Rep. TND–3603, 1966.

[2] Davies J.T. Calculation of critical velocities to maintain solids in suspension in horizontal pipes. Chemical Engineering Science 1987; 42(7) 1667-1670.

[3] Gore R.A., Crowe C.T. Effect of Particle Size on Modulating Turbulent Intensity. International Journal of Multiphase Flow 1989; 15(2) 279-285.

[4] Tsuji, Y. Morikawa, Y. LDV Measurements of an Air-Solid Two-Phase Flow in a Horizontal Pipe. Journal of Fluid Mechanics 1982; 120 385-409.

[5] Michaelides E.E. A Model for the Flow of Solid Particles in Gases. International Journal of Multiphase Flow 1984; 10(1) 61-77.

[6] Tsuji Y., Morikawa Y., Shiomi H. LDV Measurements of an Air-Solid Two-Phase Flow in a Vertical Pipe. Journal of Fluid Mechanics 1984;139 417-434.

[7] Squires K.D., Eaton J. K. Particle Response and Turbulence Modification in Isotropic Turbulence. Physics of Fluids 1990; 2 1191-1203.

[8] Yuan Z., Michaelides E.E. Turbulence Modulation in Particulate Flows - a Theoretical Approach. International Journal of Multiphase Flow 1992; 18(5) 779-785.

[9] Gidaspow D. Multiphase Flow and Fluidization: Continuum and Kinetic Theory Descriptions. Boston: Acad. Press; 1994.

[10] Cabrejos F.J, Klinzing G.E. Pickup and Saltation Mechanisms of Solid Particles in Horizontal Pneumatic Transport. Powder Technology 1994; 79(2) 173-186.

[11] Yarin L.P., Hetsroni G. Turbulence Intensity in Dilute Two-Phase Flows. Parts I, II and III International Journal of Multiphase Flow 1994; 20(1) 1-15.

[12] Cao J, Ahmadi G. Gas-Particle Two-Phase Turbulent Flow in Vertical Duct. International Journal of Multiphase Flow 1995; 21(6) 1203-1228.

[13] Crowe C.T., Gillandt I. Turbulence modulation of fluid-particle flows – a basic approach. In: Proceedings of the 3rd International Conference on Multiphase Flow, 8-12 June 1998, Lyon, France. CD-ROM.

[14] Crowe C. T. On Models for Turbulence Modulation in Fluid-Particle Flows. International Journal of Multiphase Flow 2000; 26(5) 719-727.

[15] Sommerfeld M. Analysis of Collision Effects for Turbulent Gas-Particle Flow in a Horizontal Channel. Part I: Particle Transport. International Journal of Multiphase Flow 2003; 29(4) 675-699.

[16] Kartushinsky A., Michaelides E.E. An analytical approach for the closure equations of gas-solid flows with inter-particle collisions. International Journal of Multiphase Flow 2004; 30(2) 159-180.

[17] Michaelides EE. Particles, Bubbles and Drops – Their Motion, Heat and Mass Transfer. New Jersey: World Scientific Publishers; 2006.

[18] Kartushinsky A.I., Michaelides E.E., Zaichik L.I. Comparison of the RANS and PDF Methods for Air-Particle Flows. International Journal of Multiphase Flow 2009; 35(10) 914-923.

[19] Kartushinsky A.I., Michaelides E.E., Hussainov M., Rudi Y. Effects of the Variation of Mass Loading and Particle Density in Gas-Solid Particle Flow in Pipes. Powder Technology 2009; 193(2) 176-181.

[20] Kartushinsky A.I., Michaelides E.E., Rudi Y.A., Tisler S.V., Shcheglov I.N. Numerical Simulation of Three-Dimensional Gas-Solid Particle Flow in a Horizontal Pipe. American Institute of Chemical Engineers 2011; 57(11) 2977-2988.

[21] Elghobashi S.E., Abou-Arab T.W. A Two-Equation Turbulence Model for Two-Phase Flows. Physics of Fluids 1983; 26(4) 931-938.

[22] Rizk M.A., Elghobashi S.E. A Two-Equation Turbulence Model for Dispersed Dilute Confined Two-Phase Flows. International Journal of Multiphase Flow 1989; 15(1) 119-133.

[23] Simonin O. Eulerian formulation for particle dispersion in turbulent two-phase flows. In: Sommerfeld M, Wennerberg D. (eds.) Proceedings of the 5th Workshop on Two-Phase Flow Predictions, 19-22 March 1990, Erlangen, Germany. Ju◎lich: Forschungszentrum Ju◎lich; 1990.

[24] Deutsch E., Simonin O. Large eddy simulation applied to the motion of particles in stationary homogeneous fluid turbulence. In: Michaelides EE, Fukano T, Serizawa A. (eds.) Proceedings of the 1st ASME/JSME Fluids Engineering Conference, 23-27 June 1991, Portland, USA. New York: American Society of Mechanical Engineers, Series FED; 1991.

[25] Reeks M.W. On the Continuum Equations for Dispersed Particles in Nonuniform Flows. Physics of Fluids A: Fluid Dynamics 1992; 4(6) 1290-1303.

[26] Marchioli C., Giusti A., Salvetti M.-V., Soldati A. Direct Numerical Simulation of Particle Wall Transfer and Deposition in Upward Turbulent Pipe Flow. International Journal of Multiphase Flow 2003; 29(6) 1017-1038.

[27] Schiller L., Naumann A. Über die grundlegenden Berechnungen bei der Schwerkraftaufbereitung. Zeitschrift des Vereines Deutscher Ingenieure 1933; 77(12) 318-320.

[28] Mei R. An Approximate Expression for the Shear Lift Force on a Spherical Particle at Finite Reynolds Number International Journal of Multiphase Flow 1992; 18(1) 145-147.

[29] Zaichik L.I., Alipchenkov V.M. Statistical Models for Predicting Particle Dispersion and Preferential Concentration in Turbulent Flows. International Journal of Heat and Fluid Flow 2005; 26(3) 416-430.

[30] Pope SB. Turbulent Flows. Cambridge – New York: Cambridge University Press; 2008.

[31] Perić M., Scheuerer G. CAST – A Finite Volume Method for Predicting Two-Dimensional Flow and Heat Transfer Phenomena. GRS - Technische Notiz SRR–89–01. 1989.

[32] Kartushinsky A., Michaelides E. E. Particle-Laden Gas Flow in Horizontal Channels with Collision Effects. Powder Technology 2006; 168(2) 89-103.

Chapter 3

RSTM Numerical Simulation of Channel Particulate Flow with Rough Wall

Alexander Kartushinsky, Ylo Rudi,
Medhat Hussainov, Igor Shcheglov, Sergei Tisler,
Igor Krupenski and David Stock

Additional information is available at the end of the chapter

http://dx.doi.org/10.5772/57047

1. Introduction

Turbulent gas-solid particles flows in channels have numerous engineering applications ranging from pneumatic conveying systems to coal gasifiers, chemical reactor design and are one of the most thoroughly investigated subject in the area of the particulate flows. These flows are very complex and influenced by various physical phenomena, such as particle-turbulence and particle-particle interactions, deposition, gravitational and viscous drag forces, particle rotation and lift forces etc.

The mutual effect of particles and a flow turbulence is the subject of numerous theoretical studies during several decades. These studies have reported about the influence of a gas turbulence on particles (one-way coupling) and/or particles on turbulence of a carrier gas flow (the two-way coupling) in case of high flow mass loading (the four-way coupling). The influence of particles on a gas turbulence, which consists in a turbulence attenuation or augmentation depending on the relation between the parameters of gas and particles.

There are different approaches and numerical models that describe the mutual effect of gas turbulence and particles.

The k-ε models, earlier elaborated for the turbulent particulate flows, e.g., [1-5], considered a turbulence attenuation only by the additional terms of the equations of the turbulence kinetic energy and its dissipation rate. The results obtained by these models were validated by the experimental data on the turbulent particulate free-surface flows [6].

Later on, the models [7, 8] considered both the turbulence augmentation and attenuation occurring in the pipe particulate flows depending on the flow mass loading and the Stokes number. Then, these models have been expanded for the free-surface flows. As opposed to the k-ε models, [7, 8] considered both the turbulence augmentation caused by the velocity slip between gas and particles and the turbulence attenuation due to the change of the turbulence macroscale occurred in the particulate flow as compared to the unladen flow. The given approach has been successfully tested for various pipe and channel particulate flows.

Currently, the probability dense function (PDF) approach is widely applied for the numerical modeling of the particulate flows. The PDF models, for example, [9-13] contain more complete differential transport equations, which are written for various velocity correlations and consider both the turbulence augmentation and attenuation due to the particles.

As opposed to the pipe flows, the rectangular and square channel flows, even in case of unladen flows, are considerably anisotropic with respect to the components of the turbulence energy, that is vividly expressed near the channel walls and corners being notable as for the secondary flows. In addition, the presence of particles aggravates such anisotropy. Such flows are studied by the Reynolds stress turbulence models (RSTM), which are based on the transport equations for all components of the Reynolds stress tensor and the turbulence dissipation rate. RSTM approach allows to completely analyze the influence of particles on longitudinal, radial and azimuthal components of the turbulence kinetic energy, including also possible modifications of the cross-correlation velocity moments.

A few studies based on the RSTM approach showed its good performance and capability for simulation of the complicated flows, e.g., [14], as well for the turbulent particulate flows, for example, see [15]. Recently, the nonlinear algebraic Reynolds stress model based on the PDF approach has been proposed in [16] for the gas flow laden with small heavy particles. The original equations written for each component of Reynolds stress were reduced to their general form in terms of the turbulence energy and its dissipation rate with additional effect of the particulate phase. Eventually, the model [16] operated with the k-ε solution and did not allow to analyze the particles effect on each component of the Reynolds stress.

The 3D RSTM model, being presented in this chapter, is intended to apply for a simulation of the downward turbulent particulate flow in channel of the square cross-section (the aspect ratio of 1:6) with rough walls.

In order to approve and validate the developed model, the separate investigations have been carried out. The first study was the simulation of the downward unladen gas flow in channel of the rectangular cross-section with the smooth and rough walls. The second study relates to the downward grid-generated turbulent particulate flow in the same channel with the smooth walls.

The further stage of this study will be the development of the present model for implementation to the particulate channel flow with the rough walls and the initial level of turbulence.

2. Governing equations and numerical method

The present 3D RSTM model is based on the two-way coupling k-L model [8] and applies the 3D RANS equations and the RSTM closure momentum equations.

The sketch of the computational flow domain is shown in Figure 1 for the case of the downward grid-generated turbulent particulate flow in the channel of square cross-section. Here u and u_s are the longitudinal components of velocities of gas and particles, respectively.

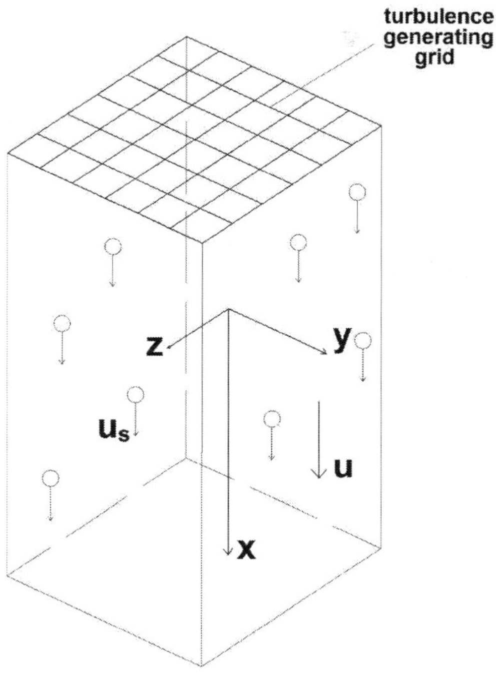

Figure 1. Downward channel grid-generated turbulent particulate flow.

2.1. Governing equations for the Reynolds stress turbulence model

The numerical simulation of the stationary incompressible 3D turbulent particulate flow in the square cross-section channel was performed by the 3D RANS model with applying of the 3D Reynolds stress turbulence model for the closure of the governing equations of gas, while the particulate phase was modeled in a frame of the 3D Euler approach with the equations closed by the two-way coupling model [8] and the eddy-viscosity concept.

The particles were brought into the developed isotropic turbulent flow set-up in channel domain, which has been preliminary computed to obtain the flow velocity field. The system of the momentum and closure equations of the gas phase are identical for the unladen while the particle-laden flows under impact of the viscous drag force. Therefore, here is only presented the system of equations of the gas phase written for the case of the particle-laden flow in the Cartesian coordinates.

3D governing equations for the stationary gas phase of the laden flow are written together with the closure equations as follows:

continuity equation:

$$\frac{\partial u}{\partial x}+\frac{\partial v}{\partial y}+\frac{\partial w}{\partial z}=0, \tag{1}$$

where u, v and w are the axial, transverse and spanwise time-averaged velocity components of the gas phase, respectively.

x-component of the momentum equation:

$$\begin{gathered}\frac{\partial u^2}{\partial x}+\frac{\partial uv}{\partial y}+\frac{\partial uw}{\partial z}=\frac{\partial}{\partial x}\left(2\nu\frac{\partial u}{\partial x}-\overline{u'^2}\right)+\frac{\partial}{\partial y}\left[\nu\left(\frac{\partial u}{\partial y}+\frac{\partial v}{\partial x}\right)-\overline{u'v'}\right]+\\+\frac{\partial}{\partial z}\left[\nu\left(\frac{\partial u}{\partial z}+\frac{\partial w}{\partial x}\right)-\overline{u'w'}\right]-\frac{\partial p}{\rho\partial x}-\alpha C_D'\frac{\left(u-u_s\right)}{\tau_p},\end{gathered} \tag{2}$$

y-component of the momentum equation:

$$\begin{gathered}\frac{\partial uv}{\partial x}+\frac{\partial v^2}{\partial y}+\frac{\partial vw}{\partial z}=\frac{\partial}{\partial x}\left[\nu\left(\frac{\partial u}{\partial y}+\frac{\partial v}{\partial x}\right)-\overline{u'v'}\right]+\frac{\partial}{\partial y}\left(2\nu\frac{\partial v}{\partial y}-\overline{v'^2}\right)+\\+\frac{\partial}{\partial z}\left[\nu\left(\frac{\partial v}{\partial z}+\frac{\partial w}{\partial y}\right)-\overline{v'w'}\right]-\frac{\partial p}{\rho\partial y}-\alpha C_D'\frac{\left(v-v_s\right)}{\tau_p},\end{gathered} \tag{3}$$

z-component of the momentum equation:

$$\begin{gathered}\frac{\partial uw}{\partial x}+\frac{\partial vw}{\partial y}+\frac{\partial w^2}{\partial z}=\frac{\partial}{\partial x}\left[\nu\left(\frac{\partial u}{\partial z}+\frac{\partial w}{\partial x}\right)-\overline{u'w'}\right]+\frac{\partial}{\partial y}\left[\nu\left(\frac{\partial v}{\partial z}+\frac{\partial w}{\partial y}\right)-\overline{v'w'}\right]\\+\frac{\partial}{\partial z}\left(2\nu\frac{\partial w}{\partial z}-\overline{w'^2}\right)-\frac{\partial p}{\rho\partial z}-\alpha C_D'\frac{\left(w-w_s\right)}{\tau_p}\end{gathered} \tag{4}$$

the transport equation of the x-normal component of the Reynolds stress:

$$\begin{aligned}
&\frac{\partial\left(u\overline{u'^2}\right)}{\partial x}+\frac{\partial\left(v\overline{u'^2}\right)}{\partial y}+\frac{\partial\left(w\overline{u'^2}\right)}{\partial z}=\frac{\partial}{\partial x}\left[\left(C_sT\overline{u'^2}+\nu\right)\frac{\partial\overline{u'^2}}{\partial x}+C_sT\left(\overline{u'v'}\frac{\partial\overline{u'^2}}{\partial y}+\overline{u'w'}\frac{\partial\overline{u'^2}}{\partial z}\right)\right]\\
&+\frac{\partial}{\partial y}\left[\left(C_sT\overline{v'^2}+\nu\right)\frac{\partial\overline{u'^2}}{\partial y}+C_sT\left(\overline{u'v'}\frac{\partial\overline{u'^2}}{\partial x}+\overline{v'w'}\frac{\partial\overline{u'^2}}{\partial z}\right)\right]\\
&\frac{\partial}{\partial z}\left[\left(C_sT\overline{w'^2}+\nu\right)\frac{\partial\overline{u'^2}}{\partial z}+C_sT\left(\overline{u'w'}\frac{\partial\overline{u'^2}}{\partial x}+\overline{v'w'}\frac{\partial\overline{u'^2}}{\partial y}\right)\right]+P_{uu}+R_{uu}+\alpha C'_D\frac{\left(u-u_s\right)^2}{\tau_p}-\varepsilon_h
\end{aligned}\tag{5}$$

the transport equation of the y-normal component of the Reynolds stress:

$$\begin{aligned}
&\frac{\partial\left(u\overline{v'^2}\right)}{\partial x}+\frac{\partial\left(v\overline{v'^2}\right)}{\partial y}+\frac{\partial\left(w\overline{v'^2}\right)}{\partial z}=\frac{\partial}{\partial x}\left[\left(C_sT\overline{u'^2}+\nu\right)\frac{\partial\overline{v'^2}}{\partial x}+C_sT\left(\overline{u'v'}\frac{\partial\overline{v'^2}}{\partial y}+\overline{u'w'}\frac{\partial\overline{v'^2}}{\partial z}\right)\right]\\
&+\frac{\partial}{\partial y}\left[\left(C_sT\overline{v'^2}+\nu\right)\frac{\partial\overline{v'^2}}{\partial y}+C_sT\left(\overline{u'v'}\frac{\partial\overline{v'^2}}{\partial x}+\overline{v'w'}\frac{\partial\overline{v'^2}}{\partial z}\right)\right]+\\
&+\frac{\partial}{\partial z}\left[\left(C_sT\overline{w'^2}+\nu\right)\frac{\partial\overline{v'^2}}{\partial z}+C_sT\left(\overline{u'w'}\frac{\partial\overline{v'^2}}{\partial x}+\overline{v'w'}\frac{\partial\overline{v'^2}}{\partial y}\right)\right]\\
&+P_{vv}+R_{vv}+\alpha C'_D\frac{\left(v-v_s\right)^2}{\tau_p}-\varepsilon_h
\end{aligned}\tag{6}$$

the transport equation of the z-normal component of the Reynolds stress:

$$\begin{aligned}
&\frac{\partial\left(u\overline{w'^2}\right)}{\partial x}+\frac{\partial\left(v\overline{w'^2}\right)}{\partial y}+\frac{\partial\left(w\overline{w'^2}\right)}{\partial z}=\frac{\partial}{\partial x}\left[\left(C_sT\overline{u'^2}+\nu\right)\frac{\partial\overline{w'^2}}{\partial x}+C_sT\left(\overline{u'v'}\frac{\partial\overline{w'^2}}{\partial y}+\overline{u'w'}\frac{\partial\overline{w^2}}{\partial z}\right)\right]\\
&+\frac{\partial}{\partial y}\left[\left(C_sT\overline{v'^2}+\nu\right)\frac{\partial\overline{w'^2}}{\partial y}+C_sT\left(\overline{u'v'}\frac{\partial\overline{w'^2}}{\partial x}+\overline{v'w'}\frac{\partial\overline{w'^2}}{\partial z}\right)\right]\\
&+\frac{\partial}{\partial z}\left[\left(C_sT\overline{w'^2}+\nu\right)\frac{\partial\overline{w'^2}}{\partial z}+C_sT\left(\overline{u'w'}\frac{\partial\overline{w'^2}}{\partial x}+\overline{v'w'}\frac{\partial\overline{w'^2}}{\partial y}\right)\right]+P_{ww}+R_{ww}+\alpha C'_D\frac{\left(w-w_s\right)^2}{\tau_p}-\varepsilon_h
\end{aligned}\tag{7}$$

the transport equation of the xy shear stress component of the Reynolds stress:

$$\begin{aligned}
&\frac{\partial\left(u\overline{u'v'}\right)}{\partial x}+\frac{\partial\left(v\overline{u'v'}\right)}{\partial y}+\frac{\partial\left(w\overline{u'v'}\right)}{\partial z}= \\
&=\frac{\partial}{\partial x}\left[\left(C_sT\overline{u'^2}+\nu\right)\frac{\partial\overline{u'v'}}{\partial x}+C_sT\left(\overline{u'v'}\frac{\partial\overline{u'v'}}{\partial y}+\overline{u'w'}\frac{\partial\overline{u'v'}}{\partial z}\right)\right]+\frac{\partial}{\partial y}\left[\left(C_sT\overline{v'^2}+\nu\right)\frac{\partial\overline{u'v'}}{\partial y},\right. \\
&\left.+C_sT\left(\overline{u'v'}\frac{\partial\overline{u'v'}}{\partial x}+\overline{v'w'}\frac{\partial\overline{u'v'}}{\partial z}\right)\right]+\frac{\partial}{\partial z}\left[\left(C_sT\overline{w'^2}+\nu\right)\frac{\partial\overline{u'v'}}{\partial z}+C_sT\left(\overline{u'w'}\frac{\partial\overline{u'v'}}{\partial x}+\overline{v'w'}\frac{\partial\overline{u'v'}}{\partial y}\right)\right]+ \\
&+P_{uv}+R_{uv}
\end{aligned} \tag{8}$$

the transport equation of the xz shear stress component of the Reynolds stress:

$$\begin{aligned}
&\frac{\partial\left(u\overline{u'w'}\right)}{\partial x}+\frac{\partial\left(v\overline{u'w'}\right)}{\partial y}+\frac{\partial\left(w\overline{u'w'}\right)}{\partial z}=\frac{\partial}{\partial x}\left[\left(C_sT\overline{u'^2}+\nu\right)\frac{\partial\overline{u'w'}}{\partial x}+C_sT\left(\overline{u'v'}\frac{\partial\overline{u'w'}}{\partial y}+\overline{u'w'}\frac{\partial\overline{u'w'}}{\partial z}\right)\right] \\
&+\frac{\partial}{\partial y}\left[\left(C_sT\overline{v'^2}+\nu\right)\frac{\partial\overline{u'w'}}{\partial y}+C_sT\left(\overline{u'v'}\frac{\partial\overline{u'w'}}{\partial x}+\overline{v'w'}\frac{\partial\overline{u'w'}}{\partial z}\right)\right] \\
&+\frac{\partial}{\partial z}\left[\left(C_sT\overline{w'^2}+\nu\right)\frac{\partial\overline{u'w'}}{\partial z}+C_sT\left(\overline{u'w'}\frac{\partial\overline{u'w'}}{\partial x}+\overline{v'w'}\frac{\partial\overline{u'w'}}{\partial y}\right)\right]+P_{uw}+R_{uw}
\end{aligned} \tag{9}$$

the transport equation of the yz shear stress component of the Reynolds stress:

$$\begin{aligned}
&\frac{\partial\left(u\overline{v'w'}\right)}{\partial x}+\frac{\partial\left(v\overline{v'w'}\right)}{\partial y}+\frac{\partial\left(w\overline{v'w'}\right)}{\partial z} \\
&=\frac{\partial}{\partial x}\left[\left(C_sT\overline{u'^2}+\nu\right)\frac{\partial\overline{v'w'}}{\partial x}+C_sT\left(\overline{u'v'}\frac{\partial\overline{v'w'}}{\partial y}+\overline{u'w'}\frac{\partial\overline{v'w'}}{\partial z}\right)\right]+\frac{\partial}{\partial y}\left[\left(C_sT\overline{v'^2}+\nu\right)\frac{\partial\overline{v'w'}}{\partial y}\right. \\
&\left.+C_sT\left(\overline{u'v'}\frac{\partial\overline{v'w'}}{\partial x}+\overline{v'w'}\frac{\partial\overline{v'w'}}{\partial z}\right)\right]+\frac{\partial}{\partial z}\left[\left(C_sT\overline{w'^2}+\nu\right)\frac{\partial\overline{v'w'}}{\partial z}+C_sT\left(\overline{u'w'}\frac{\partial\overline{v'w'}}{\partial x}+\overline{v'w'}\frac{\partial\overline{v'w'}}{\partial y}\right)\right] \\
&+P_{vw}+R_{vw}
\end{aligned} \tag{10}$$

the transport equation of the dissipation rate of the turbulence kinetic energy:

$$\frac{\partial u_0\varepsilon_0}{\partial x}+\frac{\partial v_0\varepsilon_0}{\partial y}+\frac{\partial w_0\varepsilon_0}{\partial z}=\frac{\partial}{\partial x}\left[\left(C_\varepsilon T_0\overline{u_0'^2}+\nu\right)\frac{\partial\varepsilon_0}{\partial x}+C_\varepsilon T_0\left(\overline{u_0'v_0'}\frac{\partial\varepsilon_0}{\partial y}+\overline{u_0'w_0'}\frac{\partial\varepsilon_0}{\partial z}\right)\right]$$
$$+\frac{\partial}{\partial y}\left[\left(C_\varepsilon T_0\overline{v_0'^2}+\nu\right)\frac{\partial\varepsilon_0}{\partial y}+C_\varepsilon T_0\left(\overline{u_0'v_0'}\frac{\partial\varepsilon_0}{\partial x}+\overline{v_0'w_0'}\frac{\partial\varepsilon_0}{\partial z}\right)\right]+\frac{\partial}{\partial z}\left[\left(C_\varepsilon T_0\overline{w_0'^2}+\nu\right)\frac{\partial\varepsilon_0}{\partial z}\right.\qquad(11)$$
$$\left.+C_\varepsilon T_0\left(\overline{u_0'w_0'}\frac{\partial\varepsilon_0}{\partial x}+\overline{v_0'w_0'}\frac{\partial\varepsilon_0}{\partial y}\right)\right]+C_{\varepsilon1}\frac{P\varepsilon_0}{k_0}-C_{\varepsilon2}\frac{\varepsilon_0^2}{k_0}$$

The given system of the transport equations (Eqs. 1 – 11) is based on the model [17] with applying of the numerical constants taken from [18]: C_R=1.8, C_2=0.6, C_s=0.22, C_ε=0.18, $C_{\varepsilon1}$=1.44, $C_{\varepsilon2}$=1.92. Here $T_0=\frac{k_0}{\varepsilon_0}$ and $T=\frac{k}{\varepsilon}$ are the turbulence integral time scales for the unladen and particle-laden flows, respectively. $k=0.5\left(\overline{u'^2}+\overline{v'^2}+\overline{w'^2}\right)$ and $k_0=0.5\left(\overline{u'^2_0}+\overline{v'^2_0}+\overline{w'^2_0}\right)$ are the turbulence kinetic energy of gas in the particle-laden and in the unladen flows, respectively; ε and ε_0 are the dissipation rates of the turbulence kinetic energy in the particle-laden and unladen flows, respectively; τ_p is the Stokesian particle response time, $\tau_p=\frac{\rho_p\delta^2}{18\rho\nu}$; ν is the gas viscosity; $(u-u_s)$, $(v-v_s)$ and $(w-w_s)$ are the components of the slip velocity.

The additional terms of Eqs. (2 – 7) pertain to presence of particles in the flow and contain the particle mass concentration α. The influence of particles on gas is considered by the aerodynamic drag force in the momentum equations (the last term of the right-hand sides of Eqs. 2 – 4), and by the turbulence generation and attenuation effects contained in the transport equations of components of the Reynolds stress (the penultimate and last terms of the right-hand sides of Eqs. (5 – 7), respectively). The given model applies the two-way coupling approach [8], where the turbulence generation terms are proportional to the squared slip velocity, and the turbulence attenuation terms are expressed via the hybrid length scale L_h and the hybrid dissipation rate ε_h of the particle-laden flow, where L_h is calculated as the harmonic average of the integral length scale of the unladen flow L_0 and the interparticle distance λ. Here $\lambda=\delta\left(\sqrt[3]{\pi\rho_p/6\rho\alpha}-1\right)$, $L_0=\frac{k_0^{3/2}}{\varepsilon_0}$, $L_h=\frac{2L_0\lambda}{L_0+\lambda}$, $\varepsilon_h=\frac{k^{3/2}}{L_h}$. The particles influence on the shear Reynolds stress components is considered in Eqs. (8 – 10) indirectly via the averaged velocity flow field (u, v, w).

The production terms P are determined according to [18] as follows:

$$P_{uu}=-2\left(\overline{u'^2}\frac{\partial u}{\partial x}+\overline{u'v'}\frac{\partial u}{\partial y}+\overline{u'w'}\frac{\partial u}{\partial z}\right),\qquad(12)$$

$$P_{vv} = -2\left(\overline{u'v'}\frac{\partial v}{\partial x} + \overline{v'^2}\frac{\partial v}{\partial y} + \overline{v'w'}\frac{\partial v}{\partial z}\right), \tag{13}$$

$$P_{ww} = -2\left(\overline{u'w'}\frac{\partial w}{\partial x} + \overline{v'w'}\frac{\partial w}{\partial y} + \overline{w'^2}\frac{\partial w}{\partial z}\right), \tag{14}$$

$$P_{uv} = -\left(\overline{u'^2}\frac{\partial v}{\partial x} + \overline{u'v'}\frac{\partial v}{\partial y} + \overline{u'w'}\frac{\partial v}{\partial z} + \overline{u'v'}\frac{\partial u}{\partial x} + \overline{v'^2}\frac{\partial u}{\partial y} + \overline{v'w'}\frac{\partial u}{\partial z}\right), \tag{15}$$

$$P_{uw} = -\left(\overline{u'^2}\frac{\partial w}{\partial x} + \overline{u'v'}\frac{\partial w}{\partial y} + \overline{u'w'}\frac{\partial w}{\partial z} + \overline{u'w'}\frac{\partial u}{\partial x} + \overline{v'w'}\frac{\partial u}{\partial y} + \overline{w'^2}\frac{\partial u}{\partial z}\right), \tag{16}$$

$$P_{vw} = -\left(\overline{u'v'}\frac{\partial w}{\partial x} + \overline{v'^2}\frac{\partial w}{\partial y} + \overline{v'w'}\frac{\partial w}{\partial z} + \overline{u'w'}\frac{\partial v}{\partial x} + \overline{v'w'}\frac{\partial v}{\partial y} + \overline{w'^2}\frac{\partial v}{\partial z}\right), \tag{17}$$

$$\begin{aligned} P = \frac{1}{2}\left(P_{uu} + P_{vv} + P_{ww}\right) = {} & \overline{u'^2}\frac{\partial u}{\partial x} + \overline{u'v'}\frac{\partial u}{\partial y} + \overline{u'w'}\frac{\partial u}{\partial z} + \overline{u'v'}\frac{\partial v}{\partial x} + \overline{v'^2}\frac{\partial v}{\partial y} + \overline{v'w'}\frac{\partial v}{\partial z} \\ & + \overline{u'w'}\frac{\partial w}{\partial x} + \overline{v'w'}\frac{\partial w}{\partial y} + \overline{w'^2}\frac{\partial w}{\partial z} \end{aligned} \tag{18}$$

The diffusive or second order partial differentiation over Cartesian coordinates, i.e. the first three terms in Eqs. (5 – 11) are given, e.g. in [18]. The anisotropy terms R of the normal and shear components of the Reynolds stress $\overline{u'^2}, \overline{v'^2}, \overline{w'^2}, \overline{u'v'}, \overline{u'w'}, \overline{v'w'}$, are defined by various pressure-rate-of-strain models of the isotropic turbulence written in terms of variation of constants C_R and C_2 [18] as follows:

$$R_{uu} = -\frac{(C_R - 1)}{T}\left(\overline{u'^2} - \frac{2}{3}k\right) - C_2\left(P_{uu} - \frac{2}{3}P\right), \tag{19}$$

$$R_{vv} = -\frac{(C_R - 1)}{T}\left(\overline{v'^2} - \frac{2}{3}k\right) - C_2\left(P_{vv} - \frac{2}{3}P\right), \tag{20}$$

$$R_{ww} = -\frac{(C_R - 1)}{T}\left(\overline{w'^2} - \frac{2}{3}k\right) - C_2\left(P_{ww} - \frac{2}{3}P\right), \tag{21}$$

http://dx.doi.org/10.5772/57047

$$R_{uv} = -\frac{\left(C_R - 1\right)\overline{u'v'}}{T} - C_2 P_{uv}, \tag{22}$$

$$R_{uw} = -\frac{\left(C_R - 1\right)\overline{u'w'}}{T} - C_2 P_{uw}, \tag{23}$$

$$R_{vw} = -\frac{\left(C_R - 1\right)\overline{v'w'}}{T} - C_2 P_{vw}. \tag{24}$$

The relative friction coefficient C'_D is expressed as $C'_D = 1 + 0.15\mathrm{Re}_s^{0.687}$ for the non-Stokesian streamlining of particle. The particle Reynolds number Re_s is calculated according to [19] as $\mathrm{Re}_s = \delta\sqrt{(u-u_s)^2 + (v-v_s)^2 + (w-w_s)^2} / \nu$.

3D governing equations for the particulate phase are written as follows:

the particle mass conservation equation:

$$\frac{\partial\left(\alpha u_s\right)}{\partial x} + \frac{\partial\left(\alpha v_s\right)}{\partial y} + \frac{\partial\left(\alpha w_s\right)}{\partial z} = \frac{\partial}{\partial x} D_s \frac{\partial \alpha}{\partial x} + \frac{\partial}{\partial y} D_s \frac{\partial \alpha}{\partial y} + \frac{\partial}{\partial z} D_s \frac{\partial \alpha}{\partial z}, \tag{25}$$

x-component of the momentum equation:

$$\begin{aligned} &\frac{\partial\left(\alpha u_s v_s\right)}{\partial x} + \frac{\partial\left(\alpha v_s^2\right)}{\partial y} + \frac{\partial\left(\alpha v_s w_s\right)}{\partial z} = \frac{\partial}{\partial x}\left[\alpha \nu_s \left(\frac{\partial u_s}{\partial y} + \frac{\partial v_s}{\partial x}\right)\right] + \frac{\partial}{\partial y}\alpha\left(2\nu_s \frac{\partial v_s}{\partial y} - \frac{2}{3}k_s\right) \\ &+ \frac{\partial}{\partial z}\left[\alpha \nu_s \left(\frac{\partial v_s}{\partial z} + \frac{\partial w_s}{\partial y}\right)\right] + \alpha C'_D \frac{\left(v - v_s\right)}{\tau_p} - \alpha g\left(1 - \frac{\rho}{\rho_p}\right) \end{aligned} \tag{26}$$

y-component of the momentum equation:

$$\begin{aligned} &\frac{\partial\left(\alpha u_s v_s\right)}{\partial x} + \frac{\partial\left(\alpha v_s^2\right)}{\partial y} + \frac{\partial\left(\alpha v_s w_s\right)}{\partial z} = \frac{\partial}{\partial x}\left[\alpha \nu_s \left(\frac{\partial u_s}{\partial y} + \frac{\partial v_s}{\partial x}\right)\right] + \frac{\partial}{\partial y}\varepsilon\left(2\nu_s \frac{\partial v_s}{\partial y} - \frac{2}{3}k_s\right) \\ &+ \frac{\partial}{\partial z}\left[\alpha \nu_s \left(\frac{\partial v_s}{\partial z} + \frac{\partial w_s}{\partial y}\right)\right] + \alpha C'_D \frac{\left(v - v_s\right)}{\tau_p}, \end{aligned} \tag{27}$$

z-component of the momentum equation:

$$\frac{\partial(\alpha u_s w_s)}{\partial x}+\frac{\partial(\alpha v_s w_s)}{\partial y}+\frac{\partial(\alpha w_s^2)}{\partial z}=\frac{\partial}{\partial x}\left[\alpha \nu_s\left(\frac{\partial u_s}{\partial z}+\frac{\partial w_s}{\partial x}\right)\right]+\frac{\partial}{\partial y}\left[\alpha \nu_s\left(\frac{\partial v_s}{\partial z}+\frac{\partial w_s}{\partial y}\right)\right]$$
$$+\frac{\partial}{\partial z}\alpha\left(2\nu_s\frac{\partial w_s}{\partial z}-\frac{2}{3}k_s\right)+\alpha C_D'\frac{(w-w_s)}{\tau_p}. \tag{28}$$

The closure model for the transport equations of the particulate phase was applied to the PDF model [20], where the turbulent kinetic energy of dispersed phase, the coefficients of the turbulent viscosity and turbulent diffusion of the particulate phase are determined as follows, respectively:

$$k_s=\left[1-\exp\left(-\frac{T_0}{\tau_p'}\right)\right]k,\quad \nu_s=\left(\nu_t+\frac{\tau_p' k}{3}\right)\left[1-\exp\left(-\frac{T_0}{\tau_p'}\right)\right],\quad D_s=\frac{2k}{3}\left(1+\frac{T_0}{\tau}\right)\left[1-\exp\left(-\frac{T_0}{\tau}\right)\right],$$
$$\nu_s=\left(\nu_t+\frac{\tau_p' k}{3}\right)\left[1-\exp\left(-\frac{T_0}{\tau_p'}\right)\right], \tag{29}$$

where ν_t is the turbulent viscosity, $\nu_t=0.09\frac{k_0^2}{\varepsilon_0}$ and $\tau'_p=\tau_p/C'_D$ is the particle response time with respect of correction of the particles motion to the non-Stokesian regime.

2.2. Boundary conditions for the Reynolds stress turbulence model

The grid-generated turbulent flow is vertical, and it is symmetrical with respect to the vertical axis for both y-and z-directions. Therefore, the symmetry conditions are set at the flow axis, and the wall conditions are set at the wall. In case of the rough and smooth walls the flow was asymmetrical over the y-direction and symmetrical over the z-direction.

The axisymmetric conditions are written as follows:

for z=0:

$$\frac{\partial u}{\partial z}=\frac{\partial \overline{u'^2}}{\partial z}=\frac{\partial \overline{v'^2}}{\partial z}=\frac{\partial \overline{w'^2}}{\partial z}=\frac{\partial \varepsilon}{\partial z}=\frac{\partial u_s}{\partial z}=\frac{\partial \alpha}{\partial z}=v=w=\overline{u'v'}=\overline{u'w'}=\overline{v'w'}=v_s=w_s=0; \tag{30}$$

for $z=0.5h$:

$$u^+=\frac{u}{v_*}=\begin{cases} z^+ \\ \frac{1}{æ}\ln z^+ + B_1 \end{cases}. \tag{31}$$

The wall conditions are written as follows:

for $y = 0.5h$ (smooth wall):

$$u^{+} = \frac{u}{v_{*}} = \begin{cases} y^{+} \\ \frac{1}{æ}\ln y^{+} + B_{1} \end{cases}, \tag{32}$$

for $y = -0.5h$ (rough wall):

$$u^{+} = \frac{u}{v_{*}} = \frac{1}{æ}\ln\frac{4\Delta y}{s} + B_{2};\ v = w = 0 \tag{33}$$

where h is the channel width; v_{*} is the friction velocity of gas; æ is von Karman's constant, æ =0.41; the wall coordinates y^{+} and z^{+} correspond to the transverse and spanwise directions, respectively; s is a roughness height. The friction velocity of gas v_{*} is determined according to [21] as $v_{*}=(c_{\mu}/2)^{0.25}\sqrt{k}$, where c_{μ} is the numerical constant of the k-ε model, c_{μ}=0.09; B_1=5.2 for the smooth wall and B_2=8.5 for the rough wall; Δy is the grid step of the control volume.

For the normal and shear stresses and dissipation rate of the unladen flow calculated at the wall, the boundary conditions are set based on the "wall-function" according to [18] with the following relationships for the production and dissipation terms:

for $y = 0.5h$:

$$P_{uu} = -\overline{u'v'}\frac{\partial u}{\partial y},\ P_{vv} = P_{ww} = P_{uv} = P_{uw} = P_{vw} = 0, \tag{34}$$

$$\varepsilon = \frac{2c_{\mu}^{0.75}k^{1.5}}{æ\Delta y}, \tag{35}$$

for $z = 0.5h$:

$$P_{uu} = -\overline{u'w'}\frac{\partial u}{\partial z},\ P_{vv} = P_{ww} = P_{uv} = P_{uw} = P_{vw} = 0, \tag{36}$$

$$\varepsilon = \frac{2c_{\mu}^{0.75}k^{1.5}}{æ\Delta z}. \tag{37}$$

The boundary conditions for the particulate phase are set at the wall as follows:

for $y = 0.5h$:

$$\frac{\partial u_s}{\partial y} = -\lambda u_s, \ \frac{\partial w_s}{\partial y} = -\lambda w_s, \ \frac{\partial \alpha}{\partial y} = D_s \alpha, \ v_s = 0, \tag{38}$$

for $z = 0.5h$:

$$\frac{\partial u_s}{\partial z} = -\lambda u_s; \ \frac{\partial v_s}{\partial z} = -\lambda v_s, \ \frac{\partial \alpha}{\partial z} = D_s \alpha \quad w_s = 0; \tag{39}$$

At the exit of the channel the following boundary conditions are set:

$$\begin{aligned} &\frac{\partial u}{\partial x} = \frac{\partial v}{\partial x} = \frac{\partial w}{\partial x} = \frac{\partial \overline{u'^2}}{\partial x} = \frac{\partial \overline{v'^2}}{\partial x} = \frac{\partial \overline{w'^2}}{\partial x} = \frac{\partial \overline{u'v'}}{\partial x} = \\ &= \frac{\partial \overline{u'w'}}{\partial x} = \frac{\partial \overline{v'w'}}{\partial x} = \frac{\partial \varepsilon}{\partial x} = \frac{\partial u_s}{\partial x} = \frac{\partial v_s}{\partial x} = \frac{\partial w_s}{\partial x} = \frac{\partial \alpha}{\partial x} = 0. \end{aligned} \tag{40}$$

Additionally, the initial boundary conditions are set for three specific cases:

1. the low level of the initial intensity of turbulence that usually occurs at the axis of the channel turbulent flow;

2. the high level of the initial turbulence generated by two different grids:

a. small grid of the mesh size *M*=4.8 mm;

b. large grid with mesh size of *M*=10 mm.

2.3. Numerical method

The control volume method was applied to solve the 3D partial differential equations written for the unladen flow (Eqs. 1 – 11) and the particulate phase (Eqs. 26 – 29), respectively, with taking into account the boundary conditions (Eqs. 30 – 40). The governing equations were solved using the implicit lower and upper (ILU) matrix decomposition method with the flux-blending differed-correction and upwind-differencing schemes [21]. This method is utilized for the calculations of the particulate turbulent flows in channels of the rectangular and square cross-sections. The calculations were performed in the dimensional form for all the flow conditions. The number of the control volumes was 1120000.

3. Numerical results

The validation of the present model took place in two stages.

In case of the unladen flow, the model was validated by comparison of the kinetic (normal) components of stresses with the experimental data [22] obtained for the specially constructed horizontal turbulent gas flow in the channel of rectangular cross-section (the aspect ratio of 1:6) of 54 mm width with the smooth and rough walls for the flow Reynolds number *Re*=56000 and the roughness height of 3.18 mm.

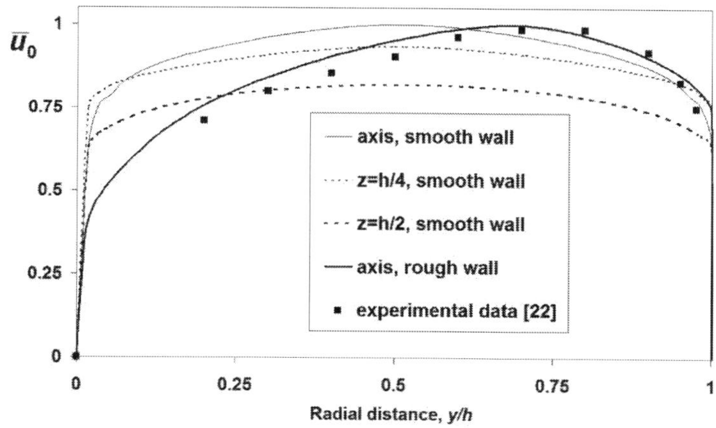

Figure 2. Numerical and experimental [22] distributions of the longitudinal component of the averaged velocity of gas over the channel cross-section.

Figure 2 shows the distributions of the longitudinal component of the averaged velocity of gas u_0 over the channel cross-section for two cases: i) the smooth walls and ii) the left wall is rough and the right wall is smooth for the mean flow velocity 15.5 m/s. Figure 3 shows the distributions of the normalized Reynolds normal stress tensor components obtained for the same conditions as Figure 2. The radial distance y/h=0 corresponds to the rough wall and y/h=1 corresponds to the smooth wall. The subscript "0" denotes the unladen flow conditions.

One can see that in case of the smooth channel walls, the mean flow velocity and the components of the turbulence kinetic energy demonstrate the representative symmetrical turbulent distributions over the cross-section of the rectangular channel. The transfer to the rough walls results in transformation of the given distributions. The maximum of the distribution of the time-averaged flow velocity moves towards the smooth wall. The similar change relates to the distributions of each component of the turbulence kinetic energy. These numerical results demonstrates the satisfactory agreement with the experimental data [22].

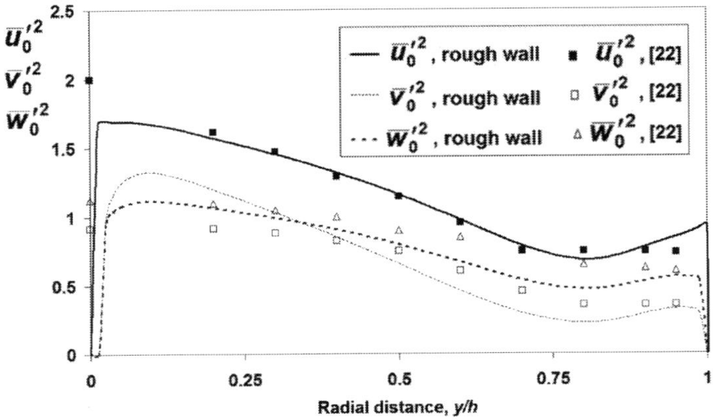

Figure 3. Numerical and experimental [22] distributions of the normalized Reynolds normal stress tensor components.

The next step of the study was the extension of the present model to the gas-solid particles grid-generated turbulent downward vertical channel flow. The experimental data [23] obtained for the channel flow of 200 mm square cross-section loaded with 700-μm glass beads of the physical density 2500 kg/m^3 was used for the model validation. The mean flow velocity was 9.5 m/s, the flow mass loading was 0.14 kg dust/kg air. The grids of the square mesh size M=4.8 and 10 mm were used for generating of the flow initial turbulence length scale.

The validity criterion was based on the satisfactory agreement of the axial turbulence decay curves occurring behind different grids in the unladen and particle-laden flows obtained by the given RSTM model and by the experiments [23]. Figure 4 demonstrates such agreement for the grid M=4.8 mm.

Figure 5 shows the decay curves calculated by the present RSTM model for the grids M=4.8 and 10 mm. As follows from Figs. 4 and 5, the pronounced turbulence enhancement by particles is observed for both grids. The character of the turbulence attenuation occurring along the flow axis agrees with the behavior of the decay curves in the grid-generated turbulent flows described in [24].

Figures 6 – 11 show the cross-section modifications of three components of the Reynolds stress, Δ_u, Δ_v, Δ_w, caused by 700-μm glass beads, calculated by the presented RSTM model at two locations of the initial period of the grid-generated turbulence decay x/M =46 and 93 as well as beyond it for $x/M \approx 200$. Here:

$$\Delta_u = \frac{\overline{u'^2} - \overline{u'^2_0}}{\overline{u'^2_0}}, \%, \quad \Delta_v = \frac{\overline{v'^2} - \overline{v'^2_0}}{\overline{v'^2_0}} \%, \quad \Delta_w = \frac{\overline{w'^2} - \overline{w'^2_0}}{\overline{w'^2_0}} \%. \tag{41}$$

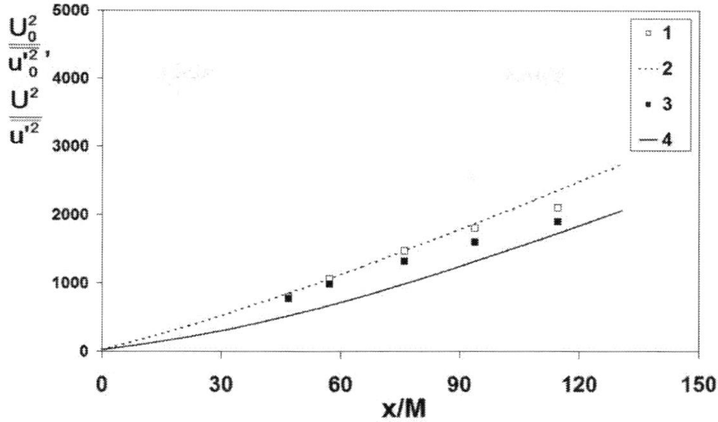

Figure 4. Axial turbulence decay behind the grid M=4.8 mm: 1 and 3 are the data [23] got for the unladen and particle-laden flows, respectively; 2 and 4 are the numerical data obtained for the same conditions.

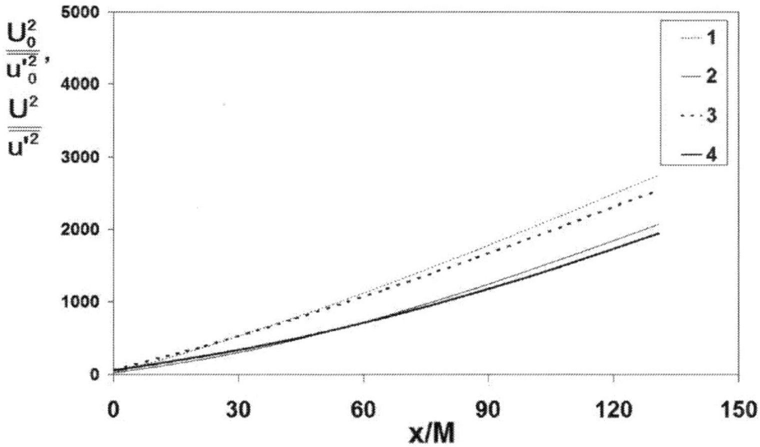

Figure 5. The calculated axial turbulence decay behind the grids: 1 and 2 are the data got for the unladen and particle-laden flow, respectively, at M=4.8 mm, 3 and 4 are the data obtained for the same conditions at M=10 mm.

One can see that the turbulence enhancement occupies over 75% of the half-width of the channel, that takes place at the initial period of the turbulence decay of the particle-laden flow as compared to the unladen flow. Along with, the distributions of Δ_u, Δ_v and Δ_w are uniform that corresponds to the initial grid-generated homogeneous isotropic turbulence, which decays downstream (s. Figures 4 and 5). The distributions of modification of Δ_u, Δ_v and Δ_w remain uniform downstream. At the same time, the cross-section extent of uniformity of distributions of components of the Reynolds stress and the degree of the particles effect on turbulence decrease, since the turbulence level decreases downstream (cf. data presented for $x/M = 46$ and 93 in Figures 6 – 11).

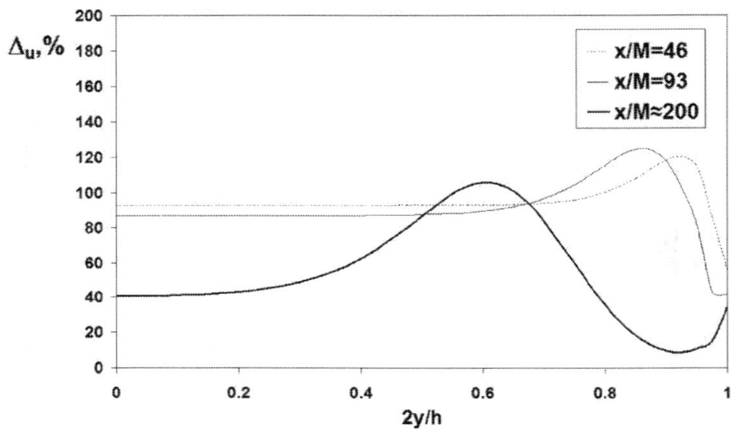

Figure 6. Effect of particles on the modification of the *x*-normal component of the Reynolds stress: *M*=4.8 mm, *z*=0.

The distributions of modification of Δ_u, Δ_v and Δ_w taken place beyond the initial period of the turbulence decay (location $x/M \approx 200$ at Figures 6 – 11) are typical of the channel turbulent particulate flow. One can see that in this case the turbulence enhancement becomes slower, since here the turbulence level is substantially smaller as compared with the initial period of decay, i.e. for $x/M < 100$ (s. Figures 4 and 5). This means that the grid-generated turbulence of the particulate flow decays downstream, and this causes the decrease of the rate of turbulence enhancement due to the particles occurred beyond the initial period of the turbulence decay. As a result, the turbulence is attenuated, that is expressed in terms of decrease of Δ_u towards the pipe wall (s. Figure 9). Such tendency has been shown qualitatively in [25].

The certain increase of Δ_u, Δ_v and Δ_w, that is observed verge towards the wall (s. Figures 6 – 11), arises from the growth of the slip velocity (s. curves 1, 2, 3 in Figure 12). The decrease of Δ_u, Δ_v and Δ_w taken place in the immediate vicinity of the wall is caused by the decrease of the length scale of the energy-containing vortices and, thus, the increase of the dissipation of the turbulence kinetic energy.

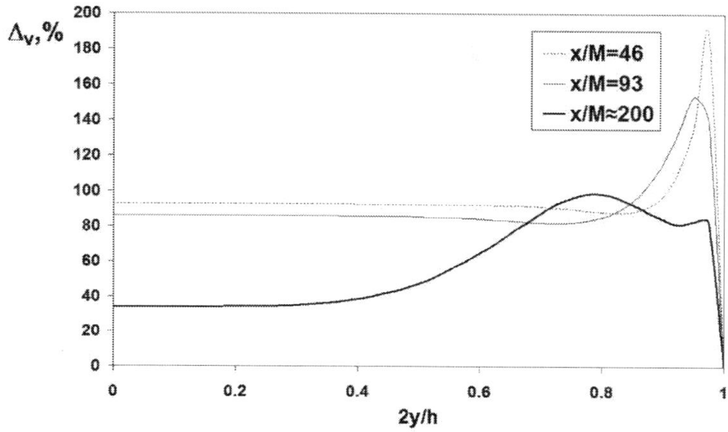

Figure 7. Effect of particles on the modification of the *y*-normal component of the Reynolds stress: *M*=4.8 mm, *z*=0.

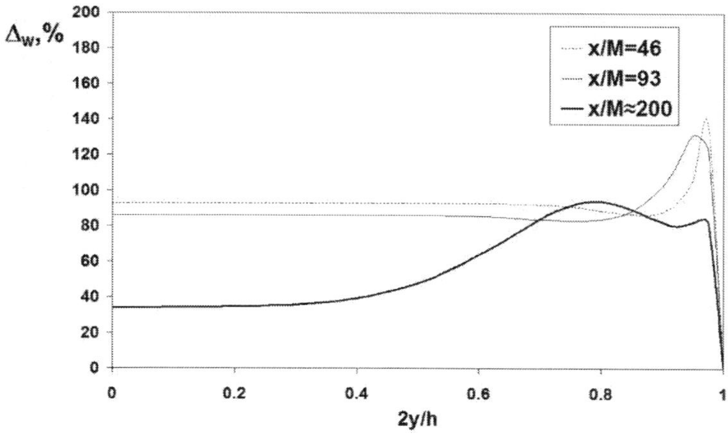

Figure 8. Effect of particles on the modification of the *z*-normal component of the Reynolds stress: *M*=4.8 mm, *z*=0.

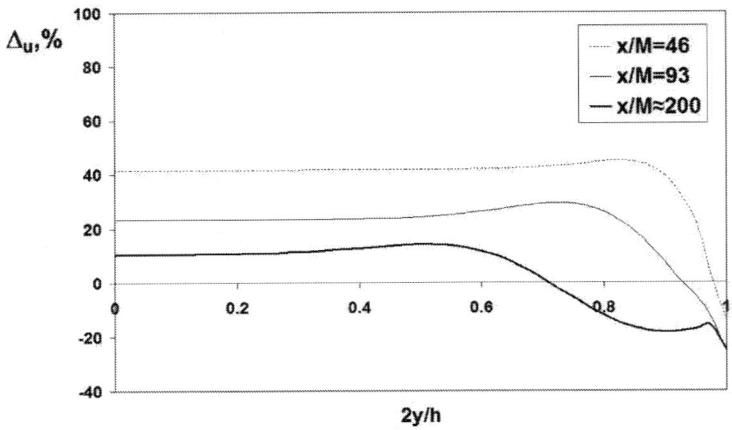

Figure 9. Effect of particles on the modification of the *x*-normal component of the Reynolds stress: M=10 mm, z=0.

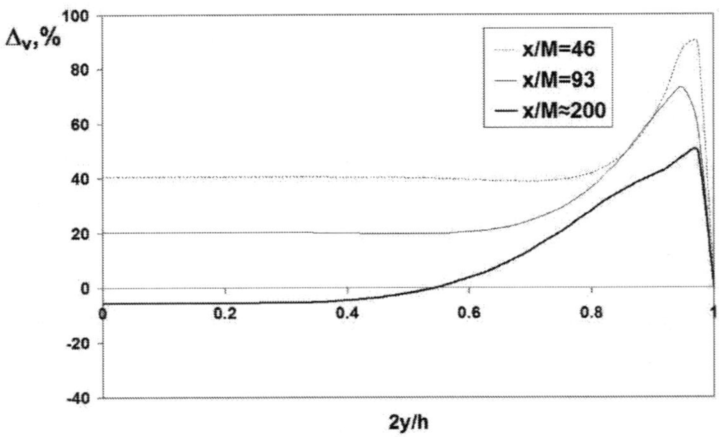

Figure 10. Effect of particles on the modification of the *y*-normal component of the Reynolds stress: M=10 mm, z=0.

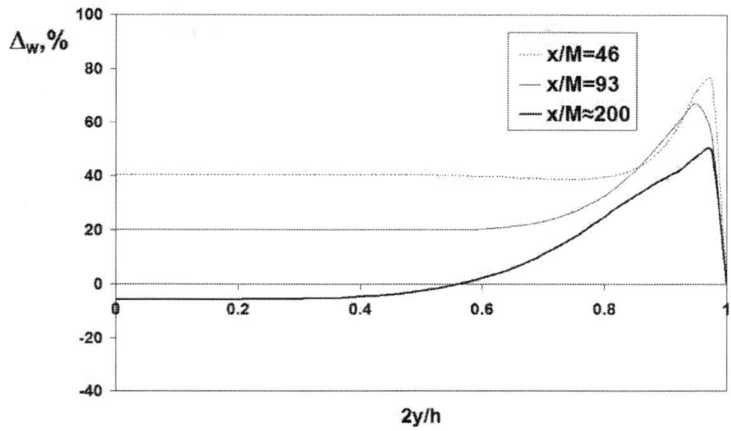

Figure 11. Effect of particles on the modification of the *z*-normal component of the Reynolds stress: *M*=10 mm, *z*=0.

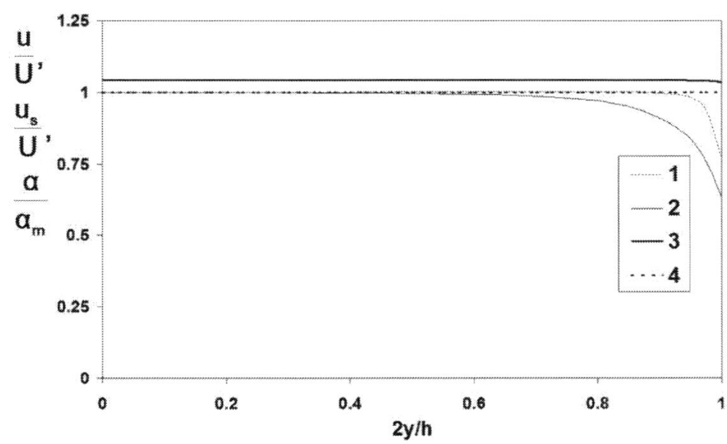

Figure 12. The cross-section distributions of the axial gas and particles velocities and particles mass concentration for the grid *M*=4.8 mm: 1 –u / U for $x / M = 46$; 2 –u / U, 3 –u_s / U and 4 –α / α_m for $x / M \approx 200$. Here α_m is the value of the mass concentration occurring at the flow axis.

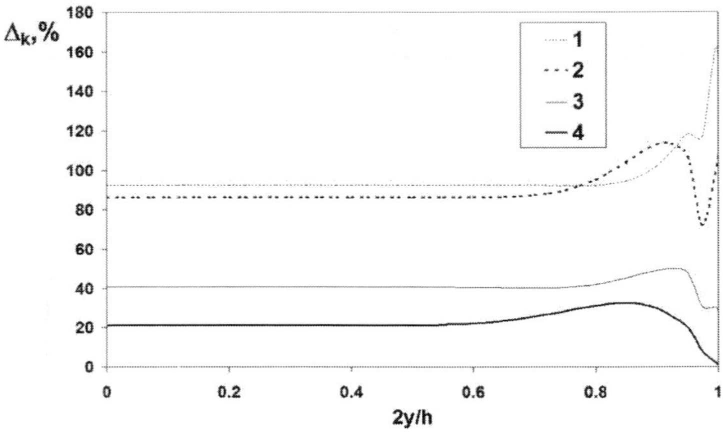

Figure 13. Effect of particles on the modification of the turbulence kinetic energy: 1 $-M = 4.8\text{mm}, x / M = 46$; 2 $-M = 4.8\text{mm}, x / M = 93$; 3 $-M = 10\text{mm}, x / M = 46$; 4 $-M = 10\text{mm}, x / M = 93$.

The analysis of Figure 13 shows that the increase of the grid mesh size results in the weaker contribution of particles to the turbulence enhancement and dissipation of the kinetic energy taking place over the cross-section for the initial period of the turbulence decay. This can be explained by the higher rate of the particles involvement into the turbulent motion due to the longer residence time that comes from the larger size of the eddies.

4. Conclusions

The RSTM model has been elaborated for the horizontal and vertical turbulent particulate flows in the channels of rectangular and square cross-sections with the smooth and rough walls.

The present RSTM model has been validated for the unladen channel gas flow with the rough wall. It satisfactorily described the experimental data on the averaged gas axial velocity and three components of the turbulence energy.

Further, the present model was applied to simulate the vertical grid-generated turbulent particulate channel flow. It considered both the enhancement and attenuation of turbulence by means of the additional terms of the transport equations of the normal Reynolds stress components. The model allowed to carry out the calculations covering the long distance of the channel length without using algebraic assumptions for various components of the Reynolds stress. The numerical results showed the effects of the particles and the mesh size of the turbulence generating grids on the turbulence modification that had been observed in experiments. It was obtained that the character of modification of all three normal components of the Reynolds stress taken place at the initial period of the turbulence decay are uniform almost all over the channel cross-sections. The increase of the grid mesh size slows down the rate of the turbulence enhancement which is caused by particles.

Acknowledgements

The work was done within the frame of the target financing under the Project SF0140070s08 (Estonia) and supported by the ETF grant Project ETF9343 (Estonia). The authors are grateful for the technical support of Computational Biology Initiative High Performance Computing Center of University of Texas at San Antonio (USA) and Texas Advanced Computing Center in Austin (USA). This study is related to the activity of the European network action COST MP1106 "Smart and green interfaces - from single bubbles and drops to industrial, environmental and biomedical applications".

Author details

Alexander Kartushinsky[1*], Ylo Rudi[1], Medhat Hussainov[1], Igor Shcheglov[1], Sergei Tisler[1], Igor Krupenski[1] and David Stock[2]

*Address all correspondence to: aleksander.kartusinski@ttu.ee

1 Research Laboratory of Multiphase Media Physics, Faculty of Science, Tallinn University of Technology, Tallinn, Estonia

2 School of Mechanical and Materials Engineering, Washington State University, Pullman, Washington, USA

References

[1] Elghobashi S.E., Abou-Arab T.W. A Two-Equation Turbulence Model for Two-Phase Flows. Physics of Fluids 1983; 26(4) 931-938.

[2] Pourahmadi F., Humphrey J.A.C. Modeling Solid-Fluid Turbulent Flows with Application to Predicting Erosive Wear. International Journal of Physicochemical Hydrodynamics 1983; 4(3) 191-219.

[3] Rizk M.A., Elghobashi S.E. A Two-Equation Turbulence Model for Dispersed Dilute Confined Two-Phase Flows. International Journal of Multiphase Flow 1989; 15(1) 119-133.

[4] Simonin O. Eulerian formulation for particle dispersion in turbulent two-phase flows. In: Sommerfeld M, Wennerberg D. (eds.) Proceedings of the 5th Workshop on Two-Phase Flow Predictions, 19-22 March 1990, Erlangen, Germany. Ju◎lich: Forschungszentrum Ju◎lich; 1990.

[5] Deutsch E., Simonin O. Large eddy simulation applied to the motion of particles in stationary homogeneous fluid turbulence. In: Michaelides EE, Fukano T, Serizawa A. (eds.) Proceedings of the 1st ASME/JSME Fluids Engineering Conference, 23-27 June 1991, Portland, USA. New York: American Society of Mechanical Engineers, Series FED; 1991.

[6] Shraiber AA, Yatsenko VP, Gavin LB, Naumov VA. Turbulent Flows in Gas Suspensions. New York: Hemisphere Pub. Corp.; 1990.

[7] Crowe C.T., Gillandt I. Turbulence modulation of fluid-particle flows – a basic approach. In: Proceedings of the 3rd International Conference on Multiphase Flow, 8-12 June 1998, Lyon, France. CD-ROM.

[8] Crowe C. T. On Models for Turbulence Modulation in Fluid-Particle Flows. International Journal of Multiphase Flow 2000; 26(5) 719-727.

[9] Reeks M.W. On a Kinetic Equation for the Transport of Particles in Turbulent flows. Physics of Fluids A: Fluid Dynamics 1991; 3(3) 446-456.

[10] Reeks M.W. On the Continuum Equations for Dispersed Particles in Nonuniform Flows. Physics of Fluids A: Fluid Dynamics 1992; 4(6) 1290-1303.

[11] Zaichik L.I., Vinberg A.A. Modeling of particle dynamics and heat transfer in turbulent flows using equations for first and second moments of velocity and temperature fluctuations. In: Durst F, Friedrich R, Launder BE, Schmidt FW, Schumann U, Whitelaw, JH. (eds.) Proceedings of the 8th International Symposium on Turbulent Shear Flows, 9-11 September 1991, Munich, Germany. Berlin: Springer-Verlag; 1993.

[12] Zaichik L.I., Fede P., Simonin O., Alipchenkov V.M. Comparison of two statistical approaches for modeling collision in bidisperse mixture of particles settling in homogeneous turbulent flows. In: Sommerfeld M. (ed.) Proceedings of the 6th International Conference on Multiphase Flow, 9-13 July 2007, Leipzig, Germany. CD-ROM.

[13] Kartushinsky A.I., Michaelides E.E., Zaichik L.I. Comparison of the RANS and PDF Methods for Air-Particle Flows. International Journal of Multiphase Flow 2009; 35(10) 914-923.

[14] Gerolymos G.A., Vallet I. Contribution to single-point-closure Reynolds-stress modeling of inhomogeneous flow. In: Proceedings of the 4th ASME/JSME Joint Fluids Summer Engineering Conference FEDSM2003, 6-10 July 2003, Honolulu, Hawaii, USA. CD-ROM.

[15] Taulbee D.B., Mashayek F., Barré C. Simulation and Reynolds Stress Modeling of Particle-Laden Turbulent Shear Flows. International Journal of Heat and Fluid Flow 1999; 20(4) 368-373.

[16] Mukin R.V., Zaichik L.I. Nonlinear Algebraic Reynolds Stress Model for Two-Phase Turbulent Flows Laden with Small Heavy Particles. International Journal of Heat and Fluid Flow 2012; 33(1) 81-91.

[17] Launder B.E., Reece G.J., Rodi W. Progress in the Development of a Reynolds-Stress Turbulence Closure. Journal of Fluid Mechanics 1975; 68(3) 537-566.

[18] Pope SB. Turbulent Flows. Cambridge – New York: Cambridge University Press; 2008.

[19] Schiller L., Naumann A. Über die grundlegenden Berechnungen bei der Schwerkraftaufbereitung. Zeitschrift des Vereines deutscher Ingenieure 1933; 77 318-320.

[20] Zaichik L.I., Alipchenkov V.M. Statistical Models for Predicting Particle Dispersion and Preferential Concentration in Turbulent Flows. International Journal of Heat and Fluid Flow 2005; 26(3) 416-430.

[21] Perić M., Scheuerer G. CAST – A Finite Volume Method for Predicting Two-Dimensional Flow and Heat Transfer Phenomena. GRS - Technische Notiz SRR–89–01. 1989

[22] Hanjalic K., Launder B.E. Fully Developed Asymmetric Flow in a Plane Channel. Journal of Fluid Mechanics 1972; 51(2) 301-335.

[23] Hussainov M., Kartushinsky A., Rudi Y., Shcheglov I., Tisler, S. Experimental Study of the Effect of Velocity Slip and Mass Loading on the Modification of Grid-Generated Turbulence in Gas-Solid Particles Flows. Proceedings of the Estonian Academy of Sciences. Engineering 2005; 11(2) 169-180.

[24] Hinze JO. Turbulence. New York: McGraw-Hill; 1975.

[25] Kartushinsky A.I., Michaelides E.E., Hussainov M., Rudi Y. Effects of the Variation of Mass Loading and Particle Density in Gas-Solid Particle Flow in Pipes. Powder Technology 2009; 193(2) 176-181.

Chapter 4

Numerical Modelling of a Cutting Arc Torch

Beatriz Mancinelli, F. O. Minotti,
Leandro Prevosto and Héctor Kelly

Additional information is available at the end of the chapter

http://dx.doi.org/10.5772/57045

1. Introduction

1.1. Thermal plasmas

Thermal plasmas are partially or strongly ionized gases, usually developed at atmospheric pressure. In fact, thermal plasmas can be generated by many methods, such as dc electrical discharges at current intensities higher than a few A and up to 10^5 A: free burning arcs, transferred arcs, or non-transferred plasma torches; ac or transient arcs (e.g., discharge lamps), circuit-breakers, or pulsed arcs; rf and microwave discharges at near-atmospheric pressure; and laser induced plasmas after the ignition and expansion phases (Gleizes et al., 2005; Boulos et al., 1994).

In this kind of plasma, the electric field remains rather weak (less than a few kVm^{-1}) and the electron number density is rather high (more than 10^{20} m^{-3}) so that the velocity distribution functions of all the types of particles can be considered as Maxwellian. The energy delivered to the plasma, in general by the Joule effect, is first picked up by the electrons because of their high mobility. The electrons transfer part of this energy to the heavy particles by elastic collisions. Due to the high electron number density, elastic collision frequencies are very high, so energy transfer is important and leads to an almost even distribution of the energy: the mean heavy particle energy is the same as the electron energy and there is thermal equilibrium among all the kinds of particles, allowing a single temperature to be defined for the plasma at a given position. In the hottest regions of thermal plasmas this mean kinetic energy is of the order of 1 eV, which corresponds to a temperature of the order of 10^4 K.

In thermal plasmas, the electrons are also most responsible for inelastic collisions, such as ionization, recombination, excitation, de-excitation, attachment, and detachment. Due to the large value of the electron density, the inelastic collision frequencies are high, and they tend to establish a statistical equilibrium among all kinds of particles; i.e. the populations of the excited atoms, molecules and ions tend to obey equilibrium laws, such as the Boltzmann and Saha laws. This situation requires one condition: the influence of radiation on the populating mechanisms of the various species must be negligible in comparison to the inelastic electron collisions. This condition is, in general, verified in the hottest regions of thermal plasmas, corresponding to the regions with high electron density values, but not in the outer regions (Ghorui et al., 2007). In spite of the weak role of radiation in the population, the experimental evidence shows that thermal plasmas emit strong amounts of radiation, particularly in the UV and visible parts of the spectrum, and they cannot be considered as black body emitters. This radiation emission, together with the presence of temperature and number density gradients within the plasmas inducing diffusion effects, shows that thermal plasmas are not in a state of thermodynamic equilibrium. Nevertheless, locally and as a first approximation, thermal plasmas can be considered to be in a state of local thermodynamic equilibrium (LTE), meaning that the particle number densities are related by equilibrium laws (because of high collision frequencies), whereas radiation is not in equilibrium with the particle distribution (Planck's law is not valid). More specifically, for thermal plasma to be considered in LTE, it has to accomplish the following requirements:

a. The different species of the plasma (atoms, ions, electrons, molecules) share a single Maxwellian distribution, characterized by a single temperature.

b. The ratio of the electrostatic energy density to pressure has to be small enough, and the temperature must be high enough, so charge carriers equilibrate through collisions the energy gained from the electric field.

c. Collisions (but not radiation) are the dominating mechanisms for ionization and excitation, and there must be micro-reversibility among collisions. Hence, Saha equilibrium and Boltzmann distribution laws are valid.

d. Spatial variations of the plasma properties are enough smooth, so a given particle that diffuses from one location to another has sufficient time to equilibrate.

1.2. Plasma cutting torch modelling

Plasma cutting is a process of metal cutting at atmospheric pressure by an arc plasma jet, where a transferred arc is generated between a cathode and a work-piece (the metal to be cut) acting as the anode (Ramakrishnan et al., 1997). Small nozzle bore, extremely high enthalpy and operation at relatively low arc current (≈ 10 ÷ 200) A are a few of the primary features of these torches (Nemchinsky & Severance, 2006). The physics involved in such arcs is very complicated. The conversion of electric energy into heat within small volumes causes high temperatures and steep gradients. Dissociation, ionization, large heat transfer rates (including losses by radiation), fluid turbulence and electromagnetic phenomena are involved. In addition, wide variations of physical properties, such as density, thermal conductivity, electric conductivity and viscosity have to be taken into account. These factors make hopeless the possibility of an analytical solution for such thermal plasmas. In the last years numerical plasma modelling has reached a state advanced enough to be of practical use in the study of cutting-arc processes (e.g., Gleizes et al., 2005).

Plasma modelling by numerical simulation in cutting torches is a powerful tool to predict the values of the fundamental physical quantities, namely the plasma temperature, the particles concentration and the fluid velocity. These numerical codes are employed to understand the relevant physical processes ruling the plasma behavior in order to interpret the experimental results of several plasma diagnostics, and ultimately to obtain optimized designs of such devices (Colombo et al., 2008). However, no complete predictive power has been possible as yet due to the complexity and variety of the processes involved. In particular, the practical use of cutting torch codes requires the introduction of some numerical coefficient whose value has to be obtained from a comparison between the model predictions and the experiment. For these reasons, the experimental validation of such models is of primary importance.

On the other hand, experimental data of cutting arcs are hard to obtain due to the harsh ambient conditions, and also because much of the plasma flow takes place in relatively small, bounded regions inaccessible to experimental probing (Nemchinsky & Severance, 2006). In practice, most of the available experimental data are related to spectroscopic (Pardo et al., 1999; Girard et al., 2006) and probe (Prevosto et al., 2008a, 2008b, 2009a) measurements in the external plasma region (the outer region between the nozzle exit and the anode, where the pressure has relatively small variations about the atmospheric value), giving information of only part of the variables involved, mostly temperatures and species concentrations. Although data on flow velocities are commonly reported for low-energy density (subsonic flow) non-transferred arc torches (e.g., Singh et al., 2000), measurement of flow velocities in cutting torches have been reported only recently by our Group (Prevosto et al., 2009b).

Because of the above quoted reasons, the experimental validation of the existing cutting torch models has been restricted to the temperature distribution in the nozzle-anode gap, together with other global parameters easy to obtain as the arc voltage and the arc chamber pressure. That experimental validation consists in obtaining a good matching with the experimental temperature values within the experimental uncertainty, which typically amounts to 10 % of the measured value (Peters et al., 2007). However, since in a cutting torch the plasma pressure is close to the atmospheric pressure, the plasma temperature is mainly determined by the energy equation (with the dominant energy loses being due to inelastic electron collisions that produce a sort of "anchorage" in the temperature), and so it is almost decoupled from the hydrodynamic flow. Hence, the calculated temperature value does not result in practice quite sensitive to changes in the numerical coefficients of the models at least within the temperature experimental uncertainty.

In high-energy density cutting torches it appears that the flow velocity is a more sensitive variable than the temperature to the modelling details. This can be understood considering the following argument. The acceleration of the flow is driven by a mostly axial pressure gradient along the torch nozzle, established between the pre-nozzle chamber and the nozzle exit. So, given the pressure profile, the velocity of each fluid element at different positions inside the nozzle depends strongly on its density, which in turn depends on the temperature and, in the high velocity, compressible regime, on the velocity itself. As inside the nozzle the radial temperature profile is very sharp, small variations of its shape, for instance its peak width, lead to appreciable changes in the radial mass distribution that reflect directly on the velocity. All this is more clearly seen and quantified using simple 1-D, two zone models in which only axial dependence is considered of an inner hot zone and an outer cold region. By assuming sonic flow at the nozzle exit, these simple 1-D models are able to predict quite reasonably the measured temperatures (within the experimental uncertainty), but give very imprecise values (100% off) of the flow velocity (Kelly et al., 2004).

The purpose of this work is to present a validation of the most frequently used plasma cutting torch models employing not only temperature but also velocity values as the experimental data to be confronted with. In order to do this, a 2-D model (similar to those proposed in the literature) was developed and applied to the same 30 A oxygen cutting torch that was used in a previous velocity measurement experiment. In this paper the plasma torch, model assumptions, governing equations, boundary conditions and the physical details of the model are presented. The calculated distributions of temperature and velocity and its comparison with the experimental data are shown.

2. Arc cutting torch

The high energy density cutting torch used in this numerical study consisted of a cathode centered above an orifice in a converging-straight copper nozzle. The cathode was made of copper (7 mm in diameter) with a hafnium tip (1.5 mm in diameter) inserted at the cathode center. A flow of oxygen gas cooled the cathode and the nozzle and was also employed as the plasma gas. The gas passed through a swirl ring to provide arc stability. The nozzle consisted in a converging-straight bore (with a converging length of 1 mm, and a bore 1 mm in diameter, 4.5 mm length) in a copper holder surrounding the cathode (with a separation of 0.5 mm between the holder and the cathode surface). To avoid plasma contamination by metal vapors from the anode (usually the work piece to be cut), a rotating steel disk with 200 mm in diameter and 15 mm thickness was used as the anode (Freton et al., 2002). In this study, the disk upper surface was located at 6 mm from the nozzle exit. The arc was transferred to the edge of the disk, and the rotating frequency of the disk was equal to 24 Hz. At this velocity, a well-stabilized arc column was obtained, and the lateral surface of the anode disc was completely not melted. Thus, practically no metal vapors from the anode were present in the arc. A scheme of the torch indicating several geometric dimensions is presented in Fig. 1.

By performing a small orifice (1 mm in diameter) on the lateral of the cathode surface the pressure in the plenum chamber (p_{ch}) was measured by connecting a pressure meter at the upper head of the cathode. The gas mass flow (dm/dt) injected in the torch was also registered. In this experiment, the arc current, the plenum pressure and the gas mass flow, were fixed to values of 30 A for the arc current, p_{ch} = 0.7 MPa and dm/dt = 0.71 g s^{-1}, respectively.

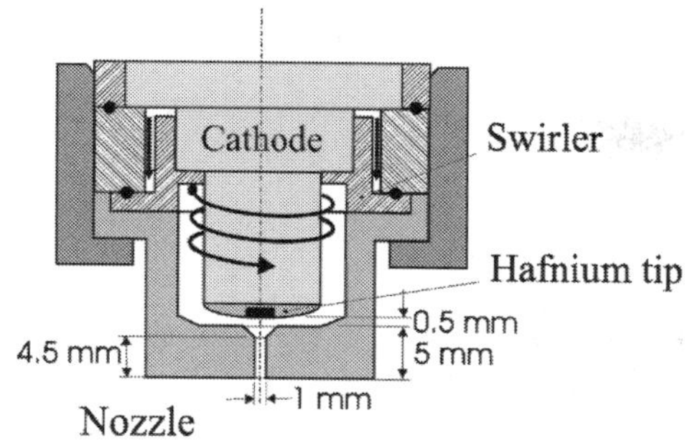

Figure 1. Schematic of the Cutting torch.

3. Mathematical model

3.1. Computational domain

The schematic of the modelled domain for the simulation is presented in Fig. 2. AC is the cathode part, including a 0.75 mm radius hafnium insert (AB). DE represents the copper nozzle. The edge of the domain EF is located at a radius of 10 R_N (Gonzalez-Aguilar at al., 1999). FG represents the anode located at 6 mm from the nozzle exit. A mass flow rate of 0.71 g s^{-1} with a vortex injection that leads to a ratio of the azimuthal to the axial inlet velocity of tan (13º) ≈ 0.23 was used at the torch inlet CD.

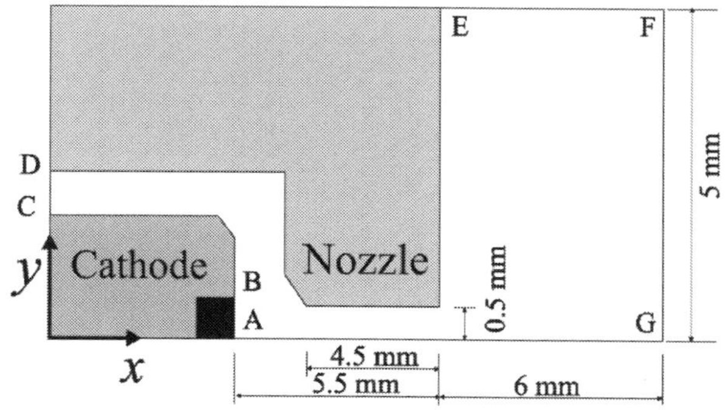

Figure 2. Cutting torch computational domain.

3.2. Model assumptions

The most frequently used cutting torch models use the LTE approximation, with the plasma flow in chemical equilibrium, and the internal energy of the fluid being characterized by a single temperature T. Other assumptions are:

a. The plasma flow is two-dimensional and axisymmetric. There are two effects that could break these assumptions. The first one is catastrophic: the double-arcing phenomenon in which a secondary arc appears from the cathode to anode passing across the nozzle (Prevosto et al., 2009c). The second one is a non-symmetric alignment of the torch. Both effects are not considered in this work.

b. At atmospheric pressure or above, the plasma is generally collision dominated: the mean free path for all species is much smaller than the macroscopic characteristic lengths. Therefore, the continuum assumption is valid; and the plasma is considered as a Newtonian fluid following Navier-Stokes equation.

c. The plasma gas is assumed to be pure oxygen in LTE with negligible concentration of metals in the plasma. The infiltration of metal atoms into the plasma can be due to the evaporation of copper and hafnium from the cathode and the nozzle. Atoms from the work-piece could also be diffused into the plasma, but generally in a negligible concentration considering the high mass flux rate of the working gas.

d. Non turbulent fluctuations are considered in the electromagnetic parameters, which results in a considerable simplification to the problem. So, for the calculations of the electromagnetic parameters the mean plasma state parameters are considered.

e. The electrodes sheath phenomena are not included in the modelling.

f. Hall currents and gravitational effects are considered negligible.

g. In the energy equation the viscous dissipation term is considered negligible.

h. The anode was considered as a porous free boundary characterized by its electrostatic potential.

3.3. Governing equations

The fluid part of the thermal plasma model can be expressed as a set of general transport equations expressed in conservative form as a balance among accumulation, net flux and production, namely:

$$\frac{\partial \psi}{\partial t} + \nabla \cdot \bar{f}_{\psi} - S_{\psi} = 0, \tag{1}$$

where Ψ is a conservative quantity, t represents time, $\bar{f}_{\psi}$ is the total (i.e., convective plus diffusive) flux of Ψ, and S_{Ψ} is the net production rate of Ψ. The set of conservation equations describing such a flow can be expressed as follows.

Total mass conservation

$$\frac{\partial \rho}{\partial t} + \nabla \cdot (\rho \bar{u}) = 0. \tag{2}$$

Momentum conservation

$$\frac{\partial(\rho\bar{u})}{\partial t} + \nabla\cdot\left(\rho\bar{u}\otimes\bar{u} + p\bar{\bar{\delta}} - \bar{\bar{\tau}}\right) - \bar{J}\times\bar{B} = 0. \tag{3}$$

Internal energy conservation

$$\frac{\partial(\rho e)}{\partial t} + \nabla\cdot(\rho\bar{u}\,e + \bar{q}) - \bar{J}\cdot\bar{E} + p\nabla\cdot\bar{u} + 4\pi\varepsilon_N\frac{p}{p_{ATM}} = 0, \tag{4}$$

where ρ represents the total mass density, $\bar{u}$ the fluid velocity (having, axial $-u_x-$, radial $-u_y-$ and azimuthal $-u_z-$ components), p the pressure, $\bar{\bar{\delta}}$ the identity tensor, $\bar{\bar{\tau}}$ the stress tensor, $\bar{J}$ the current density, $\bar{B}$ the magnetic field (only the azimuthal component was considered), e the internal energy, $\bar{q}$ the total heat flux, $\bar{E}$ the electric field and ε_N the plasma radiation net emission coefficient (NEC) (Naghizadeh-Kashani, et al., 2002).

Two further equations are required to describe the electromagnetic part of the plasma model. The first is the current continuity equation

$$\nabla\cdot\bar{J} = 0, \tag{5}$$

where

$$\bar{J} = -\sigma\nabla\phi, \tag{6}$$

and the second is one of Maxwell's equations

$$\nabla\times\bar{B} = \mu_0\bar{J}, \tag{7}$$

where σ is the electric conductivity, ϕ is the electrostatic potential and μ_0 the magnetic permeability of free space.

In (3) the stress tensor is given by

$$\tau_{i,j} = \mu_e\left(\frac{\partial u_i}{\partial x_j} + \frac{\partial u_j}{\partial x_i} - \frac{2}{3}\delta_{i,j}\frac{\partial u_l}{\partial x_l}\right), \tag{8}$$

where μ_e is the effective viscosity and the 2/3 factor in the fluid dilatation term, $\partial u_l / \partial x_l$, comes from the Stokes hypothesis for the dilatation viscosity. The total heat flux in (4) describes the heat transported by conduction and the enthalpy transport by mass diffusion, and is defined as

$$\bar{q} \equiv -\kappa_e \nabla T + \bar{\Gamma}_e h_e, \tag{9}$$

where κ_e is the effective thermal conductivity and $\bar{\Gamma}_e$ is the electron mass diffusion that can be approximated by

$$\bar{\Gamma}_e \approx -\frac{m}{e'} \bar{J}, \tag{10}$$

where e' is the elementary electric charge and m is the electron mass. Equation (10) neglects the charge transported by ions. In (9) $h_e = 5 k_B T / (2m)$ represents the specific electron enthalpy (k_B is the Boltzmann's constant).

The effective viscosity is

$$\mu_e = \mu_l + \mu_t, \tag{11}$$

and the effective thermal conductivity is

$$\kappa_e = \kappa + \frac{\mu_t C_p}{P_r}, \tag{12}$$

where C_p, μ_l and κ are the plasma specific heat at constant pressure, viscosity and thermal conductivity, respectively. The turbulent Prandtl number P_r and the turbulent viscosity μ_t are given in the section 3.5.

3.4. Thermodynamic properties and transport coefficients

The thermodynamic properties and transport coefficients data for a pure oxygen plasma in the temperature range 300 ÷ 30000 K (with a 100 K temperature intervals) and for nine different pressure values (0.1 ÷ 10 atm) were taken from (Murphy & Arundell, 1994). The source terms in (4) account for the Joule effect, the compression work, and the radiation loses $4\pi\,\varepsilon_N$, where ε_N was taken for a plasma radius of 0.5 mm (Freton et al., 2003). The NEC of pure oxygen for one atmosphere, has been multiplied by the factor p / p_{ATM} for other pressures (Zhou et al., 2009).

3.5. Turbulent model

The closure of the system equations requires extra relationships (which are commonly known as the turbulence model) to calculate the turbulent enhanced viscosity and thermal conductivity. There are in the literature turbulence models of varying degrees of sophistication: the Reynolds stress model (RSM), the k- ε model and its variants, the renormalization group (RNG) k-ε model, the RNG k- ε model taking into account the low Reynolds number effect, the realizable k- ε model and the Prandtl mixing length model (Zhou et al., 2009). The two most usual models are the Prandtl mixing length model and the k- ε model.

Following previous published models (Freton et al. 2002; Freton et al., 2003), the Prandtl mixing length model was chosen. Such length is given as:

$$l_m \equiv c\,\lambda, \tag{13}$$

where c is an adjustable parameter and λ is a local thermal radius which characterizes the boundary of the high velocity arc core, defined as the radial distance from the axis to the point at 2000 K (Yan et al., 1999). As inside the nozzle the radial temperature profile is very sharp (Prevosto et al., 2009c), λ results very close to the nozzle radius R_N. It has been found that for transferred arcs the turbulent Prandtl number can be approximated by unity (Fang et al., 1994).

$$P_r \equiv 1, \tag{14}$$

thus only the parameter c in (13) needs to be adjusted by comparing the numerical results with the experiment. The turbulent viscosity for isotropic turbulence was calculated taking into account the effect of the vortex injection (Freton et al., 2003)

$$\mu_t = \rho {l_m}^2 \left(\left(\frac{\partial u_x}{\partial y} \right)^2 + \left(y \frac{\partial}{\partial y} \left(\frac{u_z}{y} \right) \right)^2 \right)^{1/2}. \tag{15}$$

3.6. Boundary conditions

Table 1 summarizes the prescribed values of the physical quantities (or its spatial derivatives) on the boundaries shown in Fig. 2. In addition, the voltage drop between the cathode AC and the anode FG was adjusted in order that the integrated value of the axial current density on a given section corresponds to the value of the electric current of the torch. An external source term to increase the temperature was applied at the axis of the torch AG to initiate the current. A current value of 30 A was used in this study, in according to the value used in the experiments. Also, at the hafnium insert AB the maximum value of the axial current density on the axis of the geometry was limited to ≤ 170 A mm^{-2} (Freton et al., 2003). Besides, the electrostatic potential value of the nozzle DE was calculated so as to preserve the zero current balance at its surface (i.e., the nozzle is electrically floating).

Finally, at the interface between the plasma and the anode, in order to maintain the conservation of the energy flux and current intensity at this boundary, the following relations (neglecting radiation) were used to calculate the local thermal and electric conductivities

$$\left[-\kappa\left(\frac{\partial T}{\partial x}\right)\right]_{anode} = \left[-\kappa\left(\frac{\partial T}{\partial x}\right)\right]_{plasma} + J_x\left(\frac{5}{2}\frac{k_B}{e}\left(T - T_{anode}\right) + \varphi_A + \varphi_w\right), \tag{16}$$

$$\left[-\sigma\left(\frac{\partial \phi}{\partial x}\right)\right]_{anode} = \left[-\sigma\left(\frac{\partial \phi}{\partial x}\right)\right]_{plasma}, \tag{17}$$

here φ_A, φ_w and T_{anode} are the anode voltage drop, the anode work function and the anode temperature; respectively (Gleizes et al; 2005).

	p	*u*	*T*	*Φ*
AB	–	0	3500 K	–
BC	–	0	500 K	–
CD	–	mass flow 0.71 g s^{-1}	300 K	$\frac{\partial \phi}{\partial x} = 0$
DE	–	0	500 K	–
EF	1 atm	$\frac{\partial u_x}{\partial y} = \frac{\partial u_y}{\partial y} = \frac{\partial u_z}{\partial y} = 0$	300 K	$\frac{\partial \phi}{\partial y} = 0$
FG	–	$\frac{\partial u_x}{\partial x} = \frac{\partial u_y}{\partial x} = \frac{\partial u_z}{\partial x} = 0$	$\frac{\partial T}{\partial x} = 0$	$\phi = 0$
GA	–	$\frac{\partial u_x}{\partial y} = 0,\ u_y = u_z = 0$	$\frac{\partial T}{\partial y} = 0$	$\frac{\partial \phi}{\partial y} = 0$

Table 1. Model boundary conditions

3.7. Numerical aspects

The unsteady form of (1) was solved using a time-marching method (Ferziger &Perić, 2002; Fletcher, 1991). Consequently, initial conditions had to be supplied in order to complete the formulation of the problem.

For the internal flow calculations the initial pressure distribution was prescribed as a linearly decreasing function of the axial position, from a specific value at the torch inlet to the atmospheric one at the exit. The fluid temperature was set to the ambient value everywhere, while the initial fluid velocity was given taking into account the mass flow conservation. The total mass density at each position was then calculated from these initial pressure and temperature distributions using the equation of state. The electrostatic potential was set to zero initially. No initial distribution was required for the magnetic field as it is governed by an elliptic equation (equation (7)).

For the external flow, the pressure within the domain was set to the ambient value of one atmosphere initially. The initial temperature was set to the ambient value throughout the domain. The initial value of the density was then evaluated from the temperature and pressure using the equation of the state. The electrostatic potential was set to zero initially. The specific values used for these initial guesses did not impact the final converged results.

The set of governing equation was written in conservation form and discretized in time using a Taylor series first-order accuracy. These equations were then discretized in space using the finite volume method and solved with the given boundary conditions on a 81 15 non uniform internal grid and 39 47 non uniform external grid, by using the predictor-corrector algorithm (Ferziger &Perić, 2002; Fletcher, 1991). The time-step used in the time-marching algorithm was chosen so that the Courant-Friedrich-Levy criterion was fulfilled (Ferziger &Perić, 2002; Fletcher, 1991). The calculation was stopped when the following condition was achieved

$$\frac{\chi^{(t)} - \chi^{(t-1)}}{\chi^{(t)}} \leq 10^{-3}, \tag{18}$$

being $\chi^{(t)}$ the value of variable χ at the time t. This convergence criterion was found to be sufficient. Use of lower values for the convergence criterion resulted in negligible differences in the final results.

The accuracy of the calculations was tested by repeating them with a 38 × 15 internal grid and 19 × 47 external grid. The change in the plasma temperature was everywhere less than 15 %, while the changes in the axial velocity were less than 20 %. The finer grid was then used for generating the results to be presented in the following section.

4. Validation of the model

This section is devoted to the torch model validation (for the temperature and the velocity) by comparing the model results with experimental data on these quantities obtained in our Laboratory for the same cutting torch.

For the temperature, its radial profile at 3.5 mm from the nozzle exit was used. This profile was derived from electrostatic probe measurements (Prevosto et al, 2008a, 2008b, 2009a) by using a rotating Langmuir probe system; and from a Schlieren technique (Prevosto et al, 2010) by using a Z-type optical configuration with a laser as light source. Both techniques give an experimental uncertainty of ≈ 10 % in the temperature values. For the axial velocity, two axial distributions (with an experimental uncertainty of ≈ 10 %) derived from a time-of-flight technique were employed. One of the distribution corresponded to light emitted from the arc central core, while the other corresponded to an averaged emission over the whole emitting section of the arc (Prevosto et al., 2009b). The arc core velocity was obtained from spectrally filtered light fluctuations measurements using a band-pass filter (475 nm) to detect light emission fluctuations emitted only from the arc axis.

Figure 3 presents the radial profiles of the calculated temperature at 3.5 mm from the nozzle exit for $c = 0$ (i.e., laminar flow), $c = 0.08$ and $c = 0.20$. As shown, all the temperature profiles are similar, their differences being smaller than the experimental temperature uncertainty. As an example, Fig. 4 shows the comparison among the theoretical profile corresponding to $c = 0.08$ and the experimentally derived temperature profiles. It can be seen from Fig. 4 that the model results are in good agreement with the experimental data.

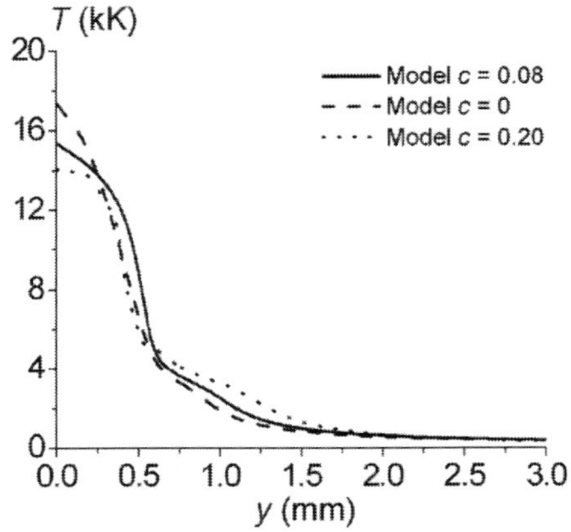

Figure 3. Radial profile of the calculated plasma temperature for $c = 0$, $c = 0.08$ and $c = 0.20$. Taken from Mancinelli et al., 2011.

The measured plasma flow velocity obtained for different axial positions (z) with and without band-pass filter, together with a visible photograph of the arc is shown in Fig. 5. The theoretical distributions of the axial velocity on the axis for the same c values presented in Fig. 3 are shown in Fig. 6. For comparison purposes, the measured values of the axial velocity corresponding to light emitted from the arc central core are also included in Fig. 6. It can be seen that the theoretical profiles are close among them at the vicinities of the nozzle exit (reflecting the well known fact of the little importance of the turbulence inside the nozzle (Gleizes et al., 2005) but soon after the scatter in the u_x values is larger than those found for the temperature, reaching about 100 % at the middle of the gap. Hence, it can be concluded that the fluid velocity strongly depends on the particular value of the turbulent parameter c. On the other hand, the theoretical profile presenting the best matching with the experimental data is that corresponding to $c = 0.08$.

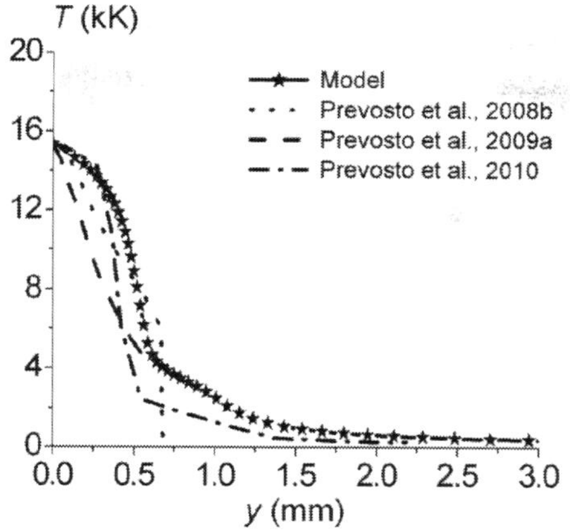

Figure 4. Radial profile of the plasma temperature predicted by the model at 3.5 mm from the nozzle exit for $c = 0.08$ together with the experimental data derived from electrostatic probes and Schlieren techniques. Taken from Mancinelli et al., 2011.

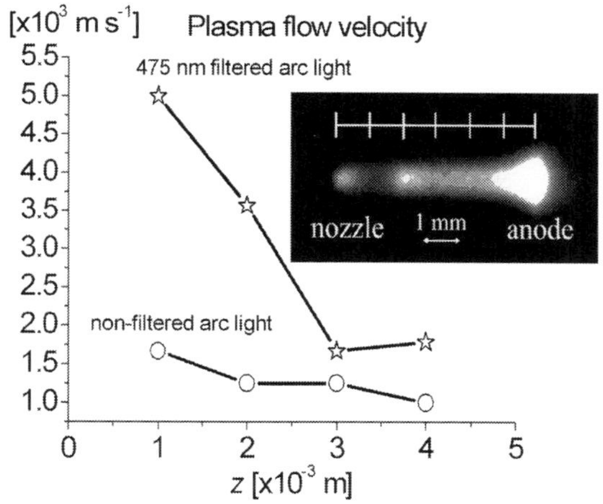

Figure 5. Measured values of the axial velocity of the arc (z corresponds to the axial coordinate measured from the nozzle exit). Taken from Prevosto et al., 2009b.

Figure 7 shows the averaged theoretical axial plasma velocity over the emitting arc cross section, defined from the arc core (axis) to the ≈ 4000 K temperature line (Prevosto et al., 2009a) for the same c values presented in Fig. 3. As before, the experimental values of u_x corresponding to an averaged emission over the whole emitting section of the arc are also included in this figure. It can be seen that the theoretical profile presenting the best matching with the experimental data is that corresponding to $c = 0.08$.

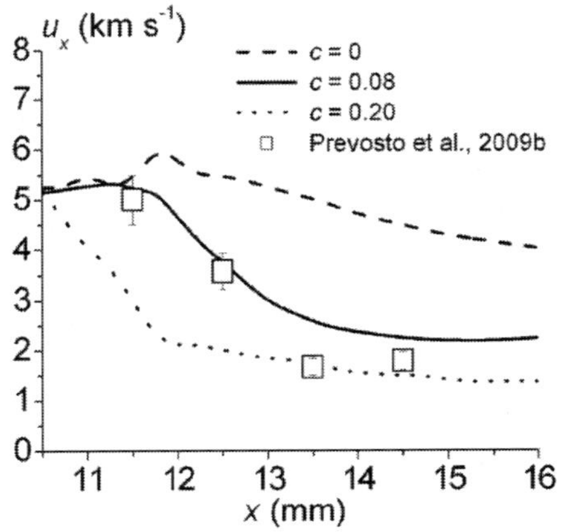

Figure 6. Comparison between calculated plasma velocity values at the axis for $c = 0$, $c = 0.08$ and $c = 0.20$, and the measured values of the axial velocity corresponding to light emitted from the arc central core. Taken from Mancinelli et al., 2011.

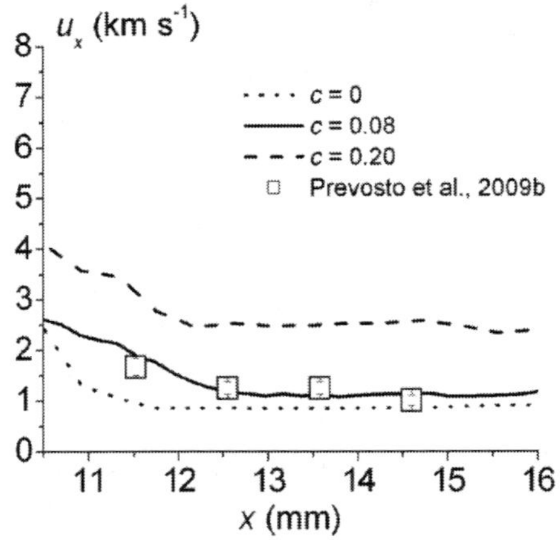

Figure 7. Averaged theoretical axial plasma velocity over the emitting arc cross section, defined from the arc core (axis) to the ≈ 4000 K temperature line for the same c values presented in Fig. 3. The experimental values corresponding to an averaged emission over the whole emitting section of the arc are also shown. Taken from Mancinelli et al., 2011.

5. Conclusions

The modelling of dc arc plasma torches is quite challenging because the plasma flow is highly nonlinear, presents strong quantity gradients and is characterized by a wide range of time and length scales.

In the last years numerical plasma modelling has reached a state advanced enough to be of practical use in the study of cutting-arc processes. However, a self-consistent description of the plasma starting from only macroscopic parameters (such as the geometry, current intensity, nature of the gas and type of employed materials, mass flow rate and/or some boundary conditions) has not yet been possible because of the lack of precise knowledge of some phenomena (electrode phenomena, radiation, turbulence, wall ablation, etc), which impose simplifications on the models. In particular, the practical use of cutting torch codes requires the introduction of some numerical coefficient whose value has to be obtained from a comparison between the model predictions and the experiment. For these reasons, the experimental validation of such models is of primary importance.

Assuming LTE conditions, the properties of the plasma that must be computed are the temperature, pressure and velocity fields. Numerical models for the plasma generated in cutting torches published during the last ten years have been validated using temperature data derived from spectroscopic measurements in the nozzle-anode gap. It has been shown in this work that the plasma temperature is not the most appropriate quantity to validate numerical codes since it is not quite sensitive to changes in the model numerical parameters. Instead, it has been shown that the plasma velocity appears to be a more adequate quantity to perform such validation.

In order to realize this validation to such a sensitive variable as the plasma velocity, a 2-D model similar to those proposed in the literature was developed and applied to the same 30 A high-energy density cutting torch that was used in the velocity measurements recently published by some of the authors. Within the experimental uncertainties, it was found that a Prandtl mixing length turbulent parameter c = 0.08 allows to reproduce both the experimental data of velocity and temperature. However, this value has to be taken with caution, since that c value depends on the actual torch geometry, gas type and arc current. It can also be concluded that the simple Prandtl mixing length model is appropriated to predict the plasma characteristics in low-current cutting torches.

Acknowledgements

This work was supported by grants from the CONICET (PIP 112/200901/00219) and Universidad Tecnológica Nacional (PID 1389).

Author details

Beatriz Mancinelli[1], F. O. Minotti[1,2], Leandro Prevosto[1] and Héctor Kelly[1,2]

1 Grupo de Descargas Eléctricas, Departamento Ing. Electromecánica, Facultad Regional Venado Tuerto (UTN), Santa Fe, Argentina

2 Instituto de Física del Plasma (CONICET), Departamento de Física, Facultad de Ciencias Exactas y Naturales (UBA) Ciudad Universitaria, Buenos Aires, Argentina

References

[1] Boulos, M.; Fauchais, P. & Pfender, E. (1994). *Thermal Plasmas, Fundamentals and Applications*, Vol1, Plenum Press, New York.

[2] Colombo, V.; Concetti, A.; Ghedini, E.; Dallavalle, S. & Vancini, M. (2008). Understanding Plasma Fluid Dynamics Inside Plasma Torches Trough Advanced Modeling. *IEEE Trans. Plasma Sci.*, 36, 389.

[3] Fang, M. T. C.; Zhuang, Q. & Guo, X. J. (1994). Current-zero behaviour of an SF_6 gas-blast arc. II. Turbulent flow. *J. Phys. D: Appl. Phys*. 27, 74.

[4] Ferziger, J. H. & Períc, M. (2002) *Computational Methods for Fluid Dynamics*, Springer-Verlag.

[5] Fletcher, C. A. J. (1991) *Computational Techniques for Fluid Dynamics* Vol 1, Springer-Verlag.

[6] Freton, P.; Gonzalez, J. J.; Gleizes, A.; Camy Peyret, F.; Caillibotte, G. & Delzenne, M. (2002). Numerical and experimental study of a plasma cutting torch. *J. Phys. D: Appl. Phys.*, 35, 115.

[7] Freton, P.; Gonzalez, J. J.; Camy Peyret, F. & Gleizes, A. (2003). Complementary experimental and theoretical approaches to the determination of the plasma characteristics in a cutting plasma torch. *J. Phys. D: Appl. Phys.*, 36, 1269.

[8] Girard, L.; Teulet, Ph.; Razafinimanana, M.; Gleizes, A.; Camy-Peyret, F.; Baillot, E. & Richard, F. (2006). Experimental study of an oxygen plasma cutting torch: I. Spectroscopic analysis of the plasma jet. *J. Phys. D: Appl. Phys.*, 39, 1543.

[9] Gleizes, A.; Gonzalez, J. J. & Freton, P. (2005). Termal Plasma Modelling *J. Phys. D: Appl. Phys*. 38, R153.

[10] Ghorui, S.; Heberlein, J. V. R. & Pfender, E. (2007). Non-equilibrium modelling of an oxygen–plasma cutting torch. *J. Phys. D: Appl. Phys.*, 40, 1966.

[11] González-Aguilar, J.; Pardo, C.; Rodríguez-Yunta, A. & García Calderón, M. A. G. (1999). A theoretical study of a cutting air plasma torch. *IEEE Trans. Plasma Sci.*, 27, 264.

[12] Guo, S.; Zhou, Q.; Guo, W. & Xu, P. (2010). Computational analysis of a double nozzle structure plasma cutting torch. *Plasma Chem. Plasma Process*, 30, 121.

[13] Kelly, H.; Minotti, F. O.; Prevosto, L. & Mancinelli, B. (2004). Hydrodynamic model for the plasma-gas flow in a cutting torch nozzle. *Brazilian J. of Phys.* 34, 1531.

[14] Mancinelli, B.; Minotti, F. O. & Kelly, H. (2011). On the use of the Prandtl mixing length model in the cutting-torch modelling. *Journal of Phys. Conf. Series* 296, 012025.

[15] Murphy, A. B. & Arundell, C. J. (1994). Transport Coefficients of Argon, Nitrogen, Oxygen, Argon-Nitrogen, and Argon-Oxygen Plasmas. *Plasma Chem. Plasma Process.* 14, 451.

[16] Naghizadeh–Kashani, Y.; Cressault, Y. & Gleizes, A. (2002). Net emission coefficient of air thermal plasmas. *J. Phys. D: Appl. Phys.*, 35, 2925.

[17] Nemchinsky, V. A. & Severance, W. S. (2006). What we know and what we do not know about plasma arc cutting. *J. Phys. D: Appl. Phys.*, 39, R423.

[18] Pardo, C.; González-Aguilar, J.; Rodríguez-Yunta, A. & Calderón, M. A. G. (1999). Spectroscopic analysis of an air plasma cutting torch. *J. Phys. D: Appl. Phys.*, 32, 2181.

[19] Peters, J.; Heberlein, J. V. R. & Lindsay, J. (2007). Spectroscopic diagnostics in a highly constricted oxygen arc. *J. Phys. D: Appl. Phys.*, 40, 3960.

[20] Prevosto, L.; Kelly, H. & Mancinelli, B. (2008). On the use of sweeping Langmuir probes in cutting arc plasmas–Part I: Experimental results. *IEEE Trans. Plasma Sci.*, 36, 263.

[21] Prevosto, L.; Kelly, H. & Minotti, F. O. (2008). On the use of sweeping Langmuir probes in cutting arc plasmas–Part II: Interpretation of the results. *IEEE Trans. Plasma Sci.*, 36, 271.

[22] Prevosto, L.; Kelly, H. & Minotti, F. O. (2009). An interpretation of Langmuir probe floating voltage signals in a cutting arc. *IEEE Trans. Plasma Sci.*, 37, 1092.

[23] Prevosto, L.; Kelly, H. and Mancinelli, B. (2009). Determination of plasma velocity from light fluctuations in a cutting torch. *J. Appl. Phys.*, 106, 053308.

[24] Prevosto, L.; Kelly, H. and Mancinelli, B. (2009). On the physical origin of the nozzle characteristic and its connection with the double-arcing phenomenon in a cutting torch. *J. Appl. Phys.*, 105, 013309.

[25] Prevosto, L.; Kelly, H. and Mancinelli, B. (2010). Schlieren technique applied to the arc temperature measurement in a high energy density cutting torch. *J. Appl. Phys.*, 107, 023304.

[26] Ramakrishnan, S.; Gershenzon, M.; Polivka, F.; Kearny, T. N. & Rogozinsky, M. W. (1997). Plasma generation for the plasma cutting process. *IEEE Trans. Plasma Sci.*, 25, 937.

[27] Singh, N.; Razafinimanana, M. & Hlinas, J. (2000). Determination of plasma velocity from light fluctuations in a dc plasma torch. J. Phys. D: Appl. Phys. 33, 275.

[28] Yan, J. D.; Nuttall, K. I. & Fang, M. T. C. (1999). A comparative study of turbulence models for SF_6 arcs in a supersonic nozzle. J. Phys. D: Appl. Phys. 32, 1401.

[29] Zhou, Q.; Li, H.; Xu, X.; Liu, F.; Guo, S.; Chang, X.; Guo, W. & Xu, P. (2009) Comparative study of turbulence models on highly constricted plasma cutting arc. *J. Phys. D: Appl. Phys*. 42, 015210.

Chapter 5

Unsteady Flowfield Characteristics Over Blunt Bodies at High Speed

R. C. Mehta

Additional information is available at the end of the chapter

http://dx.doi.org/10.5772/57050

1. Introduction

The characteristics of the unsteady flowfield over a hemisphere-cylinder model and a bulbous heat shield of a satellite launch vehicle at turbulent flow and at transonic speeds and a laminar flow over a conical spike attached to a forward facing blunt body at supersonic speed are numerically simulated by solving time-dependent compressible axisymmetric Navier-Stokes equations.

Hsieh [1] has conducted wind-tunnel tests of a hemisphere-cylinder model at zero angle of attack and freestream Mach number $M_\infty = 0.7 - 1.3$ to investigate viscous-inviscid interaction. Hsieh [2] has solved full potential equation to analyze wind-tunnel results and found that the inviscid analysis is unable to predict the external flowfield satisfactory. This is due to the fact that the shock wave-turbulent boundary layer interaction causes a separated flow between $M_\infty = 0.80 - 0.90$ on the hemisphere-cylinder model in a high speed wind-tunnel testing. The numerical simulations analyze the unsteady flow caused by shock wave-turbulent boundary layer at transonic Mach numbers.

A bulbous payload shroud is generally selected to accommodate an increased payload volume of the satellite in a launch vehicle. All launch vehicles require a heat shield to protect the satellite from aerodynamic loading, heating, aero-acoustic vibration, and other environmental conditions during the ascent phase of the flight and to provide aerodynamic forward surface. The wind-tunnel tests for Titan I – IV were conducted during 1955 to 1996 and summarized by Brower [3]. The estimation of flowfield characteristics around such a heat shield configuration is of great aerodynamic importance, as well as research interest. For the ascent flight, during the transonic speed range, their study is particular important because of such resulting phenomena as terminal shock wave movements, frequently coupled with substantial free-stream dynamic pressure. Flow induced vibrations are important design requirement of aerospace launch vehicles. Awrejcewicz, and Krysko [4] have developed numerical simulation of a cylindrical panel within transonic ideal-gas flow stream and solved dynamics for all intervals of the frequency. These parameters directly depend on the intensity of the vorticity components of the turbulence, the strength of the shock wave, and the mechanism of their interaction, all of which are implicitly linked to the specific configuration of a bulbous heat shield of a satellite launch vehicle. The numerical flow simulation over a bulbous payload shroud at transonic Mach number range is very useful to decide the geometrical configuration for minimum buffeting load and minimum aerodynamic drag requirement. The terminal shock wave of sufficient strength to interact with the boundary layer can cause flow separation and flowfield may become unstable as observed in the high speed cinematography [5]. Therefore, it is desirable to determine the location of the terminal shock wave on the heat shield and the strength of the terminal shock wave as a function of transonic Mach numbers range. The strength of the terminal shock wave and the mechanism of their interaction are related to the specific configuration of the heat shield satellite launch vehicle. Fluctuations of pressure level in shock waves and in separated flow regions can cause flow instabilities and then leads to buffeting phenomenon [6] – [7]. The features of the transonic flowfield can be delineated through the wind-tunnel data such as schlieren photographs and oil flow patterns. It is characterized by a normal or a terminal shock wave, supersonic pocket on the cylindrical region of the heat shield, shock wave/turbulent boundary layer interaction, and a separation bubble may be caused by the shock wave/turbulent boundary layer interaction on the cylindrical section of the heat shield. The main features of transonic flowfield around a bulbous heat shield are illustrated in Fig. 1. The terminal shock waves are an essential feature of transonic flow [8]. As the freestream Mach number increases from subsonic values a shock wave system appears near the shoulder. The flow is called transonic if both subsonic ($M < 1$) and supersonic ($M > 1$) regions are present in the field.

The transonic range begins when the highest Mach number reaches unity ($M = 1$) on the heat shield. The general features of the flow are as present once the sonic velocity occurs at the shoulder and remains throughout the whole transonic range. There is a local supersonic region ahead of the main shoulder shock. The near normal shock wave grows and moves downstream as the freestream Mach number increases. The difficulties to analyze the flowfield are associated with the detail design and a quantitative theoretical prediction. For the former, a sufficient wind-tunnel test data is required; the latter is due to nonlinearity of the equation governing transonic flow requires Computational Fluid Dynamics approach. In the boat-tail region, a local separation results, due to sharp discontinuity in the longitudinal of the payload shroud. The regions of flow separation impose additional complexity to aerodynamic and structural design aspects [9] – [13]. The complex flowfield at the transonic speeds is also observed during the experimental investigation of the bulbous heat shield. Experimental studies [14] – [15] have been made to understand flow behavior at transonic Mach numbers. These experimental investigations were limited to the measurement of surface pressure distribution, oil flow patterns, shadowgraphs and schlieren pictures for various heat shield models at transonic Mach number range. Recently analyses of Ares launch vehicle are carried out in the transonic speed and reported in a series of papers by Pinier [16], Piatak et al. [17] and Sekula et al. [18]. The current work reveals the paramount importance of aerodynamics at transonic Mach range.

http://dx.doi.org/10.5772/57050

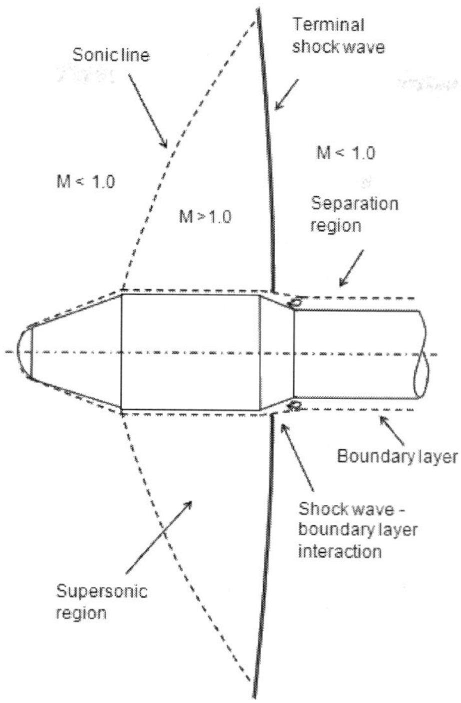

Figure 1. Schematic flowfield on bulbous heat shield at transonic Mach number.

A high-speed flow over a blunt body generates a bow shock wave in front of it, which causes a rather high surface pressure, and as a result, high aerodynamic drag. The surface pressure on the blunt body can be reduced if a conical shock wave is generated by mounting a forward facing spike. The aerospike produces a region of re-circulating separated flow that shields the blunt-nosed body from the incoming flow as shown in Fig. 2. The literature review reveals that addresses the mechanism how the unstable flow is initiated and how it persists [19] – [20]. The combination of the numerical simulations with experimental investigations has found to be a powerful tool to analyze unsteady flow and first results of a renewed investigation of the aerospike problem. The aerospike has been known since the 1950's to cause an unstable flow [21]. Wood [22] has distinguished five different types of flow regimes over spiked cones based on the semi-cone angle and flow characteristics which may correspond to the fluctuation and oscillation regimes.

Bogdonoff and Vas [23] were the first to identify the two modes of unstable axisymmetric separation, the fluctuation mode and the oscillation mode by varying flat faced and hemi-spherical blunt bodies. The flowfield problem associated with the blunt-nosed spike bodies can be distinguished by a conical blunt body with a total angles of the conical faces varied from 30⁰ to 180⁰ [22] or a hemisphere-cylinder body [24]. Kabelitz [25] has observed two distinct unsteady flow modes, namely, oscillation and pulsation [26] in the spike attached to the blunt-nosed (flat-faced) cylindrical body. Experimental studies have been focused on identifying the boundaries of the unsteady region. The flow just outside the separated shear layer approaching the body's shoulder can be turned by an attached conical shock, and then the shock structure is stable because an equilibrium condition is reached between escaping and recirculating flows in the separated region. Kistler [27] was the first to make detailed fluctuating wall pressure measurements under the separated supersonic turbulent boundary layer upstream of a forward step.

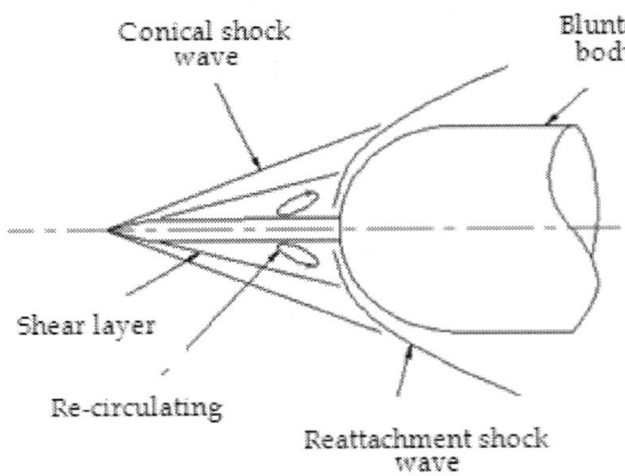

Figure 2. Schematic flowfield over spiked-blunt body.

For a range of spike lengths the flow can became unsteady with two modes of instability observed. The oscillation mode involves the motion of the fore-shock due to the spike tip. The pulsation mode features a large-scale motion of the bow shock associates with blunt body. Spike length to diameter (L/D) ratio of 0.9, half-cone angle of blunt body 70^0, $M_\infty = 2.21$, $Re_D = 0.12 \times 10^6$ for oscillation modes and L/D ratio of 1.0, half-cone angle of blunt body 90^0, $M_\infty = 6$, $Re_D = 0.13 \times 10^6$ for the pulsation modes are numerically investigated by Badcock et al. [28]. Feszty et al. [29] have conducted a computational analysis of the pulsation mode using computational fluid dynamics.

Flowfield over a conical spike attached to a blunt body is analyzed to understand the periodic oscillations of flowfield. The laminar Navier-Stokes equations are solved using multi-stage Runge-Kutta time stepping method. If the turning angle of the flow is too large to be accomplished by an attached conical shock wave, a detached strong shock is generated, which pushes high-pressure flow from the reattachment zone at the body's face into the recirculating region of the separated shear layer. This high-pressure flow that gets into the separated flow region inflates the separation bubble, and the shock structure is pumped upstream. This gives rise to self-excited shock oscillations during which the conical fore-shock wave and the accompanying shear layer oscillate laterally and their shape changes periodically from concave to convex. This type of flowfield is unsteady in nature. The separated shear layer with an inflection point in the velocity profile is inherently unstable [21], and when this hits the body at the reattachment point selective amplification of the disturbances takes place, and this would cause the surface pressure to fluctuate in the flow separation region. The point of reattachment could be shifting to and fro along the body surface because of these shock oscillations. Because of this unsteady oscillation of the separation bubble, pronounced variations in the locations of separation shock, conical shock wave ahead of the blunt cone, and the reattachment point on the blunt cone surface are observed in different models with identical freestream conditions. Panaras et al. [30] have numerically simulated unsteady flows at high speeds around spiked-blunt bodies. The experimental studies are also carried out to know the effect of variations to the spike diameter to blunt body diameter ratio.

The main aim of the present Chapter to analyze the unsteady flow characteristics and wall pressure fluctuations and oscillations over the hemisphere-cylinder, the bulbous payload shroud of a typical satellite launch vehicle and the conical spike attached to the forward facing blunt body. The numerical simulations present glimpse of the instantaneous flowfield features over various models at high speeds.

2. Governing fluid dynamics equations

The Navier-Stokes equations describe the motion of a viscous, heat conducting compressible fluid. In the Cartesian tensor notation, let x_j, be the coordinates, p, ρ, T and E the pressure, density, temperature, and total energy, and u, the velocity components. The governing fluid dynamics equations can be written as

$$\frac{\partial \rho}{\partial t}+\frac{\partial}{\partial x_j}\left(\rho u_j\right)=0 \tag{1}$$

$$\frac{\partial}{\partial t}\left(\rho u_i\right)+\frac{\partial}{\partial x_j}\left(\rho u_i u_j+\delta_{ij}p-\tau_{ij}\right)=0 \tag{2}$$

$$\frac{\partial}{\partial t}\left(\rho E\right)+\frac{\partial}{\partial x_j}\left[\left(\rho E+p\right)u_j-u_i\tau_{ij}+q_j\right]=0 \tag{3}$$

where τ_{ij} is the stress tensor, which is proportional to the rate of strain tensor and the bulk dilatation

$$\tau_{ij} = \mu\left(\frac{\partial u_i}{\partial x_j} + \frac{\partial u_j}{\partial x_i}\right) + \lambda\delta_{ij}\left(\frac{\partial u_k}{\partial x_k}\right) \tag{4}$$

Usually $\lambda = -2\mu/3$, and velocity gradient tensor can be represented as

$$\left(\frac{\partial u_i}{\partial x_j}\right) = \left[S_{ij} + \Omega_{ij}\right] \tag{5}$$

where strain rate tensor S_{ij} and rotation rate tensor Ω_{ij} can be written as

$$S_{ij} = \frac{1}{2}\left[\left(\frac{\partial u_i}{\partial x_j} + \frac{\partial u_j}{\partial x_i}\right)\right],\ \Omega_{ij} = \frac{1}{2}\left[\left(\frac{\partial u_i}{\partial x_j} - \frac{\partial u_j}{\partial x_i}\right)\right]$$

The heat flux component is

$$q_j = -k\frac{\partial T}{\partial x_j} \tag{6}$$

where k is the coefficient of heat conduction. The pressure is related to the density and energy by equation of state

$$p = (\gamma - 1)\rho\left(E - \frac{1}{2}u_i u_i\right) \tag{7}$$

in which γ is the ratio of specific heats.

Turbulent flows can be simulated by the Reynolds equations, in which statistical average are taken of rapidly fluctuating Reynolds stress terms which cannot be determined from the mean values of the velocity and density. Represent $u(t)$ at a particular location (x, y, z). Then the time average and its mean square of u is defined as

$$\bar{u} = \frac{1}{T}\int_{t_0}^{t_0+T} u dt,\ \overline{u'^2} = \frac{1}{T}\int_{t_0}^{t_0+T} u'^2 dt \tag{8}$$

where the integration interval T is chosen to be large than any significant period of the fluctuation, u'. The integrals in the above equations are independent of starting time t_0. The fluctuations are said to be statistically stationary. The root-mean-square value of u' is defined as

$$u'_{rms} = \sqrt{\overline{u'^2}} \tag{9}$$

The statistical theory needs the statistical properties of the fluctuations, such as frequency correlation. Estimates of the Reynolds stress terms must be provided by a turbulence model. The simplest turbulence models augment the molecular viscosity by an eddy viscosity, μ_t that approximately represents the effects of turbulent mixing, and is estimated with some characteristic length scale such as boundary layer thickness. Baldwin-Lomax [31] proposed algebraic or zero-equation turbulence for the outer law, eliminating boundary layer thickness and momentum thickness, in favor of a certain maximum function occurring in the boundary layer. A typical transonic flow patter over a bulbous heat shield of satellite launch vehicle is illustrated in Fig. 1. The effects of compressibility start to cause a radical change in the flow. This occurs when embedded pocket of supersonic flow appear, generally in the terminal shock wave.

3. Axisymmetric fluid dynamics equations

The one of the serious problems in transonic regime of the flight of a bulbous payload shroud is wall pressure fluctuations caused by shock wave-turbulent boundary layer interaction. A terminal shock wave of sufficient strength interacting with a boundary layer may cause flow separation and boundary layer may become unstable. The strength of the terminal shock and the mechanism of its interaction with the boundary layer are linked to a specific configuration of heat shield of a satellite launch vehicle. The shock wave turbulent boundary layer interaction unsteadiness may produce large amplitude fluctuations of the loads acting on the heat shield. The frequency band of the acoustic loads is typically in the range of several hundred Hz to several kHz. The experimental results obtained from the wind-tunnel at zero angle of incidence depict that the flow pattern remains the identical with reference to the wind-tunnel configuration even when the model is rotated. The measurements are made at two diametrically opposite locations indicate that the flow is axisymmetric. Therefore, a numerical solution of the time-dependent, compressible, turbulent, axisymmetric Reynolds-averaged Navier-Stokes equation is attempted to analyze the flow at transonic speeds over the hemisphere-cylinder and the bulbous heat shield of a typical launch vehicle. Now, Equation (1) can be written as

$$\frac{\partial \mathrm{U}}{\partial t} + \frac{\partial \mathrm{F}}{\partial x} + \frac{1}{r}\frac{\partial (r\mathrm{G})}{\partial r} + \frac{\mathrm{H}}{r} = 0 \tag{10}$$

where

$$U=\begin{bmatrix}\rho\\ \rho u\\ \rho v\\ \rho E\end{bmatrix},\ F=\begin{bmatrix}\rho u\\ \rho u^2+p-\sigma_{xx}\\ \rho uv-\tau_{rx}\\ (\rho E+p)u-u\sigma_{xx}-v\tau_{rx}+q_x\end{bmatrix},\ G=\begin{bmatrix}\rho v\\ \rho uv-\tau_{xr}\\ \rho v^2+p-\sigma_{rr}\\ (\rho E+p)v-u\tau_{xr}-v\sigma_{rr}+q_r\end{bmatrix},\ H=\begin{bmatrix}0\\ 0\\ \sigma_+\\ 0\end{bmatrix}$$

Reynolds stresses and turbulent heat fluxes in the mean flow equations are modeled by introducing an isotropic eddy viscosity, μ_t. Thus the viscous terms in the above equations become

$$\sigma_{xx}=-\frac{2}{3}(\mu+\mu_t)\nabla\cdot\phi+2(\mu+\mu_t)\frac{\partial u}{\partial x}$$

$$\sigma_{rr}=-\frac{2}{3}(\mu+\mu_t)\nabla\cdot\phi+2(\mu+\mu_t)\frac{\partial v}{\partial r}$$

$$\tau_{rx}=\tau_{xr}=(\mu+\mu_t)\left(\frac{\partial u}{\partial r}+\frac{\partial v}{\partial x}\right)$$

$$\sigma_+=-p-\frac{2}{3}(\mu+\mu_t)\nabla\cdot\phi+2(\mu+\mu_t)\frac{v}{r}$$

$$\nabla\cdot\phi=\frac{\partial u}{\partial x}+\frac{\partial v}{\partial r}+\frac{v}{r}$$

$$q_x=-cp\left(\frac{\mu}{\mathrm{Pr}}+\frac{\mu_t}{\mathrm{Pr}_t}\right)\frac{\partial T}{\partial x}$$

$$q_r=-cp\left(\frac{\mu}{\mathrm{Pr}}+\frac{\mu_t}{\mathrm{Pr}_t}\right)\frac{\partial T}{\partial r}$$

Temperature is related to pressure and density by the perfect gas Eq. (7). The coefficient of molecular viscosity is calculated according to Sutherland's law. The value of the turbulent Prandtl number Pr_t is assumed to take a constant value of 0.90. The closure of the system of equations is achieved by introducing following the algebraic turbulence model of the Baldwin-Lomax [31]

$$(\mu_0)_i=(0.4D_1 l)\rho|\omega| \tag{11}$$

where ω is the vorticity function, l the normal distance to the model wall, and D_1 is the Van Driest's damping factor

$$D_1=1-\exp\left[-\left(\frac{\rho_w|\omega|_w}{\mu_w}\right)^{0.5}\frac{l}{26}\right] \tag{12}$$

http://dx.doi.org/10.5772/57050

in the outer region

$$(\mu_0)_0 = 0.0168(1.6)F_w F_{KIF} \tag{13}$$

The coefficient of F_w is calculated as the minimum of the following two values

a. $l_{max}F_{max}$

b. $0.25l_{max}\,[(u^2+v^2)]^{0.5}/F_{max}$

The scale length l_{max} is the maximum value of l when the function $F(= l/D_1|\omega|)$ attains its maximum F_{max}. The Klebanoff intermittency correction factor is given by

$$F_{KIF} = \left[1+5.5\left(0.3\frac{l}{l_{max}}\right)^6\right]^{-1} \tag{14}$$

The effective viscosity is given by

$$\mu_t = \min(\mu_i, \mu_0) \tag{15}$$

This algebraic model, which utilizes the vorticity distribution to determine the scale lengths, has been extensively used in conjunction with the Reynolds-averaged Navier-Stokes equations [13, 32, 33].

4. Numerical scheme

4.1. Spatial discretization

To facilitate the spatial discretization in the numerical scheme, Equation (10) can be written in the integral form over a finite volume as

$$\frac{\partial}{\partial t}\int_{\Omega} \mathrm{U}d\Omega + \int_{\Gamma}(\mathrm{F}dr - \mathrm{G}dx) = \int_{\Omega} \mathrm{H}d\Omega \tag{16}$$

where Ω is the computational domain. Γ is the boundary domain. The contour integration around the boundary of the cell is taken in the anticlockwise sense.

Figure 3 depicts a typical stencil of the computing cell which has four edges *(1–4)*, four vortices *(A – D)* and a cell-centre grid point *P*. The spatial and temporal terms are decoupled using the method of lines. The flux vector is divided into the inviscid and viscous components. A cell-centered scheme is used to store the flow variables [34] – [35]. The discretization of inviscid fluxes is performed using the cell average scheme. When the integral governing Eq. (16) is applied separately to each cell in the computational domain, we obtain a set of coupled differential equations of the form

$$A_{i,j}\frac{\partial U_{i,j}}{\partial t}+Q\left(U_{i,j}\right)-V\left(U_{i,j}\right)+D\left(U_{i,j}\right)+A_{i,j}\left(U_{i,j}\right)=0 \tag{17}$$

Where $A_{i,j}$ is the area of the computational cell, $Q(\boldsymbol{U}_{i,j})$ and $V(\boldsymbol{U}_{i,j})$ are inviscid and viscous fluxes respectively, and $D(\boldsymbol{U}_{i,j})$ is the artificial dissipation flux added for numerical stability.

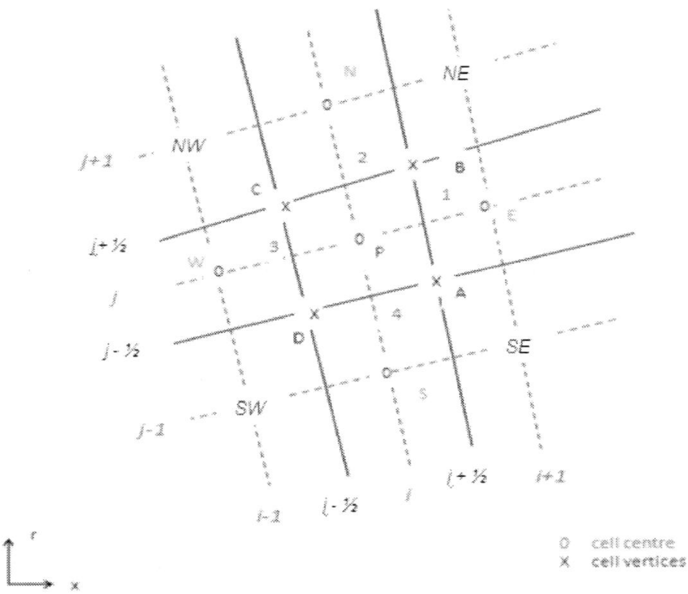

Figure 3. Stencil of the computational cell.

4.2. Artificial dissipation

In cell-centered spatial discretization schemes, such as above which is non-dissipative, therefore, artificial are added to Eq. (17). The approach of Jameson et al. [36] is adopted to construct the dissipative function $\boldsymbol{D}_{i,j}$ consisting of a blend of second and fourth differences of the vector conserved variables $\boldsymbol{U}_{i,j}$. Fourth differences are added everywhere in the flow domain where the solution is smooth, but are 'switched-off' in the region of shock waves. A term involving second differences is then 'switch-on' to damp oscillations in the vicinity of shock waves. This switching is achieved by means of a shock sensor based on the local second differences of pressure. Since the computational domain is having structured grids, the cell centers are defined by two indices *(i,j)*in these coordinate directions. The dissipation term are written in terms of differences of cell-edge values as

$$D_{i,j} = \frac{\Delta A_{i,j}\left(d_{AB} - d_{CD} + d_{BC} - d_{DA}\right)}{\Delta t_{i,j}} \tag{18}$$

where $\Delta t_{i,j}$ is the local cell-centre time step. The cell-edge components of the artificial dissipation terms are composed of first and second differences of dependent variables, e.g.

$$d_{AB} = d_{AB}^{(2)} - d_{AB}^{(4)}$$

with

$$d_{AB}^{(2)} = \varepsilon_2^{(2)}(U_{i+1,j} - U_{i,j})$$

$$d_{AB}^{(4)} = \varepsilon_2^{(4)}(U_{i+2,j} - 3U_{i+1,j} + 3U_{i,j} - U_{i-1,j})$$

The adaptive coefficients

$$\varepsilon_2^{(2)} = \kappa^{(2)} \max(\upsilon_{i+1}, \upsilon_{i,j})$$

$$\varepsilon_2^{(4)} = \max\left(0, \kappa^{(4)} - \varepsilon_2^{(2)}\right)$$

are switched on or off by use of the shock wave sensor ν, with

$$\upsilon_{i,j} = \left|\frac{p_{i+1,j} - 2p_{i,j} + p_{i-1,j}}{p_{i+1,j} + 2p_{i,j} + p_{i-1,j}}\right| \tag{19}$$

where $\kappa^{(2)}$ and $\kappa^{(4)}$ are constants, taken equal to *1/4* and *1/256* respectively. The scaling quantity $(\Delta A/\Delta t)_{i,j}$ in Eq.(18) confirms the inclusion of the cell volume in the dependent variable of Eq. (16). The blend of second and fourth differences provides third-order background dissipation in smooth regions of the flow and first-order dissipation at shock waves.

The spatial discretization can be summarized here which is employed in numerical simulations. The convective terms are nonlinear, hyperbolic and grid dependent. A structured non-overlapping quadrilateral cell is used in the numerical simulations. The diffusive terms are quasi-linear, elliptic, grid independent, cell centered use of dual control volume for evaluating the gradients at a given location. Thus, the discretized solution to the governing equations results in a set of volume-averaged state variables of mass, momentum, and energy which are balance with their area-averaged fluxes (inviscid and viscous) across the cell faces [34]. The finite volume code constructed in this manner reduces to a central difference scheme and is second-order accurate provided that the mesh is smooth enough [34]. The cell-centered spatial discretization scheme is non-dissipative; therefore, artificial dissipation terms are included as a blend of a Laplacian and biharmonic operator in a manner analogous to the second and fourth difference. The artificial dissipation term [36] was added explicitly to prevent numerical oscillations near the shock waves to damp high-frequency modes.

5. Multi-stage time-stepping scheme

The spatial discretiztion described above reduces the governing flow equations to semi-discrete ordinary differential equations. The integration is performed employing an efficient multi-stage scheme [36]. The following three-stage, time-stepping scheme is used for the numerical simulation (for clarity, the subscripts i and j are neglected here)

$$\begin{aligned} U^{(0)} &= U^{n} \\ U^{(1)} &= U^{n} - 0.6\Delta t\left(R^{(0)} - D^{(0)}\right) \\ U^{(2)} &= U^{n} - 0.6\Delta t\left(R^{(1)} - D^{(0)}\right) \\ U^{(3)} &= U^{n} - 1.0\Delta t\left(R^{(2)} - D^{(0)}\right) \\ U^{n+1} &= U^{(3)} \end{aligned} \tag{20}$$

where n is the current time level, $n + 1$ is the new time level, and residual $\boldsymbol{R}$ is the sum of the inviscid and viscous fluxes. The multi-stages time-stepping scheme has been proved to be second-order accurate in time for a linear system of one-dimensional equation [35]. The artificial dissipation is evaluated only at the first stage. The permissible time step of an explicit scheme is limited by the Courant-Friedrichs-Lewy condition, which states that a difference scheme cannot be convergent and stable approximation unless its domain of dependence contains the domain of dependence of the corresponding differential equation. A conservative choice of the Courant number is made in the simulation to achieve a stable numerical solution. A global time-step is used rather than the grid-varying time-step to numerically simulate a time-accurate solution and is computed using following expression [37]

$$(\Delta t)_{i,j} = \min\left[\frac{|u|}{\Delta x} + \frac{|v|}{\Delta r} + c\sqrt{\frac{1}{(\Delta x)^2 + (\Delta r)^2}}\right]^{-1} \tag{21}$$

where i,j are grid point as shown in Fig. 3.

http://dx.doi.org/10.5772/57050

5.1. Initial and boundary conditions

Conditions corresponding to a freestream Mach number were given as initial conditions. On the surface, no slip condition is considered together with an adiabatic wall condition. The symmetric conditions were applied on the centerline. For the transonic flow simulations, non-reflecting far field boundary conditions are applied at the outer boundary of the computational cell. For supersonic flow, all the flow variables are extrapolated at the outflow from the vector of conservative vector, *U*.

5.2. Geometrical details of the Model

Hemisphere-cylinder model

The dimension of the hemisphere-cylinder model is taken as 2.54×10^{-2} m and 25.4×10^{-2} m length.

Heat shield geometry

The maximum payload shroud diameter *D* of the model is *0.04* m and the booster diameter *d* is *0.035* m. The symbols *D* and *d* are depicted in Fig. 4. The inclination at the fore body junction is 20^0 and the total length of the shroud from the stagnation point to the boat tail is *0.083* m. The boat tail angle is 15^0 measured clock-wise from the axis with reference to the on-coming flow direction. The values of l_1/D and l_2/D are 0.96 and 1.4, respectively.

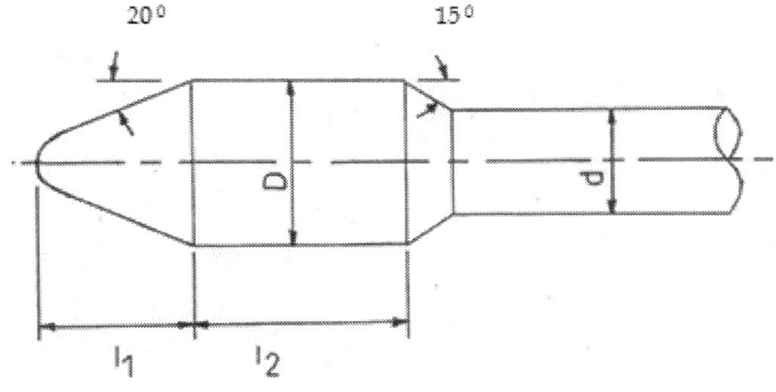

Figure 4. Geometry of the bulbous heat shield.

Spike geometry

The dimensions of the spiked-blunt body are depicted in Fig. 5. The model is axisymmetric, the main body has a hemispherical-cylinder nose, and the diameter D is 7.62×10^{-2} m. The aerospike consists of a conical part and a cylindrical part. The angle of the spike's cone is 10^0 and the diameter of the spike is 0.1D. The aerospike model has a simple stick configuration. The L/D ratios of the spike are 0.5, 1.0 and 2.0.

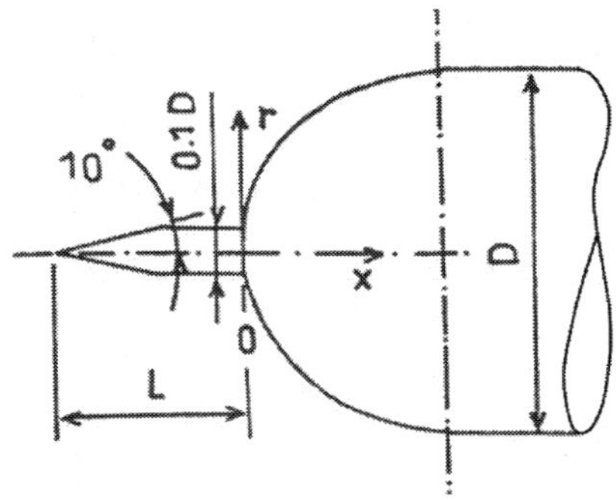

Figure 5. Dimensions of the spiked-blunt body.

5.3. Computational grid

One of the controlling factors for the numerical simulation is the proper grid arrangement. The following procedure is adopted to generate grid in the computational domain of the model. The computational region is divided into a number of non-overlapping zones. The mesh points are generated in each zone using finite element methods [38] in conjunction with the homotopy scheme [39]. The above models are defined by a number of mesh points in the cylindrical coordinate system. Using these surface points as the reference node, the normal coordinate is then described by the exponentially stretched grid points extending towards up to an outer computational boundary.

$$\begin{aligned} x_{i,j} &= x_{i,o}\left[\frac{e^{(j-1)\beta/(nr-1)}-1}{e^{\beta}-1}\right]+x_{i,w}\left[1-\frac{e^{(j-1)\beta/(nr-1)}-1}{e^{\beta}-1}\right] \\ r_{i,j} &= r_{i,o}\left[\frac{e^{(j-1)\beta/(nr-1)}-1}{e^{\beta}-1}\right]+r_{i,w}\left[1-\frac{e^{(j-1)\beta/(nr-1)}-1}{e^{\beta}-1}\right] \\ & i=1,2,3....,nx, \qquad j=1,2,3....,nr \end{aligned} \tag{22}$$

where subscripts o and w are wall and outer surface points, respectively, β is a stretching factor. nx and nr are total number of grid points in x and r directions, respectively.

The outer boundary of the computational domain is varied from 5 to 8 times the cylinder diameter, D, and the grid-stretching factor β in the radial direction varied from 1.5 to 5.0. At transonic freestream Mach number, the computational domain of dependence is unbounded, and the implementation of boundary and initial conditions become important factor for the selection of the computational region. The known physically acceptable far-field boundary conditions usually limit the flow variables to asymptotic values at large distances from the payload shroud. For the supersonic speeds, the computational domain is kept 4 to 6 times the maximum diameter *D*. Figure 6 depicts the computational grid in the physical domain of the hemisphere-cylinder, the heat shield and the conical spiked attached to the blunt body. The grid independent is carried out using the above mentioned numerical algorithm.

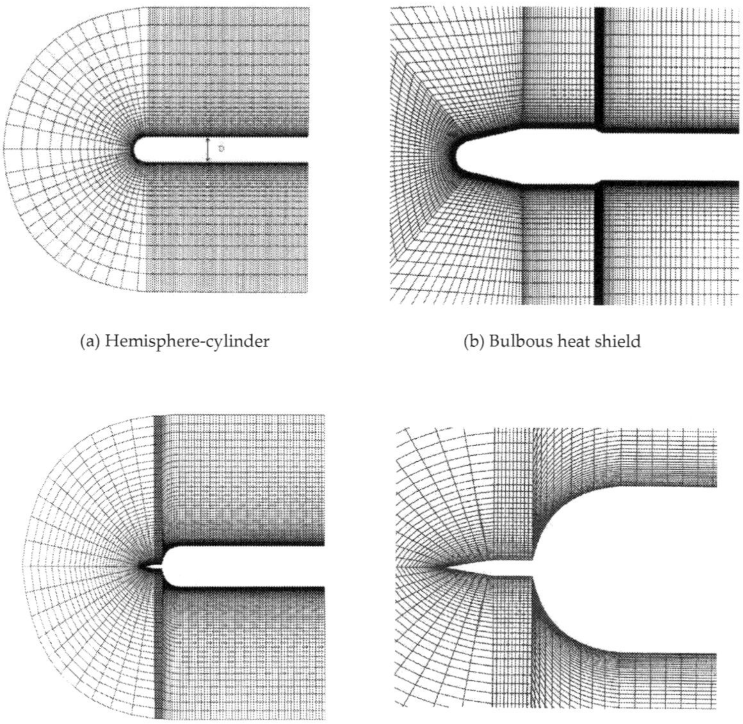

(a) Hemisphere-cylinder (b) Bulbous heat shield

(c) Spiked-blunt body (d) Close-up view of grid over spiked-blunt body

Figure 6. Computational grids.

6. Results and discussion

6.1. Hemisphere-cylinder model

A terminal shock wave of sufficient strength interacting with a boundary layer can cause flow separation and the process can become unsteady [40]. The numerical procedure described in the previous section is applied to compute the flowfield over the hemisphere-cylinder at M_∞ = *0.90* and Reynolds number 5.1×10^{6}. Figure 7 depicts the close-up view of velocity field. The strong attached flow near the hemisphere-cylinder junction and an expansion due to the hemisphere geometry makes way to a separation following a terminal shock wave accompanying with supersonic pocket. The separation and reattachment points are indicted by symbols *S* and *R*, respectively. The separation is confined to a short distance and flow reattach at x/D = 1.07 for M_∞ = 0.90. Figure 7 also shows the comparison between the numerical and the experimental results of Hsieh [1] – [2]. All the essential flowfield features of the transonic flow, such as supersonic pocket, terminal shock wave and expansion region are well captured and compare well with the shadowgraph picture.

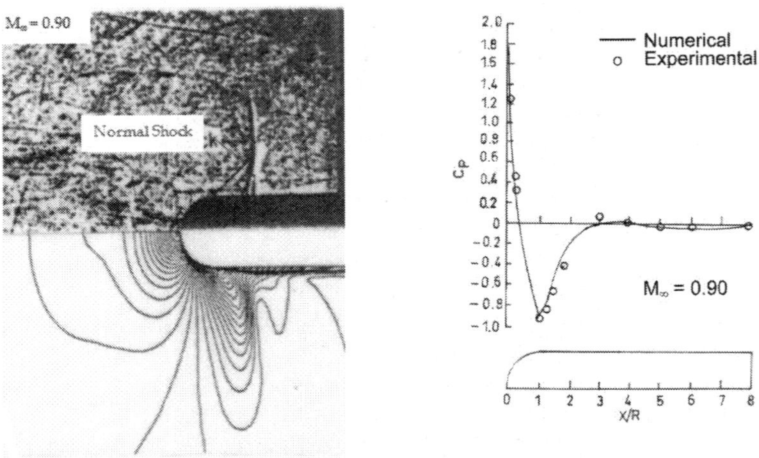

(a) Density contours and shadowgraph picture (b) Variation of surface pressure

Figure 7. Comparison of numerical with experimental results over hemisphere-cylinder model.

Once the initial phase of the computation is over 16 axial location ($x/D = 0.16$ - 2.50) along the hemisphere-cylinder measured from the stagnation point of the hemisphere are selected to study the sensitivity of the unsteadiness in the flow. Figure 8 depicts instantaneous vector plot at $M_\infty = 0.90$. The calculated surface pressure data are analyzed for the time mean, root mean pressure and, fast Fourier transform FFT [41] – [42].

http://dx.doi.org/10.5772/57050

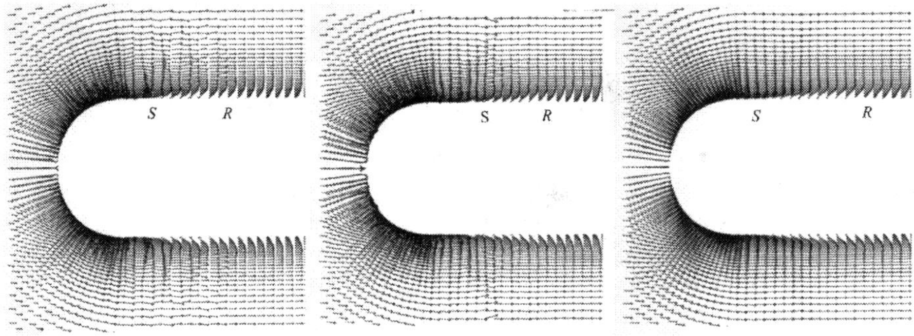

Figure 8. Instantaneous vector plot over hemisphere-cylinder at $M_\infty = 0.90$.

6.2. Spectral analysis

A spectral analysis is carried out on the computed pressure-time data for all possible modes of fluctuations employing fast Fourier transform [41], which converts the pressure history from time domain into frequency domain. Figure 9 shows the spectrum of sound pressure level SPL over the hemisphere-cylinder model. The pressure values have been converted from Pascal to decibel (dB) of surface pressure levels.

$$SPL(db) = 20\log\left[\frac{p_w(t)}{p_{ref}}\right] \tag{23}$$

The surface pressure levels are computed in terms of the pressure reference at 20×10^{-6} Pa. The frequencies for which assessment were carried out at the multiples of the fundamental frequency of 26 Hz for the hemisphere-cylinder model. A high value of SPL is found at 200 Hz at x/D = *1.7996*, *2.0660* and *2.2630*. A significant SPL of *168 dB* at about *26* Hz is found at x/D = *2.611* which may be attributed to the separated flow associated with the terminal shock. The SPL value increases gradually in the local supersonic pocket.

The function is non-periodic, a period T is to be assumed. This is dictated by the lowest or fundamental frequency that is to be considered in the analysis

$$\begin{aligned} \omega_0 &= \omega\Delta T = \frac{2\pi}{T} \\ n\omega_0 &= n\Delta\omega = \omega_n \end{aligned} \tag{24}$$

where ω is angular frequency. The period is divided into N equal intervals of Δt and the function is sampled at time $t_m = m\Delta t$. The Fast Fourier Transform FFT is a computer algorithm for calculating Discrete Fourier Transform DFT. The FFT computes in the frequency domain can be written as

$$F(\omega_n) = \frac{T}{N} \sum_{m=0}^{N-1} F(t_m) e^{i(-2\pi nm/N)} \tag{25}$$

where N is the number of data points, Δt is sampling interval and $T = N\Delta t$ is record length. The FFT offers an enormous reduction of computer time as compared to DFT.

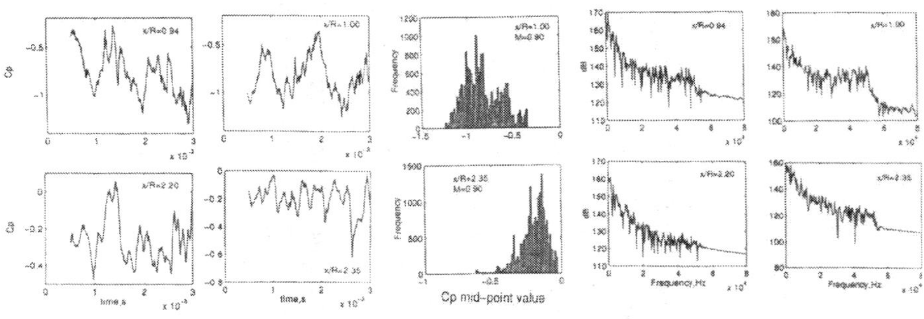

(a) Pressure coefficient fluctuations (b) Histogram (c) Spectrum of sound

Figure 9. Pressure coefficient, histogram and SPL over the hemisphere-cylinder.

6.3. Bulbous heat shield of a satellite launch vehicle

Figure 10 depicts the density contour plots for the freestream transonic Mach number of 0.80 and 0.90 for the bulbous heat shield and compare the density plots with schlieren pictures. The strength of the terminal shock wave initially increases with Mach number and later decreases. It can be observed from the figures that all of the essential flowfield features of the transonic flow, such as supersonic pocket, normal shock, and expansion and compression regions are very well captured and compare well with the schlieren pictures. The density contour plots reveal that the supersonic pocket increases with increasing freestream Mach number, and as a result, the terminal shock moves downstream with increasing freestream Mach number. It is important to mention here that the density increases ahead of the stagnation region of the heat shield moves close to the heat shield with the increasing transonic Mach number. It also depends on the cone angle of the heat shield as observed in the density contours plots of the flowfield.

The general flowfield along the payload shroud is shown in Fig. 11 for freestream Mach number of *0.80 – 1.00*. Figure 12 depicts comparison between density contours and schlieren pictures. All of the essential flow characteristics of the transonic flow, such as the supersonic

http://dx.doi.org/10.5772/57050

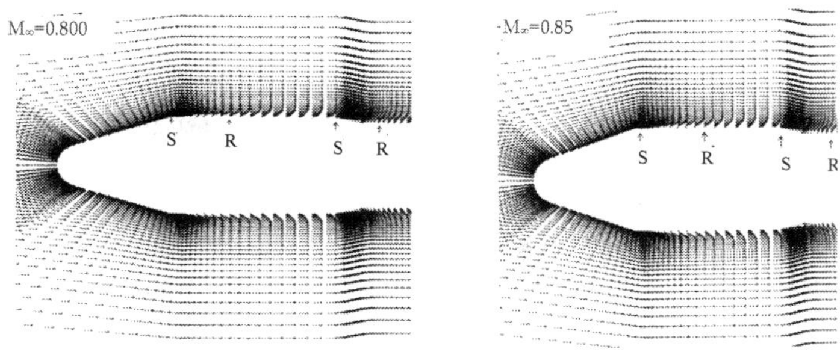

Figure 10. Velocity vector plots at transonic Mach number.

pocket, the terminal shock wave, and the expansion and compression regions, are well captured by present numerical simulations. It can be seen from the density contour plots of heat shield that the formation of the terminal shock and supersonic region over the payload shroud is a function of the geometrical parameters of the heat shield [43]. Envelope of Mach lines leads to formation of the terminal shock wave. The expansion regions of the axisymmteric supersonic flow are characterized by diverging Mach lines, whereas in the compression region they converge to form a shock wave. In the shock wave theory [8] in fact there is no "expansion shock". The flow separation on the payload shroud is caused by the terminal shock wave. The shock-induced separated flow on the cone-cylinder is not found for the heat shield with a cone angle of *15* deg. As freestream Mach number increases, the terminal shock moves downstream and the local supersonic zone increases rapidly. The terminal shock becomes so strong that, as a result of a shock wave-boundary layer interaction, boundary layer separation occurs and it is the function of shock strength, geometrical parameter of the heat shield and freestream Mach number. The density contour plots reveals that a shear layer is formed which accommodates the recirculating flow for the transonic speeds. The downstream boundary layer is found to be thick, which is nearly the boat-tail height. It is worth to mention here that the main purpose to introduce the boat-tail is to increase payload volume of a satellite launch vehicle.

The shock wave separated boundary layer and flow separation caused by boat tail geometry of heat shield generated high and low frequency pressure fluctuations. Flow induced vibrations are important issues to be taken into account the design requirement of the satellite. Shock wave separated boundary layer and flow separation caused by boat tail geometry of the heat shield generated high and low frequency pressure fluctuations. Analyses of the time-dependent flowfield feature are essential to design the bulbous heat shield of a satellite launch vehicle. Fluctuations of pressure level in shock waves and in separation areas induce flow instabilities and then structural vibration leading to the buffeting phenomenon.

In the boat-tail region, a local flow separation occurs, due to sharp discontinuity in the longitudinal curvature. The flow reattachment length $(X_r - X_c)$ is normalized by the boat-tail height *H*, where X_c is the location of the boat tail shoulder and X_r is the reattachment point. The prediction of reattachment point is the point where the axial component of the velocity along the downstream wall changes from negative to positive. The non-dimensional separation

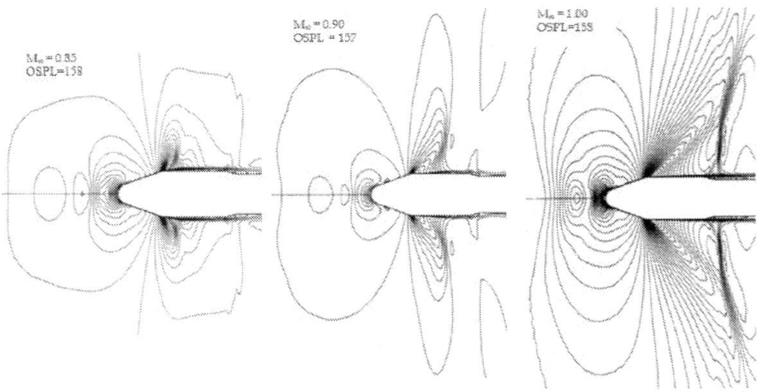

Figure 11. Density contour plots over the bulbous heat shield at transonic Mach number.

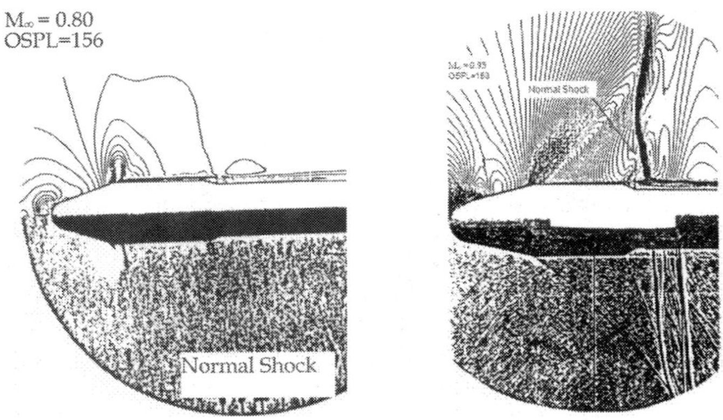

Figure 12. Comparison between density contour plots and schlieren pictures.

length $(X_r - X_c)/H$ is found *11.7* from the velocity vector plot as shown in Fig. 13(a). The location of the flow reattachment point is required to analyze the wall pressure fluctuations. The density contour plots of Fig. 11 reveal that the supersonic region increases with increasing freestream Mach number, and as a result, the terminal shock moves downstream with increasing freestream Mach number as shown in Fig. 13(b).

Once the initial phase of the computation was completed, some unsteadiness in the flow characteristics was observed. The sixteen locations (x/D) along the heat shield measured from the stagnation point are selected to study the unsteadiness of the flowfield. Figure 14 shows the instantaneous flow separation and pressure distribution at different location of the heat

http://dx.doi.org/10.5772/57050

shield. Before the analysis of the amplification factor and sound pressure levels are initiated, a statistical approach was employed to ensure that the computed data are free from transitional phase, i.e., the pressure values are representative of the numerical results, if the computation had continued for a very long period of time.

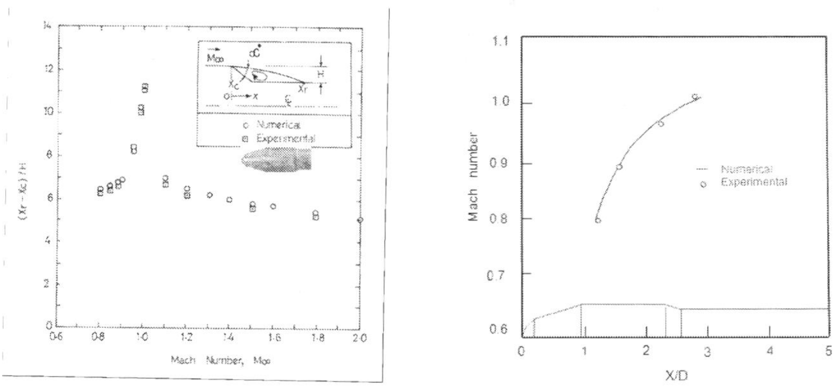

(a) Reattachment distance as a function of Mach number (b) Location of terminal shock on heat shield

Figure 13. Overall flowfield features over the bulbous heat shield.

A set of histograms of *Cp* is depicted in Fig. 15. The numerical data in the separation region and other stations exhibit a Gaussian distribution. A spectral analysis was carried out on the computed pressure data for all possible modes of oscillations using fast Fourier transform FFT of MATLAB [44]. A cyclic behaviour of the pressure coefficient is observed in the vicinity of the separation and reattachment points. From the spectrum analysis low frequency pressure fluctuations and sound pressure levels are found at freestream Mach number 0.95.

The wall pressure fluctuations may arise as an effect of unsteady pressure associated to the turbulent velocity field. The Mach variation on the flow physics is the change of the location of the intense shock wave which is originally generated on the fairing and moves towards the booster for Mach approaching unity. From the acoustic point of view, it is observed that the most critical situation correspond to $M_{\infty} = 0.80$, where a significant unsteadiness of the shock wave is observed. These behaviors can be qualitatively seen in the schlieren picture. The visualizations suggest that a shock wave is generated in the fairing region and then it moves downstream for increasing Mach. The present chapter is focalized on the transonic range of flow conditions. The characterization of the pressure fluctuations is accomplished by statistical analysis, and flow visualizations are used to the physical interpretation of the results. The overall sound pressure level is mentioned in the density contour plots. The overall sound pressure level OSPL reaches the maximum amplitude at transonic conditions.

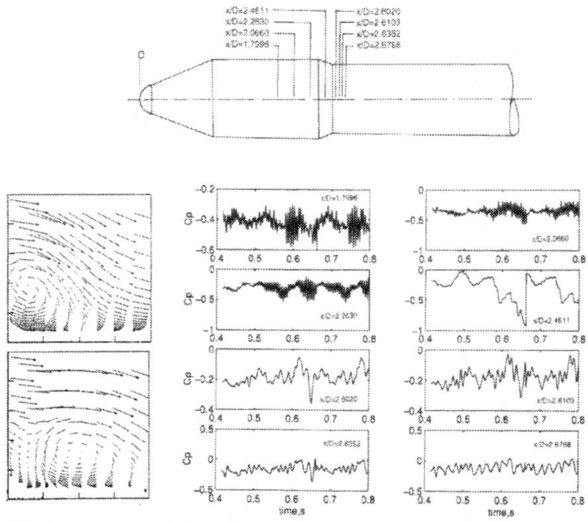

Figure 14. Velocity vector plot and fluctuations of pressure coefficient.

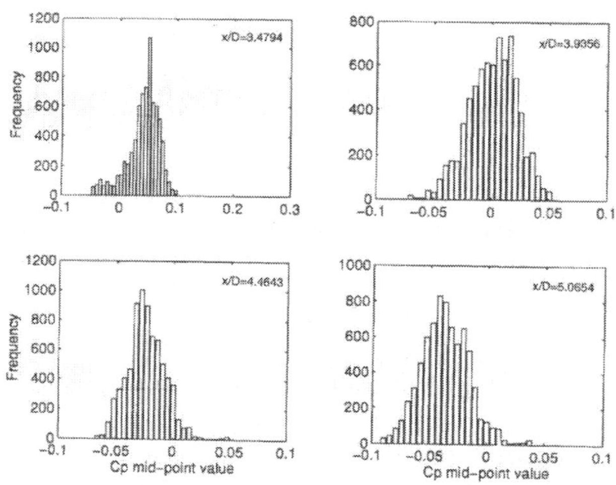

Figure 15. Histograms of pressure coefficient over the bulbous heat shield.

The numerical simulation is used to analysis the unsteady flowfield characteristics of the bulbous payload shroud.

http://dx.doi.org/10.5772/57050

6.4. Statistics analysis

A statistical approach was used in order to ensure that the data are free from transitional phase, i.e., the pressure values are representive of the data, if computational had continued for a long time. The computed surface pressure data along the shroud were analyzed for the time mean and standard deviation values using the following relations:

$$\overline{Cp} = \frac{1}{n}\sum_{i=1}^{n} Cp_i \tag{26}$$

$$\sigma_{Cp} = \sqrt{\sum_{i=1}^{n} \frac{\left(Cp_i - \overline{Cp}\right)^2}{n-1}} \tag{27}$$

The total time period $n\Delta t$ ($\Delta t = 0.8 \times 10^{-6} s$) and is considered after 47 900 time step computation is over. Higher order moments of pressure fluctuations, the skewness coefficient, and the kurtosis coefficient are expressed as

$$\sigma_{Cp} = \frac{\left[\frac{1}{n}\sum_{i=1}^{n}\left(Cp_i - \overline{Cp}\right)^3\right]}{\sigma_{Cp}^3} \tag{28}$$

$$\sigma_{Cp} = \frac{\left[\frac{1}{n}\sum_{i=1}^{n}\left(Cp_i - \overline{Cp}\right)^4\right]}{\sigma_{Cp}^4} \tag{29}$$

The skewness coefficient expresses the asymmetric of fluctuations around the mean value and the kurtosis coefficient expresses the symmetric property around the mean value. Figure 16 shows variation of mean pressure, rms, skewness, and Kurtosis coefficient.

6.5. Flowfield over the spiked-blunt body

The flow is assumed to be laminar for the spiked-blunt body, which is consistent with the experimental study of Crawford [24] and Kenworthy [45] and the numerical simulation of Yamauchi et al. [46], Hankey and Shang [47] and Badcock et al. [28]. Therefore, the turbulent viscosity μ_t is neglected in Eq. (10). The time-dependent axisymmetric compressible laminar Navier-Stokes equations are employed to analyze unsteady low over the spiked-blunt body. The coefficient of molecular viscosity μ is calculated using Sutherland's law.

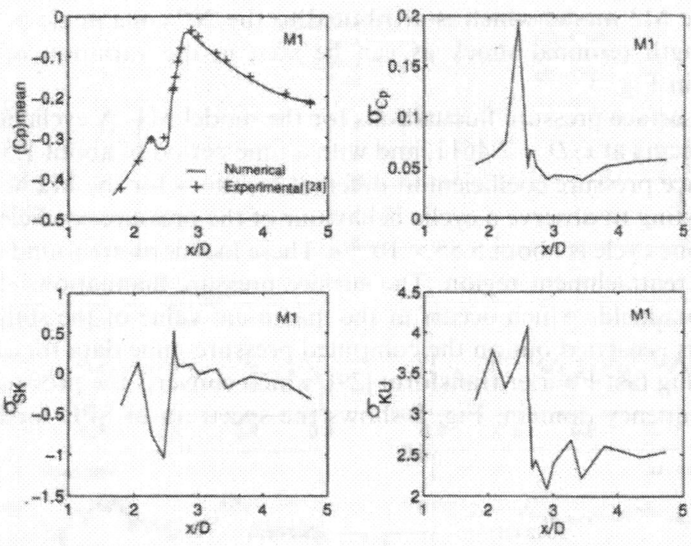

Figure 16. Variations of (a) mean pressure (b) rms (c) skewness (d) Kurtosis coefficients over the bulbous heat shield.

Figure 17 shows the enlarged view of the computed density contour and velocity plots for semi-cone angle of spike α = 10, 15, 20 and 30 deg at M_{∞} = 6.0 and *L*/*D* = 0.5. Figure 18 shows the pressure variation (*p*/*pa*) along the surface of the spiked-blunt body for different semi-cone angle of the spike. The wall pressure is normalized by freestream pressure *pa*. The *x* = *0* location is the spike/nose-tip junction. The location of the maximum pressure on the surface of the spiked-blunt body is at a body angle of about 40 deg for all the semi-cone angle of the conical spike. This location corresponds to the reattachment point. A wavy pressure distribution is observed on the spike, which may be attributed the separated flowfield behavior. The maximum pressure level is occurred at the same location on the blunt body. The flowfield can be studied using the shock polar diagram in conjunction with the Computational Fluid Dynamics approach [48]. The computed conical shock wave angles are compared with Ref. [49] and found good agreement between them.

It can be observed from the figure that interaction between the conical oblique shock wave emanating from the tip of the spike and the reattachment shock wave on the blunt body is seen. The reflected reattachment shock wave and shear layer from the interaction are seen behind the reattachment shock wave. A large separated region is observed in front of the blunt body. Flow patterns are same as that for *L*/*D* = *0.5*. When the spike is long, the angle of the conical shock wave emanating from the spike-tip decreases and flow separation occurs slightly downstream. Since the reattachment point moved backward and the spike is long, the length of the separated region extended.

http://dx.doi.org/10.5772/57050

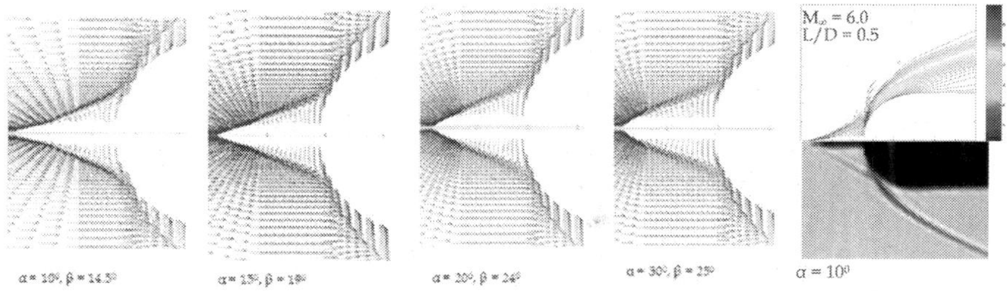

Figure 17. Enlarged view of velocity vector plot over conical spiked-blunt body.

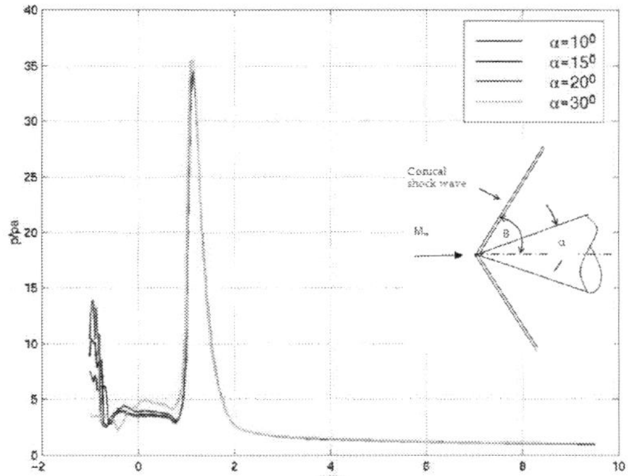

Figure 18. Pressure distributions along the spiked-blunt body.

6.6. Flow characteristics for the spiked-blunt body

Figure 19 show the enlarged view of the density contours and velocity vector plots for spike lengths of *L/D = 0.5* and the semi-cone angle of the spike 10 deg (Fig. 5) at M_∞ = 2.01, 4.15 and 6.80. It can be seen from the figures that interaction between the conical shock emanating from the tip of the spike and the reattachment shock wave on the blunt body is observed. The reflected reattachment shock wave and shear layer from the interaction are observed behind the reattachment shock wave. A large separated flow region is visible in the vector plots. In the separation region, a number of vortices exist and the velocity magnitude is very low.

Flowfield was analyzed for $M_\infty = 2.01, 4.15, 6.80$ for $L/D = 0.5$ and for the $Re = 0.14 \times 10^6$ based on the diameter of the hemispherical body D. Computed density contour plots with schlieren pictures are compared in Fig. 20 for L/D = 0.5, 1.0, 2.0 for M∞ = 6.80. The computed flowfield shows agreement with the schlieren photographs taken in the experiment by Yamauchi et al.

[46] and Crawford [24]. Figure 21 reveals the effects of ratio of *L/D* and M_ over the flow over the spiked-blunt body.

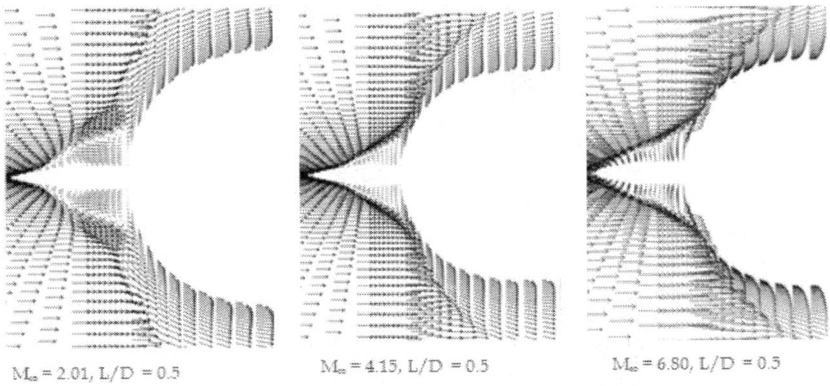

Figure 19. Enlarged views of velocity vector plots.

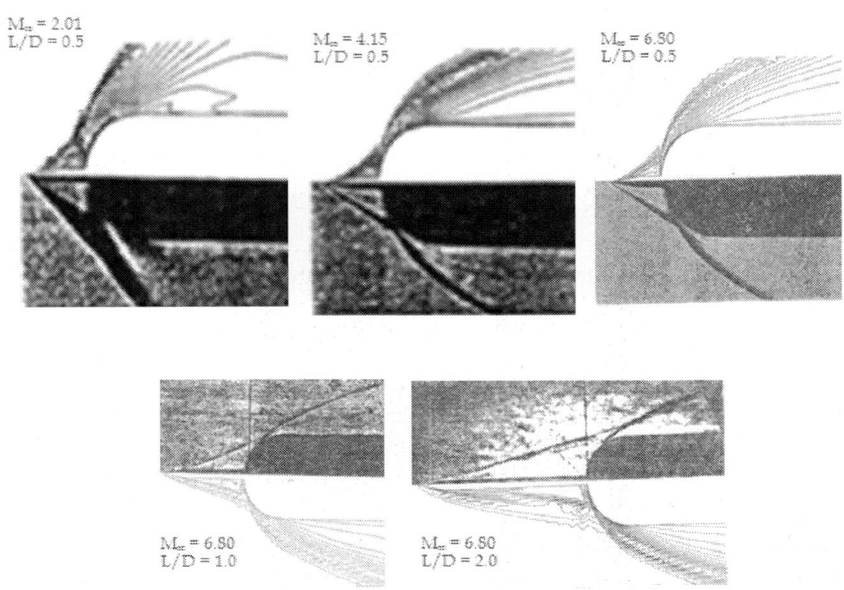

Figure 20. Comparison between density contours and schlieren photographs.

http://dx.doi.org/10.5772/57050

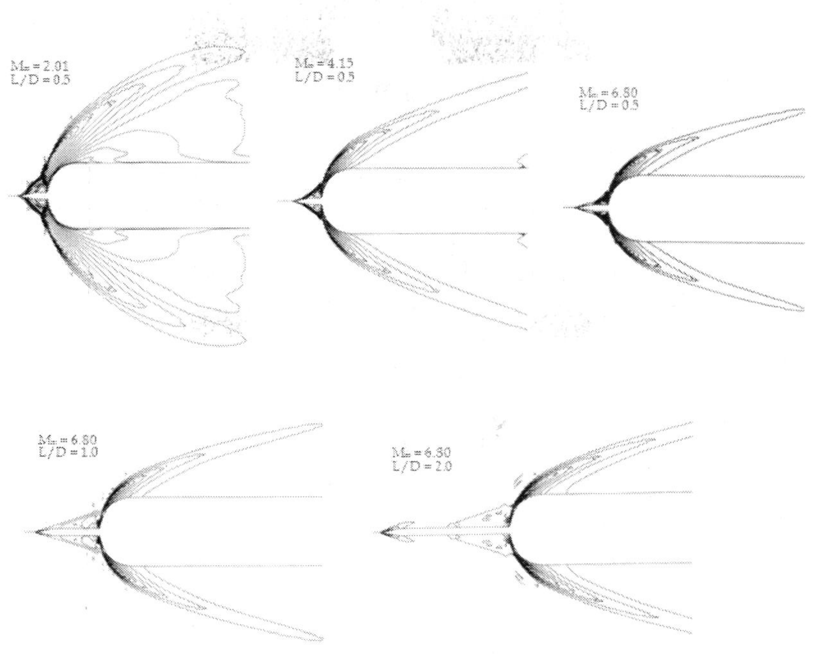

Figure 21. Density vector plots over spiked-blunt body.

Once the oscillatory motion is established in the flow, as can be visualized in the instantaneous velocity vector plots in Fig. 22, the periodic phenomenon is investigated by a spectral analysis to obtain information on the frequency and amplitude for various modes of oscillations. The time steps Δt were $5.0 \times 10^{-7} s$ taken for $M_\infty = 6.8$ and $L/D = 0.5$.

The periodic phenomenon is investigated by a spectral analysis to obtain information on the frequency and amplitude for various modes of oscillation. Figure 23 show the pressure coefficient $[Cp = 2\{(p/p_\infty) - 1\}/\gamma M_\infty^2]$ variation with respect to time on the spiked-blunt body at $M_\infty = 4.15$ and $L/D = 0.5$. The interaction of the conical shock wave emanating from the spike tip with the separation vortices governs the pressure oscillations. The pressure oscillations are found more cyclic in nature and function of the L/D ratio and M_∞. These pressure oscillations are low in amplitude and depend on the location on the spike. This unsteady behavior of the flowfield is caused by the separated region enclosed inside the reattachment.

A spectral analysis is carried out on the computed pressure history employing FFT of MATLAB [44]. The pressure amplitude versus frequency and phase plots for $L/D = 0.5$ and $M_\infty = 6.8$ are computed using pressure oscillations data $p(t)$. In the spectrum plots, there are pressure amplitude peaks of dominant frequency and multiples of the dominant frequency at various locations of the spike. The spectral analysis of the pressure reveals that the discrete frequencies of higher modes of oscillations are multiples of the principal modes.

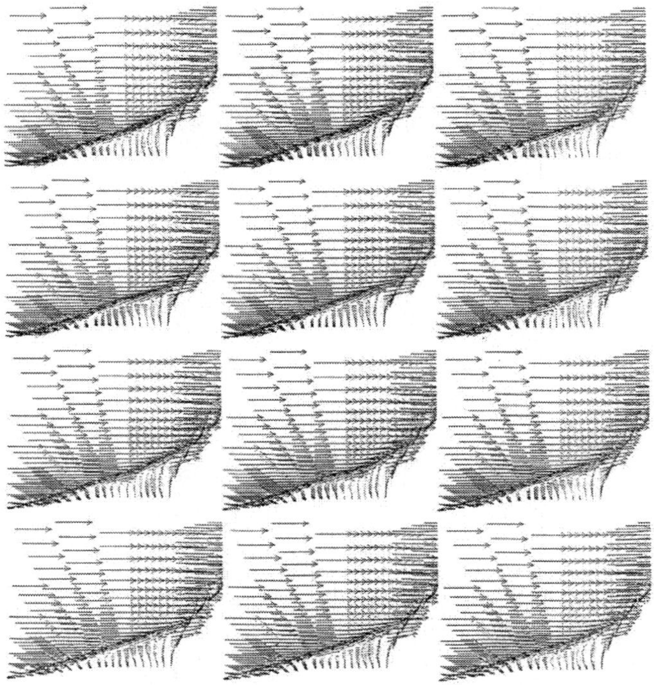

Figure 22. Instantaneous vector plot, $M_\infty = 6.8$ and L/D = 0.5.

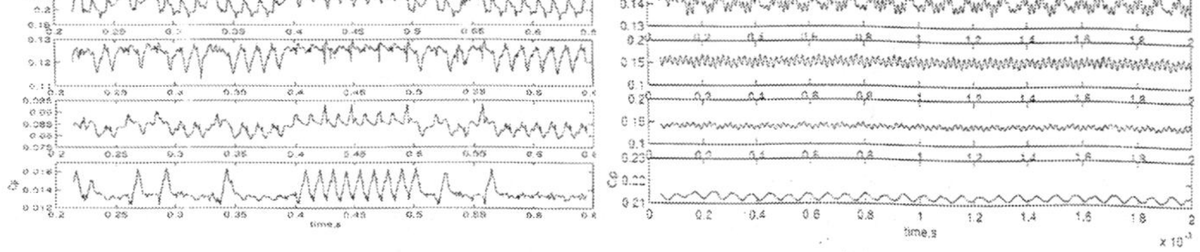

Figure 23. Pressure oscillations, $M_\infty = 4.15$ and $L/D = 0.5$.

http://dx.doi.org/10.5772/57050

Figure 24 represents the pressure amplitude versus frequency and phase plots for L/D = 0.5 and M_∞ = 6.80. In the spectrum plots, there are pr4essure amplitude peaks of dominant frequency and multiples of the dominant frequency at different stations of the spike. The spectral analysis of the pressure reveals that the discrete frequencies of higher mode of oscillation are multiples of the principal modes. The vortex pattern inside the separated region is different for different spike lengths. Therefore the second and third mode frequencies are different for different location.

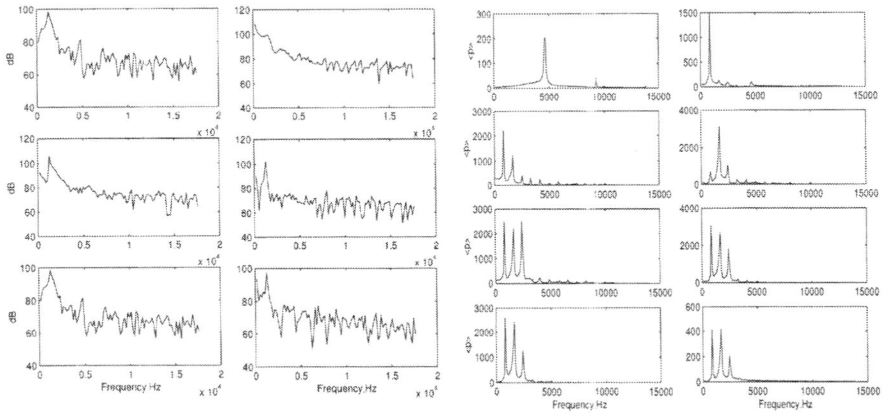

Figure 24. Spectrum of sound pressure level and pressure oscillations.

6.7. Self-excited oscillation for the spiked-blunt body

The fluid dynamics of the self-sustained oscillatory flow is analyzed using spring-mass analogy as well as the nonlinear oscillatory model. The self-excited oscillation is governed or autonomous and draws its energy from the external source by its own periodic motion. For small oscillations, energy is fed into the system and there is "negative damping" [50, 51]. For large flow oscillations, energy is taken from the system and therefore damped. The periodic pressure behavior is analogous with differential equation describing the self-sustained oscillation of Van der Pol equation [51]. Figure 25 shows [*d(Cp)/dt*] versus *Cp*. The phase plane portrait is analyzed to understand the characteristics of the oscillatory flow. The phase plane plots are computed using the time-dependent pressure data. The phase plots reveal the characteristics of the oscillatory pressure field. The motion tends to build up small oscillations and decrease for large oscillations, which indicates that the damping term is greater than zero, hence, after the initial transient, the motion becomes periodic, represented by a closed trajectory which is also called a limit cycle.

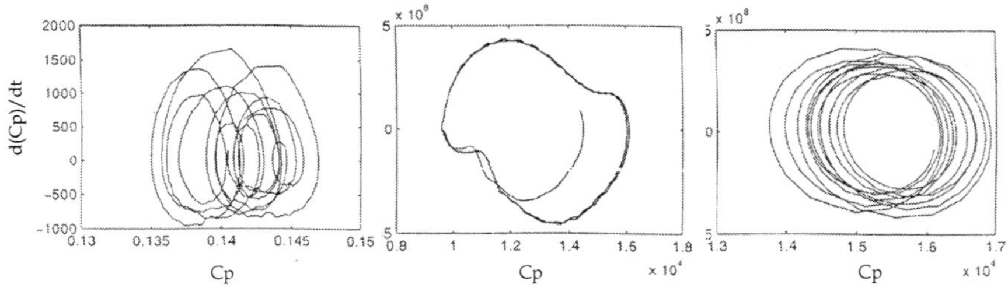

Figure 25. Phase trajectory, $M_\infty = 6.8$ and $L/D = 0.5$.

7. Conclusions

The numerical simulations are carried out over the hemisphere-cylinder model and the bulbous heat shield of a satellite launch vehicle at transonic Mach number. The time-dependent compressible axisymmetric Navier-Stokes equations are solved employing multi-stage Runge-Kutta time-stepping scheme with Baldwin-Lomax turbulence model. The pressure fluctuations are computed at different location on the model. The unsteady flowfield characteristics are analyzed using fast Fourier transform. The numerical analysis also includes the numerical flow visualization and comparison with the available experimental data.

The key concern of research into the area of protruding spikes ahead of blunt bodies is the unstable flow that has been observed to exist for particular families of blunt bodies in supersonic and hypersonic flow. The length of the spike had an impact on the frequency and mode of oscillations. In this study the spike length was the principle parameter of variation on both flat faced and hemispherical blunt bodies. To this point, the focus of numerical simulations had remained on the effects that variation to the spike length and blunt body profile had on the resulting flow. Research into spike tipped blunt bodies has typically focused on variations to two main design variables; the length of the spike relative to the diameter of the blunt body, and the geometric shape of the blunt body itself. This research has drawn conclusions about the different flow regimes and the relative spike lengths that this is observed to occur for specific flow conditions. It is the objective of this project to contribute to this understanding by analyzing the effect that variations to the spike diameter relative to the blunt body diameter have on the characteristics of the flow. The numerical analysis is extended to simulate the flow over spiked-blunt body under laminar condition. The numerical simulations captured pressure oscillations in the separation region. A limit cycle is obtained that describes the self-sustained oscillation of Van der Pol equation.

http://dx.doi.org/10.5772/57050

Nomenclature

Cp = specific heat at constant pressure

Cp = pressure coefficient

D = diameter

c = sound velocity

d = booster diameter

e = internal specific energy

E = total specific energy, $(e + 0.5(u_i u_i))$

$\boldsymbol{F}$, $\boldsymbol{G}$, $\boldsymbol{H}$ = flux vectors

L = length of spike

M = Mach number

N = number of data points

Pr = Prandtl number

p = static pressure

q_j = heat flux components

Re = Reynolds number

SPL = sound pressure level

T = temperature

t = time

u_i = velocity components

u, v = axial and radial velocity

$\boldsymbol{U}$ = conservative variables in vector form

x_j = Cartesian coordinate

x, r = axial and radial coordinate

α = semi-cone angle

β = angle of conical shock wave

γ = ratio of specific heats

δ = Kronecker delta

μ = molecular viscosity

ρ = density

σ_{ij} = viscous stress tensor

τ_{ij} = stress tensor

Δ = increment

Subscripts

D = diameter

rms = root-mean-square

t = turbulent

∞ = freestream

Superscripts

$-$ = time mean

$'$ = turbulent fluctuation

Acknowledgements

The author is indebted to his parents and Vikram Sarabhai Space Centre, Trivandrum, India for their valuable encouragement, support and contributions to build the research career.

Author details

R. C. Mehta[1,2]

Address all correspondence to: drrakhab.mehta@gmail.com

1 Department of Aeronautical Engineering, Noorul Islam University, Kumaracoil, Tamil Nadu, India

2 School of Mechanical & Aerospace Engineering, Nanyang Technological University, Singapore

References

[1] Hsieh, T. Flowfield about Hemispherical Cylinder in Transonic and Low Supersonic Mach Number Range. AIAA 75-83, 1975.

[2] Hsieh, T. Hemisphere-Cylinder in transonic flow, M_∞ = 0.7–1.0, AIAA Journal, 1975; 13:1411-1413.

[3] Brower, T. L. Titan Launch Vehicle: Ground test history. Journal of Spacecraft and Rockets, 2006; 43(1):147-160.

[4] Awrejcewicz, J. and Krysko, V.A., Nonclassical Thermoelastic Problems in Nonlinear Dynamics of Shells, Springer-Verlag, Berlin 2003, pp. 43-120.

[5] Bogdonoff, S. M. Some experimental studies of the separation of supersonic turbulent boundary layer, Heat Transfer and Fluid Mechanics Institute, University of California, Los Angles, June 1955, pp.1-23.

[6] Dotson K. W. and Engblom, W. A. Vortex Induced Vibration of a Heavy-Lift Launch Vehicle During Transonic Flight, Journal of Fluids and Structure, 2004; 19: 669-680.

[7] Camussi, R., Guj, G., Imperatore, B., Pizzicaroli, A., Perigo, D. Wall Pressure Fluctuations Induced by Transonic Boundary Layers on a Launcher Model, Aerospace Science and Technology, 2007; 11: 349-359.

[8] H. W. Liepmann and A. Roshko, Elements of Gas Dynamics, First South Asian Edition, Dover Publications, Inc., New Delhi, 2007.

[9] Ericsson, L. E. and Reding, J. P. Analysis of Flow Separation Effects on the Dynamics of a Large Space Booster, Journal of Spacecraft and Rockets, 1965; 2: 481-490.

[10] Ericsson, L. E. Steady and Unsteady Terminal Shock Aerodynamics on Cone-Cylinder Bodies, NASA CR 61560, 1967.

[11] Rainey, A. G. Progress on the Launch Vehicle Buffeting Problem, Journal of Spacecraft and Rockets, 1965; 2: 289-299.

[12] Coe, C. F. and Nute, J. B. Steady and Fluctuating Pressures at Transonic Speeds on Hammer Head Launch Vehicles, NASA TM X-778 (1962).

[13] Purohit, S. C. A Navier-Stokes Solution for Bulbous Payload Shroud, Journal of Spacecraft and Rockets, 1986; 23: 590-596.

[14] Ahmed, S. and Selvarajan, S. Investigation of Flow on a Hammer Head Nose Configuration at Transonic Speeds, AIAA 91-1711, 1991.

[15] Ramaswamy, M. A. and Rajendra, G. Experimental Investigation of Transonic Flow Past a Blunt Cone Cylinder, Journal of Spacecraft and Rockets, 1978; 15: 120-123.

[16] Pinier, J. New Aerodynamic Data Dispersion Method with Application to Launch Vehicle Design, Journal of Spacecraft and Rockets, 2012; 49: 834-863.

[17] Piatak, P. J. Sekula M. K. and Rausch, R. D. Ares Launch Vehicle Transonic Buffet Testing and Analysis Techniques, Journal of Spacecraft and Rockets, 2012; 49: 853-863.

[18] Sekula, M. K., Piatak, D. J. and Rausch, R. D. Comparison of Ares I-X Wind-Tunnel-Derived Buffet Environment with Flight Data, Journal of Spacecraft and Rockets, 2012; 49: 822-833.

[19] Panaras A.G. Pulsating Flows about Axisymmetric Concave Bodies, AIAA Journal; 1981, 19(6): 804-806.

[20] Calarese, W. and Hankey, W.L. Modes of Shock-Wave Oscillations on Spike-Tipped Bodies," AIAA Journal,1985; 23(2):185-192.

[21] Mair, W. Experiments on Separation of Boundary Layers on Probes in front of Blunt-Nosed Bodies in Supersonic Air Stream. Philosophy Magazine, 1952; 43: 695-716.

[22] Wood, C. J., Hypersonic Flow over Spiked Cones, Journal of Fluid Mechanics, 1961; 12: 614 - 624.

[23] Bogdonoff, S.M. and Vas, I.E. Preliminary Investigations of Spiked Bodies at Hypersonic Speeds, Journal of the Aero/Space Sciences, 1959; 26(2): 65-74.

[24] Crawford, D. H., Investigation of the flow over a spiked-nose hemisphere-cylinder, NASA TND-118, Dec. 1959.

[25] Kabelitz., H., Zur Stabilität Geschlossener Greznschichtablösegebeite an Konischen Drehkörpern bei Hyperschallströmung, DLR, FB: 71-77, Germany, 1971.

[26] Feszty, D., Badcock, K. J., and Richards, B. E. Driving Mechanism of High-Speed Unsteady Spiked Body Flows, Part 1 & 2, AIAA Journal, 2004; 42(1): 95-106.

[27] Kistler, A. L. Fluctuating Wall Pressure under a Separated Supersonic Flow, Journal of Acoustic Society of America; 1964; 36: 543-550.

[28] Badcock, K. J., Richards, B. E., and Woodgate, M. A. Elements of Computational Fluid Dynamics on Block Structured Grids Using Implicit Solvers, Progress in Aerospace Sciences, 2000; 36: 351-392.

[29] Feszty, D., Badcock, K.J., Richards, B.E. Driving Mechanisms of High-Speed Unsteady Spiked Body Flows, Part 1: Pulsation Mode, AIAA Journal; 2004 42(1): 95-106

[30] Panaras, D., and Drikakis, D. High Speed Unsteady Flows Around Spiked-Blunt Bodies, Journal of Fluid Mechanics, 2009; 632: 60-96.

[31] Baldwin, B. S., and Lomax, H. Thin Layer Approximation and Algebraic Model for Separated Turbulent Flow, AIAA 78-257, 1978.

[32] Purohit, S. C., Shang, J. S., and Hankey, W. L. Effects of Suction on the Wave Structure of a Three-Dimensional Turret, AIAA 83-1738, 1983.

[33] Liu, F., and Jameson, A. Multgrid Navier-Stokes Calculations for Three-Dimensional Cascades, AIAA 92-0190, 1992.

[34] Peyret, R., and Vivind, H., Computational Methods for Fluid Flows, Springer, Berlin, 1993.

[35] Blazek, J. Computational Fluid Dynamics: Principles and Applications, 1st Editon, Elsevier Science Ltd, Oxford, 2001.

[36] Jameson, A, Schmidt, W. and Turkel, E. Numerical Simulation of Euler Equations by Finite Volume Methods using Runge-Kutta Time-Stepping Scheme, AIAA 81-1259, 1981.

[37] MaCormack, R. W. Numerical Methods for Compressible Flow, Workshop-cum-Seminar on Computational Fluid Dynamics, Vikram Sarabhai Space Centre, Trivandrum, Dec. 14-21, 1981.

[38] Mehta, R. C. Block structured finite element grid generation method, Computational Fluid Dynamics Journal, 18(2)2011.

[39] Shang, J. S. Numerical simulation of wing-fuselage aerodynamic interference, AIAAJ,1984; 22(10):1345–1353.

[40] Mehta, R. C. Numerical Simulation of Wall Pressure Fluctuations on Hemisphere-Cylinder at Transonic Mach Numbers, Computational Fluid Dynamics Journal, 2000; 8(4): 511-520.

[41] E. Isaacson and H. B. Keller, Analysis of Nonlinear Methods, Wiley, New York, 1966, pp.489.

[42] Marple Jr., S. L., Digital Spectral Analysis with Applications, Prentice-Hall, Inc., NJ, USA 1987.

[43] Mehta, R. C. Influence of Geometrical Parameters of Heat Shield on Flow Characteristics at Transonic Mach Number, International Review of Aerospace Engineering, 2013; 6(1), 69-75.

[44] MATLAB User's Guide, pp. 2.47-2.51, The Math Works Inc., USA, 1992.

[45] Kenworthy, M. A. A Study of Unstable Axisymmetric Separation in High Speed Flows, Ph. D. thesis, Virginia Polytechnic Institute and State University, 1978.

[46] Yamauchi, M., Fujii, K., Tamura, Y. and Higashino, F. Numerical Investigation of Supersonic Flows Around a Spiked-blunt body, AIAA 93-0887, 1993.

[47] Hankey, W. L. and Shang, J. S. Numerical Simulation of Self Excited Oscillations in Fluid Flows, in Habashi W. G., (ed) Computational Methods in Viscous Flows, Vol. 3, Pineridge Press, Swansea, 1984, 543-582.

[48] Mehta, R. C. High Speed Flow over Spiked-blunt body and Representation of Shock Polar, Computational Fluid Dynamics Journal, 2009; 18(1:3): 22-30.

[49] Ames Research Staff, Equations, Tables and Charts for Compressible Flow, NACA report 1135, 1953.

[50] Greensite, A. L., Elements of Nonlinear Control Theory, Vol. 1, Spartan Books, New York, 1970, pp. 215–232.

[51] Kreyszig, E., Advanced Engineering Mathematics, 5th ed., Wiley, New Delhi, 1985, pp. 135.

Chapter 6

Computer Modelling of Radial-Direct Extrusion of Porous Powder Billets

Lyudmila Ryabicheva and Dmytro Usatyuk

Additional information is available at the end of the chapter

http://dx.doi.org/10.5772/57142

1. Introduction

Improving the competitiveness of engineering products related to enhancement of extrusion technologies using computer modelling of the material behaviour that allows production of high-quality products (Aliev et al., 2001; Favrot et al., 1997, Ryabicheva, 2012).

It is well known that a wide range of complex-shaped parts with flanges and spherical cavities are applied in machine-building and operating at variable loadings and high wear conditions. This is why the mentioned parts are produced of compact materials by various types of extrusion. The extrusion techniques are less used for production parts from powder materials due to presence of residual porosity and density variation. The extrusion technologies for parts with spherical cavities producing in the automotive industry have studied insufficiently. Production of parts may be carried out using various deformation schemes by selection the optimal initial shape and porosity of billets, as well as the deformation temperature. The most common process flowsheet for parts from powder materials is the scheme involving pressing of billet (compact), sintering and subsequent final stamping to obtain the necessary accuracy and density (Ryabicheva et al., 2011).

Finite element simulation is the most effective way for determination of optimal process variables of forming operations. However, simulation of extrusion of porous billets from powder materials with taking into account dependences of mechanical properties from porosity, thermal and strain rate deforming conditions does not allow to estimate the convergence of finite element method (Awrejcewicz et al., 2004; Awrejcewicz & Pyryev, 2009). Mathematical formulation of the nonlinear coupled thermal plasticity problem makes necessary implementation of advanced solution methods for systems of linear algebraic equations (Awrejcewicz et al., 2007).

This work aims on improvement a quality of automotive parts based on a theoretical analysis of the stress-strain state, temperature fields and density distribution during radial-direct extrusion of porous powder billets.

2. The mathematical model of radial direct extrusion of porous powder billets

In this chapter mathematical modelling has been conducted on the basis of plasticity theory of porous bodies and focused on sequential solving the following problems:

1. construction a system of differential equations of the nonlinear coupled thermal plasticity problem for three-dimensional model of billet-stamp system on the basis of the laws of plasticity theory of porous bodies with taking into account density distribution and other singularities of deformable porous body (Awrejcewicz et al., 2007; Ryabicheva & Orlova, 2012; Segal et al., 1981);
2. application of a finite element method for solving of nonlinear coupled thermal plasticity problem (Awrejcewicz et al., 2007, Lienhard IV & Lienhard V, 2003);
3. proving the stability of the finite element solution for the examined class of problems (Lienhard IV & Lienhard V, 2003; Awrejcewicz et al., 2007; Awrejcewicz & Pyryev, 2009);
4. formulation of the method and solving of physically nonlinear coupled thermal plasticity problem for a three-dimensional billet-stamp model of radial-direct extrusion of porous powder billets and examine the influence of temperature and deformation fields' coupling on simulation results (Awrejcewicz et al., 2007; Awrejcewicz& Pyryev, 2009; Ryabicheva, 2012);
5. verification of the results of finite element simulation by experimental investigation of radial-direct extrusion of porous powder billets (Ryabicheva et al., 2012).

The plastic potential is considered as a function of stress tensor components corresponding to smooth, convex, closed surface into the stress space (Shtern et al., 1982; Ryabicheva & Orlova, 2012). This potential may be presented in the following way (Shtern, 1981; Segal et al., 1981):

$$F = \frac{\tau^2}{\varphi} + (1+m)^2 \frac{\left(p + \frac{m}{m+1}\bar{\rho}\sigma_s\sqrt{\psi}\right)^2}{\psi} - \bar{\rho}\sigma_s, \tag{1}$$

where $p = \frac{1}{3}\sigma_{ij}\delta_{ij}$ - is the medium pressure;

$\tau = \sqrt{(\sigma_{ij} - p\delta_{ij})(\sigma_{ij} - p\delta_{ij})}$- is the intensity of shear stress;

$\varphi = (1-\theta)^2$, $\psi = \frac{2}{3}\frac{(1-\theta)^2}{\theta}$- are porosity functions;

θ - is the porosity;

$\bar{\rho}=1-\theta$- is the relative density;

m - is the parameter characterizing the degree of imperfection of the contacts in the powder billet and defining different resistance of a porous body during its testing in tension and compression. The rate of volume change resulting from the plastic deformation is presented by the expression (Shtern et al., 1982; Segal et al., 1981):

$$e \sim \frac{2(1+m)^2}{\psi} p + \frac{2m(1+m)\sigma_0}{\sqrt{\psi}}, \tag{2}$$

where σ_0 - is the flow stress of hard phase, which is a function of accumulated deformation ω and is determined by a hardening curve of powder material at uniaxial tension.

A flow stress of hard phase may be expressed as the function $\sigma=\sigma_0+K\omega^{0.5}$, where K - is the hardening coefficient. The rate of accumulating deformation in hard phase of porous body was determined on the basis of postulate of uniqueness of the dissipation function formulated by Skorokhod V.V. (Skorokhod, 1973):

$$\omega = \sqrt{1-\theta}\left(\frac{m}{1+m}\sqrt{\psi}e + \frac{\sqrt{(1+m)^2\gamma^2 + e^2\psi}}{1+m}\right), \tag{3}$$

where γ - is the shape changing rate.

The value of accumulated deformation ω is renewed by solving of differential equation (Skorokhod, 1973; Shtern et al., 1982; Segal et al., 1994):

$$\frac{d\omega}{dt} = W, \tag{4}$$

where W - is the equivalent strain rate:

$$W = \frac{1}{\sqrt{1-\Theta}}\sqrt{\psi e^2 + \varphi\gamma^2}. \tag{5}$$

The finite element method presented as a series of procedures has used for determination of distributions of stress and strain intensity, as well as density in the volume of porous billet. The first procedure is triangulation of plastically deformed body or transition from a continuum billet to its finite element counterpart. Such simulation requires implementation of extremal requirement for the functional (Shtern et al., 1982, Segal et al., 1981):

$$J(v_i(x)) = \int_{\Omega} D(e_{ij}(V_i))d\Omega + \int_{\partial\Omega_p} p_i v_i d(\partial\Omega), \tag{6}$$

where $D(e_{ij}(V_i))$ - is the dissipative function;

p_i- is the stress vector on the surface of the processed billet;

v_i- is the velocity vector on the surface of the processed billet.

The first integral in (6) is the total rate of energy dissipation, the second integral - is the power of the external stresses. For a porous body, which deforms plastically, the dissipation function $D(e_{ij}(V_i))$ may be presented by the following expression (Shtern et al., 1982):

$$D\left(e_{ij}\left(V_i\right)\right) = \frac{\sqrt{\gamma^2\phi + e^2\psi}}{\sqrt{1-\theta}}\tau_s + \frac{p_0 e}{\sqrt{1-\theta}}, \tag{7}$$

where $V_i = v(x)$, $e_{ij} = \frac{1}{2}\left(\frac{\partial v_i}{\partial x_j} + \frac{\partial v_j}{\partial x_i}\right)$, $p_0 = -\sqrt{\frac{2}{3}}\tau_s\sqrt{\psi}\frac{m}{1+m}$, τ_s- is the shear yield stress.

The stress-strain state of porous powder billet and density distribution at radial direct extrusion may be calculated using dependences (1) - (7) and specific mathematical approaches with implementation of a Hilbert space (Awrejcewicz et al., 2007) and advanced solution method for a system of linear algebraic equations obtained by finite element discretization of a volume of porous powder billet (Awrejcewicz et al., 2007, Awrejcewicz & Pyryev, 2009, Ryabicheva et al., 2012).

The technology of radial direct extrusion of forged pieces from water atomized steel powder Ancorsteel® 150 HP with a spherical cavity and small flange with the ratio $D_{flange}/D_{out} = 1.1$ has been considered.

Temperature changes by sections of billet were determined using a heat conduction law. The analysis of interaction of contact surfaces has been conducted during each loading step, so, for elements inside of billet and in contact with tool surfaces heat conduction is determined only. The Fourier heat conduction differential equation was implemented for calculation of temperature field (Lienhard IV & Lienhard V, 2003):

$$k_T\left(\frac{\partial^2 T}{\partial x^2} + \frac{\partial^2 T}{\partial y^2} + \frac{\partial^2 T}{\partial z^2}\right)dV = C\rho\frac{\partial T}{\partial \tau}dV, \tag{8}$$

where

k_T - is the summary heat conduction coefficient;

C - is the specific heat capacity;

ϱ - is the density of material;

T - is the temperature, K;

τ - is the loading time step.

The minimum of heat conduction functional is related to each loading step (Segal et al., 1981; Lienhard IV & Lienhard V, 2003):

$$Q = \iiint_V k_T \left(\frac{\partial^2 T}{\partial x^2} + \frac{\partial^2 T}{\partial y^2} + \frac{\partial^2 T}{\partial z^2} \right) dV, \tag{9}$$

The outward heat transfer between medium and surface of the billet is carrying out by convective heat transfer. The boundary conditions of the third kind have implemented on the surface of the billet (Lienhard IV & Lienhard V, 2003; Ryabicheva et al., 2012):

$$\alpha'(T_0 - T_{np}) = -\lambda' \left(\frac{\partial T}{\partial \tau'} \right). \tag{10}$$

where α' - is the heat-transfer coefficient;

λ' - is the heat conduction coefficient;

$\frac{\partial T}{\partial \tau'}$ - is the temperature gradient.

The predictor-corrector method and Arbitrary Lagrangian Eulerian (ALE) formulation were implemented for more effective solving of nonlinear coupled thermal plasticity problem and prevention of gradual distortion of mesh due to severe plastic deformations during radial-direct extrusion. The transfinite mapping method is used to create an initial mesh and remeshing (Wisselink, 2000; Stoker, 1999).

3. Initial data for modelling

Two variants of radial direct extrusion, which are different by a shape of initial billet, have been considered. The first variant of billet is the bushing with a hole and the second is the bushing with a hole and a spherical cavity in the upper butt end. The input data for simulation: the strain rate is 0.5 m/s, deformation temperature interval is 1100 - 900 °C, friction coefficient 0.2, initial porosity of powder billet is 15 %. The dimensions of billet for extrusion by the first variant: the outer diameter D_{init} is 27 mm, hole diameter 9 mm, height 31 mm, diameter of forged piece 28 mm, flange diameter 30.8 mm, height 26 mm, hole diameter 8.5 mm, die preheating temperature 200 °C. Material of stamp is die steel 5HNV GOST 5950 - 2000. The finite element model of the billet-stamp system at the beginning and the end of the extrusion is presented in Fig. 1.

Analysis of the stress-strain state and temperature field were performed in sections of billet, as shown in Fig. 2. The effective method to reduce a non-uniformity of the stress-strain state during extrusion is formation of relieving cone-shaped cavity in the initial billet (Fig. 4). According to the recommendations (Ryabicheva et al., 2011), relieving cavity for reducing of significant non-uniformity of stress-strain state in the upper end of the billet has made. The simulation scheme is presented in Fig. 3. It was assumed for simulation that the cavity depth is equal to the radius of the sphere, the cone angle was equal to 15°, 30° and 40°.

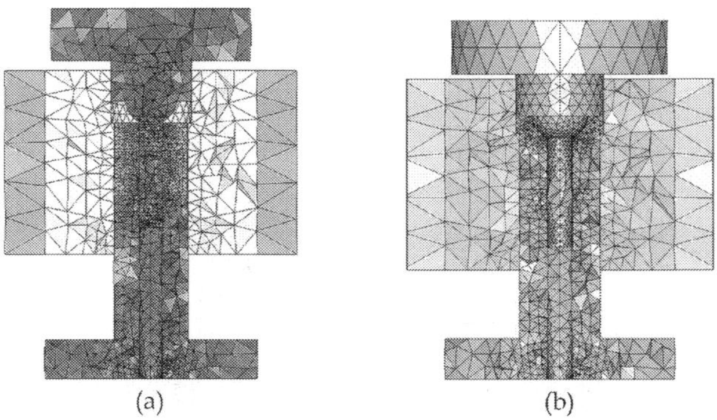

Figure 1. The model of the billet-stamp system: (a) - is the starting position, (b) - is the extrusion stage.

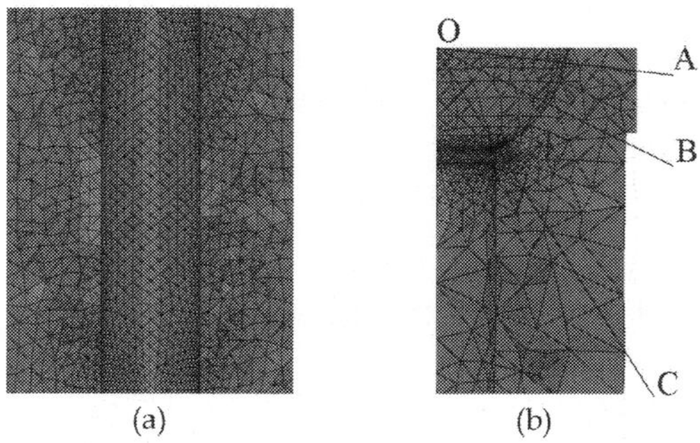

Figure 2. The model of initial billet – (a), section of forged piece for analysis of the stress-strain state – (b).

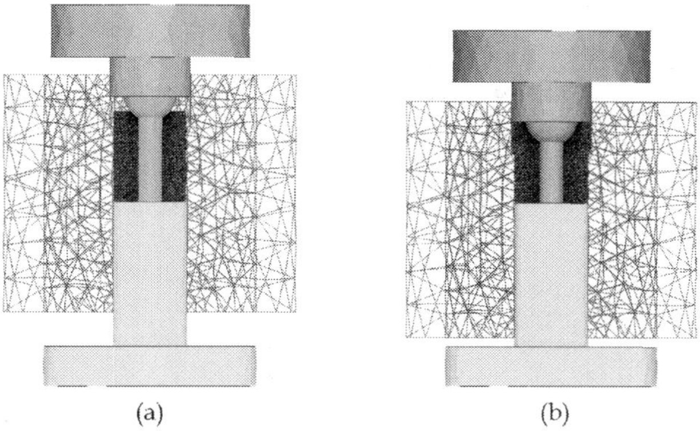

Figure 3. The model of the billet-stamp system for extrusion of billet with a relieving cavity: (a) - is the starting position, (b) - is the extrusion stage.

Drawings of initial porous powder billets are presented in Fig. 4.

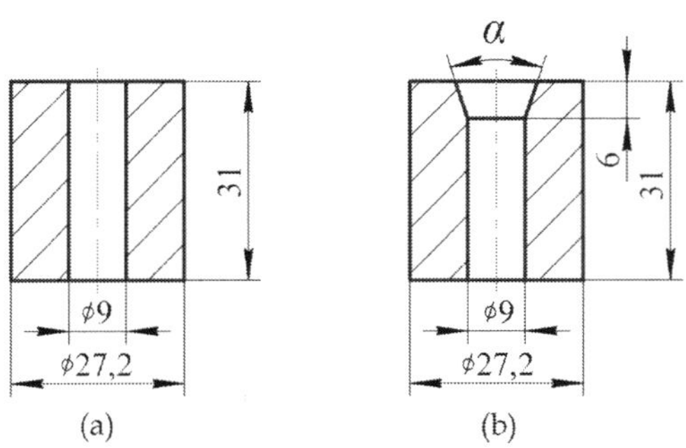

Figure 4. Drawings of initial porous powder billets: (a) - is the billet without relieving cavity; (b) - is the billet with relieving cavity.

4. Computer simulation of radial-direct extrusion of forged piece with a spherical cavity and flange from cylindrical billet with axial hole

Finite element simulation of extrusion of forged piece from cylindrical billet with a hole has shown clearly that maximum intensities of stress and deformation observed in the surface layers of the spherical cavity by sections of forged piece OA, OB and OC. These values were decreased gradually while increasing the distance from the surface of the forged piece (Fig. 5). The maximum values of the studied variables and dramatic non-uniformity of stress-strain state have been observed in the section OC, where the highest probability of defects formation established. The intensity of stress reduced to 5.28 times while growing the distance from the surface of the forged piece, the intensity of deformation decreased to 1.6 times. At a distance of 1.8 - 2.0 mm from the surface of the cavity there is a maximum of values due to overcooling of the metal in the area of transition of spherical cavity to the hole.

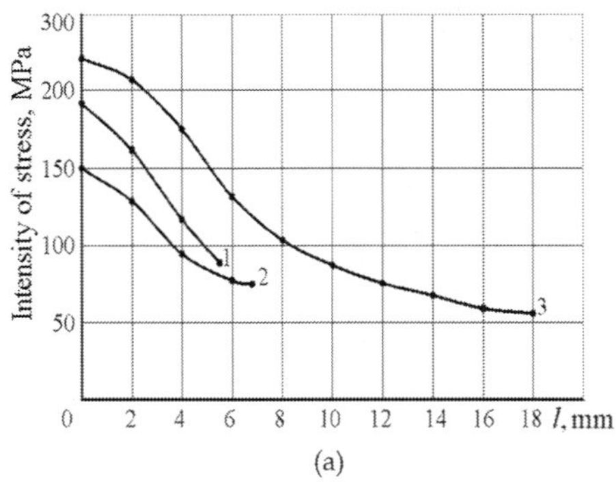

Figure 5. Distribution of the intensity of stress and intensity of deformation during extrusion of billet with a cylindrical hole in the sections: 1 - OA; 2 - OB; 3 - OC.

Non-uniformity of stress-strain state is a significant cause of non-uniformity of the temperature field (Fig. 6). The temperature rises up to 1200 °C due to the thermal effect of plastic deformation while increasing the distance from the surface of the billet. The overcooled layer is formed at the points of contact with the forging tool due to heat transfer by conduction and convection.

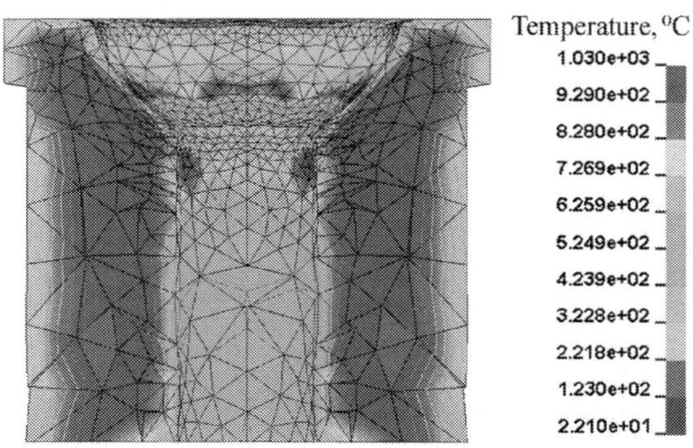

Figure 6. The temperature field of billet at extrusion of cylindrical powder billets with a hole.

Non-uniformity of temperature field and stress-strain state of forged piece creates conditions for the formation of the fold at a distance of 2 - 3 mm from the edge of the hole, which is gradually transformed into the flow-through flaw and then leads to loss of plastic equilibrium and cracking of products. The stages of flow-through flaw defect evolution (Fig. 7, a) to the fold (Fig. 7, b, c) and crack (Fig. 7, d) have been observed. The retraction of the surface layer inside of forged piece around the flaw transforms it to the fold. Later, under pressure from a punch, the cavity of fold collapses, edges sharpening and becoming stress concentrators with following initiation and propagation of crack and formation of failure.

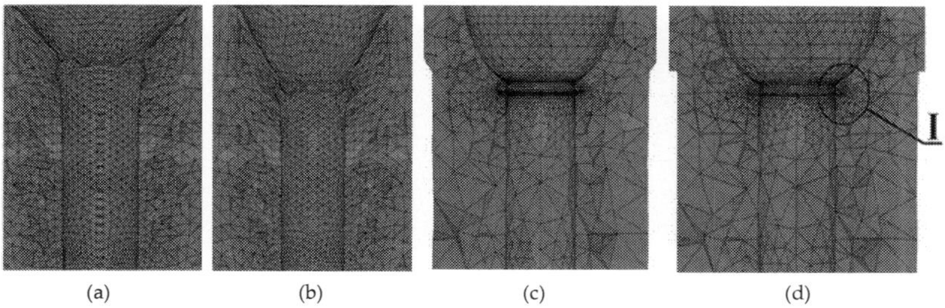

Figure 7. Evolution of flow-through flaw to a fold at extrusion of powder billets with cylindrical hole.

The stress state near the defect is significantly non-uniform (Fig. 8) and in the layers of metal adjacent to the surface of the fold, the stress intensity was about 160 - 240 MPa and the stress intensity corresponds to the lower edge of the spherical cavity surface within 180 - 250 MPa.

Estimation of stress concentration, considering the influence of temperature and strain rate conditions on properties of deformable material has provided using technical stress concentration factor a_σ with taking into account the structure and plastic properties of powder material (Skorokhod, 1985; Ryabicheva, 2012):

$$a_\sigma = \frac{\sigma_i^{\max}}{\sigma_i}, \qquad (11)$$

where $\sigma_i^{\max}$ - is the highest intensity of stress near the defect;
σ_i- is the intensity of stress under the given deforming conditions.

Stress concentration factor on the surface of forged piece $a_\sigma = 2.5 - 3.0$. After closure of the fold stress concentrator formed at its end, leading to increase in stress concentration factor a_σ up to 4.0 - 6.0, resulting formation of cracks into the forged piece. This promotes the evolution of folds in a failure, and also causes deterioration of the spherical surface in the region of its transition into the inner hole. This cracking is accompanied by stress relaxation, which leads to reduction of stress down to 70 MPa after crack propagation.

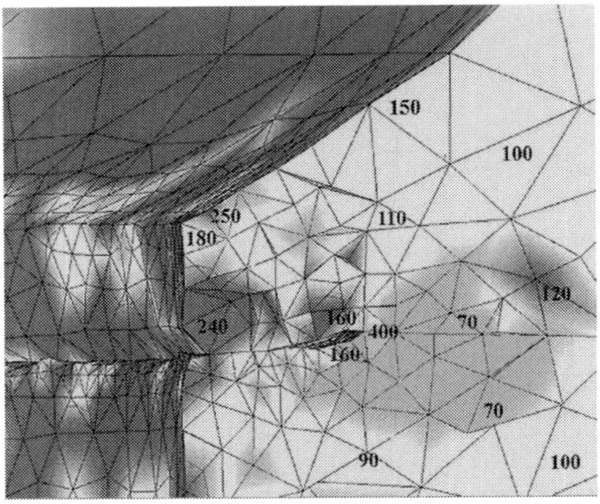

Figure 8. The stress state during the evolution of fold to crack.

The non-uniformity coefficients of stress σ_{inh} and deformations e_{inh} were implemented for estimation the non-uniformity of stress-strain state:

$$\sigma_{inh} = \frac{\sum_{j=1}^{N}\sqrt{\left(\sigma_i^{ave} - \sigma_i^j\right)^2}}{\sigma_i^{ave} N}, \quad e_{inh} = \frac{\sum_{j=1}^{N}\sqrt{\left(e_i^{ave} - e_i^j\right)^2}}{e_i^{ave} N}, \tag{12}$$

where σ_i^{ave}- is the average stress intensity in the volume of billet;

$\dot{\varepsilon}_i^{ave}$- is the average intensity of deformation in the volume of billet;

σ_i^j- is the stress intensity into a finite element j;

$\dot{\varepsilon}_i^j$- is the intensity of deformation into a finite element j;

N - is the number of finite elements inside the model.

In case of uniform deformation the values of σ_{inh} and e_{inh} are asymptotically approaching zero.

The results of analysis of non-uniformity of stress-strain state by sections of forged piece confirms that the highest non-uniformity of stress-strain state has been observed in section OC, which corresponds to retraction of surface layers of the metal during formation of flow-through flaw (Table 1).

Thus, conditions that are leading to formation of defects have established by numerical simulation of extrusion of the porous powder billet with a hole.

Section of billet	σ_{inh}	e_{inh}
OA	0.29	0.31
OB	0.33	0.36
OC	0.41	0.56

Table 1. Non-uniformity of stress-strain state by sections of forged piece

5. Computer simulation of radial-direct extrusion of forged piece with the spherical cavity and flange from cylindrical compact with axial hole and relieving cavity

The effect of the generatrix inclination angle α, radius of sphere R and size of cone-shaped relieving cavity on the non-uniformity of stress-strain state and temperature field has been investigated. The angle α was equal to 15°, 30°, 40° and sphere's radius have changed from 6 to 16 mm.

As a result of implementation the relieving cavity with α = 15°, the non-uniformity of stress-strain state decreased, in compare with extrusion of billet without the cavity, but was not completely eliminated (Fig. 9). The maximum stress intensities in the surface layers of the spherical cavity of forged piece for all three sections have found (Fig. 9, a). The intensity of stress decreases at increasing of the distance from the cavity surface, especially in the most dangerous section OC down to 52 MPa. Intensity of deformation maximized at the distance of 1.9 - 2.4 mm from the surface, indicating the risk of flow-through flaw formation, and then also decreased (Fig. 9, b).

In this case, the intensity of stress and deformation values during extrusion of billet with generatrix inclination angle of relieving cavity 15° are lower than without it.

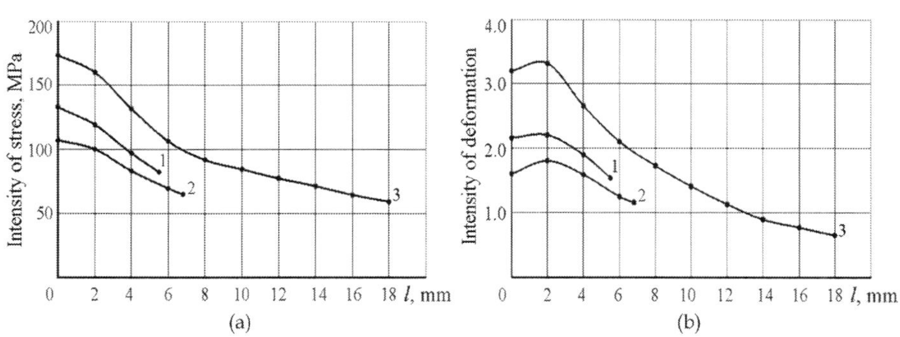

Figure 9. The distribution of the intensity of stress and intensity of deformation during extrusion of billet with relieving cavity (α = 15°): 1 - is the section OA; 2 - is the section OB; 3 - is the section OC.

Thus, implementation of compacts with the relieving cavity and α =15° was not ensured decreasing of non-uniformity of stress-strain state to an appropriate level. Consequently, in the transition region of spherical cavity in the hole during the final extrusion step a flaw is formed, but was not developed into a fold as the result of decreasing the non-uniformity of stress-strain state.

Increasing the angle α up to 30° reduces non-uniformity of stress-strain state on 30 %. The largest and smallest σ_i and e_i differ by 1.7 times and 2.1 times, respectively (Fig. 10). Parameters of stress-strain state are distributed more uniformly by sections. Consequently, a flow-through flaw was not formed in forged pieces during extrusion.

The results of analysis of non-uniformity of stress-strain state by sections of forged piece during extrusion of billets with relieving cavity at α = 15° and α = 30° are presented in Table 2.

Section of billet	σ_{inh}		e_{inh}	
	α = 15°	α = 30°	α = 15°	α = 30°
OA	0.25	0.15	0.13	0.17
OB	0.28	0.10	0.14	0.12
OC	0.33	0.13	0.23	0.15

Table 2. Evaluation of non-uniformity of stress-strain state at various values of the inclination angle of relieving cavity generatrix

The non-uniformity of stress-strain state in the sections OB and OC decreases with increasing of inclination angle of the relieving cavity generatrix that improving quality of forged piece, but does not completely eliminates defects. Further reduction of non-uniformity of stress-strain state by increasing the angle α was confirmed by simulation of radial direct extrusion of billets with spherical cavity at inclination angle α = 5 - 45° and radius of sphere R = 6 - 16 mm.

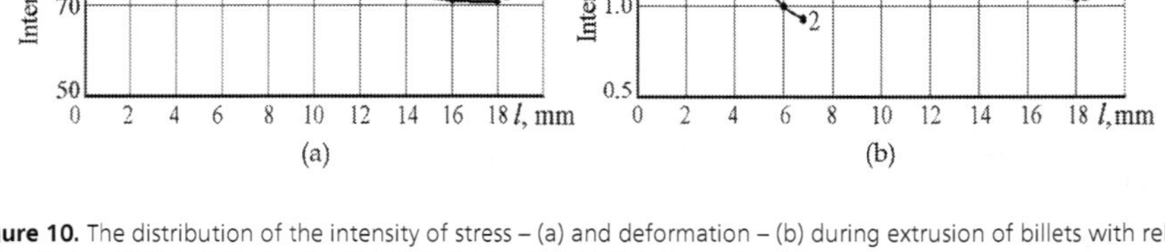

Figure 10. The distribution of the intensity of stress – (a) and deformation – (b) during extrusion of billets with relieving cavity (α = 30°): 1 - is the section OA; 2 - is the section OB; 3 - is the section OC.

http://dx.doi.org/10.5772/57142

Dependences of the intensity of stress by layers of powder material for various radii of spherical cavity R and different values of angle α are presented on Fig. 11 according to the modelling results.

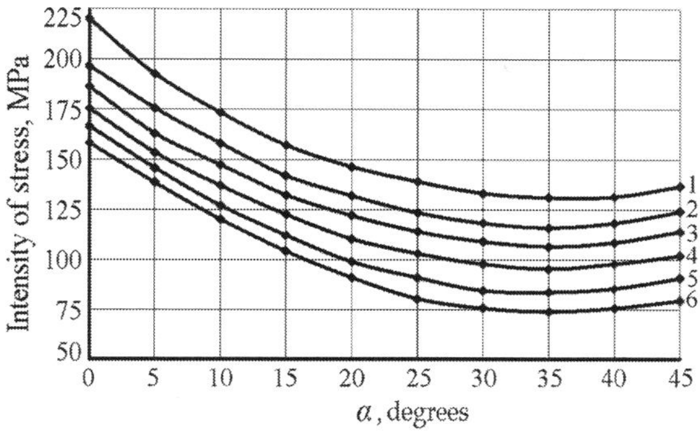

Figure 11. Dependences of maximum intensity of stress from the angle α and radius R: 1 - R = 16 mm; 2 - R = 14 mm; 3 - R = 12 mm; 4 - R = 10 mm; 5 - R = 8 mm; 6 - R = 6 mm.

Analysis of dependences has shown that intensity of stress reaches a minimum at α = 30 - 40°. The angle α is close to 40° at increasing of R, and angle α is close to 30° while decreasing of R. This means that the range of permissible values of angle α is within 30 - 40°.

Thus, to obtain the most uniform stress-strain state during radial-direct extrusion of forged pieces at D_{flange}/D_{out} = 1.1, the billet with relieving cavity (Fig. 4, b) and α = 30 - 40° may be recommended.

To verify the validity of this conclusion the distribution of stress-strain state parameters at α = 40° in three sections of forged piece are presented on Fig. 12. Retrieved reduction of non-uniformity of stress-strain state by 6-10% at extrusion, according to (9), has compared with extrusion at α = 30°.

The maximal values of the intensity of deformations are lower and shifted to deeper layers of forged piece at 2.3 - 4.0 mm. The results of the non-uniformity analysis of stress-strain state by sections of forged piece with relieving cavity angle α = 40° are presented in Table 3. The non-uniformity of stress-strain states is lower for all three sections, in compare with extrusion at α = 30°.

Therefore, extrusion of porous powder billets with relieving cavity having a generatrix inclination angle within 30 - 40° provides a uniform stress-strain state.

Improvement of the uniformity of stress-strain state by using billets with relieving cavity allows obtaining a more uniform temperature field by the section of forged piece (Fig. 13).

Thus, the comparative analysis of the radial-direct extrusion of cylindrical billets with generatrix inclination angle α within 30 - 40° has shown that the presence of relieving cavity

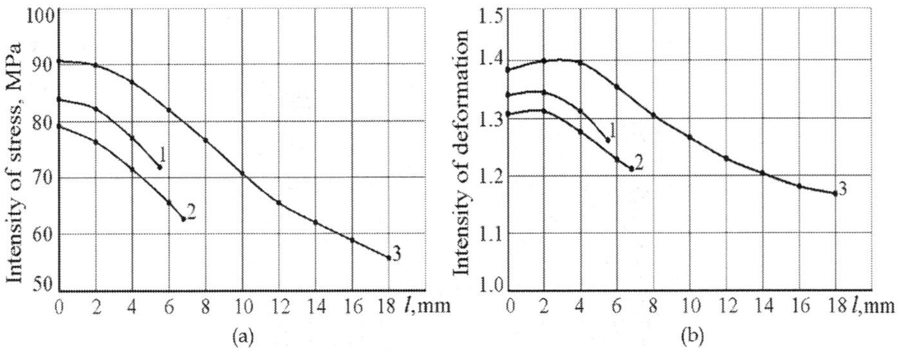

Figure 12. The distribution of the intensity of stress and intensity of deformation at extrusion of billets with relieving cavity (α = 40°): 1 - is the section OA; 2 - is the section OB; 3 - is the section OC.

increases the uniformity of the temperature field and stress-strain state. This helps to reduce the stress intensity and stress concentration factor k_σ at the edges of the cavity by 3 - 4 times.

Section of billet	σ_{inh}	e_{inh}
OA	0.08	0.01
OB	0.06	0.01
OC	0.08	0.03

Table 3. Evaluation of non-uniformity of stress-strain state at the generatrix inclination angle α = 40°

As a result, the probability of flow-through flaw formation and risk of crack propagation during extrusion have diminished rapidly.

Analysis of the density changing by the volume of forged piece was simulated for extrusion of billet with the initial porosity 15 %, outer diameter D_{out} = 27 mm and diameter of hole 9 mm. The density variation and equidensity at different conditions of radial direct extrusion of forged piece have been investigated.

The most difficult is to ensure equidensity at extrusion of flange of forged piece due to tensile stresses. Therefore, density distribution is presented by section OA (Fig. 14) where the highest probability of defects formation occurs.

The maximum density of 7.77 g/cm^3 during extrusion of billets without relieving cavity at ratio D_{flange}/D_{out} 1.1 - 1.3 (Fig. 14, a) was reached in the volume of metal adjacent to the surface of forged piece at D_{flange}/D_{out} = 1.1 that does not corresponding to the density of compact material. This is due to the increase of tensile stress, leading to a tightening of the surface layer of the metal forging deeper. Moreover, the greater a flange, the more decrease in density of metal

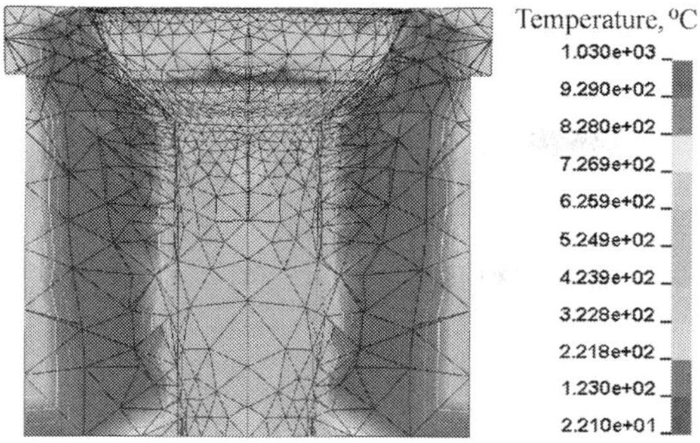

Figure 13. The temperature field of the billet at extrusion of billet with relieving cavity at α = 40°.

adjacent to the surface of sphere and in the flange. A density close to 7.83 g/cm^3 has obtained in the billet at α = 15° only at the ratio D_{flange}/D_{out} = 1.1 (Fig. 14, b).

In two other cases, it decreases by the volume of flange, but with a smaller gradient. A high density obtained for D_{flange}/D_{out} = 1.1 - 1.2 at different initial density while increasing angle α to 30° (Fig. 14, c). However, if D_{flange} / D_{out} = 1.3 the density of compact material obtained. The high density has obtained at the cavity angle α = 40° for D_{flange}/D_{out} = 1.1 - 1.2 (Fig. 13, d). It is rather difficult to change the volume of forged piece at any density for D_{flange}/D_{out} = 1.3. Pores and cracks were appeared on spherical surface of the metal due to increased loosening at radial flow of metal in the gap and on the side of flange.

Simulation of the density distribution at D_{flange}/D_{out} = 1.3 during extrusion of billets with 10 % initial porosity and inclination angle of relieving cavity generatrix 40° shown the density variation within 7.79 - 7.81 g/cm^3 that indicates a possibility to obtain the equidence and high-strength details.

6. Determination of extrusion force

One of the most important problems during development of metal forming technologies for powder billets is determination of deforming force that is necessary for reasonable choice of pressing equipment. The analytical expression of extrusion force P in polar coordinates for known average intensity of stress σ_i^{ave} on the contact surface of upper punch and powder billet or function for σ_i may be written in the following way (Wagoner & Chenot, 2001):

$$P = \iint_F \sigma_i r dr d\phi = \int_0^r dr \int_0^{2\pi} \sigma_i r d\phi, \tag{13}$$

where F - is the area of contact surface of upper punch and powder billet.

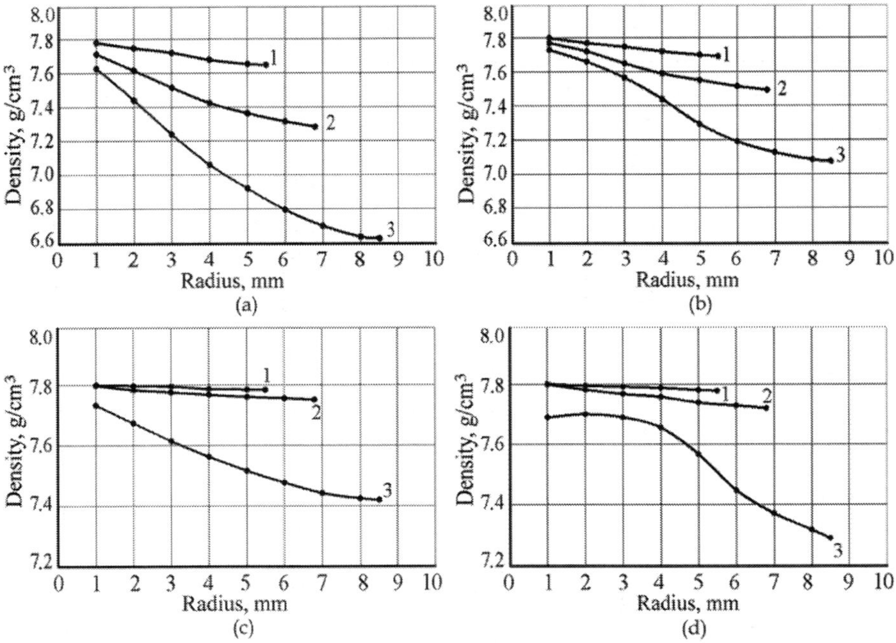

Figure 14. Density distribution by the section OA of forged piece (a) - with no relieving cavity; (b, c, d) - with the relieving cavity (generatrix inclination angle α is 15, 30, 40°, respectively): 1 - D_{flange} / D_{out} = 1.1; 2 - D_{flange} / D_{out} =1.2; 3 - D_{flange} / D_{out} = 1.3.

The expression (13) for radial-direct extrusion of forged piece with spherical cavity and central hole with accounting the modelling results may be transformed to:

$$P = \int_{D_{hole}}^{D_{flange}} \frac{1}{2} dD \int_{0}^{2\pi} \sigma_i D d\varphi = \frac{\sigma_i^{ave} \pi \left(D_{flange}^2 - D_{hole}^2 \right)}{4}, \tag{14}$$

where D_{flange} - is the outer diameter of flange;

D_{hole} - is the diameter of hole.

Values of extrusion force calculated by formula (14) at different inclination angles of generatrix of relieving cavity for D_{flange}/D_{out} = 1.1 and height of the cavity 6 mm are presented in the Table 4.

The dependence of extrusion force from the relative flange size is presented in the Table 5 (α = 40°, diameter of sphere D_{sf} = 20 mm).

α, °	σ_i^{ave}, MPa	P, kN
0	133.1	92.0
15	118.2	81.7
30	103.7	71.6
40	84.5	58.4

Table 4. Extrusion force at different inclination angles of generatrix of relieving cavity for D_{flange}/D_{out} = 1.1

D_{flange}/D_{out}	σ_i^{ave}, MPa	P, kN
1.1	84.5	58.4
1.2	106.2	89.6
1.3	127.4	124.5

Table 5. The extrusion force at different flange size, α= 40° (D_{sf} = 20 mm)

The results of computer modelling and laboratory experiments are well concordant with relative error 7 - 9 %.

7. Conclusions

In this chapter the results of computer modelling of radial direct extrusion of forged piece with the spherical cavity and small flange from a cylindrical billet with a porosity of 15 % and axial hole have shown a high non-uniformity of the stress-strain state, temperature field and density distribution by sections of forged piece that leads to appearing of defects are reported. It has been shown, among other, how the smallest non-uniformity of the stress-strain state, temperature field and maximum density indicate a possibility to obtain high-quality products.

A high-quality details with a spherical cavity and the ratio D_{flange} /D_{out} = 1.2 may be obtained from powder billets with 15 % initial porosity and relieving cavity with generatrix inclination angle 40°. Details with the ratio D_{flange} / D_{out} = 1.3 may not be produced from such billets due to the presence of cracks and non-uniformity into the flange. High-quality details with the ratio D_{flange}/D_{out} = 1.3 may be made from billets of 10 % initial porosity and relieving cavity with generatrix inclination angle within 30 - 40°.

The highest density of 7.80 - 7.83 g/cm^3 and the equidensity of flange observed in forged pieces at the ratio D_{flange}/D_{out} = 1.1 - 1.2, obtained from billets with generatrix inclination angle of relieving cavity within 30 - 40° and initial porosity of 15 %. Forged pieces with D_{flange}/D_{out} = 1.3 and density 7.79 - 7.81 g/cm^3 may be produced from powder billets with generatrix inclination angle of relieving cavity within 30 - 40° and 10 % initial porosity.

The simulation and experimental results are well concordant with relative error 7 - 9 %.

Author details

Lyudmila Ryabicheva* and Dmytro Usatyuk

Volodymyr Dahl East Ukrainian National University, Ukraine

References

[1] Awrejcewicz, J., Andrianov, I.V., Manevitch, L.I. (2004). *Asymptotical Mechanics of Thin-Walled Structures. A Handbook.* Springer-Verlag, Berlin.

[2] Awrejcewicz, J., Krysko, V.A., Krysko, A.V. (2007). *Thermodynamics of Plates and Shells.* Springer-Verlag, Berlin.

[3] Awrejcewicz, J., Pyryev, Yu. (2009). *Nonsmooth Dynamics of Contacting Thermoelastic Bodies.* Springer-Verlag, New York.

[4] Aliev, I.S., Solodun, E.M., Nosakov, A.A., and Kruger, K. (2001). *Modeling of Combined Extrusion Processes,* Nowe Technologie i Osiqgniecia w Metalurgie i Inzynierii Materialowej, II Miedzynarodowa Sesja Naukowa, Wydawnictwo Wydzialu Metalurgii i Inzynierii Materialowej Politechniki Czestochowskiej. – P. 195–200.

[5] Favrot N., Besson, J., Colin, C., Delannay, F., and Bienvenu, Y. (1997). *Modeling Sintering Deformations Occurring After Cold Compaction, Qualitative Methods for the Mechanics of Compaction,* Proceedings of the International Workshop on Modeling of Metal Powder Forming Process, Grenoble, 21-23 July. – P. 133–147.

[6] Lienhard, IV, J.H., Lienhard, V, J.H. (2003). *A Heat Transfer Textbook,* Phlogiston Press. Cambridge, Massachusetts.

[7] Ryabicheva, L.A., Tsirkin, A.T., Nikitin, Yu.N., Beloshitskij, N.V., and Lubchich, K.V. (2011). *Technologies for Production of Complex-shaped Details From Powder Materials,* Resursozberìgaûči Tehnologìï Virobnictva ta Obrobki Tiskom Materìalìv u Mašino-buduvannì, Volodymyr Dahl East Ukrainian National University, Lugansk. – P. 189–198.

[8] Ryabicheva, L., Usatyuk, D., Lyubchich, K. (2011) *Radial-direct extrusion of details with spherical cavity from powder porous billets with relieving cavity,* 8th International Congress "Machines, Technologies, Materials 2011", September 18-20, 2011, Varna, Bulgaria, V. 1. – P. 116–119.

[9] Ryabicheva, L., Orlova, Y. *Analysis of densification of porous powder billets on a basis of extended model of plastic flow,* Lugansk, Volodymyr Dahl East Ukrainian National University. No. 1(13), (2012). – P. 227–234.

[10] Ryabicheva L., Usatyuk, D., Beloshitskij, N. *Computer modelling of radial-direct extrusion of complex-shaped details.* Journal of Computer and Information Technology, Vol. 2, No. 1 (2012). – P. 91–101.

[11] Ryabicheva, L. *Modeling of direct extrusion of porous powder billets.* Advanced Materials Research, Vol. 566, (2012). – P. 267–270.

[12] Ryabicheva, L., Usatyuk, D., Ryabovol, T. (2012). *Production of high-density copper-titanium powder material by angular extrusion with back pressure,* XIII International Scientific Conference New Technologies and Achievements in Metallurgy and Material Engineering, 30 May – 1 June, 2012, Ch. 2, Czestochowa, Poland. – P. 698–701.

[13] Ryabicheva, L.(2012). *Development of the theory and production technology of machine-building parts from powder materials,* MTM'12 Conference proceedings, 18-21 September, 2012, Varna, Bulgaria.

[14] Segal, V.M., Reznikov, V.I., Kopilov, V.I., Belarus (1994). *The Plastic Structure Formation Processes in Metals,* Minsk, Nauka i Technika.

[15] Segal, V.M., Reznikov, V.I. & Malyshev, V.F. *Variational functional for a porous plastic body,* Powder Metallurgy and Metal Ceramics, Vol. 20, No. 9 (1981). – P. 604–607.

[16] Shtern, M.B., Serdyuk, G.G., and Maximenko, L.A. (1982). *Phenomenological Theories of Pressing of Powders,* Naukova Dumka.

[17] Skorokhod, V.V., Ukraine (1973). *The Rheological Basics of Sintering Theory,* Naukova Dumka.

[18] Shtern, M.B., *Development of the theory of pressing and plastic deformation of powder materials,* Powder Metallurgy and Metal Ceramics, No. 9 (1992). – P. 735–745.

[19] Shtern, M.B. *Determining equations for compressible plastic porous solids,* Powder Metallurgy and Metal Ceramics, No. 4 (1981). – P. 250–255.

[20] Skorokhod, V.V. (1985). *The topical problems of continuum theory of structural modelling of deforming processes of powders and porous bodies, rheological models and processes of deforming of porous powder and composite materials,* Naukova Dumka, Kiev. – P. 6–11.

[21] Stoker, H.C., Netherlands (1999). *Developments of the Arbitrary Lagrangian-Eulerian Method in Non-linear Solid Mechanics, Applications to Forming Processes,* Ph.D - Thesis, University of Twente, P. 23–82.

[22] Wagoner, R. H. & Chenot, J. L. (2001). *Metal Forming Analysi s, Cambridge University Press, ISBN 0-521-64267-1, Cambridge.*

[23] Wisselink, H.H., Netherlands (2000). *Analysis of Guillotining and Slitting, Finite Element Simulations,* Ph.D-Thesis, University of Twente. – P. 33–66.

Chapter 7

Numerical Simulations of Post-Critical Behaviour of Thin-Walled Load-Bearing Structures Applied in Aviation

Tomasz Kopecki

Additional information is available at the end of the chapter

http://dx.doi.org/10.5772/57218

1. Introduction

The design work on aircraft constructions, with applicable standards and requirements imposed by regulations applicable to aircraft design taken into account, represents a discipline significantly different than other fields of modern engineering. In fact, as opposed to rules commonly applicable to design of technical structures, in view of the need to limit the mass, in the case of airframe structures there is a necessity to allow phenomena involving loss of stability with respect to some of their components under the in-flight conditions.

From the historical point of view, the issue of the loss of stability was a factor significantly slowing down the progress in aviation at early stage of its development. In aspiration to ensure safety, a large group of designers adhered to the lattice structure concepts for many years. The first attempts to develop some more advanced solutions were based on the use of corrugated sheet metal as the skin material for wings and fuselages. Such solution was adopted in numerous constructions manufactured on a mass scale, e.g. Ford Trimotor or Junkers 52 (Fig. 1).

With increasing availability of more and more reliable and powerful aircraft engines and the related improvement of aircraft performance parameters, it became necessary to use smooth skin materials constituting integral components of semi-monocoque and monocoque structures. On the other hand, in striving after development of optimum constructions with the mass criterion met at the same time, it became impossible to use the sheet metal with thickness allowing to achieve critical loads with values exceeding the allowable loads.

Similarly as for other types of constructions, the principal rule involved preventing bar systems, such as stringers, frame components, or spar flanges, from buckling. In the case of the loss of stability, such elements of the structure were considered damaged.

Figure 1. Airplanes with the skin made of corrugated sheet metal: Ford Trimotor (left) and Junkers Ju-52 (right)

At the same time it has been found that the skin stability loss is not dangerous for the whole of the structure provided its character is local, i.e. it occurs within the area of skin segments limited by components of the skeleton, such as frames and stringers, and represents an elastic phenomenon.

In such situation, it has become a standard that some local buckling of airframe skin is admitted in the in-flight conditions. In the current state of the art, the rule applies mainly to isotropic materials, e.g. metals. It should be emphasized that in case when the post-buckling deformation field encompasses also components of the framing, such as bars constituting frame components or stringers, the skin buckling is considered global, and the structure is assumed to be destroyed. It can be therefore concluded that a loss of stability is of a local type when it encompasses skin segments limited with components of the framing.

Further experience collected in operation of airframes constructed with the use of the above-mentioned standard revealed another issue connected with limited operating durability of such structures. In fact, cyclic nature of loads which a plane is subjected to in the course of flight induces occurrence of fatigue phenomena which, when undiagnosed or underestimated, may lead to destruction of the structure. Examples include such aviation accidents as e.g. disasters of De Havilland Comet airplanes in the years 1953–54 or the accident occurring in the course of flight of Aloha Airlines' Boeing 737 when a fatigue-induced gap developed in the skin resulted in explosive decompression of the plane's fuselage and breaking off a large fragment of the fuselage skin (Fig. 2).

Nature and intensity of fatigue-induced changes in a structure is related to the stress distribution which, assuming admissibility of skin stability loss, means that it is necessary to carry out detailed analyses of post-buckling deformation states.

The tool that become used commonly for this purpose is the nonlinear numerical analysis based on the finite element method (FEM), allowing to represent actual deformations of thin-walled structures and the related stress distributions. However, in so far as application of FEM in linear problems became a routine in the engineering practice, and results being obtained with the use of commercial software packages are, on the whole, correct and reliable, the

Figure 2. Damaged Aloha Airlines' Boeing 737

nonlinear analysis still causes numerous problems and requires application of additional tools to verify the results.

The essence of FEM-based nonlinear numerical analysis comes down to determination of a relationship between a set of parameters determining the state of the structure, known as state parameters, and a set of control parameters related to the load. The latter can be, in general, related to and expressed by means of a single control parameter. On the other hand, the number of state parameters corresponds to the total number of degrees of freedom of the analyzed system. Such relationship is known as the equilibrium path and for a system with an arbitrary number of degrees of freedom can be interpreted as a hypersurface in the state hyperspace where the dimension of the hyperspace corresponds to the number of degrees of freedom [1-4]. The equilibrium path fulfils the matrix equation of residual forces which, for a single control parameter, has the following form:

$$\mathbf{r}(\mathbf{u},\lambda) = \mathbf{0}, \tag{1}$$

where $\mathbf{u}$ is the state vector containing components of displacements of nodes of the structure corresponding to its current geometrical configuration, λ is the control parameter representing a function of the load, and $\mathbf{r}$ is the residual vector containing non-balanced force components related to the current system deformation state.

Procedures employed in modern numerical software packages, apart from the prognostic phase allowing to determine the next point on the equilibrium path, comprise also a correction phase offering the possibility to compensate divergences between the actual equilibrium path and the solution determined in the prognostic phase, or the so-called "drift error". The correction phase consists in the use of an additional equation to be met by the system, known as the increment control equation or the equation of constraints,

$$c(\Delta \mathbf{u}_n, \Delta \lambda_n) = 0, \tag{2}$$

where increments $\Delta \mathbf{u}_n = \mathbf{u}_{n+1} - \mathbf{u}_n$ and $\Delta \lambda_n = \lambda_{n+1} - \lambda_n$ correspond to transition from state n to state $n + 1$.

In view of the large number of degrees of freedom and state parameters related to them, deformation processes are represented in practice by means of a relationship between a control parameter related to the load and a selected geometrical quantity linked to deformation of the system. The relationship is called the representative equilibrium path [5-9].

As was already mentioned above, results of FEM-based nonlinear numerical analyses require verification. Relying unquestioningly on such results alone can lead to significant errors in design processes through adopting incorrect solutions as a base for construction design assumptions. The problem consisting in arriving at incorrect deformation patterns as a result of numerical calculations is a consequence of the fact that numerical procedures employed in commercial software packets contain a large number of algorithms the course of which depends on choice of certain control parameters. These in turn follow from the applied boundary conditions, selection of prognostic procedures, correction strategies, and a number of other factors.

In view of practical impossibility to obtain appropriate solutions for complex thin-walled structures in a purely analytical way, the basic tool that can be used for verification of results nonlinear numerical analyses is the experiment, by its nature representing an undertaking relatively expensive and frequently difficult to execute.

In case of systems characterized with high degree of complexity or having geometrical singularities of any kind (e.g. cut-outs), execution of an appropriate experiments is absolutely necessary. It should be however emphasized that semi-monocoque aircraft structures include, in many cases, some typical components with characteristic, repeatable geometrical features. In such cases, it seems to be purposeful to create a base of standard solutions, containing result of experiments aimed at determination of deformation patterns of the analyzed structure for a given range of post-buckling loads justified by actual in-flight conditions. Such data could constitute a base sufficient to verify results of nonlinear numerical analyses.

2. Objective and the point of the research

Thin-walled aircraft load-carrying structures, in view of requirements applicable to them, are typically characterized with significant sophistication of the applied solutions. However, despite their advanced degree of complexity, they still have a number of characteristic features following from assumptions on which their operation is based. Thus, the loss of stability of thin-walled shell segments used in such structures is a result, in general, of a distribution of tangential stresses interpreted as a field of tensions. It can be therefore stated that post-buckling deformation patterns of a skin segments limited by components of the framing depend on factors decisive for stress distributions, i.e. proportions between dimensions of skin segments (rectangular in general), curvature radii related to these dimensions, and the load intensity [10].

Occurrence of post-buckling deformations corresponding to rapid changes in combinations of state parameters, known as bifurcation, in the case of the load only slightly exceeding the critical value, depends in great measure on geometrical imperfections and, to some extent, can exhibit random nature [11, 12]. In most cases, however, the ultimate pattern of post-buckling deformations corresponding to the maximum load is the same in each of load cycles. It is therefore possible to distinct the so-called nature of post-buckling deformations in case of structure designs characterized with specific, fixed geometrical features [13,14]. With knowledge of this nature, i.e. availability of data concerning post-buckling deformation patterns for a sufficiently broad spectrum of variants of the structure, it seems to be possible to use them as a tool for verification of results of nonlinear numerical analyses without necessity to carry out additional experiments.

In the present study, an attempt was made to determine the nature of post-buckling deformation of a characteristic fragment of the typical semi-monocoque aircraft structure by means of carrying out a series of relevant model experiments and confronting the results with the outcome of nonlinear numerical analyses performed with the use of commercial software package.

The subject of the research was a closed, semi-monocoque thin-walled cylindrical shell structure which corresponded to a fragment of an aircraft fuselage tail section (Fig. 3).

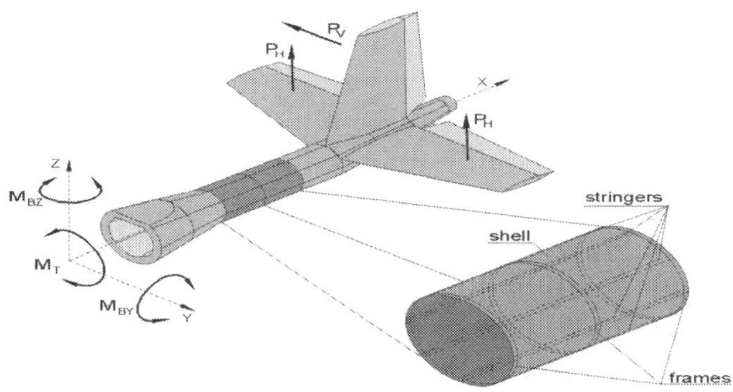

Figure 3. Examined part of the aircraft structure

In the in-flight conditions, the structure can be subjected to bending and twisting, as a result of aerodynamic forces exerted on tail control surfaces. The structure components responsible

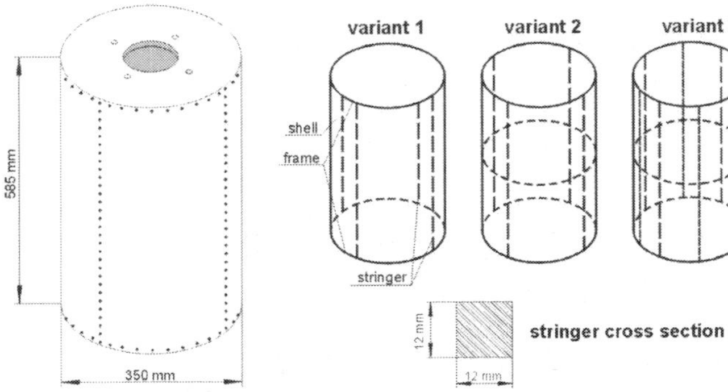

Figure 4. Geometry of the examined structure

for transfer of bending loads are the stringers, cross-sections of which are selected based on the rod stability conditions, with the safety factor provided by aircraft construction regulations taken into account. However, appropriate torsional strength of the structure and its required torsional rigidity must be ensured by the skin in which a distribution of tangential stresses is developed creating conditions favorable for the loss of stability. The distributions, as was already mentioned, depend on a number of factors of geometrical nature, related to the number of frames and stringers determining size and shape of skin segments.

To determine characteristic features of deformation of the tested structure type and examine in detail the nature of the involved phenomena, it is necessary to analyze different geometrical variants. In order to be able to use the obtained results as a universal tool supporting the design process, it would be advisable to examine as broad spectrum of such variants as possible. This study presents only a few examples of such analyses, while the fundamental objective of the work consisted in development of a methodology for creation of sets of results obtained from appropriate model experiments and their numerical representations. Comparison of representative equilibrium paths of the examined systems and convergence of deformation patterns was aimed at determination of recommendations applicable to modeling structures of that type and carrying out nonlinear FEM analyses.

3. Experimental research

The subject of the research were three variants of a thin-walled cylindrical structure, geometrical details of which are presented in Fig. 4. The first variant was a design solution representing a limiting case with particularly small number of framing components. Employing, in the next variant, an additional frame situated half length of the skin segment, and further increasing the number of stringers, corresponded to modifications possible to be employed in practice, as a result of which the size and geometrical relationships characterizing skin segments change significantly.

http://dx.doi.org/10.5772/57218

In all the cases it has been assumed that cross-sections of stringers applied in similar structures have geometrical characteristics preventing them from buckling in conditions of actual operating loads. For this reasons, their dimensions were intentionally exaggerated in model experiments.

All experimental models were made of polycarbonate for which the following material constants have been determined: $E = 3000$ MPa, $v = 0.36$. Selection of the material was dictated by its isotropic properties and low Young modulus which allowed to limit the applied loads to relatively low values.

The models were subjected to constrained torsion with the use of experimental set-up allowing to apply loads gravitationally (Fig. 5). As the representative equilibrium path, the relationship between the total angle of torsion of the structure and the torsional moment was selected. In view of the lack of possibility to register instantaneous changes of the load related to bifurcation changes of combinations of the parameters of state occurring in the structure, the presented equilibrium paths were determined for steady-state conditions as a result of which they have "smooth" courses.

As expected, in the case of the first variant of the examined structure, occurrence of post-buckling deformation had a violent nature. Magnitude of post-buckling deformations and the resulting significant value of the total angle of torsion make application of similar solution in actual aircraft impracticable. Despite the fact that the loss of stability had a local nature, deformations occurring in this case would mean loss of rigidity of the fuselage.

Figure 5. The experimental set-up

The deformation pattern as such was characterized with occurrence of folds observed in all four skin segments (Fig. 6). In the course of experiment, Atos optical scanner of GOM Optical Measuring Techniques brand was used to register the geometry of the deformed skin.

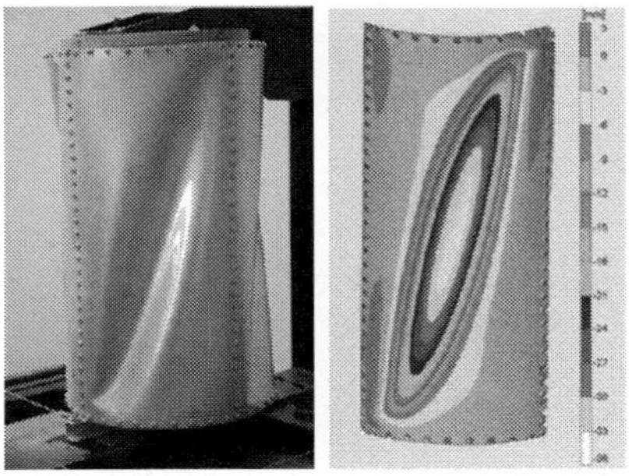

Figure 6. Advanced post-buckling deformation of the examined structure (left) and distribution of contour lines reflecting magnitude of deformations obtained by means of the projection moiré technique (right) — variant 1

In connection with a violent development of deformation, the representative equilibrium path contains a characteristic horizontal segment corresponding to a large change of state parameter combinations at virtually fixed load value (Fig. 9).

The next stage consisted in examination of the second variant of the structure in which an additional frame was employed (Fig. 4, variant 2). The change in proportions of basic skin segment dimensions resulted in occurrence of a post-buckling deformation pattern significantly different than this observed in the first case (Fig. 7).

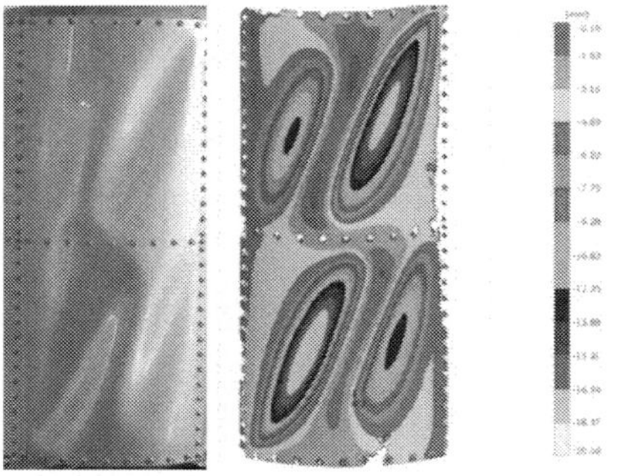

Figure 7. Advanced post-buckling deformation of the examined structure (left) and distribution of contour lines reflecting magnitude of deformations obtained by means of the projection moiré technique (right) — variant 2

Occurrence of a double fold resulted in more gentle course of the phenomenon, which manifested itself in absence of any large jump on the equilibrium path (Fig. 9). An increase of the load critical value and torsional rigidity of the system with respect to the first variant was also observed.

The third variant of the structure was a modification of the second variant reinforced with four evenly distributed additional stringers (Fig. 4, variant 3). As comparison of representative

http://dx.doi.org/10.5772/57218

equilibrium paths proves, the change of skin segment sizes and proportions as well as changed ratio of the segment dimensions and the curvature radius have brought the effect in the form of further increase of torsional rigidity of the examined structure with simultaneous small reduction of the critical load [10,12].

The pattern of post-buckling deformations has significantly changed, taking the form of single shallow folds (Fig. 8). The course of the phenomenon as such was more gentle in this case than in the variants examined earlier.

Therefore, in this case the skin stability loss resulted in development of small geometrical defects of the fuselage inducing a local drag coefficient increase; however, higher rigidity guarantees that basic aerodynamic properties of the aircraft are maintained.

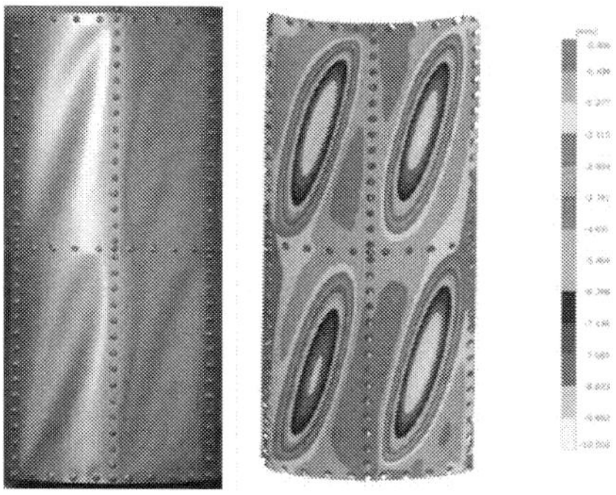

Figure 8. Advanced post-buckling deformation of the examined structure (left) and distribution of contour lines reflecting magnitude of deformations obtained by means of the projection moiré technique (right) — variant 3

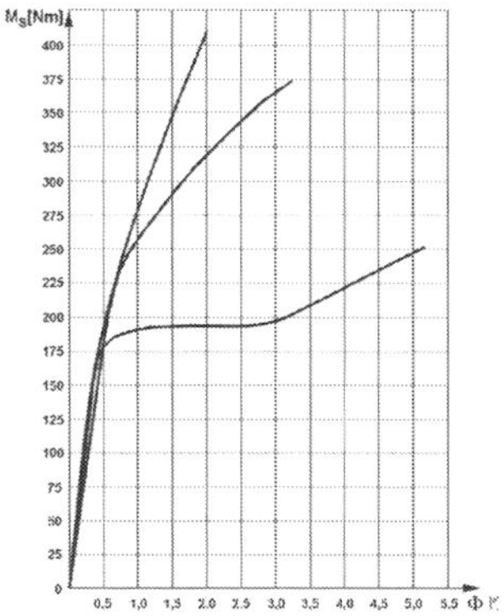

Figure 9. Comparison of representative equilibrium paths determined in the course of experimental research

4. FEM-based numerical analysis

Examining the nature of post-buckling deformations occurring in thin-walled structures with the intent to use the obtained results as a tool useful in aircraft design processes, together with carrying out appropriate experiments, it seems to be purposeful to develop recommendations concerning methods of numerical modeling of considered structures and selection of most effective numerical methods. It should be emphasized that the practice of developing dedicated software based on the finite elements method by entities dealing with aircraft structures design is a relatively rare phenomenon. As a rule, different types of routines are used available on the commercial software market.

Analyses discussed in the present study were carried out on the grounds of MSC MARC program. In all cases, the mounting of the model was reproduced by locking all degrees of freedom of selected points on the upper frame (corresponding to location of bolt joints in the experimental model) and a pair of forces was applied at appropriate points of the lower frame (corresponding to locations where the ties were attached). To represent the skin, four-node shell elements of the thin-shell type were used, with six degrees of freedom at each of the nodes and bilinear shape functions. The frames have been modeled with the use of thick-shell elements with similar properties. In case of stringers, according to software authors' recommendations, beam-type elements were employed, based on the Euler-Bernoulli model [14].

The first variant of the examined structure, in view of the observed post-buckling deformation scale and violent course of the related phenomena, turned out to be very troublesome from the point of view of FEM-based nonlinear numerical simulation. In fact, lack of ability to represent symmetry or antisymmetry of post-buckling deformation states is a characteristic feature of algorithms employed in majority of commercial software packages. In absence of geometrical imperfections of the structure, the state parameter combination change occurred only in one segment of the structure. Errors of that type follow, in general, from unreliability of algorithm used to select an appropriate equilibrium path variant after reaching a bifurcation point [15].

In order to initiate deformation patterns corresponding to actual ones, additional loads in the form of forces with small values normal to the skin applied at central points of skin segments have been introduced to the numerical model (Fig. 10). However, despite the obtained repeatability of deformation in individual segments, faulty results were obtained for a number of consecutive numerical models or solutions in the full load range were impossible to obtain.

A significant improvement of effectiveness of the analysis process and quality of the obtained results was achieved by changing the concept used to model the stringers. In successive versions of numerical models, thick-walled shell elements were used to represent these components of the structure. From among numerical models available in the software package, after a series of tests, a combination of the prognostic secant method and the strain correction method was adopted [16]. The deformation distribution obtained numerically was found satisfactory from the point of view of both qualitative and quantitative similarity to deformation patterns obtained experimentally. Also representative equilibrium paths (Fig. 12) were

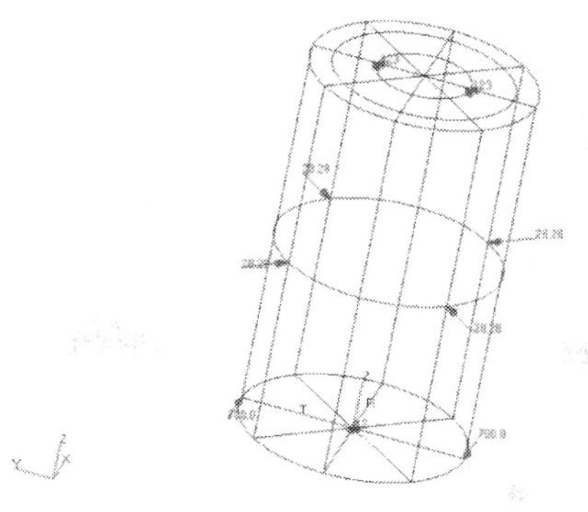

Figure 10. Geometrical model of the structure developed in MSC Patran environment with boundary conditions and load

recognized satisfactorily convergent with experimental characteristics. In line with the rule of uniqueness of solutions, according to which one and only one distribution of the reduced stress corresponds to each deformation state, the obtained reduced stress distribution can be therefore also considered reliable (Fig. 11).

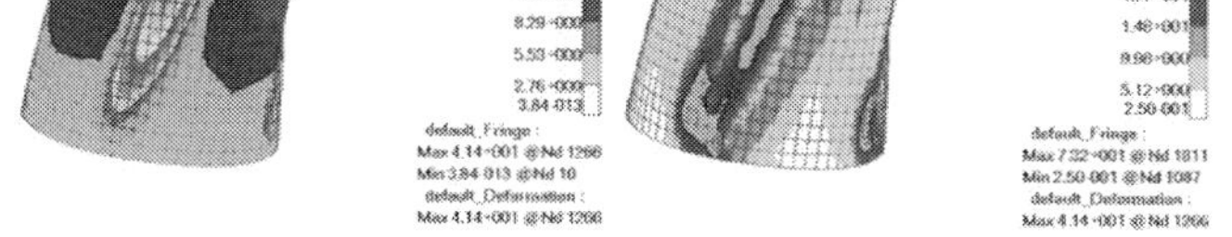

Figure 11. Displacement distribution (left) and the reduced stress according to Huber-Mises hypothesis (right) for 100% of the maximum load (stringers modeled by means of bilinear thick-walled shell elements)

When numerical models for the remaining variants of the structure were developed, the same concept as for application of constraints, loads, and additional forces initiating post-buckling deformation was adopted as in the first variant (Fig. 13).

Application of numerical methods identical to those used previously allowed to obtain post-buckling deformation distributions and the corresponding reduced stress distributions satisfactorily consistent with results of experiments (Figs. 14 and 15).

Plots of representative equilibrium paths for variants 2 and 3 (Figs. 16, 17) are characterized with significantly better conformity with experimental characteristics then in the case of variant 1. In the pre-buckling range, the consistence is almost perfect. On the other hand, for maximum loads, the error of representation of the total angle of torsion does not exceed 10%. It allows to conclude that the adopted modeling method and selection of numerical procedures turned out to be satisfactory.

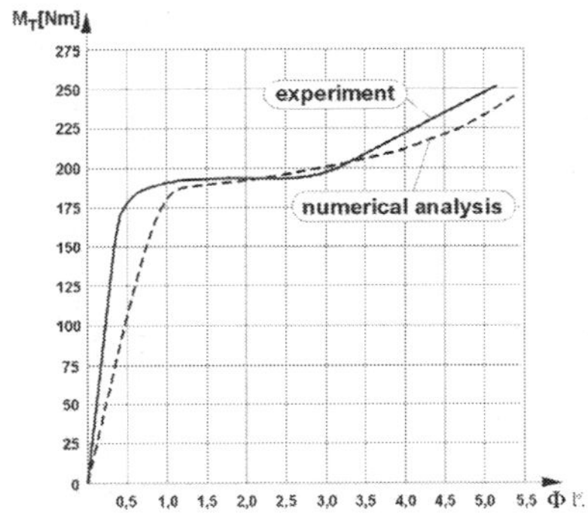

Figure 12. Comparison of representative equilibrium paths — variant 1

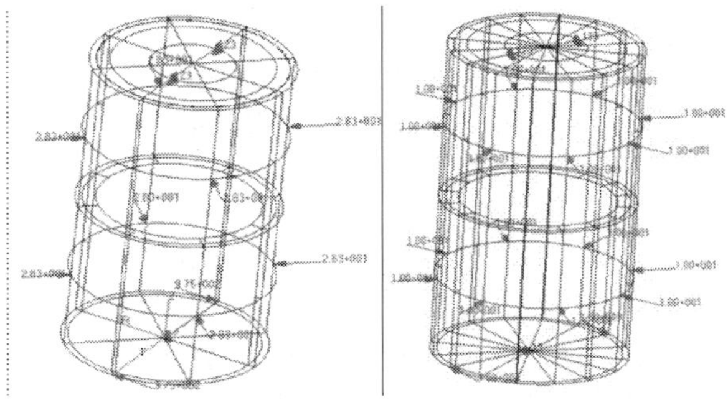

Figure 13. Geometrical models of variant 2 (left) and variant 3 (right) of the examined structure developed in MSC Patran environment, with boundary conditions and loads

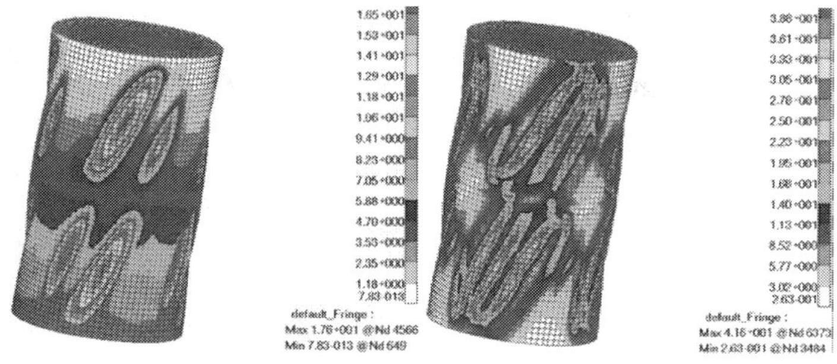

Figure 14. Distribution of the displacement (left) and the reduced stress according to Huber-Mises hypothesis (right) for 100% of the maximum load — variant 2

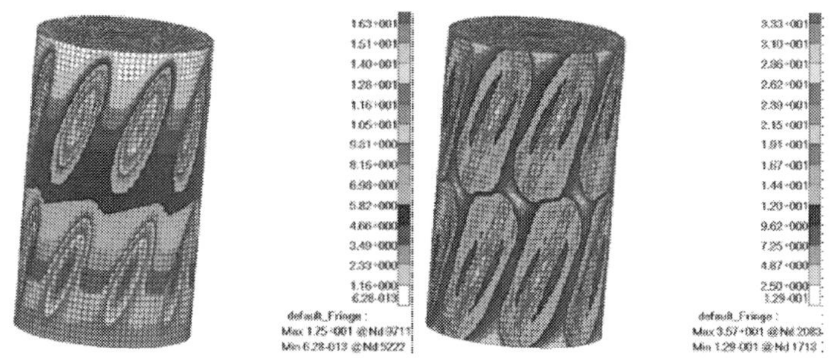

Figure 15. Distribution of the displacement (left) and the reduced stress according to Huber-Mises hypothesis (right) for 100% of the maximum load — variant 3

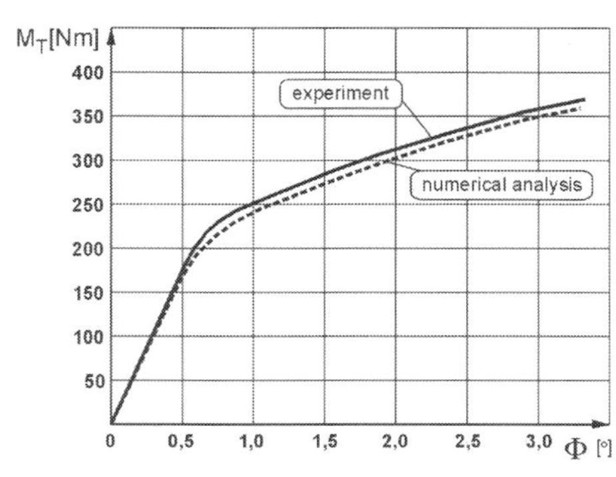

Figure 16. Comparison of representative equilibrium paths — variant 2

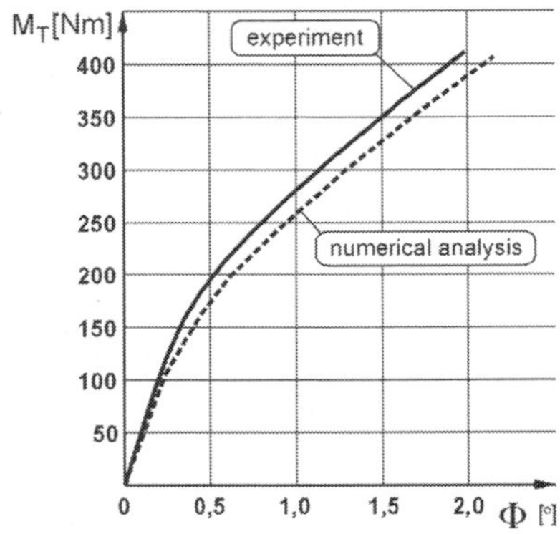

Figure 17. Comparison of representative equilibrium paths — variant 3

5. Summary and conclusions

As it was emphasized in the introduction, the research results presented in this study represent a fragment of the cycle of experiments that should be executed in order to test the whole of the physical phenomena involved in the loss of stability of the examined structure. It can be stated on the grounds of the executed experiments that construction solutions of structures of the type analyzed in this study that comprise too small quantity of framing components, are characterized with deformations far too large to be used in actual aircraft constructions. Considering the three presented variants of the thin-walled cylindrical structure, it seems that the last of them could be used in practical applications.

The fundamental observation that can be made on the grounds of relatively small number of the cases examined here is an increase of torsional rigidity of the structure with increasing number of components of the framing. The increase is caused partly by rigidity of stringers alone, however another reason consists in the change of relationship between the skin segment surface areas and their linear dimensions on one hand and the skin curvature radius on the other. Increasing the number of frames and stringers results in a decrease of average size of skin segments which, at fixed curvature radius value, is the cause of relative „flattening" of skin components. Reduction of the value following from the above-mentioned relationship limits, in a natural way, the depth of folds developed as a result of the loss of stability, and therefore also the scale of deformation. The deformation pattern, and thus also the number and relative position of the folds occurring in individual skin segments, depends also on the ratio of their linear dimensions which is decisive for the nature of the field of tensions developing in the segments [10]. To be able to call a post-buckling deformation research program the completed task, it seems to be necessary to perform a series of experiments aimed at determination of detailed relationships between ratios of geometrical parameters character-

http://dx.doi.org/10.5772/57218

izing skin segments on one hand and location of folds and the related deformations on the other which in turn determine magnitude of the structure's total angle of torsion. Realization of such research program would require application of the above-described experimental procedure to consecutive versions of the model with fixed curvature radius and different cylinder lengths, and then to another series of models with a fixed length and different diameters. This would allow to determine characteristic combinations of geometrical parameters which are connected to fundamental changes in post-buckling deformation patterns resulting in increase of torsional rigidity of the structure.

As was already noted earlier, results of experiments allow to conclude that, in general, the structure rigidity increases with increasing number of components of the structure framing. It should be however borne in mind that in the case of aircraft structures, there is an absolute necessity to strive after minimization of the mass which limits the possibility to increase the number of frames and stringers. It seems therefore to be possible to determine a limiting number of framing components above which further increase of the weight is no more justified by measurable improvement of strength and rigidity of the structure.

With a sufficiently broad range of test results being available, it would be possible to use them as a base of standards for verification of results of nonlinear numerical analyses, as the nature of post-buckling deformations, with geometrical proportions and rigidity relationships between elements of the structure maintained, is not subject to any major changes when other isotropic materials are used or other load values are applied. This was confirmed by numerical tests performed with the use of models presented here.

The main conclusion following from the presented numerical calculation cases is the necessity to strive to reduce the size of the task and avoid any numerical singularities which, in the case of nonlinear analysis, may result from using different finite element types in the model.

Despite difficulties related frequently to carrying out nonlinear numerical analyses of FEM models of thin-walled structures subjected to advanced deformation states, commercial FEM programs represent a tool allowing for effective determination of stress distributions in such states. However, one should always bear in mind the absolute necessity to verify results obtained this way, either by making use of the above-discussed base of standard solutions, or by performing an appropriate experiment.

Author details

Tomasz Kopecki*

Address all correspondence to: t_kopecki@poczta.wp.pl

* Faculty of Mechanical Engineering and Aeronautics, Rzeszów University of Technology, Rzeszów, Poland

References

[1] Marcinowski J. (1999). *Nonlinear stability of elastic shells*. Publishing House of Technical University of Wrocław, Poland

[2] Felippa C. A. (1976): *Procedures for computer analysis of large nonlinear structural system in large engineering systems*. ed. by A. Wexler, Pergamon Press, London, UK

[3] Bathe K.J. (1996). *Finite element procedures*, Prentice Hall, USA

[4] Doyle J.F. (2001). *Nonlinear analysis of thin-walled structures.* Springer-Verlag, Berlin, Germany

[5] Andrianov J., Awrejcewicz J., Manewitch L.I. (2004) *Asymptotical Mechanics of thin-walled structures.* Springer, Berlin, Germany

[6] Awrejcewicz J., Krysko V.A., Vakakis A.F. (2004) N*onlinear dynamics of continuous elastic systems.* Springer, Berlin, Germany

[7] A.V. Krysko, J. Awrejcewicz, E.S. Kuznetsova, V.A. Krysko, *Chaotic vibrations of closed cylindrical shells in a temperature field,* International Journal of Bifurcation and Chaos, 18 (5), 2008,1515-1529.

[8] A.V. Krysko, J. Awrejcewicz, E.S. Kuznetsova, V.A. Krysko, *Chaotic vibrations of closed cylindrical shells in a temperature field*, Shock and Vibration, 15 (3-4), 2008, 335-343.

[9] I.V. Andrianov, V.M. Verbonol, J. Awrejcewicz, *Buckling analysis of discretely stringer-stiffened cylindrical shells,* International Journal of Mechanical Sciences, 48, 2006, 1505-1515.

[10] Brzoska Z. (1965). *Statics and stability of bar and thin-walled structures.* PWN, Warszawa, Poland

[11] Arborcz J. (1985). *Post-buckling behavior of structures. Numerical techniques for more complicated structures.* Lecture Notes In Physics, 228, USA

[12] Kopecki T. (2010). *Advanced deformation states in thin-walled load-bearing structure design work.* Publishing House of Rzeszów University of Technology, Rzeszów, Poland

[13] Niu M. C. (1988). *Airframe structural design*. Conmilit Press Ltd., Hong Kong10] Lynch C., Murphy A., Price M., Gibson A. (2004). *The computational post buckling analysis of fuselage stiffened panels loaded in compression.* Thin-Walled Structures, 42:1445-1464, USA

[14] Mohri F., Azrar L., Potier-Ferry M. (2002). *Lateral post buckling analysis of thin-walled open section beams*. Thin-Walled Structures, 40:1013-1036, USA

[15] Rakowski G., Kacprzyk Z. (2005). *Finite elements method in structure mechanics.* Publishing House of Technical University of Warszawa, Warszawa, Poland

[16] Ramm E. (1987). *The Riks/Wempner Approach – An extension of the displacement control method in nonlinear analysis*. Pineridge Press, Swensea, UK Aben H. (1979). *Integrated photoelasticity*. Mc Graw-Hill Book Co., London, UK

Processor-in-the-Loop Simulations Applied to the Design and Evaluation of a Satellite Attitude Control

Luiz S. Martins-Filho, Adrielle C. Santana,
Ricardo O. Duarte and Gilberto Arantes Junior

Additional information is available at the end of the chapter

http://dx.doi.org/10.5772/57219

1. Introduction

The design of a controller requires a mathematic modeling followed by the adjusting of some model parameters. However to overcome the controller to a single piece of hardware, involves the codification of this mathematical based model into an appropriate firmware description suited to work correctly in a specific platform. Recently a model driven development approach, firstly defined by system engineers, has been frequently used as way to reduce the time of development of embedded systems, producing rapid and reliable product in a short time development cycle. This model driven approach is basically used for test and is known as X-In-The-Loop. These tests provide four levels of testing configurations: MIL (Model-In-The-Loop), SIL (Software-In-The-Loop), PIL (Processor-In-The-Loop) and HIL (Hardware-In-The-Loop). Each of the configuration levels provides some advances and reduces the gap in the development process that initiate with the mathematical model and ends at the firmware running in a stand-alone microprocessor platform [1].

A model-driven system approach starts from the MIL configuration, where basic simulation is performed to analyze the controller model along with the simulated plant model. The basic idea behind MIL is to generate and validate some test cases of your model in a computing high precision float pointing arithmetic platform, providing the behavior and the quality of your model under a certain computer platform. The proposal of this step is to generate the reference output test results of your controller to the following steps. Any problem with the mathematical controller model can be rapidly found and corrected, taking the MIL step a first step of development.

In Software-In-The-Loop (SIL) the model used in the MIL test is replaced by an executable code running at the same computer platform in a fixed-point arithmetic manner. This step helps the system developer to find fast some wrong memory sizing choices. Normally these two steps are made using a single integrated platform in a PC. The SIL step can be bypassed if your controller system will run in a piece of hardware that has a floating point dedicated unit in its CPU datapath.

The following test consists in the PIL (Processor-In-The-Loop) that goes beyond the PC platform. This step introduces some hardware features that permit to achieve more realistic situations where the control algorithm will run. In PIL the target processor is a non-real time environment and the communication with the external processors is given by using specific functions installed in a simulation integrated environment installed in the host PC.

PIL requires drivers to communicate the computer platform with the aimed hardware. The resulting object code generated in the PC links with other test-management functionality and is then downloaded, typically to an off-the-shelf evaluation board with the target processor. The simulation tool, running on the PC machine, then communicates with the downloaded software, typically via a serial communication link.

The PIL simulation follows the simulation tool installed in the computer send test values to the firmware installed in the processor of the evaluation board, through a serial link and waits for the processor response through the same or another communication channel.

The software real time operation cannot be tested in the PIL, this step is done by the HIL test. Although at first sight, this can be seen as a limitation, in fact this permits to break the simulation problem in two parts that can be verified before we have the certainty that the controller firmware will run correctly in the standalone processor platform. PIL permits to test if the compile optimizations effects in a non-real time execution platform with the presence of an off-the-shelf processor platform where the firmware will finally run.

As the last step of an embedded controller system development HIL is presented. HIL simulation must include electrical emulation of sensors and actuators in a real time target platform before the controller be validated with real sensors and actuators of the plant. These electrical emulations act as the interface between the plant simulation and the embedded system under test all of them in the same platform. The value of each electrically emulated sensor is controlled by the plant simulation and is read by the embedded system under test bringing a real time feedback next to the real situation that the controller will face before to be installed to control a physical plant.

Nowadays there are some model-driven platforms that allows the engineer develop the above simulation step of the controller. Latelly, Mathworks© and National Instruments© are the most known platforms. This work concentrates in presenting the development steps of an attitude control model in the MATLAB – Simulink tool from Mathworks©.

http://dx.doi.org/10.5772/57219

2. The processor in the loop (PIL) and hardware in the loop (HIL) simulation approach

In the PIL application example described in section 3, we use MATLAB/Simulink environment both for a design procedure, code generation and for perform a PIL co-simulation together with a device. In the following paragraphs we describe some works that has some relationship with our work regarding the use of a development environment, code generation and co-simulation. The focus was in works with aerospace application where we presented their proposition, the hardware and tools used as well as the co-simulation scheme done.

In [2], simulations SIL and PIL were performed to obtain an attitude determination and control system (ADCS) for the microsatellite CKUTEX from Cheng Kung University. The SIL simulation is made using the MATLAB software and after, the PIL simulation is implemented using a PIC microcontroller to the implantation of the ADCS algorithm while the satellite dynamics is implemented in NI-PXI platform and coded by Labview software. According to the authors, the attitude determination and control system that was obtained and tested, provided good results once the plant dynamic response obeyed the project specifications. In [3], the MATLAB software is used with the purpose of generate the code of an entire control system and the dynamics of two satellites (represented by two robots). In this work a physical simulator using two industrial robots is assembled for a simulation of proximity operations between satellites as *on-orbit servicing* (OOS) activities. A model of the satellites dynamics, its control, actuators and sensors (constituting the named Application Control System - ACS) is made in MATLAB/ Simulink by the tool named Real-Time Workshop (RTW). It generates a code supported by the operating system VxWorks that on the other hand, operate according this code, the monitoring and control system of the facility where the movement commands desired are sent to the robots. It is a HIL simulation where controllers, actuators, state observers, among other modeled modules in the MATLAB/Simulink can be removed of the ACS and included in their own hardware if necessary.

In [4], a true co-simulation approach is studied for control application running on a Field Programmable Gate Array processor (FPGA). The proposed approach adopts the LABVIEW Real-Time environment (from National Instruments©) to perform the simulation of an artificial satellite' dynamic model. This study simulates a reaction wheel and its control in Simulink exclusively for the controller design. Subsequently, the generated code is implemented on the FPGA. The entire system model attitude control is previously built and simulated in Simulink. The RTW generates the code that represents the satellite dynamics' mathematical model inside LABVIEW environment. In the case of the reaction wheel and its control, RTW generates the C code to simulate the dynamic model that must be adapted to the LABVIEW rules for FPGA programming.

In [5], the Simulink is used together with another MATLAB toolbox called xPC Target. This toolbox allows to perform prototyping, testing and development of real-time systems for running in general-purpose computers. The MATLAB/Simulink tools were used to generate executable code for the target computer from the model built in Simulink. The goal is to achieve simulation and real-time implementation of an algorithm integrating inertial navigation and GPS, using the validation and testing of the proposed algorithm in the FlightGear flight simulator (inside MATLAB), running on the host computer.

In order to exemplify the possibility of use of different development environment to perform SIL and PIL simulations of a satellite control system; in the work of [6], a SIL simulation is made in $MATRIX_x$ environment where is obtained and tested the control algorithm, simulated the space environment and the satellite dynamics. This same software is used to generate the controller code, that after is downloaded in the satellite processor while its model is ported to a DSP that is controlled by a computer. This computer runs the real-time simulation together with the satellite processor, controlling the actuators and sensors signals too, in a PIL simulation. An interface allows the user to interact with the simulation, monitoring and changing simulation parameters in real-time.

In the cited works, is observed as the simulations SIL, PIL and HIL can be useful in controllers project and test to aerospace applications and as this simulations can be implemented in different ways, different virtual development environments and together with several hardware platforms. The results are not only obtained much more quickly but come from tests very cheap that those made in a real platform, which is often not accessible to the researchers. Furthermore, the interaction with the user in real-time and the analysis instruments, available by co-simulation tools, make the tests much more dynamic and enables the analysis of the system response in situations more realistic.

Today there are many co-simulation tools and many are the possibilities of combination between these tools and the several processors hardware platforms. Such tools are in continuous development and making possible the coupling with several hardware platforms from different manufacturers, including additional functional facilities to become easier the task of development.

In these studies, the Simulink is used as a friendly graphical tool for systems development, design and generation of executable code for various devices and applications. The following section presents more details of a control system design procedure using the PIL approach, Simulink tools and a DSP processor.

3. Example of PIL simulation application

As an example of PIL simulation scheme, we present the application of this strategy on the attitude control problem of an artificial satellite. This case study consists of an embedded digital attitude control system (ACS) design for three axis stabilization [7]. The information obtained by the sensors is processed by a Digital Signal Processor (DSP). The controller design is based on Linear-quadratic Gaussian (LQG) optimal control approach, a well known control theory in terms of space technology applications.

3.1. The satellite attitude control problem

The mathematical model of the satellite attitude considers two reference systems: the orbital frame and the satellite body frame. The orbital frame moves jointly with the satellite. Its origin coincides with the satellite's center of the mass. The axis z_0 of the orbital frame is defined by the satellite radius vector, the axis y_0 by the orbital normal, and the axis x_0 completes a right handed coordinate frame.

The body frame (x, y, z) has its origin in the center of mass of the satellite. Their axes coincide with the satellite's principal axes of inertia. We consider the case where the nominal attitude has axes of the body frame aligned with the axes of the orbital frame [8]. The Euler angles are adopted as parameters of attitude, considering the sequence of rotations 3-2-1. In this case, the rotation matrix is given by [9].

$$R_x^X = \begin{bmatrix} \cos\psi\cos\theta & \cos\psi\cos\theta & -\sin\theta \\ -\cos\phi\sin\psi + \sin\phi\sin\theta\cos\psi & \cos\phi\cos\psi + \sin\phi\sin\theta\sin\psi & \sin\phi\cos\theta \\ \sin\phi\sin\psi + \cos\phi\sin\theta\cos\psi & -\sin\phi\cos\psi + \cos\phi\sin\theta\sin\psi & \cos\phi\cos\theta \end{bmatrix} \tag{1}$$

The kinematics equation is obtained by the time derivative of the rotation matrix equation [8], then:

$$\dot{R}(t) = S(\omega(t))R(t) \tag{2}$$

The kinematics equation can be simplified if one considers small angle maneuvers, in this case we can approximate: $\sin\phi \approx \phi$, $\sin\theta \approx \theta$, $\sin\psi \approx \psi$, $\cos\phi \approx 1$, $\cos\theta \approx 1$ and $\cos\psi \approx 1$. Moreover, the non-linear terms $(\psi\theta, \psi\phi, \theta\phi)$ are very small compared to the linear ones. The velocities are also small compared to the orbital velocity [10]. Considering those approximations the kinematic equation is given by:

$$\omega_{ib}^b = \begin{bmatrix} \dot{\phi} \\ \theta \\ \psi \end{bmatrix} + \omega_0 \begin{bmatrix} -\psi \\ -1 \\ 0 \end{bmatrix} \tag{3}$$

In this work the satellite is modeled as a rigid body. Therefore the dynamic model can be obtained with the Euler equation that describes the rotation of a rigid body [9, 11]. The dynamic equation is given by:

$$J\dot{\omega}_{ib}^b + S(\omega_{ib}^b)J\omega_{ib}^b = \tau_d^b + \tau_p^b \tag{4}$$

where J is the inertia matrix of the satellite, τ_d^b represents the torques from external perturbations acting on the satellite, and τ_p^b represent the control torques (τ_x, τ_y, τ_z), all vectors described in the body frame, ω_{ib}^{b} is the angular velocity of the body with respect to the inertial frame written in the body frame. The gravity gradient is the only external perturbation considered in this work. Its effect cannot be neglected in a low-orbit satellite; an asymmetric body subject to the Earth gravitational field will experience a torque tending to align the axis of minor inertia with the field direction. The gravity gradient torque is modeled as:

$$\tau_g^b = 3\omega_0^2 \begin{bmatrix} (J_z - J_y)\phi \\ (J_x - J_z)\theta \\ 0 \end{bmatrix} \tag{5}$$

Substituting the applied torques and the kinematic equation (Eqs. 5 and 3) into Eq. 4, and representing this dynamics in the state space form, we have [10]:

$$\begin{aligned} \dot{x} &= Ax + Bu \\ y &= Cx + Du \end{aligned} \tag{6}$$

3.1.1. The LQG control approach

The Linear Quadratic Regulator is designed upon the linearization of the dynamic model. The theory is developed for linear systems. However, the system simulation takes into consideration the complete non-linear model of the satellite. This optimal control approach consists of minimizing a quadratic cost function and computing a feedback gain matrix [12]. The optimization problem aims to obtain a control law expressed by a linear relationship between the state variable x (expressing here the Euler's angles and the angular velocities) and the control variable u (the applied torques), i.e. $u = -Kx$. The matrix of gain K is obtained by the minimization of a quadratic cost function formulated as follows:

$$J_{lqr} = \int_0^T \left(x^T Q_c x + u^T R_c u \right) dt \tag{7}$$

where Q_c and R_c are the weight matrices of state and control vectors, respectively. The value of K results from solving the algebraic matrix Riccati equation for a time-invariant system and considering an infinite horizon context:

$$A^T P + PA - PBR_c^{-1} B^T P + Q_c = 0 \tag{8}$$

where A and B are the matrices of the linearized attitude dynamic model. The optimal control gain is then given in terms of the solution P of the Riccati equation:

$$K = R^{-1} B^T P \tag{9}$$

http://dx.doi.org/10.5772/57219

Due to the presence of noises in sensors measurements and uncertainties in models, a filter is needed to obtain more reliable information about the states. For the inclusion of signals filtering, we adopted the controller design based on the theory of Linear Quadratic Gaussian control [12]. We consider in this work the presence of white noise in the observations, and that the system is observable. In the LQG problem, we want to minimize the cost function:

$$J_{lqg} = \int_0^T \left(x^T Q_f x + u^T R_f u\right) dt \tag{10}$$

where Q_f is the covariance matrix of the measurements noise, and R_f is the covariance matrix of the dynamics noise (or model uncertainties). The LQG control law determination will be given by solving two problems: setting the controller for the linear quadratic deterministic problem, and setting a Kalman-Bucy filter for optimum estimation $\hat{x}$ of state x. The formulation of the Kalman-Bucy filter is given by:

$$\hat{x} = A\hat{x} + Bu + L\ (y - C\hat{x}) \tag{11}$$

where L is the Kalman filter gain that is obtained by solving the algebraic Riccati matrix equation:

$$A^T S + SA - SCR_f^{-1} C^T S + Q_f = 0 \tag{12}$$

The gain of the optimal filter is given by $L = R_f^{-1} C^T S$. After obtaining L, it is possible to obtain the transfer function of open loop LQG controller according to [10]:

$$K_{lqg} G(s) = K(sI - A + BK + LC)^{-1} LG(s) \tag{13}$$

where $G(s) = C(s)(sI - A)^{-1} B$ is the transfer function of the attitude dynamics.

The linear quadratic controller action can be implemented using actuators such as reaction wheels and magnetic actuators for a continuous control command. However, during orbital operations, such as rapid detumbling maneuvers, the required torqueses are usually too high for reaction wheels. Therefore, on-off propulsion strategies are used for such operations [9]. The choice of cold gas jets actuation in the present study aims to test the control in a most critical situation in terms of the small attitude adjustments difficulties.

The firing of the gas jets is controlled by a pulse-width pulse-frequency modulator (PWPF) [13]. The PWPF is an interesting option for the thrusters control system due to its advantages over other types of pulse modulators. PWPF is designed to provide propulsion output proportional to the input command. The modulator optimizes the use of propellants; it provides a smoother control and increases the equipment life. The PWPF structure is shown in Fig. 1 [10].

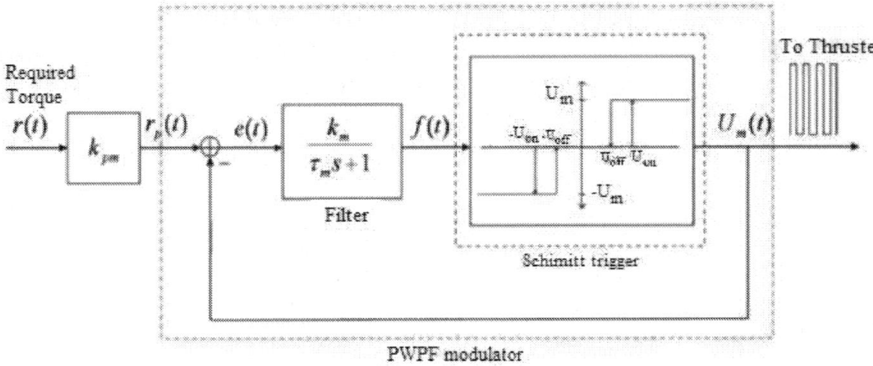

Figure 1. Scheme of the PWPF modulator.

When the positive input in the Schmitt trigger is greater than U_{on}, the trigger output is U_m. If the input falls below U_{off}, the trigger output becomes null. This response is also reflected for negative inputs. The error signal *e(t)* is the difference between the output of Schmitt trigger U_{on} and system input *r(t)*. This error is sent to a pre-filter whose input *f(t)* feeds the Schmitt trigger [10].

3.1.2. The digital LQG controller

The LQG controller, originally designed for continuous time systems, must be adapted to discrete time application. The appropriate selection of the sampling period *T* is a crucial factor in digital controller design, since if this period is too large there are problems in the signal reconstruction, and if it is too small, system instability and processing capacity problems can occur. In principle, one can believed that smaller sampling period is the best digital approximation. However, if the sampling period is too small, the controller poles approach the unit, causing instability. According to the equation mapping from *s* and *z* spaces, where, we can see that if *T* is very small, tending to zero, the poles of the controller in *z* tends to 1, which are the poles of a marginally unstable system, making the closed-loop system unstable. However, it is not necessary that *T* approaches to zero to start the problems, if it is small enough the poles at *z* cannot be anymore distinguished by the computer unit. Furthermore, small sampling periods can introduce significant distortions in the system dynamics behavior [14].

Very large sampling periods may result in violation of the rule established by the sampling theorem, which says that the sampling frequency ω_s must be twice greater than the highest signal component frequency ω_M [15]. If the condition of the theorem is not satisfied, there are information losses in the signal reconstruction. A reasonable choice for the sampling rate is 10 to 30 times the bandwidth of the system ω_B in closed loop [15]. A suggestion of [16] is to adopt a sampling frequency greater than 20 ω_B, in order to have a fairly smooth control response. In [17], the indication is to adopt the sampling period $T=1/(10f_B)$, where $f_B=\omega_B/2\pi$ and f_B is the bandwidth of the closed loop continuous system. System dynamics frequencies' analysis and recursive tuning adjustments led to the value of 10ms as a quite satisfactory value, considering the desired pointing accuracy. Furthermore, since the maximum speed of the adopted DSP core is 600MHz, a sampling period of 10ms allows the processing of the received signal and computing the control signal in the co-simulation in the interval between samples.

The design of control systems in the continuous domain is mathematically simpler and allows the use of a large set of tools. In the case of control system design in discrete domain, the mathematical problem is quite more complicated. In addition, in the continuous time domain, the visualization of the relationship between physical reality and mathematical representation of a control system is more evident. Therefore, the usual starting point for a discrete time control design is the continuous time control system study, followed by discretization procedures.

There are several methods of discretization of a given continuous time system, and they are basically divided into open loop methods and closed loop methods. In the open-loop methods the discretization essentially consists of turning the transfer function *G(s)* in *G(z)*. This transformation is performed by substituting the terms in *s* by *z* terms in order to satisfy some criterion. In the closed loop methods, the discretization of a controller function *G(s)* is obtained taking into account information from the operation of the closed-loop system, and also the knowledge of all the transfer functions involved in the system, including the plant that is is intrinsically continuous.

Several methods of discretization have been proposed and evaluated [18]. We adopted the open loop method of transformation of Tustin, also called bilinear transformation, giving satisfactory results even when compared to closed loop methods (which often have better results by taking into account the whole system), when applied to systems of low order. This method is based on the approximation of the integral represented by the factor *1/s*. The integral can be approximated by trapezoidal integration method in order to obtain:

$$s \approx \frac{2z-1}{Tz+1} \tag{14}$$

The dynamics of the satellite plant in the case of discrete control remains the same as in the continuous time case. Figure 2 illustrates the LQG controller scheme after its discretization. The main change observed in this scheme is the addition of a zero-order holder in the output signal which is sent to the satellite's block, as indicated by the output named "torque". The sensors signals are received by the "measured states" gateway. Finally, the controller subsystem was changed by the discretization in terms of its integration function.

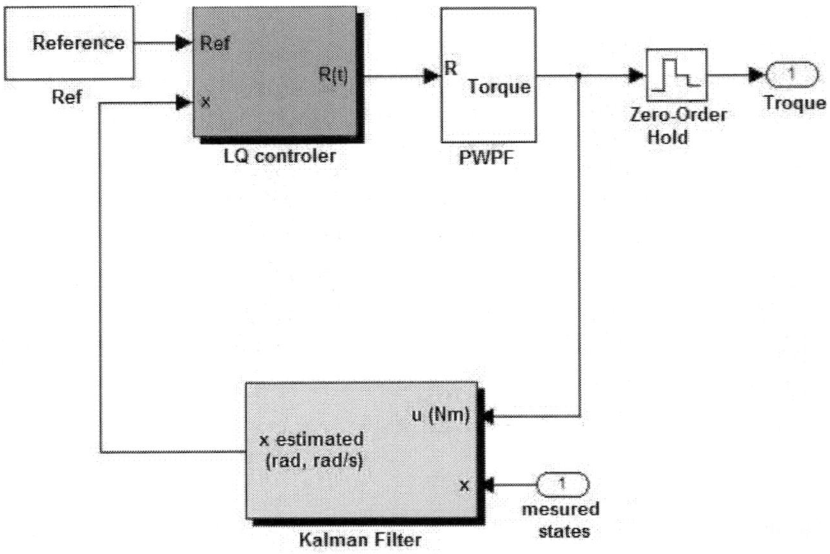

Figure 2. Scheme of the discret LQG controller.

3.2. Numerical simulations

The validation of the digital attitude controller was carried through a scheme of co-simulation, where a computer performs the simulation of the satellite's motion, in MATLAB/Simulink, using models of attitude kinematics and dynamics, and a Blackfin 537 DSP device (installed on ADSP-BF537 kit, Analog Devices) plays the digital LQG controller processing, and also the PWPF modulator [7].

The interface with the computer uses the Real-Time Workshop tool, through the Embedded IDE link, as shown in the Fig. 3.

The validation tests comprise two distinct scenarios. In the first one, the tests consider the same case studied in the precedent sections, i.e. the three axes attitude stabilization. In the second scenario, the attitude control is aimed to perform a maneuver to achieve a new orientation, i.e. a task of attitude tracking.

The co-simulation scheme is based on the computer communication with the DSP (cf. Fig. 4), which is facilitated by Simulink tool, which allows integration of several external processors, including the BF537, by creating a block *Processor-In-the-Loop* (PIL) in the simulation diagram. This communication is made possible through the interaction of the Simulink with the BF537 development environment, the Visual DSP ++ (Fig. 5).

http://dx.doi.org/10.5772/57219

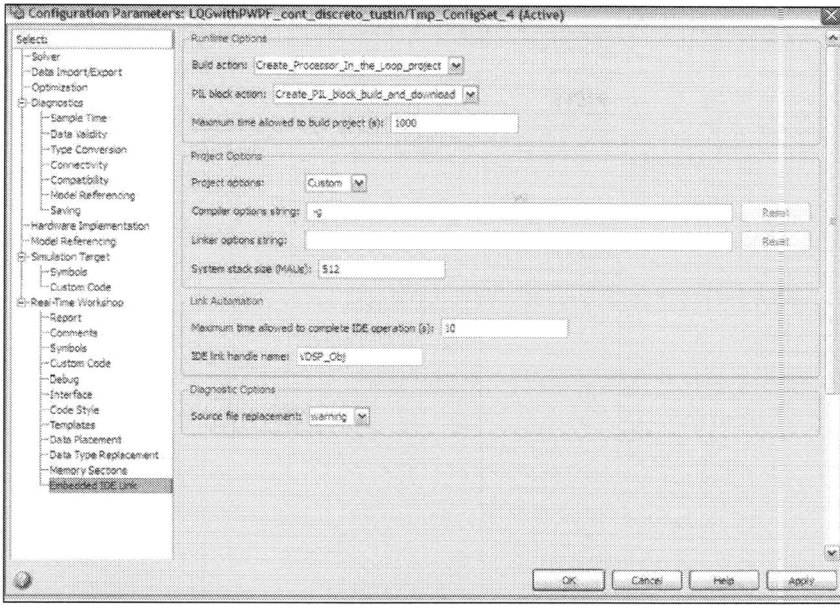

Figure 3. The PIL interface screen of the Real-Time Workshop (MATLAB/Simulink).

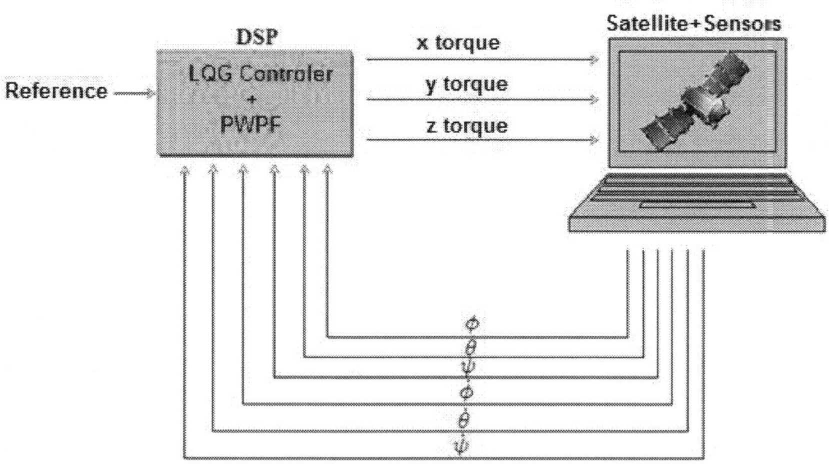

Figure 4. Co-simulation scheme: the DSP processes the LQG controller and the PWPF modulator, and computer simulates the motion of the satellite attitude.

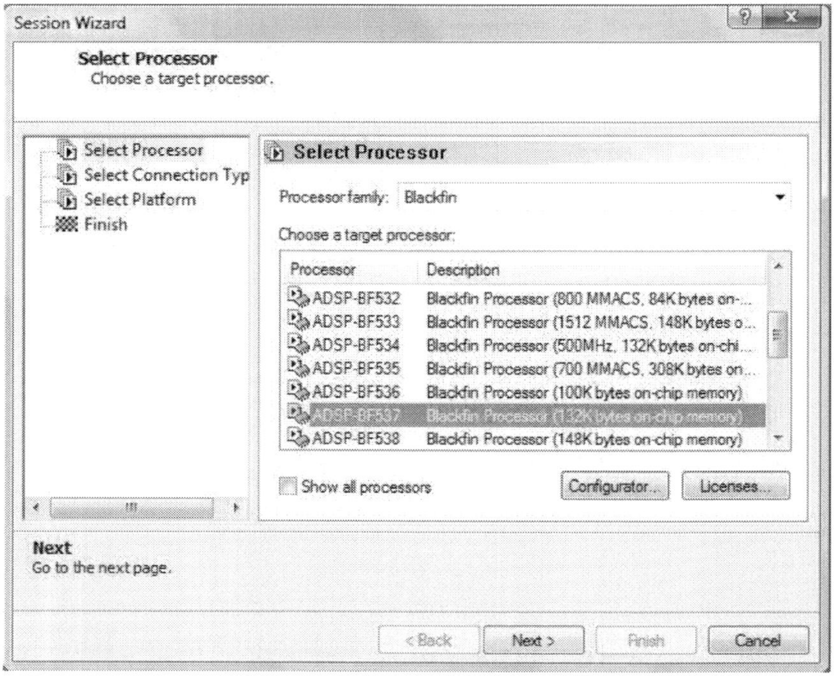

Figure 5. The session opening in Visual DSP++ environment.

The block PIL is inserted in the block diagram developed in the Simulink environment. It is responsible for the communication with the DSP, i.e. in charge of sending the information of the satellite attitude and of receiving the commands related to the control action, i.e. the gas jets driving from the PWPF modulator.

Figure 6 shows the results for the three Euler angles, of the validation tests for the case of three-axis stabilization scheme using co-simulation. The considered initial deviation is 10 degrees for each one of the three Euler angles, as in the case of the previous simulations.

A comparative analysis of the obtained results in the case of continuous LQG controller (in a simulation made only in MATLAB/ Simulink environment), and those obtained in the scheme of co-simulation (Fig. 6), can be made from a plot of the results differences. This differences plot is shown in Fig. 7.

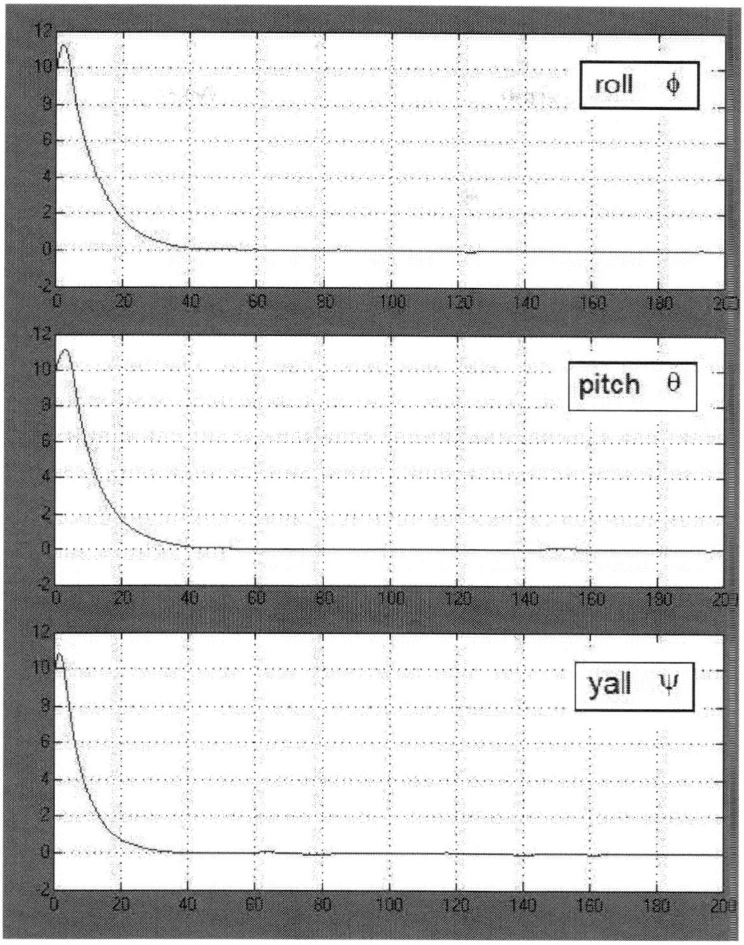

Figure 6. Co-simulation results of attitude control using a DSP (for ϕ, θ, ψ, in degrees).

The differences are smaller than 0.1 degree for the three angles. However, we cannot conclude about the better precision scenario. Both simulations met the accuracy specifications, nevertheless the simulation of continuous-time system lacks of realism for an experimental application. In fact, the small difference between the two cases shows only that the co-simulation scheme works very similarly to the idealized case, which may suggest an optimistic outcome in relation to the expectations of an experimental application.

In a second test case, the satellite is commanded to change its attitude, initially with three angles (roll, pitch, and yaw) at the same value of 10°, for a new attitude defined by the values

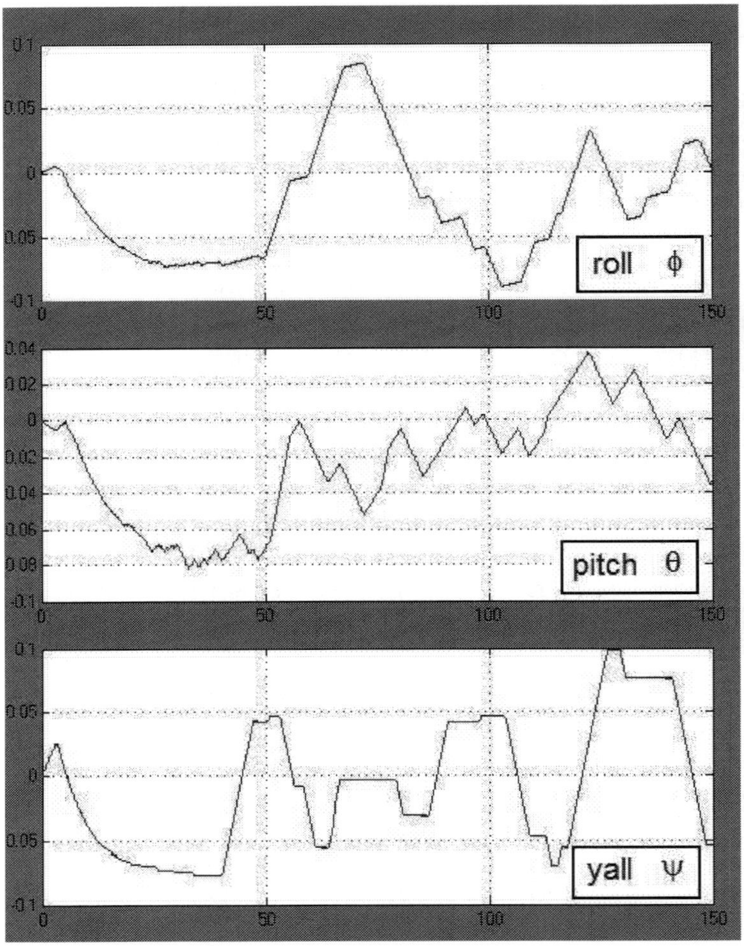

Figure 7. Difference between the simulation results of the continuous controller and co-simulation of digital control (for ϕ, θ, ψ, in degrees).

50, 60 and 45°, respectively. The results are shown in Fig. 8. It was observed that the controller performs satisfactorily its task, with tracking maneuver time of about 45 seconds. An important remark: the gap angles between initial and final attitudes are relatively large for the considered approximations in the synthesis of LQG control law. In the controller design, we adopted a linearized model for small angle values, whereas in the simulation of the motion of the satellite attitude we used nonlinear models of kinematics and dynamics. These models, in the case of large angles, exhibit very different behaviors of the linearized model, especially for higher angular velocities. It shows that the adopted controller achieves adequate performance even with this difference between models, and it presents interesting features of robustness.

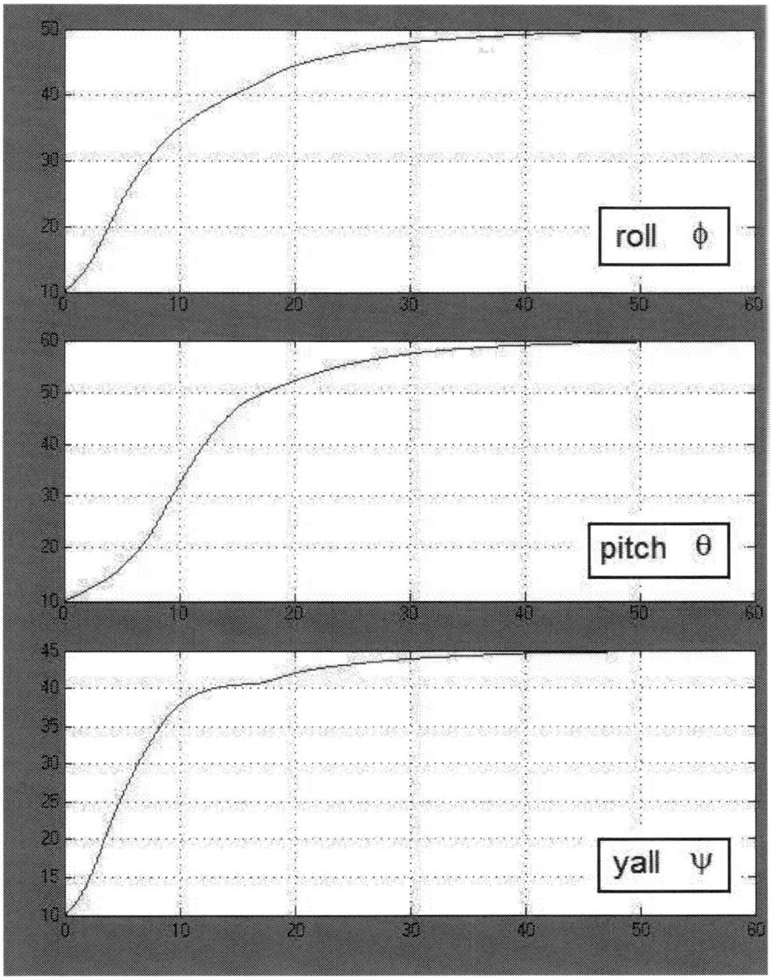

Figure 8. Co-simulation results of attitude control for the three Euler's angles, considering a tracking maneuver.

In terms of adopted sampling time, it was observed that the simulation in MATLAB/ Simulink waits the DSP processing to continue the calculations, preventing it from some problem related to the interval between two controller processing and actuation. However, there is a DSP development platform tool that allows the measurement of processing time and data traffic.

Consequently, it is possible to verify if the DSP processing time remains inferior to the maximum time period provided for sampling (10ms in this study). This tool is the *Cycle Counter*, which considers the frequency of the DSP core, 500MHz. The obtained result was processing and traffic time, much smaller than the time available due to the sampling period. It's possible to conclude that there are no problems in this application related to the aspect of the controller discretization and the use of a digital processor to perform the function of controlling and modulating the actuators.

4. Conclusion

The development of applications for embedded systems, as well the design of controllers to be performed by dedicate processors, can be immensely facilitated using the co-simulation approaches such as the Processor-In-The-Loop and Hardware-In-The-Loop. This validation scheme has been used as a way to move beyond on strictly computer simulations, opening the studies to realistic problems related to communication and exchange of data between embedded processor and controlled system, e.g. time delays, reliability of transmitted and received data, and processing time of the controller. These features are particularly useful for the design of artificial satellite embedded systems. That is the case of the example discussed here, a module function for the attitude control to be performed by an embedded digital processor.

Acknowledgements

The authors acknowledge the support of the Federal University of ABC - UFABC (Brazil), and of the *Coordenação de Aperfeiçoamento de Pessoal de Nível Superior* – CAPES / Program BJT – Science without Borders (Brazil).

Author details

Luiz S. Martins-Filho[1*], Adrielle C. Santana[2], Ricardo O. Duarte[3] and
Gilberto Arantes Junior[1]

*Address all correspondence to: luizsmf@gmail.com

1 Federal University of ABC, Brazil

2 Federal University of Ouro Preto, Brazil

3 Federal University of Minas Gerais, Brazil

http://dx.doi.org/10.5772/57219

References

[1] Shokry H, Hinchey M. Model-based verification of embedded software. Computer 2009; 2(4) 53-59.

[2] Juang JC, Chong CY, Tsai YF, Miau JJ, Tsai JR, Pan HP. Design, Implementation and Verification of Microsatellite Attitude Determination and Control Subsystem Based on Processor-in-the-loop. The 3rd Nano-Satellite Symposium: conference proceedings, Kitakyushu, Japan. 2011.

[3] Gaias G, D'Amico S, Ardeans JS, Boge T. Hardware-in-the-loop Multi-satellite Simulator for Proximity Operations. The 11th International Workshop on Simulation & EGSE facilities for Space Programmes: conference proceedings, Noordwijk, Netherlands, 2010.

[4] Seelaender G. Emulation and co-simulation of attitude control system for the PMM satellite and electro-hydraulic system for an aircraft using FPGAs. MSc. Thesis. Brazilian Institute for Space Researches, 2009.

[5] França Jr JA, Morgado JA. Real time implementation of a low-cost INS/GPS system using xPC Target. Journal of Aerospace Engineering, Sciences and Applications 2010, II(3) 29-38.

[6] Sabatini P, De Marchi E, Lupi T. Development and validation of attitude control systems using advanced off-the-shelf computer-based tools. Data Systems in Aerospace – DASIA: conference proceedings, Sevilla, Spain, 1997.

[7] Santana AC, Martins-Filho LS, Duarte RO, Arantes Jr G, Casella IRS. Satellite attitude control using a digital signal processor. Journal of Aerospace Technology and Management 2012, 4(1) 15-24.

[8] Wie HWB, Arapostathis A. Quaternion feedback regulator for spacecraft eigenaxis rotations. Journal of Guidance Control and Dynamics 1989 12(3) 375-380.

[9] Shuster, M.D. A survey of attitude representations. The Journal of the Astronautical Sciences 1993 41(4) 439-517.

[10] Arantes Jr G, Martins-Filho LS, Santana AC. Optimal on-off attitude control for the Brazilian multi-mission platform satellite. Mathematical Problems in Engineering V. 2009, ID 750945.

[11] Awrejcewicz J, Koruba Z. Classical Mechanics. Applied Mechanics and Mechatronics. New York: Springer, 2012.

[12] Dorato P, Abdallah CT, Cerone V. Linear Quadratic Control: an Introduction. New Jersey, USA: Prentice Hall, 1998.

[13] Buck NV. Minimum vibration maneuvers using input shaping and pulse-width, pulse-frequency modulated thruster control. MSc. Thesis. Monterey Naval Postgraduate School, 1996.

[14] Smith SW. The Scientist and Engineer's Guide to Digital Signal Processing. San Diego, California, USA: California Technical Publishing, 1997.

[15] Åstrom KJ, Witternmark B. Computer Controlled Systems: Theory and Design, New Jersey, USA: Prentice Hall, 1997.

[16] Franklin GF, Powell JD, Workman ML. Digital Control of Dynamic Systems, Manio Park, California, USA: Addison Wesley Longman, 1998.

[17] Dorf RC, Bishop RH. Modern Control Systems. Upper Saddle River, New Jersey, EUA: Pearson Prentice Hall, 2008.

[18] Soares PMOR. Discretization of continuous controllers. MSc Thesis. University of Porto, 1996.

Chapter 9

Application of the Liu and Murakami Damage Model for Creep Crack Growth Predictions in Power Plant Steels

Christopher J. Hyde, Wei Sun, Thomas H. Hyde,
Mohammed Saber and Adib A. Becker

Additional information is available at the end of the chapter

http://dx.doi.org/10.5772/57052

1. Introduction

Components in power plant, chemical plant, manufacturing processes, aero-engines, etc. may operate at temperatures which are high enough for creep to occur [1]. Such components may contain cracks or must be assumed to contain cracks as part of design life or remaining life analyses which are required [2]. In order to perform these analyses a number of approaches have been used, based on, for example, a fracture mechanics approach [3], or a continuum damage mechanics approach [4, 5, 6]. This paper is related to the use of the damage mechanics approach. In particular the methods used to obtain the material constants in the multiaxial form of the creep damage and creep strain equations are described. Most of the constants are obtained by fitting to uniaxial creep data; this is a well-established method [7]. However, in this paper, the determination of the multiaxial stress state parameter, α [8], is based on results from compact tension (CT) tests; this approach is novel and results in properties which are particularly suited for predicting creep crack growth in components, where the crack growth is defined by a damage parameter, ω. When this damage parameter reaches a critical value (0.99 chosen for the presented work) the material is regarded as 'completely damaged' and hence a void or crack growth is assumed to be present. A previously used technique for obtaining the multiaxial stress state parameter, based on the notch strengthening which usually occurs in Bridgman notch [9] creep rupture tests, relative to corresponding uniaxial tests, does not closely represent the stress states and constraint which occur at crack tips. The validity of the method proposed has been established by comparing finite element predictions of creep crack growth in thumbnail cracked specimens with experimental data [7] using the material constants obtained from uniaxial creep and CT creep test results.

The material chosen for the investigation is a 316 stainless steel and a P91 steel because of the ready availability of uniaxial creep, uniaxial creep rupture, compact tension creep crack growth and thumbnail creep crack growth data at temperatures of 600°C and 650°C, respectively. The particular form of damage equation chosen for the investigation is that proposed by Liu and Murakami [6]. By comparison with the more commonly used Kachanov damage equations [4], it was found that the Liu and Murakami equations do not cause the time steps in the finite element analyses to become impractically small [10] and unlike the Kachanov equations, they produce results which are relatively insensitive to element size near the crack tip. These aspects are covered further in the paper.

2. Experimental testing

Two materials have been used for the experimental testing presented, namely P91 steel and 316 stainless steel. The modified 9Cr (P91) steel was initially developed in the US in the early 1980s and was introduced to UK power plants in the early 1990s, to replace some of the components made from low alloy ferritic steels, as its high creep strength allows the use of thinner walled components, which will be less prone to thermal fatigue cracking. The 316 stainless steel is also a creep resistant steel, which is widely used in power plants at high temperature. Table I shows the chemical composition of the P91 steel and 316 stainless steel. All tests for P91 were performed at 650°C [11] and all tests for 316 stainless steel were performed at 600°C [10].

	Cr	Ni	Mo	Mn	Si	Cu	V	Co	S	C	Nb	N	Fe
P91	8.74	-	0.98	0.36	0.022	0.08	0.21	-	-	0.11	0.12	0.048	Balance
316	16.8	11.8	2.15	1.42	0.5	0.49	0.08	0.07	0.03	0.02	0.02	-	Balance

Table 1. Chemical composition (wt %) of P91 and 316 Stainless Steel

Three main specimen types have been used in order to obtain the experimental data shown in this paper, namely, uniaxial specimens, compact tension (CT) crack growth and thumbnail crack growth creep specimens, as shown in Figure 1, Figure 2 and Figure 3, respectively. Testing was also carried out using side-grooved CT specimens (see Figure 4) for P91. Tunnelling behaviour was observed for the plain specimens and relatively uniform creep crack growth fronts were observed for the side grooved specimens.

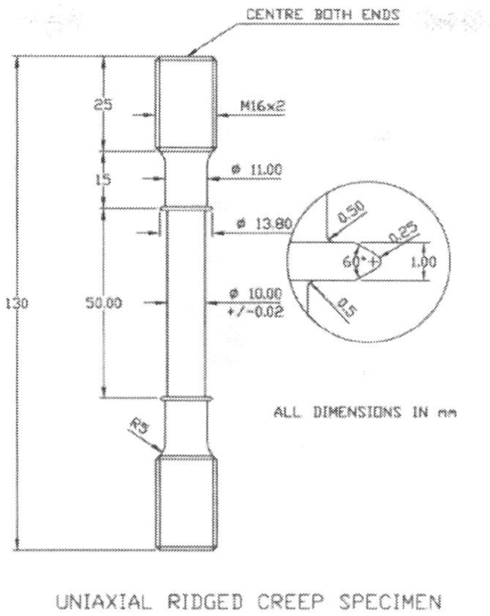

Figure 1. Uniaxial creep specimen geometry (dimensions in mm).

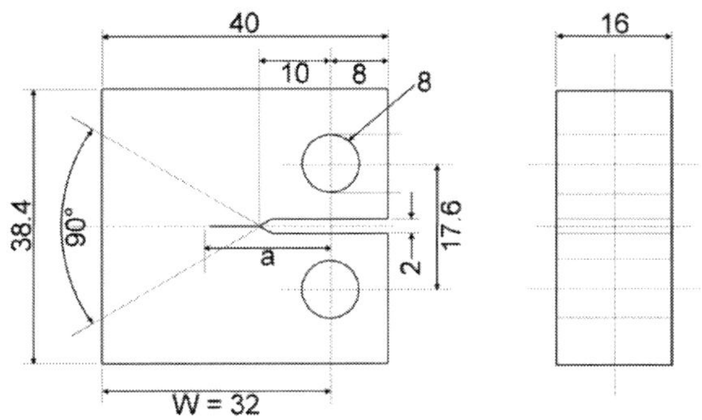

Figure 2. CT specimen geometry (dimensions in mm).

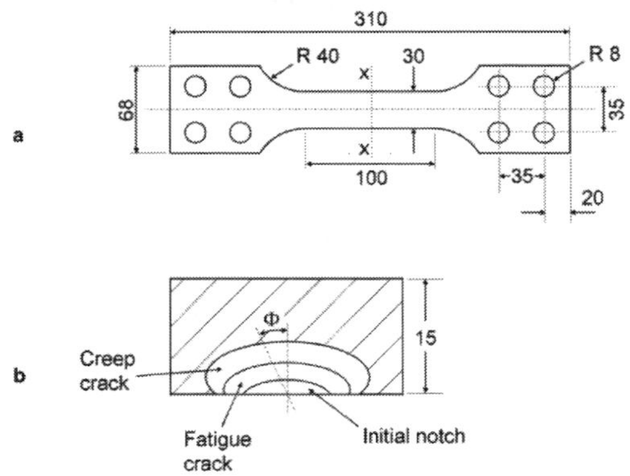

Figure 3. Thumbnail crack specimen (a) geometry, and (b) crack profile (dimensions in mm).

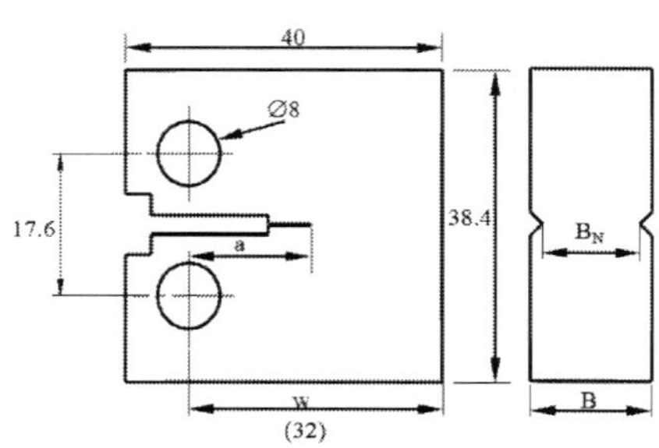

Figure 4. Side-grooved CT specimen (dimensions in mm).

3. Liu and Murakami creep damage model

3.1. Definition of the model

The governing equations for the Liu and Murakami creep damage model are shown by equations (1), (2) and (3).

http://dx.doi.org/10.5772/57352

$$\dot{\varepsilon}_{eq}^{c} = \frac{3}{2} A \sigma_{eq}{}^{n} \frac{S_{ij}}{\sigma_{eq}} \exp\left(\frac{2(n+1)}{\pi\sqrt{1+3/n}} \cdot \left(\frac{\sigma_1}{\sigma_{eq}} \right) . \omega^{3/2} \right) \tag{1}$$

$$\dot{\omega} = B \frac{\left(1 - e^{-q_2}\right)}{q_2} \sigma_r{}^{\chi} e^{q_2 \omega} \tag{2}$$

$$\sigma_r = \alpha\sigma_1 + (1-\alpha)\sigma_{eq} \tag{3}$$

where A, n, B, q_2 and χ are material constants. σ_r is the rupture stress, ε_{eq}^{c} and σ_{eq} are the equivalent strain and equivalent stress, respectively, σ_1 is the maximum principle stress, S_{ij} is the deviatoric stress and ω is the damage variable [10]. When the damage value reaches a critical value (0.99 within the present work), crack growth is assumed to have occurred into the regions where this has happened. The derivation of the uniaxial form of these equations can be seen in [10].

3.2. Determination of the material constants

The required material constants shown in equations (1) and (2), i.e. A, n, B, χ and q_2, can be determined from uniaxial creep data as detailed in [12] and a creep tip relevant value of the multiaxiality constant, α, can be determined from CT creep crack growth data as detailed in [10].

3.2.1. Uniaxial constants

From equation (1) the relationship between the minimum strain rate and stress can be given by [10]:

$$\log\left(\dot{\varepsilon}^{c}\right) = n\log(\sigma) + \log(A) \tag{4}$$

Therefore, using experimental uniaxial creep data to plot $\log(\dot{\varepsilon}^{c})$ vs. $\log(\sigma)$ and fitting a straight line of best fit through this data allows the identification of n from the gradient and A from the y-axis intercept. An example of this plot is shown in Figure 5, for 316 stainless steel, at 600°C. From equation (2) [10]:

$$\log\left(t_f\right) = -\chi\log(\sigma) + \log\left(\frac{1}{B}\right) \tag{5}$$

Therefore, plotting $\log(t_f)$ vs. $\log(\sigma)$ using data obtained from uniaxial experiments, allows the identification of both χ, from the gradient of the straight line of best fit and B, from the y-intercept. Figure 6 shows an example of this plot for uniaxial, 316 stainless steel data at 600°C.

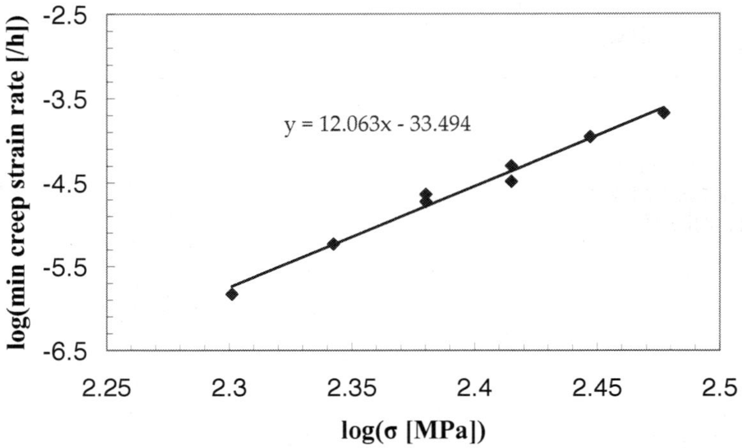

Figure 5. Linear fit to creep strain rate vs. σ on a log-log scale for 316 stainless steel at 600°C.

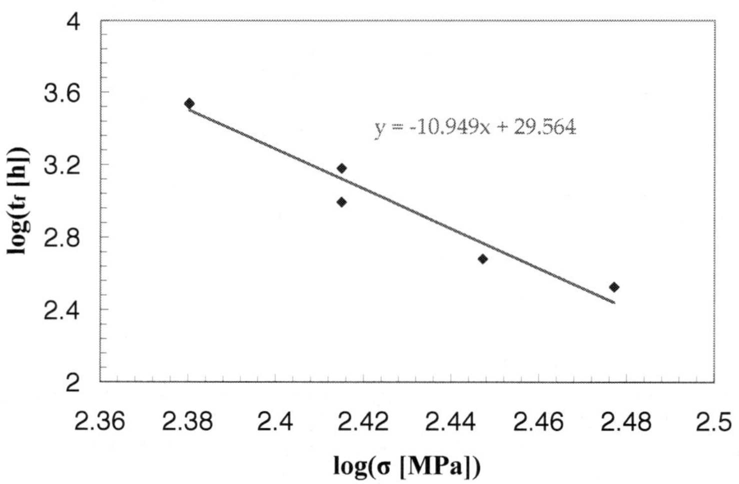

Figure 6. Linear fit to $\log(t_f)$ vs. $\log(\sigma)$ for 316 stainless steel at 600°C.

http://dx.doi.org/10.5772/57052

In order to obtain q_2, a curve fitting process is used on the ε^c vs. time data in order to determine the value of q_2 which is the optimum fit at all stress levels. In order to plot ε^c vs. time using the model, ε^c must first be found as a function of t [10]. This equation is as follows:

$$\dot{\varepsilon}^c = A\sigma^n \exp\left(\frac{2(n+1)}{\pi\sqrt{1+3/n}} \cdot \left(-\frac{\ln\left(1-B\left(1-e^{-q_2}\right)\sigma^{\chi}t\right)}{q_2} \right)^{3/2} \right) \tag{6}$$

An example of this plot using uniaxial creep data for 316 stainless steel, at 600°C, is shown by Figure 7.

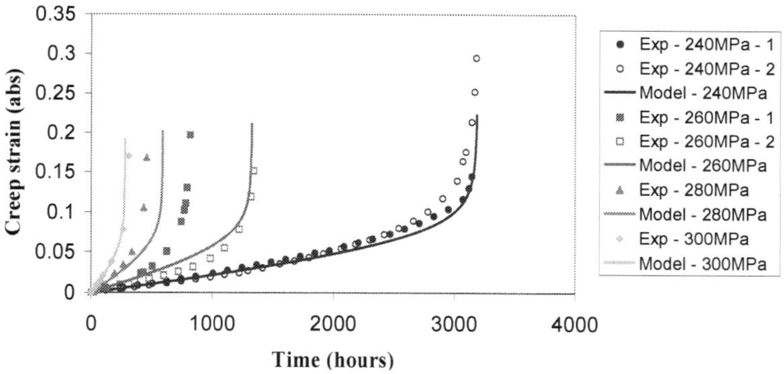

Figure 7. Comparison of the Liu and Murakami creep damage model to uniaxial, experimental creep data for 316 stainless steel at 600°C.

3.2.2. Multiaxiality parameter, α

Equation (3) is used for the rupture stress, σ_r, within the model to include the multiaxial stress effect. Within this equation is the material constant, α, which is not required for the uniaxial condition. However, if a multiaxial stress condition exists, the α value is required. It can be obtained from equation (2) that [10]:

$$t_f = \frac{1}{B\left(\alpha\sigma_1 + (1-\alpha)\sigma_{eq}\right)^{\chi}} \tag{7}$$

It can therefore be seen that the failure time is dependent on this multiaxial constant, α. Therefore, experimental data can be used in order to obtain the value of α. A series of finite element (FE) modelling of the conditions of the experimental tests are then carried out using the material properties (A, n, B, χ, and q_2) obtained from the corresponding uniaxial test data, together with a different α-value for each calculation. The α-value which results in the same failure time as that of the experimental test is taken to be the material α-value. The average α-value for a range of load levels applied in the experiments gives a more accurate estimate for the α -value. The process is capable of giving α-values which can be used with confidence when the triaxial stress state within the specimen is similar to that in the components for which damage zones and failure times are to be determined. Therefore for a crack tip (crack growth) condition, crack growth experimental data is used. A series of FE calculations, to predict the creep crack growth in the experimental CT specimens, as shown in Figure 8, were carried out for the experimental test durations, using the same load levels. The results of the time to the final crack length measured in an experimental test are plotted against α, and the experimental value of time to this given crack length, t_a, used to interpolate for the material α value. An example of this plot for a 316 stainless steel CT specimen geometry subjected to a load of 7.48kN, at 600°C, is shown by Figure 9. The application of the experimental t_a-value and reading of the material α–value is indicated by the dashed line.

3.3. Material constants

The material constants obtained for P91 and 316 stainless steels are given in Table 2.

	A	n	B	χ	q_2	α
P91	1.09×10^{-20}	8.462	2.95×10^{-16}	6.789	3.2	0.313
316	1.47×10^{-29}	10.147	2.73×10^{-30}	10.949	6.35	0.478

Table 2. Material Constants in Damage Equations for P91 at 650°C and 316 Stainless Steel at 600°C (σ in MPa and t in h).

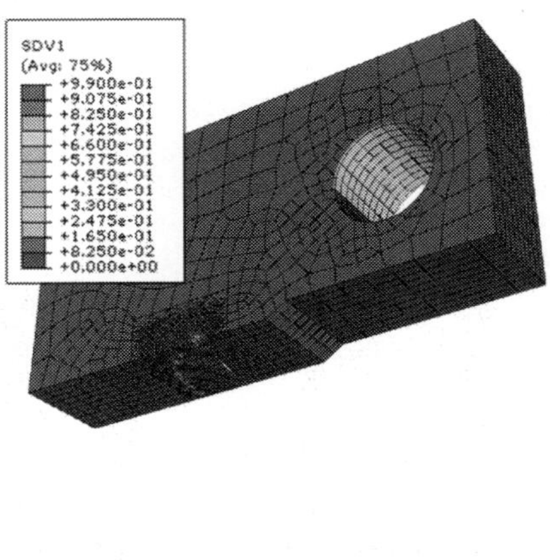

Figure 8. CT specimen FE mesh.

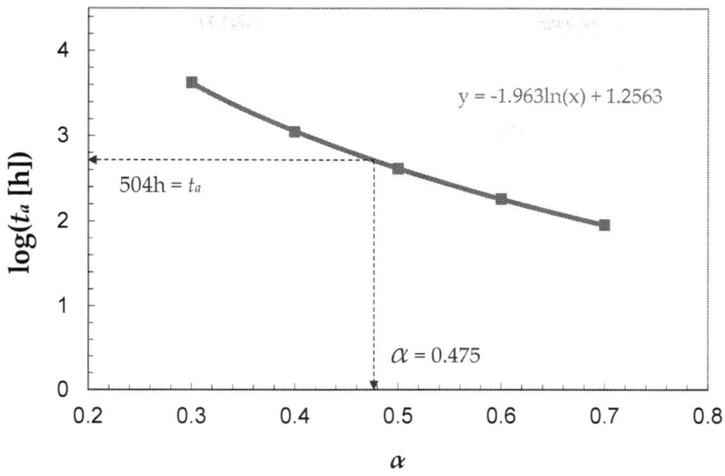

Figure 9. Typical α determination graph for 316 stainless steel from CT test data, using a logarithmic fitting.

3.4. Predictive capability of the model

3.4.1. P91 at 650˚C

A typical three-dimensional FE mesh and 0.99 damage (crack) zone for the CT specimen geometry is shown in (plain CT specimen), where due to two planes of symmetry in a CT specimen, only one quarter of the specimen has been modelled, with the appropriate boundary conditions applied [11]. Testing and modelling has been carried out for P91 at 650˚C for both plain and side-grooved CT specimens (see Figure 2 and Figure 4), with the model constants being calculated as shown in section 3.2. Figure 10 shows an example of a tested CT specimen of each type and shows the difference in the corresponding characteristic crack front shapes. Examples of FE creep crack growth modelling of P91 CT specimens using the damage mechanics approach are illustrated in Figure 10 and Figure 11. Figure 10 shows the damage contours, at times close to fracture, of a plain specimen and a side-grooved specimen. It can be seen from Figure 10 that the tunnelling effect observed in the plain specimens and the essentially uniform crack growth observed in the side-grooved specimens, as shown in Figure 10, have been reasonably accurately reproduced by the FE analyses. In addition and more importantly, as can be seen in Figure 11, the FE damage modelling has reasonably accurately predicted the creep crack growth behaviour for the P91 CT specimens, when compared with the corresponding experimental results.

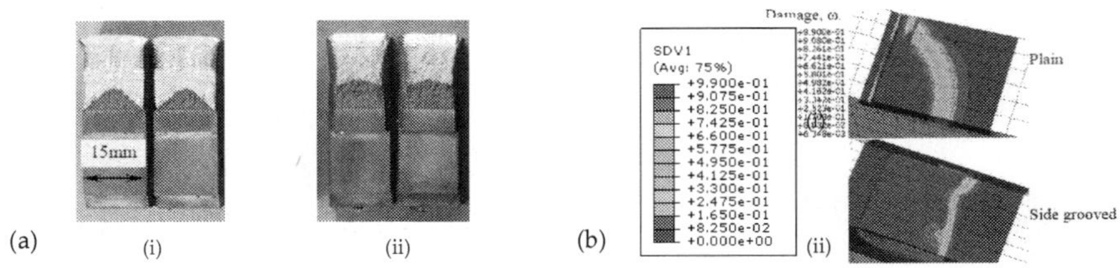

Figure 10. Examples of creep profiles for P91 at 650°C at times close to failure (a) Experimental CT specimen photographs and (b) FE damage contours [(i) plain (P = 5kN) and (ii) side-grooved (P = 3.6kN)].

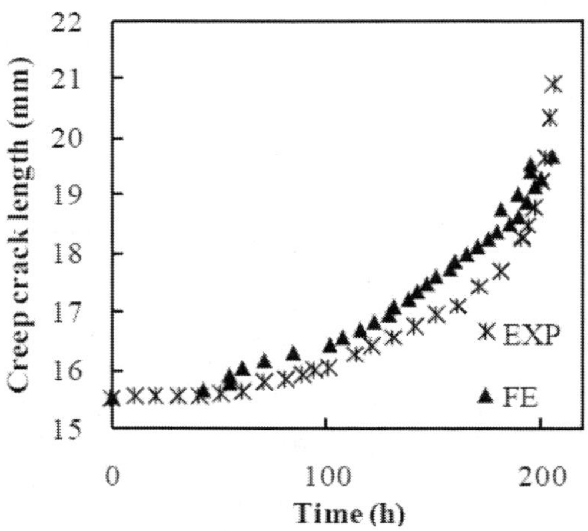

Figure 11. Predicted creep crack growth compared to experimental results for a P91 CT specimen (side-grooved, P = 3.6kN).

3.4.2. 316 stainless steel at 600°C

The comparisons of the experimental and FE creep crack growths for three plain CT specimens, each subjected to a different test load, are shown in Figure 12, from which it can be seen that the crack front shapes, as well as the extents of creep crack growth, were accurately predicted.

http://dx.doi.org/10.5772/57052

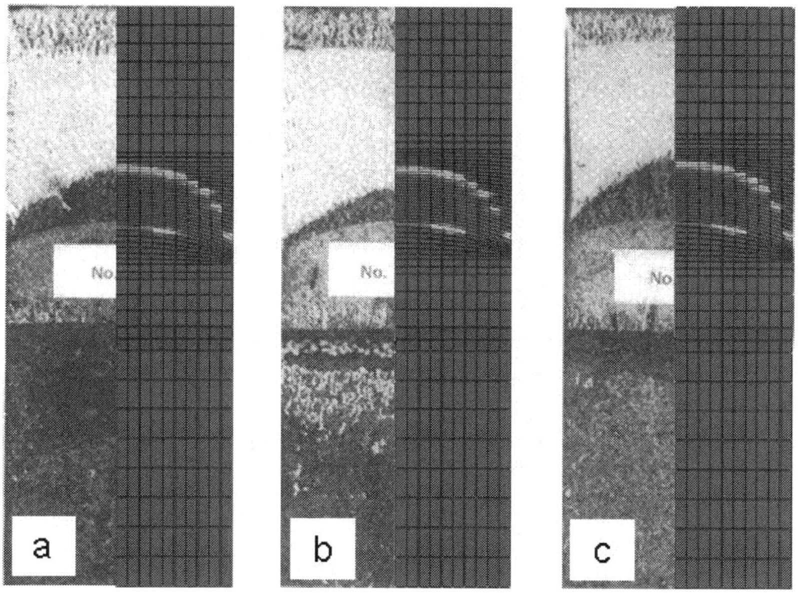

Figure 12. Tested specimen photo to FE damage contour comparisons (a) 8.522kN (b) 6.977kN (c) 7.476kN.

As the multiaxial constant, α, was determined using the CT crack growth data, it is to some extent not surprising that the FE crack growth predictions correspond well to this experimental data, with all of the other material constants having been determined using data from uniaxial creep data. However, similar simulations have been performed for thumbnail crack geometries using the same constants as for the CT specimen and can therefore be considered as 'pure prediction'. Figure 13 shows an example of the 3-dimensional mesh (and 0.99 damage (crack) zone) used for the thumbnail crack growth simulations. As with the CT specimens, due to two planes of symmetry in a thumbnail crack specimen, only one quarter of the specimen has been modelled, with the appropriate boundary conditions applied [10].

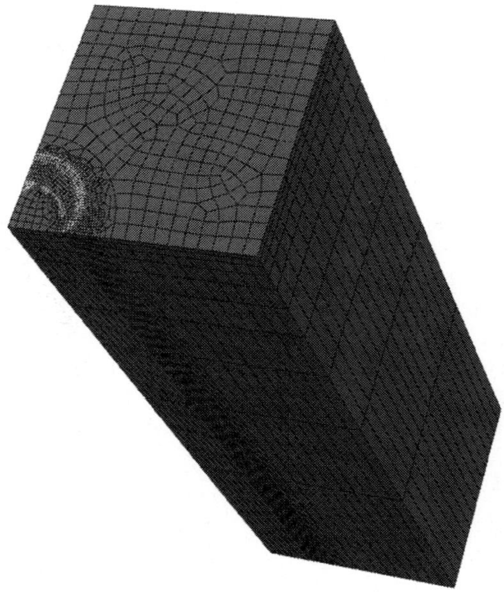

Figure 13. thumbnail crack specimen FE mesh.

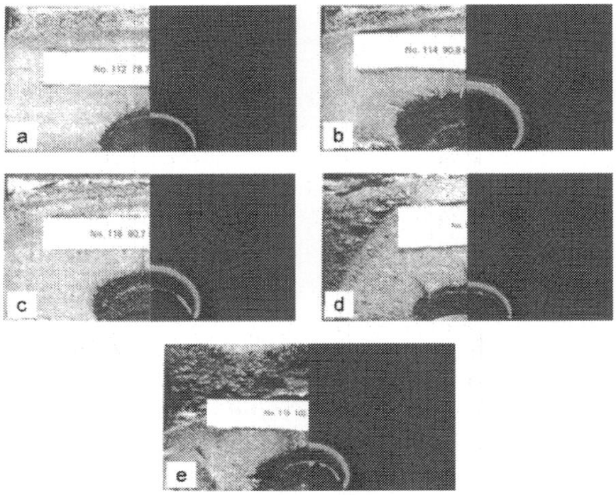

Figure 14. Tested specimen photo to FE damage contour comparisons (a) 78.7kN (b) 90.8kN (c) 90.7kN (d) 91.7kN (e) 102.3kN.

The comparisons of the experimental and FE creep crack growths for five thumbnail specimens, each subjected to a different test load, are shown in Figure 14, from which it can be seen that similarly to the CT predictions, the crack front shapes, as well as the extents of creep crack growth were accurately predicted.

4. Discussion and future work

A comprehensive procedure for the determination of the material constants for the Liu and Murakami creep damage model, based on experimental data, has been described. Particular attention has been given to ensuring a constant of multiaxiality value (α) which is highly appropriate to crack tip conditions. These constants have been applied, for a 316 stainless steel at 600°C and a P91 steel at 650°C, to a user subroutine for the Liu and Murakami model which has been used in conjunction with Finite Element package ABAQUS, in order to provide numerical predictions for creep crack growth in both compact tension specimen and thumbnail specimen geometries. Comparisons of the model predictions to corresponding experimental data for multiple specimen geometries, in terms of both crack growth and final crack length/profile, show extremely close correlation.

Also shown is the effect that side-grooves have on the crack profile in a CT specimen and the ability of the Liu and Murakami creep damage model to predict this more uniform crack profile observed in side-grooved CT specimens.

Nomenclature

Roman symbols

A Liu and Murakami Creep Law Coefficient

B Liu and Murakami Creep Law Coefficient

n Liu and Murakami Creep Law Constant

P Load

q_2 Liu and Murakami Creep Law Constant

S_{ij} Deviatoric Stress

t_a Time to Crack Length, a

t_f Failure Time

T Temperature

Greek symbols

α Multiaxiality Constant

$\dot{\varepsilon}_{eq}^{c}$ Equivalent Creep Strain Rate

σ_{eq} Equivalent Stress

σ_r Rupture Stress

σ_1 Maximum Principal Stress

χ Liu and Murakami Creep Law Constant

ω Damage

Abbreviations

CT Compact Tension

FE Finite Element

Acknowledgements

The authors would like to thank Dennis Cooper, Brian Webster and Shane Maskill for their assistance with the experimental work.

Author details

Christopher J. Hyde[1*], Wei Sun[1], Thomas H. Hyde[1], Mohammed Saber[2] and Adib A. Becker[1]

*Address all correspondence to: christopher.hyde@nottingham.ac.uk

1 Department of Mechanical, Materials and Manufacturing Engineering, University of Nottingham, Nottingham, UK

2 Department of Production and Mechanical Design, Faculty of Engineering, University of Port Said, Port Said, Egypt

References

[1] R. K. Penny and D. L. Marriott, “Design for Creep”, *McGraw-Hill*, Liverpool, 1971.

[2] T. H. Hyde, W. Sun and A. A. Becker, "Creep crack growth in welds: A damage mechanics approach to predicting initiation and growth of circumferential cracks in CrMoV weldments", *Int. J. Pres. Ves. & Piping*, 2001; 78, 765-771.

[3] B. Dogan and B. Ptrovski, "Creep crack growth of high temperature weldment." *International Journal of Pressure Vessel and Piping*, 2001, 78, 795-805.

[4] L. M. Kachanov, "The time to failure under creep condition", *Izv. Akad. Nauk., SSSR. Tekh. Nauk*, 1958, 8, 26-31.

[5] Y. N. Robotnov, "Creep Problems of Structural Members", *North-Holland*, 1969.

[6] Y. Lui and S. Murakami, "Damage localization of conventional creep damage models and proposition of a new model for creep damage analysis", *JSME International Journal*, 1998, 41, 57-65.

[7] T. H. Hyde, "Creep crack growth in 316 stainless steel at 600°C", *High Temperature Technology*, 1988, 6(2), 51-61.

[8] D. R. Hayhurst and C. J. Morrison, "Development of continuum damage in the creep rupture of notched bars", *Phil. Trans. R. Soc. Lond. (A)*, 1984, 311, 103-129.

[9] G. A. Webster, S. R. Holdsworth, M. S. Loveday, I. J. Perrin, K. Nikbin, H. Purper, R. P. Skelton, and M. W. Spindler, "A code of practice for conducting notched bar creep rupture tests and for interpreting the data", *J. Fatigue and Fatigue of Eng. Materials and Struct*, 2004, 24, 319-342.

[10] C. J. Hyde, T. H. Hyde, W. Sun and A. A. Becker, "Damage mechanics based predictions of creep crack growth in 316 stainless steel", *Engineering Fracture Mechanics*, 2010, 77(12), 2385-2402.

[11] T. H. Hyde, M. Saber and W. Sun, "Testing and modelling of creep crack growth in compact tension specimens from a P91 weld at 650°C," *Engng. Frac. Mech*, 2010, 77(15), 2946-2957.

[12] T. H. Hyde and W. Sun, "Determining high temperature properties of weld materials," *JSME Int. J. of Solids Mechanics & Material Eng, Series A*, 2000, 43(4), 408-414.

Chapter 10

Large-eddy simulation of turbulent flows with applications to atmospheric boundary layer research

Hao Lu

Additional information is available at the end of the chapter

http://dx.doi.org/10.5772/57051

1. Introduction

In 1932, the British physicist Sir Horace Lamb, in an address to the British Association for the Advancement of Science, reportedly said, "I am an old man now, and when I die and go to heaven there are two matters on which I hope for enlightenment. One is quantum electrodynamics, and the other is the turbulent motion of fluids. And about the former I am rather optimistic."

Why then is the problem of turbulence so difficult? One reason is that the governing equations of turbulence are nonlinear partial differential equations, and appear to be insoluble. There are only partial proofs for the existence, uniqueness and regularity of solutions. What is more, these proofs correspond to simplified cases. It is not clear whether the equations themselves have some hidden randomness, or just the solutions. And if the latter, is it a consequence of the equations, or a consequence of the initial conditions?

With increased computing power over the last three decades, researchers can numerically solve the governing equations to obtain a complete description of a turbulent flow, where the flow variable (e.g., velocity, temperature, and pressure) is expressed as a function of space and time. The direct numerical simulation (DNS) of turbulence is the most straightforward approach to the solution of turbulent flows; however, DNS of high-Reynolds-number flow like atmospheric boundary layer (ABL) is not possible with today's computer resources. Large-eddy simulation (LES) has been introduced to simulate turbulence since the 1960s [82]. In LES, the large-scale motions of the flow are calculated, while the effects of the smaller scales are modeled through the use of a sub-grid scale (SGS) model. The main advantage of LES over computationally cheaper Reynolds-averaged Navier-Stokes (RANS) is the increased level of detail that LES can deliver [e.g., 80]. While RANS provides "averaged" results, LES can potentially provide the kind of high-resolution spatial and temporal information needed for applications.

The ABL is the lowest part of the atmosphere which is in direct interaction with the Earth's surface and responds to surface forcing with time scales of one hour or less. It is a highly turbulent boundary-layer flow with a Reynolds number of order $Re \sim 10^8$ or higher. The ABL flow has a huge continuous range of turbulent eddy scales, ranging from the integral scale, on the order of $L \sim O(1\,\text{km})$, down to the Kolmogorov viscous dissipation scale $\eta \sim O(1\,\text{mm})$. Prediction of ABL flow is complicated by the often strong temporal and spatial variability of the land-surface characteristics (e.g., surface temperature and aerodynamic roughness). Moreover, land surfaces are often characterized by complex topography, which is in many cases multifractal [79], as well as spatial heterogeneity of aerodynamic roughness and temperature associated with different land-cover types. This leads to highly non-linear interactions between the complexity of the land surfaces and the ABL flow.

Accurate modeling turbulent transport of momentum and scalars in ABL is of great importance to forecast weather, climate, air pollution, wind loads on structures, and wind energy resources. Of special relevance are the seminal works of Deardorff, who first performed actual LESs of channel flow [23] and ABL flow [24]. In the last decades, LES has become a powerful tool to study turbulent transport and mixing in the ABL. Numerical simulations have been used to investigate the impact of different surface types (homogeneous, heterogeneous, flat, complex topography) on turbulent fluxes of momentum and scalars, such as temperature, water vapor and pollutants [e.g., 1, 2, 11, 25, 48, 55, 72, 87, 96, 99]. Recently, LES studies of the interaction between ABL turbulence and wind turbines, and the interference effects among wind turbines have been carried out, in order to understand the impact of wind farms on local meteorology as well as to optimize the design (turbine siting) of wind energy projects [e.g., 16, 36, 37, 59, 78, 97].

However, there are still some open issues that need to be addressed in order to make LES a more accurate tool for turbulence simulations. The main weakness of LES is associated with our limited ability to accurately account for the dynamics that are not explicitly resolved in the simulations (because they occur at scales smaller than the grid size). Here, we present a summary of our recent efforts to improve subgrid-scale parameterizations and, thus, to make LES a more reliable tool to study turbulent flows.

2. LES governing equations

Along with laminar-turbulent transition, turbulence parameterization constitutes the most critical part of flow modeling [68, 80]. In high-Reynolds-number turbulent flows computational limitations impose the choice of a grid size Δ_{grid} substantially larger than the smallest scale of motion. In LES, the separation of scales between resolved and unresolved scales is achieved by filtering (with a spatial filter of characteristic size $\widetilde{\Delta} \gtrsim \Delta_{grid}$) the equations describing the transport of mass, momentum and scalar quantities. In particular, the filtered equations (using the Boussinesq approximation) governing continuity, conservation of momentum and scalar transport are

$$\frac{\partial \widetilde{u}_i}{\partial x_i} = 0\,, \tag{1}$$

$$\frac{\partial \widetilde{u}_i}{\partial t} + \frac{\partial \widetilde{u}_i \widetilde{u}_j}{\partial x_j} = -\frac{\partial \widetilde{p}}{\partial x_i} - \frac{\partial \tau_{ij}}{\partial x_j} + \nu \frac{\partial^2 \widetilde{u}_i}{\partial x_j \partial x_j} + \widetilde{f}_i\,, \tag{2}$$

$$\frac{\partial \widetilde{\theta}}{\partial t} + \widetilde{u}_i \frac{\partial \widetilde{\theta}}{\partial x_i} = -\frac{\partial q_i}{\partial x_i} + \kappa \frac{\partial^2 \widetilde{\theta}}{\partial x_i \partial x_i}\,, \tag{3}$$

http://dx.doi.org/10.5772/57051

where $(\widetilde{u}_1, \widetilde{u}_2, \widetilde{u}_3) = (\widetilde{u}, \widetilde{v}, \widetilde{w})$ are the components of the resolved velocity field, $\widetilde{\theta}$ is the resolved scalar, $\widetilde{p}$ is the effective pressure, ν is the kinematic viscosity, κ is the scalar diffusivity, and $\widetilde{f}_i$ is a forcing term. In the stable/unstable ABL flow, the buoyancy force and the Coriolis force would be included as $\widetilde{f}_i = \delta_{i3} g \frac{\widetilde{\theta} - \langle \widetilde{\theta} \rangle_H}{\theta_0} + f_c \varepsilon_{ij3} \widetilde{u}_j$, where $\widetilde{\theta}$ represents the resolved potential temperature, θ_0 is the reference temperature, $\langle \cdot \rangle_H$ denotes a horizontal average, g is the gravitational acceleration, f_c is the Coriolis parameter, δ_{ij} is the Kronecker delta, and ε_{ijk} is the alternating unit tensor. In homogeneous rotating turbulence, the Coriolis force would be included as $\widetilde{f}_i = -2\varepsilon_{ij3} \Omega_j \widetilde{u}_k$, and without loss of generality, we would chose $\overrightarrow{\Omega} = (0, 0, \Omega)$. The effects of the sub-grid scales on the evolution of $\widetilde{u}_i$ and $\widetilde{\theta}$ appears in the SGS stress τ_{ij} and the SGS flux q_i, respectively. They are defined as

$$\tau_{ij} = \widetilde{u_i u_j} - \widetilde{u}_i \widetilde{u}_j, \qquad \text{and} \qquad q_i = \widetilde{u_i \theta} - \widetilde{u}_i \widetilde{\theta}. \tag{4}$$

SGS models are needed to parameterize τ_{ij} and q_i as a function of the resolved velocity and scalar fields.

3. Subgrid-scale modeling

This section provides a brief overview of standard eddy-viscosity/diffusivity models. On the basis of some mathematical and physical constraints, we developed a new nonlinear approach.

3.1. Standard eddy-viscosity/diffusivity models

Base on the Boussinesq hypothesis [14], a common class of SGS models, eddy-viscosity/diffusivity model, parameterizes the SGS stress' deviatoric part and the SGS flux as

$$\tau_{ij} - \frac{1}{3}\delta_{ij}\tau_{kk} = -2\nu_{sgs}\widetilde{S}_{ij}, \qquad \text{and} \qquad q_i = -\frac{\nu_{sgs}}{Sc_{sgs}}\frac{\partial \widetilde{\theta}}{\partial x_i}, \tag{5}$$

where $\widetilde{S}_{ij} = \frac{1}{2}\left(\frac{\partial \widetilde{u}_i}{\partial x_j} + \frac{\partial \widetilde{u}_j}{\partial x_i}\right)$ is the resolved (filtered) strain rate tensor, ν_{sgs} is the SGS eddy viscosity and Sc_{sgs} is the SGS Schmidt number. Several different models have been used to determine the eddy viscosity. The most common one was introduced by Smagorinsky [32] by assuming a local equilibrium between production and dissipation of SGS kinetic energy. The Smagorinsky model computes the eddy viscosity as

$$\nu_{sgs} = \left(C_S \widetilde{\Delta}\right)^2 \left|\widetilde{S}\right|, \tag{6}$$

where $\left|\widetilde{S}\right| = \left(2\widetilde{S}_{ij}\widetilde{S}_{ij}\right)^{\frac{1}{2}}$ is the strain rate, and C_S is a non-dimensional parameter called Smagorinsky coefficient. In isotropic turbulence, if a cut-off filter is used in the inertial subrange and the filter scale $\widetilde{\Delta}$ is equal to the grid size, then $C_s \approx 0.17$ and $Sc_{sgs} \approx 0.5$ [6, 53]. However, flow anisotropy, particularly the presence of a strong mean shear near the surface in high-Reynolds-number ABLs, makes the optimum values of those coefficients depart from their isotropic counterparts [e.g., 13, 46, 77]. [45] have also shown that the optimal value of the Smagorinsky coefficient decreases with increasing atmospheric stability in order to account for the reduction of characteristic length scales associated with thermal stratification. A common practice is to specify the coefficients in an *ad-hoc* fashion. The *ad-hoc* damping function proposed by Mason and Thomson [65] can be rewritten [76] as: $C_s = \left(C_0^{-n} + \left(\kappa \left(\frac{z}{\tilde{\Delta}} + \frac{z_0}{\tilde{\Delta}} \right) \right)^{-n} \right)^{-1/n}$, where n is an adjustable parameter, and studies [e.g., 5, 65, 76] have reported that this formulation with values of C_0 ranging from 0.1 to 0.3, and $n = 1, 2,$ or 3 can deliver a more realistic logarithmic velocity profile in the surface layer than does the standard Smagorinsky model using a constant coefficient. Studies [e.g., 5, 63, 65] have found the range of Sc_{sgs} is from 0.33 to 0.7.

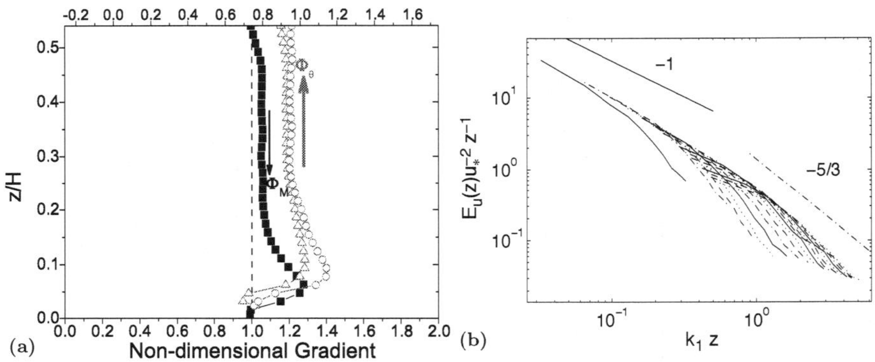

Figure 1. ((a) Vertical distribution of non-dimensional gradient of the mean streamwise velocity ($\Phi_M = \frac{\kappa z}{u_*} \frac{d<\tilde{u}>}{dz}$) and scalar concentration ($\Phi_\theta = \frac{\kappa z}{\theta_*} \frac{\partial<\tilde{\theta}>}{\partial z}$) obtained using standard eddy-viscosity/diffusivity models (■ shows Φ_M using $C_0 = 0.17$ and $n = 1$, △ shows Φ_θ using $Sc_{sgs} = 0.5$, and ◯ shows Φ_θ using $Sc_{sgs} = 0.7$, figure is modified from[60]); the dashed line corresponds to the classical similarity profile; (b) averaged non-dimensional 1-D spectra of the streamwise velocity obtained using the traditional Smagorinsky model with the constant coefficient $C_s = 0.17$.

Despite the popularity of the eddy-viscosity/diffusivity models, they are known to have important limitations:

(1) The eddy-viscosity/diffusivity closure assumes a one-to-one correlation between the exact SGS terms and the eddy-viscosity/diffusivity term, and locally employs the same eddy-viscosity/diffusivity for all directions. *A-priori* studies using experimental data and DNS data have shown that eddy-viscosity SGS models cannot capture the local characteristics of the SGS fluxes [21, 29, 32, 56, 61, 68, 69, 81]. For example, the underlying assumption of strain rates being aligned with the SGS stress tensor is found to be unrealistic (see 32 and the references therein). Field studies have also shown that the correlation between measured (in the field) and modeled SGS stresses (using the eddy-viscosity model) is very low (about 20 %) [75, 77]. Moreover, the fully dissipative nature of the model precludes backscatter, or negative SGS dissipation (energy transfer from unresolved to resolved scales), which has been reported in *a-priori* studies.

(2) For complex flows, it may not be possible to find a universal coefficient that is appropriate for the entire domain at all times. For instance, using the theoretical values in LES of boundary-layer turbulence, the Smagorinsky model yields too much transfer of energy and scalar variance from resolved to subgrid scales near the ground [64, 76]. This excessive SGS dissipation leads to unrealistic mean velocity and scalar profiles, with excessive non-dimensional mean shear and scalar gradients (Fig. 1(a)). The overestimation of the SGS dissipation leads also to velocity spectra (Fig. 1(b)) that decay too rapidly in the near-ground region [76]. Note that the normalized spectra do not show the collapse as found in experimental studies [40, 73].

(3) In anisotropic turbulence there can be a net transfer of kinetic energy from small to large scales [17, 84, 85]. The Smagorinsky model is by construction dissipative. For numerical stability, this is a desirable characteristic of the model. However, the actual SGS stress may also provide opportunities for inverse energy transfer. Studies of Khanna and Brasseur [43], Juneja and Brasseur [39], and Porté-Agel et al. [76] have showed that on coarse grids the Smagorinsky model may induce large errors because it is not able to account for the strong flow anisotropy in the near-wall region. Moreover, eddy-viscosity models do not have the same rotation transformation properties as the actual SGS stress tensor, which is not material frame indifferent (MFI). Recent studies [33, 47, 61, 62] revisited the importance of the MFI-consistency of the modeled SGS stresses. In LES of mesoscale and large-scale atmospheric turbulence including planetary rotation, the Smagorinsky model induces extra errors, yields excessive dissipation at large scales, and thus delivers unsatisfactory results, such as the failure of capturing large-scale cyclone/anti-cyclone asymmetry in favor of cyclone [62].

3.2. A new nonlinear formulation

To overcome some critical weaknesses of eddy-viscosity/diffusivity models, such as low correlations between the exact SGS terms and the modeling terms, modeling errors regarding the strong flow anisotropies, and a common issue of the early eddy-viscosity/diffusivity models that, in the context of ABL flows, the mean wind and temperature profiles in the surface layer differ from the Monin-Obukhov similarity forms [e.g., 15, 88] as shown in figure 1(a), a nonlinear SGS approach has been introduced and tested [57, 58, 60]. The new closure is based on gradient models, which, different than eddy-viscosity/diffusivity models, are derived from the Taylor series expansions of the SGS terms that appear in the filtered conservation equations, do not locally assume the same eddy viscosity/diffusivity for all directions, and make no use of prior knowledge of the interactions between the resolved motions and the SGS motions. At *a-priori* level, gradient models generally predict the structure of the exact SGS terms much more accurately than eddy-viscosity/diffusivity models (and therefore are better able to capture anisotropic effects and disequilibrium, e.g., 32, 56, 61, 62, 77). These features make gradient models attractive. However, when implemented in LESs, they are not able to produce the correct levels of the SGS energy production (energy transfer between resolved and SGS scales), and as a result, simulations often become numerically unstable as reported in a variety of contexts [e.g., 80].

Many schemes have been proposed for resolving this insufficient-dissipation issue relative to gradient models. Bardina et al. [8] proposed a mixed procedure; and later on, Vreman et al. [94, 95] achieved the mixing of the gradient form with eddy-viscosities, and showed that mixed gradient models can capture disequilibrium. In LES of rotating turbulence, to overcome the weakness that the traditional eddy viscosity $(-2\nu_{sgs}\widetilde{S}_{ij})$ is too dissipative at large scales, which may hinder kinetic energy from transferring to large scales, Lu et al. [62] considered a hyper-viscosity term $(+\nu_u \nabla^2 \widetilde{S}_{ij})$ as suggested by previous researchers [9, 26]. The new mixed nonlinear model is defined as

$$\tau_{ij} = 2k_{sgs}\left(\frac{G_{ij}}{G_{kk}}\right) + \nu_u \nabla^2 \widetilde{S}_{ij} \,, \tag{7}$$

where $G_{ij} = \frac{\widetilde{\Delta}^2}{12}\frac{\partial \widetilde{u}_i}{\partial x_k}\frac{\partial \widetilde{u}_j}{\partial x_k}$ for the isotropic grid, and the hyper-viscosity magnitude ν_u can be calculated by either $\nu_u = C_s' \Delta^4 |\widetilde{S}|$ or $\nu_u = C_k' \Delta^3 \sqrt{k_{sgs}}$. Note that C_s' and C_k' can be determined by dynamic procedures, for the sake of simplicity, an empirical constant $C_k' = 0.008$ has been adopted. The development of this new nonlinear model also shows the importance of anisotropy and MFI-consistent requirements for SGS models in rotating system. At last, an approximation for k_{sgs} is obtained solving the transport equation

$$\frac{\partial k_{sgs}}{\partial t} + \widetilde{u}_j \frac{\partial k_{sgs}}{\partial x_j} = -\tau_{ij}\frac{\partial \widetilde{u}_i}{\partial x_j} - C_\varepsilon \frac{k_{sgs}^{3/2}}{\Delta} + \frac{\partial}{\partial x_j}\left[\left(\frac{\nu_k}{\sigma_k} + \nu\right)\frac{\partial k_{sgs}}{\partial x_j}\right] \,. \tag{8}$$

Here, the three terms on the right-hand side represent, respectively, the production, the dissipation, and the diffusion. The constants are typically chosen as $C_k = 0.05$, $C_\varepsilon = 1.0$ and $\sigma_k = 1.0$ based on previous studies [e.g., 44, 100].

Liu et al. [56] revisited this energy cascade issue and recommended another meaningful choice, a clipping procedure, to control the amplitude of backward cascade induced by the model. Inconveniently, Vreman et al. [95] have reported that their coupling of the gradient model with the clipping procedure still does not provide sufficient SGS dissipation in simulations of mixing layer flows.

Integrate the clipping procedure and the model of Pomraning and Rutland [74] and Lu et al. [61, 62], a simple SGS formulation for the LES of ABL flows has been proposed. The new algebraic nonlinear models for the SGS stress tensor and for the SGS flux vector can be written as

$$\tau_{ij} = 2k_{sgs}\left(\frac{\widetilde{G}_{ij}}{\widetilde{G}_{kk}}\right) \,, \quad \text{and} \quad q_i = |\mathbf{q}|\left(\frac{\widetilde{G}_{\theta,i}}{|\widetilde{\mathbf{G}}_\theta|}\right) \,. \tag{9}$$

The method separates the modeling into two elements: the normalized gradient term serves to model the structure (relative magnitude of each component); and a separate model is needed for the magnitudes. To account for the grid anisotropy in the study ($\widetilde{\Delta}_x$, $\widetilde{\Delta}_y$ and $\widetilde{\Delta}_z$ are not equal), it is defined that $\widetilde{G}_{ij} = \frac{\widetilde{\Delta}_x^2}{12}\frac{\partial \widetilde{u}_i}{\partial x}\frac{\partial \widetilde{u}_j}{\partial x} + \frac{\widetilde{\Delta}_y^2}{12}\frac{\partial \widetilde{u}_i}{\partial y}\frac{\partial \widetilde{u}_j}{\partial y} + \frac{\widetilde{\Delta}_z^2}{12}\frac{\partial \widetilde{u}_i}{\partial z}\frac{\partial \widetilde{u}_j}{\partial z}$, and $\widetilde{G}_{\theta,i} = \frac{\widetilde{\Delta}_x^2}{12}\frac{\partial \widetilde{u}_i}{\partial x}\frac{\partial \widetilde{\theta}}{\partial x} + \frac{\widetilde{\Delta}_y^2}{12}\frac{\partial \widetilde{u}_i}{\partial y}\frac{\partial \widetilde{\theta}}{\partial y} + \frac{\widetilde{\Delta}_z^2}{12}\frac{\partial \widetilde{u}_i}{\partial z}\frac{\partial \widetilde{\theta}}{\partial z}$, and the gradient vector's magnitude is computed using the Euclidean norm $|\widetilde{\mathbf{G}}_\theta| = \sqrt{\widetilde{G}_{\theta,1}^2 + \widetilde{G}_{\theta,2}^2 + \widetilde{G}_{\theta,3}^2}$. To close the approach, it is required to evaluate the SGS kinetic energy, $k_{sgs} = \frac{1}{2}\tau_{ii}$, and the magnitude of the SGS flux vector, $|\mathbf{q}|$. Even though a previous approach [20] places much emphasis on the scalar field, it is desirable, owing to the definition of the SGS flux vector, that the SGS flux magnitude encompasses both the velocity and the scalar fields. Therefore, it is proposed to model the flux magnitude as the multiplication of an SGS velocity scale and an SGS scalar concentration scale, $|\mathbf{q}| = u_{sgs}\theta_{sgs}$. It is straightforward to assume that the SGS velocity scale is proportional to the square root of the SGS kinetic energy, $u_{sgs} = C\sqrt{k_{sgs}}$. The value of k_{sgs} is evaluated by using the resolved velocities on the basis of the local equilibrium hypothesis, which assumes a balance between the SGS kinetic energy production P ($P = -\tau_{ij}\frac{\partial \widetilde{u}_i}{\partial x_j} = -\tau_{ij}\widetilde{S}_{ij}$, where $\widetilde{S}_{ij} = \frac{1}{2}\left(\frac{\partial \widetilde{u}_i}{\partial x_j} + \frac{\partial \widetilde{u}_j}{\partial x_i}\right)$ is the resolved strain rate tensor) and dissipation rate ε. A classical evaluation of kinetic energy dissipation is $\varepsilon = C_\varepsilon \frac{k_{sgs}^{3/2}}{\widetilde{\Delta}}$. Simulations allow for no local energy transfer from unresolved to resolved scales, a step that is consistent with the non-negative value of the dissipation rate; this leads to

$$k_{sgs} = H(P)\frac{4\widetilde{\Delta}^2}{C_\varepsilon^2}\left(-\frac{\widetilde{G}_{ij}}{\widetilde{G}_{kk}}\widetilde{S}_{ij}\right)^2, \tag{10}$$

where $H(x)$ is the Heaviside step function defined as $H(x) = 0$ if $x < 0$ and $H(x) = 1$ if $x \geq 0$. The local equilibrium hypothesis assumes a balance between the SGS scalar variance production, $P_\theta = -q_i\frac{\partial \widetilde{\theta}}{\partial x_i}$, and the SGS scalar variance dissipation rate ε_θ. A classical evaluation of the SGS scalar variance dissipation rate is $\varepsilon_\theta = C_{\varepsilon\theta}\frac{\theta_{sgs}^2 u_{sgs}}{\widetilde{\Delta}}$. Using the proposed model formulation together with the local equilibrium hypothesis, one obtains $\theta_{sgs} = \frac{\widetilde{\Delta}}{C_{\varepsilon\theta}}\left(-\frac{\widetilde{G}_{\theta,i}}{|\widetilde{\mathbf{G}}_\theta|}\frac{\partial \widetilde{\theta}}{\partial x_i}\right)$. The clipping procedure assumes the SGS scalar variance production and the dissipation rate are always non-negative $\theta_{sgs} = H(P_\theta)\frac{\widetilde{\Delta}}{C_{\varepsilon\theta}}\left(-\frac{\widetilde{G}_{\theta,i}}{|\widetilde{\mathbf{G}}_\theta|}\frac{\partial \widetilde{\theta}}{\partial x_i}\right)$. Although a dynamic procedure [28, 54] might serve to determine the model coefficients C_ε and $C_{\varepsilon\theta}$, for simplicity, a simple method for determining a constant value has been adopted. To model the SGS scalar variance dissipation, Jiménez et al. [38] assumed that the SGS scalar mixing time is proportional to the SGS turbulent characteristic time, $\frac{\theta_{sgs}^2}{\varepsilon_\theta} \propto \frac{k_{sgs}}{\varepsilon}$. Tests have shown that the Schmidt number (or the Prandtl number depending on the physical significance of the scalar field) leads to satisfactory results. Using the model $\varepsilon_\theta = \frac{1}{Sc}\frac{\theta_{sgs}^2\varepsilon}{k_{sgs}}$, one obtains the following equation for the magnitude of the SGS flux

$$|\mathbf{q}| = H(P_\theta)H(P)\frac{1}{Sc}\frac{2\widetilde{\Delta}^2}{C_{\varepsilon\theta}^2}\left(-\frac{\widetilde{G}_{\theta,i}}{|\widetilde{\mathbf{G}}_\theta|}\frac{\partial \widetilde{\theta}}{\partial x_i}\right)\left(-\frac{\widetilde{G}_{ij}}{\widetilde{G}_{kk}}\widetilde{S}_{ij}\right). \tag{11}$$

Also, the coefficient can be derived as $C_{\varepsilon\theta} = \frac{1}{Sc}\frac{C_\varepsilon}{C}$. When adopting (as this study has done) $Sc = 0.71$ (the Prandtl number of air near 20°C), $C_\varepsilon = 1$, and $C = \sqrt{2}$ (with $u_{sgs} = \sqrt{(\widetilde{u_i u_i} - \widetilde{u}_i\widetilde{u}_i)} = \sqrt{2k_{sgs}}$), one obtains $C_{\varepsilon\theta} = 1.0$.

3.3. Model performance in atmospheric boundary layer flows

The new algebraic nonlinear closure (Eqn. (9)) is assessed through a systematic comparison with well-established empirical formulations and theoretical predictions of a variety of flow statistics in a neutral atmospheric boundary layer (see 58 for more details) and a a stable boundary layer (see 11, 60 for more details). Obtained from different resolution simulations of the neutral ABL case, figure 2 shows the values of the nondimensional vertical gradients of the resolved streamwise velocity as a function of vertical position, $\Phi_M = \frac{\kappa z}{u_*}\frac{\partial <\widetilde{u}>}{\partial z}$, and the scalar counterpart, the values of the nondimensional vertical gradients of the mean resolved scalar concentration as a function of vertical position, $\Phi_\theta = \frac{\kappa z}{\theta_*}\frac{\partial <\widetilde{\theta}>}{\partial z}$. On the basis of experimental results and dimensional analysis [e.g., 15, 88, 93], it has been found in neutral cases that $\Phi_M = 1$, and $\Phi_\theta = 0.74$ for all z in the surface layer. The new closure yields the value of Φ_M that remains close to 1 (indicative of the expected logarithmic velocity profile), and the value of Φ_θ that remains close to 0.74. Further, figure 3 shows the nondimensional one-dimensional spectra of the simulated streamwise velocity and the nondimensional one-dimensional power spectra of the resolved scalar concentration obtained from the 128^3 simulation using the new closure, computed at different heights. In the inertial subrange ($k_1 z \gtrsim 1$) all the normalized spectra are in good agreement with the $-5/3$ power-law scaling.

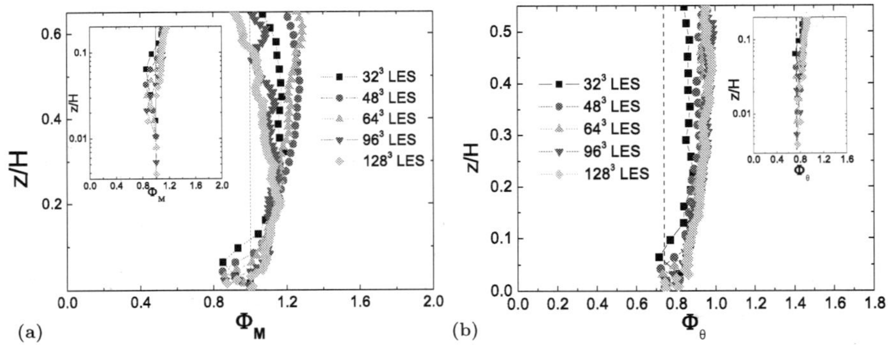

Figure 2. Nondimensional vertical gradients of (a) the mean resolved streamwise velocity and (b) the mean resolved scalar concentration obtained from the simulations of a neutral ABL case. Figure is modified from Lu and Porté-Agel [58, 60].

Stable boundary layers (SBLs) are relatively shallow and are characterized by strong vertical shear and a relatively high wind near the top of the boundary layer, thus are particularly challenging to simulate accurately. Φ_M and Φ_θ are key parameters for surface parameterizations in large-scale models and assessment of a SGS model. Owing to the existence of non-zero mean spanwise velocity component, the definition equation is modified as $\Phi_M = \frac{\kappa z}{u_*}\sqrt{\left(\frac{\partial <\widetilde{u}>}{\partial z}\right)^2 + \left(\frac{\partial <\widetilde{v}>}{\partial z}\right)^2}$. In the surface layer, Φ_M and Φ_θ are usually parameterized as functions of z/L, where L is the Obukhov length. For instance, the well-known linear relations [15, 88]

http://dx.doi.org/10.5772/57051

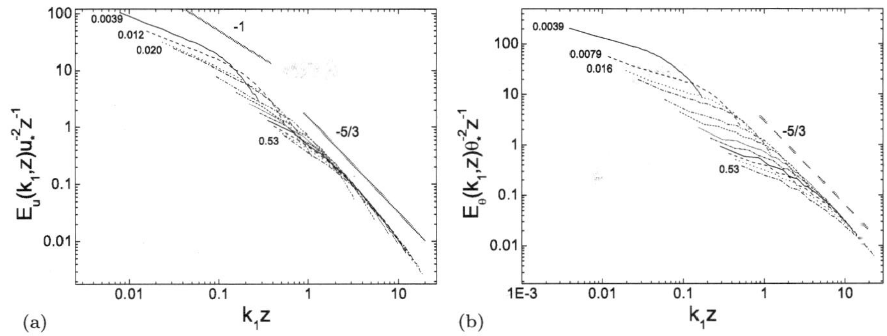

Figure 3. Averaged non-dimensional 1-D spectra of (a) the streamwise velocity and (b) the resolved scalar concentration obtained from the 128^3 simulation of a neutral ABL case. Figure is modified from Lu and Porté-Agel [58, 60].

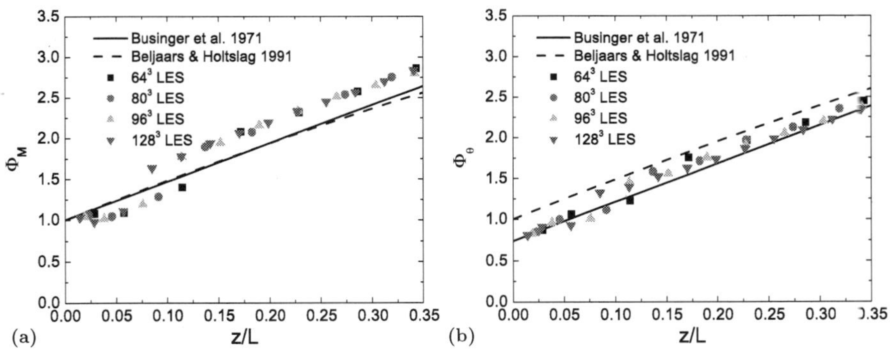

Figure 4. Nondimensional (a) velocity gradient and (b) temperature gradient at different resolution simulations of a stable ABL case. The solid and dashed lines correspond to the formulations according to equations (12) and (13). Figure is modified from Lu and Porté-Agel [60].

$$\Phi_M = 1 + 4.7\frac{z}{L}, \qquad \Phi_\theta = 0.74 + 4.7\frac{z}{L}, \tag{12}$$

and nonlinear relations derived from Beljaars and Holtslag [12]

$$\Phi_M = 1 + \frac{z}{L}\left(a + be^{-\frac{dz}{L}}\left(1 + c - \frac{dz}{L}\right)\right), \; \Phi_\theta = 1 + \frac{z}{L}\left(a\sqrt{1 + \frac{2}{3}\frac{az}{L}} + be^{-\frac{dz}{L}}\left(1 + c - \frac{dz}{L}\right)\right), \tag{13}$$

where the coefficients are $a = 1$, $b = 2/3$, $c = 5$ and $d = 0.35$. These formulations are plotted along with the LES Φ_M and Φ_θ results as functions of z/L in figure 4. It is evident that all of our simulation results agree quite well with the empirical relations. In the bulk of the surface layer the results have better agreement with equation (12) than equation (13).

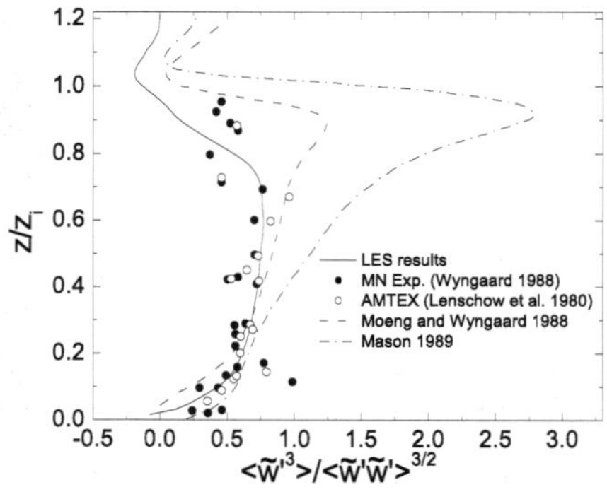

Figure 5. Nondimensional skewness of vertical velocity in an unstable ABL flow.

In unstable ABL flows, the land surface is warmer than the surrounding air, in response to solar heating. The warmer land surface leads to a positive (upward) heat flux, which creates a thermal instability and generates turbulence. Vertical-velocity skewness in an unstable ABL flow is indicative of the structure of the motion, when a positive value means that updrafts are narrower than surrounding downdrafts. A number of puzzling features of the vertical-velocity skewness are found in observations and LES of the unstable ABL. Figure 5 includes the vertical-velocity skewness derived from observations (the Minnesota experiment, 98, and AMTEX, 51) and from LESs. There is fairly good agreement over the lower portion of the convective ABL; however in the upper portion, previous LESs [63, 70, 71] indicate a further increase of the vertical-velocity skewness while the observations show a nearly constant value. The new closure, evidently, predicts much more accurate vertical-velocity skewness.

3.4. Model performance in rotating and isotropic turbulences

It has been noted that rotating turbulence with a moderate Rossby number below an $O(1)$ critical value accompanies asymmetry in favor of large scale cyclonic vortical columns [e.g. 83, 84]. This cyclone/anti-cyclone asymmetry is widely observable in atmospheric science. The direction of rotation of large scale wind flow (e.g., hurricanes & typhoons) is counterclockwise in the northern hemispheres (clockwise in the south). It is interesting to note that small scale rotating turbulent flows in the atmosphere, in which the direct influence of planetary Coriolis effect is inconsequential, are usually triggered by large scale cyclonical storms, and approximately more than 90% of tornadoes rotate in a cyclonic direction. Figure 6 shows that rotating turbulence captures this asymmetry, and a quasi two-dimensional flow - in other words, reduced variations along the rotation axis [e.g. 17, 18, 61, 62, 83].

Figure 7(a) shows the 3D & 2D kinetic energy spectra in a statistically steady state obtained from the new mixed nonlinear model (Eqn. (7)) at the resolution of 64^3. The flow is forced at large scales, and $Ro^{\omega_3} = 0.12$. The new model facilitates the two-dimensionalization process resulting in very close 3D & 2D energy spectra at large scales, $k <\sim 7$. All other examined models fail to deliver this quasi 2D structure at large scales.

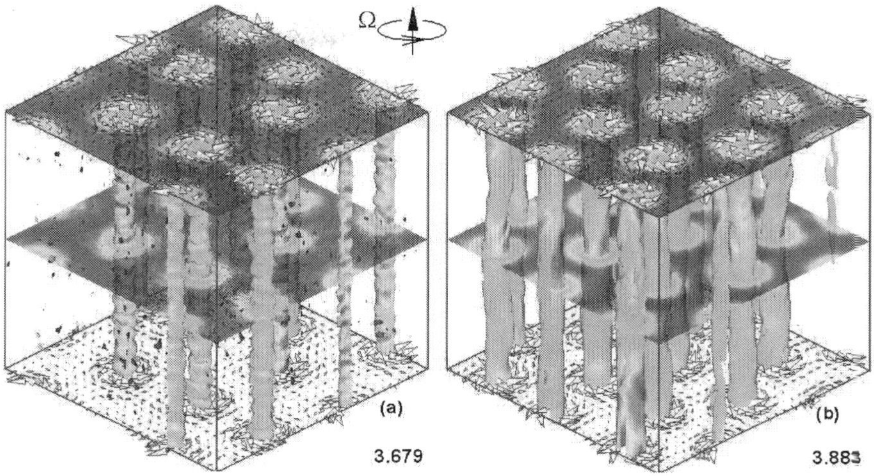

Figure 6. Cyclonic two-dimensional coherent structures appearing in rotating turbulence as indicated by iso-surfaces of vorticity, planar contours of kinetic energy and velocity vectors: (a) statistically steady state of small scale forced rotating case. (b) statistically steady state of large scale forced rotating case. Figure is adapted from Lu et al. [61].

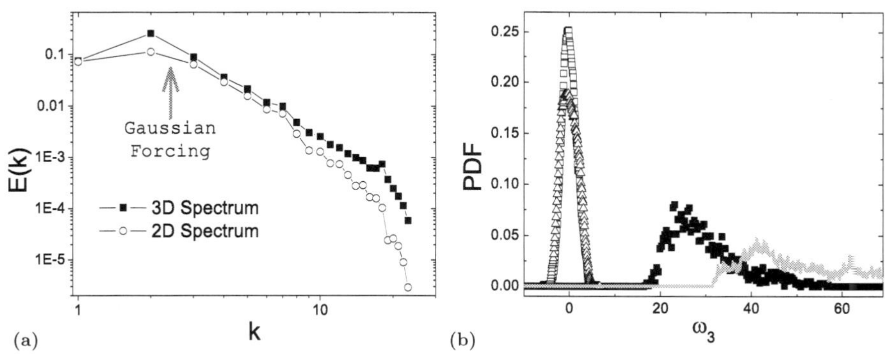

Figure 7. Assessment of the 64^3 LES of large scale forced rotating turbulence at statistically steady state: (a) 3D & 2D kinetic energy spectra obtained from the new nonlinear mixed model; (b) PDF of ω_3 obtained from the filtered DNS (gray line), the Smagorinsky model (△), the mixed scale-similarity model (□) and the new model (■). Figure is modified from Lu et al. [62].

In order to examine the cyclonic/anti-cyclonic asymmetry, vortex regions rather than the whole domain are concentrated. The vortex regions can be identified using the criterion $\lambda_2 < 0$[1] for a vortex region [35], and points with $\lambda_2 < (1/6)\min(\lambda_2) < 0$ are sampled to obtain the probability density function $PDF(\omega_3)$. Figure 7(b) compares the Smagorinsky model, the mixed scale-similarity model and the new model with respect to the (PDF) of ω_3.

[1] λ_2 is the second large eigenvalue of tensor $S_{im}S_{mj} + \Omega_{im}\Omega_{mj}$, where $\Omega_{ij} = \frac{1}{2}(\partial u_i/\partial x_j - \partial u_j/\partial x_i)$

The new model successfully delivers the cyclonic/anti-cyclonic asymmetry (the dominance of positive ω_3 vortices); others fail to do so.

Figure 8 examines the 64^3 intermediate scale forced large eddy simulations with $Ro^{\omega_3} = 0.16$. As shown in figure 8(a), the new model dissipates the kinetic energy at small scales and captures the reverse energy transfer to large scales. Figure 8(b) compares SGS models with respect to $PDF(\omega_3)$, and shows that the new model is capable of delivering the cyclonic/anti-cyclonic asymmetry.

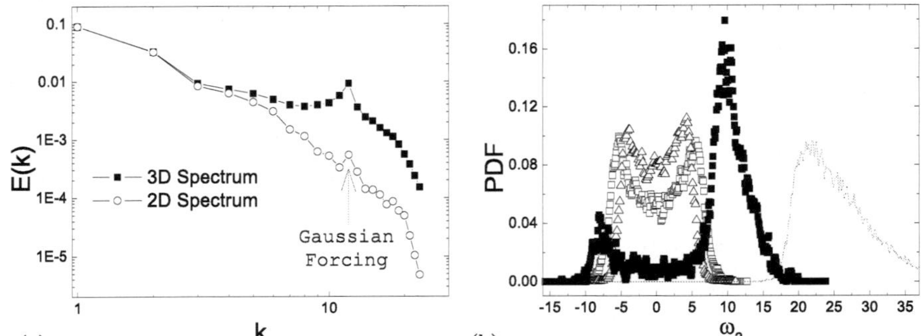

(a) (b)

Figure 8. Assessment of the 64^3 LES of small scale forced rotating turbulence at statistically steady state: (a) 3D & 2D kinetic energy spectra obtained from the new nonlinear mixed model; (b) PDF of ω_3 obtained from the filtered DNS (gray line), the Smagorinsky model (△), the mixed scale-similarity model (□) and the new model (■). Figure is modified from Lu et al. [62].

A direct numerical simulation case has been simulated at the University of Wisconsin-Madison by means of decaying, and has been adopted in model assessment studies [57, 61, 62]. The initial Taylor micro-scale Reynolds number (Re_λ) is approximately 85. Thus, the 128^3 DNS has resolved the flow of all scales, and the DNS results can be used to verify the accuracy of SGS models and identify their problems. Figure 9(a) shows the evolution of the resolved kinetic energy (normalized by its initial value) obtained from DNS and LESs. The decaying case starts at $Re_\lambda = 85$, and is beyond the capability of 64^3 simulation (typically $Re_\lambda \sim 50$). The total resolved kinetic energy obtained from the 64^3 simulation without a model, which simply omits τ_{ij}, yields the worst prediction. In order to obtain proper kinetic energy decay rates, turbulence modeling is needed for coarser grids. It is clear that the results obtained using the new algebraic nonlinear model are in the excellent agreement with the filtered DNS results.

The Smagorinsky model yields a higher kinetic energy decay rate than that is found in the filtered DNS results. Figure 9(b) shows that using the Smagorinsky model, kinetic energy at small scales is dissipated excessively. By construction, the standard gradient model allows for energy "backscatter." However, over a period of time, it yields a lower kinetic energy decay rate, and kinetic energy at small scales is accumulating (cannot be dissipated effectively). As its revision, the new algebraic model has shown significant improvement in energy-spectrum accuracy.

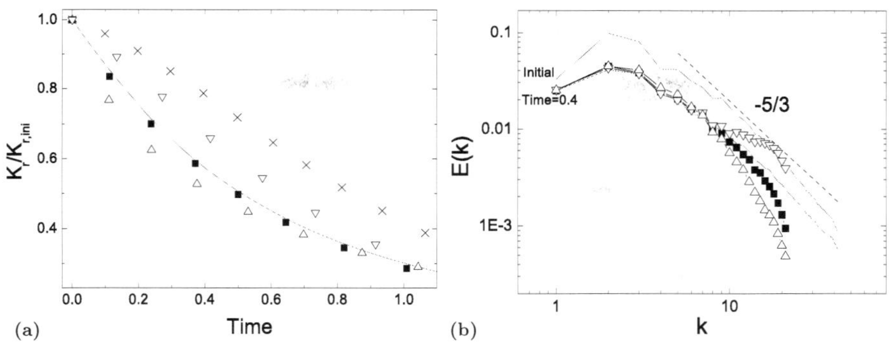

Figure 9. (a) Evolution of resolved kinetic energy; (b) comparison of energy spectra at $t = 0.4$ (normalized using initial eddy turnover time). The gray line represents the results from the filtered DNS, the × represents the results from simulation without a model, the △ represents the results from the Smagorinsky model, the ▽ represents the results from the standard gradient model, and the ■ represents the results from the new model. Figure is modified from Lu [57].

For further testing of the new algebraic model, two high-Reynolds-number cases were conducted. Regarding the first case, the original simulation was performed at the Johns Hopkins University using 1024 grid points in each direction [52]. The database contains a 1024^4 space-time history of an incompressible isotropic turbulent flow in 3D. The initial condition for decaying LES runs, downloaded from "turbulence.pha.jhu.edu" at time equals 2 without space interpolation, bears $Re_\lambda = 430$. A direct numerical simulation of decay was lacking; thus comparisons could be performed only against statistical theories of turbulence. Figure 10(a) shows the kinetic energy spectra obtained from the 128^3 LES at different times. They follow the $-5/3$ power-law behavior until the dissipation range starts to be captured through LES at a late period, and importantly, there are no improper accumulations of kinetic energy at small scales.

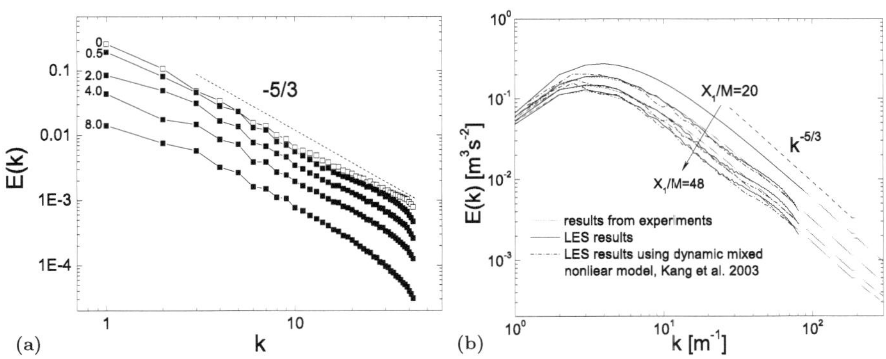

Figure 10. Energy spectra obtained from the LES (a) starting from high-Reynolds-number DNS data; Figure is modified from [57] (b) starting from high-Reynolds-number wind-tunnel measured spectrum, and the gray lines represent the results from measurement, the solid lines represent the results from the new model, and the dash-dotted lines represent the results from the standard dynamic mixed nonlinear model.

The second high-Reynolds-number is based on measurements of nearly isotropic turbulence downstream of an active grid [41]. The initial Taylor micro-scale Reynolds number (Re_λ) is approximately 720. The new model is implemented in LES of decaying isotropic turbulence with initial conditions that match the measured energy spectra at $x_1/M = 20$. Figure 10(b) shows energy spectra at different times, for comparison, the results obtained using the standard dynamic nonlinear mixed model [41] were also included in the plot. The new model clearly gives more accurate results at small scales that $k > 6\,\mathrm{m}^{-1}$.

4. Wind energy applications

With the fast growing number of wind farms being installed worldwide, the interaction between ABL turbulence and wind-turbine wakes, and its effects on energy production and dynamic loading on downwind turbines, have become important issues in the wind energy and atmospheric sciences communities [92]. Optimizing the design of wind energy projects (placement of isolated wind turbines or layout of wind farms) requires the prediction of atmospheric turbulence and its interactions with wind turbines at a wide range of spatial and temporal scales. As a result, during the last decade, numerical modeling of wind-turbine wakes has become increasingly popular. Most of the previous studies of ABL flow through isolated wind turbines or wind farms have parameterized the turbulence using a RANS approach [3, 4, 30, 42]. Only recently there have been some efforts to apply LES to simulate wind-turbine wakes [16, 36, 37, 59, 78, 97]. In addition to the above-mentioned challenges in LES of the ABL, the accuracy of LES for wind energy applications hinges also on our ability to parameterize the forces induced by the turbines on the flow. These forces are responsible for the development of the turbine wake.

4.1. Wind-turbine parameterizations

Figure 11(a) shows a typical three-blade horizontal axis upwind wind turbine, which usually exhibits much better power efficiency than other types of wind turbines [66]. The actuator line method [ALM, 34, 86, 91] combines a three-dimensional flow solver with a technique in which body forces are distributed radially along lines, which represent the blades of the wind turbine.

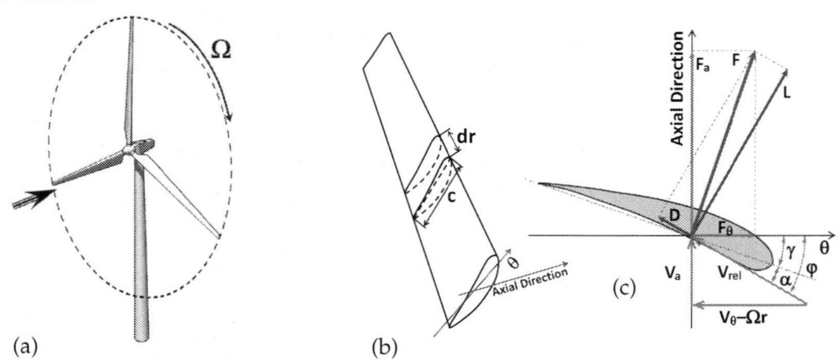

Figure 11. Schematic of the actuator line model: (a) three-dimensional view of a wind turbine; (b) a discretized blade; and (c) cross-section airfoil element showing velocities and force vectors.

Figure 11(b) shows one discretized element of a blade, and figure 11(c) shows a cross-sectional element at radius r defining the airfoil in the (θ, x) plane, where x is the axial direction. With the tangential and axial velocities of the incident flow denoted as V_θ and V_a, respectively, the local velocity relative to the rotating blade is given as $\mathbf{V}_{rel} = (V_\theta - \Omega r, V_a)$. The angle of attack is defined as $\alpha = \varphi - \gamma$, where $\varphi = tan^{-1}(V_a/(\Omega r - V_\theta))$ is the angle between $\mathbf{V}_{rel}$ and the rotor plane, and γ is the local pitch angle. The turbine-induced force per radial unit length is given by the following equation

$$\mathbf{f} = \frac{\mathbf{dF}}{dr} = \frac{1}{2}\rho V_{rel}^2 c(C_L \mathbf{e}_L + C_D \mathbf{e}_D) , \tag{14}$$

where $C_L = C_L(\alpha, Re)$ and $C_D = C_D(\alpha, Re)$ are the lift coefficient and the drag coefficient, respectively, ρ is the air density, c is the chord length, and $\mathbf{e}_L$ and $\mathbf{e}_D$ denote the unit vectors in the directions of the lift and the drag, respectively. The flow of interest is essentially inviscid, and viscous effects from the boundary layer of blade are introduced only as integrated quantities through the use of airfoil data. The airfoil data and subsequent loading are determined by computing local angles of attack from the movement of the blades and the local flow field. The model enables us to study in detail the dynamics of the wake and the tip vortices and their influence on the induced velocities in the rotor plane. The applied blade forces are distributed smoothly to avoid singular behavior and numerical instability. In practice, the aerodynamic blade forces are distributed along and away from the actuator lines in a three-dimensional Gaussian manner through the convolution of the computed local load, $\mathbf{f}$, and a regularization kernel η_ϵ as shown below

$$\mathbf{f}_\epsilon = \mathbf{f} \otimes \eta_\epsilon , \qquad \eta_\epsilon = \frac{1}{\epsilon^3 \pi^{3/2}} \exp\left(-\frac{d^2}{\epsilon^2}\right) , \tag{15}$$

where d is the distance between grid points and points at the actuator line, and ϵ is a parameter that serves to adjust the concentration of the regularized load. The value of this regularization parameter, ϵ, is typically on the order of $1 - 3$ grid sizes and should be as small as possible so that the turbine-induced force is distributed over an area representing the chord distribution and does not affect the wake structure. However, small values will deliver significant numerical oscillations; thus, as a trade-off between numerical stability and accuracy [34, 90], it is set to be 1.5 times of the grid size in the rotor plane.

The main advantage of representing the blades by airfoil data is that many fewer grid points are needed to capture the influence of the blades than would be needed for simulating the actual geometry of the blades. Therefore, the ALM is well suited for wake studies since grid points can be concentrated in a larger part of the wake while keeping the computing costs at a reasonable level. Moreover, the ALM encompasses blade motions as well as their mixing mechanism, which is crucial for simulating more realistic wind-turbine wakes and achieving improved predictions with respect to the standard actuator disk model [7, 78, 97]. However, the ALM does not resolve detailed flows on blade surfaces and relies on tabulated two-dimensional airfoil data for providing lift and drag coefficients. This makes it dependent on both the quality of airfoil data and the method used to model the influence of dynamically changing angles of attack and stall.

4.2. Turbine model testing

Validation of LES of wind turbine wakes is complicated by the difficulties associated with measuring turbulence in the field at the spatial and temporal resolution required for the validation of numerical models. Wind-tunnel experiments provide high-resolution spatial and temporal information characterization of the turbulent flow under controlled stationary inflow conditions and offer a valuable alternative to study the turbulent flow and vortical structures in wind-turbine wakes. Simulation results are compared with the high-resolution velocity measurements collected in the wake of a 3-blade miniature wind turbine placed in the Saint Anthony Falls Laboratory atmospheric boundary-layer wind tunnel. The miniature turbine adopted in the experimental study of Chamorro and Porté-Agel [19] consists of a 3-blade GWS/EP-6030x3 rotor attached to the small DC generator motor. In the simulations, the lift and drag coefficients of blade are determined based on a previous experimental study by Sunada et al. [89]. The computation domain has a height $L_z = 0.46\,\text{m}$. The horizontal computational domain spans a distance $L_x = 4.5\,\text{m} = 30D$ in the streamwise direction and $L_y = L_z$ in the spanwise direction, where $D = 0.15\,\text{m}$ denotes the turbine diameter. A wind turbine, which has a hub height $H_{hub} = 0.125\,\text{m}$, is placed in the middle of the computational domain at $6D$ measuring from the upstream boundary. The resolution of the simulation is $N_x \times N_y \times N_z = 192 \times 64 \times 64$. The spatial distributions of key turbulence statistics, including time-averaged axial velocity, axial velocity variance and turbulent shear stress, are used to characterize wind-turbine wakes. Readers may find a detailed discussion of this wind-turbine wake in Porté-Agel et al. [78], Wu and Porté-Agel [97].

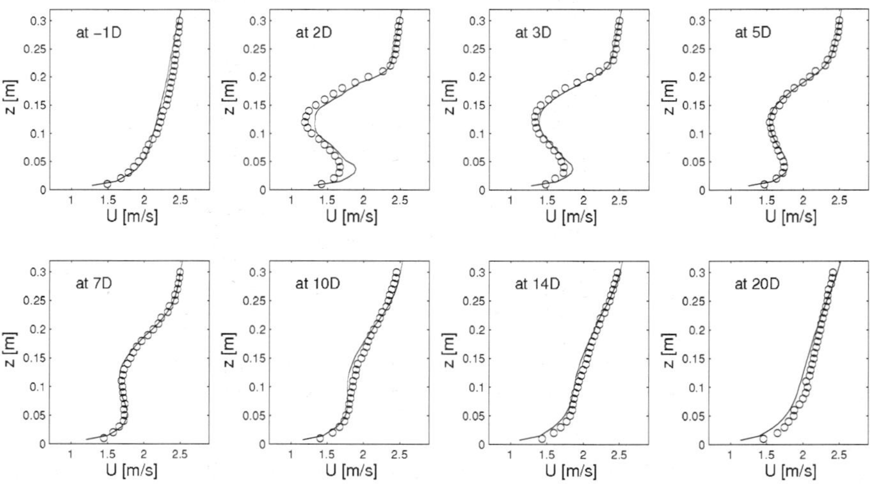

Figure 12. Time-averaged streamwise velocity at different downwind distances. o: results from wind-tunnel measurements; solid line: results from simulations using the ALM.

Figure 12 shows the measured and simulated time-averaged streamwise velocity profiles at selected downwind locations (x/D=2, 3, 5, 7, 10, 14, 20), together with the incoming (x/D=-1) flow velocity profile. LES with the ALM yields mean velocity profiles that are in good agreement with the measurements in the turbine wake. There is a clear evidence of the effect of the turbine extracting momentum from the incoming flow and producing a wake immediately downwind. As expected the velocity deficit is largest near the turbine and it becomes smaller as the wake expands and entrains surrounding air. Nonetheless, the effect of the wake is still noticeable even in the far wake, at distances as large as x/D=20.

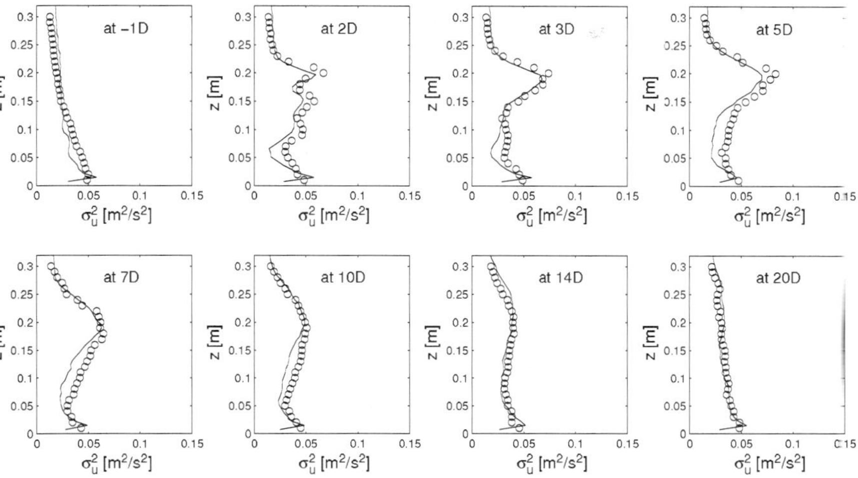

Figure 13. Axial velocity variance at different downwind distances. o: results from wind-tunnel measurements; solid line: results from simulations using the ALM.

Figure 13 compares the measured and simulated axial velocity variances at selected locations. The turbulence profiles obtained using the ALM are in acceptable agreement with the wind-tunnel measurements. The results show a strong enhancement of the turbulence (compared with the relatively low turbulence levels in the incoming flow) at the top-tip level. The maximum turbulence is found at that level and at a normalized distance of approximately 3< x/D <5. It is important to point out that this is within the typical range of distances between adjacent wind turbines in wind farms and, therefore, it should be considered when calculating wind loads on the turbines.

Further, due to the non-uniform (logarithmic) mean velocity profile of the incoming boundary-layer flow, it is found that a non-axisymmetric distribution of the mean velocity profile and, consequently, of the mean shear in the turbine wake. In particular, the strongest shear is found at the top-tip level. The turbulence distribution and the maximum enhancement of turbulence occurs at the top-tip level can be explained considering the non-axisymmetric distribution of velocity profiles and the fact that the mean shear and associated turbulence kinetic energy production are maximum at the top-tip height. It contrasts with the axisymmetry of the turbulence statistics reported by previous studies in the case of wakes of turbines placed in free-stream flows [22, 67, 91], and demonstrates the substantial influence of the incoming flow on the structure and dynamics of wind-turbine wakes.

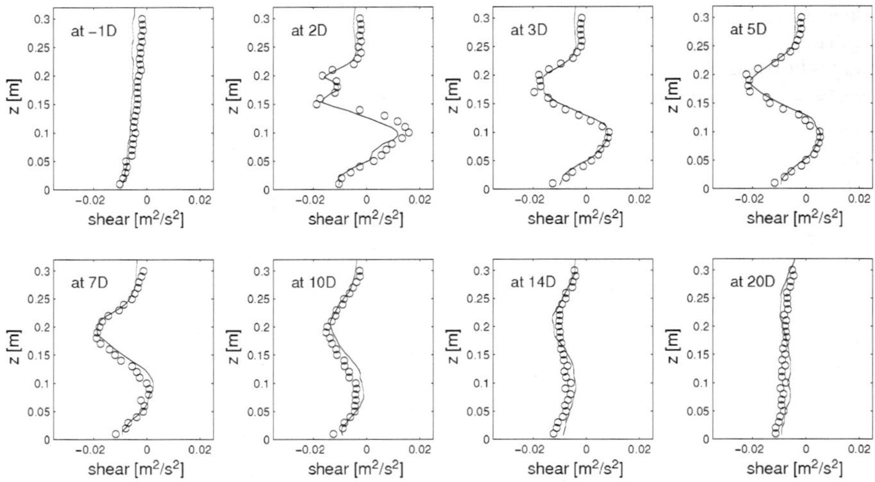

Figure 14. Kinematic shear stress at different downwind distances. o: results from wind-tunnel measurements; solid line: results from simulations using the ALM.

Figure 14 compares the measured and simulated total shear stress (summation of the resolved part and the SGS part) at selected locations. Again results obtained using the ALM are in good agreement with the wind-tunnel measurements. It is clear that the turbine introduces stresses that are locally much larger in magnitude than the stresses in the incoming flow. In the near-wake region, a region above the turbine hub bears large negative stress and a lower region bears large positive stress. As the wake grows with downwind distance, the relative change becomes smaller. Also, similar to the other turbulence statistics, the change in kinematic stress with respect to the incoming flow is not negligible until the far-wake at a distance of x/D=20.

4.3. A wind farm in a stable boundary layer

Of special interest for wind-energy applications is the study of the stable boundary layer, which typically develops during the night in mid-latitudes, and also during the day in cold regions (e.g., polar regions). Under these conditions, the surface is colder than the surrounding air, the flow stratifies and turbulence is generated by shear and destroyed by dissipation and negative buoyancy. Near the top of the boundary layer, the wind can become super-geostrophic and form the so-called low-level jet. Moreover, the Coriolis effect associated with planetary rotation leads to a change of wind direction with height. This creates an additional lateral shear, which is considerable for large-sized wind turbines. As a result, compared with daytime boundary layers, stable boundary layers provide not only larger energy potential, but also larger structural fatigue loads associated with strong vertical and lateral shear.

In order to reduce uncertainties when studying the effects of a wind farm on a SBL, it is important to start with a SBL case, without wind turbines, that has been well established and tested with LES. Such case was launched for an LES inter-comparison study as part of the

Global Energy and Water Cycle Experiment Atmospheric Boundary Layer Study (GABLS) initiative [11]. It represents a typical quasi-equilibrium moderately SBL, similar to those commonly observed over polar regions and equilibrium nighttime conditions over land in mid-latitudes. The GABLS case is used here as a baseline case (no-turbine case).

To study the effect of a wind farm on the GABLS case [59], a V112-3.0MW wind turbine is "immersed" (using the ALM) in the GABLS domain such that the wind-turbine center is located at $x_c = 80\,\mathrm{m}$, $y_c = 280\,\mathrm{m}$, and $z_c = 119\,\mathrm{m}$ (hub height). This wind turbine has a rotor diameter of $D = 112\,\mathrm{m}$, and rotates at 8 RPM, corresponding to a tip speed ratio of approximately 7 for an optimal performance at a free-stream wind speed of approximately 6 m/s. Three blades consist of Risø-P airfoil. Like in the original GABLS case, the vertical height of the computational domain is $L_z = 400\,\mathrm{m}$. The domain size in the y-direction is fixed to be $L_y = 5D = 560\,\mathrm{m}$, and two x-direction dimensions corresponding two typical wind-turbine spacings that are studied: (i) $L_x = 8D = 896\,\mathrm{m}$ (the corresponding LES is abbreviated as the 8D case); (ii) $L_x = 5D = 560\,\mathrm{m}$ (the corresponding LES is abbreviated as the 5D case). Periodic boundary conditions are applied horizontally to simulate an infinitely large wind farm. It should be noted that the baseline case (without turbines) attains a quasi-steady state in 8 - 9h [10, 11]. Therefore, in order to examine the wind-turbine effects relative to the baseline case, the wind turbine is only introduced in the last hour of simulation.

Figure 15 shows the time evolutions of the boundary height, the surface momentum flux and the surface buoyancy flux. Data are saved each 15 seconds. When wind turbines are installed, there exists a significant increase of the boundary-layer height. Specifically, over the last 15 min, the 8D case yields a SBL height of approximately 225 m (increased $\approx 28\%$), and the 5D case yields a SBL height of approximately 250 m (increased $\approx 43\%$). The current simulation results support the tendency that smaller wind-turbine spacing yields larger boundary-layer increases. Further, the magnitudes of the surface momentum flux and the surface buoyancy flux decrease with time. Specifically, over the last 15 min, the 8D case yields a momentum-flux magnitude of approximately $0.05\,\mathrm{m^2/s^2}$ (reduced $\approx 30\%$), corresponding to a friction velocity of 0.23 m/s; the 5D case yields a momentum-flux magnitude of approximately $0.043\,\mathrm{m^2/s^2}$ (reduced $\approx 40\%$), corresponding to a friction velocity of 0.21 m/s. The 8D case yields a buoyancy-flux magnitude of approximately $-3.8 \times 10^{-4}\,\mathrm{m^2/s^3}$ (reduced $\approx 15\%$), corresponding to a heat flux of $-13.5\,\mathrm{W/m^2}$; the 5D case yields a buoyancy-flux magnitude of approximately $-3.2 \times 10^{-4}\,\mathrm{m^2/s^3}$ (reduced $\approx 28\%$), corresponding to a heat flux of $-11.4\,\mathrm{W/m^2}$. It is interesting to note that it takes some time before wind turbines are able to affect surface fluxes. This delay in the change of the fluxes is likely associated to the time it takes for the multiple wakes to expand horizontally and affect the entire surface area. Overall, the reduced surface heat flux phenomenon obtained from the current research is consistent with the results from low-resolution wind-farm simulations performed by [7]. The reduced surface momentum and heat flux magnitudes indicate a reduction in the level of turbulent mixing and transport near the surface. Regarding the overall thermal-energy budget, this reduced heat flux is consistent with the increase of air temperature in the boundary layer as shown later in figure 17(b).

Figure 16(a) shows the formation (initial stages) of blade-induced three-dimensional helicoidal tip vortices, detected using $|\omega|$-definition (0.3 times of the maximum vorticity, 35) in the 5D case. Due to the strong shear and non-uniformity of the incoming boundary-layer flow, helicoidal vortices are stretched as they travel faster at the top tip level compared with

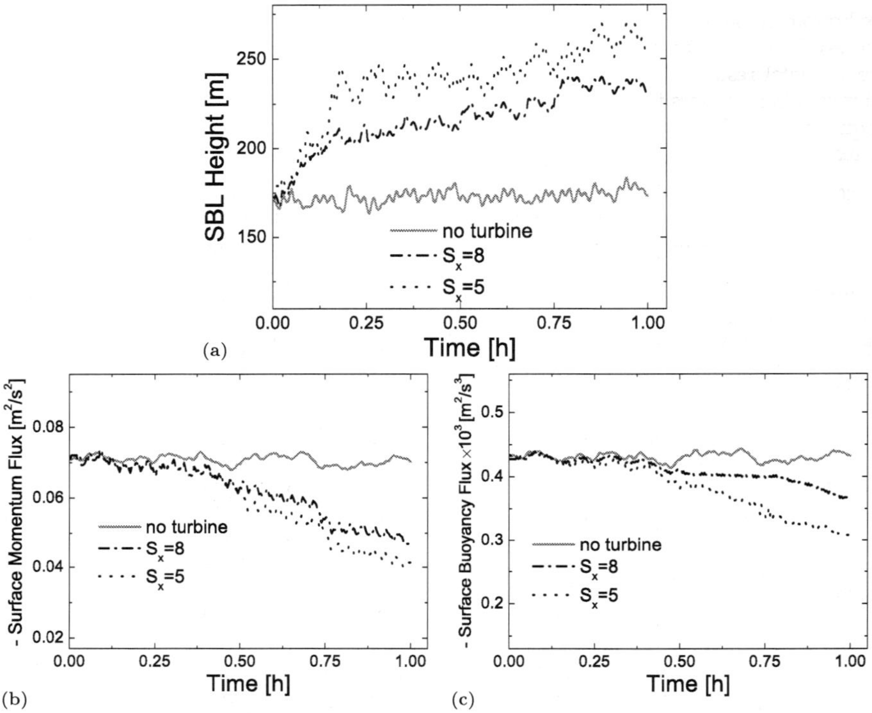

Figure 15. Evolutions of (a) stable boundary-layer height; (b) surface momentum flux; and (b) surface buoyancy flux. Solid lines: results obtained from the baseline case; dashed lines: results obtained from the 8D case; dash dotted lines: results obtained from the 5D case. Figure is modified from Lu and Porté-Agel [59].

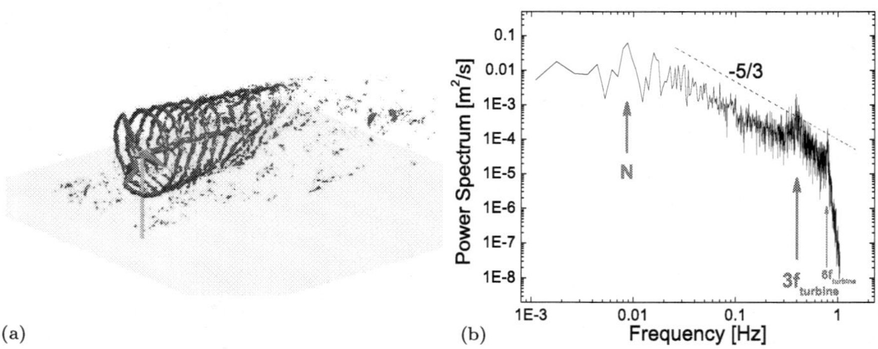

Figure 16. (a) Iso-surface of vorticity showing the three-dimensional structures of a instantaneous field of the 5D case at t=30s; (b) Power spectrum sampled at the location $(x_c + 0.5D, y_c, z_c + 0.5D)$ over the last 15min of the 5D case. Figure is modified from Lu and Porté-Agel [59].

the bottom tip level. Figure 16(b) shows the kinetic energy power spectrum sampled over the last 15 min at 0.5D downwind of the wind-turbine top tip height. Consistent with experimental results [e.g., 19], a clear peak, coinciding with three times the frequency of rotor rotation, appears in the near-wake region. The power spectra also show the buoyancy frequency as well as the inertial subrange. As expected, the power spectrum drops at a scale corresponding to the resolution of the LES.

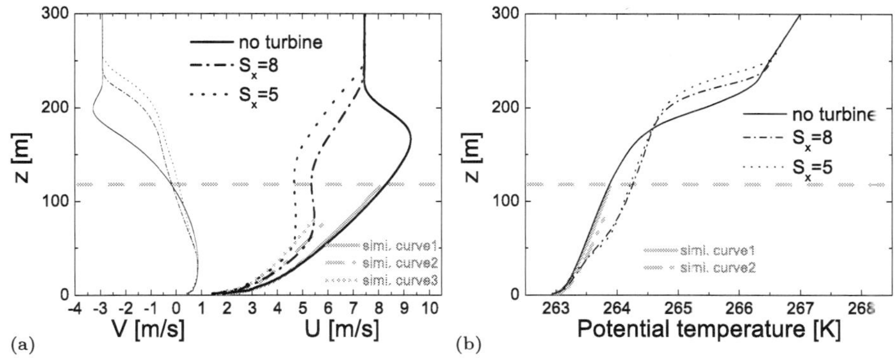

Figure 17. Vertical distribution of mean (a) x-direction velocity U and y-direction velocity V, and (b) potential temperature. Gray dash dotted lines show Monin-Obukhov similarity curves. Figure is modified from Lu and Porté-Agel [59].

Figure 17(a) shows the mean profiles of wind speeds, and figure 17(b) shows the mean potential temperatures. In agreement with other studies [e.g., 27], when wind turbines are installed, there is a significant increase of the boundary height. The baseline case clearly shows a super-geostrophic nocturnal jet peaking near the top of the boundary layer. However, the extraction of energy by the turbines, leads to a distortion of the velocity field (compared with the baseline case) and an elimination of the low-level jet in the wind farm simulations. Also, as expected, the closer the distance between the wind turbines, the larger extraction of kinetic energy from the mean flow. Further, compared to the potential temperature profile from the baseline case, blade motions enhance the vertical mixing and transfer more thermal energy from higher levels to lower levels. This leads to an increase of temperature below the top tip level and a decrease between the tip-height and the SBL height. Interestingly, the two wind-turbine simulations deliver almost identical potential temperature profiles, which indicates that wind-turbine effects on scalars are relatively weaker than their effects on momentum.

A typical design lifetime of modern wind turbines is 20 years. However, many have been dismantled after only a few years of service owing to unsuccessful designs and siting arrangements. The primary cause of failure is that, in a wind farm, the effects of accumulated wakes can lead to increased fatigue loads on wind turbines. Here, study focuses on the turbulent velocity fluctuation, which is directly relevant to the fatigue load. Figure 18 shows vertical profiles of the turbulent kinetic energy for selected downwind locations ($x/D = 1,2,3,$ and 4). The baseline case results are consistent with other GABLS cases [10]. In the current scenario, turbulence in the wake is notably persistent because each turbine generates turbulence which compensates for the tendency of decay. When wind

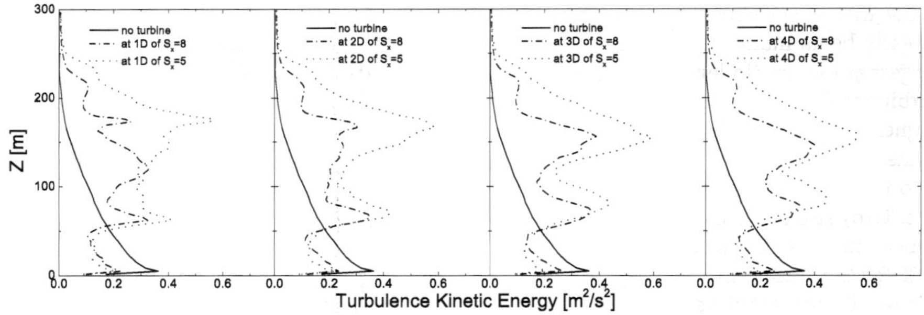

Figure 18. Vertical distribution of turbulent kinetic energy (measured over the last 15 min) obtained from the baseline case (solid), the 8D case (dashed) and the 5D case (dash dotted) through the axis of the turbine at different downwind locations. Figure is modified from Lu and Porté-Agel [59].

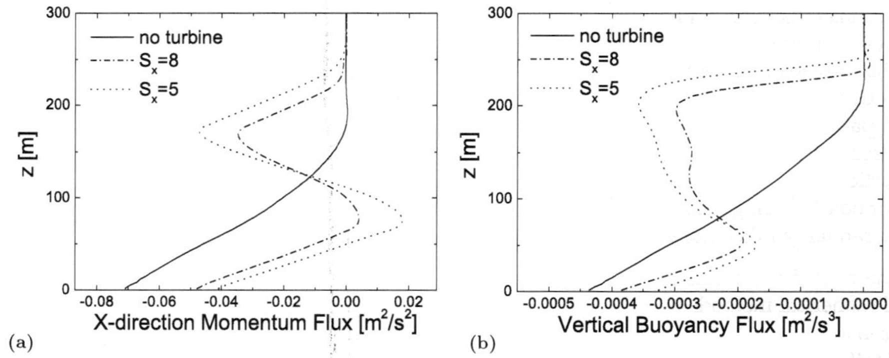

Figure 19. Vertical distributions of (a) x-direction momentum flux and (b) buoyancy flux. Figure is modified from Lu and Porté-Agel [59].

turbines are placed in the boundary layer, turbulence is reduced below the turbine bottom and significantly enhanced in the wake region; this observation agrees with single turbine experimental results [19]. As revealed in other researches on wind-turbine wakes in shear flows including experiments [19, 92] and simulations [90], the large values of turbulence intensity are found at both the top-tip and bottom-tip levels, and the turbulence intensity above the hub-height is generally larger than that below the hub-height. It is argued that this is due to the enhancement in mean shear at the top-tip level.

Besides extracting kinetic energy and generating turbulence, wind-turbine blade motions also mix fluid parcels. The investigation of fluxes is of interest because local meteorology is considerably affected by the overall exchanges of momentum, heat, moisture, etc. Figure 19 shows the vertical distributions of mean total (resolved part plus SGS part) vertical flux of axial momentum and heat. The results obtained from the baseline case are consistent with previous GABLS LES studies [10, 11]. Also in agreement with other studies [19], our results show that when wind turbines are immersed in a non-uniform boundary-layer flow that already bears momentum exchanges (negative flux), the magnitude of the negative flux is largest at the top-tip level due to an enhanced vertical mixing of momentum induced by the turbine wakes at that height. This strong mixing and entrainment of relatively warm air (with higher potential virtual temperature) from the free atmosphere, induced by the wind-turbine wakes, leads also to a strong enhancement of the negative heat flux at the top-tip level. It is also important to note that, consistent with the results as shown in figure 15, figures 19(a) and 19(b) also show that the magnitude of the surface momentum and heat fluxes undergo substantial reductions with respect to the no-turbine base case. This reduction is larger than 30% for the surface momentum flux, and larger than 15% for the surface heat flux. Overall, the results presented here indicate that large wind-farms have the potential to impact local meteorology.

5. Prospects for the future

This chapter gives an overview of our recent research efforts aimed at improving parameterizations and making LES a more reliable technique to planetary boundary layer research. Large-eddy simulation has shown its capabilities in simulations of high-Reynolds-number flows that, at present, could not be solved by DNS. It has been proved to be very useful in understanding the turbulent exchange in atmosphere and ultimately in parameterization improvement in traditional meteorological models; and also it assists theoreticians and weather/climate modelers with reliable information about the averaged vertical structure of the ABL, as well as with better estimations of key ABL parameters. The outlook for using LES in planetary boundary layer modeling is very good. The number of high-quality LES studies is rapidly increasing.

The need for accurate simulation has provided much of the impetus for the development of numerical methods in turbulence research. The proposed new nonlinear formulation has been examined in LESs of several types of turbulent flows. The new SGS closure presents a significant improvement with respect to simple eddy-viscosity/diffusivity-type models, also delivers more accurate representation of the energy cascade in the inertial sub-range.

Possible future model modifications of the new SGS closure include the development of dynamic and scale-dependent dynamic procedures to optimize the values of the model coefficients using information of the resolved scales. Moreover, one could develop and assess more advanced modifications (e.g., one-equation models), which could offer alternatives to relax some of the model assumptions.

Further, the next stage of wind-energy application will encompass more realistic physics and a variety of atmospheric conditions. These include the consideration of other inflow and surface boundary conditions, wind-farm configurations, and the effects of topography, air moisture, and the like. Future studies will use the LES framework to further study the effects of wind-farm size, atmospheric stability (neutral, convective and stable), topography, and wind-farm configuration. Also, there is a need for reliable coupling of LES with weather models to account for the effects of large-scale atmospheric forcing.

Author details

Hao Lu*

*Address all corespodance to: hao.lu@live.com

Wind Engineering and Renewable Energy Laboratory (WIRE), School of Architecture, Civil and Environmental Engineering, Swiss Federal Institute of Technology - Lausanne (EPFL), Switzerland

References

[1] Albertson, J. D. and Parlange, M. B. (1999a). Natural integration of scalar fluxes from complex terrain. *Advan. Water Resour.*, 23:239–252.

[2] Albertson, J. D. and Parlange, M. B. (1999b). Surface length scales and shear stress: Implications for land-atmosphere interaction over complex terrain. *Water Resour. Res.*, 35:2121–2132.

[3] Alinot, C. and Masson, C. (2002). Aerodynamic simulations of wind turbines operating in atmospheric boundary layer with various thermal stratifications. *ASME Wind Energy Symposium*, AIAA:2002–42.

[4] Ammara, I., Leclerc, C., and Masson, C. (2002). A viscous three-dimensional differential/actuator-disk method for the aerodynamic analysis of wind farms. *J. Sol. Energy Eng.*, 124:345–356.

[5] Andren, A., Brown, A. R., Graf, J., Mason, P. J., Moeng, C.-H., Nieuwstadt, F. T. M., and Schumann, U. (1994). Large-eddy simulation of a neutrally stratified boundary layer: A comparison of four computer codes. *Q. J. R. Meteorol. Soc.*, 120(520):1457–1484.

[6] Antonopoulos-Domis, M. (1981). Large-eddy simulation of a passive scalar in isotropic turbulence. *J. Fluid Mech.*, 104:55–79.

[7] Baidya Roy, S., Pacala, S. W., and Walko, R. L. (2004). Can large wind farms affect local meteorology? *J. Geophys. Res.*, 109:1–6.

[8] Bardina, J., Ferziger, J. H., and Reynolds, W. C. (1980). Improved subgrid scale models for large eddy simulation. *AIAA Paper No. 80-1357.*

[9] Basdevant, C. and Sadourny, R. (1983). Modélisation des échelles virtuelles dans la simulation numérique des éecoulements turbulents bidimensionels. *J. Méc. Théor. Appl., Numéro Spéc.*, pages 243–269.

[10] Basu, S. and Porté-Agel, F. (2006). Large-eddy simulation of stably stratified atmospheric boundary layer turbulence: A scale-dependent dynamic modeling approach. *J. Atmos. Sci.*, 63:2074–2091.

[11] Beare, R. J., MacVean, M. K., Holtslag, A. A. M., Cuxart, J., Esau, I., Golaz, J.-C., Jimenez, M. A., Khairoutdinov, M., Kosovic, B., Lewellen, D., Lund, T. S., Lundquist, J. K., Mccabe,

A., Moene, A. F., Noh, Y., Raasch, S., and Sullivan, P. (2006). An intercomparison of large-eddy simulations of the stable boundary layer. *Boundary Layer Meteorol.*, 118:247–272.

[12] Beljaars, A. C. M. and Holtslag, A. A. M. (1991). Flux parameterization over land surfaces for atmospheric models. *J. Appl. Meteorol.*, 30:327–341.

[13] Bou-Zeid, E., Vercauteren, N., Parlange, M. B., and Meneveau, C. (2008). Scale dependence of subgrid-scale model coefficients: an a priori study. *Phys. Fluids*, 20.

[14] Boussinesq, J. (1877). Théorie de l'écoulement tourbillant. *Acad. Sci. Inst. Fr., Paris*, 23:46–50.

[15] Businger, J. A., Wynagaard, J. C., Izumi, Y., and Bradley, E. F. (1971). Flux-profile relationships in the atmospheric surface layer. *J. Atmos. Sci.*, 28:181–189.

[16] Calaf, M., Meneveau, C., and Meyers, J. (2010). Large eddy simulation study of fully developed wind-turbine array boundary layers. *Phys. Fluids*, 22.

[17] Cambon, C., Mansour, N. N., and Godeferd, F. S. (1997). Energy transfer in rotating turbulence. *J. Fluid Mech.*, 337:303–332.

[18] Cambon, C., Mansour, N. N., and Squires, K. D. (1994). Anisotropic structure of homogeneous turbulence subjected to uniform rotation. *Proceeding of the Summer Program*, pages 397–420.

[19] Chamorro, L. P. and Porté-Agel, F. (2009). A wind-tunnel investigation of wind-turbine wakes: Boundary-layer turbulence effects. *Boundary Layer Meteorol.*, 132(1):129–149.

[20] Chumakov, S. G. and Rutland, C. J. (2005). Dynamic structure subgrid-scale models for large eddy simulation. *Int. J. Numer. Meth. Fluids*, 47:911–923.

[21] Clark, R. A., Ferziger, J. H., and Reynolds, W. C. (1979). Evaluation of subgrid-scale models using an accurately simulated turbulent flow. *J. Fluid Mech.*, 91(1):1–16.

[22] Crespo, A. and Hernández, J. (1996). Turbulence characteristics in wind-turbine wakes. *J. Wind Eng. Ind. Aerodyn.*, 61:71–85.

[23] Deardorff, J. W. (1970). A numerical study of three-dimensional turbulent channel flow at large Reynolds numbers. *J. Fluid Mech.*, 41:453–480.

[24] Deardorff, J. W. (1972). Numerical investigation of neutral and unstable planetary boundary layers. *J. Atmos. Sci.*, 29:91–115.

[25] Fedorovich, E. and Conzemius, R. (2008). Effects of wind shear on the atmospheric convective boundary layer structure and evolution. *Adv. Geophys.*, 56:114–141.

[26] Ferziger, J. H. (2000). Large eddy simulation - a short course. Stanford University.

[27] Frandsen, S., Barthelmie, R., Pryor, S., Rathmann, O., Larsen, S., Hojstrup, J., and Thogersen, M. (2006). Analytical modelling of wind speed de cit in large offshore wind farms. *Wind Energ.*, pages 39–53.

[28] Germano, M., Piomelli, U., and Cabot, W. H. (1991). A dynamic subgrid-scale eddy viscosity model. *Phys. Fluids A*, 3(7):1760–1765.

[29] Geurts, B. J. and Holm, D. D. (2003). Regularization modeling for large-eddy simulation. *Phys. Fluids*, 15:L13–L16.

[30] Gómez-Elvira, R., Crespo, A., Migoya, E., and Manuel F. Hernández, J. (2005). Anisotropy of turbulence in wind turbine wakes. *J. Wind. Eng. Ind. Aerodyn.*, 93:797–814.

[31] Helmis, C. G., Papadopoulos, K. H., Asimakopoulos, D. N., Papageorgas, P. G., and Soilemes, A. T. (1995). An experimental study of the near wake structure of a wind turbine operating over complex terrain. *Solar Energy*, 54:413–428.

[32] Higgins, C. W., Parlange, M. B., and Meneveau, C. (2003). Alignment trends of velocity gradients and subgrid-scale fluxes in the turbulent atmospheric boundary layer. *Boundary Layer Meteorol.*, 109:59–83.

[33] Horiuti, K. (2006). Transformation properties of dynamic subgrid-sale models in a frame of reference undergoing rotation. *J. Turbul.*, 7(16):1–27.

[34] Ivanell, S., Sørensen, J. N., Mikkelsen, R., and Henningson, D. (2009). Analysis of numerically generated wake structures. *Wind Energ.*, 12:63–80.

[35] Jeong, J. and Hussain, F. (1995). On the identification of a vortex. *J. Fluid Mech.*, 285:69–94.

[36] Jimenez, A., Crespo, A., Migoya, E., and Garcia, J. (2007). Advances in large-eddy simulation of a wind turbine wake. *J. Phys.: Conf. Ser.*, 75:012041.

[37] Jimenez, A., Crespo, A., Migoya, E., and Garcia, J. (2008). Large-eddy simulation of spectral coherence in a wind turbine wake. *Environ. Res. Lett.*, 3:015004.

[38] Jiménez, C., Ducros, F., Cuenot, B., and Bédat, B. (2001). Subgrid scale variance and dissipation of a scalar field in large eddy simulations. *Phys. Fluids*, 13(6):1748–1754.

[39] Juneja, A. and Brasseur, J. G. (1999). Characteristics of subgrid-resolved-scale dynamics in anisotropic turbulence, with application to rough-wall boundary layers. *Phys. Fluids*, 11(10):3054–3068.

[40] Kader, B. A. and Yaglom, A. M. (1991). Spectra and correlation functions of surface layer atmospheric turbulence in unstable thermal stratification. *Turbulence and Coherent Structures, edited by O. Metais and M. Lesieur, Kluwer Academic, Norwell, Mass*, page 450.

[41] Kang, H. S., Chester, S., and Meneveau, C. (2003). Decaying turbulence in an active-grid-generated flow and comparisons with large-eddy simulation. *J. Fluid Mech.*, 480:129–160.

[42] Kasmi, A. E. and Masson, C. (2008). An extended κ - ϵ model for turbulent flow through horizontal-axis wind turbines. *J. Wind. Eng. Ind. Aerodyn.*, 96:103–122.

http://dx.doi.org/10.5772/57051

[43] Khanna, S. and Brasseur, J. G. (1998). Three-dimensional buoyancy- and shear-induced local structure of the atmospheric boundary layer. *J. Atmos. Sci.*, 55:710–743.

[44] Kim, W.-W. and Menon, S. (1995). A new dynamic one-equation subgrid-scale model for large eddy simulations. *AIAA Paper 1995-356*.

[45] Kleissl, J., Kumar, V., Meneveau, C., and Parlange, M. B. (2006). Numerical study of dynamic smagorinsky models in large-eddy simulation of the atmospheric boundary layer: Validation in stable and unstable conditions. *Water. Resour. Res.*, 42:W06D10.

[46] Kleissl, J., Meneveau, C., and Parlange, M. B. (2003). On the magnitude and variability of subgrid-scale eddy-diffusion coefficients in the atmospheric surface layer. *J. Atmos. Sci.*, 60:2372–2388.

[47] Kobayashi, H. and Shimomura, Y. (2001). The performance of dynamic subgrid-scale models in the large eddy simulation of rotating homogeneous turbulence. *Phys. Fluids*, 13(8):2350–2360.

[48] Kumar, V., Kleissl, J., Meneveau, C., and Parlange, M. B. (2006). Large-eddy simulation of a diurnal cycle of the atmospheric boundary layer: Atmospheric stability and scaling issues. *Water. Resour. Res.*, 42(6):W06D09.

[49] Laursen, J., Enevoldsen, P., and Hjort, S. (2007). 3D CFD rotor computations of a multi megawatt HAWT rotor. *European Wind Energy Conference, Milan, Italy*.

[50] Leloudas, G. (2006). Optimization of wind turbines with respect to noise. Master's thesis, Masters Thesis Project, MEK, DTU.

[51] Lenschow, D. H., Wyngaard, J. C., and Pennell, W. T. (1980). Mean-field and second-moment budgets in a baroclinic, convective boundary layer. *J. Atmos. Sci.*, 37:1313Ű1326.

[52] Li, Y., Perlman, E., Wan, M., Yang, Y., Meneveau, C., Burns, R., Chen, S., Szalay, A., and Eyink, G. (2008). A public turbulence database cluster and applications to study Lagrangian evolution of velocity increments in turbulence. *J. Turbul.*, 9(31).

[53] Lilly, D. K. (1967). The representation of small-scale turbulence in numerical simulation experiments. *Proc. IBM Sci. Com. Symp. Environmental Sciences (Yorktown Heights, N Y.)*, page 167.

[54] Lilly, D. K. (1992). A proposed modification of the Germano subgrid-scale closure method. *Phys. Fluids*, 4(3):633–635.

[55] Lin, C. and Glendening, W. (2002). Large eddy simulation of an inhomogeneous atmospheric boundary layer under neutral conditions. *J. Atmos. Sci.*, 59:2479–2497.

[56] Liu, S., Meneveau, C., and Katz, J. (1994). On the properties of similarity subgrid-scale models as deduced from measurements in a turbulent jet. *J. Fluid Mech.*, 275:83–119.

[57] Lu, H. (2011). Assessment of the modulated gradient model in decaying isotropic turbulence. *Theor. Appl. Mech. Lett.*, 1:041004.

[58] Lu, H. and Porté-Agel, F. (2010). A modulated gradient model for large-eddy simulation: application to a neutral atmospheric boundary layer. *Phys. Fluids*, 22:015109.

[59] Lu, H. and Porté-Agel, F. (2011). Large-eddy simulation of a very large wind farm in a stable atmospheric boundary layer. *Phys. Fluids*, 23:065101.

[60] Lu, H. and Porté-Agel, F. (2013). A modulated gradient model for scalar transport in large-eddy simulation of the atmospheric boundary layer. *Phys. Fluids*.

[61] Lu, H., Rutland, C. J., and Smith, L. M. (2007). A-priori tests of one-equation LES modeling of rotating turbulence. *J. Turbul.*, 8(37):1–27.

[62] Lu, H., Rutland, C. J., and Smith, L. M. (2008). A posteriori tests of one-equation LES modeling of rotating turbulence. *Int. J. Mod. Phys. C*, 19:1949–1964.

[63] Mason, P. J. (1989). Large-eddy simulation of the convective atmospheric boundary layer. *J. Atmos. Sci.*, 46(11):1492–1516.

[64] Mason, P. J. (1994). Large-eddy simulation: a critical review of the technique. *Q. J. R. Meteorol. Soc.*, 120:1–26.

[65] Mason, P. J. and Thomson, D. J. (1992). Stochastic backscatter in large-eddy simulations of boundary layers. *J. Fluid Mech.*, 242:51–78.

[66] Mathew, S. (2006). *Wind energy: fundamentals, resource analysis and economics.* Springer-Verlag, Berlin Heidelberg.

[67] Medici, D. and Alfredsson, P. H. (2006). Measurements on a wind turbine wake: 3d effects and bluff body vortex shedding. *Wind Energ.*, 9:219–236.

[68] Meneveau, C. and Katz, J. (2000). Scale-invariance and turbulence models for large-eddy simulation. *Annu. Rev. Fluid Mech.*, 32:1–32.

[69] Menon, S., Yeung, P.-K., and Kim, W.-W. (1996). Effect of subgrid models on the computed interscale energy transfer in isotropic turbulence. *Comp. Fluids*, 25(2):165–180.

[70] Moeng, C.-H. and Rotunno, R. (1990). Vertical-velocity skewness in the buoyancy-driven boundary layer. *J. Atmos. Sci.*, 47:1149–1162.

[71] Moeng, C.-H. and Wyngaard, J. C. (1988). Spectral analysis of large-eddy simulations of the convective boundary layer. *J. Atmos. Sci.*, 45:3575–3587.

[72] Patton, E. G., Sullivan, P. P., and Moeng, C.-H. (2005). The influence of idealized heterogeneity on wet and dry planetary boundary layers coupled to the land surface. *J. Atmos. Sci.*, 62(7):2078–2097.

[73] Perry, A. E., Henbest, S., and Chong, M. S. (1986). A theoretical and experimental study of wall turbulence. *J. Fluid Mech.*, 165:163–199.

[74] Pomraning, E. and Rutland, C. J. (2002). Dynamic one-equation nonviscosity large-eddy simulation model. *AIAA J.*, 40(4):689–701.

[75] Porté-Agel, F. (2004). A scale-dependent dynamic model for scalar transport in large-eddy simulations of the atmospheric boundary layer. *Boundary Layer Meteorol.*, 112:81–105.

[76] Porté-Agel, F., Meneveau, C., and Parlange, M. B. (2000). A scale-dependent dynamic model for large-eddy simulation: application to a neutral atmospheric boundary layer. *J. Fluid Mech.*, 415:261–284.

[77] Porté-Agel, F., Meneveau, C., Parlange, M. B., and Eichinger, W. E. (2001). A priori field study of the subgrid-scale heat fluxes and dissipation in the atmospheric surface layer. *J. Atmos. Sci.*, 58:2673–2698.

[78] Porté-Agel, F., Wu, Y.-T., Lu, H., and Conzemius, R. (2011). Large-eddy simulation of atmospheric boundary layer flow through wind turbines and wind farms. *J. Wind Eng. Ind. Aerodyn.*, 99(4):154–168.

[79] Rodriguez-Iturbe, I. and Rinaldo, A. (1997). *Fractal river networks: chance and self-organization*. Cambridge University Press, New York.

[80] Sagaut, P. (2006). *Large eddy simulation for incompressible flows*. Springer-Verlag, Berlin Heidelberg, 3rd edition.

[81] Sarghini, F., Piomelli, U., and Balaras, E. (1999). Scale-similar models for large-eddy simulations. *Phys. Fluids*, 11(6):1596–1607.

[82] Smagorinsky, J. (1963). General circulation experiments with the primitive equations: I. the basic experiment. *Mon. Weather Rev.*, 91(3):99–164.

[83] Smith, L. M. and Lee, Y. (2005). On near resonances and symmetry breaking in forced rotating flows at moderate rossby number. *J. Fluid Mech.*, 535:111–142.

[84] Smith, L. M. and Waleffe, F. (1999). Transfer of energy to two-dimensional large scales in forced, rotating three-dimensional turbulence. *Phys. Fluids*, 11(6):1608–1622.

[85] Smith, L. M. and Waleffe, F. (2002). Generation of slow large scales in forced rotating stratified turbulence. *J. Fluid Mech.*, 451:145–168.

[86] Sørensen, J. N. and Shen, W. Z. (2002). Numerical modeling of wind turbine wakes. *J. Fluids Eng.*, 124:393–399.

[87] Stoll, R. and Porté-Agel, F. (2009). Surface heterogeneity effects on regional-scale fluxes in stable boundary layers: surface temperature transitions. *J. Atmos. Sci.*, 66(2):412–431.

[88] Stull, R. B. (1988). *An introduction to Boundary-Layer Meteorology*. Kluwer Academic Publishers.

[89] Sunada, S., Sakaguchi, A., and Kawachi, K. (1997). Airfoil section characteristics at a low reynolds number. *J. Fluids Eng.*, 119:129–135.

[90] Troldborg, N. (2008). *Actuator Line Modeling of Wind Turbine Wakes*. PhD thesis, Dept. of Mechanical Engineering, Technical Univ. of Denmark.

[91] Troldborg, N., Sørensen, J. N., and Mikkelsen, R. (2007). Actuator line simulation of wake of wind turbine operating in turbulent inflow. *J. of Phys.: Conf. Series*, 75.

[92] Vermeer, L. J., Sørensen, J. N., and Crespo, A. (2003). Wind turbine wake aerodynamics. *Progress Aero. Sci.*, 39:467–510.

[93] von Kármán, T. (1931). Mechanical similitude and turbulence. *Tech. Mem., No. 611, Washington D.C., NACA*.

[94] Vreman, B., Geurts, B., and Kuerten, H. (1996). Large-eddy simulation of the temporal mixing layer using the Clark model. *Theor. Comput. Fluid Dyn.*, 8:309–324.

[95] Vreman, B., Geurts, B., and Kuerten, H. (1997). Large-eddy simulation of the turbulent mixing layer. *J. Fluid Mech.*, 339:357–390.

[96] Wan, F., Porté-Agel, F., and Stoll, R. (2007). Evaluation of dynamic subgrid-scale models in large-eddy simulations of neutral turbulent flow over a two-dimensional sinusoidal hill. *Atmos. Env.*, 41(13):2719–2728.

[97] Wu, Y.-T. and Porté-Agel, F. (2011). Large-eddy simulation of wind-turbine wakes: Evaluation of turbine parameterizations. *Boundary-Layer Meteorol.*, 138(3):345–366.

[98] Wyngaard, J. (1988). *Lectures on air pollution modeling*, chapter "Structure of the PBL". edited by A. Venkatram and J. Wyngaard, American Meteorological Society, Boston.

[99] Xie, Z.-T. and Castro, I. P. (2009). Large-eddy simulation for flow and dispersion in urban streets. *Atmos. Environ.*, 43(13):2174–2185.

[100] Yoshizawa, A. and Horiuti, K. (1985). A statistically-derived subgrid-scale kinetic energy model for the large-eddy simulation of turbulent flows. *J. Phys. Soc. Jpn.*, 54(8):2834–2839.

[34] Ivanell, S., Sørensen, J. N., Mikkelsen, R., and Henningson, D. (2009). Analysis of numerically generated wake structures. *Wind Energ.*, 12:63–80.

[35] Jeong, J. and Hussain, F. (1995). On the identification of a vortex. *J. Fluid Mech.*, 285:69–94.

[36] Jimenez, A., Crespo, A., Migoya, E., and Garcia, J. (2007). Advances in large-eddy simulation of a wind turbine wake. *J. Phys.: Conf. Ser.*, 75:012041.

[37] Jimenez, A., Crespo, A., Migoya, E., and Garcia, J. (2008). Large-eddy simulation of spectral coherence in a wind turbine wake. *Environ. Res. Lett.*, 3:015004.

[38] Jiménez, C., Ducros, F., Cuenot, B., and Bédat, B. (2001). Subgrid scale variance and dissipation of a scalar field in large eddy simulations. *Phys. Fluids*, 13(6):1748–1754.

[39] Juneja, A. and Brasseur, J. G. (1999). Characteristics of subgrid-resolved-scale dynamics in anisotropic turbulence, with application to rough-wall boundary layers. *Phys. Fluids*, 11(10):3054–3068.

[40] Kader, B. A. and Yaglom, A. M. (1991). Spectra and correlation functions of surface layer atmospheric turbulence in unstable thermal stratification. *Turbulence and Coherent Structures, edited by O. Metais and M. Lesieur, Kluwer Academic, Norwell, Mass*, page 450.

[41] Kang, H. S., Chester, S., and Meneveau, C. (2003). Decaying turbulence in an active-grid-generated flow and comparisons with large-eddy simulation. *J. Fluid Mech.*, 480:129–160.

[42] Kasmi, A. E. and Masson, C. (2008). An extended κ - ϵ model for turbulent flow through horizontal-axis wind turbines. *J. Wind. Eng. Ind. Aerodyn.*, 96:103–122.

[43] Khanna, S. and Brasseur, J. G. (1998). Three-dimensional buoyancy- and shear-induced local structure of the atmospheric boundary layer. *J. Atmos. Sci.*, 55:710–743.

[44] Kim, W.-W. and Menon, S. (1995). A new dynamic one-equation subgrid-scale model for large eddy simulations. *AIAA Paper 1995-356*.

[45] Kleissl, J., Kumar, V., Meneveau, C., and Parlange, M. B. (2006). Numerical study of dynamic smagorinsky models in large-eddy simulation of the atmospheric boundary layer: Validation in stable and unstable conditions. *Water. Resour. Res.*, 42:W06D10.

[46] Kleissl, J., Meneveau, C., and Parlange, M. B. (2003). On the magnitude and variability of subgrid-scale eddy-diffusion coefficients in the atmospheric surface layer. *J. Atmos. Sci.*, 60:2372–2388.

[47] Kobayashi, H. and Shimomura, Y. (2001). The performance of dynamic subgrid-scale models in the large eddy simulation of rotating homogeneous turbulence. *Phys. Fluids*, 13(8):2350–2360.

[48] Kumar, V., Kleissl, J., Meneveau, C., and Parlange, M. B. (2006). Large-eddy simulation of a diurnal cycle of the atmospheric boundary layer: Atmospheric stability and scaling issues. *Water. Resour. Res.*, 42(6):W06D09.

[49] Laursen, J., Enevoldsen, P., and Hjort, S. (2007). 3D CFD rotor computations of a multi megawatt HAWT rotor. *European Wind Energy Conference, Milan, Italy.*

[50] Leloudas, G. (2006). Optimization of wind turbines with respect to noise. Master's thesis, Masters Thesis Project, MEK, DTU.

[51] Lenschow, D. H., Wyngaard, J. C., and Pennell, W. T. (1980). Mean-field and second-moment budgets in a baroclinic, convective boundary layer. *J. Atmos. Sci.*, 37:1313Ű1326.

[52] Li, Y., Perlman, E., Wan, M., Yang, Y., Meneveau, C., Burns, R., Chen, S., Szalay, A., and Eyink, G. (2008). A public turbulence database cluster and applications to study Lagrangian evolution of velocity increments in turbulence. *J. Turbul.*, 9(31).

[53] Lilly, D. K. (1967). The representation of small-scale turbulence in numerical simulation experiments. *Proc. IBM Sci. Com. Symp. Environmental Sciences (Yorktown Heights, N.Y.)*, page 167.

[54] Lilly, D. K. (1992). A proposed modification of the Germano subgrid-scale closure method. *Phys. Fluids*, 4(3):633–635.

[55] Lin, C. and Glendening, W. (2002). Large eddy simulation of an inhomogeneous atmospheric boundary layer under neutral conditions. *J. Atmos. Sci.*, 59:2479–2497.

[56] Liu, S., Meneveau, C., and Katz, J. (1994). On the properties of similarity subgrid-scale models as deduced from measurements in a turbulent jet. *J. Fluid Mech.*, 275:83–119.

[57] Lu, H. (2011). Assessment of the modulated gradient model in decaying isotropic turbulence. *Theor. Appl. Mech. Lett.*, 1:041004.

[58] Lu, H. and Porté-Agel, F. (2010). A modulated gradient model for large-eddy simulation: application to a neutral atmospheric boundary layer. *Phys. Fluids*, 22:015109.

[59] Lu, H. and Porté-Agel, F. (2011). Large-eddy simulation of a very large wind farm in a stable atmospheric boundary layer. *Phys. Fluids*, 23:065101.

[60] Lu, H. and Porté-Agel, F. (2013). A modulated gradient model for scalar transport in large-eddy simulation of the atmospheric boundary layer. *Phys. Fluids.*

[61] Lu, H., Rutland, C. J., and Smith, L. M. (2007). A-priori tests of one-equation LES modeling of rotating turbulence. *J. Turbul.*, 8(37):1–27.

[62] Lu, H., Rutland, C. J., and Smith, L. M. (2008). A posteriori tests of one-equation LES modeling of rotating turbulence. *Int. J. Mod. Phys. C*, 19:1949–1964.

[63] Mason, P. J. (1989). Large-eddy simulation of the convective atmospheric boundary layer. *J. Atmos. Sci.*, 46(11):1492–1516.

[64] Mason, P. J. (1994). Large-eddy simulation: a critical review of the technique. *Q. J. R. Meteorol. Soc.*, 120:1–26.

[65] Mason, P. J. and Thomson, D. J. (1992). Stochastic backscatter in large-eddy simulations of boundary layers. *J. Fluid Mech.*, 242:51–78.

[66] Mathew, S. (2006). *Wind energy: fundamentals, resource analysis and economics*. Springer-Verlag, Berlin Heidelberg.

[67] Medici, D. and Alfredsson, P. H. (2006). Measurements on a wind turbine wake: 3d effects and bluff body vortex shedding. *Wind Energ.*, 9:219–236.

[68] Meneveau, C. and Katz, J. (2000). Scale-invariance and turbulence models for large-eddy simulation. *Annu. Rev. Fluid Mech.*, 32:1–32.

[69] Menon, S., Yeung, P.-K., and Kim, W.-W. (1996). Effect of subgrid models on the computed interscale energy transfer in isotropic turbulence. *Comp. Fluids*, 25(2):165–180.

[70] Moeng, C.-H. and Rotunno, R. (1990). Vertical-velocity skewness in the buoyancy-driven boundary layer. *J. Atmos. Sci.*, 47:1149–1162.

[71] Moeng, C.-H. and Wyngaard, J. C. (1988). Spectral analysis of large-eddy simulations of the convective boundary layer. *J. Atmos. Sci.*, 45:3575–3587.

[72] Patton, E. G., Sullivan, P. P., and Moeng, C.-H. (2005). The influence of idealized heterogeneity on wet and dry planetary boundary layers coupled to the land surface. *J. Atmos. Sci.*, 62(7):2078–2097.

[73] Perry, A. E., Henbest, S., and Chong, M. S. (1986). A theoretical and experimental study of wall turbulence. *J. Fluid Mech.*, 165:163–199.

[74] Pomraning, E. and Rutland, C. J. (2002). Dynamic one-equation nonviscosity large-eddy simulation model. *AIAA J.*, 40(4):689–701.

[75] Porté-Agel, F. (2004). A scale-dependent dynamic model for scalar transport in large-eddy simulations of the atmospheric boundary layer. *Boundary Layer Meteorol.*, 112:81–105.

[76] Porté-Agel, F., Meneveau, C., and Parlange, M. B. (2000). A scale-dependent dynamic model for large-eddy simulation: application to a neutral atmospheric boundary layer. *J. Fluid Mech.*, 415:261–284.

[77] Porté-Agel, F., Meneveau, C., Parlange, M. B., and Eichinger, W. E. (2001). A priori field study of the subgrid-scale heat fluxes and dissipation in the atmospheric surface layer. *J. Atmos. Sci.*, 58:2673–2698.

[78] Porté-Agel, F., Wu, Y.-T., Lu, H., and Conzemius, R. (2011). Large-eddy simulation of atmospheric boundary layer flow through wind turbines and wind farms. *J. Wind Eng. Ind. Aerodyn.*, 99(4):154–168.

[79] Rodriguez-Iturbe, I. and Rinaldo, A. (1997). *Fractal river networks: chance and self-organization*. Cambridge University Press, New York.

[80] Sagaut, P. (2006). *Large eddy simulation for incompressible flows*. Springer-Verlag, Berlin Heidelberg, 3rd edition.

[81] Sarghini, F., Piomelli, U., and Balaras, E. (1999). Scale-similar models for large-eddy simulations. *Phys. Fluids*, 11(6):1596–1607.

[82] Smagorinsky, J. (1963). General circulation experiments with the primitive equations: I. the basic experiment. *Mon. Weather Rev.*, 91(3):99–164.

[83] Smith, L. M. and Lee, Y. (2005). On near resonances and symmetry breaking in forced rotating flows at moderate rossby number. *J. Fluid Mech.*, 535:111–142.

[84] Smith, L. M. and Waleffe, F. (1999). Transfer of energy to two-dimensional large scales in forced, rotating three-dimensional turbulence. *Phys. Fluids*, 11(6):1608–1622.

[85] Smith, L. M. and Waleffe, F. (2002). Generation of slow large scales in forced rotating stratified turbulence. *J. Fluid Mech.*, 451:145–168.

[86] Sørensen, J. N. and Shen, W. Z. (2002). Numerical modeling of wind turbine wakes. *J. Fluids Eng.*, 124:393–399.

[87] Stoll, R. and Porté-Agel, F. (2009). Surface heterogeneity effects on regional-scale fluxes in stable boundary layers: surface temperature transitions. *J. Atmos. Sci.*, 66(2):412–431.

[88] Stull, R. B. (1988). *An introduction to Boundary-Layer Meteorology*. Kluwer Academic Publishers.

[89] Sunada, S., Sakaguchi, A., and Kawachi, K. (1997). Airfoil section characteristics at a low reynolds number. *J. Fluids Eng.*, 119:129–135.

[90] Troldborg, N. (2008). *Actuator Line Modeling of Wind Turbine Wakes*. PhD thesis, Dept. of Mechanical Engineering, Technical Univ. of Denmark.

[91] Troldborg, N., Sørensen, J. N., and Mikkelsen, R. (2007). Actuator line simulation of wake of wind turbine operating in turbulent inflow. *J. of Phys.: Conf. Series*, 75.

[92] Vermeer, L. J., Sørensen, J. N., and Crespo, A. (2003). Wind turbine wake aerodynamics. *Progress Aero. Sci.*, 39:467–510.

[93] von Kármán, T. (1931). Mechanical similitude and turbulence. *Tech. Mem., No. 611, Washington D.C., NACA*.

[94] Vreman, B., Geurts, B., and Kuerten, H. (1996). Large-eddy simulation of the temporal mixing layer using the Clark model. *Theor. Comput. Fluid Dyn.*, 8:309–324.

[95] Vreman, B., Geurts, B., and Kuerten, H. (1997). Large-eddy simulation of the turbulent mixing layer. *J. Fluid Mech.*, 339:357–390.

[96] Wan, F., Porté-Agel, F., and Stoll, R. (2007). Evaluation of dynamic subgrid-scale models in large-eddy simulations of neutral turbulent flow over a two-dimensional sinusoidal hill. *Atmos. Env.*, 41(13):2719–2728.

[97] Wu, Y.-T. and Porté-Agel, F. (2011). Large-eddy simulation of wind-turbine wakes: Evaluation of turbine parameterizations. *Boundary-Layer Meteorol.*, 138(3):345–366.

[98] Wyngaard, J. (1988). *Lectures on air pollution modeling*, chapter "Structure of the PBL". edited by A. Venkatram and J. Wyngaard, American Meteorological Society, Boston.

[99] Xie, Z.-T. and Castro, I. P. (2009). Large-eddy simulation for flow and dispersion in urban streets. *Atmos. Environ.*, 43(13):2174–2185.

[100] Yoshizawa, A. and Horiuti, K. (1985). A statistically-derived subgrid-scale kinetic energy model for the large-eddy simulation of turbulent flows. *J. Phys. Soc. Jpn.*, 54(8):2834–2839.

Chapter 11

Investigation of Sensitivity to Heavy-Ion Irradiation of Junctionless Double-Gate MOSFETs by 3-D Numerical Simulation

Daniela Munteanu and Jean-Luc Autran

Additional information is available at the end of the chapter

http://dx.doi.org/10.5772/57048

1. Introduction

Microelectronics industry has experienced tremendous progress in the last forty years, especially with regard to the evolution of the products (i.e. integrated circuits) performances, and at the same time, concerning the drastic reduction of manufacturing costs by elementary function integrated. So far, this considerable growth of the semiconductor industry has been due to its technological capability to constantly miniaturize the elementary components of circuits, namely the MOSFET (metal-oxide-semiconductor field effect transistor), the basic building block of VLSI (very large scale integration) integrated circuits. The continuous decrease of the silicon surface used by these elementary components has kept the race integration at the rhythm dictated by the famous "Moore's Law", which states that the number transistors per integrated circuit doubles every 18 to 24 months [1]. However, the conventional bulk MOSFET scaling down encountered this last decade serious physical and technological limitations, mainly related to the gate oxide (SiO_2) leakage currents [2-3], the large increase of parasitic short channel effects and the dramatic mobility reduction [4] due to highly doped silicon substrates precisely used to reduce these short channel effects. Technological solutions have been proposed in order to continue to use the "bulk solution" until the 32-28 nm ITRS nodes [5]. Most of these solutions have then introduced high-permittivity gate dielectric stacks (to reduce the gate leakage [1], [6], midgap metal gate (to suppress the Silicon gate polydepletion-induced parasitic capacitances) and strained silicon channel (to increase carrier mobility) [7]. However, in parallel to these efforts, alternative solutions to replace the conventional bulk MOSFET architecture have been proposed and studied in the recent literature. These options are numerous and can be classified in general according to three main directions: (i) the use of new materials in the continuity of the "bulk solution", allowing increasing

MOSFET performances due to their dielectric properties (permittivity), electrostatic immunity (SOI materials), mechanical (strain), or transport (mobility) properties; (ii) the complete change of the device architecture (e.g. Multiple-Gate devices, Silicon nanowires MOSFET) allowing better electrostatic control, and, as a result, intrinsic channels with higher mobilities and currents; (iii) the exploitation of certain new physical phenomena that appear at the nanometer scale, such as quantum ballistic transport, substrate orientation or modifications of the material band structure in devices/wires with nanometer dimensions [8-9].

As the MOSFET is scaling down, the sensitivity of the integrated circuits to radiation coming from the natural space or present in the terrestrial environment has been found to seriously increase [10-13]. In nowadays ultra-scaled devices, natural radiation is inducing one of the highest failure rates of all reliability concerns for devices and circuits entering in the area of nanoelectronics [5],[14]. In particular, ultra-scaled memory integrated circuits have been found to be more sensitive to single-event-upset (SEU) and digital devices more subjected to digital single-event transient (DSETs). This sensitivity is a direct consequence of the reduction of device dimensions and spacing within memory cells combined with the reduction of supply voltage and node capacitance, resulting in a decrease of both the critical charge (i.e. the minimum amount of charge required to induce the flipping of the logic state) and the sensitive area (i.e. the minimum collection area inside which a given particle can deposit enough charge to induce the flipping of the cell) [13]-[15].

As explained before, among the technological solutions to replace the bulk MOSFET, it was envisaged to completely change the device architecture, making then possible a better electrostatic control of the channel by the gate. MOSFETs designed with Double-Gate (DGFET) configuration are now widely recognized as one of the most promising solutions to meet the requirements of the roadmap at the nanometer scale [16]-[20]. These structures present a very good control of parasitic short channel effects (SCE) and drain-induced barrier lowering (DIBL) resulting from an improved electrostatic coupling between the conduction channel and the gate electrodes [20]-[22]. The constraints on the channel doping can then be greatly reduced in these devices, which can be designed with an intrinsic film. Parasitic doping level fluctuation effects are then eliminated and, in the same time, the carrier mobility and drain current are increased [23]. The intrinsic films are also characterized by a high probability of ballistic transport in the channel [24]-[28], which could additionally reinforce the electrical performances of DGFET.

Recently, a new concept of field-effect MOS transistor without junctions (called junctionless MOSFET) has been proposed [29]-[34] and experimentally validated. A junctionless MOSFET is a transistor having the same type of semiconductor throughout the entire silicon film, including the source, channel and drain regions. A Double-Gate junctionless MOSFET (JL-DGFET) contains a heavily doped silicon film sandwiched between two gate electrodes connected together. The two gates are used to deplete the silicon film (resp. to accumulate majority carriers from the doped silicon layer) and then to turn off (resp. to turn on) the device. This is a very interesting transistor, particularly from a technological point-of-view, because its fabrication is simplified compared to the conventional process (there are no doping gradients in the device [31] and no semiconductor-type inversion). The off-state current of these devices is no longer degraded by the leakage current of the reversely-biased source-channel and channel-drain diodes, but is uniquely controlled by the gate. This could be very attractive for ultra-short devices, typically for deca-nanometer channel lengths, for which the off-state current could be reduced.

Although standard DGFETs with junctions, also called inversion-mode (IM) DGFETs, and JL-DGFETs are very similar, the operating principle of the junctionless devices is quite different from that of IM-DGFETs. The conventional IM-DGFET is normally in the off state at V_G=0 V; the source-channel and channel-drain junctions are reversely biased and the current in the transistor is off. A voltage must be applied on the gate to turn on the transistor. The vertical electric field created across the gate insulator attracts minority carriers at the silicon/insulator interface to create an inversion (conduction) channel and then these carriers flow from source to drain through this channel. Thus, in IM-DGFET transistor, the electric field is the highest when the transistor is in the on-state and the lowest in the off-state. In contrast to IM-DGFET, the electric field is high in the off-state for JL-DGFET and very low in the on-state [31]. The junctionless transistor is normally on-state and the current flows into the channel which extends throughout the entire silicon film [32]. In this transistor, the work function difference between the gate and the doped silicon film leads to a positive flat-band voltage. Therefore, in the on-state, the junctionless transistor is under flat-band conditions and the transverse electric field is zero [32]. The conduction takes place in the film volume unlike conventional devices where the conduction takes place at the silicon/insulator interface. Thus, even at high gate voltages, the majority carriers flow mainly through the film volume and not at the interface. This can be beneficial for the carrier mobility because the impact of the surface roughness is reduced. In order to switch-off the transistor, a low gate voltage has to be applied on the gates; the vertical electric field increases and depletes the film, which cuts-off the transistor (in contrast to IM-DGFET where the high electric field is used to create an inversion layer at the interface).

From a radiation-hardness point-of-view, the high doping level in the silicon film of JL-DGFET could have a negative impact on its immunity to single-events, because the floating-body effects are expected to be strong. Then, in spite of its double-gate configuration, JL-DGFET should be more sensitive to radiation than IM-DGFET where the channel is intrinsic. The transient response of the IM-DGFET devices under heavy-ion irradiation has been studied by 3-D numerical simulation in [35]-[38]. These previous studies show that IM-DGFET shows a better resistance to radiation than Fully Depleted SOI transistors (FDSOI) with single-gate, due to the enhanced control of the film potential by the two connected gates which reduces the floating-body effects. The bipolar amplification of JL-DGFET was studied in [39] and compared to that of IM-DGFET with similar geometrical parameters. In that work, we have shown that JL-DGFET is characterized by a higher bipolar gain than IM-DGFET, due to worse radiation hardness. However, in that preliminary work we have not analyzed in depth the radiation sensitivity of JL-DGFET, especially the dependence on the position of the ion strike in the channel. Similarly, the impact of time parameters of the ion track on the transient response of these devices has not been addressed.

In the present work, we investigated by 3-D numerical simulation the sensitivity to single-event of JL-DGFET and we compared the JL-DGFET behavior with that of more conventional inversion-mode devices, IM-DGFET and FDSOI. The effect of an ion strike on the main internal electrical parameters inside the structure (potential and carrier density) and on the drain current transient is investigated. JL-DGFET is compared with IM-DGFET and FDSOI in terms of collected charge and bipolar amplification. The impact on the transient response of several parameters of the ion track (such as the characteristic time and the track radius), as well as of the position of the ion strike along the channel and of the film doping level is addressed. Our simulations show that JL-DGFET may be more resistant to heavy-ion radiation (i.e. may have a lower bipolar gain) than IM-DGFET and FDSOI for some particular configurations (specific ion LET values and ion-impact locations along the channel between the source and drain contacts).

The chapter is organized as follows. In section 2 we describe in detail the simulated devices and the simulation models used in this work. The static operation of JL-DGFET, IM-DGFET and FDSOI is presented in section 3. The transient response of JL-DGFET for ions striking in the middle of the channel (at equal distance from the source and drain contacts) is detailed in section 4. In particular, we compare JL-DGFET, IM-DGFET and FDSOI in terms of electron density, electrostatic potential, drain current transient and bipolar amplification. Section 5 addresses the impact of heavy-ion track parameters (ion track characteristic time, track radius and ion strike location between source and drain contact) on the JL-DGFET transient response. The JL-DGFET behavior is systematically compared with that of IM-DGFET and FDSOI structures. Finally, section 6 presents the influence of the silicon film doping level on the bipolar amplification in JL-DGFET.

2. Simulation details

2.1. Description of the simulated devices

Figure 1 shows the schematic 3-D description of the simulated devices. Planar IM-DGFET structures are based on real devices reported in [40]. These devices are designed with 20 nm channel length, 100 nm gate width, 6 nm-thick silicon film and 1 nm-thick gate oxide. The channel is intrinsic; the source/drain regions are highly n-type doped and the doping profile in these regions is uniform. The transition between the channel and the highly–doped source/drain regions is characterized by an abrupt doping profile. JL-DGFET have the same geometrical dimensions, but the silicon film is uniformly n-type doped at 10^{19} cm^{-3}. In this device there are no highly-doped source/drain regions, as shown in Fig. 1(a). In addition, the channel thickness has to be sufficiently small in order to make possible the complete depletion of the silicon film and to be able to cut-off the device [29]. This condition is satisfied for the doping level and the film thickness considered here. The two gates are connected together in IM-DGFET and JL-DGFET. The silicon film in FDSOI devices has the same geometrical parameters and doping profiles as the silicon film of IM-DGFET. However, only a single gate controls the electrostatic potential and the current flow in the film of FDSOI. A 10 nm-thick buried oxide and a thick silicon substrate lowly-doped at 10^{16} cm^{-3} have been also considered in FDSOI. The very thin buried oxide is necessary to minimize the short channel effects in these devices. All devices were calibrated to meet the requirements of the ITRS Low Power technology node corresponding to the year 2015 [5]. To facilitate comparison, the gates work function has been refined to achieve the same off-state current (I_{OFF}) for all devices.

2.2. Simulation models

Numerical simulations in 3 dimensions (3-D) were carried out with the DESSIS module of the commercial simulator Synopsis [41]. We considered in the simulation physical models such as Shockley-Read-Hall (SRH) and Auger recombination models, as well as the Fermi-Dirac carrier statistics. In the SRH recombination model, carrier lifetimes depend on the doping level [41-43]. The model of the effective intrinsic density includes a doping-dependent band-gap narrowing (Slotboom's model [41]) and a lattice temperature-dependent band gap The carrier transport model used in the simulation is the hydrodynamic model which includes the energy balance equations for electrons, holes and lattice. We also used models for impact ionization and carrier mobility depending on the carrier energy calculated by the hydrodynamic model. The mobility model also takes into account the dependence of mobility with normal electric field (through the Lombardi's model [41]), temperature and channel doping. The physical parameters of the models used in the simulation (in particular the carrier mobility) are not calibrated on experimental data, but realistic values are considered in the simulation. The parameters and models chosen in this way were then used for the simulation of drain current transients induced by the energetic particle striking the sensitive area of the device. The transistors were simulated in the off-state (most sensitive case) under V_G=0 V and V_D=0.75 V.

Transient simulations have been performed considering an ion track with a Gaussian shape and a very narrow radius of 20 nm, in order to facilitate comparison with experimental and simulation results reported in references [35] and [44]. In addition, we performed in section 5.2 simulations with different track radii in order to discuss the influence of the track radius on the radiation sensitivity of the three devices simulated here. The ion track has a Gaussian time dependence centered on t=10 ps, with a characteristic time of 2 ps. We chose this characteristic time value because a good agreement was obtained in a previous study [35] between the simulation and experimental data. However, it is clear that, if we change the characteristic time of the Gaussian distribution, the transient current will be modified. Nevertheless, it is not sure that the radiation resistance of the device and its bipolar amplification will change. To clarify this point, additional simulations with different characteristic time will be presented in section 5.1. The linear energy transfer (LET) value is kept constant along the ion track; this is justified by the very short ion-track length (equal to the silicon film thickness, 6 nm).

The ion strikes the device in a vertical incidence perpendicular to the gate, as shown in Fig. 1. In a first step, we considered that the ion strikes in the middle of the channel (at equal distance from the source and drain contacts). In a second step, we will consider several locations for the ion impact between the source and the drain, in order to investigate the sensitivity of the device to the ion strike position (section 5.3). In most cases the ion track is not entirely contained in the active area of the device, which requires accurately calculating the charge deposited by

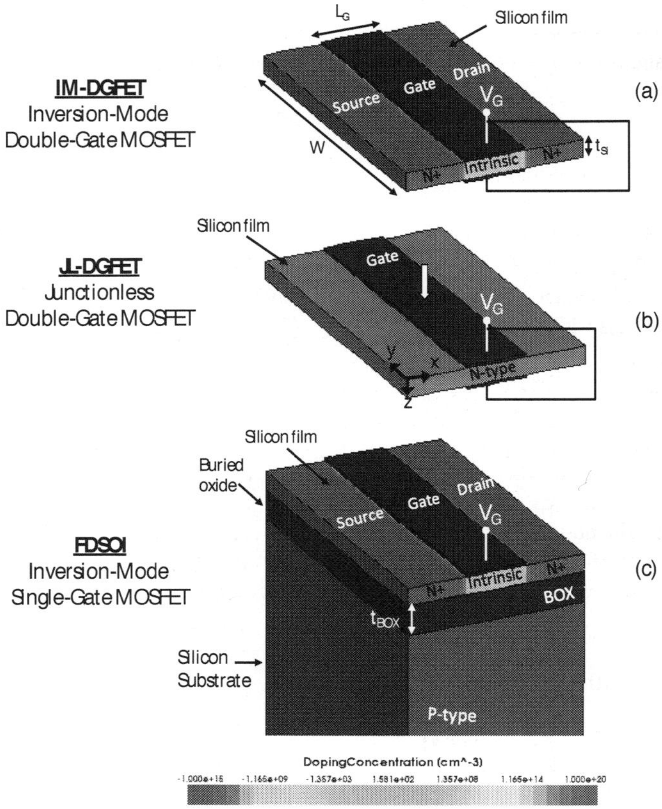

Figure 1. Schematic description of the simulated JL-DGFET (a), IM-DGFET (b), and FDSOI (c) structures considered in this work. The doping level distribution in each device is shown and the main geometrical parameters are defined. For a better view, the spacers and isolation oxide are not shown. The position of the ion strike is indicated by the arrow; the ion strikes vertically in the middle of the channel and in a direction parallel to the z axis.

the ion in the device. The deposited charge is then obtained in each case taking into account the Gaussian distribution of the ion track, the 3-D geometry of the silicon film and the exact location of the ion strike. The deposited carriers are rapidly transported (mainly by drift and diffusion mechanisms [37]) and collected by the drain contact. A part of these carriers can be recombined by carrier recombination mechanisms; the deposited charge can also be amplified by bipolar amplification mechanism. This phenomenon is specific to partially-depleted SOI (PDSOI) devices, but also exists in FDSOI [45]-[46] and double-gate transistors [37]. The charge collected at the drain contact, following the ion strike, results in a drain current transient, which is further used to accurately calculate the collected charge (by integrating the drain current on the duration of the transient). The bipolar amplification of the charge deposited by the ion is

http://dx.doi.org/10.5772/57048

obtained by calculating the ratio between the collected and the deposited charges. The bipolar amplification is a key-parameter that characterizes the device sensitivity to ionizing particles, and gives insights on the radiation-hardness of circuits based on this type of device.

3. Static operation

The simulated steady-state drain current characteristics of JL-DGFET, IM-DGFET and FDSOI are plotted in Fig. 2. The three devices have the same off-state current, but different subthreshold swings and on-state currents. While Double-Gate devices (both JL-DGFET and IM-DGFET) have near ideal subthreshold swings (65 mV/dec), FDSOI has a much higher subthreshold swing (90 mV/dec) because the single-gate configuration reduces the control by the gate of the channel potential and increases the parasitic short-channel effects compared to a double-gate configuration. The highest on-state current is obtained in IM-DGFET, due to the combination of a double-gate structure and an intrinsic channel; this structure has the advantage to maximize the carrier mobility. In JL-DGFET the highly-doped silicon film degrades the mobility and then, the on-state current is the lowest in spite of a double-gate configuration. The on-state current in FDSOI is situated between those of IM-DGFET and JL-DGFET: it is lower than in IM-DGFET because only a single gate controls the channel, but it is higher than in JL-DGFET since the channel is intrinsic and the mobility is enhanced.

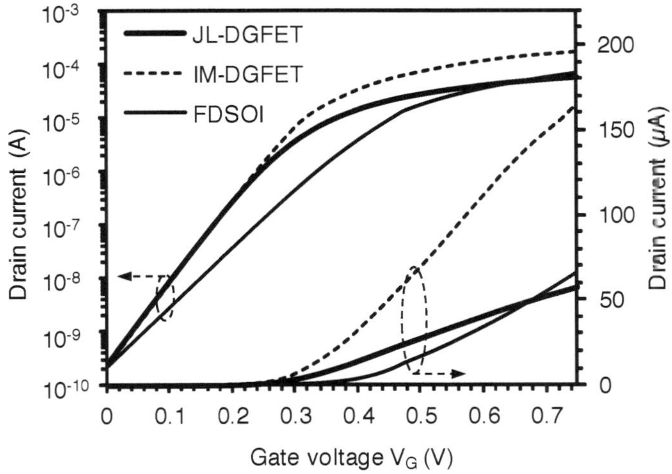

Figure 2. Drain current as a function of gate voltage for JL-DGFET, IM-DGFET and FDSOI. The gate workfunction for each device has been finely tuned to obtain the same off-state current for all devices. Characteristics simulated for V_D=0.75 V.

4. Transient operation

The 3-D distributions of the carrier density simulated before and after the ion strike are shown in Fig. 3 for JL-DGFET, IM-DGFET and FDSOI. The 2-D profile of the electrostatic in a cross-section (plane x-z in Fig. 1) corresponding to the middle of the channel is plotted in Fig. 4.

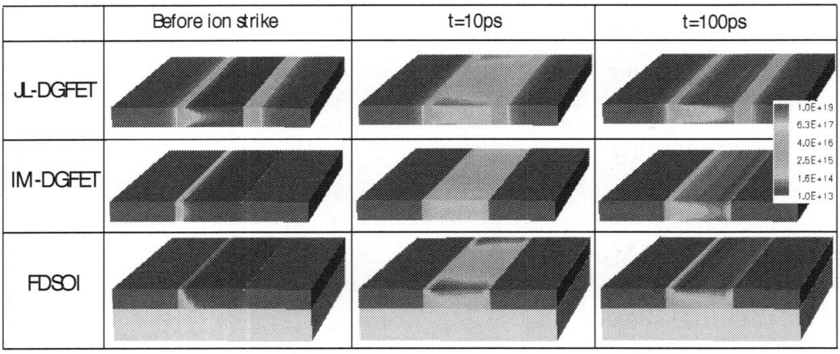

Figure 3. D profiles of electron density in JL-DGFET, IM-DGFET and FDSOI before the ion strike, at t=10 ps (maximum charge generation) and at t=100 ps. The values of the electron density are in cm^{-3}. For a better view of the film, gate material, spacers and isolation oxide are not shown. The ion strike LET is 0.1 MeV/(mg/cm^2), V_G=0 V, V_D=0.75 V.

As shown in Fig. 3, the density profiles are strongly affected by the ion strike in the three devices. As expected, the charge density on the y axis is symmetrical with respect to the middle of the film in double-gate devices and it is asymmetrical in FDSOI. At maximum deposited charge (t=10 ps), the electron density sharply increases compared to the steady state; after t=10 ps, the electron density decreases with time due to charge transport and carrier recombination mechanisms.

The ion strike not only disturbs the charge density, but also the electrostatic potential (Fig. 4) and induces a transient current which can be visualized at the drain contact. Simulated drain current transients due to the ion strike are reported in Fig. 5 for LET=0.1 MeV/(mg/cm^2). The "prompt" components of the current transients are almost identical for the three devices; on the contrary, the transient tails, representing the slow discharge component (due to floating-body effects and carrier recombination mechanisms) are very different. FDSOI shows the longest transient tail indicating the presence of stronger floating-body effects than in double-gate devices. This is confirmed by the bipolar amplification which is plotted as a function of the ion-strike LET in Fig. 6. For LET=0.1 MeV/(mg/cm^2), the bipolar gain is higher in FDSOI than in JL-DGFET and IM-DGFET. IM-DGFET shows the lowest bipolar gain owing to its double-gate configuration and its intrinsic channel. In spite of its double-gate structure, JL-DGFET has a higher bipolar gain than IM-DGFET essentially because the highly-doped silicon film enhances the floating-body effects; however, at low LET values the bipolar amplification of JL-DGFET is lower than that of single-gate FDSOI.

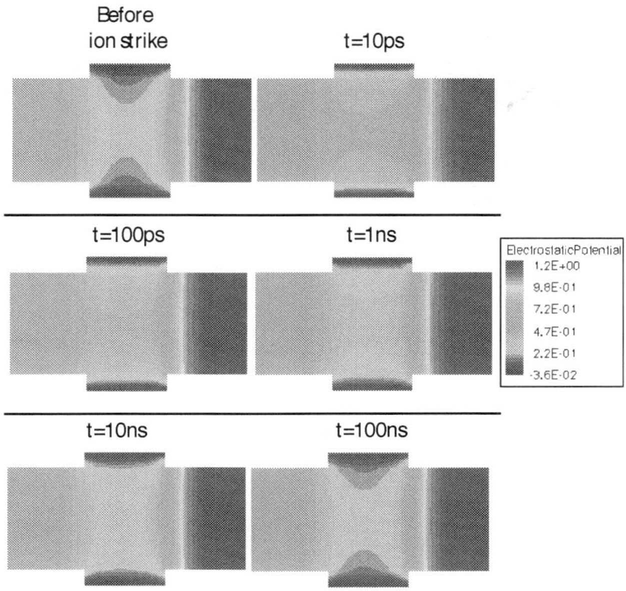

Figure 4. D profiles of the electrostatic potential (in V) within the JL-DGFET structure at different times before and after the ion strike. For a better view of the silicon film, the gate material, spacers and isolation oxide are not shown. LET=0.1 MeV/(mg/cm²), V_G=0 V and V_D=0.75 V.

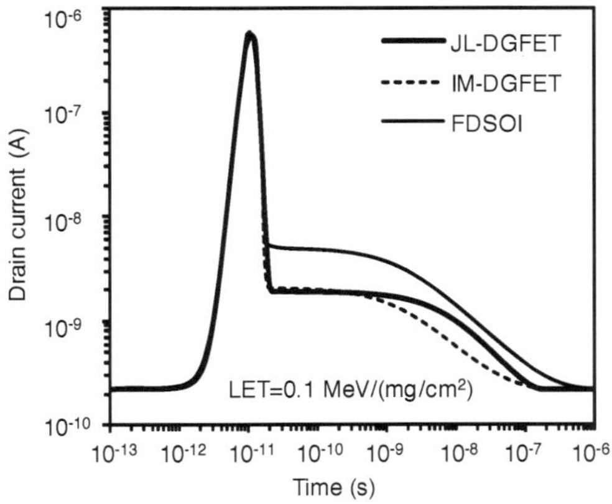

Figure 5. Drain current transients in JL-DGFET, IM-DGFET and FDSOI. All the transistors are biased in the off-state. LET=0.1 MeV/(mg/cm²).

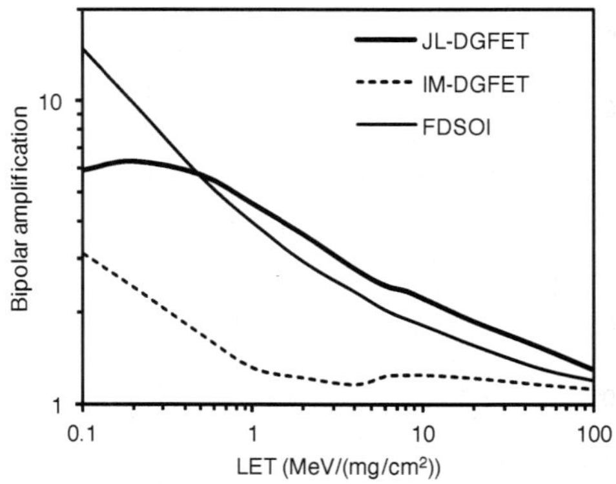

Figure 6. Bipolar gain versus the ion-strike LET in JL-DGFET, IM-DGFET and FDSOI. The ion strikes vertically in the middle of the channel between the source and drain contacts.

We recall here that in simulations presented in Fig. 6 the ion strikes the devices in the middle of the channel. We will see in section 5 that, for particular LET values, the bipolar amplification of JL-DGFET may be lower than that of IM-DGFET and FDSOI if the ion strikes the channel in other particular locations, along the x axis, between the source and drain contacts.

5. Impact of heavy-ion track parameters on the transistor transient response

In this section we study in detail the impact of several ion track parameters as well as the influence of the ion-strike location along the channel on the bipolar amplification of the three devices considered in this work. We change one parameter at a time in order to decorrelate the effects induced on the transient current and bipolar gain.

5.1. Ion track characteristic time

We begin with the characteristic time of the Gaussian time dependence of the ion track, s_hi. This parameter has a large influence on the transient current. For all previous simulations we used s_hi=2 ps since, as stated before, a very good agreement was found in a previous work between simulations and experimental data. To illustrate the impact of s_hi on the transient current and bipolar gain, we performed additional simulations with s_hi=0.5 ps. In these simulations the ion strikes in the middle of the channel and all other simulation parameters are unchanged (the same as those defined in section 2.2). Figure 7 shows the current transients obtained with s_hi=2 ps and s_hi=0.5 ps in JL-DGFET. As expected, the "prompt" component of the drain current transient is much narrower for s_hi=0.5 ps that for s_hi=2 ps. However, the transient tail is the same in both cases, which is normal, since the transient tail is essentially governed by the floating-body effects and the recombination mechanisms taking place in the device and does not depend on the time parameters of the ion track.

http://dx.doi.org/10.5772/57048

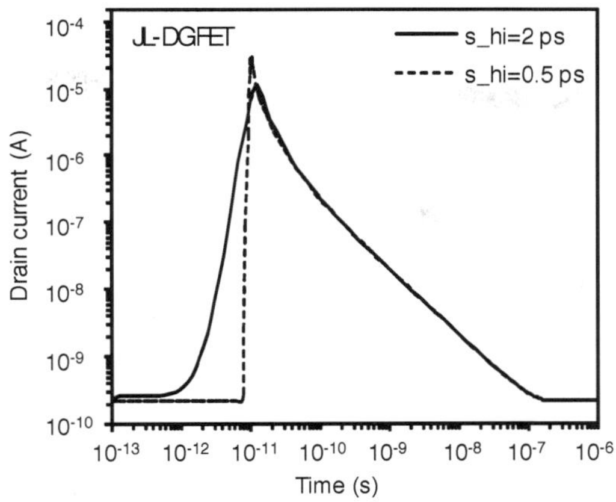

Figure 7. Drain current transients in JL-DGFET for two characteristic times of the Gaussian time dependence of the ion track. LET=1 MeV/(mg/cm^2), V_G=0 V and V_D=0.75 V.

Unlike the transient current, bipolar amplification is only slightly influenced by the value of s_hi. Figure 8 shows that the gain bipolar in JL-DGFET is always higher than that of IM-DGFET (for all LET values). Compared to FDSOI, JL-DGFET is more interesting for very low LET (lower than 0.5 MeV/(mg/cm2)) where FDSOI has a stronger bipolar gain. However, for intermediate and high LET, the bipolar gain of JL-DGFET becomes slightly higher than that of FDSOI.

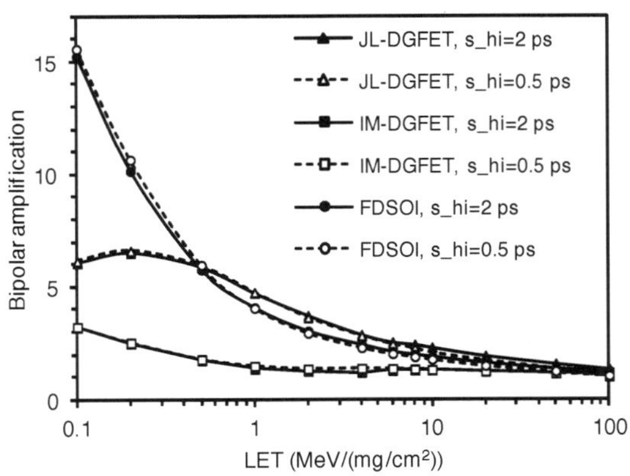

Figure 8. Bipolar amplification versus the ion-strike LET in JL-DGFET, IM-DGFET and FDSOI for two characteristic times of the Gaussian time dependence of the ion track.

5.2. Ion track radius

We have also analyzed the impact of the ion track radius on the JL-DGET transient response. For the previous analysis a very narrow (20 nm) was considered in order to facilitate the comparison with experimental and simulation results in [35] and [44]. In the following, we show simulation results performed with a larger characteristic radius r=70 nm and we compare them with results obtained at r=20 nm. The purpose of this study is to determine if the value of the ion track radius changes the conclusions regarding the increased single-event susceptibly of JL-DGFET compared to IM-DGFET. Our simulation results show that for both JL-DGFET and IM-DGFET, the current peak is higher when considering a narrow radius, mainly because more charge is deposited in the channel region of the device than in the source/drain region. This is confirmed by the collected charge which decreases when the ion track radius increases. The bipolar gain calculated for all devices considering r=70 nm is plotted in Fig. 9; results obtained for r=20 nm are also reported. Figure 9 shows that when the track radius increases the bipolar gain is only slightly modified for IM-DGFET. For JL-DGFET the bipolar gain at low LET is lower for r=70 nm than for r=20 nm, probably due to the lower deposited charge. However, at high LET the bipolar gain for r=70 nm is very similar to that obtained for r=20 nm. In spite of these variations of the collected charge and bipolar gain when the ion track radius increases, the previous trends and conclusions concerning the JL-DGFET transient response to heavy ion radiation are not changed. In the case of a larger radius the bipolar gain changes for all devices, but the bipolar amplification of JL-DGFET is still higher than that of IM-DGFET (for all LET values). These results are consistent with simulation data obtained in [39]. Compared to FDSOI, the bipolar amplification of JL-DGFET is weaker for LET values less than 1 MeV/(mg/cm^2), and becomes slightly higher for LET>1 MeV/(mg/cm^2).

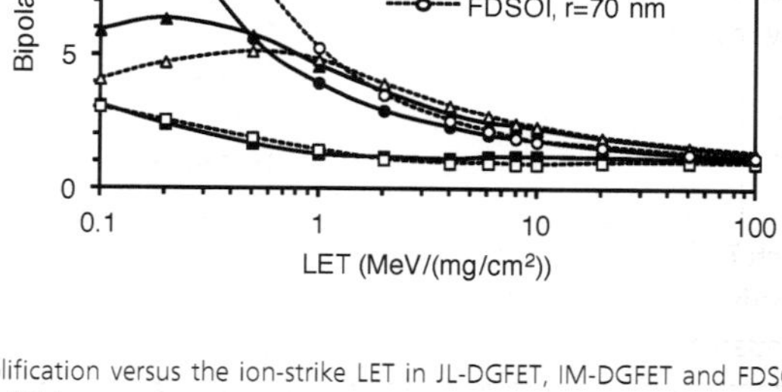

Figure 9. Bipolar amplification versus the ion-strike LET in JL-DGFET, IM-DGFET and FDSOI for two radii of the ion track. V_G=0 V and V_D=0.75 V.

5.3. Ion strike location between source and drain contacts

Until now we have considered that the ion hits the device in the middle of the channel. In this part we are changing the location of the ion strike along the channel (x-axis) in order to study the impact of this position on the radiation sensitivity of JL-DGFET compared to that of IM-DGFET and FDSOI. In the following, the track radius is 20 nm, s_hi=2 ps and all other parameters are those defined in section 2.2. Several locations of ion strike are considered between the source contact (x=0) and the drain contact (x=60 nm), as shown in Fig. 10.

The 3-D profile of the heavy-ion charge density in the entire silicon film (the same for all three devices) is shown in this figure for an ion strike in x=10 nm. For this particular location, as shown in Fig. 10, the ion track is not entirely contained on the silicon film. This is also the case for other locations, which requires a specific calculation of the deposited charge. For each location, the current transient is simulated and the collected charge is extracted from this transient. Finally, the bipolar gain is calculated at a given LET for each x value.

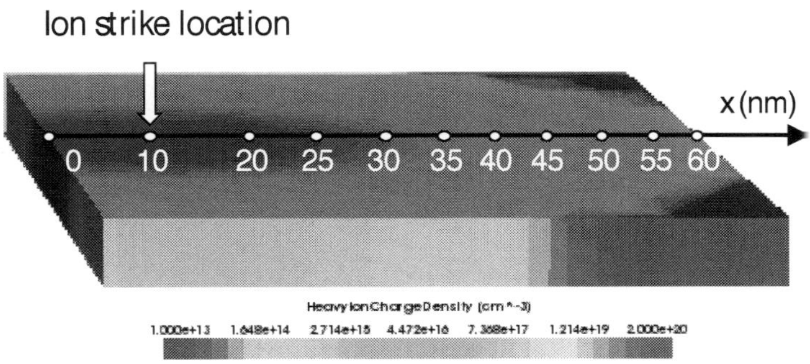

Figure 10. D profiles of the heavy-ion charge density in the silicon film of JL-DGFET for an ion strike at x=10 nm and LET=2 MeV/(mg/cm^2). The values of the heavy-ion charge density are in cm^{-3}. For a better view of the film gate material, spacers and isolation oxide are not shown. The position of the ion strike is indicated by the arrow. Other positions for the ion strike considered in this work are also indicated.

For simulations considering the ion strike in the middle of the channel (x=30 nm), we saw that JL-DGFET always shows a higher bipolar gain than IM-DGFET (for all LET values). In addition, the bipolar gain of JL-DGFET is also higher than that of FDSOI for intermediate and high LET. The purpose of this section is to verify whether these conclusions also apply to other locations of the ion strike along the channel. The collected charge as a function of the x location is shown in Fig. 11 for both very low and very high LET values. The deposited charge, calculated for each x location and each LET, is also reported in this figure to facilitate the comparison. The deposited charge is maximum in the middle of the channel and decreases towards the sides of the silicon film, because a smaller part of ion track is contained in the active region when the ion strike position moves towards the source or drain contacts. At very low LET=0.2 MeV/(mg/cm^2) and for all x locations, the lowest collected charge is obtained for IM-DGFET and the highest collected charge for FDSOI (Fig. 11(a)). This result shows that the trend obtained for x=30 nm is confirmed for all other locations. For all devices, the collected charge has a bell-shaped profile with a maximum around the middle of the channel (where the deposited charge is the highest) and two minima at the source and drain contacts (where the deposited charge is the lowest). The collected charge is always higher than the deposited charge for all x locations, which indicates a strong bipolar amplification. The behavior is quite different for LET=80 MeV/(mg/cm^2), as shown in Fig. 11(b). For ion strikes located between the source contact and the middle of the channel, the collected charge is higher for JL-DGFET than that of FDSOI and IM-DGFET. It is also interesting to note that for x locations situated between the source contact (x=0) and the middle of the channel, the collected charge is lower than the deposited charge. This indicates that the bipolar amplification is very low and there is a strong recombination of the deposited charge in the device. Beyond x=30 nm, the collected charge for JL-DGFET decreases and becomes lower than that of IM-DGFET and FDSOI. These results show that for a high LET, the trends obtained for ion strikes in the middle of the channel are no longer valid for ion strikes located in the vicinity of the drain region, beyond x=30 nm. In addition, these results show, for the first time, that JL-DGFET is able to collect a smaller amount of charge than IM-DGFET for these specific values of x location and LET.

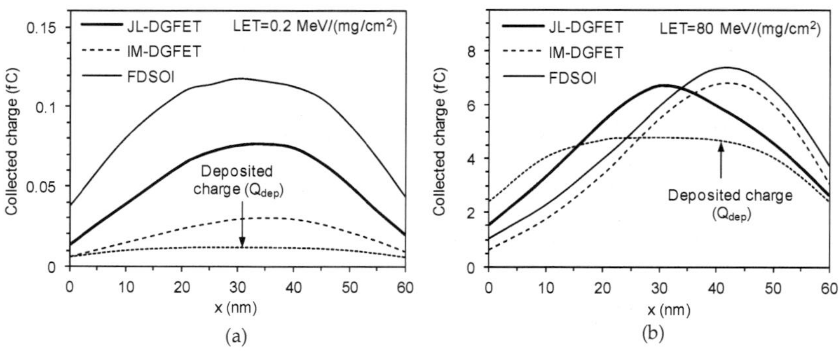

Figure 11. Collected charge as function of the x location in IM-DGFET, JL-DGFET and FDSOI. The deposited charge is also plotted for comparison. (a) LET=0.2 MeV/(mg/cm^2) and (b) LET=80 MeV/(mg/cm^2).

To confirm these new findings and highlight the range of LET for which these observations are valid, we calculated the bipolar gain as a function of x for different LET values. Figure 12(a) shows, as expected, that at LET=0.2 MeV/(mg/cm^2) the bipolar gain of FDSOI is the highest and the gain of JL-DGFET is situated between that of FDSOI and IM-DGFET. JL-DGFET is therefore more resistant to radiations than FDSOI, but IM-DGFET remains the most interesting device for low LET. This trend continues when LET increases until LET values around 0.5 MeV/(mg/cm^2). For LET values between 0.5 MeV/(mg/cm^2) and 20 MeV/(mg/cm^2) (approximately), JL-DGFET shows the highest bipolar gain for all x locations, IM-DGFET always having the lowest gain. The bipolar gain of JL-DGFET is slightly higher than that of FDSOI for x locations beyond 40 nm. The trend changes for LET values above 20 MeV/(mg/cm^2). This can be visualized in Fig. 12(b) which shows the bipolar amplification for LET=30 MeV/(mg/cm^2). Finally, Fig. 13 shows the bipolar amplification as a function of x location for LET=80 MeV/(mg/cm^2). Although for x less than 30 nm IM-DGFET remains the most interesting device in terms of radiation resistance, for x location beyond about 30 nm, the bipolar gain of JL-DGFET becomes the lowest.

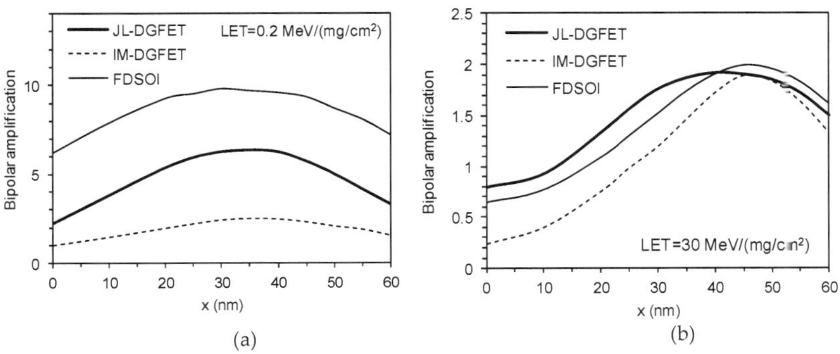

Figure 12. Bipolar amplification as a function of the x position of the ion strike in JL-DGFET, IM-DGFET and FDSOI for (a) LET=0.2 MeV/(mg/cm^2) and (b) LET=30 MeV/(mg/cm^2).

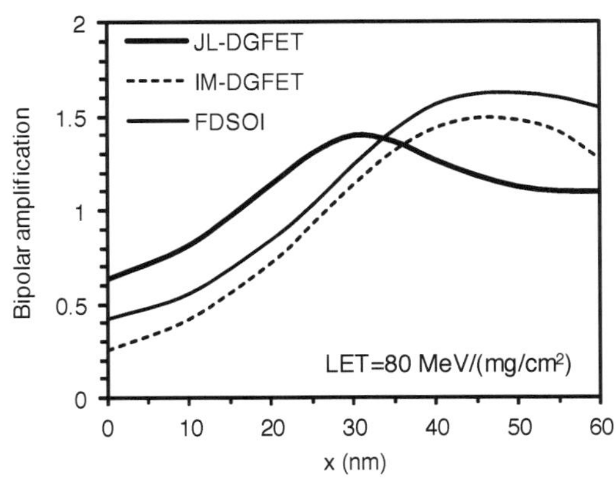

Figure 13. Bipolar amplification as a function of the x position of the ion strike in JL-DGFET, IM-DGFET and FDSOI for LET=80 MeV/(mg/cm^2).

We summarize these results in Table 1, indicating for each range of values the device having the lowest bipolar gain:

a. for ion strike locations in the first part of the channel (between the source contact and the middle of the channel) IM-DGFET has the lowest bipolar amplification for all LET values.

b. for x locations beyond the middle of the channel:

- for LET<20 MeV/(mg/cm^2), the bipolar gain of IM-DGFET is always the smallest.
- for LET>20 MeV/(mg/cm^2), JL-DGFET has the lowest bipolar gain; the JL-DGFET becomes more resistant to radiation than IM-DGFET and FDSOI.

In addition, compared to FDSOI, JL-DGFET is also more resistant to radiation for LET<0.5 MeV/(mg/cm^2) and all x locations. These results show that there are LET ranges and specific ion-strike locations for which JL-DGFET can be more interesting in terms of radiation hardness than more conventional inversion-mode devices such as FDSOI and IM-DGFET.

Ion strike location x	LET values	Lowest bipolar gain
Between source contact and middle of the channel	All LET values	IM-DGFET
Beyond the middle of the channel	< 20 MeV/(mg/cm^2)	IM-DGFET
	> 20 MeV/(mg/cm^2)	JL-DGFET

Table 1. Simulation results summary indicating the device characterized by the lowest bipolar gain as function of the ion strike location and LET values.

Finally, we compared our results with experimental and simulation results published in Ref. [35]; the purpose is to validate a part of our previous results showing that JL-DGFET could have a lower radiation sensitivity than inversion-mode devices such as IM-DGFET and FDSOI for ion strikes near the drain and ion LET values higher than 20 MeV/(mg/cm^2). In [35] we investigated the transient response of inversion-mode FD single-gate SOI MOSFET designed with 80 and 50 nm gate length, 11 nm-thick silicon film and intrinsic channel. In that work we found an excellent agreement between experimental bipolar gain values (measured by heavy ions experiments) and simulated bipolar gain obtained with 3-D numerical simulation. The results were also consistent with experimental data obtained by pulsed laser irradiation performed on 80 nm gate length FD SOI MOSFETs fabricated with the same technology [44]. In [35] the ion strikes in a location situated in the drain region, location equivalent to x=50 nm in the present work. For this reason, we plot in Fig. 14, the bipolar gain for JL-DGFET, IM-DGFET and FDSOI for a ion strike at x=50 nm and ion LET values between 10 and 100 MeV/(mg/cm^2). The experimental and simulation data from [35] are also reported in Fig. 14. This figure indicates that the bipolar gain in JL-DGFET is lower than the experimental and simulated bipolar gain in FD SOI 80 nm and FD SOI 50 nm. The comparison is not easy because the silicon film thickness and the channel length are not the same in JL-DGFET and FD SOI devices measured in [35]. However, these experimental data confirm our simulation results concerning JL-DGFET, which shows lower bipolar amplification than IM-DGFET and FDSOI for ion strikes near the drain and ion LET values higher than 20 MeV/(mg/cm²).

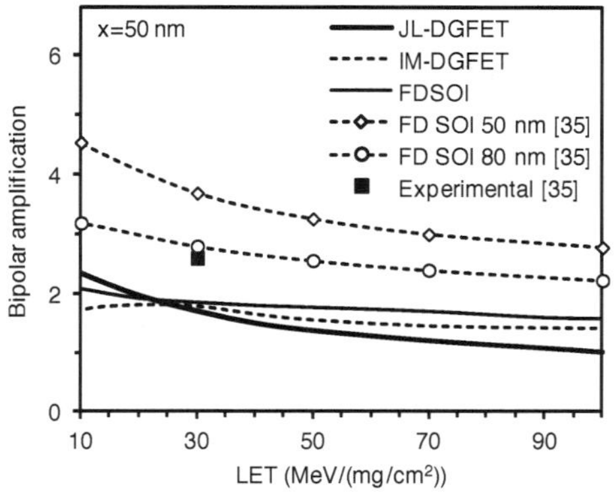

Figure 14. Bipolar amplification vs. LET in JL-DGFET, IM-DGFET and FDSOI for an ion strike at x=50 nm and comparison with experimental and simulated data obtained in [35] for FD SOI MOSFET.

6. Impact of film doping level on the JL-DGFET transient response

For JL-DGFET, we also investigated the impact of channel doping level on the drain current transient and bipolar amplification. Three channel doping levels have been considered in simulation: 1×10^{19}, 2×10^{19} and 3×10^{19} cm^{-3}. In JL-DGFET the channel thickness has to be sufficiently small in order to be able to fully deplete the channel of carriers and to turn the device off [29]. The higher the channel doping level, the smaller the film thickness needs to be. This condition is satisfied for all the doping levels and the film thickness considered here. All devices have been calibrated to fill the ITRS Low-Power requirements for the technology node corresponding to the year 2015 [5]. In order to facilitate the comparison, the gate work-function has been finely tuned to obtain the same off-state current (I_{OFF}) for all devices.

When the channel doping increase, the floating body effects are enhanced and the drain current transient is longer, as shown in Fig. 15. Both the collected charge (Fig. 16) and bipolar amplification (Fig. 17) increase with the channel doping. Impact ionization is also larger for higher doping levels, which additionally contribute to enhance the bipolar amplification. Very high values of the bipolar gain are found for a channel doping of 3×10^{19} cm^{-3}, but these values are reduced when a larger ion track radius is considered in simulation. Finally, at very high LET the electric field collapses and the bipolar gain decreases below 2.5 for all devices.

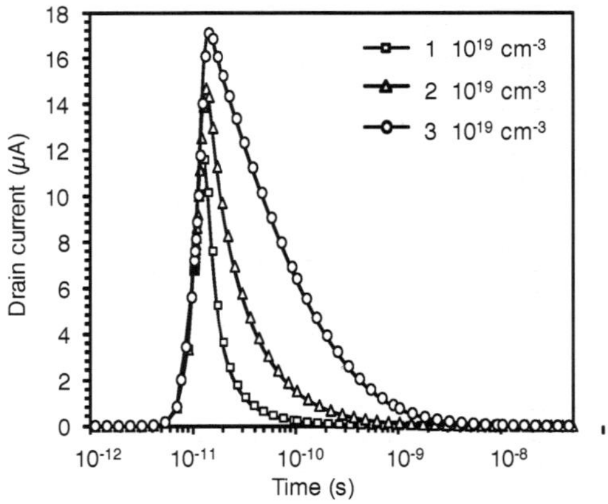

Figure 15. Drain current transient in JL-DGFET for different film doping levels. The incident ion LET is 1 MeV/(mg/cm^2). V_G=0 V and V_D=0.75 V.

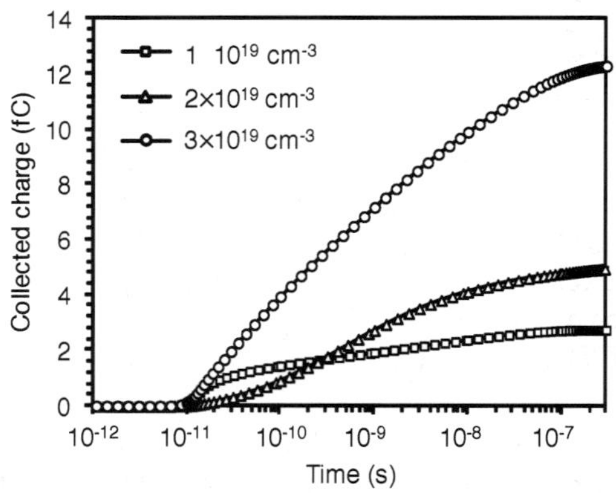

Figure 16. Collected charge in JL-DGFET for different film doping levels. The incident ion LET is 1 MeV/(mg/cm^2). V_G=0 V and V_D=0.75 V.

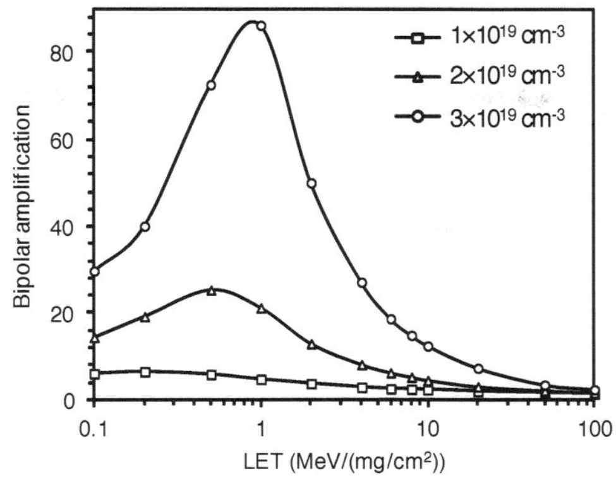

Figure 17. Bipolar amplification as function of LET in JL-DGFET for different film doping levels. V_G=0 V and V_D=0.75 V.

7. Conclusion

In conclusion, this chapter presented a detailed investigation of the radiation sensitivity of JL-DGFET by 3-D numerical simulation. In particular, the bipolar gain of JL-DGFET has been compared with that of more conventional inversion-mode devices such as FDSOI and IM-DGFET. We have firstly shown that for an ion strike in the middle of the channel, IM-DGFET shows a lower bipolar gain than JL-DGFET and FDSOI (for all LET values). We also studied the impact of various parameters of the ion track (characteristic time and track radius) on the drain current transient and bipolar gain of JL-DGFET. Our results show that modifying these parameters does not change the previous conclusion, the bipolar gain of IM-DGFET being always smaller than those of JL-DGFET and FDSOI. However, a thorough study of the bipolar gain as a function of the ion strike position along the channel showed that JL-DGFET has a lower bipolar gain than IM-DGFET and FDSOI for some particular conditions, precisely for LET values superior to 20 MeV/(mg/cm^2) and ion strike positions between the middle of the channel and the drain contact. These results are also confirmed by already published experimental and simulation data obtained on FD SOI MOSFETs with longer channels. JL-DGFET is also better than FDSOI for low LET values below 0.5 MeV/(mg/cm^2) (for all ion strike positions).

Author details

Daniela Munteanu and Jean-Luc Autran

CNRS & Aix-Marseille University, Marseille, France

References

[1] Moore GE. Electronics 1965;38, 19. see also : http://www.intel.com/research/silicon/mooreslaw.htm

[2] Gusev EP, Narayanan V, Frank MM. Advanced high-k dielectric stacks with polySi and metal gates: Recent progress and current challenges. IBM Journal of Research and Development 2006;50(4/5), 387-410.

[3] Taur Y, Buchanan D, Chen W, Frank D, Ismail K, Lo S-H, Sai-Halasz G, Viswanathan R, Wann H-JC, Wind S, Wong H-S. CMOS scaling into the nanometer regime. Proceedings of IEEE 1997;85 486–504.

[4] Fischetti MV, Laux SE. Long-Range Coulomb Interactions in Small Si Devices. Part I: Performance and Reliability. Journal of Applied Physics 2001;89(2) 1205-1231.

[5] ITRS 2012. International Technology Roadmap for Semiconductors. Available online: http://public.itrs.net.

[6] Houssa M. Fundamental and Technological Aspects of High-k Gate Dielectrics. Institute of Physics, London, 2004.

[7] Rim K, Hoyt JL, Gibbons JF. Transconductance Enhancement in Deep Submicron Strained-Si 12-MOSFETs. In: International Electron Devices Meeting Technical Digest 1998, pp. 707–710, Washington, USA.

[8] Haensch W, Nowak EJ, Dennard RH, Solomon PM, Bryant A, Dokumaci OH, Kumar A, Wang X, Johnson JB, Fischetti MV. Silicon CMOS devices beyond scaling. IBM Journal of Research and Development 2006;50(4/5) 339-361.

[9] Hiramoto T., Saitoh M., and Tsutsui G., Emerging nanoscale Silicon devices taking advantage of nanostructure physics. IBM Journal of Research and Development 2006;50(4/5) 411-418.

[10] Dodd PE. Device Simulation of Charge Collection and Single-Event Upset. IEEE Transactions on Nuclear Science 1996;43(2) 561-575.

[11] Dodd PE, Massengill LW. Basic mechanisms and modeling of single-event upset in digital microelectronics. IEEE Transactions on Nuclear Science 2003; 50(3) 583-602.

[12] Dodd PE. Physics-Based Simulation of Single-Event Effects. IEEE Transactions on Device and Materials Reliability 2005;5(3) 343-357.

[13] Baumann RC. Radiation-Induced Soft Errors in Advanced Semiconductor Technologies. IEEE Transactions on Device and Materials Reliability 2005;5(3) 305-316.

[14] Mitra S, Sanda P, Seifert N. Soft Errors: Technology Trends, System Effects and Protection Techniques. In: Proceedings of IEEE VLSI Test Symposium, 2008.

[15] Roche P. Year-in-Review on radiation-induced Soft Error Rate. In: IEEE International Reliability Physics Symposium 2006, San Jose, USA.

[16] Colinge JP. Multiple-gate SOI MOSFETs. Solid-State Electronics 2004;48(6)897-905.

[17] Park JT, Colinge JP. Multiple-gate SOI MOSFETs: device design guidelines. IEEE Transactions on Electron Devices 2002;49(12) 2222-2229.

[18] Harrison S, Coronel P, Cros A, Cerutti R, Leverd F, Beverina A, Wacquez R, Bustos J, Delille D, Tavel B, Barge D, Bienacel J, Samson MP, Martin F, Maitrejean S, Munteanu D, Autran JL, Skotnicki T. Poly-gate replacement through contact hole (PRETCH): A new method for high-K/metal gate and multi-oxide implementation on chip. In: International Electron Devices Meeting Technical Digest 2004, pp. 291-294.

[19] Ernst T, Munteanu D, Cristoloveanu S, Ouisse T, Horiguchi S, Ono Y, Takahashi Y, Murase K. Investigation of SOI MOSFETs with Ultimate Thickness. Microelectronic Engineering 1999;48(1-4) 339-342.

[20] Munteanu D, Autran JL, Harrison S. Quantum short-channel compact model for the threshold voltage in Double-Gate MOSFETs with high-k permittivity gate dielectrics. Journal of Non-Crystalline Solids 2005;351(21-23) 1911-1918.

[21] Munteanu D, Autran JL, Harrison S, Nehari K, Tintori O, Skotnicki T. Compact Model of the Quantum Short-Channel Threshold Voltage in Symmetric Double-Gate MOSFET. Molecular Simulation 2005;31(12) 831-837.

[22] Moreau M, Munteanu D, Autran JL. Simulation Analysis of Quantum Confinement and Short-Channel Effects in Independent Double-Gate Metal-Oxide-Semiconductor Field-Effect Transistors. Japanese Journal of Applied Physics 2008;47 7013-7018.

[23] Hisamoto D. FD/DG-SOI MOSFET-A viable approach to overcoming the device scaling limit. In: International Electron Devices Meeting Technical Digest 2001, pp. 429-432.

[24] Barral V, Poiroux T, Vinet M, Widiez J, Previtali B, Grosgeorges P, Le Carval G, Barraud S, Autran JL, Munteanu D, Deleonibus S. Experimental determination of the channel backscattering coefficient on 10-70 nm-metal-gate Double-Gate transistors. Solid State Electronics 2007;51(4) 537-542.

[25] Martinie S, Le Carval G, Munteanu D, Soliveres S, Autran JL. Impact of ballistic and quasi-ballistic transport on performances of Double-Gate MOSFET-based circuits. IEEE Transactions on Electron Devices 2008;55(9) 2443-2453.

[26] Barral V, Poiroux T, Munteanu D, Autran JL, Deleonibus S. Experimental investigation on the Quasi-Ballistic Transport: Part II-Backscattering coefficient extraction and link with the mobility. IEEE Transactions on Electron Devices 2009;56(3) 420-430.

[27] Munteanu D, Autran JL. Two-dimensional Modeling of Quantum Ballistic Transport in Ultimate Double-Gate SOI Devices. Solid State Electronics 2003;47 1219-1225.

[28] Autran JL, Munteanu D. Simulation of electron transport in nanoscale independent-gate DG devices using a full 2D Green's function approach. Journal of Computational and Theoretical Nanoscience 2008;5 1120–1127.

[29] Lee C-W, Afzalian A, Akhavan ND, Yan R, Ferain I, Colinge JP. Junctionless multigate field-effect transistor. Applied Physics Letters 2009;94 053511.

[30] Colinge JP, Lee C-W, Afzalian A, Akhavan ND, Yan R, Ferain I, Razavi P, O'Neill B, Blake A, White M, Kelleher A-M, McCarthy B, Murphy R. Nanowire transistors without junctions. Nature Nanotechnology 2010;5.

[31] Kranti A, Yan R, Lee C-W, Ferain I, Yu R, Akhavan ND, Razavi P, Colinge JP. Junctionless Nanowire Transistor (JNT): Properties and Design Guidelines. In: proceedings of the European Solid State Device Research Conf. (ESSDERC) 2010, pp. 357-360.

[32] Colinge JP, Lee C-W, Ferain I, Akhavan ND, Yan R, Razavi P, Yu R, Nazarov AN, Doria RT. Reduced electric field in junctionless transistors. Applied Physics Letters 2009;96 073510.

[33] Chen C-Y, Lin J-T, Chiang M-H, Kim K. High-Performance Ultra-Low Power Junctionless Nanowire FET on SOI Substrate in Subthreshold Logic Application. In Proceeding of the IEEE SOI Conference, 2010.

[34] Lee C-W, Borne A, Ferain I, Afzalian A, Yan R, Akhavan ND, Razavi P, Colinge JP. High Temperature Performance of Silicon Junctionless MOSFETs. IEEE Transactions on Electron Devices 2010;53(3) 620-625.

[35] Munteanu D, Ferlet-Cavrois V, Autran JL, Paillet P, Baggio J, Faynot O, Jahan C, Tosti L. Investigation of Quantum Effects in Ultra-Thin Body Single- and Double-Gate Devices Submitted to Heavy Ion Irradiation. IEEE Transactions on Nuclear Science 2006;53(6) 3363-3371.

[36] Munteanu D, Autran JL, Ferlet-Cavrois V, Paillet P, Baggio J, Castellani K. 3-D Quantum Numerical Simulation of Single-Event Transients in Multiple-Gate Nanowire MOSFETs. IEEE Transactions on Nuclear Science 2007;54(4) 994-1001.

[37] Munteanu D, Autran JL. Modeling and Simulation of Single-Event Effects in Digital Devices and ICs. IEEE Transactions on Nuclear Science 2008;55(4) 1854-1878.

[38] Munteanu D, Autran JL. 3-D Simulation Analysis of Bipolar Amplification in Planar Double-Gate and FinFET with Independent Gates. IEEE Transactions on Nuclear Science 2009;56(4) 2083-2090.

[39] Munteanu D, Autran JL. 3-D Numerical Simulation of Bipolar Amplification in Junctionless Double-Gate MOSFETs Under Heavy-Ion Irradiation. IEEE Transactions on Nuclear Science 2012;59(4) 773-780.

[40] Vinet M, Poiroux T, Widiez J, Lolivier J, Previtali B, Vizioz C, Guillaumot B, Le Tiec Y, Besson P, Biasse B, Allain F, Cassé M, Lafond D, Hartmann J-M, Morand Y, Chiar-

oni J, Deleonibus S. Bonded Planar Double-Metal-Gate NMOS Transistors Down to 10 nm. IEEE Electron Device Letters 2005;26(5) 317-319.

[41] Synopsys Sentaurus TCAD tools. Available online: http://www.synopsys.com/products/tcad/tcad.html

[42] Munteanu D, Weiser D, Cristoloveanu S, Faynot O, Pelloie JL, Fossum JG. Generation-Recombination Transient Effects in Partially Depleted SOI Transistors: Systematic Experiments and Simulations. IEEE Transactions on Electron Devices 1998;45(8) 1678-1683.

[43] Munteanu D, Ionescu AM. Modeling of Drain Current Overshoot and Recombination Lifetime Extraction in Floating-Body Submicron SOI MOSFETs. IEEE Transactions on Electron Devices 2002;49(7) 1198-1205.

[44] Ferlet-Cavrois V, Paillet P, McMorrow D, Torres A, Gaillardin M, Melinger JS, Knudson AR, Campbell AB, Schwank JR, Vizkelethy G, Shaneyfelt MR, Hirose K, Faynot O, Jahan C, Tosti L. Direct Measurement of Transient Pulses Induced by Laser Irradiation in Deca-Nanometer SOI Devices. IEEE Transactions on Nuclear Science 2005;52(6) 2104.

[45] Ferlet-Cavrois V, Marcandella C, Giraud G, Gasiot G, Colladant T, Musseau O, Fenouillet C, du Port de Pontcharra J. Characterization of the parasitic bipolar amplification in SOI technologies submitted to transient irradiation. IEEE Transactions on Nuclear Science 2002;49(3) 1456-1461.

[46] Ferlet-Cavrois V, Vizkelethy G, Paillet P, Torres A, Schwank JR, Shaneyfelt MR, Baggio J, du Port de Pontcharra J, Tosti L. Charge Enhancement Effect in NMOS Bulk Transistors Induced by Heavy Ion Irradiation-Comparison With SOI. IEEE Transactions on Nuclear Science 2004;51(6) 3255-3262.

Chapter 12

Stimulated Raman Scattering with a Relativistic Vlasov-Maxwell Code: Cascades of Nonstationary Nonlinear Kinetic Interactions

Magdi Shoucri and Bedros Afeyan

Additional information is available at the end of the chapter

http://dx.doi.org/10.5772/57476

1. Introduction

In laser fusion, hundreds of laser beams propagate through underdense coronal (ablator material) plasmas surrounding the Deuterium-Tritium (fusion fuel) filled target. At least tens of targets would have to be irradiated in succession per second for laser fusion energy cycle economics to be viable with modest or high (50-100) gain targets. The propagation of multiple laser beams in this coronal plasma and the subsequent energy deposition must be well controlled to achieve thermonuclear ignition and significant gain [1]. Because of high laser intensities and long plasma scalelengths, the underdense plasma environment is invariably the scene of nonlinear coherent processes which are detrimental to laser fusion. This is because they can lead to backscattering losses, hot electron preheating and implosion non-uniformity. Considerable attention has been given to parametric instabilities or nonlinear optical processes in plasmas (for an entry level introduction, see [2]). The linear theory of such instabilities is well understood (see [3-6] for high frequency parametric instabilities involving electron plasma waves (EPW)) but the nonlinear kinetic theory is still rich with mysteries to be uncovered (for an introduction with some advanced elements see the recent text in [7]). This is because kinetic effects add new dimensions of velocity space dynamics, changing the distribution functions strongly (away from a dull Maxwellian) and making the resonant wave-wave interaction picture much more intricate via wave-particle and particle-particle interactions (see [8,9] for an older perspective, and [10] for a more in depth and modern one). In particular, trapping, untrapping and retrapping of (a sufficiently large number of) particles makes the *transient* behaviour well beyond the reach of nonlinear knob-kludged fluid models. Coherent, phase sensitive, nonlocal memory effects, disparate scales and bursty or intermittent structures, all make predictions difficult, toy models irrelevant, and useful simulations very challenging. In particular, the initiation of large backscattering, for instance, may depend on many processes that precede that growth in leading the distribution function away from a Maxwellian, which, had it not changed, would not have allowed backscattering growth at all.

In the present work, we apply an Eulerian Vlasov code for the numerical simulation of the one-dimensional (1D) relativistic Vlasov-Maxwell equations, to study the laser-plasma interaction process known as stimulated Raman scattering (SRS). The Eulerian Vlasov code we use was presented and applied in several references [11-16]. The numerical scheme applies a direct solution method of the Vlasov equation as a partial differential equation in phase-space without dimensional splitting. The numerical scheme is based on a 2D advection technique, of second-order accuracy in time-step. The distribution function is advanced in time by interpolating in 2D along the phase space characteristic using a tensor product of cubic *B*-spline. Interest in Eulerian grid-based solvers associated with the method of characteristics for the numerical simulation of the Vlasov equation comes from the very low noise levels inherent in these codes, which allow us to study accurately nonlinear physics in low density regions of phase-space (see also [17]), without being inundated by numerical artifacts.

Besides SRBS, and SRFS, which is the analogous Raman forward scattering instability, other high frequency instabilities may occur at least kinetically when modified distribution functions exist (see [5,6,18-20]). In the family of such structures, which are beyond the scope of fluid models, are stimulated scattering off Electron Acoustic Waves (EAW) and Kinetic Electrostatic Electron Nonlinear (KEEN) waves. These stimulated processes are therefore called SEAS and SKEENS. There are also Beam Acoustic Modes (BAM) having been identified as possibly being linked to SRBS nonlinear evolution and saturation (see for instance [21-23]). A different perspective has also been promulgated under the heading of transient enhanced instability levels attributed to rapidly changing distribution functions which diminish damping rates and thus allow larger levels of SRS than would be expected in models ignoring transient tracking of distribution functions. These come under the heading of inflationary models of SRS.

Of these, KEEN waves have the interesting feature that they do not require a pre-flattened (zero slope at the phase velocity of the wave) distribution function and are not steady-state, time-independent solutions. In other words, they are not BGK modes (see for instance [8,9]). On the other hand, EAWs and nonlinear EPWs are BGK modes. In contrast, KEEN waves involve multiple phase-locked harmonics which produce a steepened multi-mode electric field pattern that can throw particles a good distance ahead as untrapped particles which then may become retrapped and help maintain an overall wave amplitude that is not in strict local equilibrium with the plasma particle distribution. The slope of the averaged distribution function need not be zero anywhere (a necessity for EPW and EAW and BGK modes, or for stationarity) and there is no infinitesimal amplitude version of KEEN waves which are nonlinearly strongly modified phase space distribution function states. They were discovered by Afeyan *et al.* in 2002 while performing ponderomotively driven Vlasov-Poisson simulations, and while trying to explore the limits of resonance physics of EAWs. The latter were found to be of measure zero compared to KEEN waves. This was first published in the proceedings of the 2003 IFSA meeting [18].

Returning to the choice of a Vlasov code over a PIC code, say, we offer this argument. If some violent rapidly and strongly driven regime is adopted in a PIC simulation, say, solely to render the initial conditions of an underesolved model less troubling, then all such intricate physics (as found here) might go unnoticed. Or if all diagnostics that can be afforded after massively parallel and data distributed simulations only look at time averaged or time integrated quantities, again, the transient and exciting initiation processes might go unnoticed or obscured by much larger final state signatures. This is what we avoid here, and it appears the sequence of events in time that are revealed here have not been seen before by PIC or Vlasov code studies.

What causes the pre-distortion of distribution functions can easily be missed or miscalculated if coarse means of tracking the fine scale structures of phase space are adopted. This is an inherent risk in PIC codes. Typical practitioners tend to emphasize very rapidly imposed and large amplitude perturbations since otherwise they would risk drowning in slowly brewing, artificial-noise generated physics. Even with Vlasov codes, the important transient kinetic physics can be easily missed if the backscattered process is strongly promoted over all other processes by seeding it externally and artificially. Not allowing the plasma to develop its own response as it sees fit, when confronted with a high intensity laser and in the presence of thermal level plasma fluctuations, leads to blocking many phase space pathways of self-organization beyond just the backscattering channel. Instead of just stimulated Raman backscattering (SRBS), in a plasma at a given density and temperature (for sufficiently large wave vector-Debye length product values for stimulated Raman backscattering electron plasma waves, SRBS EPWs), one may also expect Raman forward scatter (SRFS), especially when the wavenumber of a small perturbation imposed in the plasma as an initial condition in the transverse field, corresponds to SRFS. We may then expect to see Kinetic Electrostatic Electron Nonlinear (KEEN) waves [18-20] driven by the pump beating with the backscattering portion of the imposed standing wave initial condition perturbation at the SRFS wavenumber. We observe that only after stimulated KEEN wave scattering, SKEENS, has caused sufficient KEEN wave growth, and the background distribution function sufficiently flattened, that Raman backscatter finally can develop in earnest. This is a novel scenario of SRBS initiation and entrenched entanglement with KEEN waves which coevolve even though eventually SRBS having the far superior growth rate outstrips the KEEN wave influence reaching even more nonlinear states later in time with positive slopes in the electron distribution function and the accompanying chaotic, bursty behaviour.

In this chapter we report new results that show that SRFS is first driven in such plasmas before SRBS can grow from small perturbations that do not directly seed it. We will show that SRFS will give rise to the excitation of KEEN waves due to the opposite direction wavenumber of the SRFS wave that was seeded by the initial scattered standing wave light field. This is then amplified by the pump through the SKEENS process. This then drives KEEN waves into their characteristic multiple-harmonic phase-locked structure and steepened electric field profiles which facilitate retrapping of particles that escape any given potential well as the overall electrostatic field adjusts to all these waves being driven and amplified. The back of the simulation box is where these processes coexist most markedly. In the middle of the simulation box, SRBS finally grows after KEEN waves reach that area and change the local distribution function by softening it. SRBS eventually swallows up the KEEN wave and dominates since its growth rate is far higher. This new scenario confirms that nonlinear trapping evolution of SRBS is not just a question of EPWs but also of KEEN waves and SKEENS and that SRFS wavenumber perturbations can initiate the latter if a standing wave already exists much before SRBS can occur. The later evolution of all these processes is very complicated still involving positive slope electron distribution functions which will then accelerate the self-destruction of these modes and render the picture even more transient, intermittent and chaotic. We stop the simulations short of that eventuality where even Brillouin scatter begins to occur and dynamics and predictions become more challenging to track requiring ion acoustic waves and fluid saturation of SRS as well via Langmuir decay instability, etc.

Nonlocal and collective kinetic effects are involved in this physics. A direct Vlasov solver, capable of resolving these kinetic processes, is used here to address some aspects of the scattering properties of SRS and SKEENS. The code evolves relativistically both electrons and ions. In Vlasov codes used to simulate these problems, noise and other numerical fluctuations are very low for the SRBS to grow from, therefore it is usual in several simulations to stimulate artificially the counter-propagating daughter light wave at a low level as an injected seed, in order to enhance the SRBS growth and to allow the saturation phase to be reached rapidly. This saturation results from the competition of non-linear effects which include frequency shift, pump depletion, damping reduction, trapped particle instability, spatiotemporal chaos, among others. A detailed study of the resulting distribution function obtained at saturation has been presented, for instance, in Strozzi *et al*, 2007, which showed that the stage following saturation involved the transformation of Raman Langmuir waves into a set of beam acoustic modes or BAM (see also [24,25]), and an EAW appears at this stage with a weak reflected light that phase-matches for scattering off this mode, a process called electron acoustic scatter (EAS). SEAS has been experimentally observed in [26,27], and has been reported in simulations of plasmas overdense to SRBS and at relativistic pump intensities [11,28], and has been also observed in underdense Vlasov simulations [29]. Distinguishing between BAMs and EAWs is discussed in the literature, see for instance [22,29]. We will avoid this discussion, because they play secondary roles in the results presented here. For the parameters we are using, which involves strongly damped electron plasma waves, our simulations are dominated by SRFS, SKEENS and SRBS, in that order. It is the purpose of the present work to study these three processes and their mutual interactions, SRFS, SKEENS and SRBS which arise during the SRS dynamics process, and which appear in the early stage which precedes the saturation of the SRBS. To avoid any interference from artificially distorted distribution functions or imposed seeding, we start the code from an initial Maxwellian distribution, and the system evolves under the influence of a pump light wave which provides fluctuations from which SRS develops, without any additional imposed initial perturbation except for a standing wave at the resonant wavenumber of SRFS. This then develops SRFS but also drives SKEENS at the backscattering portion beating with the pump electrostatic ponderomotive field which seeds a KEEN wave directly. We do not seed the counter-propagating daughter light wave to stimulate the growth of the SRBS. We identify in the early phase of the Raman interaction a backscattered light that phase-matches for scattering off a KEEN wave, and which precedes the growth and saturation of the SRBS process. These SKEENS events arise during the Raman physics, from the initial Maxwellian distribution. The signature of this KEEN wave is clearly identified in the electron distribution function phase-space, and the evolution of the system until the appearance of the growth and the saturation of the SRBS process will be followed. Possible effect of this SKEENS on the initiation and subsequent saturation of the SRBS process will be discussed.

2. The relevant equations of the Eulerian Vlasov code and the numerical scheme

We study this current problem by using an Eulerian Vlasov code for the numerical solution of the one-dimensional (1D) relativistic Vlasov-Maxwell equations. The relevant equations for the Eulerian Vlasov formulation are those previously presented in references [12-15] for instance. We present here these equations in order to fix the notation. Time t is normalized to the inverse plasma frequency ω_p^{-1}, length is normalized to $l_0 = c\omega_p^{-1}$, velocity and momentum are normalized respectively to the velocity of light c and to $M_e c$, where M_e is the electron mass and c is the velocity of light. We have the following Vlasov equations for the electrons and the ions distribution functions $f_{e,i}(x, p_{xe,i}, t)$:

$$\frac{\partial f_{e,i}}{\partial t} + \frac{p_{xe,i}}{\mu_{e,i}\gamma_{e,i}}\frac{\partial f_{e,i}}{\partial x} + (\mp E_x - \frac{1}{2\mu_{e,i}\gamma_{e,i}}\frac{\partial a_\perp^2}{\partial x})\frac{\partial f_{e,i}}{\partial p_{xe,i}} = 0 \tag{1}$$

where $\gamma_{e,i} = (1 + (p_{xe,i} / \mu_{e,i})^2 + (a_\perp / \mu_{e,i})^2)^{1/2}$.

(the upper sign in Eq.(1) is for the electron equation and the lower sign for the ion equation, and subscripts e or i denote electrons or ions, respectively). In our normalized units $\mu_e = 1$ and $\mu_i = M_i / M_e$ is the ratio of ion to electron masses.

$$E_x = -\frac{\partial \phi}{\partial x} \text{and}\, \vec{E}_\perp = -\frac{\partial \vec{a}_\perp}{\partial t} \tag{2}$$

and ϕ is given by Poisson's equation, which is given here by:

$$\frac{\partial^2 \phi}{\partial x^2} = \int f_e(x, p_{xe}) dp_{xe} - \int f_i(x, p_{xi}) dp_{xi} \tag{3}$$

The transverse electromagnetic fields E_y, B_z for the linearly polarized wave obey Maxwell's equations. Defining $E^{\pm} = E_y \pm B_z$, we have:

$$(\frac{\partial}{\partial t} \pm \frac{\partial}{\partial x})E^{\pm} = -J_y. \tag{4}$$

In our normalized units we have the following expressions for the normal current densities:

$$\vec{J}_{\perp} = \vec{J}_{\perp e} + \vec{J}_{\perp i} \;; \qquad \vec{J}_{\perp e,i} = -\frac{\vec{a}_{\perp}}{\mu_{e,i}} \int_{-\infty}^{+\infty} \frac{f_{e,i}}{\gamma_{e,i}} d\, p_{xe,i}.$$

The longitudinal electric field is calculated from Ampère's equation: $\partial E_x / \partial t = -J_x$ where

$$J_x = \frac{1}{\mu_i} \int_{-\infty}^{+\infty} \frac{p_{xi}}{\gamma_i} f_i \, dp_{xi} - \frac{1}{\mu_e} \int_{-\infty}^{+\infty} \frac{p_{xe}}{\gamma_e} f_e \, dp_{xe} \tag{5}$$

Test runs were made in which Poisson's equation was used instead of Ampère's equation to obtain the longitudinal electric field, with identical results.

The Eulerian Vlasov code we use to solve Eqs.(1-5) was recently presented and applied in [11-16] for instance. We outline the main steps for the numerical solution of Eq.(1), using an Eulerian scheme. Given $f_{e,i}^{n}$ at mesh points at time $t = n\Delta t$ (we stress here that the subscript i denotes the ion distribution function), we calculate the new value $f_{e,i}^{n+1}$ at the grid points j_x, and j_p corresponding to the mesh points (x_{j_x}, $p_{xe,i\, j_p}$) by writing that the distribution function is constant along the characteristics. The characteristics equations for Eq.(1) are given by:

$$\begin{aligned} \frac{dx}{dt} &= m_{e,i} \frac{p_{xe,i}}{\gamma_{e,i}} = V_{xe,i}(x, p_{xe,i}) \\ \frac{dp_{xe,i}}{dt} &= \mp E_x - \frac{m_{e,i}}{2\gamma_{e,i}} \frac{\partial a_{\perp}^2}{\partial x} = V_{p_{xe,i}}(x, p_{xe,i}). \end{aligned} \tag{6}$$

We assume that at the time $t_{n+1} \equiv t_n + \Delta t$, x is at the grid point j_x, and $p_{xe,i}$ is at the grid point j_p. The following leapfrog scheme can be written for the solution of (6):

$$\frac{x_{j_x} - x(t_n)}{\Delta t} = V_{xe,i}(x^{n+1/2}, p_{xe,i}^{n+1/2}) = V_{xe,i}(\frac{x_{j_x} + x(t_n)}{2}, \frac{p_{xe,ij_p} + p_{xe,i}(t_n)}{2}) \tag{7}$$

$$\frac{p_{xe,ij_p} - p_{xe,i}(t_n)}{\Delta t} = V_{p_{xe,i}}(x^{n+1/2}, p_{xe,i}^{n+1/2}) = V_{p_{xe,i}}(\frac{x_{j_x} + x(t_n)}{2}, \frac{p_{xe,ij_p} + p_{xe,i}(t_n)}{2}) \tag{8}$$

http://dx.doi.org/10.5772/57476

where $(x(t_n),\ p_{xe,i}(t_n))$ is the point where the characteristic is originating at t_n (not necessarily a grid point).

Put

$$\Delta_{xe,i} = \frac{x_{j_x} - x(t_n)}{2} \quad ; \ \Delta_{p_{xe,i}} = \frac{p_{xe,ij_p} - p_{xe,i}(t_n)}{2}. \tag{9}$$

Equations (7) and (8) can be rewritten as:

$$\Delta_{xe,i} = \frac{\Delta t}{2} V_{xe,i}(x_{j_x} - \Delta_{xe,i}, p_{xe,ij_p} - \Delta_{p_{xe,i}}). \tag{10}$$

$$\Delta_{p_{xe,i}} = \frac{\Delta t}{2} V_{p_{xe,i}}(x_{j_x} - \Delta_{xe,i}, p_{xe,ij_p} - \Delta_{p_{xe,i}}) \tag{11}$$

Which are implicit equations for $\Delta_{xe,i}$ and $\Delta_{p_{xe,i}}$ and are solved by iteration. This iteration is effected as follows. We rewrite Eqs.(10,11) in the vectorial form:

$$\Delta_{\mathbf{X}e,i} = \frac{\Delta t}{2} \mathbf{V}_{e,i}\left(\mathbf{X}_{e,i} - \Delta_{\mathbf{X}e,i}, t_{n+1/2}\right) \tag{12}$$

$\mathbf{X}_{e,i}$ is the two dimensional vector $\mathbf{X}_{e,i} = (x,\ p_{xe,i})$, and $\Delta_{\mathbf{X}\,e,i} = (\Delta_{xe,i},\ \Delta_{p_{xe,i}})$ is the two dimensional vector in Eq.(12) and $\mathbf{V}_{e,i} = \left(V_{xe,i}^{n+1/2},\ V_{p_{xe,i}}^{n+1/2}\right)$. Eq.(12) for $\Delta_{\mathbf{X}\,e,i}$ is implicit and is solved iteratively by writing: $\Delta_{\mathbf{X}\,e,i}^{k+1} = \frac{\Delta t}{2} \mathbf{V}_{e,i}(\mathbf{X}_{e,i} - \Delta_{\mathbf{X}\,e,i}^{k}, t_{n+1/2})$, where we start the iteration with $\Delta_{\mathbf{X}\,e,}^{0} = 0$ for k=0. Usually two or three iterations are sufficient to get a good convergence. The shifted values in Eqs.(10,11) are calculated by a two-dimensional interpolation using a tensor product of cubic *B*-splines [30]. We now write that the distribution function is constant along the characteristics. Then $f_{e,i}^{n+1}$ is calculated from $f_{e,i}^{n}$ from the relation :

$$f_{e,i}^{n+1}(x_{j_x}, p_{xe,ij_p}) = f_{e,i}^{n}(x(t_n), p_{xe,i}(t_n)) = f_{e,i}^{n}(x_{j_x} - 2\Delta_{xe,i}, p_{xe,i} - 2\Delta_{p_{xe,i}}). \tag{13}$$

Again the shifted values in Eq.(13) are calculated with a two-dimensional interpolation using a tensor product of cubic *B*-splines. Details have been presented in [30]. These methods compared favourably with other Eulerian methods for the numerical solution of the Vlasov equation [31].

The numerical scheme to advance Eq.(1) from time t_n to t_{n+1} necessitates the knowledge of the electromagnetic field $E^{\pm}$ at time $t_{n+1/2}$. This is done using a centered scheme where we integrate Eq.(4) exactly along the vacuum characteristics with $\Delta x = \Delta t$, to calculate $E^{\pm n+1/2}$ as follows:

$$E^{\pm}(x \pm \Delta t, t_{n+1/2}) = E^{\pm}(x, t_{n-1/2}) - \Delta t J_y(x \pm \Delta t / 2, t_n) \tag{14}$$

with $J_y(x \pm \Delta t / 2, t_n) = \dfrac{J_y(x \pm \Delta x,\ t_n) + J_y(x,\ t_n)}{2}$

From Eq.(2) we also have $\vec{a}_{\perp}^{\,n+1} = \vec{a}_{\perp}^{\,n} - \Delta t \vec{E}_{\perp}^{\,n+1/2}$, from which we calculate $\vec{a}_{\perp}^{\,n+1/2} = (\vec{a}_{\perp}^{\,n+1} + \vec{a}_{\perp}^{\,n}) / 2$. To calculate $E_x^{n+1/2}$, we use Ampère's equation: $\dfrac{\partial E_x}{\partial t} = -J_x$, from which $E_x^{n+1/2} = E_x^{n-1/2} - \Delta t J_x^n$.

3. The relevant parameters

We use a fine resolution grid in phase-space, with $N = 60000$ grid points in space, and 512 grid points in momentum space for the electrons and 256 grid points in momentum space for the ions (extrema of the electron momentum are ±0.5, and ±15 for the ion momentum). The initial distribution functions for the electrons and the ions are Maxwellian. The maximum of the density is normalized to n=0.0825n_{cr}, where n_{cr} is the critical density. The electron temperature is T_e =2 keV. The ions have a temperature T_i = 0.5 keV. Ions are allowed to move, especially to adjust the sheath structure at the boundaries on both sides, but we noted at the end of the simulations beginning traces of stimulated Brillouin backscattering, which remained at a very weak level, and therefore ion dynamics can be ignored in the results we are presenting [This is not logical. Ion dynamics affects SRS saturation by creating IAW mediated LDI and similar instabilities. Given that EPW and KEEN waves live in these simulations, it is incorrect to assume a priori that IAWs could play no role. The only exception to this would be that you ran for a very short time in which case the results are not demonstrative of real situations which occur over 100s of ps at the very least at these intensities]. The initial flat profile of the uniform plasma with the density n_e=n_i=1 (normalized to n) extends over a length $L_p = 1122.56 c / \omega_{pe}$. On either side of the slab the densities are smoothly brought down to zero through a parabolic profile of length $L_{edge} = 7.81 c / \omega_{pe}$. An extra vacuum region of length $L_{vac} = 16.81 c / \omega_{pe}$ exists on each side of the slab, for a total length of the system of $L = 1171.89 c / \omega_{pe}$. In our normalized units $\Delta x = \Delta t$.

A characteristic parameter of laser beams is the normalized vector potential or quiver momentum $|\vec{a}_{\perp}| = |e\vec{A}_{\perp} / M_e c| = a_0$, where $\vec{A}_{\perp}$ is the vector potential of the wave. We chose for the amplitude of the vector potential a_0=0.025. For the linearly polarized wave

$a_0^2 = I\lambda_0^2 / 1.368x10^{18}$, I is the laser intensity in W/cm², and λ_0 the laser wavelength in microns. The frequencies are normalized to the plasma frequency ω_{pe}, and the pump wave frequency ω_0 of the injected laser beam is such that $\omega_0/\omega_{pe} = 1/\sqrt{n/n_{cr}}$, which corresponds to $\omega_0 = 3.481$ (normalized to ω_{pe}). Hydrogen ions are used with M_i/M_e=1836. A forward propagating linearly polarized wave is injected in the domain at the left boundary at x=0 with $E^+ = 2E_0\cos(\omega_0 t)$, $E_0 = \omega_0 a_0$ in our units and $E^- = 0$ (no small seed is applied as E^-). (Note that if we choose to normalize time to ω_0^{-1} and length to c/ω_0, then in the results we present in this paper the normalized time and length should be multiplied by ω_0, and the electric field should be divided by ω_0, so that in this case we would have $E_0 = a_0$).

The frequency and wavenumber (ω_0, k_0) of the pump wave are related by the relation $\omega_0^2 = \omega_{pe}^2 + k_0^2 c^2$, or in normalized units $\omega_0^2 = 1 + k_0^2$, from which k_0=3.3343. For SRS, or the coupling of a pump light wave to a daughter light wave and an electron plasma wave, the values of the electron plasma wavenumber k_{eB} associated with the SRBS, and k_{eF} associated with the SRFS are roots of the equation [32]:

$$\left[(15\Omega/4-6)\right]K^4 + (\mu + 3\Omega - 3)K^2 - 2\mu^{1/2}\left[\Omega^2 - 1 + (5/2\mu)\right]^{1/2} K + 2\Omega - 1 - (5/2\mu)(\Omega - 1) = 0 \quad (15)$$

with $K = k_e\lambda_{De}$ and $\Omega = \omega_0$ (normalized to ω_{pe}). For the present problem we have the following parameters $\mu = m_e c^2/\kappa T_e = c^2/v_{te}^2 = 1/(0.04424\sqrt{T_e})^2 = 255.8$ for T_e = 2 keV. The resulting roots are $k_{eB}\lambda_{De} = 0.3377$ for the plasma mode associated with the SRBS, and $k_{eF}\lambda_{De} = 0.0666$ for the plasma mode associated with the SRFS. As discussed in Bers *et al.*, 2009, for these parameters the SRBS plasma wave is heavily damped, and the damping of the SRFS plasma wave is negligible. The heavily damped regime with $k\lambda_{De} > 0.29$ is called the kinetic regime (Kline *et al.*, 2005). In our normalized units the Debye length $\lambda_{De} = v_{te}/c = 0.04424\sqrt{T_e}$ (normalized to c/ω_{pe} in our units), so $\lambda_{De} = 0.06256$ for T_e = 2 keV. We finally get $k_{eB} = 0.3377/\lambda_{De} = 5.398$ for the SRBS plasma wave, and $k_{eF} = 0.0666/\lambda_{De} = 1.0645$ for the SRFS plasma wave. The corresponding frequencies for the SRBS plasma wave and the SRFS plasma wave are solutions of the equation [32]:

$$\omega^2 \approx 1 + 3k^2\lambda_{De}^2/\omega^2 + 15k^4\lambda_{De}^4/\omega^4 - 5/(2\mu) \quad (16)$$

Equation (16) has the following roots: ω_{eB}=1.178 for the SRBS and ω_{eF}=1.0066 for the SRFS. The selection rules give the following results for the forward scattered electromagnetic wave (ω_{sF}, k_{sF}) and the backward scattered electromagnetic wave (ω_{sB}, k_{sB}):

$$\omega_{sB} = \omega_0 - \omega_{eB} = 3.481 - 1.178 = 2.303; \; \omega_{sF} = \omega_0 - \omega_{eF} = 3.481 - 1.0066 = 2.4744 \quad (17)$$

$$k_{sB} = k_{eB} - k_0 = 5.398 - 3.3343 = 2.0637;\\ k_{sF} = k_0 - k_{eF} = 3.3343 - 1.0645 = 2.2698 \tag{18}$$

The results in Eqs.(17-18) obey the dispersion relation for the electromagnetic wave: $1 + k_{sF}^2 = 6.152 = \omega_{sF}^2$ (from which we get $\omega_{sF} = 2.480$), and $1 + k_{sB}^2 = 5.2588 = \omega_{sB}^2$ (from which we get 2.293). These results are very close to what is calculated in Eq.(17).

4. Results

We follow the evolution of the system with a close look to the evolution in two regions of the domain, a first one at about a quarter of the length in the domain, and a second one closer to the center of the domain. We will point out important differences in the initial evolution of the spectra between these two regions depending on the level of the round-off errors which now act as a perturbation in the noiseless Vlasov code. So the initial evolution of the SRFS and SRBS is not uniform through the domain, and consequently this affect the initial evolution of the KEEN waves which, as we shall show, develops from the beginning of the Raman scattering.

4.1. Evolution of the system in the first quarter of the length of the plasma domain

For the parameters used in these simulations, the SRFS plasma mode with $k_{eF}\lambda_{De} = 0.0666$ is very weakly damped [32]. No seed or initial perturbation is added to stimulate the heavily damped SRBS mode with $k_{eB}\lambda_{De} = 0.3377$. We present in Figure(1a-2a) and Figure(4,top left) a contour plot of the electron distribution function at a position x between $x \in (280,300)$, at about a quarter of the length of the domain, at a time t= 351, 468 and 761 respectively. We see in these figures a modulation with wavelength $\lambda_{eF} = 2\pi / k_{eF} = 5.925$, which is the weakly damped forward scattered mode. Figure (2a) and Figure (4,top left) shows small vortices appearing around $p_{xe} = 0.183$. The phase velocity of the SRBS plasma wave $\upsilon_{eB} = \omega_{eB} / k_{eB} = 0.218$, corresponding to a momentum $p_{eB} = \upsilon_{eB}\gamma_{eB} = 0.2233$ (where in this case the relativistic factor $\gamma_{eB} = 1 \big/ \sqrt{1 - \upsilon_{eB}^2}$), is different from the position of the observed small vorticities appearing around $p_{xe} = 0.183$ in Fig.(2a) and Figure(4,top left). To identify the spatial modes present in Figures(1a-2a), we present in Figure (1c-2c) the spatial Fourier transform of the longitudinal electric field at the time t=351 and 468 respectively, in the domain $x \in (250,410)$. We identify the dominant mode with $k_{eF} = 1.06$ of the SRFS plasma wave. Since we have a linear polarization, we have in the longitudinal perturbation a mode present with $2k_0 = 6.674$ (at twice the wavenumber of the pump, appearing at 6.676 in our results in Figure (1c)). This is due to the fact that if we have a linearly polarized wave: $\vec{E} = (0, E_y, 0)$, we can write in a linear analysis with $E_y = E_0 \cos(\psi)$, $\psi = (kx - \omega t)$, and Faraday's law is:

$$\frac{\partial \vec{B}}{\partial t} = (0,0,-\frac{\partial E_y}{\partial x}) \tag{19}$$

Then $\vec{B}=(0,0,B_z)$ with $B_z=B_0\cos(\psi)$, and $B_0=E_0k/\omega$. From $\vec{E}_\perp=-\partial\vec{a}_\perp/\partial t$ and $\vec{p}_\perp=\vec{a}_\perp$, we get $\vec{p}=(0,p_y,0)$, with $p_y=-p_0\sin(\psi)$, and $p_0=E_0/\omega$. The longitudinal Lorentz force is $p_yB_z=-\frac{1}{2}k p_0^2\sin(2\psi)$. This drives a longitudinal response at the 2nd harmonic of the laser wave.

We note in Figs.(1c) a mode with a wavenumber 5.616. These results are confirmed in Figure (3), where we present the spatial Fourier modes at the time t=527 in the same domain $x\in(250,410)$, and where the mode with a wavenumber 5.616 appears with its growing harmonics at 11.232 and 16.81. This mode at k_{KEEN}=5.616 is different from the value of k_{eB}=5.398 for the SRBS plasma wave, and will be further discussed and identified as a KEEN wave, responsible for the small vortices we see in Figure (2a) and Figure (4,top left). We show on a logarithmic scale in Figure (1b) the distribution function around p_{xe}=0.183, spatially averaged over a length $\lambda_{KEEN}=2\pi/k_{KEEN}$=1.118 (which is the width of the small vortices we see in Figure (2a) and Figure (4,top left)) around x=280. At this stage at time t=351, it shows on a logarithmic scale the straight line of a Maxwellian. However, in Figure (2b) at time t=468, and in Figure (4,bottom right) at time t=761, the distribution function shows a slightly distorted (but not fully flattened) distribution function, which lower the damping rate and which can facilitate the excitation of the mode around p_{xe}=0.183. The entire distribution function, spatially averaged over a length λ_{KEEN}=1.118 around x=280, is shown at time t=751 in Figure (4,bottom left). Figure (4,top right) shows a plot of the longitudinal electric field in $x\in(280,300)$, showing a wavelength $\lambda_{eF}=2\pi/k_{eF}$=5.925 with a small modulation with λ_{KEEN}=1.118.

Figure (5) presents the spatial Fourier spectrum at time t=761 in $x\in(250,410)$. We note in Figure (5a) for the longitudinal wave, the mode with a wavenumber 5.616 has now developed important harmonics at 11.232 and 16.81. We also identify the dominant mode with k_{eF}=1.06 of the SRFS plasma wave. Since we have a linear polarization, we have in the longitudinal perturbation a mode present with $2k_0$=6.676 (at twice the wavenumber of the pump).

At this stage, we look in Figure (5b) to the wavenumber spectrum of the forward electromagnetic wave E^+ in the domain $x\in(250,410)$. We identify the dominant pump wave, appearing at k_0=3.338 (3.334 in our theoretical results). We can also identify the contribution of the SRFS plasma wave at k_{sF}=2.277 (2.2698 in our theoretical results in Eq.(18)). We have also a small peak at k_{AS}=4.398, which corresponds to the anti-Stokes coupling $k_{AS}=k_0+k_{e-AS}$= 3.334 + 1.064 = 4.398 in our theoretical results (k_{e-AS}=1.064 is the plasma wavenumber for the anti-Stokes coupling, already present in the wide dominant peak k_{eF}=1.06 in Figure (5a)). The frequency ω_{AS}=4.51 of the anti-Stokes wave is calculated from the relation $\omega_{AS}^2=1+k_{AS}^2$, in close agreement with the value calculated from the relation $\omega_{AS}=$

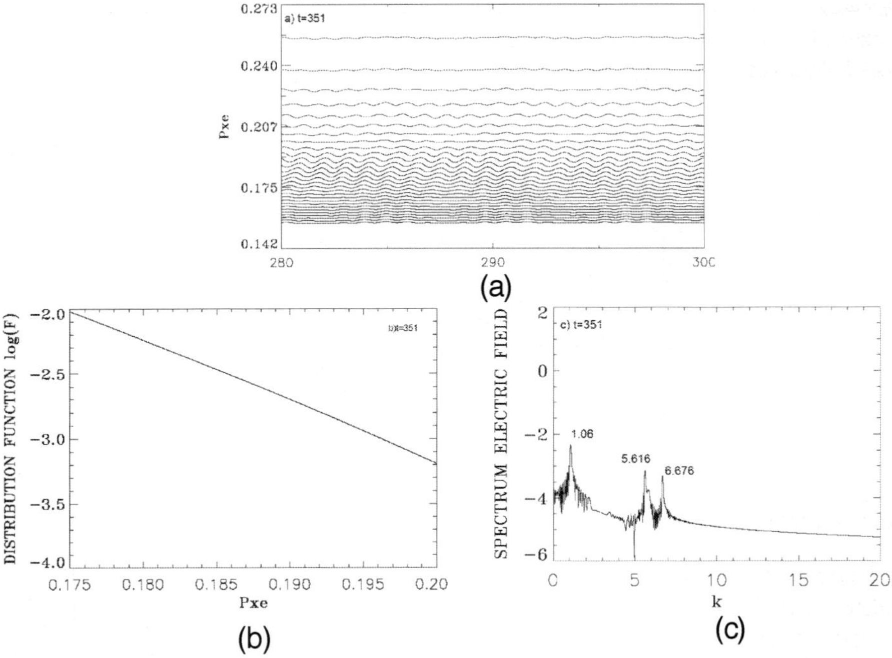

Figure 1. a) Contour plot of the electron distribution function in $x \in (280,300)$at t=351; b) Distribution function at t=351, spatially averaged around x=280 over a length of $\lambda_{KEEN} = 1.118$; 1c) Spatial Fourier spectrum at time t= 351 in $x \in (250,410)$.

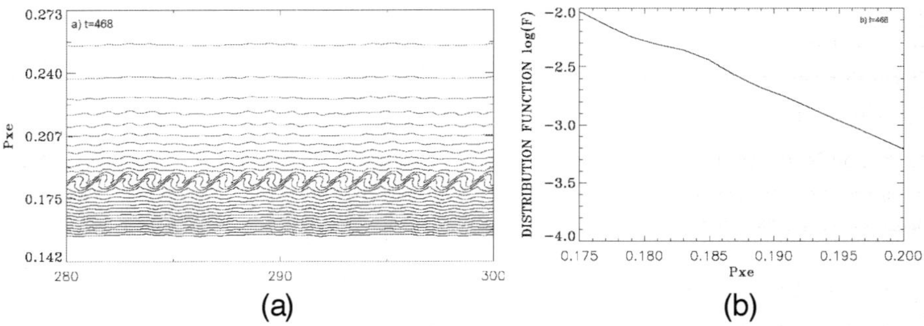

Figure 2. a) Contour plot of the electron distribution function in $x \in (280,300)$ at t=468; b) Distribution function at t=468, spatially averaged around x=280 over a length of $\lambda_{KEEN} = 1.118$

$\omega_0 + \omega_{e-AS} = 3.481 + 1.0066 = 4.487$, where the frequency $\omega_{e-AS} = 1.0066$ associated with the anti-Stokes plasma wave is essentially the same as the already excited SRFS plasma wave at $\omega_{eF} = 1.0066$. These frequencies will be verified when studying the spectrum in Figure (6,7).

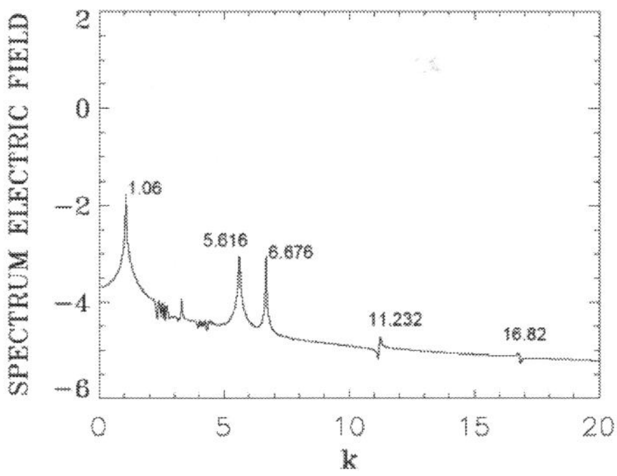

Figure 3. Spatial Fourier spectrum at the time t=527 in $x \in (250,410)$

In free space, the forward propagating wave E^+ and the backward propagating wave E^- are strictly decoupled. In a plasma, there is a very weak coupling between E^+ and E^- due to the nonlinearity of the medium. So the wavenumbers spectrum of E^- in Figure (5c) shows the same peaks at 3.338, 2.2778, 4.398 as in Figure (5b), but at a much lower level (the peak at 4.398 is barely visible, and the peak at 3.338 corresponding to the pump is almost two orders of magnitude smaller in Figure (5c) compared to Figure (5b)), with the exception of the peak at 2.277 which is reaching almost the same level in Figure (5c) as in Figure(5b). This peak of the backward wave at 2.277 in Fig.(5c) couples with the forward direction pump in Figure (5b) at 3.338 to give $k_0 = -k_{sF} + k_{KEEN}$, or a plasma wavenumber $k_{KEEN} = 3.338 + 2.277 = 5.615$ (which is the peak we identified before appearing at 5.616 in Figures (1c,2c,5a)). We have identified this mode as belonging to the KEEN wave (Afeyan *et al.*, 2004 and Afeyan *et al.*, 2013a-f) when discussing above the spectrum. The frequency ω_{KEEN} of this mode verifies $\omega_0 = \omega_{sF} + \omega_{KEEN}$, or ω_{KEEN} = 3.481 – 2.474= 1.007, and the phase velocity $v_{KEEN} = \omega_{KEEN} / k_{KEEN}$ = 0.18, which corresponds to a momentum $p_{KEEN} = v_{KEEN}\gamma_{KEEN} = v_{KEEN} / \sqrt{1 - v_{KEEN}^2} = 0.183$, which is where the small vortices appearing in Figs.(2-4) are located. These vortices are similar to what is presented for instance in references [18-20].

We present in Figure (6a) the frequency spectrum of the forward propagating wave E^+ recorded at the position x=300 between t_1=664 and t_2=824. We identify the pump frequency ω_0=3.495 (ω_0=3.481 in our theoretical results), and two small peaks for the forward scattered mode ω_{sF} =2.474 (see Eq.(17)), and the anti-Stokes mode $\omega_{AS} = 4.487 = \omega_0 + \omega_{e-AS} = 3.481 + 1.0066$.

Figure (6b) shows the frequency spectrum of the backward wave E^- at the same position x=300, during the same time. It shows the peaks with the forward wave at 3.495 (at much lower level than in Figure (6a)) and at 2.474 (at essentially the same level as the SRFS mode in Figure (6a)), and a small peak for the weakly growing heavily damped SRBS wave at ω_{sB}=2.28 (2.30 in our theoretical results). So the coupling $\omega_0=\omega_{sF}+\omega_{KEEN}, k_0=-k_{sF}+k_{KEEN}$ has resulted in an KEEN wave at (ω_{KEEN} =1.007,k_{KEEN} =5.616) which creates the small vortices we see in Figure (2a) and Figure (4a) around p_{KEEN} =0.183, and has resulted in a stimulation of the backward light wave appearing at (ω =2.474,k =2.277) in Figure (6b) and in Figure (5c) respectively. Since the kinetic enhancement of the backward scattering is one of the main point in the investigation of Raman scattering, since it can remove a substantial amount of energy from the pump laser propagating through the plasma, we have here an example of a stimulated backward wave at the wavenumber and frequency of the SRFS wave, which is excited before the SRBS wave through the coupling with the KEEN wave at (ω_{KEEN},k_{KEEN}). The wave at (ω_{KEEN},k_{KEEN}) is trapping a population of electrons at the phase velocity of the wave as in Figure (2a) and in Figure (4a,left). The slope of the distribution function is not flattened at the phase velocity of the KEEN wave, but it is reduced as shown in Figure (4b,right), which allows the wave to be less damped, and to exist and to trap a population of electrons which supports the KEEN wave, and allows it to propagate, as long as the stimulation of the pump is present through the coupling with a backward wave.

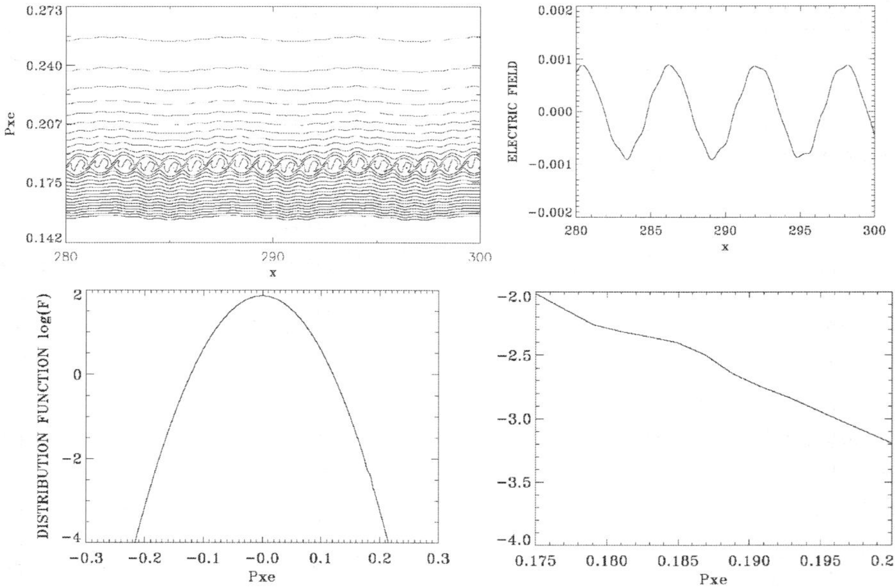

Figure 4. Top left: Contour plot of the electron distribution function in $x \in (280,300)$ at t=761. Top right: Plot of the longitudinal electric field in $x \in (280,300)$. Bottom: Distribution function at t=761, spatially averaged around x=280 over a length of λ_{KEEN} = 1.118

http://dx.doi.org/10.5772/57476

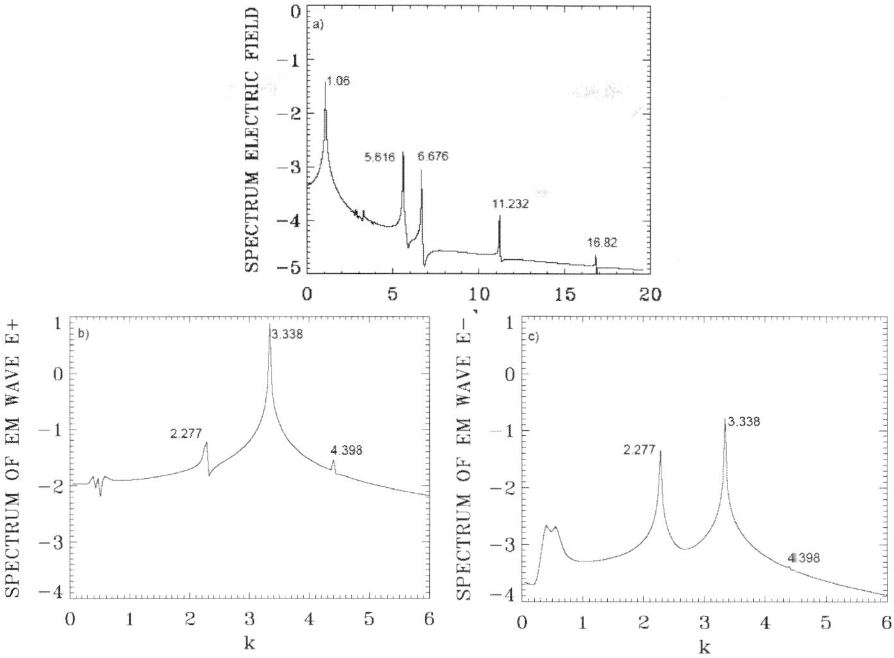

Figure 5. Spatial Fourier spectrum at the time t=761in $x \in (250,410)$ for: a) the longitudinal plasma wave; b) the forward electromagnetic wave E^+; c) the backward electromagnetic wave E^-.

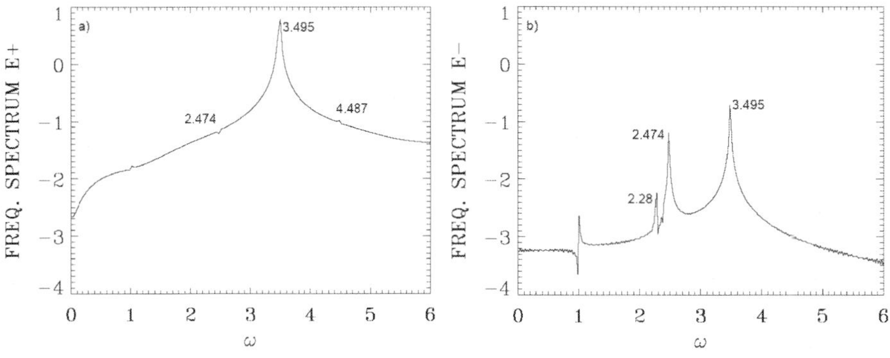

Figure 6. Frequency spectrum: a) forward propagating wave E^+; b) backward propagating wave E^-

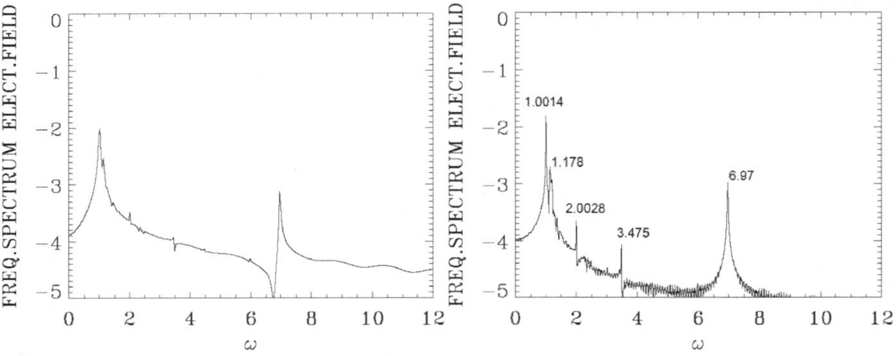

Figure 7. Frequency spectrum for the longitudinal electric field.

Figure (7,left) shows the frequency spectrum for the longitudinal electric field recorded at the position x=300, during the same time between t_1=664 and t_2=824 as in Figure (6), and Figure (7,right) shows the frequency spectrum at the same position, but between t_1=664 and t_2=984. The comparison emphasizes the growth of the modes present during this phase. We can identify the mode for the SRFS plasma wave $\omega_{eF}=1.0014$ (1.006 in our theoretical results, see Eq.(17), which is also the peak at the KEEN wave ω_{KEEN}), and its harmonic at 2.0028. A smaller peak at 1.178 is for the SRBS plasma wave, heavily damped and which is still slowly growing, appears in Figure (7,right). We also note the mode at the harmonic of the pump $2\,\omega_0$ = 6.95 (see discussion around Eq.(19)), and its sub-harmonic at the pump frequency ω_0=3.475. In Figure (7), we are still in the phase where the SRFS $k_0=k_{sF}+k_{eF}$ is coupling the pump with the forward scattered wave, and the KEEN wave $k_0=-k_{sF}+k_{KEEN}$ is coupling the pump with the backward wave at $-k_{sF}$, and are dominating, as shown in Figure (4). We can also write $2k_0=k_{eF}+k_{KEEN}$, but $2k_0$= 6.676 is also present in Figure (5a) as the harmonic of the pump as previously explained, further forcing the SKEENS oscillation at k_{KEEN} =5.615 and the SRFS at k_{eF} =1.06.

We have so far shown in this early stage, that the excitation of the KEEN wave and the forward scattering are dominating. We present in Figure (8) the contour plots of the distribution function for $x\in(300,339)$, for t=761, 937 and 966. We see at t=761 in Figure (8a) the same pattern as in Figure (4, top left). However, in Figures (8b,c) we see a mode coming from the right, and propagating to the left while growing, which is the SRBS plasma wave with k_{eB}=5.398 and ω_{eB}=1.178. We will discuss later where and when this mode is generated. Indeed in Figure (7,right), where the frequency spectrum is obtained by extending the time domain from t_1=664 to t_2=984, we see the mode at ω_{eB}=1.178 appearing.

In Figure (9a) we present in the wavenumber spectrum of the longitudinal electric field in the domain $x \in (250,410)$ at t=879 (to be compared with Figure (5a)). We note that the SRBS plasma peak at k_{eB}=5.398 has grown, and eclipsing the KEEN wave peak at k_{KEEN} =5.61. We also see the persistence of the harmonic of the mode k_{KEEN} =5.61 at 11.2. Figure (9c) shows the wavenumber spectrum of the backward wave E^-, in the same domain $x \in (250,410)$, at t=879. We see the now growing backscattered wave at k_{sB}=2.08 (2.06 in our theoretical results), and the modes at 2.238 and 3.338. The signature of the now growing backscattered wave is seen in the wavenumber spectrum of the forward wave E^+ in Figure (9b) at k_{sB}=2.05, together with the forward pump at k_0=3.338, the forward scattered wave at k_{sF} =2.2778, and the anti-Stokes mode at k_{AS}=4.398. Figure (10a) shows a contour plot of the distribution function in the domain $x \in (320,339)$ at t=1289, in the final stage close to saturation. Figures (10b) and (10c) shows the spatially averaged distribution function over one wavelength of the SRBS plasma wave, $\lambda_{eB}=2\pi / k_{eB}=1.16$, which is essentially the width of a vortex in Figure (10a)), at the left edge of the domain in Figure (10b), and in the middle of the domain of Figure (10c) respectively. We see a bump, with a minimum at the phase velocity of the SRBS plasma wave. With k_{eB}=5.398, ω_{eB}=1.178, this corresponds to a phase velocity $v_{eB}=\omega_{eB} / k_{eB}=0.218$ and to a momentum $p_{eB}=v_{eB}\gamma_{eB}$=0.2233, which corresponds to the position of the local minimum we see in Figure (10b) and Figure (10c), and which corresponds also to about the position of the center of the big vortices in Figure (10a).

There is also a local maximum on the bumpy plateau. We look in Figure (11a) to the wavenumber spectrum of the longitudinal electric field at t=1289, close to saturation, in the domain $x \in (250,410)$. We still observe the modes previously discussed, the SRFS plasma wave at k_{eF} =1.06, and the SRBS plasma wave at k_{eB}=5.38 is now dominant, the harmonic of the pump wave at 6.676 is still present, but the modes at 10.799 and 16.18 are harmonics of the now dominant SBRS plasma wave at k_{eB}=5.38 (compare with Figure (5a)). We also see sidebands developing, which is common when positive slopes of the distribution function are formed [33]. Detailed analysis of the eigen-frequencies of the distribution functions with a shape similar to what is presented in Figure (10b) and Figure (10c) has been discussed in details in [22], where BAM and EAW have been identified. The growth of these modes will lead to the fusion of the vortices but they missed KEEN wave contributions and SKEENS processes which we have seen in the SRS physics we present here. Detailed studies at this stage is beyond the scope of the present work, since an accurate study in this case requires a fine grid in velocity space for the proper treatment of the trapped particles effects and of the merging of the vortices. We note however a peak in Figure (11a) at k=4.32. The associated frequency from Eq.(16) is ω=1.11 (we note the broad frequency spectrum in Figure (12a)), which corresponds to a phase velocity $v_\varphi=\omega / k=0.25$, and to a momentum $p_\varphi=v_\varphi\gamma=0.265$, which corresponds to the local maximum in the middle of the bumpy plateau. We also have in Fig.(11a) a peak at k=3.33, which corresponds from Eq.(16) to a frequency ω=1.065, and to a phase velocity $v_\varphi=\omega / k=0.32$ and to a momemtum p_φ=0.339. This corresponds to the second local minimum we see on the bumpy plateau in Figure (10).

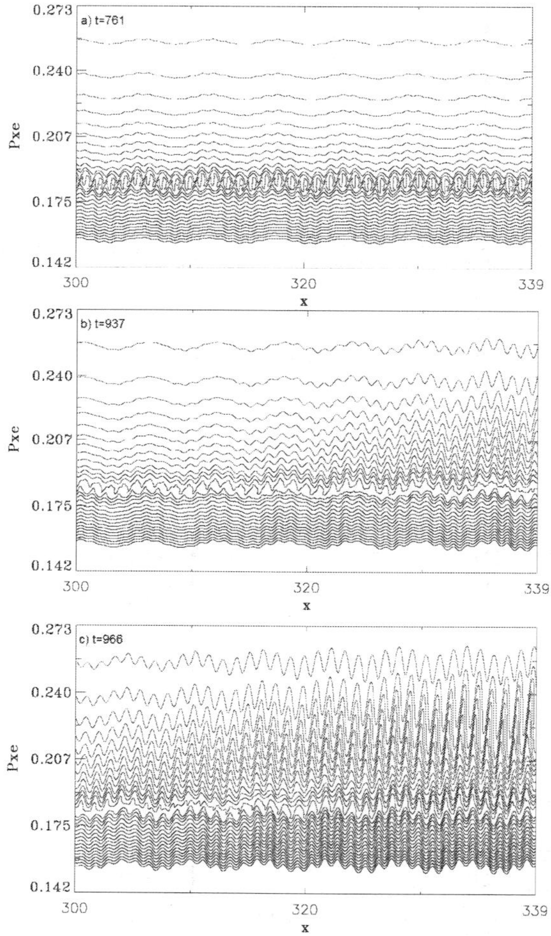

Figure 8. Contour plots of the distribution function for $x \in (300,339)$, at: a) t=761; b) t=937; c) t= 966.

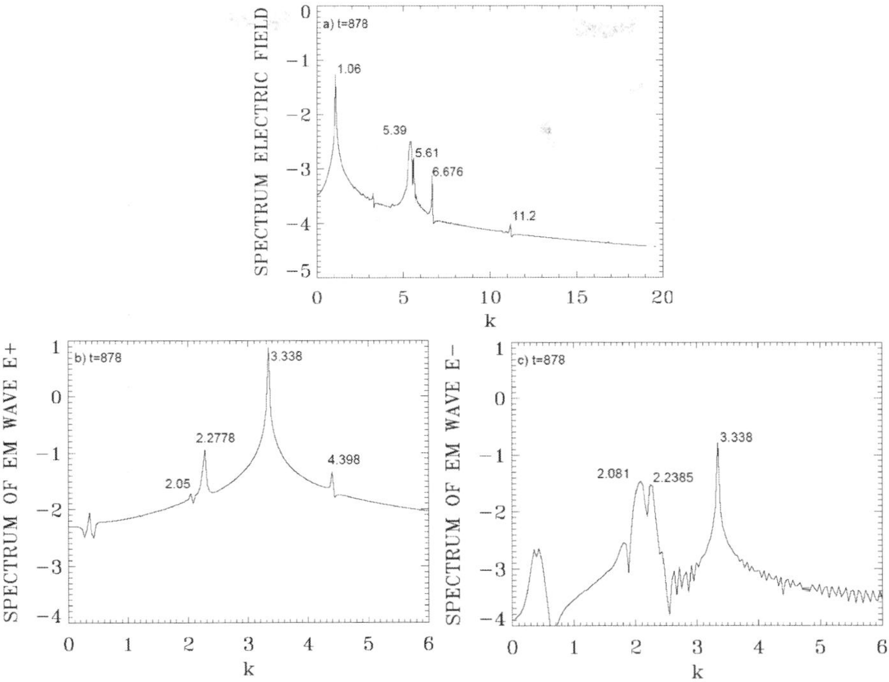

Figure 9. Spatial Fourier spectrum at the time t=878 in $x \in (250,410)$ for: a) the longitudinal plasma wave; b) the forward electromagnetic wave E^+; c) the backward electromagnetic wave E^-.

In Figure (11c) we present the wavenumber spectrum for the backward wave E^- at t= 1289, in the domain $x \in (250,410)$, which shows the now dominant backward mode at k_{sB}=2.042, and a trace of the pump wave at k_0=3.338, and of the anti-Stokes mode at 4.398. And in Figure (11b) we present the spectrum of the forward wave E^+ in the domain $x \in (250,410)$. We see the peak of the pump wave at k_0=3.338. We also see a peak at 2.042 which corresponds to the peak in Figure (11c). We have the peak of the forward scattered mode at k_{sF}=2.277, and the peak for the anti-Stokes k_{AS}=4.398. There is a small peak appearing at 8.718, which grew after the growth of the mode at k_{sB}=2.042 in Figure (11c). We can write 8.718= 10.8-2.042 (k_{sB}=2.042) or 8.718=6.676+2.042, which also happens to be at the harmonic of the anti-Stokes at 4.398. These results belong to the further evolution of the nonlinear stage which is beyond the scope of this work.

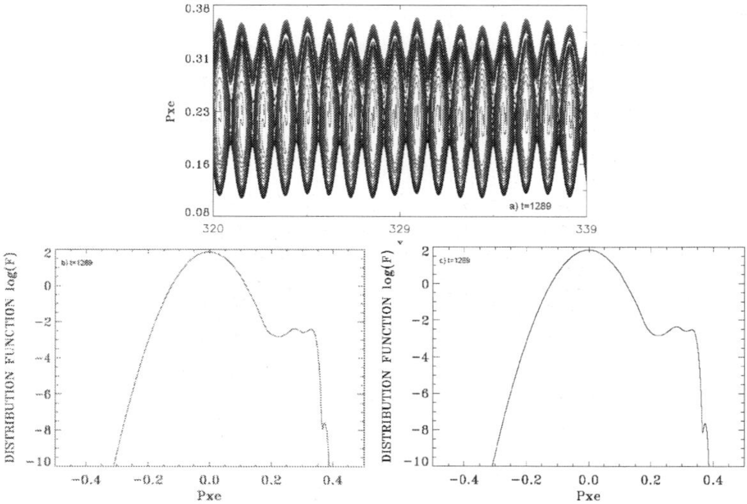

Figure 10. At t=1289: a) contour plot of the distribution function in the domain $x \in (320,339)$; b) averaged distribution function at x=320; c) averaged distribution function at x=329.

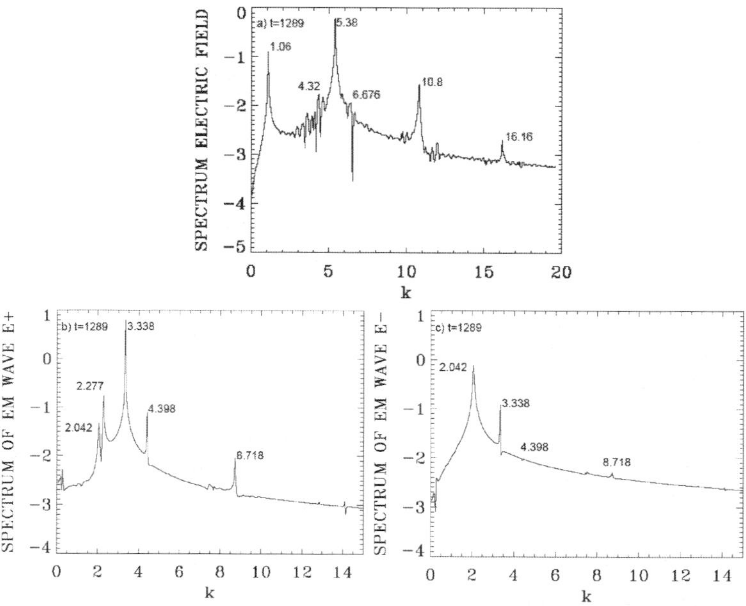

Figure 11. Spatial Fourier spectrum at the time t=1289 in $x \in (250,410)$ for: a) the longitudinal plasma wave; b) the forward electromagnetic wave E^+; c) the backward electromagnetic wave E^-.

We present in Figure (12) the frequency spectra between t_1=1132 and t_2=1292, at the position x=300. The dominant peak in Figure (12a) is now for the SRBS plasma wave at ω_{eB}=1.178. However, this peak is broad and includes peaks at 1.006 of the SRFS plasma wave ω_{eF} and the KEEN wave ω_{KEEN}. The other peaks are at 2.356, 3.534 (these peaks are very close to second and third harmonic of the now dominant SRBS plasma wave at ω_{eB}=1.178). We have also a peak at 4.55, and the peak at the harmonic of the pump at $2\omega_0$= 6.951. In Figure (12c) we see the now dominant backward mode at ω_{sB}=2.277, and the trace of the pump at 3.495 The trace of the anti-Stokes mode is negligible. In Figure (12b) we identify the pump wave in the forward direction at ω_0=3.495, and the trace of the backward wave at 2.277. The anti-Stokes peak at ω_{AS} =4.487 appears negligible. The broad spectrum at 2.277 in Figure (12b,c) would also include the SRFS peak at 2.474.

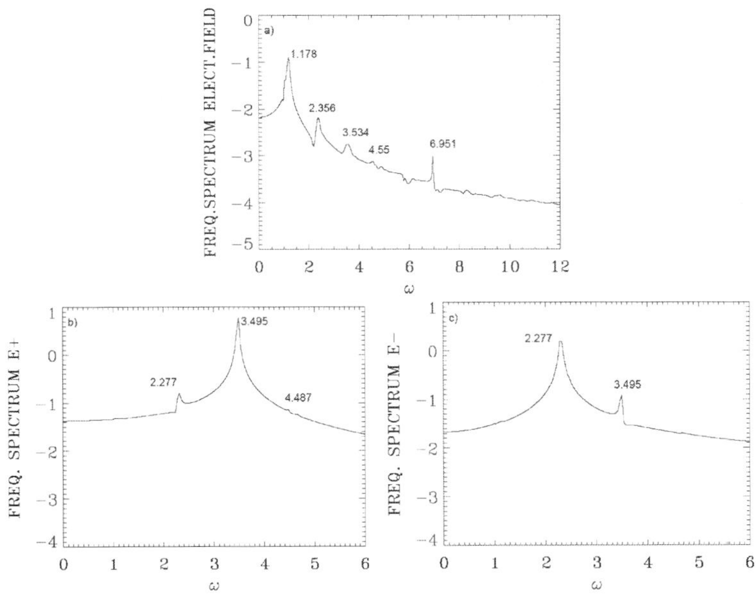

Figure 12. Frequency spectrum recorded at x=300, between t_1=1132 and t_2=1292 : a) longitudinal plasma wave; b) forward propagating wave E^+; c) backward propagating wave E^-

4.2. Evolution of the system around the center of the domain

We present in Figure (13) a plot of the longitudinal electric field at t=761 (at the time we present the spectrum in Figure (5), after about 39000 time steps). The maximum of the electric field in Figure (13) is between x=400 or x=500. We look in Figure (14) to the phase-space contour plot of the electron distribution function in $x \in (500,519)$. We see the small vortices of the KEEN wave similar to what has been presented and discussed in Figure (4) at the same time. However, Figure (14) shows the presence of the growing SRBS plasma wave absent from Figure (4). The reason is that at that time, the round-off errors in the region around x=400 or x=500 have reached a sufficiently high level to act as a perturbation, which stimulates the growth of the SRBS plasma wave, at the same time as the SKEENS we have identified and studied in section 4.1.

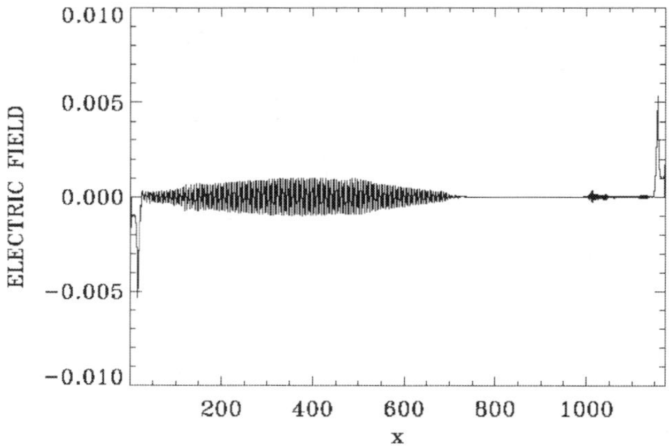

Figure 13. Plot of the longitudinal electric field at t=761.

In Figure (15) we present in the domain $x \in (380,619)$, at t=820, the phase-space contour plots of the electron distribution function. We note the rapid growth of the SRBS plasma wave, in addition to the SKEENS. We observe in Figures (15a,b) the same pattern as in Figures.(8a,b). In Figure (15a), we see the dominant modes excited are the SRFS plasma wave with $k_{eF} = 1.0645$ (wavelength $\lambda_{sF} = 5.9$), and the KEEN wave associated with the small vortices with $k_{KEEN} = 5.616$ (with a wavelength $\lambda_{eA} = 1.118$). These small vortices have a phase velocity υ_{KEEN} = $\omega_{KEEN} / k_{KEEN} = 0.18$, which corresponds to a momentum $p_{KEEN} = \upsilon_{KEEN} \Big/ \sqrt{1-\upsilon_{KEEN}^2} = 0.183$, as previously discussed for Figure (4,top left). Again these vortices are similar to what is presented in [18] for ponderomotively driven KEEN waves (see also [19-20]). Figure (15b) shows the SRBS plasma wave with $k_{eB} = 5.39$ propagating from right to left. If we follow the different frames in Figure (15), we see that the heavily damped SRBS plasma wave with $k_{eB} = 5.39$ seems to have been excited around $x = 500$, at a time and position where it is stimulated by the now substantial level reached by the round-off errors. From this position, the excited SRBS plasma wave will propagate to the left and to the right, as in Figure (15), excited by the round-off errors perturbation, which now are growing to the left and to the right around $x = 500$. It is this backward propagating plasma wave that we see appearing in the domain $x \in (300,339)$ in Figures (8b,c).

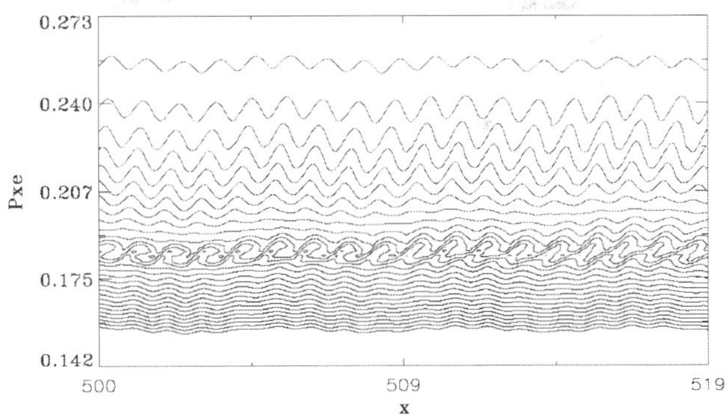

Figure 14. Phase-space contour plot of the electron distribution function in $x \in (500,519)$, at t=761.

So the pattern of excitation of the modes to the right of the domain, for instance in $x \in (460,619)$ in Figure (15) is now different from what has been observed to the left, in $x \in (380,520)$ in Figure (15) for instance or in Figure (4, top left). The wavenumber spectrum for the longitudinal electric field in the domain $x \in (400,560)$ at t=820, during the period of the growth, is given in Figure (16). It shows similar peaks as in Figure (5a), with the exception that now the SBRS plasma wave at k_{eB}=5.38 dominates with respect to the KEEN wave peak at 5.61, with its harmonics at 11.27 and 16.77. The wavenumber spectrum of the backward wave E^-, shows a peak of the backward scattered wave with k_{sB}=2.042, ($k_0 = -k_{sB} + k_{eB}$) much higher than the peak of the wave at 2.277 (compare with Figure (5c)). We also have peaks at 3.338 and 4.398, excited by the coupling with the modes with the same wavenumbers for the forward mode pump with k_0=3.338, and the small peak at 4.398 for the anti-Stokes wave (similar to what has been discussed for Figure(5)). The frequency spectra shows the frequencies of the growing modes, close to what we observe in Figures (6,7). A more complete description of the spectra is given in the end.

Figure (17) shows the longitudinal electric field profile at t=1289. We finally present in Figures (18,19) the wavenumber and frequency spectra at t=1289, at the end of the simulation, in the domain $x \in (400,560)$. Figure (18) should be compared to Figure (11). We still observe the modes previously discussed, the SRFS plasma wave at k_{eF} =1.06, the now dominant SRBS plasma wave at k_{eB}=5.39, the harmonic of the pump wave at $2\omega_0$ =6.676, and the harmonics of the now dominant SRBS plasma mode k_{eB} at 10.799 and 16.18. We also see sidebands developing, which is common when positive slopes of the distribution function are formed [33].

In Figure (18b,c) we present the wavenumber spectrum of the longitudinal electric field, the forward wave E^+ and the backward wave E^-, toward the end of the simulation at t= 1289, in

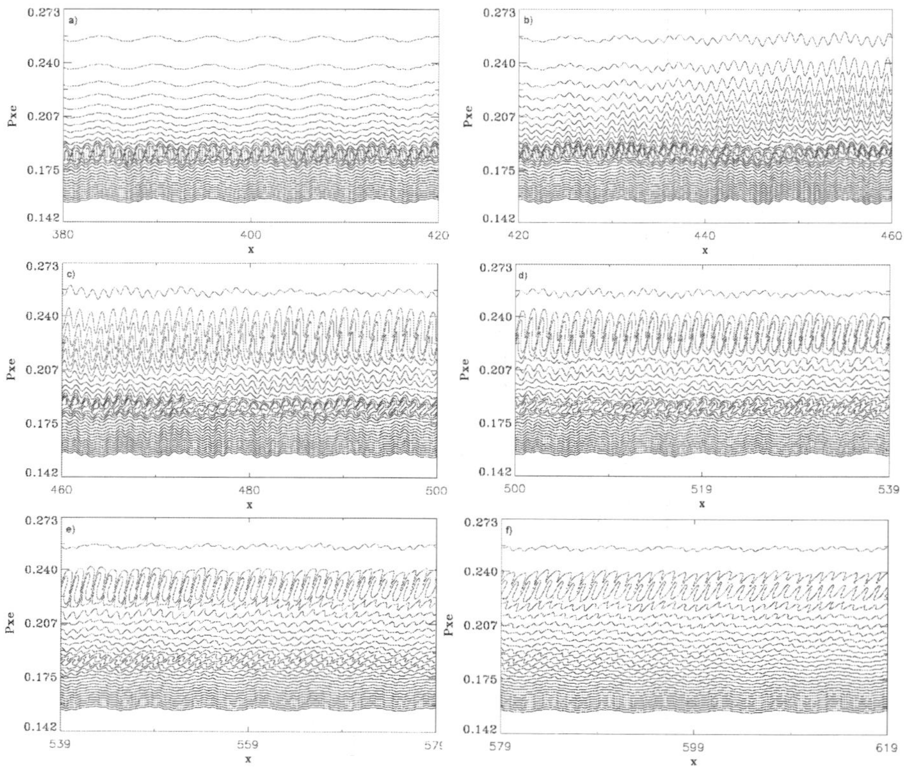

Figure 15. Phase-space contour plot of the electron distribution function in $x \in (380,619)$ at t=820.

the domain $x \in (400,560)$. We see in Figure (18c) for the wavenumber spectrum for the backward wave E^- the dominant backward mode at k_{sB}=2.042, and the trace of the pump wave at k_0=3.338. We see a small peak of the forward scattered mode at 2.277 which corresponds to the peak in Figure (18b). We also see in Figure (18b) the peak of the forward scattered mode at k_{sF} =2.277, the peak for the anti-Stokes k_{AS} =4.3985, and the peak of the pump at k_0=3.338. The small peak at 2.042 corresponds to the dominant backward mode at k_{sB}=2.042 in Figure (18c). There is a small peak at 8.718 which grew after the growth of the mode at k_{sB}=2.042 in Figure (18c). This mode can be the result of a forced oscillation. We can write 8.7= 10.76-2.042 (k_{sB}=2.042), which is a coupling with the harmonic of the SRBS plasma wave at $2k_{eB}$=10.78, or 8.718=6.676+2.042, which involves a coupling with $2k_0$=6.676 (the plasma wave excited at the harmonic of the pump). Note also that the mode at 8.718 is close to the harmonic of the anti-Stokes excited at 4.398.

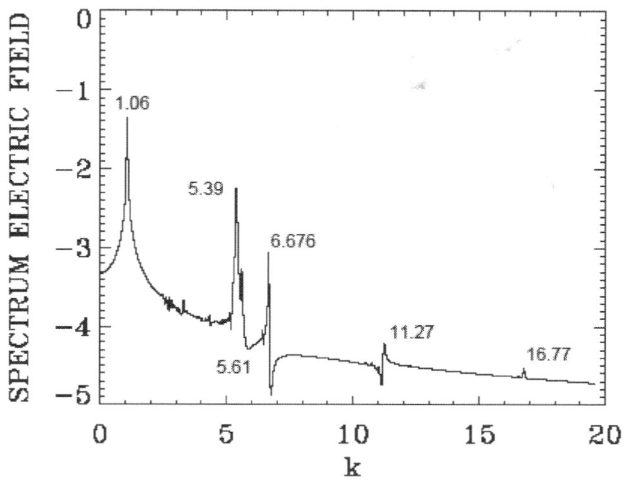

Figure 16. The wavenumber spectrum in the domain $x \in (400,560)$ at t=820, for the longitudinal electric field.

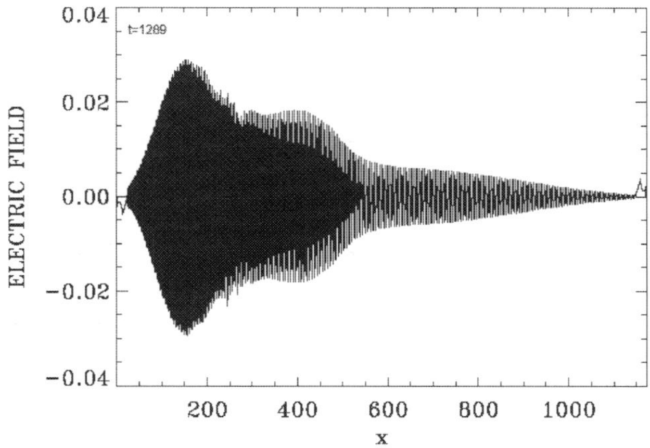

Figure 17. Longitudinal electric field profile at t=1289.

To identify the frequency spectra at the end of the simulation, we present in Figure (19) the frequency spectra between t_1=1113 and t_2=1273, at the position x=450. We identify in Fig. (19a) the local peak at ω_{eF}=1.0014 of the SRFS plasma wave (1.006 in our theoretical value). The dominant peak is for the SRBS plasma wave at ω_{eB}=1.178. The other peaks are at 0.1767, 2.18, and 2.356, 3.534, 4.732 (these last three very close to second, third harmonic and fourth harmonic of ω_{eB}=1.178). We have also a peak at the harmonic of the pump $2\omega_0$= 6.951. In Fig. (19c) we see the now dominant backward scattered mode at ω_{sB}=2.277, and the trace of the pump at 3.495. The trace of the anti-Stokes is negligible. In Figure (19b) we see the pump wave, dominant in the forward direction, at ω_0=3.495, and the trace of the backward wave at 2.277. We see also the forward scattered mode at 2.474. The anti-Stokes peak at ω_{AS}=4.487 appears negligible. In our normalized units (velocity normalized to the velocity of light) υ_T/c=0.06256 at T_e=2keV. With ω =0.176, we get k =2.169, very close to the peak at 2.14 in Figure (18a), which is close to the harmonic of 1.06 in Figure (18a).

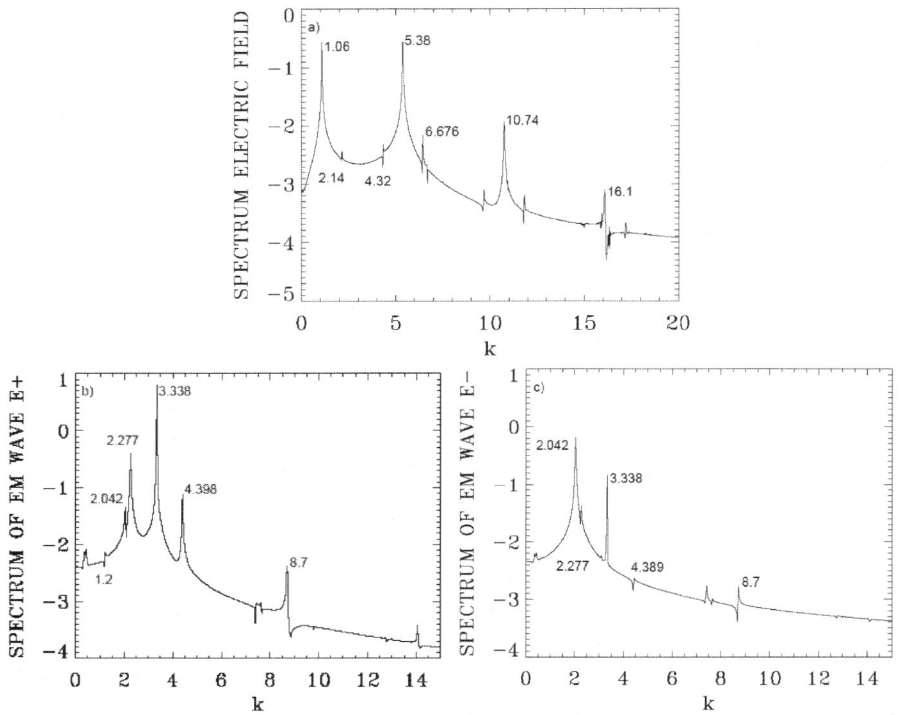

Figure 18. The wavenumber spectra in the domain $x \in (400,560)$ at t=1289, for: a) the longitudinal electric field; b) the forward propagating wave E^+; c) the backward propagating wave E^-.

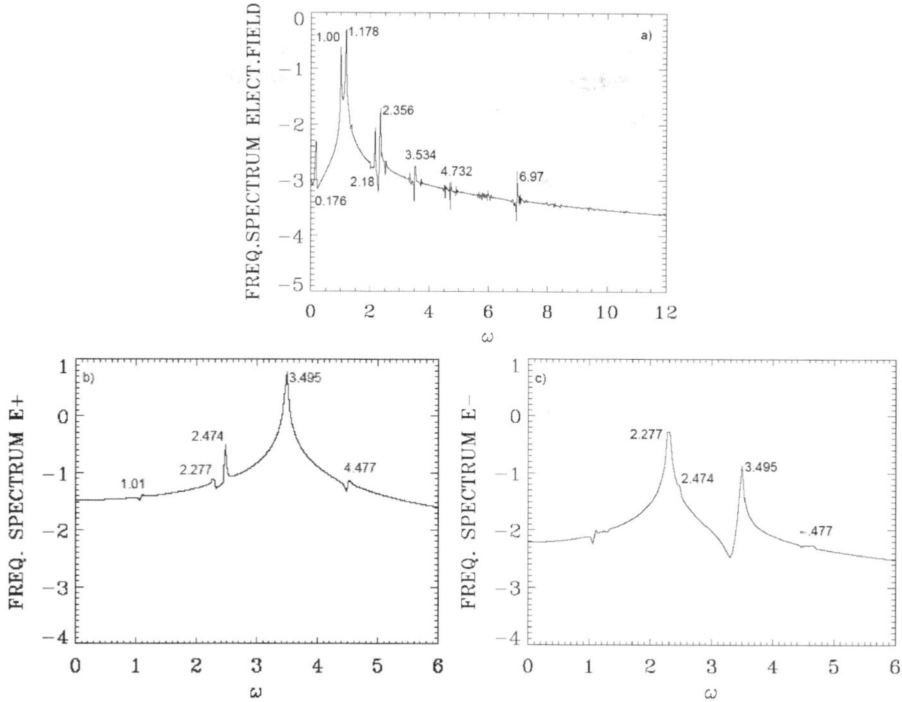

Figure 19. Frequency spectra recorded at the position x=450, between t_1=1113 and t_2=1273 for: a) the longitudinal electric field; b) the forward propagating wave E^+; c) the backward propagating wave E^-.

5. Conclusion

In laser fusion, the coupling and propagation of the laser beams in the plasma surrounding the pellet can be the scene of nonlinear processes such as parametric instabilities, which must be well understood and controlled to keep them at low levels, since they are detrimental to laser fusion because they can lead to losses of energy and illumination uniformity. Recent publications [22,23,34-40] have identified the need for a deeper understanding of laser-plasma interactions, and the importance of a kinetic treatment of the plasma, particularly in the regimes currently being approached by the new generation of lasers, and for the treatment of modes such as KEEN waves [18-20], even newer horizons are opened up. The old picture of EPWs and their evolution is now replaced by a much richer scenario of multiple harmonic waves transiently trapping, untrapping and retrapping paricle distributions that maintain the wave on average but without the need for flat distribution functions as in the canonical BGK mode setting of lore.

We showed for the first time in this study that a seemless transition occurs from Raman forward scatter, to the standing wave excited KEEN wave very near the backscattering plasma wave so that the distribution function is strongly modified by the KEEN wave before the EPW can be excited in SRBS. For the parameters we have investigated, the SRBS process is preceded by KEEN waves and then competes with SKEENS for supremacy and eventual merging. This rich physics was not observed when strong seeding of the backscattered wave prevented any detection of these intermediate processes.

The accurate representation and evolution of the particles distribution function provided by the Eulerian Vlasov code offers a powerful tool to study highly nonlinear nonstationary processes in high energy density plasmas. We have uncovered some distinctive features of KEEN waves participating in the Raman process, using a 1D Eulerian Vlasov-Maxwell code that relativistically evolves both ions and electrons. To avoid any interference from artificially distorted distribution functions or imposed linear wave seeding, we start the code from an initial Maxwellian distribution, and a very weak scattered light field standing wave pattern which is enough to trigger both SRFS and then SKEENS. The system evolves under the influence of a pump light wave which provides fluctuations from which SRBS eventually develops. We identify in the early phase of the Raman interaction a reflected light that matches the backscattering of the pump laser off a KEEN wave whose fundamental harmonic has the same wavelength as the forward scattered light, and its appearance precedes the growth and saturation of SRBS. The evolution of the system is however modified with the results presented in section 4.2, close to the center of the simulation domain. In this region, the round-off errors have reached a level where they act as a perturbation, leading to the simultaneous appearance and growth of the SRBS process, in addition to the KEEN wave (see Figure (14)). So we have two distinct evolution scenarios of Raman scattering in the domain we study. To the right of the region $x \in (500,519)$ in Figure (14), we see a simultaneous growth of the SRBS plasma wave and the KEEN wave (see Figure (15)). And to the left of the region $x \in (500,519)$, the growth of the round-off errors acting as a perturbation leads to the appearance of SRBS plasma waves moving to the left in the backward direction. This is where the KEEN wave has already reached saturation, causing heating and relative flattening of the electron distribution function, which shows a structure with a trapped population of electrons. Note the harmonic structure associated with the SRBS mode $\omega_{eB}=1.178$, $k_{eB}=5.38$ in Figures (11a,12a). Recent publications have pointed to the importance of 2D and 3D effects for a rigorous theory of SRS saturation [41]. This is beyond the scope of the present work. We have restricted our study to the initial phase of the evolution of Raman scattering, and we have shown that in this case scattering off a KEEN wave can produce a backward wave which contributes to the inflation of the Raman signal well before the SRBS starts growing on its own.

In future studies, we propose to investigate the physics of the interaction between SKEENS and SRBS, but eliminating the need for SRFS initiation. This can be achieved by driving the KEEN wave directly by the ponderomotive force generated by the beating of the pump and the appropriate seed electromagnetic wave. Driving KEEN waves directly and electromagnetically generalizes the work of Afeyan et al. [18-20] which has been based on the Vlasov-

Poisson system of equations. We expect to find interesting resonances, even with KEEN waves that have significantly lower phase velocities than the electron plasma waves. The work here showed the coevolution of SKEENS and SRBS for electrostatic waves whose phase velocities were so close that their vortical structures in phase-space directly overlapped and were eventually mixed.

Acknowledgements

The authors are grateful to the Centre de calcul scientifique de l'IREQ (CASIR) for computer time for the simulations presented in this work. BA would like to acknowledge the financial assistance of DOE OFES HEDP program through a subcontract via UCSD.

Author details

Magdi Shoucri[1] and Bedros Afeyan[2]

1 Institut de recherche Hydro-Québec (IREQ), Varennes, Québec, Canada

2 Polymath Research Inc., Pleasanton, CA, USA

References

[1] Atzeni S, Meyer-ter-Vehn J. The Physics of Inertial Fusion. Oxford; 2004.

[2] Kruer W L. The Physics of Laser Plasma Interactions. Westview; 2003.

[3] Afeyan B, Williams E A. Variational Approach to Parametric Instabilities in Inhomogeneous Plasmas I: Two Model Problems. Phys. Plasmas 1997; 4, 3788.

[4] Afeyan B, Williams E A. Variational Approach to Parametric Instabilities in Inhomogeneous Plasmas II: Stimulated Raman Scattering. Phys. Plasmas 1997; 4, 3803.

[5] Afeyan B, Williams E A. Variational Approach to Parametric Instabilities in Inhomogeneous Plasmas III: Two-Plasmon Decay. Phys. Plasmas 1997; 4, 3827.

[6] Afeyan B, Williams E.A. Variational Approach to Parametric Instabilities in Inhomogeneous Plasmas IV: The mixed polarization high-frequency instability. Phys. Plasmas 1997; 4, 3845.

[7] Kono M, Skoric M M. Nonlinear Physics of Plasmas. Springer; 2010

[8] Sagdeev R Z, Galeev A A. Nonlinear Plasma Theory. W. A. Benjamin; 1969

[9] Davidson D C. Methods of Nonlinear Plasma Theory. Academic Press; 1972

[10] Elskens Y, Escande D. Microscopic Dynamics of Plasmas and Chaos. IoP; 2003

[11] Shoucri M. Numerical Simulation of Intense Laser-Plasma Interaction using an Eulerian Vlasov Code. Proc. 34th EPS Conf. Plasma Phys., Warsaw. ECA Vol. 31F, P-2.007; 2007

[12] Shoucri M. Numerical Solution of Hyperbolic Differential Equations. New York: Nova Science Publishers; 2008

[13] Shoucri M. Numerical Simulation of Wake-Field Acceleration Using an Eulerian Vlasov Code. Commun. Comp. Phys. 2008; 4, 703-718

[14] Shoucri M. The application of the Method of Characteristics for the Numerical Solution of Hyperbolic Differential Equations. In: Numerical Simulation Research Progress. S.P. Colombo & C.L. Rizzo (Ed.). New York: Nova Science Publishers; 2009

[15] Shoucri M. Numerical Solution of the Relativistic Vlasov-Maxwell Equations for the Study of the interaction of a High Intensity Laser Beam Normally Incident on an Overdense Plasma. In: Eulerian Codes for the Numerical Solution of the Kinetic Equations of Plasmas. M. Shoucri (Ed.). New York: Nova Science Publishers; 2011

[16] Shoucri M. Ion Acceleration and Plasma JET Formation in the Interaction of an Intense Laser Beam Normally Incident on an Overdense Plasma: a Vlasov Code Simulation. Comp. Sci. Disc. 2012; 5, 014005/1-19

[17] Cordier S, Goudon Th, Gutnic M, Sonnendrucker E. Numerical Methods for Hyperbolic and Kinetic Problems. European Mathematical Society; 2005

[18] Afeyan B et al. Kinetic Electrostatic Electron Nonlinear (KEEN) Waves and their Interactions Driven by the Ponderomotive force of crossing laser beams. Proc. International Fusion Sciences and Applications. B Hammel, D Meyerhofer, J. Meyer-ter-Vehn, H Azechi (Eds.). American Nuclear Society, pp. 213. arXiv:1210.8105; 2004

[19] Afeyan B, Charbonneau-Lefort M, Won K, Savchenko V, Shoucri M. The Generation of Self-Organization of Ponderomotively Driven Kinetic Electrostatic Electron Nonlinear (KEEN) Waves in High Energy Density Plasmas. To be submitted to Phys. Rev. Lett. 2014

[20] Afeyan B, Dodhy A, Mehrenberger M., Sonnendrucker E. Long Time Evolution of KEEN Waves Excited with Low Levels Ponderomotive Drive. To be submitted to Phys. Rev. E 2014

[21] Strozzi D J, Shoucri M M, Bers A, Williams E A, Langdon A B. Vlasov Simulations of Trapping and Inhomogeneity in Raman Scattering. J. Plasma Phys. 2006; 72, 1299-1302

[22] Strozzi D J, Williams E A, Langdon A B, Bers A. Kinetic Enhancement of Raman Backscatter, and Electron Acoustic Thomson Scatter. Phys. Plasmas 2007; 14, 013104/1-13

[23] Strozzi D J, Williams E A, Langdon A B, Bers A, Brunner S. Eulerian-Lagrangian Kinetic Simulations of Laser-Plasma Interactions. In: Eulerian Codes for the Numerical Solution of the Kinetic Equations of Plasmas. M. Shoucri (Ed.). New York: Nova Science Publishers; 2010

[24] Yin L, Daughton W, Albright B J, Bezerrides B, DuBois D F, Kindel J M,Vu H X. Nonlinear Development of Stimulated Raman Scattering from Electrostatic Modes Excited by Self-Consistent non-Maxwellian Velocity Distribution. Phys. Rev. E 2006; 73, 025401/1-4

[25] Vu H X, Yin L, DuBois D F, Bezzerides B, Dodd E S. Nonlinear, Spectral Signatures and Spatiotemporal Behavior of Stimulated Raman Scattering from Single Laser Speckles. Phys. Rev. Lett. 2005; 95, 245003/1-4

[26] Montgomery D S, Focia R J, Rose H A, Russel D A, Cobble J A, Fernandez J C, Johnson R P, Phys. Rev. Lett. 2001; 87, 155001/1-4

[27] Montgomery D S, Cobble J A, Fernandez J C, Focia R J, Johnson R P, Renard-LeGalloudec R P, Rose H A, Russel D A. Phys. Plasmas 2002; 9, 2311

[28] Nikolic L, Skoric M M, Ishiguro S, Sato T. Phys. Rev. E 2002; 66, 036404

[29] Sircombe N J, Arber T D, Dendy R O. Aspects of Electron Acoustic Wave Physics in Laser Backscatter from Plasmas. Plasma Phys. Controlled Fusion 2006; 48, 1141-1153

[30] Shoucri M. Integration of the Vlasov Equation along Characteristics in One and Two Dimensions. Comp. Phys. Comm. 2003; 154, 65-75

[31] Pohn E, Shoucri M, Kamelander G. Eulerian Vlasov Codes. Comp. Phys. Comm. 2005; 166, 81-93

[32] Bers A, Shkarofsky I P, Shoucri M. Relativistic Landau Damping of Electron Plasma Waves in Stimulated Raman Scattering. Phys. Plasmas 2009; 16, 022104/1-6

[33] Shoucri M. The Sidebands Instability. J. Plasma Phys. 2006; 72, 861-864

[34] Brunner S, Valeo E J. Phys. Rev. Lett., 2004; 93, 145003/1-4

[35] Labaune C, Bandulet H, Depierreux S, Lewis K, Michel P, Michard A, Baldis H A, Hulin S, Pesme D, Hüller S, Tikhonchuk V, Riconda C, Weber S. Laser-Plasma Interaction Experiments in the Context of Inertial Fusion. Plasma Phys. Control. Fusion 2004; 46, B301-B312

[36] Vu H X, DuBois D F, Bezerrides B. Kinetic Inflation of Stimulated Raman Backscatter in Regimes of High Linear Landau Damping. Phys. Plasmas 2002; 9, 1745-1763

[37] Valentini F, O'Neil T M, Dubin D.H.E. Excitation of Nonlinear Electron Acoustic Waves. Phys. Plasmas 2006; 13, 052303/1-7

[38] Kline J L, Montgomery D S, Bezerrides B, Cobble J A, DuBois D F, Johnson R P, Rose H A, Yin L, Vu H X. Observation of a Transition from Fluid to Kinetic Nonlinearities for Langmuir Waves Driven by Stimulated Raman Backscatter. Phys. Rev. Lett. 2005; 94, 175003/1-4

[39] Bénisti D, Gremillet L. Nonlinear Plasma Response to a Slowly-Varying Electrostatic Wave, and Application to Stimulated Raman Scattering. Phys. Plasmas 2007; 14, 042304

[40] Rousseaux C, Baton S D, Bénisti D, Gremillet L, Adam J C, Héron A, Strozzi D J, Amiranoff F. Experimental Evidence of Predominantly Transverse Electron Plasma Waves Driven by Stimulated Raman Scattering of Picosecond Laser Pulses. Phys. Rev. Lett. 2009; 102, 185003/1-4

Tracking Mean Field Dynamics by Synchronous Computations of Recurrent Multilayer Perceptrons

Jiann-Ming Wu, Jung-Chao Ban and
Chun-Chang Wu

Additional information is available at the end of the chapter

http://dx.doi.org/10.5772/57217

1. Introduction

Mean field dynamics have been extensively applied for organizing neural networks in the field of computational neuroscience, since Hopfield pioneered collective decisions of interconnected processing elements for combinatorial optimization [1–6] and memory association [7, 8]. Both nonlinear transfer functions and synapses in a Hopfield neural network are a subsequence of mean field dynamics that characterize the mean configuration of a large scaled physical system at thermal equilibrium in the field of statistical mechanism. In the past decades, the mean field dynamics has been extensively applied for deriving interactive neural dynamics of solving complex tasks, such as combinatorial optimization [4, 6, 9], self-organization [10], clustering analysis [11][12], independent component analysis [13], and regression [14][15].

Mean field equations characterize feasible configurations for problem solving. Let $s_i \in \{-1, 1\}$ denote a binary random variable for modeling a stochastic two-alternative processing element and $\mathbf{s} = \{s_i\}_i$ represent a configuration for problem solving. The feasibility of **s** to the attacked problem is inversely quantified by an energy function $E(\mathbf{s})$. Minimizing $E(\mathbf{s})$ with respect to **s** means to seek the optimal solution. Under the Boltzmann assumption, the joint probability of all s_i is proportional to $exp(-\beta E(\mathbf{s}))$, where β denotes the inverse of a temperature-like parameter. As in previous works [4][5][6], the Kullback-Leibler divergence between the product of marginal probabilities and the joint probability of all s_i induces a tractable free energy function ψ that depends on the expectation of s_i, denoted by $\langle s_i \rangle$, for all i.

The following mean field dynamics exactly characterize the saddle point of a typical tractable free energy function,

$$u_i = -\frac{\partial E(\langle \mathbf{s} \rangle)}{\partial \langle s_i \rangle} \tag{1}$$

$$\langle s_i \rangle = f(u_i) \equiv \tanh(\beta u_i) \tag{2}$$

where u_i denotes an external field, $f \equiv \tanh$ is a sigmoid-like transfer function and $\langle s_i \rangle$ denotes the mean activation. In previous works [4][6], E is quadratic and u_i measures a weight sum of activations other than $\langle s_i \rangle$, such as

$$u_i = \sum_{j \neq i} w_{ij} \left\langle s_j \right\rangle + c_i \tag{3}$$

where w_{ij} denotes the synapse that connects neural processing elements i and j. For fixed β, equation (2) defines the transfer function of interconnected processing elements and equation (3) sketches synapses. The realized information processes are distributed and with computational features of fault tolerance and collective decision. All interconnected processing elements in a Hopfield neural network asynchronously operate to seek a stable configuration under an annealing process [6] that carefully scheduling β from sufficiently small to large values.

At each intermediate β, a stable configuration means a result of minimizing the mean energy function against maximizing the entropy for emulating thermal equilibrium of statistical mechanism. At the end of the annealing process, by equation (2), $\langle s_i \rangle \in \{-1, 1\}$ and the mean configuration $\langle \mathbf{s} \rangle$ is a vector of N binary values, well representing a feasible solution for problem solving. Empirical results in previous works [4][6] have extensively shown that the physical-like annealing process guarantees effectiveness and reliability of seeking the global or near global minimum of $E(\mathbf{s})$ for problem solving. In previous works [15–18], mean field dynamics have been extended for multi-state Potts modeling and applied for unsupervised learning and supervised learning of neural networks toward solving self organization, independent component analysis, function approximation and discriminate analysis.

However from the perspective of numerical simulations, asynchronous operation of interconnected processing elements means one-by-one sequential updating of neural variables. It is more efficient to simulate synchronous and parallel updating of neural variables by vector codes. Multilayer perceptrons or Adalines have been organized for parallel and synchronous processes. Significant computational features include synchronous data transmission and parallel signal processes through multilayer perceptrons. A network of multilayer perceptrons is typically composed of input, hidden, output layers as well as inter-connections among consecutive layers. The input $\mathbf{x} \in R^d$ transmits through interconnections to form external fields,

$$h = A\mathbf{x} + \mathbf{c}, \tag{4}$$

and the nonlinear transfer function translates h to activations of hidden units,

$$\mathbf{v} = F(h) = [f(h_1), ..., f(h_M)]^T, \tag{5}$$

which is multiplied by a matrix of posterior weights, denoted by R, to form the network output

$$\mathbf{y} = R\mathbf{v} \tag{6}$$

http://dx.doi.org/10.5772/57217

Equations (4)-(6) describe synchronous data transmissions and parallel signal processes, by which it only takes three time clocks to translate $\mathbf{x}$ to $\mathbf{y}$.

A recurrent network of multilayer perceptrons is further equipped with circular connections from the output to input layers. By feedback circular connections, the current output becomes the network input at the upcoming time step. Let R be an identity matrix. Setting $\mathbf{x}$ to $\mathbf{y}_n$ and $\mathbf{y}$ to $\mathbf{y}_{n+1}$ leads to the following recursive function realized by recurrent multilayer perceptrons

$$\mathbf{y}_{n+1} = F(A\mathbf{y}_n) \tag{7}$$

Since perceptrons and adalines perform post-nonlinear projection, the organized multilayer neural network realizes a high dimensional nonlinear mapping from the input domain to the output range, which has been shown significant for solving complex tasks against traditional linear systems. Recurrent multilayer perceptrons perform parallel and synchronous computations for realizing the behavior of MIMO (multiple input multiple output recurrent relation or characterizing nonlinear autoregression of time series. Recurrent multilayer perceptrons have been applied for nonlinear autoregressive modeling of chaotic time series prediction [19] and financial time series [20].

This work applies recurrent multilayer perceptrons for tracking mean field dynamics by synchronous and parallel computations. A systematic approach is proposed for translating mean field dynamics (1) and (2) to the nonlinear recursive function (7) such that recurrent multilayer perceptrons can track the saddle point of ψ by parallel and synchronous computations. The strategy is to introduce time delays and auxiliary variables for expanding local memories of storing individual states, and translate loosely coupled or densely coupled first order mean field equations to a system of post-nonlinear recursive functions, which can be evaluated directly by iterative synchronous computations of recurrent multilayer perceptrons.

Section 2 applies parallel and synchronous computations of recurrent multilayer perceptrons for tracking mean field dynamics. Asynchronous updating of tracking linear dynamics and mean field dynamics is translated to equivalent synchronous updating. Section 3 applies the transformation to derive synchronous updating of tracking mean field dynamics for solving graph bisection problem and verifies the proposed approach by numerical simulations. Section 4 further presents a hybrid of asynchronous and synchronous processes for tracking sparse large scaled mean field dynamics of sparse connectivity for problem solving.

2. Synchronous computation of tracking mean field dynamics

By asynchronous updating at each time step numerical simulations select one processing element and refine its mean activation under fixed mean activations of the others. Let $\psi_i(\langle s_i \rangle)$ denote ψ with fixed $\left\langle s_j \right\rangle, j \neq i$,

$$\psi_i(\langle s_i \rangle) = h_i \langle s_i \rangle + c_i - \left[\frac{1+\langle s_i \rangle}{2} \log \frac{1+\langle s_i \rangle}{2} + \frac{1-\langle s_i \rangle}{2} \log \frac{1-\langle s_i \rangle}{2} \right], \tag{8}$$

where $\beta = 1$ is considered. $\langle s_i \rangle = \tanh(h_i)$ minimizes the above equation. $\psi_i(\langle s_i \rangle)$ is an approximation to the one-dimensional function obtained by cutting functional surface of ψ along the direction of $\langle s_i \rangle$ for fixed $\left\langle s_j \right\rangle, j \neq i$. By asynchronous updating the coefficient h_i of the linear term in equation (8) always maintains an instance determined by fixing most recently updated mean activations. Asynchronous updating is represented by

$$\langle s_i \rangle \leftarrow f\left(\sum_{j \neq i} w_{ij} \left\langle s_j \right\rangle + c_i\right). \tag{9}$$

The asynchronous cutting and approximating strategy is very different from synchronous updating that directly combines equations (2) and (3) for all i, such as

$$\langle s \rangle \leftarrow \tanh(W \langle s \rangle) + c \tag{10}$$

where W collects all w_{ij}. By synchronous updating, all h_i use the copy formed by all mean activations synchronously determined at the previous step. Numerical simulations have verified synchronous updating based on equation (10) infeasible for relaxing of mean field dynamics.

2.1. Linear system

Let f be a linear function and the asynchronous updating rule (9) is equivalent to

$$x_i \leftarrow \sum_{j \neq i} a_{ij} x_j + c_i \tag{11}$$

where $A = [a_{ij}]$ is a $N \times N$ matrix with $a_{ii} = 0$, $\forall i = 1, \cdots, N$. To facilitate our presentation, we first give an example with $N = 4$ for illustration. Figure 1 shows data flow of asynchronous updating (11), where directed edges indicate the latest mean activations employed for updating. Each time asynchronous updating insists on revising only one mean activation. Without losing generality, consecutive steps of updating mean activations can be listed as follows,

$$\begin{aligned}
x_1[k+1] &= 0 + a_{12}x_2[k] + a_{13}x_3[k] + a_{14}x_4[k] + c_1 \\
x_2[k+2] &= a_{21}x_1[k+1] + 0 + a_{23}x_3[k] + a_{24}x_4[k] + c_2 \\
x_3[k+3] &= a_{31}x_1[k+1] + a_{32}x_2[k+2] + 0 + a_{34}x_4[k] + c_3 \\
x_4[k+4] &= a_{41}x_1[k+1] + a_{42}x_2[k+2] + a_{43}x_3[k+3] + 0 + c_4
\end{aligned} \tag{12}$$

The system (12) is translated to synchronous updating by replacing k with $k-1$, $k-2$, $k-3$ and $k-4$ respectively in the four rows of equation (13)

$$\begin{aligned}
x_1[k] &= 0 + a_{12}x_2[k-1] + a_{13}x_3[k-1] + a_{14}x_4[k-1] + c_1 \\
x_2[k] &= a_{21}x_1[k-1] + 0 + a_{23}x_3[k-2] + a_{24}x_4[k-2] + c_2 \\
x_3[k] &= a_{31}x_1[k-2] + a_{32}x_2[k-1] + 0 + a_{34}x_4[k-3] + c_3 \\
x_4[k] &= a_{41}x_1[k-3] + a_{42}x_2[k-2] + a_{43}x_3[k-1] + 0 + c_4
\end{aligned} \tag{13}$$

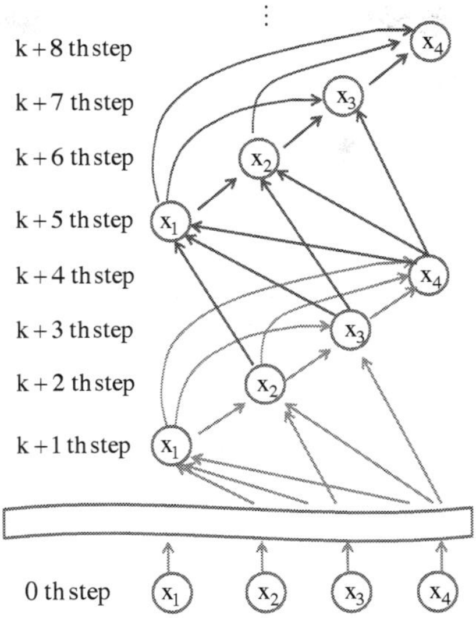

Figure 1. Asynchronous update.

for $k \geq 3$. The matrix form is expressed by

$$\mathbf{x}[k] = B\mathbf{u}[k] + \mathbf{c} \tag{14}$$

where $\mathbf{x}[k] = (x_1[k], \cdots, x_4[k])^T$ and

$$\mathbf{u}[k] = \begin{pmatrix} \mathbf{x}[k-1] \\ \mathbf{x}[k-2] \\ \mathbf{x}[k-3] \end{pmatrix},$$

T denotes transpose and

$$B = \left[\begin{array}{cccc|cccc|cccc} 0 & a_{12} & a_{13} & a_{14} & 0 & 0 & 0 & 0 & 0 & 0 & 0 & 0 \\ a_{21} & 0 & 0 & 0 & 0 & 0 & a_{23} & a_{24} & 0 & 0 & 0 & 0 \\ 0 & a_{32} & 0 & 0 & a_{31} & 0 & 0 & 0 & 0 & 0 & 0 & a_{34} \\ 0 & 0 & a_{42} & 0 & 0 & a_{42} & 0 & 0 & a_{41} & 0 & 0 & 0 \end{array}\right]$$

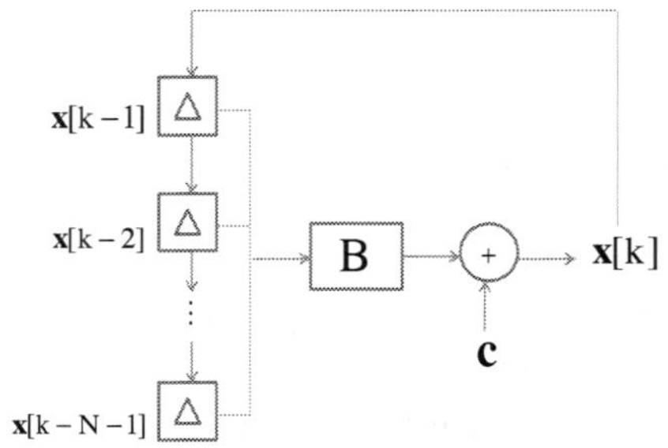

Figure 2. A linear recurrent system for synchronous computations. The triangle denotes time delay.

For initialization, $\mathbf{x}[0]$ is copied three times to form $\mathbf{u}[N]$ where $N = 4$. Figure 2 shows a recurrent linear network for synchronous computations of equation (14). The circular connection transmits the current output to the input layer at the upcoming step. In general, $\mathbf{u}[k]$ is given by

$$\mathbf{u}[k] = \begin{pmatrix} \mathbf{x}[k-1] \\ \mathbf{x}[k-2] \\ \vdots \\ \mathbf{x}[k-N+1] \end{pmatrix}$$

which concatenates $N-1$ consecutive steps of mean activations and $B = [B_1 B_2 \cdots B_{N-1}]$ is composed of $N-1$ submatrices. Figure 3 and 4 show the structure of matrices $\{B_n\}_{n=1}^{N-1}$. Distinct colors represent nonzero entries. Figure 5 shows the flow chart of creating matrix B. Figure 6 shows the flow chart of simulating asynchronous updating by linear recurrent computations where repmat is a matlab bulit-in function for matrix replication.

2.2. Mean field dynamics

Asynchronous updating (11) can be regarded as a special case of asynchronous updating (9) of mean field dynamics. Let f denote a post-nonlinear function and $v_i = \langle s_i \rangle$ for general situations. Synchronous parallel updating is explored for emulating asynchronous updating (9) for tracking mean field dynamics.

Asynchronous updating rule is rewritten as follows,

$$v_i \leftarrow f\left(\beta\left[\sum_{j\neq i} w_{ij} v_j + c_i\right]\right) \equiv g(v_1, \cdots, v_N, c_i)$$

http://dx.doi.org/10.5772/57217

$$B_1 = \begin{bmatrix} 0 & a_{12} & a_{13} & a_{14} & a_{15} & a_{16} & a_{17} & a_{18} \\ a_{21} & 0 & 0 & 0 & 0 & 0 & 0 & 0 \\ 0 & a_{32} & 0 & 0 & 0 & 0 & 0 & 0 \\ 0 & 0 & a_{43} & 0 & 0 & 0 & 0 & 0 \\ 0 & 0 & 0 & a_{54} & 0 & 0 & 0 & 0 \\ 0 & 0 & 0 & 0 & a_{65} & 0 & 0 & 0 \\ 0 & 0 & 0 & 0 & 0 & a_{76} & 0 & 0 \\ 0 & 0 & 0 & 0 & 0 & 0 & a_{87} & 0 \end{bmatrix} \quad B_3 = \begin{bmatrix} 0 & 0 & 0 & 0 & 0 & 0 & 0 & 0 \\ 0 & 0 & 0 & 0 & 0 & 0 & 0 & 0 \\ 0 & 0 & 0 & a_{34} & a_{35} & a_{36} & a_{37} & a_{38} \\ a_{41} & 0 & 0 & 0 & 0 & 0 & 0 & 0 \\ 0 & a_{52} & 0 & 0 & 0 & 0 & 0 & 0 \\ 0 & 0 & a_{63} & 0 & 0 & 0 & 0 & 0 \\ 0 & 0 & 0 & a_{74} & 0 & 0 & 0 & 0 \\ 0 & 0 & 0 & 0 & a_{85} & 0 & 0 & 0 \end{bmatrix}$$

$$\vdots$$

$$B_2 = \begin{bmatrix} 0 & 0 & 0 & 0 & 0 & 0 & 0 & 0 \\ 0 & 0 & a_{23} & a_{24} & a_{25} & a_{26} & a_{27} & a_{28} \\ a_{31} & 0 & 0 & 0 & 0 & 0 & 0 & 0 \\ 0 & a_{42} & 0 & 0 & 0 & 0 & 0 & 0 \\ 0 & 0 & a_{53} & 0 & 0 & 0 & 0 & 0 \\ 0 & 0 & 0 & a_{64} & 0 & 0 & 0 & 0 \\ 0 & 0 & 0 & 0 & a_{75} & 0 & 0 & 0 \\ 0 & 0 & 0 & 0 & 0 & a_{86} & 0 & 0 \end{bmatrix} \quad B_7 = \begin{bmatrix} 0 & 0 & 0 & 0 & 0 & 0 & 0 & 0 \\ 0 & 0 & 0 & 0 & 0 & 0 & 0 & 0 \\ 0 & 0 & 0 & 0 & 0 & 0 & 0 & 0 \\ 0 & 0 & 0 & 0 & 0 & 0 & 0 & 0 \\ 0 & 0 & 0 & 0 & 0 & 0 & 0 & 0 \\ 0 & 0 & 0 & 0 & 0 & 0 & 0 & 0 \\ 0 & 0 & 0 & 0 & 0 & 0 & 0 & a_{78} \\ a_{81} & 0 & 0 & 0 & 0 & 0 & 0 & 0 \end{bmatrix}$$

Figure 3. The representation of matrix $\{B_k\}_{k=1}^{7}$ for $N = 8$.

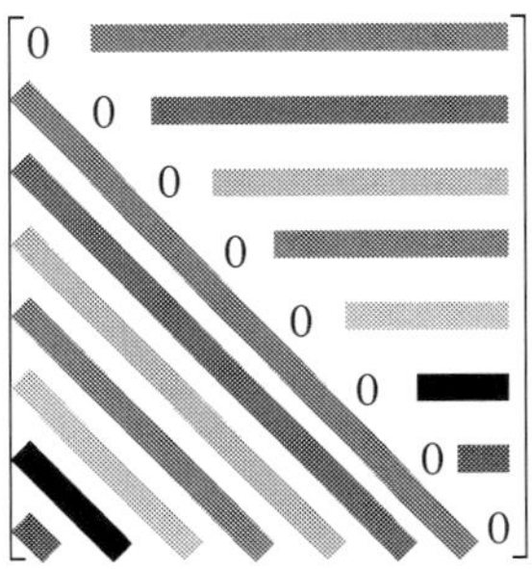

Figure 4. A diagram for illustrating the structure of $\{B_k\}_{k=1}^{7}$.

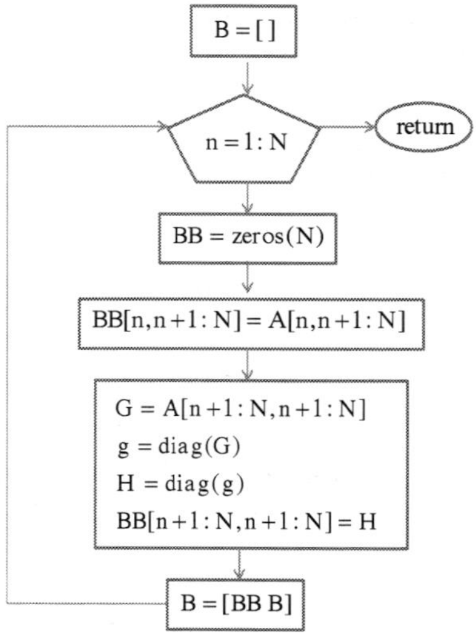

Figure 5. The flow chart of forming B.

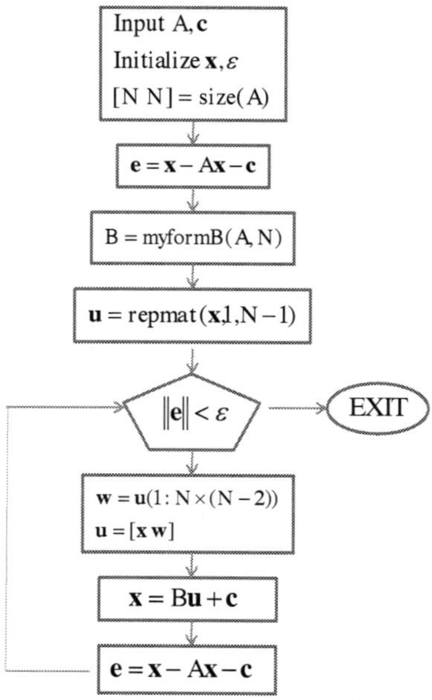

Figure 6. The flow chart of solving linear system by synchronous parallel computations.

http://dx.doi.org/10.5772/57217

where $v_i = \langle s_i \rangle$. Let $\mathbf{v}[0] = (v_1[0], v_2[0], \cdots, v_N[0])$ denote the initial mean configuration. The leave-one-out asynchronous updating is expressed as

$$\begin{aligned}
v_1[k+1] &= g(v_2[k], v_3[k], v_4[k], \cdots, v_N[k], c_1) \\
v_2[k+2] &= g(v_1[k+1], v_3[k], v_4[k], \cdots, v_N[k], c_2) \\
v_3[k+3] &= g(v_1[k+1], v[k+2], v_4[k], \cdots, v_N[k], c_3) \\
&\vdots \\
v_n[k+n] &= g(v_1[k+1], v_2[k+2], \cdots, v_{n-1}[k+n-1], v_{n+1}[k], \cdots, v_N[k], c_n \\
&\vdots \\
v_N[k+N] &= g(v_1[k+1], v_2[k+2], v_3[k+3], \cdots, v_{N-1}[k+N-1], c_N)
\end{aligned} \tag{15}$$

where $v_i[k]$ is the instance of v_i at the kth step for $k \geq 0$ and c_i is a constant. The mean activation of each processing element is asynchronously updated. The system (15) is translated to synchronous updating by replacing index $k+n$ with k in the row of updating v_n

$$\begin{aligned}
v_1[k] &= g(v_2[k-1], v_3[k-1], v_4[k-1], \cdots, v_N[k-1], c_1) \\
v_2[k] &= g(v_1[k-1], v_3[k-2], v_4[k-2], \cdots, v_N[k-2], c_2) \\
v_3[k] &= g(v_1[k-2], v_2[k-1], v_4[k-3], \cdots, v_N[k-3], c_3) \\
&\vdots \\
v_n[k] &= g(v_1[k-n+1], v_2[k-n+2], \cdots, v_{n-1}[k-1], v_{n+1}[k-n], \cdots, v_N[k-n], c_n) \\
&\vdots \\
v_N[k] &= g(v_1[k-N+1], v_2[k-N+2], v_3[k-N+3], \cdots, v_{N-1}[k-1], c_N)
\end{aligned} \tag{16}$$

where $k \geq N$.

The matrix B can be determined by the flow chart in figure 5 for translating mean field dynamics to the following form

$$\mathbf{v}[k] = \tanh(\beta B \mathbf{u}[k]) \tag{17}$$

where

$$\mathbf{u}[k] = \begin{pmatrix} \mathbf{v}[k-1] \\ \mathbf{v}[k-2] \\ \vdots \\ \mathbf{v}[k-N+1] \end{pmatrix}$$

and

$$\mathbf{v}[k] = (v_1[k], v_2[k], \cdots, v_N[k])^T$$

denotes the mean configuration at the kth step.

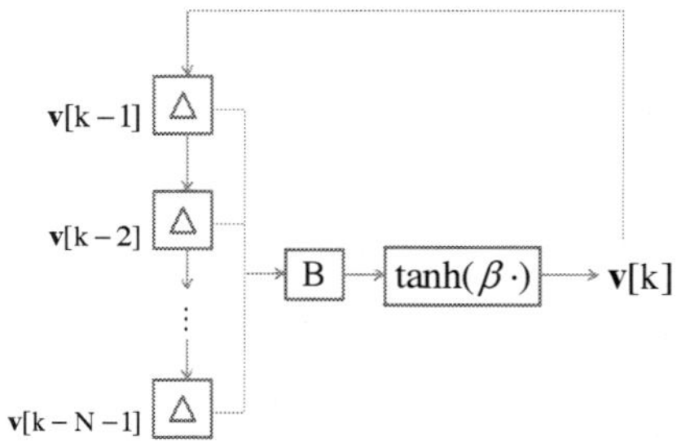

Figure 7. Nonlinear recurrent multilayer perceptrons.

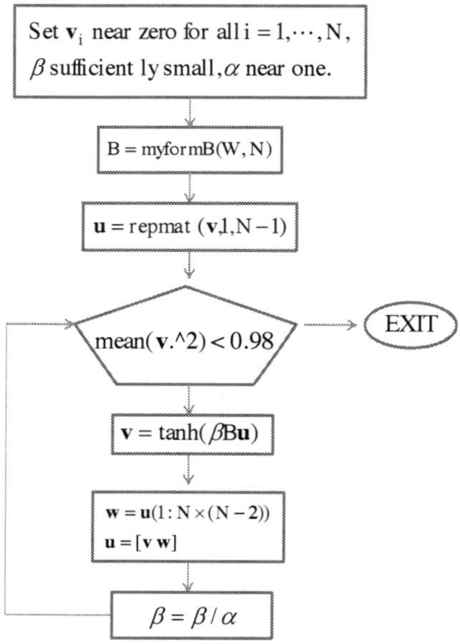

Figure 8. The flow chart of synchronous evolutionary simulations of mean field dynamics.

The structure of MIMO recurrent multilayer perceptrons is shown in Figure 7. The derived recurrent multilayer perceptrons track mean field dynamics by parallel and synchronous computations. As in the previous work [6], an annealing process is employed to schedule β from sufficiently small to large values for problem solving. Figure 8 shows the flow chart of simulating synchronous and parallel computations of recurrent multilayer perceptrons for tracking mean field dynamics.

http://dx.doi.org/10.5772/57217

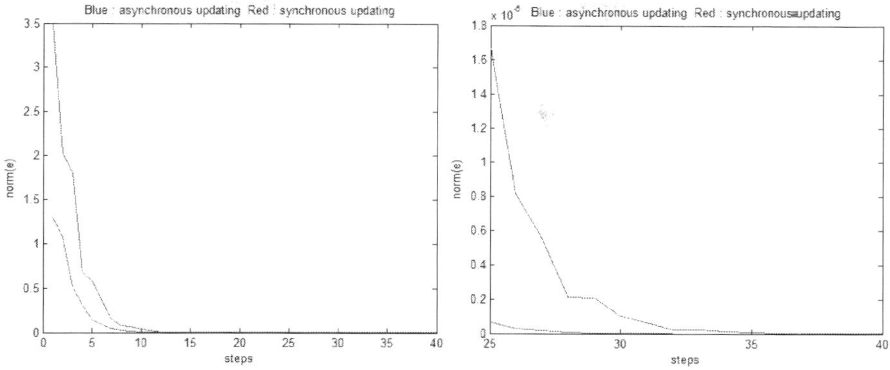

(a) (b)

Figure 9. Errors of asynchronous update and asynchronous update along time steps.

3. Numerical simulation

3.1. Solving linear systems

The linear recurrent relation (14) is verified by numerical simulations for solving the following linear system,

$$\begin{array}{rcrcrcrcrcr} x_1 &=& 0 &+& \frac{1}{10}x_2 &-& \frac{1}{5}x_3 &+& 0x_4 &+& \frac{3}{5} \\ x_2 &=& \frac{1}{11}x_1 &+& 0 &+& \frac{1}{11}x_3 &-& \frac{3}{11}x_4 &+& \frac{25}{11} \\ x_3 &=& -\frac{1}{5}x_1 &+& \frac{1}{10}x_2 &+& 0 &-& \frac{1}{10}x_4 &-& \frac{11}{10} \\ x_4 &=& 0 &-& -\frac{3}{8}x_2 &+& \frac{1}{8}x_3 &+& 0 &+& \frac{15}{8} \end{array}$$

The flow charts in figures 5 and 6 are implemented in Matlab codes. The initial value $\mathbf{x}[0] = [x_1[0], x_2[0], x_3[0], x_4[0]]$ is sampled from the hypercube $[-1,1]^4$ uniformly. The experiment simultaneously simulates asynchronous updating (11) and synchronous updating (14) of linear recurrence. Both asynchronous updating and synchronous updating attain the numerical solution $[1.0404, 1.991, -1.2067, 0.9775]^T$. Figure 9(a) shows errors of asynchronous updating and synchronous updating along time steps and (b) shows errors after the 25th step. The numerical results show the error of asynchronous updating coverages slower than that of synchronous updating. This illustrates the advantage of synchronous updating. When parallel computations like vector codes are employed, synchronous updating is more efficient than asynchronous updating for numerical simulations.

3.2. Graph bisection problem

The graph bisection problem [4] is stated to partition N nodes into two equal sets such that net edges crossing two sets in size is minimized. Let $s_i \in \{-1, 1\}$ denote the membership of the ith node to two non-overlapping sets and T_{ij} denote the connectivity, where

$$T_{ij} = \begin{cases} 1, \text{ if nodes } i \text{ and } j \text{ are connected} \\ 0, \text{ otherwise} \end{cases}$$

s_i denotes the partition of node i to two disjoint subsets. Node i is in one subset if $s_i = 1$ and belongs to the other if $s_i = -1$. As in [4], $E(\mathbf{s})$ for problem solving is given by ,

$$E(\mathbf{s}) = -\frac{1}{2}\sum_{i=1}^{N}\sum_{j \neq i}^{N} T_{ij}s_i s_j + \frac{a}{2}\left(\sum_{i=1}^{N} s_i\right)^2 \tag{18}$$

where a is the Lagrange multiplier which forces $\sum_{i=1}^{N} s_i$ to zero. $T_{ij}s_is_j$ is zero if T_{ij} =0. Otherwise, it is 1 if nodes i and j belong the same subset and -1 if node i belongs to one set and node j to the other. Therefore, the first term quantifies the number of net edges crossing two subsets. The last forces equal cut. As in Appendix A, $E(s)$ can be rewritten as

$$E(s) = -\frac{1}{2}\sum_{i=1}^{N}\sum_{j \neq i}^{N} W_{ij}s_i s_j \tag{19}$$

where $W_{ij} = T_{ij} - A$ and $W_{ii} = 0$.

We further explore the performances of synchronous updating by annealed recurrent multilayer perceptrons for graph bisection. In our simulations, each connection T_{ij} between nodes i and j is set to one if a uniform random number within $(0, 1)$ less than 0.2 is generated, and zero otherwise. The parameter a is 2. The halting condition is set to $\chi(\mathbf{v}) > 0.99$ where

$$\chi(\mathbf{v}) = \frac{1}{N}\sum_{i=1}^{N} v_i^2.$$

The temperature-like parameter β is always scheduled from sufficiently low to high values.

Figure 10 shows the convergence of annealed asynchronous updating (9) and annealed synchronous updating (17) for tracking mean field dynamics of solving a 100-nodes graph bisection problem, where the blue and red curves respectively show the change of the stability and $1/\beta$ along time steps. Figure 11 shows the change of cutsize and free energy by blue and red curve, respectively. The histograms of cutsize obtained by 50 executions of annealed asynchronous updating and annealed synchronous updating are plotted in Figure 12, where the mean of cutsize by annealed synchronous updating is 361.84, which is compatible to 358.5 of annealed asynchronous updating.

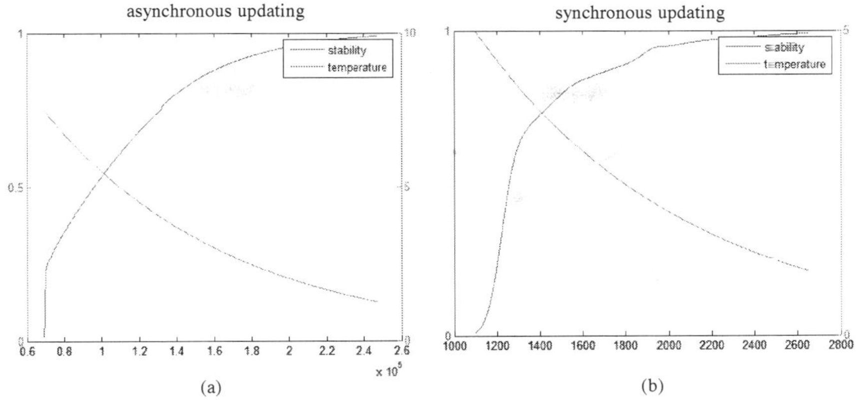

Figure 10. The change of the stability and $1/\beta$ for solving graph bisection problem by synchronous update and asynchronous update.

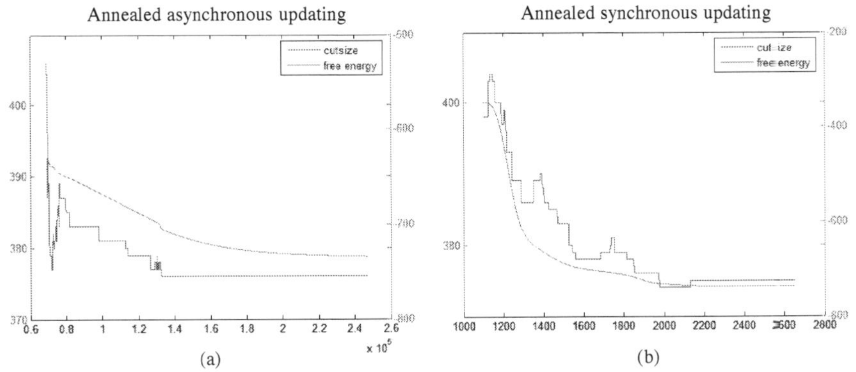

Figure 11. The change of cutsize and free energy for solving graph bisection problem by synchronous update and asynchronous update.

4. Parallel and distributed processes of tracking mean field dynamics of sparse connectivity

This section discusses the case of sparse interconnection among processing units. In the case, a processing connects only with processing units in a small neighborhood. Sparsely interconnected processing units are partitioned to K clusters such that the cutting size of interconnections crossing distinct clusters is minimized. This formulates a typical problem of K-set partition to a sparse graph. Mean field dynamics for K-set graph partition has been proposed in [6]. As argued previously, parallel and synchronous computations by recurrent multilayer perceptrons can be obtained for tracking mean field dynamics of resolving K-set graph partition. Let $\{S_k\}_{k=1}^{K}$ be the partitioned K clusters of sparsely interconnected

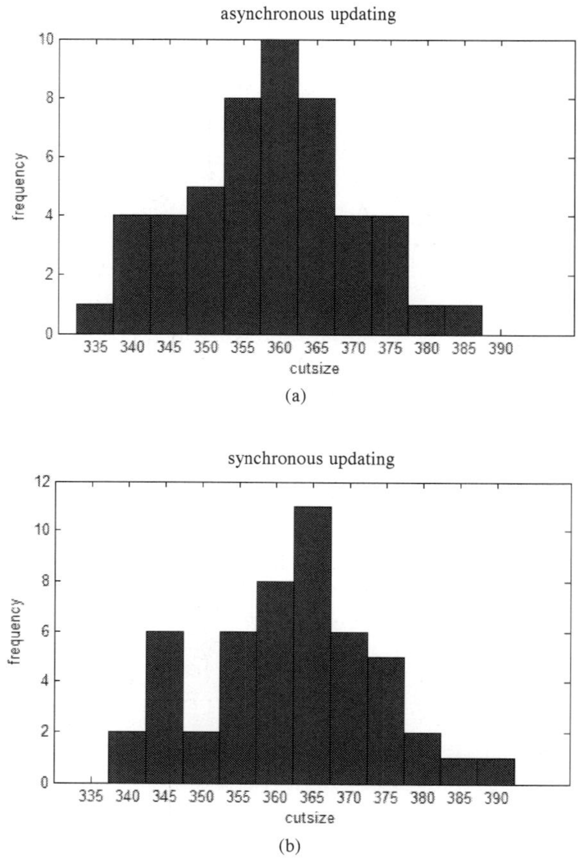

Figure 12. The histograms of cutsize obtained by 50 executions of synchronous update and asynchronous update.

processing units and $\mathbf{c}_k$ be the outer-input of processing units in S_k. $\mathbf{c}_k$ contains nonzero elements if there exists a processing unit in S_k that is connected with units not in S_k and those nonzero elements are determined by mean activations of processing units outside S_k. After K-set graph partition, all nodes are reindexed according to $\{S_k\}_{k=1}^{K}$. Ideally, there is dense connectivity among processing units inside each S_k and sparse connectivity among $\{S_k\}_{k=1}^{K}$ through $\{\mathbf{c}_k\}_{k=1}^{K}$ as illustrated in Figure 13.

In each cluster S_k when there is a processing unit connecting to processing units outside S_k according to the approach in section 2, all processing units inside S_k are evaluated directly by synchronous computations for fixed $\mathbf{c}_k$. The approach which combines synchronous update of mean activations in side each S_k and sequential update among $\{S_k\}_{k=1}^{K}$ is proposed for

http://dx.doi.org/10.5772/57217

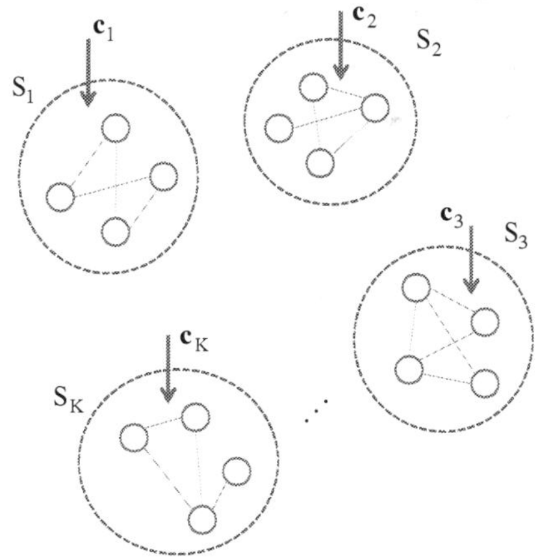

Figure 13. Partition of all nodes into K clusters to attain dense interconnection in each cluster.

tracking mean field dynamics sparse connectivity. The idea follows parallel and distributed processes. This approach decomposes a large system to several sparsely connected small systems, updates mean activations inside each small system synchronously and updates decomposed systems sequentially. Suppose that each S_k has the same number of nodes. The size of nodes in S_k is $|S_k| = \frac{N}{K} \ll N$. Figure 14 shows the flow chart of the proposed approach. The halting condition states to compare the stability $\chi(\mathbf{v})$ with a threshold. An example with $N = 12$ for illustrating decomposition of a sparse system to three small systems is given in Appendix C.

5. Conclusions

This paper has proposed a novel approach for tracking mean field dynamics by synchronous computations of recurrent multilayer perceptrons. The strategy is to introduce time delays and auxiliary variables and constructs equivalent recursive relations. This strategy essentially constructs recurrent multilayer perceptrons for tracking densely coupled mean field dynamics. The proposed approach is also extended to deal with large-scale sparsely interconnected mean field dynamics. In the beginning, all processing units are partitioned into K clusters by solving graph partition. The task is decomposed to K sub-tasks of synchronous computations and different clusters are sparsely connected by outer-inputs. The work combines synchronous updating inside each cluster with sequential updating among K clusters.

Numerical simulations show that the proposed approach has successfully translated mean field equations of solving the graph bisection problem to a system of post-nonlinear recursive functions, and verified the consistency between the original mean field equations and corresponding recurrent computations.

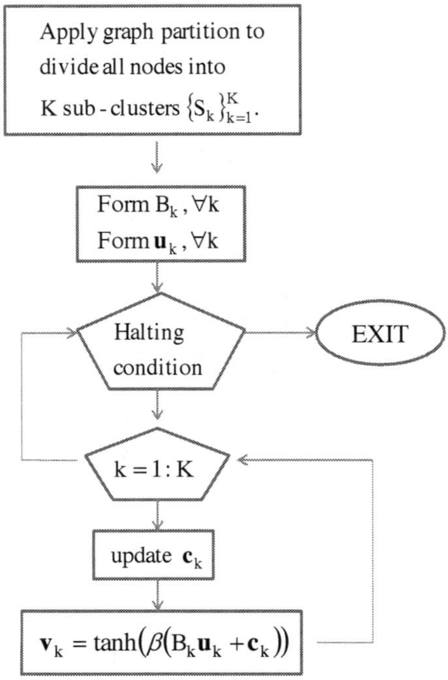

Figure 14. The flow chart of parallel and distributed processes for tracking mean field dynamics of sparse connectivity.

6. Appendix

6.1. Appendix A. Rewriting energy function of graph bisection problem

$$
\begin{aligned}
E(S) &= -\frac{1}{2}\sum_{i=1}^{N}\sum_{j\neq i}^{N} T_{ij}s_is_j + \frac{A}{2}\left(\sum_{i=1}^{N} s_i\right)^2 \\
&= -\frac{1}{2}\sum_{i=1}^{N}\sum_{j\neq i}^{N} T_{ij}s_is_j + \frac{A}{2}\left(\sum_{i=1}^{N} s_i^2 + \sum_{i=1}^{N}\sum_{j\neq i}^{N} s_is_j\right) \\
&= -\frac{1}{2}\sum_{i=1}^{N}\sum_{j\neq i}^{N}(T_{ij} - A)s_is_j + \frac{A}{2}\left(\sum_{i=1}^{N} s_i^2\right) \\
&= -\frac{1}{2}\sum_{i=1}^{N}\sum_{j\neq i}^{N}(T_{ij} - A)s_is_j + \frac{A}{2}N
\end{aligned}
$$

Let $W_{ij} = T_{ij} - A$ where $W_{ii} = 0$. Since $\frac{A}{2}N$ is a constant, the energy function is rewritten as

$$E(S) = -\frac{1}{2}\sum_{i=1}^{N}\sum_{j\neq i}^{N} W_{ij}s_i s_j$$

6.2. Appendix B. An example decomposing sparse interconnection

A linear system is given by

$$\begin{aligned}
x_1 &= 0 + a_{12}x_2 + a_{13}x_3 + 0 + 0 + 0 + 0 + 0 + 0 \\
x_2 &= a_{21}x_1 + 0 + a_{23}x_3 + 0 + 0 + 0 + 0 + 0 + 0 \\
x_3 &= a_{31}x_1 + a_{32}x_2 + 0 + 0 + 0 + 0 + 0 + a_{38}x_8 + 0 \\
x_4 &= 0 + 0 + 0 + 0 + a_{45}x_5 + a_{46}x_6 + 0 + 0 + 0 \\
x_5 &= 0 + 0 + 0 + a_{54}x_4 + 0 + a_{56}x_6 + 0 + 0 + 0 \\
x_6 &= 0 + a_{62}x_2 + 0 + a_{64}x_4 + a_{65}x_5 + 0 + 0 + 0 + 0 \\
x_7 &= a_{71}x_1 + 0 + 0 + 0 + 0 + 0 + 0 + a_{78}x_8 + a_{79}x_9 \\
x_8 &= 0 + 0 + 0 + 0 + 0 + 0 + a_{87}x_7 + 0 + a_{89}x_9 \\
x_9 &= 0 + 0 + 0 + 0 + 0 + 0 + a_{97}x_7 + a_{98}x_8 + 0
\end{aligned}$$

Let

$$A = \begin{bmatrix} A_{11} & A_{12} & A_{13} \\ A_{21} & A_{22} & A_{23} \\ A_{31} & A_{32} & A_{33} \end{bmatrix} = \begin{bmatrix}
0 & a_{12}x_2 & a_{13}x_3 & 0 & 0 & 0 & 0 & 0 & 0 \\
a_{21}x_1 & 0 & a_{23}x_3 & 0 & 0 & 0 & 0 & 0 & 0 \\
a_{31}x_1 & a_{32}x_2 & 0 & 0 & 0 & 0 & 0 & a_{38}x_8 & 0 \\
0 & 0 & 0 & 0 & a_{45}x_5 & a_{46}x_6 & 0 & 0 & 0 \\
0 & 0 & 0 & a_{54}x_4 & 0 & a_{56}x_6 & 0 & 0 & 0 \\
0 & a_{62}x_2 & 0 & a_{64}x_4 & a_{65}x_5 & 0 & 0 & 0 & 0 \\
a_{71}x_1 & 0 & 0 & 0 & 0 & 0 & 0 & a_{78}x_8 & a_{79}x_9 \\
0 & 0 & 0 & 0 & 0 & 0 & a_{87}x_7 & 0 & a_{89}x_9 \\
0 & 0 & 0 & 0 & 0 & 0 & a_{97}x_7 & a_{98}x_8 & 0
\end{bmatrix}$$

be a sparse matrix and

$$\begin{aligned}
S_1 &= \{x_1, x_2, x_3\} \\
S_2 &= \{x_4, x_5, x_6\} \\
S_3 &= \{x_7, x_8, x_9\} \\
\mathbf{v}_1 &= [x_1\ x_2\ x_3]^T \\
\mathbf{v}_2 &= [x_4\ x_5\ x_6]^T \\
\mathbf{v}_3 &= [x_7\ x_8\ x_9]^T
\end{aligned}$$

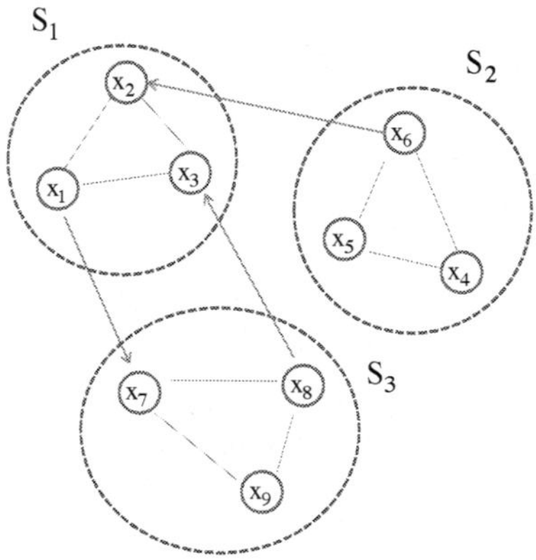

Figure 15. Dense interconnection in each cluster and sparse interconnection among three clusters.

Based on graph partition of $K = 3$, the system $\mathbf{x} = A\mathbf{x}$ has dense interconnection of S_k, $\forall k = 1, 2, 3$ and sparse interconnection among $\{S_k\}_{k=1}^{3}$ as shown in Figure 15. Let

$$
\begin{aligned}
d_1 &= d_2 = d_4 = d_5 = d_8 = d_9 = 0 \\
d_3 &= a_{38}x_8 \\
d_6 &= a_{62}x_2 \\
d_7 &= a_{71}x_1
\end{aligned}
$$

and $\mathbf{c}_1 = [d_1\ d_2\ d_3]^T$, $\mathbf{c}_2 = [d_4\ d_5\ d_6]^T$ and $\mathbf{c}_3 = [d_7\ d_8\ d_9]^T$ be the outer-input of three clusters $\{S_k\}_{k=1}^{3}$. d_i is nonzero if there is a node x_j connected to x_i with weight $a_{ij} \neq 0$ where x_i and x_j belong to different clusters. Therefore, the updating rule of $\{\mathbf{c}_k\}_{k=1}^{3}$ is

$$\mathbf{c}_k = \sum_{j \neq k}^{3} A_{kj}\mathbf{v}_j$$

Author details

Jiann-Ming Wu*, Jung-Chao Ban and Chun-Chang Wu

*Address all correspondence to: jmwu@livemail.tw

Department of Applied Mathematics, National Dong Hwa University, Shoufeng, Taiwan

http://dx.doi.org/10.5772/57217

References

[1] J. J. Hopfield, "Neural networks and physical systems with emergent collective computational abilities", Proceedings of the National Academy of Sciences 79:2554-2558, 1982.

[2] J. J. Hopfield, "Neurons with graded response have collective computational properties like those of two-state neurons", Proceedings of the National Academy of Sciences 81: 3088-3092, 1984.

[3] J. J. Hopfield and D. W. Tank, "Neural computation of decisions in optimization problems," Biol. Cybern., vol. 52, p. 141, 1985.

[4] C. Peterson and B. Söerberg, "A new method for mapping optimization problems onto neural network," Int. J. Neural Syst., vol. 1, p. 3, 1989.

[5] J. M. Wu, "Potts models with two sets of interactive dynamics," Neurocomput., vol. 34, pp. 55–77, Sept. 2000.

[6] J. M. Wu, "Annealing by Two Sets of Interactive Dynamics," IEEE Trans. on Systems Man and Cybernetics Part B-Cybernetics 34 (3): 1519-1525, Jun 2004.

[7] R. J. McEliece, E. C. Posner, E. R. Rodemich, and S. S. Venkatesh, "The capacity of the Hopfield associative memory," IEEE Truns. Inform. Theory, vol. IT-33, pp. 1-33, July 1987

[8] T. Isokawa, H. Nishimura, N. Kamiura, and N. Matsui, "Associative memory in quaternionic Hopfield neural network," Int. J. Neural Syst., vol. 18, no. 2, pp. 135–145, 2008

[9] D. W. Tank and J. J. Hopfield, "Collective computation in neuronlike circuits," Sci. Amer., vol. 257, no. 6, pp. 104–115, 1987

[10] C. Y. Liou and J. M.Wu, "Self-organization using Potts models," Neural Netw., vol. 9, no. 4, pp. 671–684, 1996.

[11] K. Rose, E. Gurewitz, and G. C. Fox, "Statistical mechanics and phase transitions in clustering," Phys. Rev. Lett., vol. 65, no. 8, pp. 945–948, 1990

[12] K. Rose, "Constrained clustering as an optimization method," IEEE Trans. Pattern Anal. Machine Intell., vol. 15, pp. 785–794, Aug. 1993.

[13] J. M. Wu and S. J. Chiu, "Independent component analysis using Potts models," IEEE Trans. Neural Networks, vol. 12, pp. 202–211, Mar. 2001.

[14] A. V. Rao, D. J. Miller, K. Rose, and A. Gersho, "A deterministic annealing approach for parsimonious design of piecewise regression models," IEEE Trans. Pattern Anal. Machine Intell., vol. 21, pp.169–173, Feb. 1999.

[15] J. M. Wu, Z. H. Lin and P. H. Hsu, "Function approximation using generalized adalines," IEEE Trans. On Neural Networks,Vol.17 No.3, 541-558, May 2006

[16] J. M. Wu, "Fetal electrocardiogram extraction by annealed expectation maximization," Neurocomputing 71, pp 1500-1514, 2008

[17] J. M. Wu, "Multilayer Potts perceptrons with Levenberg-Marquardt learning", accepted by IEEE Trans. on Neural Networks, 2008

[18] J. M. Wu, M.H. Chen, Lin Z.H., "Independent component analysis based on marginal density estimation using weighted Parzen windows", accepted by Neural Networks, 2008

[19] Dudul SV, "Prediction of Lorenz chaotic attractor using two layer perceptron neural network," Applied Soft Computing 2005; 5:333–355

[20] G. Peter Zhang, "Time series forecasting using a hybrid ARIMA and neural network model," Neurocomputing 50 (2003) 159 – 175.

Chapter 14

Methods for Blind Estimation of Speckle Variance in SAR Images: Simulation Results and Verification for Real-Life Data

Sergey Abramov, Victoriya Abramova,
Vladimir Lukin, Nikolay Ponomarenko, Benoit Vozel,
Kacem Chehdi, Karen Egiazarian and Jaakko Astola

Additional information is available at the end of the chapter

http://dx.doi.org/10.5772/57040

1. Introduction

Blind estimation of noise characteristics (BENC), such as noise type, its statistics and spectrum, has become an actual practical task for various image processing applications (Vozel et al., 2009). There are several reasons for this. First, noise is one of the main factors degrading and determining the quality of images of different types: grayscale and color optical (Liu et al., 2008; Foi et al., 2007; Plataniotis&Venetsanopoulos, 2000), component images in certain sub-bands of hyperspectral remote sensing data (Aiazzi et al., 2006), radar and ultrasound medical images (Lin et al., 2010; Oliver&Quegan, 2004), etc. Second, information on noise characteristics is valuable and widely exploited in most of stages of image processing. For example, it is used in edge detection for threshold setting (Davies, 2000), image filtering (Touzi, 2002; Lee et al., 2009) including denoising techniques based on orthogonal transforms (Mallat, 1998; Sendur&Selesnick, 2002; Egiazarian et al., 1999), image reconstruction (Katsaggelos, 1991), lossy compression of noisy images (Bekhtin, 2011), non-reference assessment of image visual quality (Choi et al., 2009), etc. Third, although there can be initial assumptions on noise type and a range of variations of its statistical parameters, these parameters can be quite different even for a given imaging system depending upon conditions of its operation. The requirements to information accuracy on noise parameters are rather strict, e.g., variance of pure additive or pure multiplicative noise has to be known or pre-estimated with a relative error not larger than ±20% (Abramov et al., 2004). Thus, it is often desirable to estimate noise characteristics for a given image.

Besides, amount of images offered by various imaging systems increases enormously. Therefore, it becomes difficult to evaluate noise characteristics in an interactive manner since this requires time, perfect skills, and availability of the corresponding software. Moreover, there are practical situations and applications for which it is impossible to find a highly qualified expert to perform the task of evaluation of the noise characteristics. The examples are estimation of noise characteristics in remote sensing images on-board satellites (Van Zyl et al., 2009). BENC can be also useful even if an expert is involved to analysis of the noise characteristics. This happens, e.g., if a newly designed and manufactured imaging system is verified to check do the main properties of the noise present in the formed images conform expected (forecasted) ones. Then, the output estimates of BENC can be compared to the outcomes of the expert analysis and support (control) each other.

There are quite many known methods of BENC designed so far. A few of them can operate on images corrupted by a general type of signal-dependent noise (Liu et al., 2008). Most of known BENC methods are able to deal only with a particular type of noise under assumption that the noise type is known a priori or pre-determined in an automatic manner (Vozel et al., 2009). The case of pure additive noise has been studied more thoroughly in literature (see Vozel et al. 2009; Zoran&Weiss, 2009; Abramov et al., 2008; Lukin et al. 2007, and references therein). Some of these methods can be, after certain modifications, applied to estimation of multiplicative noise variance. These modifications basically relate to either application of logarithmic type homomorphic transform or a special approach to form local estimates of multiplicative noise relative variance as a normalization of local variance estimates by squared local mean (Vozel et al. 2009). However, quite many BENC methods exploit local estimate scatter-plots and line (curve) fitting into them to evaluate multiplicative noise variance (Lee et al., 1992; Ramponi&d'Alvise, 1999). Note that a multiplicative noise is typical for radar imagery, in particular, images acquired by synthetic aperture radars (SARs) where coherent principles of image forming are employed (Solbo&Eltoft, 2004; Oliver&Quegan, 2004). Speckle is a specific noise-like phenomenon arising in formed images and it is known to be the dominant factor degrading their quality (Oliver&Quegan, 2004). For many operations of radar (and ultrasound) image processing, the characteristics of the speckle are to be known in advance or pre-estimated (Lee et al., 2009; Solbo&Eltoft, 2008).

One can argue that there are many practical situations when speckle characteristics such as the (relative) variance of the multiplicative noise (or the efficient number of looks) and the speckle distribution law are known in advance or can be predicted from theory (Oliver&Quegan, 2004). This holds if a given SAR operates in a known mode (e.g. forms one-look amplitude images) and the operation parameters are stable. Then, it is enough to carry out a preliminary analysis of several images acquired by this SAR manually (in interactive mode) to be sure that the aforementioned characteristics (parameters) conform theory and are stable enough.

However, in many practical situations, it is worth applying BENC, sometimes in addition to an interactive analysis. First, suppose that a new SAR is tested and it is desirable to know whether or not it provides the desired (forecasted, expected) characteristics. Second, one might deal with SAR images for which full description of the imaging mode used is absent (Lee et

http://dx.doi.org/10.5772/57040

al., 1992; Ramponi&d'Alvise, 1999). Third, although it is assumed that the multi-look mode of image formation allows decreasing the speckle variance by the number of looks, this is not absolutely true and, in practice, noise reduction is not as efficient as ideally predicted (Anfinsen et al., 2009; Foucher et al., 2000).

Therefore, two important questions arise: what is the accuracy of the existing blind estimation methods and what BENC to apply? To our best knowledge, there are no studies dealing with intensive testing of BENC with application to speckle (our conference paper (Lukin et al., 2011) seems to be one of the first attempts in this direction). By intensive testing we mean the use of tens of different images having different content and/or many realizations of speckle for both single and multi-look modes. There are several reasons why such testing has not been carried out yet. The main reason is the absence of the test radar images commonly accepted by the radar data processing community. We have to stress here that it is quite difficult to create test SAR images since one has to find an answer to many particular questions as what terrain and objects to simulate, what model of the carrier trajectory and its instabilities to use, to consider moving objects or not, what is SNR in radar receiver input, what kind of received signal processing is used (Dogan&Kartal, 2010; Di Martino et al., 2012), etc. Another reason is that, maybe, designers of BENC for speckle have been satisfied by accuracy of the obtained estimates for a limited set of processed images and have not tried applying their methods to a wider variety of data.

Experience obtained recently in testing BENCs for additive and signal dependent noise cases (Vozel et al., 2009; Abramov et al., 2011; Lukin et al., 2009b) clearly demonstrates the following. First, whilst a given method can produce an acceptable accuracy for many tested images, there can be a few test images (usually highly textural ones and/or with clipping effects) for which abnormal (unacceptable) estimates are obtained. Just to these images one has to pay more attention in attempts to improve a methods' performance. Second, a spatial correlation of noise present in most of real life images and often ignored in a design and testing of many BENC techniques can considerably influence an accuracy of estimation methods (Abramov et al., 2008). Recall that a spatial correlation of speckle is a feature typical for SAR images (Solbo&Eltoft, 2008, Lukin et al., 2008; Lukin et al., 2009; Ponomarenko et al., 2011) which is not often taken into account in SAR image simulations.

Thus, we come to a necessity to perform intensive testing of BENC methods without having a set of standard test images. Our idea then is to create a set of test SAR images with a priori known characteristics of the speckle similar to those ones observed in practice. In this sense, TerraSAR-X images can be a good choice (in Section 2, we explain this in detail). Note that quite many of them are now available in the convenient form and their amount is rapidly growing (see http://www.infoterra.de/free-sample-data). Then, it becomes possible to test BENCs for simulated data (Section 3) and to predict what could happen in practice. These predictions are then verified for the considered methods for high quality data provided by TerraSAR-X data (Section 4) to offer practical recommendations on the BENC method selection and setting its parameters. Finally, conclusions follow.

2. Basic properties of speckle and its modeling

Speckle is a typical example for which pure multiplicative model is usually exploited (Touzi, 2002; Oliver&Quegan, 2004). This means that a dependence of signal dependent noise variance on true value $\sigma_{sd}^2 = f(I^{tr})$ is monotonically increasing proportionally to squared (true value). Speckle is not Gaussian and its probability density function (PDF) depends upon a way of image forming (amplitude or intensity) and number of looks (Oliver&Quegan, 2004). PDF of the speckle considerably differs from Gaussian if a single-look imaging mode is used and it is either Rayleigh (for amplitude images) or negative exponential (for intensity images) for the case of fully developed speckle. If multi-look imaging mode is applied, the speckle PDF becomes closer to Gaussian and depends upon the number of looks.

To get an imagination on fully developed speckle PDF, consider real-life data produced by TerraSAR-X imager. Its attractive feature is that data (images) are freely available at the aforementioned site. These data have full description of parameters of the imaging system operation mode used for obtaining each presented image. Large size images (thousands to thousands pixels) for many different areas of the Earth are offered. Furthermore, a brief description of a territory, observed effects and cover types is given. This allows selecting and processing data with different numbers of looks, properties of a sensed terrain, a desired polarization, etc. Fragments of certain size as 512x512 pixels can be easily cut from large size data arrays and studied more thoroughly. Another positive feature is that single-look images are presented in the complex valued form. This allows obtaining single-look images in aforementioned forms (representations). It also makes possible to analyze distributions of real and imaginary part values for image fragments, etc. While considering single-look SAR images in this paper, we use amplitude images since it is the most common form and it provides convenient representation for visual analysis.

One more advantage is that TerraSAR-X is a high quality system designed by specialists from German Aerospace Agency DLR who have large experience in creation and management of spaceborne SAR systems (Herrmann et al., 2005). The TerraSAR-X imager provides a stability of noise characteristics and practical absence of an additive noise in formed images. Later, it will be explained why this is so important for further analysis.

To partly corroborate conformity of theory and practice for single-look SAR images, we have manually cropped several sub-arrays of complex valued data that correspond to homogeneous terrain regions. The histogram of real (in-phase) part values for one such a fragment is presented in Fig. 1(a) where sample data mean is close to zero. The histogram for imaginary (quadrature) part is very similar. Gaussianity tests hold for both data sub-arrays. The histogram of the amplitude single-look image for the same fragment is represented in Fig. 1(b). Since both components of complex valued data are Gaussian with approximately the same variance, the amplitude values obey Rayleigh distribution. This one more time shows that for single-look amplitude images speckle can be simulated as pure multiplicative noise having Rayleigh PDF. Using modern simulation tools as, e.g., Matlab, this can be done easily, at least, for the case of independent identically distributed (i.i.d.), i.e. spatially uncorrelated speckle.

The histogram in Fig. 1(b) also shows one more aspect important for simulations. Speckle image values can be by 3...4 times larger than mean (which is close to I^{tr} in homogeneous image regions). Then, if the values of I^{tr} are modelled as 8-bit data, the noisy values can be outside the limits 0…255 and, therefore, 16-bit representation of a simulated noisy image is to be used to preserve statistics of the speckle. In Section 3, we will show what might happen to the estimates provided by BENCs if clipping effects take place for simulated noisy SAR images, i.e. if they are represented as 8-bit data.

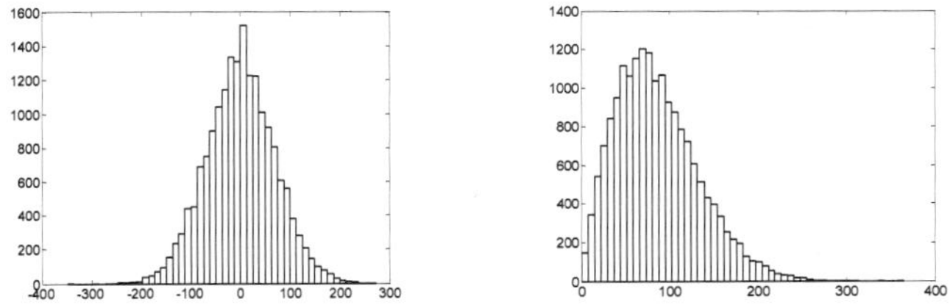

(a) (b)

Figure 1. Histograms of distributions for in-phase component (a) and amplitude (b) of complex-valued data in image homogeneous region

To additionally analyze statistics of the speckle, we have also tested several manually cropped homogeneous regions in different single-look images that correspond to either rather large (about 70x70 pixels) agricultural fields and water surface. The estimated speckle variance $\hat{\sigma}_\mu^2 = \sum_{Ghom} (I_{ij} - \hat{I}_{Gmean})^2 \Big/ \hat{I}_{Gmean}^2$, $\hat{I}_{Gmean} = \sum_{Ghom} I_{ij}$ (I_{ij} is an ij-th image pixel, G_{hom} is a selected homogeneous region) has varied from 0.265 to 0.285. This is in a good agreement with a theoretically stated $\sigma_\mu^2 = 0.273$ for Rayleigh distributed speckle in amplitude single-look SAR images. Higher order moments (skewness and kurtosis) for the studied homogeneous image regions are also in appropriate agreement with the theory (Oliver&Quegan, 2004). This means that for both simulated and real-life single-look amplitude SAR images any BENC should provide estimates of speckle variance close enough to 0.273.

To consider and simulate speckle more adequately, we have also analyzed spatial correlation of speckle using TerraSAR-X data. This has been done in three different ways. First, standard 2D autocorrelation function (ACF) estimates have been obtained for 32x32 pixels size homogeneous fragments. They have been inspected visually and have demonstrated the absence of far correlation and the presence of essential correlation for neighboring pixels in single-look amplitude images (see example in Fig. 2(a)). It is interesting that even higher correlation for neighboring pixels has been observed for multi-look images (see example in Fig. 2(b)). There are also ACF side lobes for azimuth direction that, most probably, arise due to peculiarities of the SAR response to a point target.

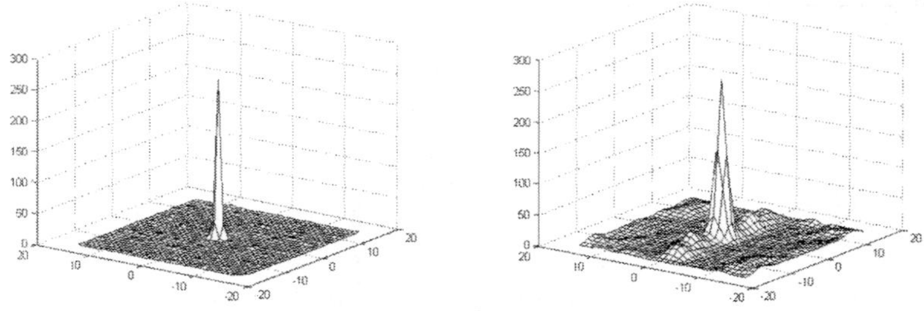

(a) (b)

Figure 2. ACF estimates for 32x32 pixel homogeneous fragments in single-look (a) and multi-look (b) TerraSAR-X images

Second, we have analyzed a normalized 8x8 DCT spectrum estimates obtained in a blind manner (Ponomarenko et al., 2010) for several considered images. These estimates also clearly indicate that speckle is spatially correlated, i.e., not i.i.d. (Lukin et al., 2011).

Third, we have also calculated a parameter r (Uss et al., 2012) able to indicate spatial correlation of noise for any type of signal dependent noise with spatially stationary spectral characteristics. For determination of r, two local estimates of noise variance are derived for each 8x8 pixel block with its left upper corner defined by indices l and m. The first estimate is calculated in the spatial domain

$$\hat{\sigma}^2_{lm}=\sum_{i=l}^{l+7}\sum_{j=m}^{m+7}(I_{ij}-\hat{\bar{I}}_{lm})^2/63,\ \hat{\bar{I}}_{lm}=\sum_{i=l}^{l+7}\sum_{j=m}^{m+7}I_{ij}/64, \tag{1}$$

and the second estimate is calculated in the DCT domain as

$$(\hat{\sigma}^{sp}_{lm})^2=(1.483 med(|D^{lm}_{qs}|))^2 \tag{2}$$

where D^{lm}_{qs}, $q=0, ..., 7$, $s=0, ..., 7$ except $q=s=0$ are DCT coefficients of lm-th block of a given image. Then, the ratio $R_{lm}=\hat{\sigma}_{lm}/\hat{\sigma}^{sp}_{lm}$ is calculated for each block. After this, the histogram of these ratios for all blocks is formed and its mode r is determined by the method (Lukin et al., 2007). For all considered real-life SAR images, the value of r was larger than 1.05 (Lukin et al., 2011b) for single-look SAR images and considerably larger for multi-look ones. This additionally gives an evidence in favor of the hypothesis that speckle is spatially correlated. Thus, we can state that speckle is spatially correlated in the considered TerraSAR-X images, both single- and multi-look ones. Then, this effect should be taken into account in simulations.

To simulate single- and multi-look SAR images, we have used four aerial optical images as I^{tr} (all test images are of size 512x512pixels). These four images are presented in Fig. 3. Positive features of these images allowing to use them in simulation of SAR data are the following.

First, these images have practically no self-noise that could later influence blind estimation of speckle statistics.

Figure 3. Noise-free (true) test images used for simulating SAR images

Second, these are the images of natural scenes and, thus, they contain large quasi-homogeneous regions, edges with different contrasts, various textures and small-sized targets

Note that we have simulated speckle with the same statistics for all pixels ignoring the fact that for small-sized targets it might differ from speckle in homogeneous image regions. This simplification is explained by the following two reasons. First, more complicated models of speckle are required for small-sized targets. Second, the percentage of pixels occupied by small-sized targets is quite small in real-life images (Lee et al., 2009) and local estimates of noise statistics in the corresponding scanning windows are anyway abnormal. Thus, these local estimates are "ignored" by the BENCs considered below which are robust (see Section 3 for more details).

Fig. 4 gives two examples of noisy test image with fully developed speckle (single look). For one of them (Fig. 4(a)) speckle is i.i.d. whilst for the second (Fig. 4(b)) speckle is spatially correlated (see details of its simulation below). Even visual analysis of these two noisy images allows noticing the difference in speckle spatial correlation. As it will become clear from the visual analysis of real-life SAR images presented later in Section 4, the case shown in Fig. 4(b) is much closer to practice.

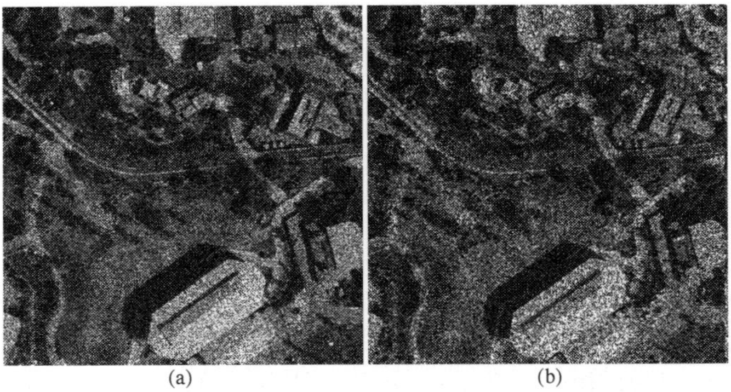

Figure 4. The first test image corrupted by i.i.d. (a) and spatially correlated (b) speckle

Thus, from a practical point of view, it is more reasonable to simulate spatially correlated speckle. This can be done in different ways. In our study, we have employed the following simulation algorithm:

1. Generate 2D array of a required size $I_{\rm Im} \times J_{\rm Im}$ for Gaussian zero mean spatially correlated noise (GCN – Gaussian correlated noise) with a desired spatial spectrum (this is a standard task solution of which is omitted).

2. Transform the 2D GCN data array into 1D array C of size K=$I_{\rm Im} \times J_{\rm Im}$ in a pre-selected way, e.g., by row-by-row scanning.

3. Generate 1D array B of i.i.d. Rayleigh distributed unity mean random variables of size K= $I_{\rm Im} \times J_{\rm Im}$.

4. For the array C, form an array of indices CI in such a manner that CI(1) is the index of the element in C which is the largest, CI(2) is the index of the element in C which is the second largest, and so on. Finally, CI(K) is the last element of the array CI which is the index of the smallest element of C.

5. Similarly, form an index array BI for the array B.

6. For k=1..K make valid the condition C(CI(i))=B(BI(i)). Then, noise with Gaussian distribution is replaced by noise with the required distribution (Rayleigh in our case).

7. The obtained array C is transformed to 2D array RES of size K=$I_{\rm Im} \times J_{\rm Im}$ in the way inverse to it has been done in step 2.

The source code in Matlab that realizes the described algorithm is presented below:

```
C=GCN(:);
B=random('rayleigh',1,1,M*N)/1.26;
[CC,CI]=sort(C);
[BB,BI]=sort(B);
C(CI)=B(BI);
RES=reshape(C,M,N);
```

Here M, N correspond to I_{Im} and J_{Im} (that is to the simulated image size), and all other notations are the same as described above. The obtained 2D array has a Rayleigh distribution and has practically the same spatial correlation properties as GCN. Then the values of RES(i,j) are pixel-wise multiplied by I_{ij}^{true} to obtain the corresponding speckle values I_{ij}^{n}, $i=1, ...I_{Im}$, $j=1, ..., J_{Im}$.

The image presented in Fig. 4(b) has been obtained in the way described above. Moreover, this allows getting multi-look images if several realizations of the speckle with desired spectrum are generated and then averaged.

3. Considered blind estimation techniques and their accuracy analysis for simulated data

Describing the considered BENC methods, one should keep in mind that blind estimates of speckle characteristics obtained for a given method can differ from each other due to the following factors:

- properties and parameters (if they can be varied or user defined) of a method applied;
- method robustness with respect to outliers;
- content of an analyzed image;
- an observed speckle realization in the considered image;
- clipping effects (if they take place).

Because of this, we first describe BENCs used in our studies and the main principles put into their basis. Then, simulation results are presented for simulated single- and multi-look SAR images, and the analysis of these results is performed.

3.1. Considered BENCs

As it has been mentioned in Introduction, there are two basic approaches to blind estimation of σ_{μ}^{2}. The first approach presumes forming local estimates of speckle variance and robust processing of the obtained local estimates. The second approach is based on obtaining a scatter-plot and robust regression line fitting into it.

Let us start from considering the former approach. It consists of the following stages. At the first stage, an analyzed image is divided into non-overlapping or overlapping blocks and local estimates are obtained as

$$\hat{\sigma}^2_{\mu\ lm} = \sum_{i=l}^{l+N-1} \sum_{j=m}^{m+N-1} (I_{ij} - \hat{\bar{I}}_{lm})^2 / ((N^2-1)\hat{\bar{I}}^2_{lm}),\ \hat{\bar{I}}_{lm} = \sum_{i=l}^{l+N-1} \sum_{j=m}^{m+N-1} I_{ij} / N^2, \tag{3}$$

where N denotes the block size under assumption that it has a square shape. According to a previous experience (Abramov et al., 2008), N is recommended to be from 5 till 9; N=5 is usually enough for i.i.d. noise whilst it is better to set N equal to 7, 8 or 9 for spatially correlated noise.

To understand the operation principles of the first group of methods, it can be useful to look at distributions of the local estimates (3). As examples, the two distributions of local estimates $\hat{\sigma}^2_{\mu\ lm}$ for the two real-life (TerraSAR-X) single-look elementary images (presented in Fig. 5(a) and Fig. 5(b)) are shown in Figs. 6(a) and 6(b), respectively (N=7 and non-overlapping blocks are used). It is easy to see that both distributions characterized by histograms have modes close to 0.273. Meanwhile, the percentages of "normal" local estimates (3) that produce quasi-Gaussian parts of distributions are considerably different – look at maximal values in histograms. Suppose that normal local estimates are those ones smaller than 0.5. Then, the probability p of occurrence of "normal" local estimates is approximately equal to 0.6 for the histogram in Fig. 6(a) and to 0.9 for the histogram in Fig. 6(b). For other tested real-life single-look images (in particular, those ones shown in Fig. 7(a) and 7(b)), the estimated values of p are from 0.55 till 0.9. The same holds for the simulated test images presented in the previous Section.

Besides, the distributions in Fig. 6 differ by heaviness of the right-hand tail. Recall that this tail stems from the presence of the so-called "abnormal" local estimates (3) that are obtained in heterogeneous image blocks (Vozel et al., 2009). For the elementary images that have a simpler structure (Figures 5(b) and 7), the tail heaviness is considerably less (see Fig. 7(b)).

The property that the distributions have maxima with the mode close to the true value of σ^2_μ has been put into the basis of several BENC methods for estimation of noise variance (Vozel et al., 2009). The task is then to find the distribution mode automatically, robustly and with a high enough accuracy. For this purpose, it is possible to exploit robust mode finders such as a sample myriad, bootstrapping and minimal inter-quantile distance with properly (adaptively) set parameters. Since an improved minimal inter-quantile distance estimator provides the best accuracy (Lukin et al., 2007), we use it in our further studies. The technique based on obtaining the set of local estimates according to (3) and estimation of its mode by the improved minimal inter-quantile distance estimator (Lukin et al., 2007) is further referred as **Method 1.** A variable parameter of this method is the block size.

http://dx.doi.org/10.5772/57040

(a) (b)

Figure 5. Two elementary single look amplitude SAR images for Rosenheim region

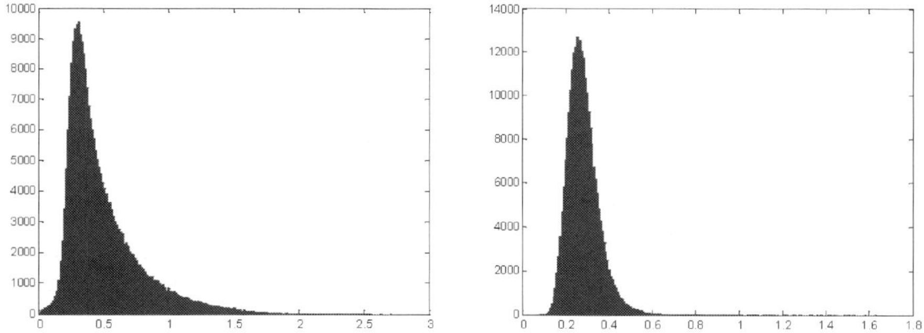

(a) (b)

Figure 6. Histograms of local estimates (3) for the elementary images in Fig. 5(a) andFig. 5(b)

The second group of BENC methods, as it has been mentioned above, is based on scatter-plots. A traditional way of scatter-plot representation for signal-dependent noise is the following. For each block, a point in Cartesian system is obtained where its Y coordinate corresponds to a local variance estimate $Y = \hat{\sigma}^2_{loc}$ and a local mean estimate is its argument (X axis coordinate $X = \bar{I}_{loc}$). An example of such a scatter-plot for the image in Fig. 5(b) is presented in Fig. 8(a). A curve $\hat{\sigma}^2_{loc} = \sigma^2_{\mu} \bar{I}_{loc}$ is depicted in this scatter-plot. It is seen that it goes through the centers of the main clusters of this scatter-plot (the cluster centers are indicated by red squares) where the clusters are formed by normal local estimates (see details below). However, there are also quite many points that are located far away from this curve and cluster centers. These points correspond to abnormal local estimates obtained in heterogeneous blocks. This means that if one presumes to fit a polynomial type curve $\hat{\sigma}^2_{loc} = D\bar{I}_{loc}$ and then to obtain $\hat{\sigma}^2_{\mu} = D$, where D is the parameter of the fitted curve, the method of curve fitting should be robust with respect to outliers.

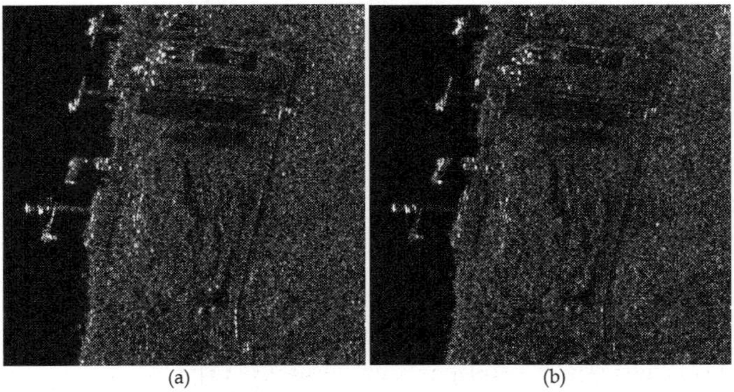

Figure 7. The 512x512 pixels elementary single-look amplitude SAR images of Indonesia for (a) HH and (b) VV polarizations

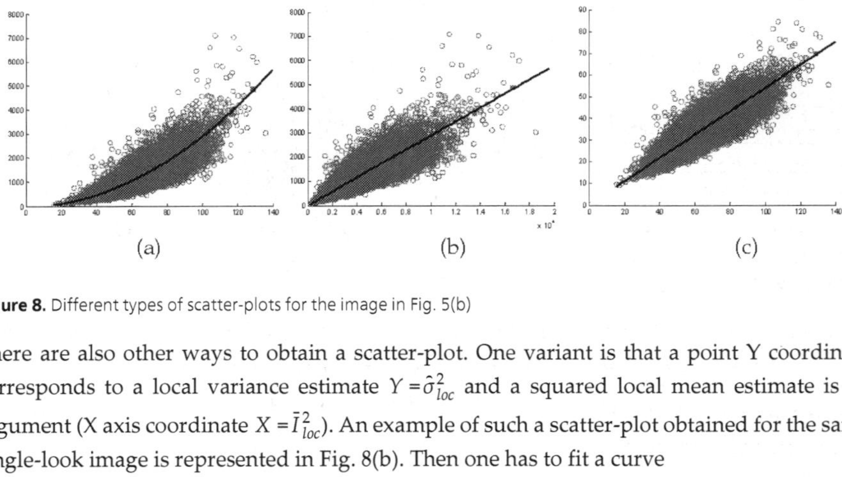

Figure 8. Different types of scatter-plots for the image in Fig. 5(b)

There are also other ways to obtain a scatter-plot. One variant is that a point Y coordinate corresponds to a local variance estimate $Y = \hat{\sigma}^2_{loc}$ and a squared local mean estimate is its argument (X axis coordinate $X = \bar{I}^2_{loc}$). An example of such a scatter-plot obtained for the same single-look image is represented in Fig. 8(b). Then one has to fit a curve

$$\hat{\sigma}^2_{loc} = E\bar{I}^2_{loc} \tag{4}$$

i.e. straight line where the estimate $\hat{\sigma}^2_{\mu} = E$, E is the parameter of the fitted line. Another option is to obtain a scatter-plot in such a way that a point coordinate Y relates to a local standard deviation estimate $Y = \hat{\sigma}_{loc}$ where its argument (X axis coordinate $X = \bar{I}_{loc}$) is the corresponding

http://dx.doi.org/10.5772/57040

local mean estimate. Then one has $\hat{\sigma}_{loc} = F\bar{I}_{loc}$ where F is the fitted straight line parameter that serves as the estimate $\hat{\sigma}_{\mu}$. This kind of a scatter-plot is shown in Fig. 8(c) for the same single-look SAR image. Visual analysis of the scatter-plots in Figs. 8(b) and 8(c) shows that for them there are also some clusters of normal local estimates whereas abnormal estimates are present as well. An advantage of the latter two approaches is that it is, in general, simpler to fit a straight line than a higher order polynomial. In particular, there are standard means for this purpose as, e.g., the Matlab version of robustfit method (DuMouchel&O'Brien, 1989). For methods analyzed below, we have used the approach based on (6).

Finally, there are also methods that exploit scatter-plot data to find cluster centers and curve (line) fitting using these scatter-plot centers (Zabrodina et al., 2011; Abramov et al., 2011). Cluster centers are indicated by red color dots in scatter-plots in Fig. 8. The cluster center coordinates relate to $Y_q = \hat{\sigma}^2_{norm\ q}$, $X_q = \hat{\bar{I}}_{norm\ q}$, $q = 1, \ldots, Q_{cl}$ where $\hat{\sigma}^2_{norm\ q}$ is the estimate of distribution mode of local variance estimates for a q-th cluster basically based on normal local estimates, $\hat{\bar{I}}_{norm\ q}$ denotes the estimate of distribution mode of the local mean estimates for this cluster, and Q_{cl} is the number of clusters. Clusters are obtained by a simple division of the scatter-plot horizontal axis to a fixed number of intervals (we recommend to use ten intervals). The estimates of distribution modes for each cluster are obtained by the improved minimal inter-quantile distance estimator (Lukin et al., 2007).

There is the straight line fitted into the cluster centers in Figs. 8(b) and 8(c). In this case, robustness with respect to abnormal local estimates is provided indirectly due to robust methods used for finding cluster centers. However, there can be also abnormal cluster centers. To reduce their influence, special techniques as RANSAC or double weighting (DW) LMSE fit can be applied (Zabrodina et al., 2011). Taking into account the comparison results (Abramov et al., 2011; Zabrodina et al., 2011), below we consider only the DW curve fitting to scatter-plot since this method, on the average, provides the best results. It is possible to use different sizes of blocks for local variance and local mean estimation in blocks. Below we study 5x5 and 7x7 pixel blocks. The technique based on forming a scatter-plot, its division into fixed number of clusters, finding cluster centers using mode estimation and DW line fitting is referred below as **Method 2**.

There are also other techniques based on curve fitting into cluster centers with improved robustness with respect to outliers. First, cluster centers can be determined without image pre-segmentation (as for the **Method 2** described above) and with pre-segmentation and further processing of the obtained segmentation map (Lukin et al., 2010). The result of image pre-segmentation is used in two ways. First, the number of image segments gives the number of clusters in the scatter-plot in a straightforward manner. Second, this information used for further image block discrimination into (probably) homogeneous and heterogeneous (Abramov et al., 2008; Lukin et al., 2010) allows diminishing the influence of abnormal errors on coordinate estimation of cluster centers. The next stages of the processing procedure are almost the same as in **Method 2**. However, **Method 3** also takes into account that the position of the last cluster(s) (the rightmost one(s)) can be erroneous due to clipping effects. They act so that the corresponding local estimates occur smaller than they should be in the case of clipping absence. Then, an approach to improve estimation accuracy is to reject the rightmost cluster center(s) from further consideration. A practical rule for cluster rejection can be the following: if $\bar{I}_{norm\,q} > \max(I_{ij})/4$, $i=1, ..., I_{Im}$, $j=1, ..., J_{Im}$, then this cluster has to be rejected. This rule takes into account the fact that for Rayleigh distribution a random variable can be, with a small probability, by 3…4 times larger than the distribution mean.

3.2. Analysis of simulation results

Let us analyze the obtained simulation results. The main properties and accuracy characteristics of the aforementioned methods based on finding a distribution mode have been intensively studied for the case of additive noise (Lukin et al., 2007). Although the multiplicative noise case is considered here, the conclusions drawn for the additive case might be still valid for **Method 1**. Recall that one of the main conclusions drawn in (Lukin et al., 2007) is that the final blind estimate of noise variance $\hat{\sigma}^2_{fin}$ can be biased where the bias is mostly positive (i.e., the estimates are larger than the true value). The absolute value of bias is larger for images with more complex structure for which the parameter p introduced above is smaller.

Another conclusion is that the estimation bias (denoted as Δ_μ for the multiplicative noise case) usually contributes more to aggregate error $\varepsilon^2 = \Delta_\mu^2 + \theta_\mu^2$, where θ_μ^2 denotes the variance of blind estimation of σ_μ^2. Here $\Delta_\mu = |\langle\hat{\sigma}_\mu^2\rangle - \sigma_\mu^2|$ and $\theta_\mu^2 = \langle(\hat{\sigma}_\mu^2 - \langle\hat{\sigma}_\mu^2\rangle)^2\rangle$ where notation $\langle\bullet\rangle$ means averaging by realizations.

Let us check are these conclusions valid for the multiplicative noise case. Usually variance θ_μ^2 is determined for a large number of realizations of the artificially added noise that corrupts a given test noise-free image. Thus, we have simulated 200 realizations of i.i.d. speckle with Rayleigh distribution. The obtained simulation results are presented in Table 1. Analysis shows that estimation bias is also positive for all four test images and for both studied sizes of blocks. The values of θ_μ^2 are of the order 10^{-6}. Thus, they are two magnitude order less than squared bias and have negligible contribution to ε^2. This shows that, in fact, it is possible to analyze only the estimation bias or even the estimates obtained for only one realization of the speckle. At least, this is possible for the test images of the considered size of 512x512 pixels or larger (θ_μ^2 decreases if a processed image size increases).

One more conclusion that follows from data analysis for **Method 1** in Table 1 is that the use of the block size 7x7 leads to more biased and, on the average, larger estimates than if 5x5 blocks are used. Nevertheless, the estimates for the fully developed speckle with $\sigma_\mu^2=0.273$ are within the required limits (Vozel et al., 2009) from 0.8x0.273=0.218 to 1.2x0.273=0.328 with high probability (it is equal to $\Delta_\mu \le 0.055$).

Consider now data for **Method 2**. They are, mostly, more biased than for **Method 1** for the same test image and block size (see data in Table 1). Moreover, the values of θ_μ^2 and, thus, ε^2 are also sufficiently larger. However, estimation accuracy is still mainly determined by the estimation bias and, therefore, it is possible to consider only one realization of the speckle in

Method	5x5 overlapping blocks			7x7 overlapping blocks		
	Δ_μ	$\theta_\mu^2 \bullet 10^{-6}$	$\varepsilon^2 \bullet 10^{-4}$	Δ_μ	$\theta_\mu^2 \bullet 10^{-6}$	$\varepsilon^2 \bullet 10^{-4}$
			Image Fr01			
Method 1	0.017	1.39	2.95	0.031	2.05	9.47
Method 2	0.034	19.46	11.71	0.042	20.64	17.53
Method 3	-0.008	48.17	1.06	-0.003	53.07	0.60
			Image Fr02			
Method 1	0.015	1.48	2.23	0.028	1.96	7.41
Method 2	0.030	10.60	8.99	0.042	9.99	17.58
Method 3	-0.008	57.63	1.27	-0.003	42.87	0.50
			Image Fr03			
Method 1	0.014	1.05	1.90	0.027	1.35	7.31
Method 2	0.032	16.01	10.49	0.045	8.51	19.93
Method 3	-0.010	31.94	1.31	-0.003	34.08	0.41
			Image Fr04			
Method 1	0.012	1.04	1.47	0.025	1.22	6.25
Method 2	0.016	50.39	3.11	0.017	33.40	3.30
Method 3	0.001	23.49	0.24	0.011	28.63	1.39

Table 1. Accuracy data for the considered test images corrupted by i.i.d. speckle (single-look case)

analysis of estimation accuracy. The results for 5x5 blocks for **Method 2** are slightly better than for 7x7 pixel blocks. Hence, the use of 5x5 pixel blocks is the better choice for the case of i.i.d. speckle.

Finally, let us analyse data for **Method 3** (see Table 1). This method produces estimates that have very small absolute values of bias which is mostly negative for both 5x5 and 7x7 pixel blocks. The values of θ_μ^2 are smaller than for **Method 2** but larger than for **Method 1**. However, due to small bias, **Method 3** provides the smallest ε^2 among the studied BENCs and thus, can be considered as the most accurate. The results for 5x5 and 7x7 block sizes are comparable and both block sizes can be recommended for practical use.

We have also obtained simulation results for 4-look test images corrupted by i.i.d. speckle (theoretical σ_μ^2 is equal to 0.273/4=0.068). They are the following. For the first test image, estimation bias is 0.0101, 0.0100 and 0.0005 for **Method 1**, **Method 2**, and **Method 3**, respectively. The values of θ_μ^2 are equal to 0.21x10^{-6}, 2.71x10^{-6}, and 2.73x10^{-6} for these three methods. Finally, the values of ε^2 are 1.028 x10^{-4}, 1.027x10^{-4}, and 0.030x10^{-4}, respectively. The results for other three test images are similar. Thus, we can state that **Method 3** again produces the best accuracy and the influence of estimation variance θ_{μ}^{2} can be ignored in further studies. One more observation is that the values of ε^{2} for multi-look test images have become smaller than for single-look test images. This does not mean that accuracy has improved since, in fact, accuracy has to be characterized not by ε^{2} but by $\varepsilon/\sigma_{\mu}^{2}$. In fact, accuracy characterized by $\varepsilon/\sigma_{\mu}^{2}$ has the tendency to make worse if σ_{μ}^{2} diminishes. This means that it is more difficult to accurately estimate speckle variance σ_{μ}^{2} for multi-look SAR images than for single-look ones.

Consider now the case of spatially correlated noise. We have carried out preliminary simulations and established that estimation bias contributes considerably more than estimation variance to the ε^{2}. Thus, below we present only the errors determined as the difference between the obtained estimate $\hat{\sigma}_{\mu}^{2}$ and the true value σ_{μ}^{2} for single (only one) realization. The simulation results for single-look images are collected in Table 2.

Method	Method 1		Method 2		Method 3	
Block size	**5x5**	**7x7**	**5x5**	**7x7**	**5x5**	**7x7**
Image Fr01	-0.0097	0.0178	0.0056	0.0041	-0.0348	-0.0138
Image Fr02	-0.0107	0.0148	-0.0070	0.0282	-0.0207	-0.0206
Image Fr03	-0.0089	0.0151	-0.0059	0.0305	-0.0194	-0.0116
Image Fr04	-0.0142	0.0103	0.0019	0.0355	-0.0408	-0.0294

Table 2. The values of $\hat{\sigma}_{\mu}^{2}$-σ_{μ}^{2} for the test single-look images corrupted by spatially correlated noise (σ_{μ}^{2}=0.273)

An interesting observation that follows from data analysis in Table 2 is that the differences are mostly negative, at least, for 5x5 block size, i.e. speckle variance is underestimated. This can be explained as follows. One factor that influences blind estimation is distribution mode position. Normal local estimates in blocks that form this mode are mostly smaller than σ_{μ}^{2} (Lukin et al., 2011b). Because of this, speckle variance estimates tend to smaller values for **Method 1**, cluster centers tend to smaller values for **Method 2** and **Method 3** as well. Another factor is the method robustness with respect to abnormal local estimates which are, recall, larger than normal estimates. These abnormal local estimates „draw" the final estimates to another side, i.e. „force" them to be larger. Thus, these two factors partly compensate each other. Since **Method 3** is more robust with respect to outliers (a large part of them is rejected due to pre-segmentation), this method provides smaller estimates $\hat{\sigma}_{\mu}^{2}$.

As it can be also seen from analysis of data in Table 2, the estimates $\hat{\sigma}_{\mu}^{2}$ for 7x7 blocks are larger than the corresponding estimates for 5x5 blocks. This is because mode position for normal local estimates shifts to right (to larger values) if the block size increases. This effects have been illustrated for spatially correlated speckle (Lukin et al., 2011b) and for spatially correlated additive noise (Abramov et al., 2008). Then, the final estimates for all BENCs also increase.

Analysis shows that it is worth using the block size 7x7 pixels for **Method 3** which is the most accurate according to simulation data.

Finally, simulation results for four-look test images corrupted by spatially correlated speckle are represented in Table 3. The data are presented as $\hat{\sigma}_{\mu}^{2}$ -σ_{μ}^{2} similarly to the previous case σ_{μ}^{2} =0.068. Overestimation is observed for **Method 1** for all four test images and overestimation is larger for 7x7 blocks. Even larger overestimation takes place for **Method 2**, especially if 7x7 blocks are used. **Method 3** usually produces small under-estimation, the errors are, on the average, the smallest among the considered BENCs and 7x7 block size seems to be a proper choice.

Method	Method 1		Method 2		Method 3	
Block size	5x5	7x7	5x5	7x7	5x5	7x7
Image Fr01	0.0025	0.0081	0.0063	0.0104	-0.0067	-0.0070
Image Fr02	0.0009	0.0055	0.0027	0.0103	-0.0076	-0.0031
Image Fr03	0.0037	0.0099	0.0042	0.0127	-0.0075	-0.0015
Image Fr04	0.0038	0.0096	0.0004	0.0109	-0.0071	0.0013

Table 3. The values of $\hat{\sigma}_{\mu}^{2}$ -σ_{μ}^{2} for the test four-look images corrupted by spatially correlated noise (σ_{μ}^{2}=0.068)

4. Verification results for real-life SAR images

First, we will verify our BENCs for the single-look real-life TerraSAR-X images presented in Figures 5 and 7. The obtained data will be considered in subsection 4.1. Besides, in subsection 4.2, we will verify our BENCs for multi-look SAR images of urban area in Canada (Toronto) (these images are presented later). All of them are acquired for HH polarization. As it is stated in file description, approximate number of looks is about 6. Thus, the expected $\sigma_{\mu}^{2} \approx 0.273/6 \approx 0.045$. Similarly, assuming σ_{μ}^{2}=0.045 for multi-look data, we can get the limits 0.036…0.054 for blind estimates that can be considered appropriate in practice. Let us keep these limits in mind in further analysis.

4.1. Verification results for single-look SAR images

Let us start from data obtained for **Method 1**. The estimates for block sizes 5x5, 7x7 and 9x9 pixels are collected in Table 4. We decided to analyse 9x9 blocks (not exploited in simulations) to understand practical tendencies and to be sure in our recommendations. Analysis shows that the estimates for 9x9 blocks are larger than for 7x7 and 5x5 blocks. Moreover, for the image in Fig. 5(a) the blind estimate is outside the desired limits. This happens because this image has complex structure and a large percentage of local estimates are abnormal. Although **Method 1** is robust with respect to outliers, its robustness is not enough to keep the blind estimate within the required limits.

Concerning other blind estimates, they all are within the required limits. For three of four real-life images, 7x7 block size is the best choice from the viewpoint of estimation accuracy.

Image presented in Figure	Block size		
	5x5	7x7	9x9
5(a)	0.292	0.322	0.348
5(b)	0.250	0.265	0.274
7(a)	0.240	0.270	0.283
7(b)	0.241	0.269	0.277

Table 4. Blind estimates of speckle variance for single-look real-life SAR images obtained by Method 1

Let us consider the results for two other BENC methods, both based on scatter-plots. Here we consider only the case of 7x7 blocks according to recommendations given in the previous Section. The estimates obtained by the **Method 2** for single-look images (Figs. 5 and 7) are, within the required limits (see data in Table 5) for three of four processed images. The only exception is again the image in Fig. 5(a), due to complexity of its structure. In general, the estimates for the **Method 2** are larger and less accurate than for the **Method 1** (see data in Table 4) for 7x7 blocks. We have the following explanation for that. It is quite difficult to provide unbiased estimates of cluster centers especially for those clusters that contain a relatively small number of points. Then, biasedness of cluster center estimates leads to final overestimation of speckle variance for **Method 2.**

Table 5 also contains blind estimates obtained by **Method 3**. All the estimates are within the required limits and they are, in general, more accurate than for other two methods. These conclusions also follow from analysis carried out by us for twenty 512x512 fragments of real-life SAR images (the data for 12 images are presented in Lukin et al., 2011b).

One more advantage of **Method 3** is that it is able to cope with image clipping effects. Note that clipping effects can arise due to limited range of image representation or incorrect scaling (Foi, 2009).

An example of such scatter-plot obtained as (6) for image with clipping effects is given in Fig. 9. Straight line shows the true position of the line to be fitted. As it is seen, there are three clusters (that correspond to large means) positions which are erroneous (vertical coordinates are considerably smaller than they should be). Although line fitting method is robust, the presence of a large percentage of such clusters can lead to essential errors in blind estimation.

4.2. Verification results for multi-look SAR images

The real-life six-look SAR images used in verification tests are given in Fig. 10. From visual inspection, the image in Fig. 10(d) seems to have more complex structures whilst other three images have quite large quasi-homogeneous regions. Let us see how this will influence blind estimates.

http://dx.doi.org/10.5772/57040

Image presented in Figure	Used method	
	Method 2, 7x7 blocks	Method 3, 7x7 blocks
5(a)	0.353	0.296
5(b)	0.289	0.259
7(a)	0.315	0.255
7(b)	0.315	0.266

Table 5. Blind estimates of speckle variance for single-look real-life SAR images obtained by Method 2 and Method 3

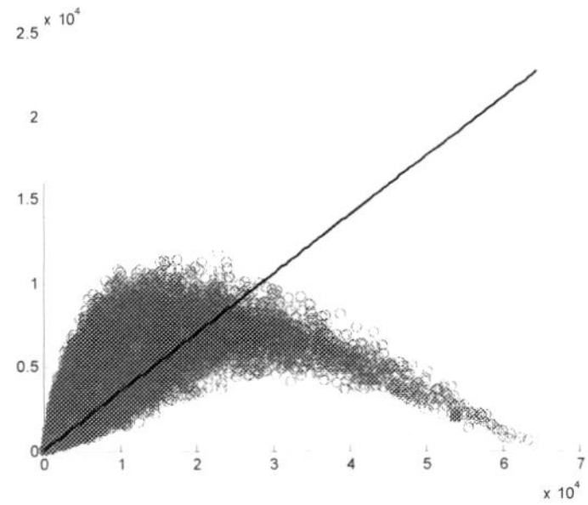

Figure 9. Scatter-plot for image with clipping effects

The obtained blind estimates for **Method 1** (three block sizes) are collected in Table 6. As it is seen, for 5x5 blocks they are mostly smaller than desired (the lower margin is 0.036), for 7x7 blocks all estimates are within the required limits (from 0.036 to 0.054), and two out of four estimates are larger than desired 0.054) for 9x9 blocks. Thus, 7x7 blocks are again the proper choice for **Method 1**. We would like to stress also that the estimate for the most complex image in Fig. 10(d) is always the largest for any given block size. To our experience, this is due to the influence of image content (large percentage of abnormal local estimates).

Image presented in Figure	Block size		
	5x5	7x7	9x9
10(a)	0.033	0.042	0.043
10(b)	0.034	0.048	0.055
10(c)	0.033	0.045	0.051
10(d)	0.038	0.053	0.061

Table 6. Blind estimates of speckle variance for six-look real-life SAR images obtained by Method 1

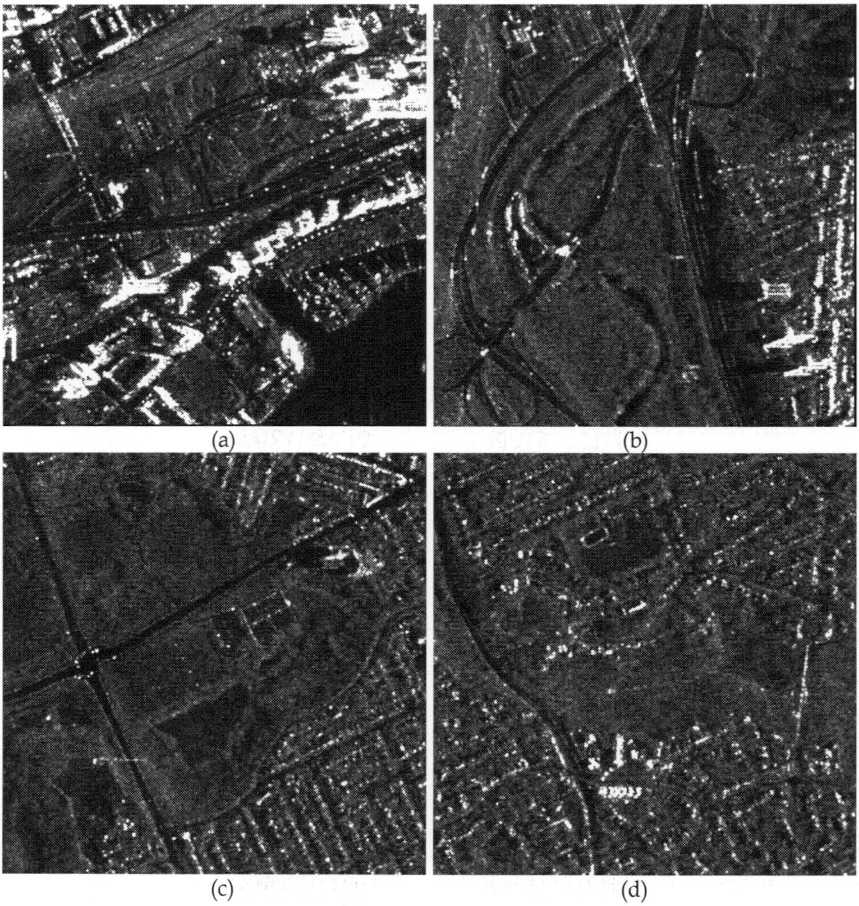

Figure 10. Multi-look SAR elementary images (512x512 pixels) of urban region in Canada

Finally, **Methods 2** and **3** have been verified for six-look images. The estimates are presented in Table 7 for 7x7 blocks. **Method 2** produces obvious overestimation (only one estimate is within the required interval and other ones exceed the upper limit). In turn, **Method 3** provides all four estimates accurate enough although underestimation is observed for all four processed images. Thus, **Method 3** operating in 7x7 blocks provides the best or nearly the best accuracy for all considered simulated and real-life images.

The presented results clearly show that for estimation techniques based on scatter-plots and robust fitting it is often not enough to carry out robust fitting. Image pre-processing able to partly remove local estimates expected to be abnormal (due to block heterogeneity or to presence of clipping effects) is desirable. Such pre-processing might include image pre-segmentation which in our experiments has been performed by unsupervised variational classification through image multi-thresholding (Klaine et al., 2005). Its advantage is that pre-processing is quite fast. This allows obtaining blind estimates quite quickly since other operations (obtaining of local estimates and robust regression) are also very fast.

Image presented in Figure	Used method	
	Method 2, 7x7 blocks	Method 3, 7x7 blocks
10(a)	0.051	0.041
10(b)	0.061	0.038
10(c)	0.089	0.036
10(d)	0.094	0.044

Table 7. Blind estimates of speckle variance for six-look real-life SAR images obtained by Method 2 and Method 3

5. Conclusions and future work

Some aspects of SAR image simulation have been considered. In particular, it has been stressed that spatial correlation of speckle is to be taken into account. One algorithm to do this is described.

Three methods for blind estimation of noise statistical characteristics in SAR images have been first tested for simulated images. It has been shown that there are several factors influencing their performance. These factors are image content (complexity), the method used and its parameters. It is not always possible to provide blind estimates within desired limits especially for highly textural (complex structure) images. Then, these methods have been verified for real life TerraSAR-X images of limited size of 512x512 pixels. Preliminary tests have clearly demonstrated the presence of essential spatial correlation of speckle, especially for multi-look images. This is taken into account in setting parameters of BENC methods. The block size of 7x7 pixels is recommended for practical use.

The BENC methods based on scatter-plots without image pre-processing produce, on the average, worse accuracy than the method based on mode determination for local estimates' distribution. If pre-processing is applied, BENC methods (as **Method 3**) are able to produce acceptable accuracy for most images. Estimation accuracy for single-look images is mostly acceptable. However, there are more problems with speckle variance estimation for multi-look images. Thus, in future, special attention should be paid to considering multi-look image case. In this sense, the methods based in obtaining noise-informative maps (Uss et al. 2011; Uss et al., 2012) seem to be attractive although they are not so fast as the methods considered above.

This work has been partly supported by French-Ukrainian program Dnipro (PHC DNIPRO 2013, PROJET N° 28370QL).

Author details

Sergey Abramov[1], Victoriya Abramova[1], Vladimir Lukin[1], Nikolay Ponomarenko[1], Benoit Vozel[2], Kacem Chehdi[2], Karen Egiazarian[3] and Jaakko Astola[3]

1 National Aerospace University, Ukraine

2 University of Rennes 1, France

3 Tampere University of Technology, Finland

References

[1] Abramov S., Lukin V., Ponomarenko N., Egiazarian K., & Pogrebnyak O. (2004). Influence of multiplicative noise variance evaluation accuracy on MM-band SLAR image filtering efficiency. *Proceedings of MSMW 2004*, Vol. 1, pp. 250-252, Kharkov, Ukraine, June 2004

[2] Abramov S., Lukin V., Vozel B., Chehdi K., & Astola J. (2008). Segmentation-based method for blind evaluation of noise variance in images, *Journal of Applied Remote Sensing*, Vol. 2(1), No. 023533, (August 13, 2008), DOI:10.1117/1.2977788

[3] Abramov S., Zabrodina V., Lukin V., Vozel B., Chehdi K., & Astola J. (2011). Methods for Blind Estimation of the Variance of Mixed Noise and Their Performance Analysis, In: *Numerical Analysis – Theory and Applications*, Ed. J. Awrejcewicz, pp. 49-70, InTech, Austria, ISBN 978-953-307-389-7

[4] Aiazzi B., Alparone L., Barducci A., Baronti S., Marcoinni P., Pippi I., & Selva M. (2006). Noise modelling and estimation of hyperspectral data from airborne imaging spectrometers. *Annals of Geophysics*, Vol. 49, No. 1, February 2006

[5] Anfinsen S.N., Doulgeris A.P., & Eltoft T. (2009). Estimation of the Equivalent Number of Looks in Polarimetric Synthetic Aperture Radar Imagery, *IEEE Transactions on Geoscience and Remote Sensing*, Vol. 47, No. 11, pp. 3795-3809

[6] Bekhtin Yu. S. (2011). Adaptive Wavelet Codec for Noisy Image Compression, *Proc. of the 9-th East-West Design and Test Symp.*, Sevastopol, Ukraine, Sept., 2011, pp. 184-188

[7] Choi M.G., Jung J.H., & Jeon J.W. (2009). No-reference Image Quality Assessment Using Blur and Noise, *World Academy of Science, Engineering and Technology*, Vol. 50, pp. 163-167

[8] Davies E.R. (2000). *Image Processing for the Food Industry*, World Scientific, ISBN 9810240228

[9] Di Martino G., Poderico M., Poggi G., Riccio D., & Verdoliva L. (2012). SAR Image Simulation for the Assessment of Despeckling Techniques, *Proceedings of IGARSS*, Munich, Germany, July 2012, pp. 1797-1800

[10] Dogan O., & Kartal M. (2010). Time Domain SAR Raw Data Simulation of Distributed Targets, *EURASIP Journal on Advances in Signal Processing*, Article ID 784815

[11] DuMouchel W. & O'Brien F. (1989). Integrating a Robust Option into a Multiple Regression Computing Environment in Computing Science and Statistics. *Proc. of the 21st Symposium on the Interface*, pp. 297-301, American Statistical Association, Alexandria, VA

[12] Egiazarian K., Astola J., Helsingius M., & Kuosmanen P. (1999). Adaptive denoising and lossy compression of images in transform domain. *Journal of Electronic Imaging*, Vol. 8(3), pp. 233-245, DOI:10.1117/1.482673

[13] Foi A., Trimeche M., Katkovnik V., & Egiazarian K. (2007). Practical Poissonian-Gaussian Noise Modeling and Fitting for Single Image Raw Data. *IEEE Transactions on Image Processing*, Vol. 17, No. 10, pp. 1737-1754

[14] Foi A. (2009). Clipped Noisy Images: Heteroskedastic Modeling and Practical Denoising. *Signal Processing*, Vol. 89, No. 12, pp. 2609-2629

[15] Foucher S., Boucher J.-M., & Benie G. B. (2000). Maximum likelihood estimation of the number of looks in SAR images, Proc. of Int. Conf. Microwave, Radar Wireless Communication, Wroclaw, Poland, May 2000, Vol. 2, pp. 657–660

[16] Herrmann J., Faller N., Kern A., & Weber M. (2005). INFOTERRA GMBH Initiatives Commercial Exploitation of TerraSAR-X, *Proc. of ISPRS Hannover Workshop*, Hannover, Germany, May 2005

[17] Katsaggelos A.K. (Ed.). (1991). *Digital Image Restoration*, Springer-Verlag, New York

[18] Klaine L., Vozel B., & Chehdi K. (2005). Unsupervised Variational Classification Through Image Multi-Thresholding. *Proc. of the 13th EUSIPCO Conference*, Antalya, Turkey

[19] Lee J.-S., Hoppel K., & Mango S.A. (1992). Unsupervised Estimation of Speckle Noise in Radar Images, *Int. Journal of Imaging Systems and Technology*. Vol. 4, pp. 298-305

[20] Lee J.-S., Wen J.H., Ainsworth T.I., Chen K.S., & Chen A.J. (2009). Improved sigma filter for speckle filtering of SAR imagery, *IEEE Transactions on Geoscience and Remote Sensing* Vol. 47(1), pp. 202–213

[21] Lin C.H., Sun Y.N., & Lin C.J. (2010). A Motion Compounding Technique for Speckle Reduction in Ultrasound Images, *Journal of Digital Imaging*, Vol. 23(3), pp. 246–257

[22] Liu C., Szeliski R., Kang S.B., Zitnick C.L., & Freeman W.T. (2008). Automatic estimation and removal of noise from a single image. *IEEE Transactions on Pattern Analysis and Machine Intelligence*, Vol. 30, No 2, pp. 299-314

[23] Lukin V., Abramov S., Zelensky A., Astola J., Vozel B., & Chehdi K. (2007). Improved minimal inter-quantile distance method for blind estimation of noise variance in images, *Proc. SPIE 6748 of Image and Signal Processing for Remote Sensing XIII*, 67481I October 24, 2007, DOI:10.1117/12.738006

[24] Lukin V., Ponomarenko N., Egiazarian K., & Astola J. (2008). Adaptive DCT-based filtering of images corrupted by spatially correlated noise, *Proc. SPIE 6812 of Image Processing: Algorithms and Systems VI*, 68120W, San Jose, USA, January 2008, DOI: 10.1117/12.764893

[25] Lukin V., Abramov S., Ponomarenko N., Uss M., Vozel B., Chehdi K., & Astola J. (2009a). Processing of images based on blind evaluation of noise type and characteristics. *Proceedings of SPIE Symposium on Remote Sensing*, Vol. 7477, Berlin, Germany, September 2009

[26] Lukin V.V., Abramov S.K., Uss M.L., Marusiy I.A., Ponomarenko N.N., Zelensky A.A., Vozel B., & Chehdi K. (2009b). Testing of methods for blind estimation of noise variance on large image database, In: *Practical Aspects of Digital Signal Processing*, Shahty, Russia, Retrieved from <http://k504.xai.edu.ua/html/prepods/lukin/BookCh1.pdf>

[27] Lukin V., Abramov S., Popov A., Eltsov P., Vozel B., & Chehdi K. (2010). A method for automatic blind estimation of additive noise variance in digital images, *Telecomunicaions and Radio Engineering*, Vol. 69(19), pp. 1681-1702

[28] Lukin V., Abramov S., Ponomarenko N., Uss M., Zriakhov M., Vozel B., Chehdi K., & Astola J. (2011). Methods and Automatic Procedures for Processing Images Based on Blind Evaluation of Noise Type and Characteristics. *SPIE Journal on Advances in Remote Sensing*, DOI: 10.1117/1.3539768

[29] Lukin V.V., Abramov S.K., Fevralev D.V., Ponomarenko N.N., Egiazarian K.O., Astola J.T., Vozel B., & Chehdi K. (2011b). Performance evaluation for Blind Methods of Noise Characteristics Estimation for TerraSAR-X Images, *Proc. SPIE 8180 of Image and Signal Processing for Remote Sensing XVII*, 81800X, Prague, Czech Republic, September 2011, DOI:10.1117/12.897730

[30] Mallat S. (1998). *A Wavelet tour of signal processing*, Academic Press, San Diego

[31] Oliver C. & Quegan S. (2004). *Understanding Synthetic Aperture Radar Images*, SciTech Publishing

[32] Plataniotis K.N. & Venetsanopoulos A.N. (2000). *Color Image Processing and Applications*, Springer-Verlag, NY

[33] Ponomarenko N.N., Lukin V.V., Egiazarian K.O., & Astola J.T. (2010). A method for blind estimation of spatially correlated noise characteristics, *Proc. SPIE 7532 of Image Processing: Algorithms and Systems VIII*, 753208, San Jose, USA, January 2010, DOI: 10.1117/12.847986

[34] Ponomarenko N.N., Lukin V.V., & Egiazarian K.O. (2011). Visually Lossless Compression of Synthetic Aperture Radar Images, *Proceedings of ICATT*, Kiev, Ukraine, September 2011, pp. 263-265

[35] Ramponi G. & D'Alvise R. (1999). Automatic Estimation of the Noise Variance in SAR Images for Use in Speckle Filtering, *Proceedings of EEE-EURASIP Workshop on Nonlinear Signal and Image Processing*, Vol. 2, pp. 835-838, Antalya, Turkey

[36] Sendur L. & Selesnick I.W. (2002). Bivariate shrinkage with local variance estimation. *IEEE Signal Processing Letters*, Vol. 9, No. 12, pp. 438-441

[37] Solbo S. & Eltoft T. (2004). Homomorphic Wavelet-based Statistical Despeckling of SAR Images. *IEEE Trans. on Geosc. and Remote Sensing*, Vol. GRS-42, No. 4, pp. 711-721

[38] Solbo S. & Eltoft T. (2008). A Stationary Wavelet-Domain Wiener Filter for Correlated Speckle, *IEEE Trans. on Geoscience and Remote Sensing*, Vol. 46(4), pp. 1219-1230

[39] Touzi R. (2002). A Review of Speckle Filtering in the Context of Estimation Theory. *IEEE Transactions on Geoscience and Remote Sensing*, Vol. 40, No. 11, pp. 2392-2404

[40] Uss M., Vozel B., Lukin V., & Chehdi K. (2011). Local Signal-Dependent Noise Variance Estimation from Hyperspectral Textural Images. *IEEE Journal of Selected Topics in Signal Processing*, Vol. 5, No. 2, DOI: 10.1109/JSTSP.2010.2104312

[41] Uss M., Vozel B., Lukin V., & Chehdi K. (2012). Maximum Likelihood Estimation of Spartially Correlated Signal-Dependent Noise in Hyperspectral Images, *Optical Engineering*, Vol. 51, No 11, DOI: 10.1117/1.OE.51.11.111712

[42] Van Zyl Marais I., Steyn W.H., & du Preez J.A. (2009). On-board image quality assessment for a small low Earth orbit satellite, *Proc. of the 7th IAA Symp. on Small Satellites for Earth Observation*, Berlin, Germany, May 2009

[43] Vozel B., Abramov S., Chehdi K., Lukin V., Ponomarenko N., Uss M., & Astola J. (2009). Blind methods for noise evaluation in multi-component images, In: *Multivariate Image Processing*, pp. 263-295, France

[44] Zabrodina V., Abramov S., Lukin V., Astola J., Vozel B., & Chehdi K. (2011). Blind Estimation of mixed noise parameters in images using robust regression curve fitting, *Proc. of 19th European Signal Processing Conference EUSIPCO2011*, Barcelona, Spain, August 2009, pp. 1135 – 1139, ISSN 2076-1465

[45] Zoran D. & Weiss Y. (2009). Scale Invariance and Noise in Natural Images, *Proc. of IEEE 12th International Conference on Computer Vision ICCV*, Kyoto, Japan, September 2009, pp. 2209-2216, DOI:10.1109/ICCV.2009.5459476

Chapter 15

Spectral Study with Automatic Formant Extraction to Improve Non-native Pronunciation of English Vowels

R. Munoz-Luna, A. Jurado-Navas and
L. Taillefer de Haya

Additional information is available at the end of the chapter

http://dx.doi.org/10.5772/57221

1. Introduction

The purpose of this paper is to develop the frequency domain of the study started in [1]. In particular, we present an algorithm which obtains the first two formants ($F1$ and $F2$) of a vowel segment. These two elements are most often enough to disambiguate an English vowel, being crucial for non-native speakers' oral training. $F1$ and $F2$, corresponding to mouth opening and tongue position respectively, provide the necessary information for a proficient pronunciation. The phonological information rendered by $F1$ and $F2$ frequency contents produces an algorithm which can help non-native students of English in positioning their tongue and lips.

2. State of the art

The most widely cited experiment on vowel perception and acoustics is a simple one conducted at Bell Telephone Laboratories [2]. In that paper, authors recorded repetitions of ten vowels in /h V d/ context uttered by 33 men, 28 women, and 15 children. From these recordings, the first three formant frequencies ($F1 - F3$) as well as the fundamental frequency ($F0$) were extracted. Nevertheless, there was considerable formant frequency variability among participants, and formant frequency patterns overlapped substantially.

Formant frequencies have been already well-studied in both American and British English vowels [2–7]. On another note, remarkable numerical investigations were performed by Jan Awrejcewicz involving vocal cord oscillations and primary resonances [8, 9] and other particular effects as stability and bifurcation phenomena [10].

As far as phonology teaching is concerned, Pavón implemented a software programme [1] as a learning tool for his university students of English. One of Pavón's software applications is the fact that users can record a specific phoneme and compare it with an already existing phoneme in his software programme. This sound comparison results in a graphical degree of similarity expressed as percentages, showing the resemblance between user and programme sound waves.

Nevertheless, as Pavón himself states, this is an approximate value and it depends on recording conditions (e.g. room noise and external variables), which make an indicative result. Although the idea is conceptually good, a frequency domain analysis is required in order to draw out the degree of resemblance between users' wave forms and those included in the system. On the one hand, software programmes do not distinguish between male and female voice recordings even though fundamental frequencies and formants are different in both cases. Women present peak energy in higher frequencies when talking, and Pavón's software only includes female recordings. On a different matter, time domain comparisons are not significant: results are very often meaningless.

For this reason, this paper attempts to improve the afore-mentioned software including a frequency domain analysis by means of fundamental frequency and $F1$, $F2$ identification. This would allow a more significant comparison between users' recordings and programme audio database. At the same time, depending on formant position, learners will receive information on mouth opening and tongue positioning according to each vowel sound. Consequently, we are making use of authors' previous research on audio signal processing [11], knowledge on communication channels [12], numerical methods [13], analytical modelling [14] and English applied linguistics [15]. This theoretical framework backs up a useful tool for students of English who want to autonomously improve their pronunciation of English vowels.

Finally, we are only focusing on vocalic sounds since not all human sounds offer well-defined formants. Vowels, on their part, do have distinct formants and their study complements oral language teaching, in this case, of the English language.

3. Organs of speech

Vowels are the result of glottal source, supraglottal tract and their filtering effects. Same quality vowels have similar spectral shapes, without regard to the source fundamental frequency (this is a variable that changes considerably depending on the speaker's age, sex and emotions). The air coming from the lungs supplies the necessary energy to produce sounds. Thanks to vocal cords vibration, the rate of air flow through the glottis generates a complex periodic wave. Glottal source waves and spectrum vary depending on the type of phonation. The differences in the waveform are due to the different amount of time that the vocal folds are open during a glottal cycle. Figure 1 shows the organs of speech in a cross-section:

The fundamental frequency, $F0$, also called the glottal frequency of the vocal fold vibration,S is dependent on several factors such as mass, length and tension of the folds which are interrelated in a fairly complicated way. These are typical values for $F0$ (during normal speech production, voicing frequency varies over an octave):

- adult male voice: 125 Hz.
- adult female voice: 220 Hz.
- child voice: 300 Hz

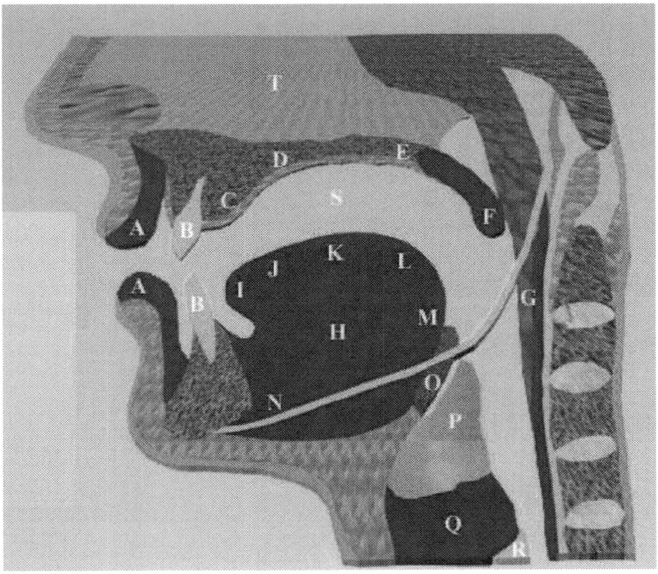

Figure 1. Organ of speech: A. Lips, B. Teeth, C. Teeth ridge, D. Hard palate, E. Soft palate, F. Uvula, G. Pharynx, H. Tongue body, I. Tongue tip, J. Blade, K. Tongue front, L. Back of the tongue, M. Tongue root, N. Jaw, O. Epiglottis, P. Thyroid cartilage, Q. Cricothyroid cartilage, R. Trachea, S. Oral cavity, T. Nasal cavity. Figure taken from [1].

Vocal tract filter selectively passes energy in the harmonics of the source. The size/shape of the vocal tract determines the amount of energy that is used in oral speech. For each vocalic sound, the so-called formants describe their characteristic resonance. In fact, the vocal tract transfer function for a particular vowel is defined by formant bandwidth and frequency. We can model the acoustic properties of the vocal tract as a tube open at one end, which is the mouth, and closed at the glottis. Assuming this tube uniformity, resonant frequencies can be calculated with the following formula:

$$F_n = \frac{(2n-1)c}{4L}, \tag{1}$$

where n is the number of the formant, c is the speed of sound, and L is the length of the tube. However, we also need to consider acoustic constrictions in the vocal tract. One way of modelling the acoustic properties of vowels is to represent the vocal tract as a concatenation of tubes [16]. An alternative approach is known as perturbation theory, which deals with vocalic acoustics in terms of relationship between air pressure and speed [17].

3.1. Formant frequencies of the vowels

First formant frequency ($F1$) is traditionally influenced by the shape of the vocal tract. $F1$ is inversely related to tongue height: low vowels have high $F1$ and high vowels have low

$F1$. On the other hand, second formant frequency ($F2$) corresponds to length and size of the speaker's oral cavity; in this case, front vowels have high $F2$ whereas back vowels have low $F2$; the formant frequencies decrease through the cardinal vowels, where the cardinal vowels can be consulted at [18]. Nevertheless, these relationships are not straightforward since there are other factors influencing sound production (e.g. lip rounding, tongue retroflexion, among others).

Articulatory properties of vowels are determined by these $F1$ and $F2$ formants in such a way that one is plotted against the other. Because of the inverse relationship between articulatory parameters and formant frequencies, zero frequency is at the top right corner. In Fig. 2 [1], we have displayed where English vowels are pronounced inside the oral cavity:

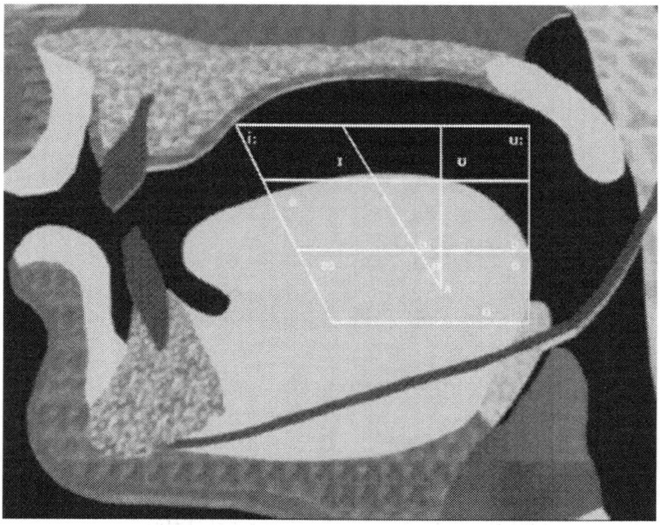

Figure 2. Vowel trapezium inserted in the oral cavity, indicating tongue movements for the pronunciation of the different vocalic phonemes [1].

4. Methodology

In this section, we present the algorithm implemented to find the frequency and amplitude of the first formants during any vowel-like segment. In order to analyse any speech fragment, a time-frequency analysis is needed. Short-time Fourier transforms (STFT), constant-Q [19] and wavelet transforms are some of the most commonly employed solutions in several systems. In this paper, the main idea is based on a previous work [20], tested on a large number of utterances produced by several different speakers; McCandless's discovery was found to be extremely successful. This algorithm is combined with some other ideas already developed by authors [11] in the context of polyphonic piano recordings.

We should remark that this manuscript comes to complement the work initiated in [1], so the recordings accepted by our system consists of only one vowel each, unlike the one presented in [20]. The latter developed a completely automatic algorithm which was meant to yield

http://dx.doi.org/10.5772/57221

the first three formants during all voiced sounds in continuous unrestricted speech. For this reason, the algorithm developed in this paper can be implemented more easily and productively.

4.1. Data acquisition and preprocessing

This stage consists in the recording of a vowel file. The audio data was kept in a WAV file at a sample rate of 44.1 kHz. The system accepts a monaural file as well as a stereophonic one. Then, the digitized signal is low-pass filtered in order to eliminate high frequency components.

4.2. Onset detection and temporal segmentation: windowing

As in [11], our system divides the vowel-segment into temporal slots and, afterwards, a frequency analysis of each slot is done. This temporal segmentation is based on the detection of onsets, so the system is prepared for detecting when a phoneme starts in the recording. This information makes it possible to discard frames whose total spectral energy is below a threshold for silence, and that must not be processed by the system.

After that, a Hamming window [13, Eq. 56] is applied to the segmented signal so that the extreme samples of the segments had less weight that the central samples. In this paper, we use a M-points Hamming window symmetric about the point $M/2$ of the form

$$w[n] = \begin{cases} 0.54 - 0.46\cos(2\pi n/M), & 0 \leq n \leq M, \\ 0, & \text{otherwise}; \end{cases} \tag{2}$$

owing to it is optimized to minimize the maximum (nearest) side lobe.

4.3. Sliding window procedure

A sliding window procedure [11] is employed to detect any increases in energy that exceed a certain threshold. This threshold has been selected to characterize the appearance of an onset. Rectangular windows that contain 4096 samples ($\approx$ 92.8 ms) of the signal to analyze are employed. The number of samples is chosen to be a power of two so that a fast Fourier algorithm can be employed to compute all values of the discrete Fourier transforms (DFTs) when performing a frequency analysis of the vowel-segment. Thus, the number of arithmetical operations required will be substantially reduced. Moreover, the character quasi-periodic and quasi-stationary of speech in that interval is seen as an additional justification for the size of these blocks, and will be of great utility in further upgrades of this system.

For any 4096 samples segmentation, a peak-picking method as the one employed in [20] was developed to extract formants. The justification of having the recording divided into frames of 92.8 ms is to detect such formants easily. Peaks can appear and dissapear from one frame to the next one due to resonances in the vocal tract and due to nasalizations, and the segmentation of the recording in frames of 4096 samples allows to successfully detect formants despite the mentioned fact of nasalizations.

In general, this latter effect presents a special problem because the nasalization is just a resonance of the nasal tract (it can be seen as a pole in the transfer function) whereas the oral tract is a closed side branch, which causes zeros (minimun energy in the spectrum). Frequently, the second formant, $F2$ is greatly reduced in amplitude, because of a nearby zero; and, in fact, often there is no peak corresponding to $F2$. In particular, the nasalization of a vowel is a problem of similar nature. In this case, the nasal cavity is an open side branch, causing extra zeros and extra poles. In a nasalized front vowel, typically, there is an extra small peak slightly above the first formant in frequency. In a nasalized back vowel, the apparent bandwidth of $F1$ becomes quite wide, because of a nearby zero, and sometimes there is no peak for $F1$. We will show this effect in the results included through this paper.

For each frame, a $N-$FFT is employed to compute all values of the DFTs. If the number of samples of the last frame is not a power of two, it is required to first zero-pad such a last frame previous to compute the FFT of the sequence [13]. As an interesting remark, for the computation of all N values of a DFT using the definition, the number of arithmetical operations required is approximately N^2, while the amount of computation is approximately proportional to $N \log_2 N$ for the same result to be computed by an FFT algorithm [21].

4.4. Processing of each frame: formant extraction

In this case, same steps as in [20] are developed. For each frame, fundamental frequency is first detected. Normally, it is always obtained as the peak with maximum energy. In our paper, all the tests were carried out by adult females, so fundamental frequencies were detected between 190-240 Hz in all cases, depending of the vowel produced by women. Tests have been restricted to women because the previous system implemented by Pavón in [1] was released with solely recordings of women. We must stress that, according to the signal processing problem, recordings obtained from women or recording produced by men are exactly the same problem, and the treatment and the way to solve both of them would be exactly the same.

Secondly, as in [11], we eliminate harmonics of fundamental frequency in each frame except, if we find a peak with higher energy placed in a potential harmonic. The constraint we impose in this step is that the amplitude of a peak placed in the frequency corresponding to the n-th harmonic must be lower than the amplitud of the peak positioned in the frequency corresponding to the $n-1$-th harmonic, with $n \leq 1$, where, in this notation, the 0-harmonic frequency is the fundamental frequency.

As a third step, our system fetches peaks finding the frequencies and amplitude of possible formants in the region from 150 to 3400 Hz. By executing this step in each 4096-sample frame, the system can detect peaks that appear, peak mergers as well as peak cancellations due to pernicious effect of the resonances and nasalizations commented above. Hence, we can take advantage of a very important feature in voice signals: the no continuity, i.e., how frequency formants can change from frame to frame, and new peaks can appear in a frame and disappear in the next one. A complete analysis of the voice signal without segmentation would entail, in many occasions, an error in the estimation of the formants, because some formants would not have enough energy to be detected.

After doing that, our system has selected some candidates to be the formants in each frame. One particular feature in the analysis of each frame is that the fundamental frequency is

http://dx.doi.org/10.5772/57221

moved to lower frequencies in subsequent frames. This fact let us obtain the bandwidth of this fundamental frequency for a most effective harmonic elimination. A final smoothing may be accomplished at each voiced frame in the same way as proposed by McCandless, to yield the formant tracks. The interpolated and smoothed values are valid if they are not too "different" from the original.

Finally, if any formant is not achieved, for instance, due to it has been merged with another one, an enhancement procedure is included using linear prediction analysis [20] employing, for this case, the linear prediction filter coefficients routine (*lpc.m*) included in MATLAB, based on an autocorrelation method of autoregressive (AR) modeling, as the one implemented in [12], to find the filter coefficients. Once the coefficients, a_k, are available, we can obtain in a straight manner the approximated spectrum by simply evaluating the magnitude of the transfer function, $H(f)$ of the filter represented by the coefficients a_k, at N equally spaced samples along the unit circle [20]:

$$H(f) = a_0 - \sum_{k=1}^{p} a_k \exp\left(-j2\pi nk/N\right) \tag{3}$$

For this purpose, the system can employ the function

```
filter([0, -a_k(2:end)], 1,xn);
```

as a previous step, where `a_k` are the coefficients, a_k, of the transfer function, `xn` is the original audio recording, and $n = 0, 1..., N-1$. As indicated in [20], two closely spaced formants frequently merge into one spectral peak, and cannot be resolved on the unit circle even with infinite resolution. However, they can often be separated by simply recomputing the spectrum on a circle of radius, r, less than 1. This amounts to reevaluating $H(f)$ at $x = r\exp j(2\pi n/N)$, r < 1. Because the contour comes in closer to the two poles, their peaks are enhanced, and a separation can be effected. Hence, by the estimated characters of linear prediction coding spectrum, in the region that the energy of signals is strong, i.e. the region closing to the peak value of the spectrum, the linear prediction coding spectrum is closing to the signal spectrum. However in the region that the energy of signals is weak, i.e. the region closing to the vale of the spectrum, both spectrums are significantly different. So to check the peak values of the linear prediction spectrum can confirm the formant.

5. Results and discussions

In this section, we are showing some results offered by the implemented system. As we have commented above, tests and recordings have been carried out in adult females, following the original system by [1], which was resealed in 2001. Nevertheless, we must remark that the signal processing problem would be identical in the case of males and children; the automatic formant extraction method would not change. After the process described in Section 3, , the system would have selected frequency peaks as candidate formants in each recording. The formant frequencies of vowels produced by males would be surely moved to lower frequencies in relation to the formant frequencies of vowels produced by women (see [4], for instance).

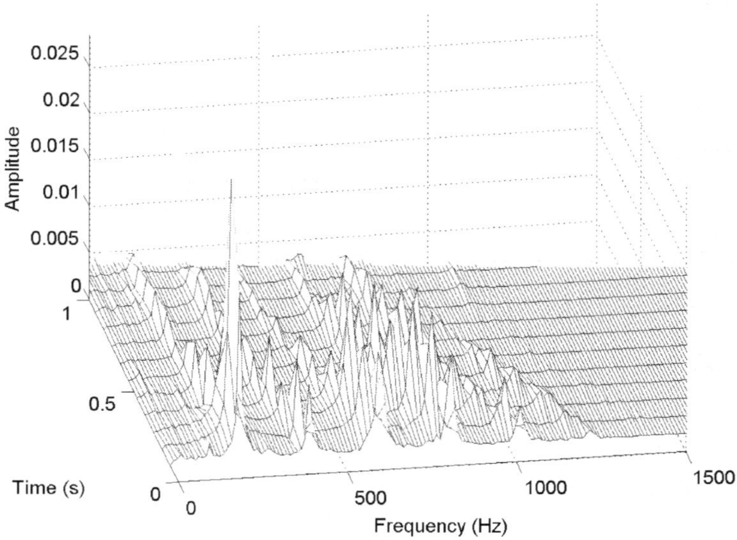

Figure 3. Time-varying spectral representation derived of a wrong-pronounced vowel number 5 = /a:/ by a woman of 29 years old.

In addition, the algorithm presented in this paper is based on the one by [20], which is effective in formant extraction during all vowel-like segments of continuous speech. In our particular case, voice recordings are even simpler, since they contain just a vowel sound, following the original system implemented by Pavón [1]. Our system compares users' recordings to those already included in its database, those latter which are the students' references in English learning. This algorithm will show users how to position their jaws and tongues for a correct vowel pronunciation by analysing formant frequency shift in vowels uttered by users in comparison to already-recorded model formants. This association comes with the relationship between $F1$, $F2$ and articulatory means. Consequently, there is a direct connection between first formant rising frequency and mouth opening: the higher $F1$ frequency is, the more open the vowel, and vice versa. Moreover, there is also a direct association between tongue backward movement and $F2$ frequency lowering: high $F2$ frequencies imply front vowels and vice versa. These conclusions can be verified in the results offered by [3, 4], especially in Table V in [4]). These authors confirm the correlation between first formant frequencies and vowel type (e.g. open, close, front and back).

As a significant result, we analyse a 29 year old female trying to pronounce vowel number 5 [18]. Initially, she does not position her mouth and tongue appropriately, being her mouth opening not wide enough. In addition, her tongue position is not so back as required. In Fig. 3 the temporal evolution of the spectrum derived when trying to pronounce the vowel number 5 [18] = /a:/ is displayed.

http://dx.doi.org/10.5772/57221

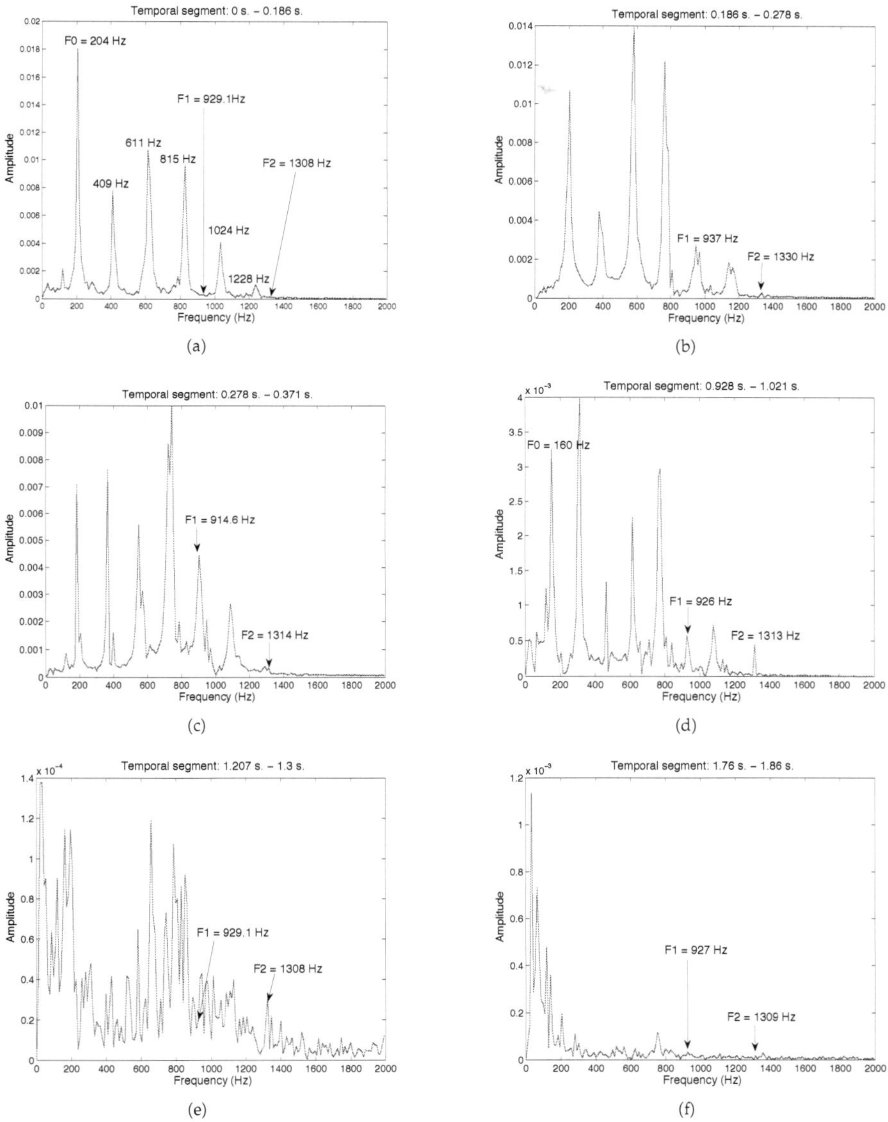

Figure 4. Spectra of different temporal segments after applying the sliding window procedure of a wrong-pronounced vocal number 5 = /a:/ by a woman of 29 years old. (a) 0 - 92.8 ms, (b) 0.186 - 0.278 s, (c) 0.278 - 0.371 s, (d) 0.928 - 1.021 s, (e) 1.207-1.3 s, (f) 1.76 - 1.86 s.

Now, in Fig. 4, we show some spectrums obtained from different temporal segments after applying the sliding window procedure detailed in previous section. As indicated above, any temporal segment is of approximately 92.8 ms. In particular, we are showing the following intervals: 0 - 92.8 ms (Fig. 4.a), 0.186 - 0.278 s (Fig. 4.b), 0.278 - 0.371 s (Fig. 4.c), 0.928 - 1.021 s (Fig. 4.d), 1.207-1.3 s (Fig. 4.e), 1.76 - 1.86 s (Fig. 4.f). We can clearly see the evolution of different peaks in the spectrum. Most of them are harmonics from the fundamental frequency ($F0 = 201.9Hz$). For instance, in Fig. 4.a, the fundamental frequency is placed in 204 Hz. Peaks at 409, 611, 815 1024 and 1228 Hz are considered the first five harmonics of $F0$. Through Fig. 4, we can see the evolution of the formants ($F1$ and $F2$) in each of the temporal segments. Even although these formants could have a low level of energy (above all in the second formant), the system operates successfully, as can be observed in Fig. 5.b. There, the system concludes that, for this recording of a 29 year old woman, the fundamental frequency is detected at 201.9 Hz, whereas the first two formants are positioned at 929.1 Hz and 1308 Hz, respectively. A peak at 872 Hz was also present, but it was discarded by the system after checking it is a harmonic of the 175.3 Hz-spurious peak. Finally, the spectrum of the whole recording (2.64 s in time, after detecting the onset of the vowel and rejecting the samples before the onset) is included in Fig. 5.a.

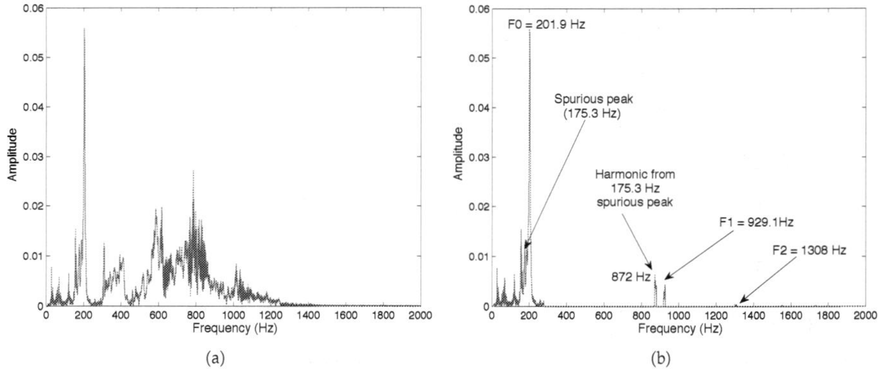

Figure 5. Spectrum of the whole recording (a), and amplitudes of fundamental frequency and frequencies of the two first formants (b).

At this stage, our system compares formant positions coming from this female recording to original recordings in [1]. According to Pavón, formants are placed at 940 and 1540 Hz, respectively. Therefore, this female subject has not achieved the correct articulatory mode or articulatory point. More specifically, her mouth is closer than required, and that is why $F1$ appears moved leftwards, from 940 Hz to 926 Hz. If $F1$ frequency had been higher, we would have had a too wide mouth opening. On the other hand, the articulatory point is not correct either: $F2$ appears at 1306 Hz, which is a much lower frequency than the 1540 Hz indicated in [1]. In this case, the subject has uttered vowel number 5 with a too backwards tongue position, while the system suggests a more central one. On the contrary, if her tongue had been more fronted, $F2$ could be detected in frequencies higher than 1540 Hz. The evolution of the first formant frequencies for each English vowel appears in Table V in [4], for American English vowels, and in [3], for British English.

http://dx.doi.org/10.5772/57221

Thanks to the corrections suggested by our system, the subject uttered vowel number 5 again, with the result shown in Fig. 6. As in the previous case, we are depicting in detail some time segments resulting from sliding window procedure described above. As indicated, any temporal segment is of approximately 92.8 ms. In this case, we are showing the following intervals: 0 - 92.8 ms (Fig. 7.a), 0.371 - 0.464 s (Fig. 7.b), 0.464 - 0.557 s (Fig. 7.c), 0.835 - 0.928 s (Fig. 7.d), 0.928 - 1.021 s (Fig. 7.e), 1.02 - 1.115 s (Fig. 7.f)

In this case, gesture corrections pointed out by our system allow the speaker to approach the target vowel sound. As we can see in Fig. 8.b, $F1$ and $F2$ are 934 and 1495 Hz, respectively, being $F1 = 940$ Hz and $F2 = 1540$ Hz the referential frequencies recorded in the system. Consequently, this new recording is closer to the adequate pronunciation range of vowel number 5. If we accept a +-5% error range, the speaker's new pronunciation can be considered correct since the system error calculation is the following:

$$\text{Error in F1 (\%)} = \frac{|934 - 940|}{940} = 0.6\%. \tag{4}$$

$$\text{Error in F2 (\%)} = \frac{|1495 - 1540|}{1540} = 2.92\%. \tag{5}$$

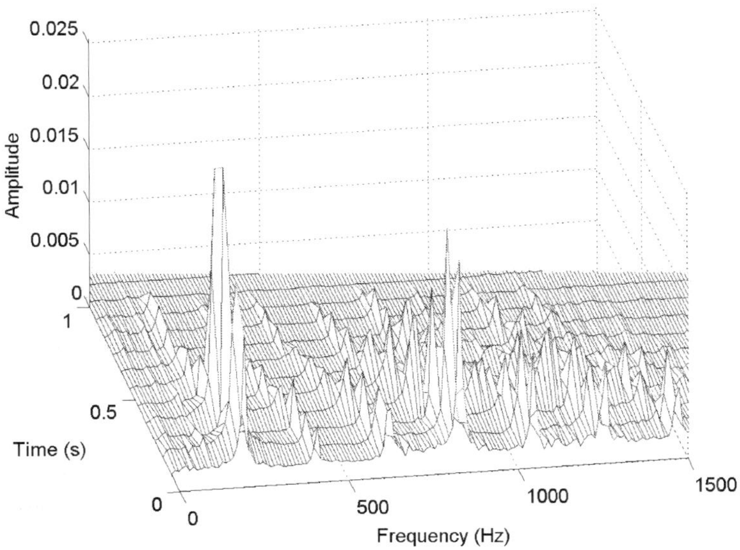

Figure 6. Time-varying spectral representation derived of vocal number 5 = /a:/.

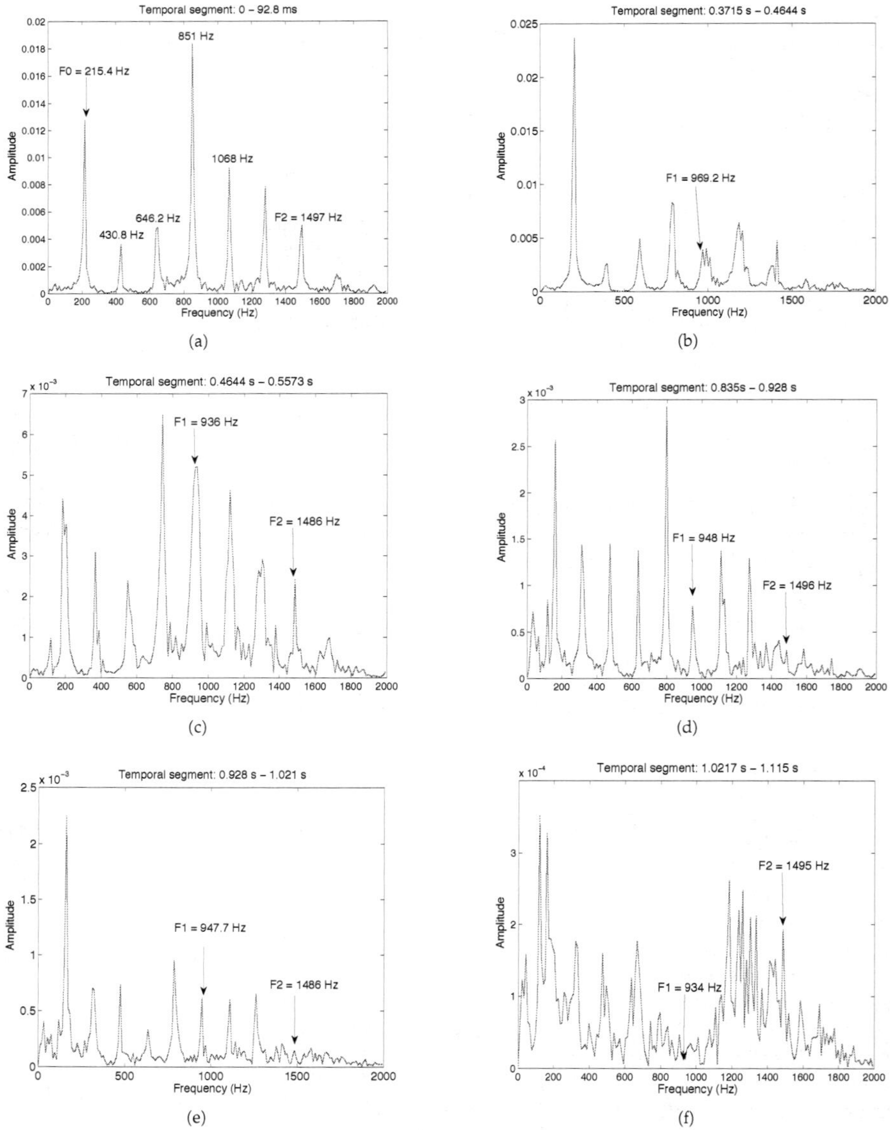

Figure 7. Spectra of different temporal segments after applying the sliding window procedure of a well-pronounced vocal number 5 = /a:/ by a woman of 29 years old.. (a) 0 - 92.8 ms, (b) 0.371 - 0.464 s, (c) 0.464 - 0.557 s, (d) 0.835 - 0.928 s, (e) 0.928 - 1.021 s, (f) 1.021 - 1.115 s

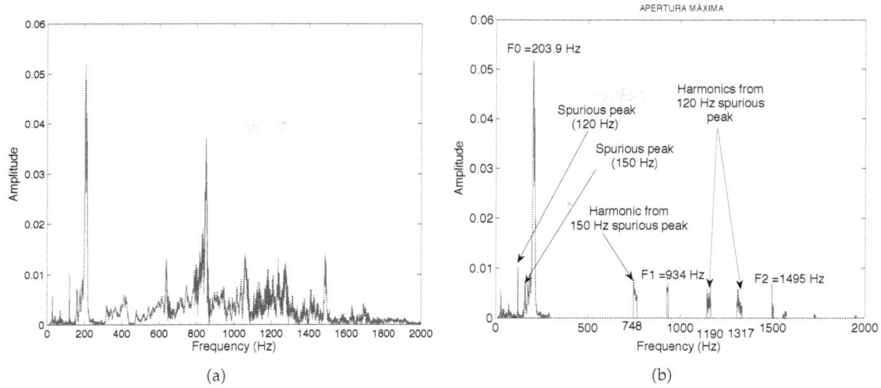

Figure 8. Spectrum of the whole recording (a), and amplitudes of fundamental frequency and frequencies of the two first formants (b).

With respect to vowel duration, our system does not pay attention to this feature because we understand that any user can distinguish a long duration with respect to a short duration of any vowel recording included in the system.

Finally, as in [20], the success of the automatic formant extraction algorithm is even higher than in McCandless's work because vowels are given to the system in an isolated manner and not in a sentence. Only when the formant was too strongly cancelled by a nearby zero (in nasals and nasalized vowels), or a peak merger was not resolve, the system does not achieve the correct result, but represent only a 10-15 percent of the total cases.

6. Concluding remarks

In this paper we have improved the tool implemented in [1], which consists in a software system for the teaching of English phonology. Pavón's contribution allows phoneme recordings, which are later on compared to similar sounds in the system. However, it offers a comparison based on the time domain, which is certainly not significant when providing help for learning a second language pronunciation. Moreover, it includes female voice recordings only, so male users (and children) would not obtain a significant result. Taking into account that Pavón's original idea is very good for those students who lack listening and pronunciation skills, this paper describes a new procedure to be added to the previous system and which is based on a frequency domain analysis. In this way, by means of a formant detection algorithm based on [20] and [11], the system can offer a more realistic contribution to the teaching of English pronunciation and phonology. F1 and F2 indicate oral cavity opening and tongue position respectively, and so the system specifies whether students have to open or close their mouths and which tongue part must be particularly employed in each vowel sound. As [1] makes use of female voice recordings only, our subjects are female adults. However, our formant detection algorithm would work with male and children voices equally. Male and children native' speakers are required for reference in order to have their voices recorded and can be employed to appropriately compare with male and children non-native users of our system.

Acknowledgments

The authors are grateful for financial support from the Junta de Andalucía (research group "Communications Engineering (TIC-0102)").

Author details

R. Munoz-Luna[1], A. Jurado-Navas[2], and L. Taillefer de Haya[1]

1 Department of English, French and German Philologies. Faculty of Humanities. University of Málaga, Spain

2 Communications Engineering Department, University of Málaga, Spain

References

[1] Pavón, V. Sistema software para la contribución a la docencia de la fonética inglesa, v. 1.0, vocales y consonantes, 2001. [CD-ROM] Universidad de Córdoba, Servicio de Publicaciones, 2001.

[2] Peterson, G.E., Barney, H.L. Control methods used in a study of vowels. Journal of the Acoustical Society of America 1952; 24(2) 175–184.

[3] Deterding, D.. The formants of monophthong vowels in Standard Southern British English pronunciation. Journal of the International Phonetic Association 1997; 27(1-2) 47–55.

[4] Hilenbrand, J., Getty-M., L. A., Clark, J., Wheeler, K. Acoustic characteristics of American English vowels. Journal of the Acoustical Society of America 1995; 97(5) 3099–3111.

[5] Bauer, L. Tracing phonetic change in the received pronunciation of British English. Journal of Phonetics 1985; 13(3)61–81.

[6] Di Benedetto, M. G. Frequency and time variations of the first formant: properties relevant to the perception of vowel height. Journal of the Acoustical Society of America 1989; 86(1) 67–77.

[7] Hilenbrand, J., Gayvert, R. T. Vowel classification based on fundamental frequency and formant frequencies. Journal of Speech and Hearing Research 1993; 36(4) 694–700.

[8] Awrejcewicz, J. Bifurcation portrait of the human vocal cord oscillations. Journal of Sound and Vibration 1990; 136(1) 151–156.

[9] Awrejcewicz, J. Numerical analysis of the oscillations of human vocal cords. Nonlinear Dynamics 1991; 2(1) 35–52.

[10] Awrejcewicz, J. Numerical investigations of the constant and periodic motions of the human vocal cords including stability and bifurcation phenomena. Journal of Dynamics and Stability of Systems 1990; 5(1) 11–28.

[11] Barbancho-Pérez, I., Jurado-Navas, A., Barbancho-Pérez, A., Tardón, L. Transcription of piano recordings. Elsevier Applied Acoustics 2004; 65(12) 1261–1287.

[12] Jurado-Navas, A., Puerta-Notario, A. Generation of correlated scintillations on atmospheric optical communications. Journal of Optical Communications and Networking 2009; 1(5) 452–462.

[13] Jurado-Navas, A., Garrido-Balsells, J. M., Castillo-Vázquez, M., Puerta-Notario, A. A computationally efficient numerical simulation for generating atmospheric optical scintillations. In: Awrejcewicz J. (ed.) Numerical simulations of physical and engineering processes Rijeka: Intech; 2011. p. 157 - 180.

[14] Jurado-Navas, A., Garrido-Balsells, J. M., Paris, J. F., Castillo-Vázquez, M., Puerta-Notario, A. Impact of pointing errors on the performance of generalized atmospheric optical channels. Optics Express 2012; 20(11) 12550–12562.

[15] Taillefer de Haya, L., Silva Ros, M. T. New technologies in English Applied Linguistics. In: Proceedings of the 30th International AEDEAN Conference, Huelva, Ed. María Losada Friend et al. Huelva: U de Huelva, 2007.

[16] Fant, G. Acoustic Theory of Speech Production. The Hague: Mouton; 1960.

[17] Chiba, T., Kajiyama, M. The Vowel: Its Nature and Structure. Tokyo: Kaiseikan; 1941.

[18] IPA, The International Phonetic Association. http:www.langsci.ucl.ac.ukipa (accessed 20 May 2013).

[19] Brown, J. C. Calculation of a constant Q spectral transform. Journal of the Acoustical Society of America 1991; 89(1) 425–434.

[20] McCandless, S.S. An algorithm for automatic formant extraction using linear prediction spectra. IEEE Transactions on Acoustics, Speech, and Signal Processing 1974; 2(2) 135–141.

[21] Oppenheim, A.V. Discrete-Time Signal Processing. Upper Saddle River, New Jersey, USA: Prentice-Hall, 2nd edition; 1999.

Chapter 16

Experimental Determinations and Numerical Simulations of the Effects of Electromagnetic Interferences into the Overhead Power Lines with Double Circuit, Operating with a Disconnected Circuit

Flavius Dan Surianu

Additional information is available at the end of the chapter

http://dx.doi.org/10.5772/57044

1. Introduction

The goal of finding methods and ways of warning and protecting the operating personnel, who perform maintenance programs on high voltage overhead power lines with double circuit, operating with a disconnected circuit, requires accurate knowledge of the electric and magnetic coupling mechanism as well as the voltages induced by these types of coupling at low frequency (50-60 Hz).

The experiments performed over the last 60 years in specialized laboratories around the world showed that low-frequency electromagnetic fields (50 Hz) generated by the overhead power lines affect both the functioning of electrical devices and equipments in the neighborhood and the health of living organisms in the area.

The experimental researches have showed that electromagnetic interferences of disturbing electromagnetic fields created by high voltage overhead power lines manifests itself mainly by two types of influences on the objects in the area, including the neighboring power lines, namely:

- Electrical influences produced by capacitive couplings between the phase conductors of electric three-phase lines and objects or neighboring power lines;
- Magnetic influences realized through the inductive couplings between the loops formed by the conductors of the neighboring parallel electric circuits and the earth.

The two types of influences are expressed, physically, through the values of the voltages induced in the elements of the electric conductor placed near the high voltage active power lines [1].

The accurate knowledge of these induced voltages, both electrically and magnetically, is necessary for searching the ways of reducing the adverse effects that these voltages produce and especially for ensuring the protection of the operating staff [2].

In practice, there are several ways of determining the electromagnetic values of the interferences of the high voltage overhead power lines, namely:

- Measurements on the ground with specialized measuring instruments. This method has a special importance for establishing some relative values and therefore it can be considered as a reference for the other methods. But this method has disadvantages related to the very limited possibilities to achieve, physically, different operating regimes in the real conditions. This method can also lead to the occurrence of relatively large errors produced by the measuring instruments. We have to consider the impossible of taking measurements in all the points of the proximate area of the power lines.
- Experimental determinations in high voltage specialized laboratories, using physical models that simulate, on an appropriate scale, the real situations on the ground. The method allows, theoretically, of realizing any operating regime of the power lines, being intuitive in terms of physical phenomena, but it is affected by errors due to the specific laboratory conditions of the realization of the physical model because some conditions imposed by the physical parameters of the objective reality (temperature, pressure, humidity, dielectric rigidity of the atmosphere, electrical permittivity and magnetic permeability of the environment) are neglected or circumvented.
- Mathematical modeling of the electromagnetic interferences using some modern ultra fast computing software which allows of obtaining through calculation the values of the electromagnetic values for any power line, at any point in the space around it in any operating regime. Mathematical modeling, although quick and easy in apply, has an inconvenience, namely: it doesn't offer reliability unless the results it produces are comparable to those obtained by at least one of the other two experimental methods mentioned above.

It means that a realistic research requires, along with the advantages of mathematical modeling and numerical simulation of electromagnetic phenomena from the objective reality the necessity to validate them through experiments so that the mathematical models should be able to confer reliability on the instruments used for the accurate representation of the natural phenomena of electromagnetic interferences. Taking into account these observations, we are presenting, comparatively, the results obtained by the author through measurements on the ground of the voltages induced electrically and magnetically in the disconnected circuits of 220 kV power lines with double circuit, from the Banat area – Romania, with the results obtained through mathematical modeling and numerical simulation of the voltages induced through capacitive and inductive couplings in the measuring points of the respective power line conductors. The concordance of the mathematical simulation results with those determined experimentally allow of validating the mathematical models which become, therefore, useful tools for the professionals in electric power systems.

2. A practical method for measuring on the ground the voltages induced by the overhead power lines

In the case of high voltage overhead power lines with double circuit having one of the electrical circuits disconnected for maintenance or repair, the active electrical circuit will induce electromotive voltages and will force the electric currents induced in the disconnected electric circuit, threatening the technical staff working on the respective line [3-5,7].

Considering this phenomenon, between years 2006 - 2009, the author measured on the ground the voltages induced in the 220 kV power lines with double circuit from the Banat area - Romania. These measurements were aimed at determining the level of electromagnetic stress which appears in a disconnected circuit, when in parallel with it there is the second circuit which is operating in normal regime. Experimentally, there has been established that immediately after disconnecting the circuit, although it is disconnected and insulated from the earth, the voltages induced through electric (capacitive) coupling appear on each phase and at the moment when the short-circuit devices are closed, the voltages induced through electric coupling become null and voltages induced through magnetic (inductive) coupling appear and they force the appearance of currents induced in the loops formed by each of the three phases of the disconnected circuit and the earth.

Given the appearance of two types of disturbances affecting the disconnected power line, the measurements must firstly take into account the determination of the voltages induced through electric (capacitive) coupling on each of the three phases, and then, that of the voltages induced by magnetic (inductive) coupling in the three loops of the disconnected circuit and connected to the ground through short-circuit devices, at one of its ends.

There are several methods of determining the induced voltages, but we have opted for using classical measurement apparatuses accessible to everybody, namely an electrostatic voltmeter, with a scale of up to 30 kV, a common voltmeter with a scale up to 2.5 kV and Ditz pliers ammeter, which is sensitive enough.

For measuring the voltages induced electrically and magnetically by the active circuit into the power lines of the disconnected circuits, the following two methods have been adopted [6]:

a. If the three-phase circuit conductors of the disconnected lines are not grounded through short-circuit devices, thus they being insulated from the ground, the disconnected circuit conductors will have a much lower potential than the active circuit conductor placed in close proximity. In this case, between the active circuit conductors and the disconnected circuit conductors there will take place electric (capacitive) couplings, the conductors playing the role of armature of the huge condenser having the air as a dielectric medium. Depending on the intensity of the electric coupling (depending on the distance between the conductor and the length of parallel lines), the potentials of the disconnected circuit phases will change when compared with the ground potential. A possible measurement of these potentials (voltages induced through capacitive coupling) is shown in figure 1.

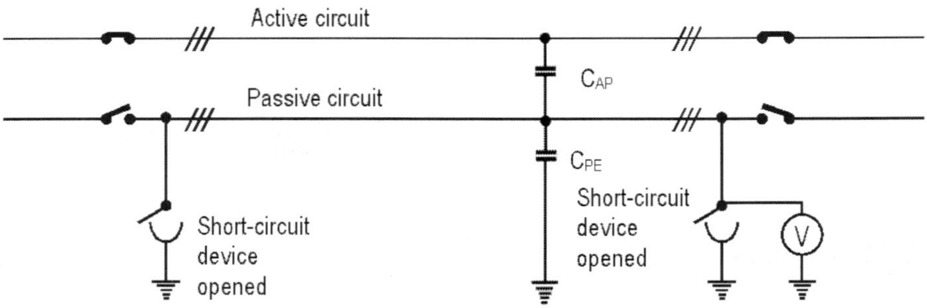

Figure 1. Measuring the voltages induced by the electric (capacitive) coupling in the disconnected circuit conductors of a high voltage overhead power line with double circuit.

b. If the disconnected three-phase circuit conductors are grounded at both ends through short-circuit devices, three loops are basically being formed, in which the intense electromagnetic fields of the load currents of the active circuit will induce electromotive voltages, forcing the closing of the induced currents, this coupling being magnetic (figure 2).

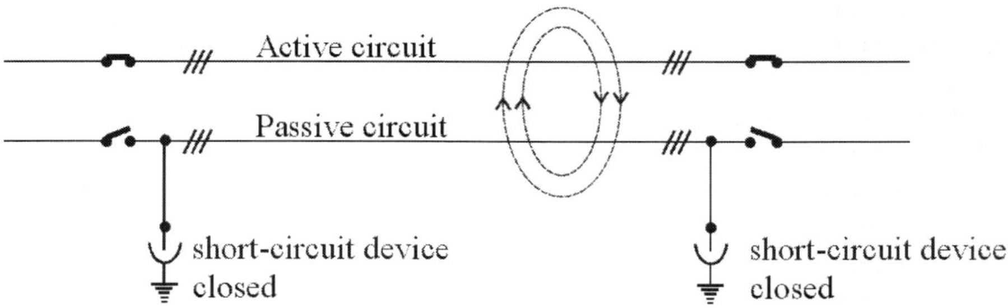

Figure 2. The magnetic coupling between the active circuit and the disconnected circuit of a high voltage overhead power line with double circuit.

In this situation, in order to measure the induced voltages in the three phases of the disconnected circuit, there need to be opened the short-circuit devices from one of the ends of the line and install a voltmeter, as shown in figure 3.

In the Banat area- Romania, which consists of four districts, there are several overhead lines of 220 kV, which operate in parallel on a structure of double circuit metal pillars, on different distances supplying many consumers of different types. Depending on the power transferred on these lines, if there is a disconnected circuit, there will appear voltages induced in the

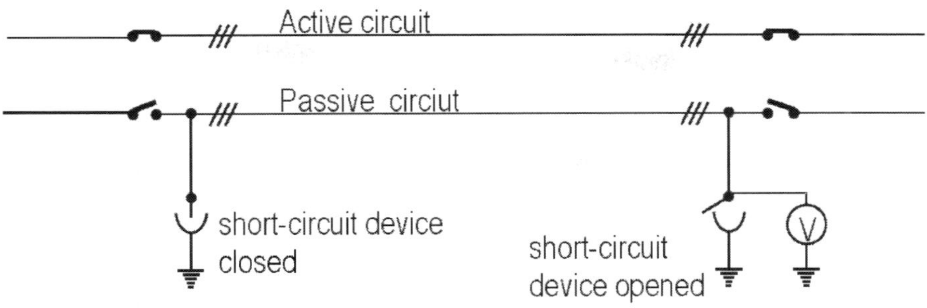

Figure 3. Measuring the voltages induced by the magnetic (inductive) coupling in the disconnected circuit of a high voltage overhead power line with double circuit.

disconnected circuit both through electric and magnetic coupling, and these voltages must be known. The worst cases are those in which the active circuit is very long and supplies consumers requiring high power consumption.

In figure 4 there is presented the configuration of 220 kV overhead power lines with double circuit, from the Banat area – Romania.

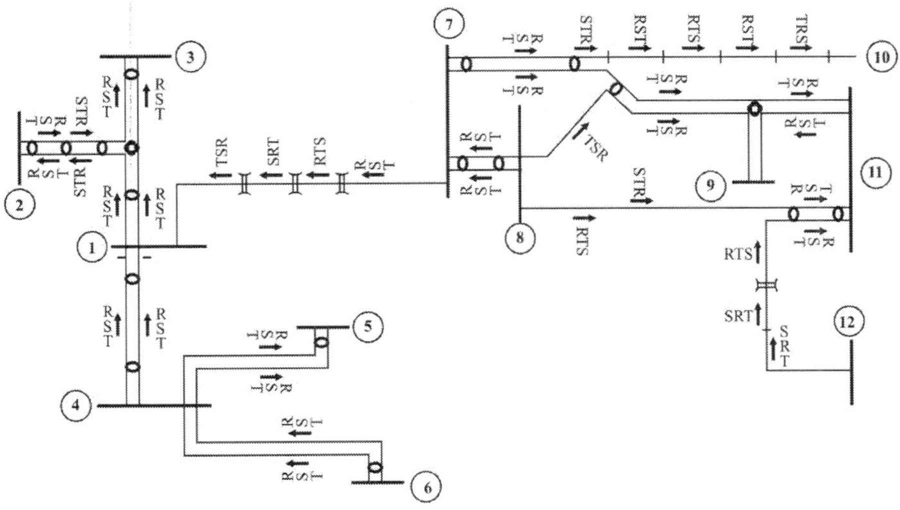

Figure 4. Configuration of 220 kV overhead power lines from the Banat area - Romania

Since the metal supporting pillars for most of the lines have the same configuration, in Table 1 there are given their main geometrical parameters corresponding to the generalized geometrical distances presented in figure 5.

Nr. crt.	Pillar type	H (m)	a1 (m)	h1(m)	h2 (m)	d1 (m)	d2 (m)	d3 (m)	λ_{iz} (m)	f_{max} (m)	h_g (m)
1	Sn 220.201	41,4	6,4	6,5	6,5	5,0	8,0	5,0	2,541	14,0	5,459
2	Sn 220.202	41,4	6,4	6,5	6,5	5,0	8,0	5,0	2,541	14,0	5,459
3	Sn 220.204	42,5	5,5	6,5	6,5	4,5	8,0	5,0	2,541	14,0	7,459
4	Sn 220.205	42,5	5,5	6,5	6,5	4,5	8,0	5,0	2,541	14,0	7,459
5	Ss 220.205	44,9	6,9	8,0	8,0	5,5	9,5	5,5	2,541	14,0	5,459
6	Ss 220.206	46,0	6,0	8,0	8,0	4,75	9,25	5,25	2,541	14,0	7,459

Table 1. The dimensions of the supporting pillars for 220 kV overhead power lines with double circuit.

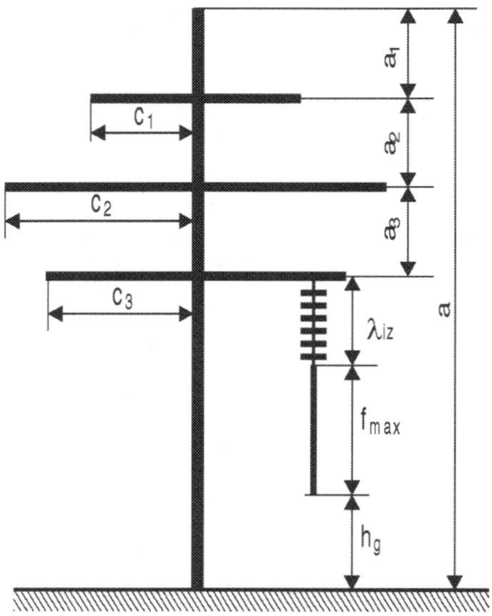

Figure 5. Schematic geometrical representation of a supporting pillar

The active conductors of the power lines are steel-aluminium with standard sections of 400 mm^2 or 450 mm^2, these being specified for each power line separately.

In order to perform measurements of the voltages induced there was previously required to establish the measuring program, with well defined steps, to be able to protect the operating staff against the exposure to the high voltage effects. This program has included all the necessary measures to be taken in case of working under voltage and it was spread out over the following steps:

a. Specification of the initial state of the overhead high voltage power line with double circuit, on which measurements are to be carried out, indicating the exact situation of the two circuits of the power lines, namely:

- Circuit A – set into operation;
- Circuit B – non- operating, grounded through short-circuit devices at both ends.

b. For each measurement, the following conditions of protection must be respected:

- The leader of the team must be equipped with overalls, high voltage electro-insulated boots, protective helmet and high voltage electro-insulated gloves.
- The modification of the measuring range of the apparatus is made only after disconnecting the measuring circuit by removing the electro-insulated rod from the circuit being measured;
- The reading of the measuring apparatus is done remotely by an operator equipped accordingly (work under high voltage).
- The cables of the measuring apparatus will be placed at a distance from the operator.

c. The measurement of the voltages induced through the two types of coupling into the conductors of the disconnected circuit is realized according to the following procedures:

- Connect to the ground the cable of the electrostatic voltmeter and then connect it to the grounding clamp of the apparatus;
- Connect one end of the active cable to the measuring clamp of the electrostatic voltmeter;
- Connect the other end of the active cable to the electro-insulated rod
- For measuring the voltages induced by electric coupling, the short-circuit devices of the disconnected circuit of the power lines have to be open at both ends and for measuring the voltage induced by magnetic coupling, the short-circuit devices of the disconnected circuit are opened only at the end where the measuring is performed.
- The voltages induced on the three-phase disconnected circuit are measured successively by touching, with the electro-insulated rod the connections of the phase conductors to the short-circuit devices.

Based on the diagram shown in Fig. 4, there have been determined sub stations in which the measures are performed, according to the number of the outputs of 220 kV lines, with double circuit:

- Substation 11 – with connections to substation 7, 8 and 12;
- Substation 2 - with connections to substation 3 and 1;
- Substation 4 - with connections to substation 5, 1 and 6;

- Substation 7 - with connections to substation 1, 8, 10 and 11;
- Substation 9 - with connections to substation 8 and 11.

The results of the measurements carried out according to the program described above are synthetically, presented in Table 2, for the voltages induced through electric (capacitive) coupling and in Table 3, for the voltages induced by the magnetic (inductive) coupling.

Overhead power line	Circuit A [km]	Circuit B [km]	Active circuit voltage	Voltage induced electrically (capacitive) measured in the disconnected circuit		
			U [kV]	U_R [kV]	U_S [kV]	U_T [kV]
7 - 11	49.876	25.455	237.5	8.87	2.7	4.4
8 - 9 maximum load	25.455	11.249	236.9	12.7	20.2	18.3
8 - 9	25.455	11.249	236.9	12.7	20.2	12.3
11 - 12	16.688	43.897	225	1.9	3.35	2.35
9 - 11	25.455	7.422	236.8	19.4	23.4	18.2
4 - 6	116..550	116..550	228 225 232	10.4	3.6	5.1
7 - 8	18.675	18.675	237	8.9	4.42	6.25
4 - 5	30.730	30.730	226.5	3.03	7.94	5.9
4 - 1	72.867	72.867	234	11.1	3.7	5.4
1 - 2	53.719	24.620	230 235 225	6.55	5.82	5.41
2 - 3	53.719	55.173	230 235 225	8.2	2.8	4.2

Table 2. The voltages induced through electric (capacitive) coupling in 220 kV overhead power lines, with double circuit, having circuit B disconnected.

Observing Table 2 and Table 3 there has been stated that:

- In the case of the lines where no phase transposition has been performed, the voltage induced through magnetic (inductive) coupling is the largest on the phase placed the highest from the ground;
- In the case of the middle phase, at most of the lines, the induced voltage is the lowest;

Overhead power line	Length of A circuit [km]	Length of B circuit [km]	Active circuit voltage	Active circuit current	Magnetically induced voltage measured in the disconnected B circuit			Transferred power and voltage – current phase shift			
			U [kV]	I [A]	U_R [V]	U_S [V]	U_T [V]	P [MW]	Q [MVar]	cos φ	φ [rad]
7 - 11	49.876	25.455	237.5	265.75	320	21	120	107	22	0.9795	0.2028
8 - 9 maximum load	25.455	11.249	236.9	156.9	68	10.2	39	50	40	0.781	0.6745
8 - 9	25.455	11.249	236.9	74.826	34	10.2	18.5	24.9	17.9	0.812	0.6232
11 - 12	16.688	43.897	225	181.68	120	26	122	5	5	0.707	0.7855
9 - 11	25.455	7.422	236.8	92.542	11	4.3	13.2	28.5	25	0.7518	0.72
4 - 6	116.550	116.550	228 225 232	440 480 460	1400	400	1440	182	7.354	0.98	0.2003
7 - 8	18.675	18.675	237	71.77	63.6	13	42	29	5	0.985	0.1734
4 - 5	30.730	30.730	226.5	14.54	20.8	3.6	17	0	5.7	0	1.57
4 - 1	72.867	72.867	234	497.03	1020	400	940	200	22	0.988	0.155
1 - 2	53.719	24.620	230 235 225	212 237 218	180	71	1260	50	10.15	0.98	0.2003
2 - 3	53.719	55.173	230 235 225	212 237 218	310	80	270	50	10.15	0.98	0.2003

Table 3. Voltages induced through magnetic (inductive) coupling in 220 kV overhead power lines, with double circuit, with circuit B disconnected.

- All the voltages induced by capacitive coupling are very high and dangerous for the operating staff.
- The length of the parallel distance between the active line (inductor) and the disconnected one (armature) influences the values of the voltage induced, regardless of the type of electromagnetic coupling. To observe this phenomenon, there have been drawn the curves of the voltages induced, depending on the length of their parallel portions; there have been drawn curves for voltages induced both through electric (capacitive) coupling, $U_E = f(l)$ and for magnetic (inductive) coupling, $U_M = f(l)$. The resulted curves are shown in fig. 6 and fig. 7.

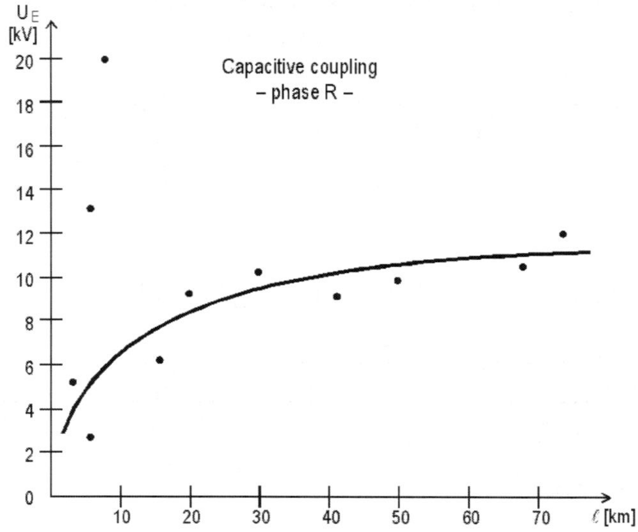

Figure 6. The variation of the voltages induced through capacitive coupling depending on the length of their parallel portions.

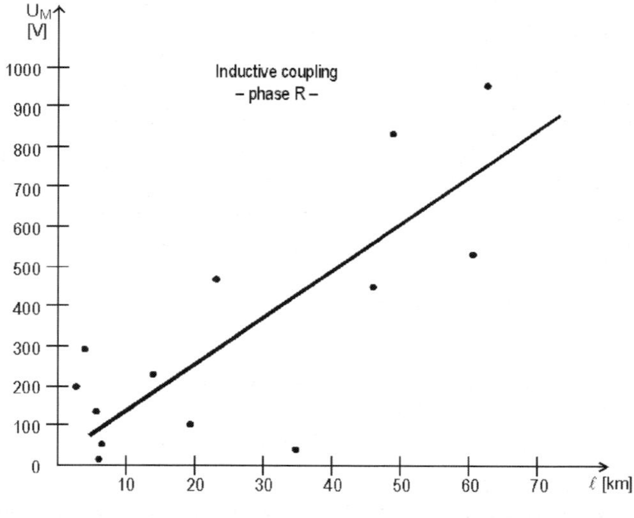

Figure 7. The variation of the voltages induced through inductive coupling depending on the length of their parallel portions.

From the analysis of figures 6 and 7 there has been observed that on small distances, of up to about 20 km, where there is parallelism between the two electric circuits located on the same pillars of the double-circuit, the length influences very little the induced voltage. On these distances, a number of other causes are more important. At distances longer than 20 km, the value of the voltage induced by both the electric (capacitive) and magnetic (inductive) coupling has a linear increasing trend along with the increasing of the length of the parallel distance.

3. The mathematical models for determining the induced voltages

The data obtained from measurements on the ground represent an advantage for conceiving mathematical models, because the results obtained through mathematical modeling can be managed comparing with the real ones. This fact has lain at the basis of designing the mathematical models, trying to imitate, as realistically as possible, the physical phenomena that occur in nature.

It should also be mentioned that, at low frequencies, the couplings of the electromagnetic interferences between sources and victims can be separated, through different experiments, into electric couplings and magnetic couplings, respectively. Mathematical modeling should take into account this observation that leads to achieving, separately, two different models, one for electric and one for magnetic phenomena [8, 9].

But regardless of the type of electromagnetic coupling, the values of induced voltages are dependent on both the geometry of the power lines and the power running on these lines and therefore the mathematical models must include, primarily, the geometric calculation of the supporting pillars of the high voltage overhead power lines with double circuit and the determination of their capacities and, respectively, the mutual inductances between the conductors of the power line with double circuit. The geometric, electric and magnetic parameters represent equation coefficients through which there are determined the voltages induced electrically and magnetically in the conductors of the disconnected circuit of the high voltage power line with double circuit.

3.1. Determination of the geometric parameters of the supporting pillars of the high voltage overhead power lines with double circuit

The calculation of the geometrical parameters of the supporting pillars of the high voltage overhead power lines with double circuit must consider the distances between the conductors of the double circuit, the distances between conductors and their images in the earth and the maximum arrow formed by the conductors of the power line in a standard horizontal opening, as shown in Fig.8, a and b.

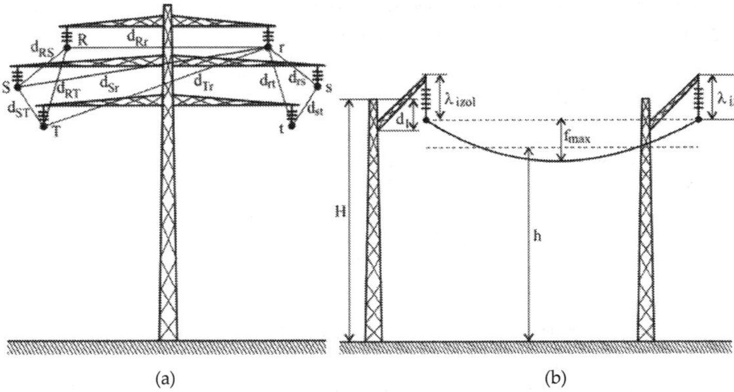

Figure 8. Explanation of the determination of the geometrical parameters of the high voltage overhead power lines with double circuit. a) The geometrical parameters of the pillar; b) Determination of the average height of the conductors from the ground.

The geometric calculation of the supporting pillar of the high voltage overhead power line with double circuit is made using the following algorithm:

a. The average distance between the conductors and the return path through the ground is obtained by taking into account the resistivity of the soil, with the expression:

$$D_{CP} = 550\sqrt{\frac{\rho}{f}} \tag{1}$$

where ρ - resistivity of the soil and f - the frequency of the power line voltage.

b. The average height of the power line conductor from the ground level results from:

$$h_k = H - a_1 - \lambda_{izk} - \frac{2}{3} f_{\max k} \tag{2}$$

c. The vertical and horizontal distances of the active conductors, for each type of pillar presented in table 1, are determined by the following expressions:

$$\begin{aligned} d_{RS} &= d_{rs} = \sqrt{h_1^2 + (d_2 - d_1)^2} \\ d_{ST} &= d_{st} = \sqrt{h_2^2 + (d_2 - d_3)^2} \\ d_{RT} &= d_{rt} = \sqrt{(h_1 + h_2)^2 + (d_3 - d_1)^2} \end{aligned} \tag{3}$$

d. The distances between the conductors of the two circuits of the power line with double circuit result from the following expressions:

$$
\begin{aligned}
& d_{Rr} = 2d_1; \qquad d_{Ss} = 2d_2; \qquad d_{Tt} = 2d_3 \\
& d_{Sr} = d_{Rs} = \sqrt{h_1^2 + \left(2d_2 - d_1\right)^2} \\
& d_{Ts} = d_{St} = \sqrt{h_2^2 + \left(2d_2 - d_3\right)^2} \\
& d_{Tr} = d_{Rt} = \sqrt{\left(h_1 + h_2\right)^2 + \left(2d_3 - d_1\right)^2}
\end{aligned}
\tag{4}
$$

3.2. The mathematical modeling of the electric (capacitive) coupling

In the case of electric (capacitive) coupling, the high voltage overhead power line with double circuit represents a complex set of capacities which are formed due to the differences in potential both between the active circuit phases, because of the different values of the voltage phasers of the three-phases at any moment and between the potentials of the conductors of the active circuit and those of the disconnected circuit and that insulated from the earth. The assembly of capacities which are formed is shown in Fig. 9.

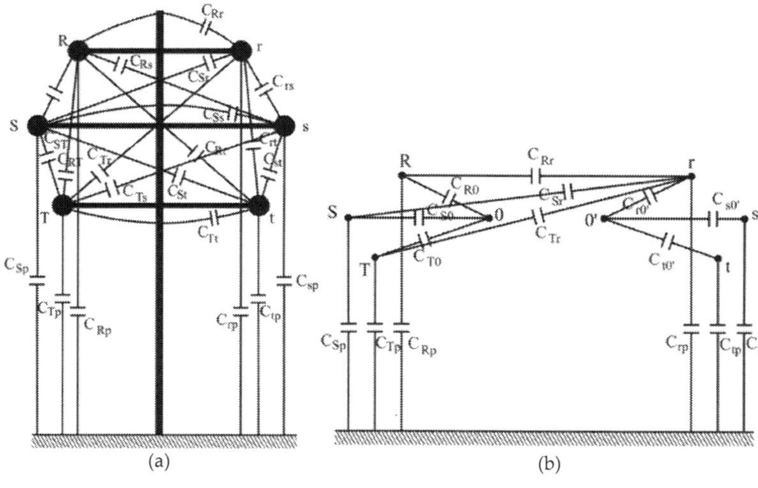

Figure 9. The set of capacities formed between the active circuit (RST) and the disconnected one (rst). a) Capacities formed between the two circuits; b) The equivalent capacities for a phase of the disconnected circuit.

The values of the partial capacities between phases and between the phases and the ground are calculated by the following expressions:

- For partial capacities between phases:

$$C_{ik} = \frac{2\pi\varepsilon_0 l}{\ln\frac{d_{ik}}{r_0}} \tag{5}$$

- For partial capacities between the phases and the ground:

$$C_{pi} = \frac{2\pi\varepsilon_0 l}{\ln\left(\frac{2h_i}{r_0}\right)} \tag{6}$$

where: l - is the length of power line, d_{ik} - the distances between the phase conductors, according to relations (3) and (4), and r_0 - the radius of the phase conductor.

By transforming the phase capacities connected in delta connection (Fig. 9 a) into the equivalent capacities in Y-connection (Fig. 9 b), the null potential of the two Y-connections are equal with the null potential of the ground and thus the phase capacities are placed in parallel with the phase capacities versus the ground. There results the electrostatic equivalent scheme shown in Fig. 10:

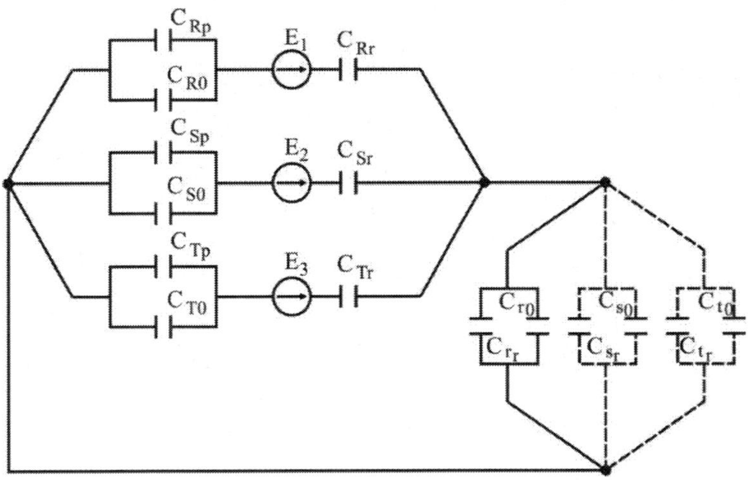

Figure 10. The electrical scheme of the capacitive coupling between the two circuits of the power line.

This electrical scheme represents a set of circuits having as passive elements only condensers, and solving of such a problem supposes using Kirchhoff's theorems either for determining the electric charge of the condensers or determining the voltages at which these condensers are being charged. But, in this particular case, there are known neither the electric charges of the condensers, nor the voltages at which these condensers are loading. In order to solve this complicated problem we have used analogies between the electric network, which contains only condensers and the electric network containing only resistors. Thus, if the relation for voltage drop, U, between the armatures of a condenser of capacitance C loaded with electric charge Q and voltage drop U, at the hubs of a resistor of resistance R run by currents of intensity I, there results:

$$U = \frac{Q}{C}, \text{ respectively}: U = R \cdot I,$$

which allows of the establishment of the following correspondences: value $\frac{1}{C}$ is analogous to value R, and value Q is analogous to value I and, as to voltage U, in order to have the same sense in both cases, the sense of current I has to correspond to the sense of electrostatic field E between the condenser armatures, as shown in Fig.11.

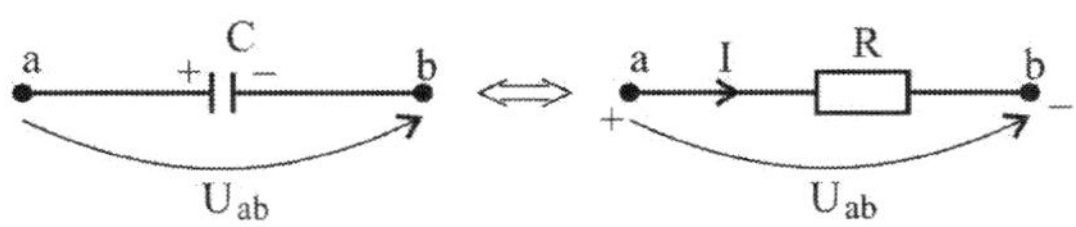

Figure 11. The correspondence between the analogous values of the theory of electrostatics and that of electro-kinetics.

Based on the analogies between the electrostatic and electro-kinetics values, there has been designed the equivalent electro-kinetics scheme, as shown in Fig. 12.

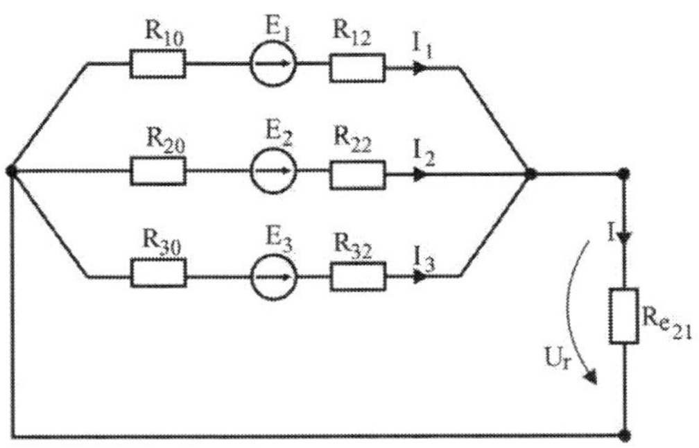

Figure 12. The analogous electro-kinetics scheme of the electric (capacitive) coupling for a phase of the disconnected circuit.

In order to determine the voltages induced through the electric (capacitive) coupling there can be applied the method of Kirchhoff's theorems in the case of the analogous electro-kinetics scheme in Fig. 12. The following system of equations result, where the currents of the edge circuits are unknown.

$$\begin{aligned} & E_1 - E_2 = (R_{10} + R_{12}) \cdot I_1 - (R_{20} + R_{22}) \cdot I_2 \\ & E_2 - E_3 = (R_{20} + R_{22}) \cdot I_2 - (R_{30} + R_{32}) \cdot I_3 \\ & E_3 = (R_{30} + R_{32}) \cdot I_3 + R_e \cdot I \\ & I_1 + I_2 + I_3 = I \end{aligned} \tag{7}$$

After solving system of equations (7), considering the analogies $I \equiv Q$ and$R_{ei} \equiv \frac{1}{C_{i0} + C_{ip}}$, there results the value of the voltage induced electrically in each of the three conductors of the disconnected circuit of the high voltage overhead power line with double circuit, namely:

$$U_{fi} = R_{ei} \cdot I_i, \text{ respectively } U_{fi} = \frac{Q_i}{C_{i0} + C_{ip}} \tag{8}$$

There should be mentioned that the analogies between electrostatic and electro-kinetics values are valid only in the case of d. c. circuits. But, in the present case, the analyzed circuits are in a. c. because voltage sources E_1, E_2 and E_3 are sinusoidal alternative voltages, having expressions:

$$\begin{aligned} & E_1 = \sqrt{2} \cdot U_{fR} \sin(\omega \cdot t + \phi) \\ & E_2 = \sqrt{2} \cdot U_{fS} \sin\left(\omega \cdot t + \phi - \frac{2 \cdot \pi}{3}\right) \\ & E_3 = \sqrt{2} \cdot U_{fT} \sin\left(\omega \cdot t + \phi - \frac{4 \cdot \pi}{3}\right) \end{aligned} \tag{9}$$

where $\omega = 2 \cdot \pi \cdot f$ - is the angular frequency of the sinusoidal wave of the phase voltage and $\phi = 0$ is the initial phase difference, considered null because the relative positions of the voltage phasers versus the fixed reference axis of the phasers are not known.

For the analogies presented above be valid, "time" must to be considered a constant. But time, $t = const.$, represents the very moment of measuring the capacitive voltage induced for each phase of the disconnected circuit. Therefore it is necessary to know the measuring moment of the voltage induced for each of the three phases, separately. To determine the measuring moment there has been considered a period of the sinusoidal voltage wave, which at the frequency of $f = 50\ Hz$ has duration $T = 0.02$ seconds. Duration T, of the sinusoidal voltage wave has been divided into 100 discrete and constant time intervals, each $\Delta t = 0.0002$ seconds and thus, through the digitization of time, the variable values of the alternative current circuit have been transformed into constant values on small time intervals, Δt_k, where: $k = 1...100$, for which the analogies mentioned above become valid.

Knowing, by measuring the voltages induced electrically in the conductors of the disconnected circuit, if there are assigned 2 ÷ 3 time interval values, Δt_k, and if we use a calculation program realized in MATHCAD, from relations (9), there result immediately the calculation values of the voltages induced electrically (capacitive). These values are given in table 4, comparatively with the measured values. The measured values and those obtained through calculation are very close, this fact demonstrating the validity of the mathematical model developed and used for determining the voltages induced electrically in the circuits of the disconnected power lines.

Overhead power line	Circuit A [km]	Circuit B [km]	Active circuit voltage	Measured voltage induced electrically in the disconnected circuit			Calculated voltage induced electrically in the disconnected circuit		
			U [kV]	U_R [kV]	U_S [kV]	U_T [kV]	E_r [kV]	E_s [kV]	E_t [kV]
7 - 11	49.876	25.455	237.5	8.87	2.7	4.4	**8.823**	**2.755**	**4.415**
8 - 9 maximum load	25.455	11.249	236.9	12.7	20.2	18.3	**12.643**	**20.324**	**12.278**
8 - 9	25.455	11.249	236.9	12.7	20.2	12.3	**12.726**	**20.324**	**12.278**
11 - 12	16.688	43.897	225	1.9	3.35	2.35	**1.845**	**3.419**	**2.427**
9 - 11	25.455	7.422	236.8	19.4	23.4	18.2	**19.433**	**23.259**	**17.906**
4 - 6	116.550	116.550	228 225 232	10.4	3.6	5.1	**10.422**	**3.619**	**4.948**
7 - 8	18.675	18.675	237	8.9	4.42	6.25	**9.076**	**4.573**	**6.278**
4 - 5	30.730	30.730	226.5	3.03	7.94	5.9	**3.154**	**7.998**	**5.876**
4 - 1	72.867	72.867	234	11.1	3.7	5.4	**11.221**	**3.768**	**4.798**
1 - 2	53.719	24.620	230 235 225	6.55	5.82	5.41	**6.582**	**5.865**	**5.452**
2 - 3	53.719	55.173	230 235 225	8.2	2.8	4.2	**8.206**	**2.845**	**4.210**

Table 4. Comparison between the measured voltages induced electrically and the calculated ones.

The mathematical model presented above also allows of the determination of the maximum values of the voltages induced electrically in each of the phases of the disconnected circuit by assigning to "time" discrete values around the maximum of the sinusoidal function of the inductor voltage.

Another important observation is required, namely, that for each phase of the disconnected circuit there has been adopted a different value for the digitized time because the measurements have been made separately for each of the three phases of the respective circuit.

3.3. The mathematical modeling of the magnetic (inductive) coupling

The magnetic (inductive) coupling is generated by the electric currents varying in time running through the three conductors of the active circuit of the high voltage overhead power line with double circuit and creating variable magnetic fields which induce electromotive voltages in the conductors of the disconnected circuit. The mathematical expressions of the electric currents running through the conductors of the active circuit are given by relations (10), namely:

$$\begin{aligned} i_R &= \sqrt{2}\cdot I_{fR}\sin(\omega\cdot t+\varphi) \\ i_S &= \sqrt{2}\cdot I_{fS}\sin\left(\omega\cdot t+\varphi-\frac{2\pi}{3}\right) \\ i_T &= \sqrt{2}\cdot I_{fT}\sin\left(\omega\cdot t+\varphi-\frac{4\pi}{3}\right) \end{aligned} \tag{10}$$

where φ represents the phase shift between the voltages and the currents of the active circuit and the phase shift is known because powers P and Q which charge the active circuit are known. (Table 2).

In the mathematical model called "network model", the magnetic (inductive) coupling can be represented by the mutual inductance between the conductors of the two circuits having the general expression:

$$M_{12}=\frac{\mu_0}{4\pi}\int_0^l\frac{dl_1dl_2}{\sqrt{(l_1-l_2)^2+d_{12}^2}} \tag{11}$$

where, $l_1$and l_2 are the lengths of two conductors in parallel and d_{12} is the distance between them.

After the expansion in series of the radical and neglecting the superior rank terms, relation (11) becomes:

$$M_{ik}=\frac{\mu_0}{2\pi}\cdot l\cdot\ln\left(\frac{D_{cp}}{d_{ik}}\right)\text{, where } i\in(R,S,T)\text{,respectively } k\in(r,s,t) \tag{12}$$

But, as the electromotive voltage induced in each of the three conductors of the disconnected circuit represents the contribution of all the three magnetic inductive fields generated by the variable currents of the active circuit, the mathematical expression for each phase of the disconnected circuit will be:

$$\begin{aligned} U_r &= -j\cdot\omega\cdot\left(i_R\cdot M_{Rr}+i_S\cdot M_{Sr}+i_T\cdot M_{Tr}\right)\\ U_s &= -j\cdot\omega\cdot\left(i_R\cdot M_{Rs}+i_S\cdot M_{Ss}+i_T\cdot M_{Ts}\right)\\ U_t &= -j\cdot\omega\cdot\left(i_R\cdot M_{Rt}+i_S\cdot M_{St}+i_T\cdot M_{Tt}\right)\end{aligned} \tag{13}$$

Overhead power line	Circuit [km]A	Circuit [km]B	Active circuit voltage	Active circuit current	Measured voltage induced magnetically in the disconnected circuit			Calculated voltage induced magnetically in the disconnected circuit		
			U [kV]	I [A]	U_R [V]	U_S [V]	U_T [V]	Ur [V]	Us [V]	Ut [V]
7 - 11	49.876	25.455	237.5	265.75	320	21	120	**317.193**	**21.014**	**120.452**
8 - 9 maximum load	25.455	11.249	236.9	156.9	68	10.2	39	**67.888**	**10.365**	**39.073**
8 - 9	25.455	11.249	236.9	74.826	34	10.2	18.5	**33.415**	**7.18**	**18.808**
11 - 12	16.688	43.897	225	181.68	120	26	122	**120.222**	**25.88**	**120.363**
9 - 11	25.455	7.422	236.8	92.542	11	4.3	13.2	**11.279**	**4.28**	**13.584**
4 - 6	116.550	116.550	228 225 232	440 480 460	1400	400	1440	**1401**	**404.28**	**1444**
7 - 8	18.675	18.675	237	71.77	63.6	13	42	**62.844**	**13.182**	**42.529**
4 - 5	30.730	30.730	226.5	14.54	20.8	3.6	17	**20.862**	**3.671**	**17.091**
4 - 1	72.867	72.867	234	497.03	1020	400	940	**1021**	**357.93**	**941.014**
1 - 2	53.719	24.620	230 235 225	212 237 218	180	71	1260	**181.052**	**71.05**	**1261**
2 - 3	53.719	55.173	230 235 225	212 237 218	310	80	270	**311.44**	**81.009**	**270.174**

Table 5. Comparison between the measured voltages induced by magnetic coupling and the calculated ones

This simple calculation algorithm has lain at the basis of designing the calculation program in MATHCAD, by means of which there were determined analytically, the voltages induced through magnetic (inductive) coupling in the disconnected circuits of 220 kV power lines with double circuit from the Banat area – Romania. The results are presented in Table 5, in comparison with the values of the voltages measured on the ground..

This case brings about an important observation. Considering phase shift φ, between voltages and currents, through which the charging with power of the inductor circuit is indirectly expressed, the mathematical model has required the representation of the currents through momentary values instead of effective ones. But this leads to an additional unknown, which is time, t, namely the measuring moment of the voltages induced for each phase. It means that this case also requires the digitization of period $T = 0.02$ seconds in 100 time intervals, $\Delta t_k = 0.0002$ seconds and the search of the moment in which the measurement of the voltage induced through magnetic coupling for each of the phases of the disconnected circuit was performed.

Comparing the measured values of the voltages induced through magnetic (inductive) coupling with the calculated ones there has been observed a very good concordance, which demonstrates an appropriate mathematical approach of the physical phenomena which lead to the magnetic (inductive) coupling between the conductors of the high voltage overhead power lines.

4. Conclusions

a. In all of the cases, the middle phase of the disconnected circuit of the high voltage overhead power lines with double circuit has got the lowest value for the voltage induced. It has been proved by both the measurements on the ground and the mathematical modeling. The explanation for the electric coupling lies in the longest distance between the phases of the active circuit and the middle phase of the disconnected circuit. As to the magnetic (inductive) coupling, the effect is due to the vector summation of the intensities of the inductor magnetic fields..

b. In the case of the power lines where the transposition of the phases has not been performed, the voltage induced through magnetic (inductive) coupling is the highest on the upper phase. This phenomenon is explained by the fact that the respective conductor – earth loop has the largest surface. This means that if all the protection conductors of each of the pillars were grounded there would be realized a large number of conductor – earth loops (equal with the number of openings) which would capture a part of the inductor magnetic flux, particularly that of the upper phase, thereby reducing the voltages induced through magnetic (inductive) coupling.

c. All the voltages induced through electric (capacitive) coupling have got very high values, which are dangerous for the operating staff. By being grounded, the power lines are discharged of this high potential, but there appear voltages induced through magnetic (inductive) coupling, they being high enough to be dangerous, too. Therefore, we consider that, in the case of circuits separated from the ground in a galvanic way, the operating staff have to obey the protection rules regarding working under high voltage.

d. If the grounding loops are closed at both ends through short-circuit devices, the voltages induced through magnetic (inductive) coupling can force high electric currents, which are very dangerous for the operating staff.

e. Besides a number of other factors (including weather) which influence the voltages induced electrically or magnetically, an important factor is the length of the portions of parallelism between the active line and the disconnected one. For lengths of parallelism greater than 20 km, the value of the voltages induced increases, practically, linearly with the length of the portion of parallelism, a phenomenon observed in figures 6 and 7.

f. The original mathematical models, designed to simulate the phenomena of electric and magnetic coupling between the conductors of the high voltage overhead power lines with double circuit lead to results very close to those obtained directly through measurements on the ground, in real operating circumstances. Therefore the mathematical models are useful instruments for studying the phenomena of electromagnetic interferences at low frequency in the case of power lines operating on parallel neighboring paths.

Author details

Flavius Dan Surianu

Politechnica University of Timisoara, Romania

References

[1] Surianu F.D. Electromagnetic Compatibility. Applies in Electric Power Systems. (in Romanian) Orizonturi Universitare, ISBN 973-638-244-3, ISBN 978-973-638-244-4, Timisoara, Romania;

[2] Surianu F.D. An apparatus for signalizing the induced currents in the disconnected circuits of double circuit h.v. overhead lines, Scientific Bull. of Politehnica University of Timisoara, Romania, Serie Energetics, Tom 50(64), Fasc.1-2, Nov., 2007, ISSN 1582-7194, pp. 615-620;

[3] Munteanu C., Topa V., Muresan T., Costin A.M., Electromagnetic Interferences between HV Power Lines and RBS Antennas Mounted on HV Tower, Proceedings of the 6th International Symposium on Electromagnetic Compatibility, EMC Europe, 2009, Eindhoven, Holland, pp. 878-881;

[4] TTU-T and CIGRE, Protection Measure for Radio Base Stations Sited on Power Line Towers, Recommendation K 57, 2003;

[5] Kenedy Aliila Greyson, Anant Oonsivilai, Identifying Critical Measurements in Power System Network, Proceedings of The 8th WSEAS International Conference on

Electric Power Systems, High Voltage, Electric Machines (POWER '08), Venice, Italy, 21-23 November, 2008, ISSN 1790-5117, ISBN 978-960-474-026-0, pp. 61-66;

[6] Surianu F.D., Measurements on the Ground and Mathematical Modeling of Voltages Induced by High Voltage Overhead Power Lines Working on Parallel and Narrow Routes, Proceedings of WSEAS International Conference on Electric Power Systems, High Voltages, Electric Machines, Genova, Italy, 17-19 Oct., 2009, ISSN 1790-5117, ISBN 978-960-474-130-4, pp. 51-58;

[7] Surianu F.D., Olariu A., Technical solution to alert the working staff to the dangerous values of the currents induced in the conductors of the disconnected circuit of a double circuit overhead power line, Proceedings of 45th International Universities' Power Engineering Conference (UPEC), 2010, Cardiff, United Kingdom, pp.1-4;

[8] Vatau D., Surianu F.D., Bianu A.E., Olariu A., Bota V., Considerations on the Electromagnetic Pollution Produced by High Voltage Power Plants, WSEAS Proceedings of the European Computing Conference, 28-30 April, 2011, Paris, France, ISBN: 978-960-474-297-4, pp. 182-186.

[9] Hemmady S., Antonsen T.M., Ott E. Jr.,Anlage S.M., Statistical Prediction and Measurement of Induced Voltages on Components Within Complicated Enclosures: A Wave-Chaotic Approach, IEEE Transactions on Electromagnetic Comparibility, August 2012, Volume 54, Number 4, IEMCAE, ISSN 0018-9375, pp. 758-771.

Chapter 17

Computational Modeling and Monte Carlo Simulation of Soft Errors in Flash Memories

Jean-Luc Autran, Daniela Munteanu,
Gilles Gasiot and Philippe Roche

Additional information is available at the end of the chapter

http://dx.doi.org/10.5772/57220

1. Introduction

As CMOS technologies are scaling down, the susceptibility of integrated circuits (IC's) to radiation coming from space or present in the terrestrial environment has been found to seriously increase [1]. Until now, radiation effects in IC's have mainly been an issue for space or avionics applications. At ground level and in nowadays ultra-scaled devices, natural atmospheric radiation principally induces Single event effects (SEE), which has been identified to induce one of the highest failure rates of all reliability concerns for devices and circuits entering in the area of nano-electronics [2]. SEE's are the result of the interaction of highly energetic particles, such as protons, neutrons, alpha particles, or heavy ions, with the sensitive region(s) of a microelectronic device or circuit. A single event may perturb the device/circuit operation (e.g., reverse or flip the data state of a memory cell, latch, flip-flop, etc.) or definitively damage the circuit (e.g. gate oxide rupture, destructive latch-up events) [3].

Among all integrated circuits used in many application areas for which a high reliability level is required (medical, space, automotive, networking, nuclear), non-volatile memories are known for their relative robustness to single events, even if the different components of a flash memory circuit (on one hand the memory cell array, on the other hand the peripheral control circuitry) exhibit distinct levels of radiation sensitivity. In addition, the specific question of their sensitivity to the terrestrial radiation environment has been little studied until now. Cellere et al. [4-5] and Gerardin et al. [6-7] have been the first to clearly state, using accelerated tests, that atmospheric neutron induced soft error occurrence is possible in flash memories, although with extremely low probabilities at ground level. A vey recent study by Just et al. [8], based for the first time on real-time tests performed in a mountain altitude natural environment, has concluded in a similar way: natural atmospheric radiation at ground level can induce soft-errors in flash memories, typically several decades below the soft-error rate (SER) of static RAM (SRAM) of comparable technological nodes.

In this context, we recently developed a numerical simulation code capable of computing the SER of floating-gate flash memories. Our simulation platform named TIARA-G4 and described in Ref. [9], has been adapted to flash memory architectures (TIARA-G4 NVM release for "Non-Volatile Memories") by modifying the device/circuit 3D geometries and by implementing a model for charge loss from the floating gates induced by ionizing particles. This chapter presents in detail our modeling and simulation approach as well as the code validation by comparison of numerical results with experimental data reported in [8].

The chapter is organized as follows: in Section II, we briefly introduce some basic knowledge about the architecture and electrical operation of floating gate flash memories. Section III also briefly reviews the current comprehension of radiation effects in floating-gate memories. The objective of these two first sections is to introduce for a non-specialist reader the technical background necessary for a good understanding of the second part of this chapter more specifically dedicated to computational modeling and Monte Carlo simulation issues. In Section IV, we detail our modeling and simulation approach based on the adaptation of our TIARA-G4 simulation platform [9] to flash memory architectures. Finally, in Section V, we expose the simulation results and compare them to experimental results obtained on a large collection of memories exposed to natural radiation.

2. Flash memory architectures and electrical operation

This paragraph provides a brief introduction to the architecture and operating principles of floating gate flash memories at both device and circuit levels. Flash memory is an electronic non-volatile storage device that can be electrically erased and reprogrammed; it offers fast read access times, as fast as dynamic RAM, although not as fast as static RAM or ROM. Flash memories are used in a wide variety of electronic devices for general storage, configuration data storage or data transfer. Modern flash memories store logical information in an array of memory cells built from floating-gate transistors. In traditional single-level cell devices, each cell stores only one bit of information. Some newer flash memory, known as multi-level cell devices can store more than one bit per cell by choosing between multiple levels of electrical charge to apply to the floating gates of its cells.

As illustrated in Fig. 1, the memory cell consists of a single n-channel transistor with a control-gate (CG) and an electrically isolated polysilicon floating gate (FG). The two gates are separated by an oxide-nitride-oxide dielectric stack (ONO), often called "inter-poly oxide". Data can be stored in the cell by adding or removing electrons in the FG, which induces changes of the threshold voltage of the cell transistor. Charge injection into the floating-gate through the tunnel oxide (TO) is governed by the electrical signals applied on the control-gate owing to the electrostatic coupling existing between the two gates. Indeed, the electrostatic potential of the FG (V_{FG}, see Fig. 2 left) is directly determined by the potential of the CG and the amount of electrical charge stored in the FG. These operations require high voltage signals produced

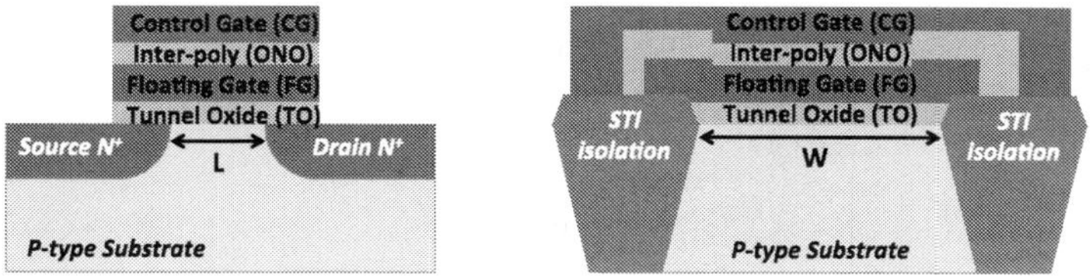

Figure 1. Schematic cross-sections of a floating-gate transistor, acting as the elementary memory element in a flash memory circuit, along its length (left) and its width (right).

on-chip using special DC-to-DC converters (charge pumps) that uses capacitors as energy storage elements to create higher voltages from the circuit external supply voltage. Two threshold voltage levels (V_T^0 and V_T^1, see Fig. 2 right) are considered to store one bit of information in the cell. The difference between the two levels, ΔV_T, is directly linked to the variation of the charge amount in the FG and to the coupling capacitance between CG and FG electrodes. A reference voltage value V_T^{REF}, intermediate between V_T^0 and V_T^1 is considered as a demarcation level between the two logical states "0" and "1" (Fig. 2 right).

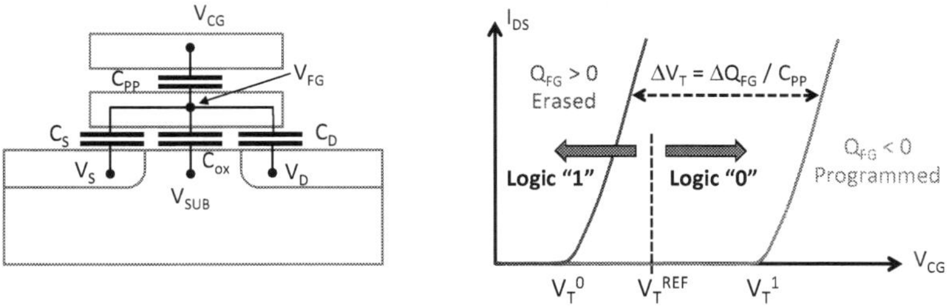

Figure 2. Left: Equivalent capacitance network of the floating-gate transistor with four terminals and definition of the main voltage and capacitance values. Right: Electrical characteristics $I_{DS}(V_{CG})$ of the floating-gate transistor with two different values of the floating-gate charge corresponding to erased and programmed states.

To form dense circuits with storage capacities up to several millions or billions of bits, elementary memory cells are arranged in matrix, i.e. in rows and columns. In addition, cells are generally grouped to form a hierarchical organization of increasing size: groups, blocks, pages, etc. Lines, called "wordlines" are connected to the control gates and columns, called "bit-lines", are connected to the drain terminals. Around the matrix memory is the peripheral control circuitry composed of additional circuits for decoding cell addresses, generating high voltage signals (charge pumps), reading cells (sense amplifiers) and managing circuit information. There are two main types of circuit architectures at the memory plan level, called NOR and NAND gate flash memories, each corresponds to a certain manner to associate several cells. The construction and the operation of NOR and NAND flash memories are briefly described in the following.

- **NOR architecture:** The organization of the NOR gate flash, shown in Fig. 3(a) is the following: several cells are connected to a bit line; each cell has the source terminal connected directly to ground, and the drain terminal is connected directly to a bit line. The drain contacts of individual transistors connected to the bitline are shared between two adjacent cells. This setting of elementary devices is called "NOR flash" because it operates as a NOR gate. The default state of a single-level NOR flash cell is logically equivalent to a binary "1" value: when a suitable voltage is applied on the control gate the current flows through the channel and the bitline voltage is pulled down. The programming operation of a NOR flash cell (i.e. setting to a binary "0" value) is done by injection of hot carriers from the channel. The high current, required by this mechanism, limits the parallelism of the operation (only some cells can be programmed in same time) [10]. The programming procedure is the following: a voltage increase (typically > 5 V) is applied to the control gate which turns on the channel and the electrons can flow from source to drain (for an n-channel MOS transistor). The source-drain current is sufficiently high so that a certain number of electrons of high energy are able to pass through the insulating layer on the floating gate by hot electrons injection mechanism. The erasing operation of a NOR flash cell (resetting it to the "1" state) is done by Fowler-Nordheim (FN) mechanism. For this purpose, a large voltage of the opposite polarity is applied between the control gate and the source terminal, pulling out the electrons from the floating gate by FN tunneling. This organization of the NOR flash allows a fast random access (approximately 100 ns). The programming operation is carried out at block level, and is much slower (approximately 5 μs). The erasing operation is carried out on the level of block and is even slower, typically 200 ms [10]. Taking into account these characteristics, the NOR flash is used principally as a read-only memory mainly for code storage, for which the random access time is important, but where the programming/erasing operations are rarely carried out [10]. In the NOR architecture, the manufacturer guarantees that all individual bits are functional and meet retention and endurance specifications, as explained in [10]; no implementation of Error Correction Code (ECC) is needed from the user side. In some cases (e.g., multi-level architecture), an internal ECC, totally transparent to the user, may be present. NOR devices typically have separate buses for addresses and data [10].

- **NAND architecture:** The organization of the NAND gate flash is shown in Fig. 3(b). In this configuration, several groups of floating-gate transistors are connected in series. These groups are then connected via some additional transistors to a NOR-style bit line array in the same way that single transistors are linked in NOR flash. Due to this arrangement, the bit line is pulled low only if all word lines are pulled high (above the threshold voltage of the transistors). This organization of elementary transistors is called NAND flash because transistors are connected in a way which is similar to a NAND gate. Compared to NOR flash, replacing single transistors with serial-linked groups adds an extra level of addressing. As explained in [10], the series arrangement and the great level of parallelism, which is achieved with this organization thanks to the low program/erase currents, give rise to a poor random access time but a very good serial access. Programming of the NAND flash is performed by FN tunneling at the page level (which is typically a few kBytes) and is carried out in about 0.2 ms [10]. The erasing operation is performed at the block level (typically a few MBytes) and takes about 2 ms [10]. Block erasure is carried out also by FN tunneling, but by using opposite polarity. Thanks to these characteristics flash NAND is adapted better for the data storage, where the problems of latency are minor and the random access time is not very important. In this configuration, the use of external ECC is mandatory (which increases the latency), because the manufacturer does not guarantee each single bit and the commercial devices may contain a few defective blocks [10].

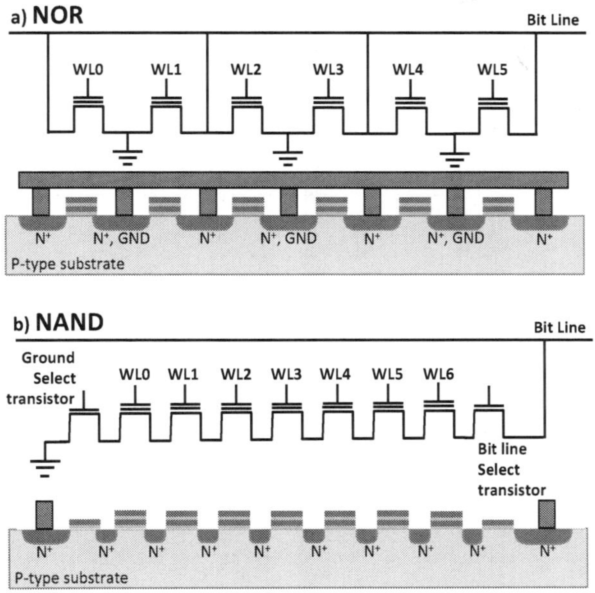

Figure 3. Schematic representations of NOR and NAND architectures.

3. Radiation effects in floating-gate memories

Floating-gate memories are sensitive to ionizing radiation, both to total ionizing dose (TID) and single event effects (SEEs). Very schematically, ionizing radiation induces charge loss in the floating-gate and charge trapping in the different dielectric layers of the transistor stack; it can also generate interface states. The induced current transients and such parasitic charges and defects cause degradation of circuit functionality and/or loss of logical information stored in the FG array in addition to possible global circuit performance degradation. Detailed results of both TID and SEEs in flash memories are available in recent papers or review presentations [4-7,10-13].

In this study, we will exclusively focus on soft-errors induced by atmospheric neutrons in the FG array of flash memories. SEEs in FG memories are due to highly energetic particles that directly (heavy ions) or indirectly (neutrons) induce charge loss from the FG. Other effects may be possible, such as Single Event Functional Interruptions (SEFI) or destructive events (Single Event Gate Rupture – SEGR) at the level of the FG array or in the peripheral circuitry. Note that SEEs only affect FG cells impacted by at least one particle whereas TID uniformly impacts the programmed FG cells.

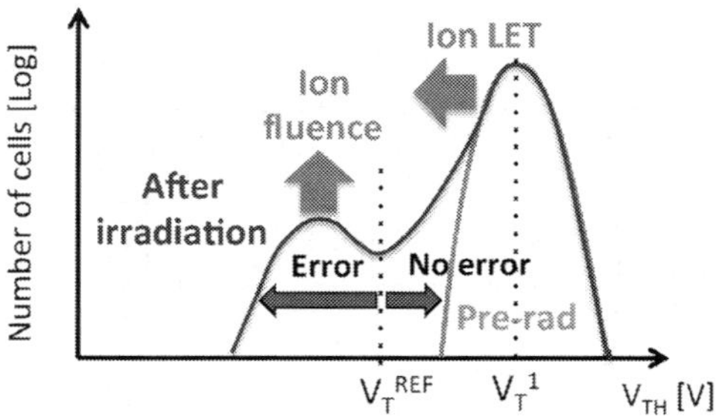

Figure 4. Schematic illustration of the effects of highly ionizing particle irradiation on the threshold voltage distributions of a floating gate array. Adapted from Paccagnella et al. [12].

Neutrons are not ionizing (they not directly create e^-/h^+ pairs in the matter) and specifically due to their neutral character, they can penetrate deeply into the chip atomic structure. Only the resulting products of the neutron-silicon (or other atoms of the circuit, O, W, Al, etc.) collisions are ionizing and, by consequence, only the impact of such secondary products on the FG can result in charge loss. This is the reason why, in the following, we will focus on the underlying physical mechanisms of charge loss induced by ionizing particles, but the link with atmospheric neutrons remains evident.

Figure 4 illustrates the effects of ionizing-particle irradiation on the threshold voltage distributions of a large array of FG devices. Before irradiation, threshold voltages of individual cells are distributed following a typical Gaussian distribution, sharply centered on the programmed value V_T^1. A secondary peak and a tail appear after irradiation: these structures correspond to all cells that have been hit by incident ionizing particles. The position (V_T shift) of the peak with respect to the initial distribution gives the average threshold voltage shift: it is directly linked to the ion Linear Energy Transfer (LET) and to the electric field in the tunnel oxide. The height of the peak is related to the irradiation fluence. Finally, the tail is related to all memory cells for which the V_T values are intermediate between the secondary peak and the initial distribution. Of course, all cells, initially programmed at V_T^1 and having their post-irradiation V_T value below V_T^{REF}, have been upset.

In their IRPS 2008 paper [14], Butt and Alam reviewed several models of charge loss due to a radiation particle strike. Different physical mechanisms have been proposed in the literature for the modeling of the charge loss from floating gates after single radiation particles strikes.

The authors summarized these earlier models and underlined theirs strengths and limitations; such classical models include the trap assisted tunneling (TAT), the conductive pipe model, the generation-recombination-transport in oxide and the electron emission. The most important limitation of these approaches is their failure to quantitatively predict the charge loss on the basis of a set of physics-based equations without any fitting parameter and/or phenomenological assumption. The authors have then proposed a new model, called Transient Carrier Flux (TCF) model, which quantitatively explains the observed charge loss in FG memories irradiated with heavy ions. Figure 5 illustrates all these different physical mechanisms and models, which are shortly detailed in the following.

1. **Generation/Recombination/Transport in Oxide:** The ion strike produces hot holes in the tunnel oxide or inter-poly dielectric and a certain fraction of these hot holes are not recombined in the prompt recombination phase. This model considers that the not-recombined holes [15] may drift into the floating gate. This may be possible since the negative electron charge stored on the floating gate itself produces an electrical field across the oxide which attracts holes. These holes that drift in FG are recombined with electrons stored in FG and cause a reduction in the negative charge on the floating gate. At the same time, the electrons produced by the ionizing particle are quickly transported to the silicon bulk or to the control gate due to their high mobility. However, this model lacks sufficient experimental validation because it does not agree quantitatively with data loss measured in FG Flash memory cells [16]. Indeed, the number of holes that survive the prompt recombination after a heavy ion strike in a 10 nm tunnel oxide is less than 100, while the data show that the charge loss is a few thousand electrons [14].

2. **Electron Emission:** This phenomenon was originally proposed by Snyder et al. as one of the main mechanisms of charge loss in FG EEPROM cells under gamma ray irradiation [17]. The charge loss is explained by the fact that electrons stored in the floating gate can gain energy from ionizing radiation and can be emitted over the oxide barrier in the control gate or in the silicon substrate. This mechanism is also called photoemission. The emission over the oxide has been empirically modeled. However, this mechanism has not been physically modeled or extended heavy ions or to other particles [14]. Moreover, in this model, the photoemission is limited only to electrons stored in the floating gate which has no physical justification [14]. In fact, an ionizing particle strike can generate a number of electrons much larger than the net number of electrons stored in the floating gate. Some of the electrons generated by the particle strike may have enough energy to be emitted over the oxide barriers [14].

3. **Trap Assisted Tunneling (TAT):** This mechanism is one of the most important causes of oxide wear out due to electrical stress of program/erased cycles of a FG cell. When an ionizing particle strikes the cell, defects are created in the tunnel oxide. These defects may provide a percolation path for the electrons which can thus pass by tunneling effect through the tunnel oxide; therefore, this mechanism is called trap assisted tunneling (TAT). It has been shown that TAT is responsible for retention problems in at least a certain percentage of irradiated devices [14]. However, a very long time is required to discharge a FG cell by TAT mechanism (a few hours to a few weeks) [16]. Therefore, the TAT

mechanism cannot be responsible for SEU in FG cell taking into account that SEU data are taken immediately after the cell irradiation and then do not change with time [14]. TAT may nevertheless result in hard errors that cause retention problems of FG cell.

4. **Conductive Pipe Model:** This model has been proposed by Cellere et al. to explain the charge loss due to heavy ions strikes [15], [18]. This model assumes that the dense plasma of e-h pairs generated by the ion strike creates a temporary very thin (~ 10 nm) conductive path in the tunnel oxide during a short time (sub picosecond) after the strike. This is accompanied by the local lowering of the oxide energy barrier, which allows the electrons stored in the floating gate to pass through this conducting pipe. This phenomenological model reproduces well the experimental data of charge loss. However, there is a lack of physical explanation of the mechanisms governing both the resistance of the conductive path and the oxide barrier lowering [14].

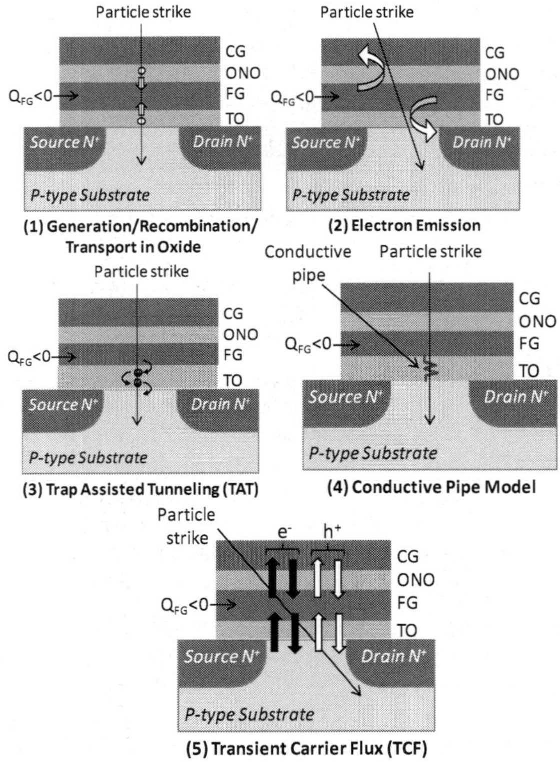

Figure 5. Schematic illustration of different models of charge loss due to a radiation particle strike. Adapted from Butt et Alam [14].

5. **Transient-Carrier-Flux (TCF) model:** This model was proposed by Butt and Alam [14] to explain the charge loss due to a SEU in FG memory cells. In this model it is assumed that the dominant physical mechanism that causes the FG charge loss due to a particle strike is the net flux of hot carriers flowing within a short time (~ ps) over the oxide barrier at the FG/oxide interfaces. After a particle strike, a dense cluster of hot electron-hole pairs are generated with carriers having broad energy distributions which return to thermal equilibrium in a time ~ 1 ps [14]. The tail of the high energy distribution induces a transient carrier flow in and out of the floating gate over the tunnel and inter-poly oxides. In case of a zero electric field in the oxide, the incoming and outgoing carrier flow balances each other at both oxide/FG interfaces and therefore the net flux is zero. On the contrary, in the programmed state, the electron negative charge stored in the floating gate induces a relatively high electric field in the oxide. Due to this electric field the electrons flux leaving the floating gate is greater than the electron flux entering the floating gate. In addition, the incoming holes flux is greater than the holes flux exiting the floating gate. The net flux therefore causes a reduction of the number of electrons stored in the floating gate. A small imbalance between the incoming and outgoing fluxes may be sufficient to disturb the state of the memory cell for which the tolerance of charge loss can be 100 electrons or less [14]. Butt and Alam validated their model by numerical simulations using a high-energy particle physics based toolkit - Geant4 for the generation and initial energy distributions in the high energy range (~10eV - ~ keVs). The hydrodynamic model coupled with Monte Carlo simulations was used for carrier relaxation in low energy (< 10eV) range, in order to accurately take into account the energy relaxation due to phonon scattering and impact ionization [14]. The transient fluxes of hot carriers flowing in and out the floating gate over the barrier oxides are calculated by solving self-consistently a system of equations including the transmission probability through the oxides and the Poisson equation, until carriers relax and reach the thermal equilibrium. These fluxes are then used to obtain the charge loss in flash memory cells due to alpha particles and cosmic neutron strikes. Butt and Alam finally demonstrated that the TCF model is in very good agreement with experimental data from Ref. [16], as will be shown later in Section 4.2.

4. Modeling and simulation of non-volatile memories using TIARA-G4 platform

In this section, we describe in details our modeling and numerical simulation approaches to compute the SER related to the floating-gate array of a flash memory circuit.

4.1. Description of TIARA-G4 NVM platform

The Tool Suite for Radiation Reliability Assessment (TIARA) platform has been developed these last years conjointly at Aix-Marseille University (IM2NP laboratory) and at STMicroelectronics (Central R&D, Crolles). The last version of the code has been called TIARA-G4 in reference to the fact that it is totally rewritten in C++ using Geant4 classes and libraries and compiled as a full Geant4 application [19]. This major evolution of TIARA allows us to consider now all the complexity of a given integrated circuit in terms of materials, doping and 3D geometry, using the Virtual Geometry Model (VGM [20]) factory and interface with both Geant4 for calculation and Root [21] for visualization. Up to now, TIARA-G4 has been used to simulate the interaction of Geant4 particles (including high energy and thermal neutrons, protons, muons, alpha-particles and heavy ions) with various SRAM and Flip-Flop architectures [9].

Figure 6 shows a schematic of the new TIARA-G4 NVM simulation flow structured into several independent modules and integrating new dedicated modules/subroutines to floating-gate NVM devices. In particular, we wrote a new cell/circuit construction model to reproduce the flash chip geometry (floating-gate array) with high fidelity. A second dedicated module implementing a physical model for radiation-induced charge loss from the floating-gate has been also developed, as detailed in paragraph 4.2.

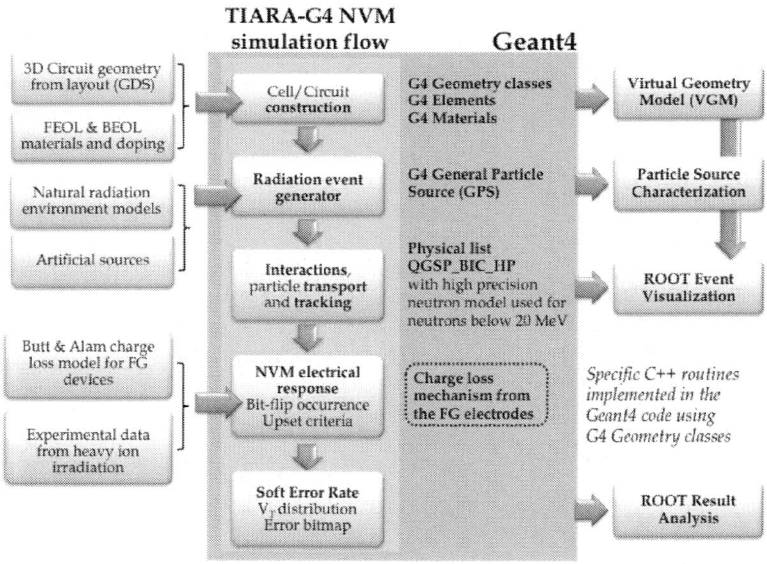

Figure 6. Schematics of the TIARA-G4 NVM simulation flow showing the different code inputs and outputs and the links with Geant4 classes, libraries, models or external modules and visualization tools.

To test the capability of the code to consider a real geometry, we based our developments on a NOR floating-gate flash memory architecture designed and fabricated by STMicroelectronics using a 90 nm CMOS process. This process is based on a Boro-Phospho-Silicate Glass (BPSG)-free Back-End Of Line (BEOL) which eliminates the major source of ^{10}B in the circuits and drastically reduces the possible interaction between ^{10}B and low – thermal energy neutrons

[22]. Figure 7(a) shows a TEM cross-section of the floating-gate devices along the transistor channel and Figure 7(b) shows a portion of the cell array layout at metal1/metal2 level. The elementary memory cell has an area of 0.18 μm². In TIARA-G4 NVM, the different transistor domains have been modeled as simple axis-aligned box volumes (Geant4 elements) of different materials (silicon, silicon dioxide, ONO and back-end-of-line stack), as illustrated in Figure 7(c) for a portion of the memory array. Figure 7(d) also shows a larger view of the array with different particle tracks interacting with certain floating-gate stacks.

4.2. Physical model considered

In complement to geometrical aspects, we also implemented in TIARA-G4 NVM a new module describing the charge loss from floating gates after single radiation particles strikes. From the review of the different available models in literature presented in Section 3, our initial choice was to adopt the full physical model of the Transient Carrier Flux (TCF) proposed by Butt and Alam [14]. The original approach of these authors is therefore based on complex simulations, in particular for the computation of carrier relaxation in the low energy (< 10eV) range, using coupled hydrodynamic and Monte Carlo simulations in order to correctly account for energy relaxation due to phonon scattering and impact ionization. This requires outsourcing from the main code the calculation of the charge loss from FG as a function of the incident particle properties.

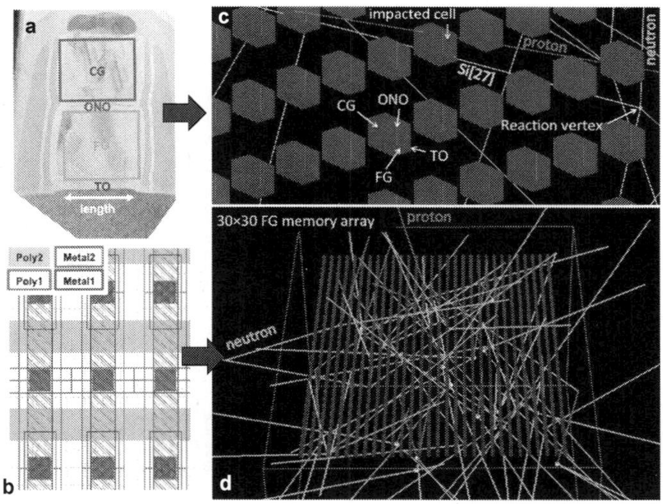

Figure 7. nm NOR floating-gate flash memory architecture considered in this work. (a) TEM cross-section of the floating-gate transistor geometry along the transistor channel and (b) layout of the cell array at metal1/metal2 level. (c) and (d): ROOT screenshots of a TIARA-G4 simulation showing detailed (c) and global (d) views of the memory array and different particle tracks resulting from atmospheric neutrons interaction with circuit materials. For a better view at FG cell level, all BEOL materials (6 metal levels), silicon substrate and intra-cell silicon and dielectrics are not shown.

An example of Butt and Alam's simulations is illustrated in Figure 8. Simulated curves very well reproduce experimental data without any fitting parameter (data extracted from Fig. 12 of Ref. [14]). From a practical point-of-view and in absence of a relatively simple computational solution to implement the Butt and Alam's model, we adopted a pragmatic approach assuming that an ionizing particle of LET striking the FG produces a Number of Electron Loss given by the following analytical function:

$$NEL = A \times LET^2 + B \times LET \tag{1}$$

Figure 8 shows that Eq. (1) is able to very well reproduce data. Of course, fitting coefficients A and B must be carefully evaluated for each device considered for the simulation from experimental measurements (heavy ion irradiation) or complementary numerical simulation using the Butt and Alam's complete computational procedure. The next release of TIARA-G4 NVM will integrate such an external dedicated module to confer to the code the capability to simulate a wide variety of NVM devices.

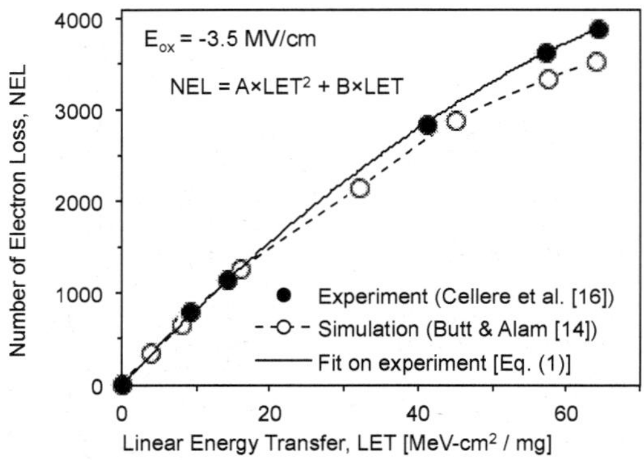

Figure 8. Number of electron loss (NEL) as a function of the particle LET for device T3 of Ref. [16] under an oxide electric field of 3.5 MV/cm. Simulation results from Butt & Alam (Ref. [14]) are also reported. The full line corresponds to the fitting function (1) on experi-mental data.

In the particular case of the present study and by chance, Figure 8 is based on data from Cellere et al. who precisely worked on STMicoelectronics FG arrays. It has been found that device T3 in Ref. [16] is technologically very close to our circuit, with the same thicknesses for the different layers composing both the FEOL and BEOL stacks. In order to consider values given by Eq. (1) to our memory devices, we introduced a scaling factor coefficient to take into account the difference in the dimensions of the floating gate polysilicon electrodes between devices considered in Fig. 8 and the present memory cell architecture (simple ratio of the volumes). Without any other calibration, we use in the following Eq. (1) to directly derive the threshold voltage shift resulting from a single particle strike in the FG domain using:

$$\Delta V_T = \frac{q \times NEL}{C_{pp}} \tag{2}$$

where C_{pp} is the coupling capacitance between the FG and CG electrodes (see Fig. 2 left).

5. Results and discussion

This last section presents the numerical simulations performed with TIARA-G4 NVM for the 90 nm NOR floating-gate flash memory architecture previously described. In a second part, we report experimental measurements obtained from the direct exposition of a large number of circuits to natural radiation. These two sets of data are finally compared and discussed in the last part of this section. It is important to notice that, in the following, all numerical results concerning the characterization and the simulation of the 90 nm flash circuit have been normalized by a common arbitrary scaling factor for confidentiality reasons imposed by the semiconductor manufacturer.

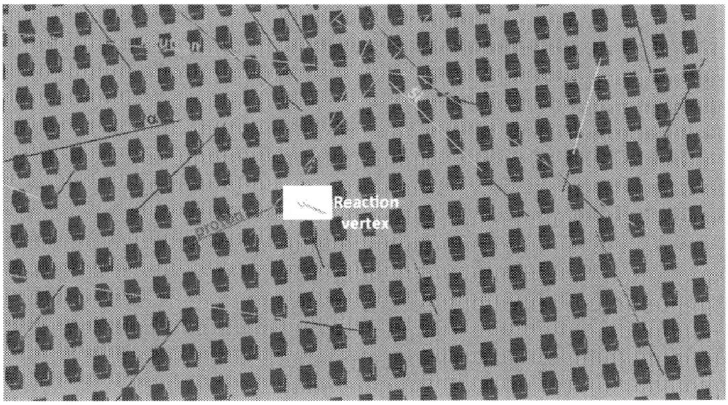

Figure 9. ROOT screenshots of a TIARA-G4 simulation showing several hundred of memory cells and different particle tracks resulting from atmospheric neutrons interaction with circuit materials. All BEOL materials, intra-cell silicon and dielectrics are not shown, silicon substrate is represented in yellow.

5.1. Numerical simulations

Using TIARA-G4 NVM, we performed extensive Monte Carlo simulations on large arrays of memory cells (up to 10^5 cells) considering the JEDEC atmospheric neutron source for high-energy incident neutrons above 1 MeV [23]. Other simulations have been also performed using a random generation of alpha particles inside the silicon material for mimicking the presence of ^{238}U contamination at ppb-level (we considered in this case the eight alpha-particle emitters of the ^{238}U decay chain) [24].

Two simulation screenshots are shown in Figure 7(c) and (d) in the case of a reduced matrix of 30×30 cells (considered for a better view). A larger simulation view is shown in Figure 9 for several hundred cells. They illustrate the interaction of atmospheric neutrons with the circuit materials and the way in which the neutron-induced secondary particles can impact the memory cells (direct strikes on the FG electrodes). A large part of the events are induced by secondary particles generated in the proximity of the FEOL/BEOL interface and predominantly by protons and silicon recoil nuclei. The BEOL stack is found to contribute marginally (< 2%) to the total SER in spite of the presence of several layers and vias of high density materials (W, Cu, Ta).

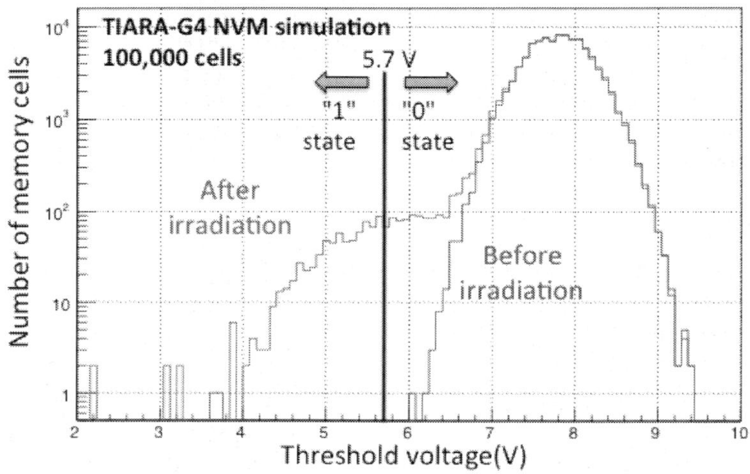

Figure 10. Distributions of V_T values computed by TIARA-G4 NVM for a population of 100,000 memory cells before and after irradiation with atmospheric neutrons.

Figure 10 shows the simulated V_T distributions for 10^5 cells before and after irradiation. The initial distribution corresponds to a Gaussian distribution with the mean and standard deviation values calibrated on experimental data (see 5.2, Fig. 13). The final distribution is the result of 10^9 incident JEDEC neutrons on the cell matrix, which corresponds to 50×10^6 h (i.e. more than 5700 years!) under natural atmospheric radiation at New-York City (NYC), the reference location defined by a high energy neutron flux of 20 n/cm²/h (neutron energies above 1 MeV). One can observe the emergence of a typical neutron-induced tail on a large domain of V_T values below 7 V. This tail indicates that the V_T value has sufficiently decreased for a certain number of cells to appear outside the Gaussian distribution. Among them, some cells have shifted below the sense value fixed at 5.7 V: their state has thus changed from a logical point-of-view ($0 \rightarrow 1$ transition) and their number must be taken into account for the evaluation of the neutron-SER. For the other cells of the distribution tail, ΔV_T values are not sufficient to decrease their V_T below 5.7 V but large enough to shift the cells outside the initial curve.

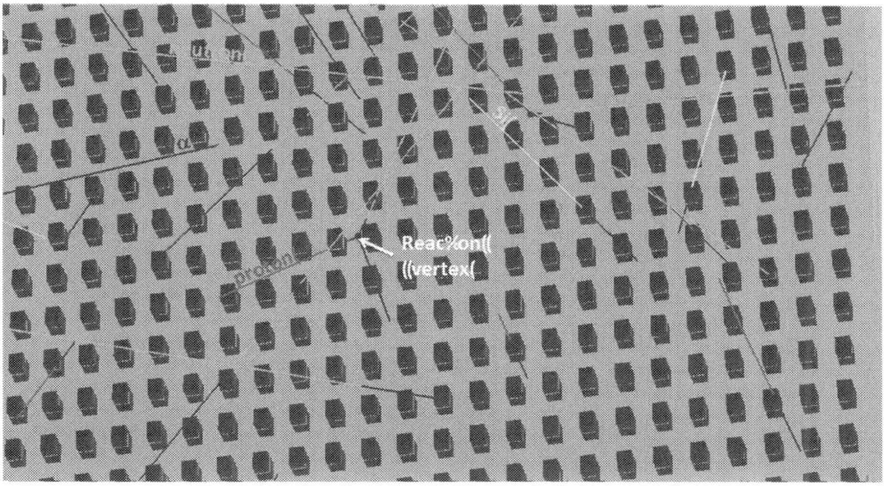

Figure 11. Distributions of ΔV_T values extracted from data of Fig. 10.

In complement to Figure 10, Figure 11 shows the threshold voltage shift distribution for all the cells of the simulated array. The peak at $\Delta V_T = 0$ V indicates that the great majority of the cells have not been impacted during the simulation run. For $\Delta V_T > 0$ V, the distribution is decreasing when ΔV_T increases. This directly reflects (cf. Eqs. (1) and (2)) the LET distribution of the secondary particles (i.e. neutron byproducts) striking the floating gates: the lightest particles (protons, alphas) with low LET values (typically below 1.5 MeV.cm^2/mg) induce a large number of events characterized by a small or moderate ΔV_T shift (<1 V); on the contrary, particles with the highest LET values, much less numerous, induce the largest ΔV_T (> 3V). From the number of cells verifying $V_T < 5.7$ V after irradiation, the neutron-SER at sea-level has been numerically evaluated to 7.7 (in arbitrary unit taking into account the common arbitrary scaling factor for confidentiality reasons). This value is expressed for the reference location (NYC).

For the alpha-SER, a value of 0.12 (a.u.) has been obtained considering a concentration of 0.2 ppb of ^{238}U uniformly distributed in the volume of circuit materials at both FEOL and BEOL levels. This concentration was directly deduced from experimental emissivity measurements (see below).

5.2. Experimental characterization and results

In parallel to this work of modeling and numerical simulation, previously described, we launched an experimental verification procedure to estimate the circuit SER from direct measurements. For this, we considered a large collection of NOR floating-gate flash memory circuits fabricated by STMicroelectronics using a 90 nm CMOS process. Circuits have been directly operated and characterized at wafer-level.

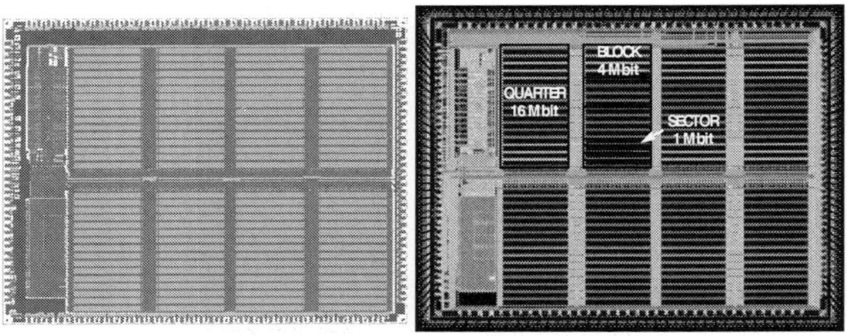

Figure 12. Layout (left) and die (right) of the ANNA test chip (area 9.230x7.044mm^2) fabricated by STMicroelectronics in CMOS 90 nm technology. The memory array is segmented into 32 blocks of 4 Mbits or 128 sectors of 1 Mbits (total capacity of 128 Mbits per chip).

The test chip, named "macrocell ANNA" and shown in Figure 12, is a 128 Mbit array of memory cells organized in 1 Mbit sectors, 4 Mbit blocks and 16 Mbit quarters without ECC. Several tens of macrocells are available per test wafer (200 mm wafers); more than 50 Gbits (~20 wafers) were used and fully characterized for the present experiment.

The test began by an initial wafer-level characterization at ST-Rousset (near Marseille) of all the circuits using a high performance tester (Verigy® V93000 platform). The test platform uses high precision voltage sources and parameter analyzers calibrated before each measurement campaign: the accuracy on V_T extraction is guaranteed to be less than 10 mV. Memory arrays have been written (all "0" pattern) and then read several times, allowing the compilation of a reference threshold voltage (V_T) mapping for all the test chips, cell per cell and wafer per wafer. The corresponding numerical data have been stored on a hard disk bay. During this initial characterization, all the wafers were also submitted to a 24h bake at 250°C followed by a new V_T characterization in order to identify (and thus to eliminate) all the test chips exhibiting electrical instabilities and/or abnormal FG charge loss. Figure 13 shows a typical V_T distribution, sharply centered around 7.8 V for a population of memory cells corresponding to all functional test chips for a series of five wafers (same technological lot). The reproducibility (i.e. repeatability) of such an electrical characterization has been attested by the fact that repeated measurements on the same wafer show exactly the same V_T distribution within measurement margins (< 10 mV), cell per cell.

In addition to this initial electrical characterization, we also performed alpha-emissivity measurements at wafer-level using a XIA UltraLo-1800 alpha-particle counter. Figure 14 shows the results of this characterization, in terms of emissivity and measurement error (Fig. 14 left) and of energy distribution (Fig. 14 right) of the emitted alpha particles from the fully processed wafers. An emissivity level of 0.0013 α/cm^2/h was measured, which corresponds to a concentration of 0.2 ppb of ^{238}U uniformly distributed in the volume of circuit materials at both FEOL and BEOL levels. Such a correspondence has been estimated using a reverse α-particle emissivity analytical modeling recently developed [25].

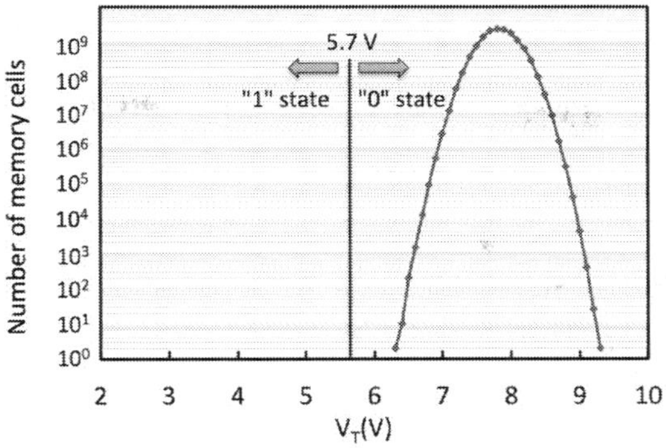

Figure 13. Initial distribution of the measured threshold voltage V_T values for all the programmed FG memory cells (all "0" pattern) related to a series of 5 wafers.

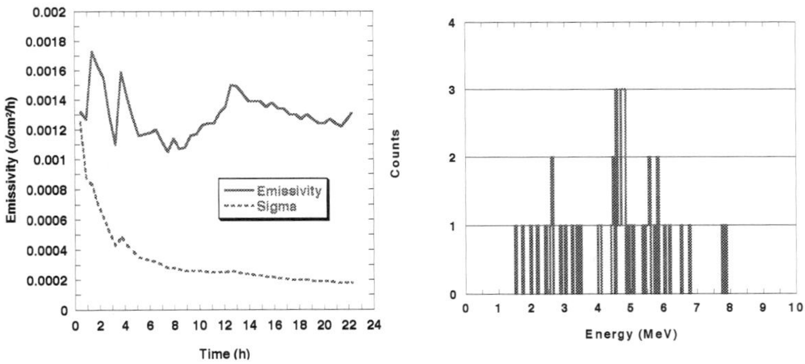

Figure 14. Alpha-particle emissivity characterization of 90 nm flash memory wafers using a XIA UltraLo-1800 alpha-particle counter. Left: emissivity and measurement error sigma as a function of measurement duration. Right: energy distribution of the detected alpha particles emitted from the surface of the wafers (fully-processed wafers).

After the initial characterization, approximately one half of the total number of wafers was stored in Rousset and the second half was delivered to an altitude test site by express mail and exposed to natural radiation. Figure 15 shows the flowchart of this test method that illustrates the sequencing of the different characterization and wafer transportation steps. Two different radiation environments have thus been considered: the first one at sea-level in Rousset for reference and the second one in altitude on the ASTEP platform [26]. The two sites are characterized by a relative atmospheric neutron flux of 1.04 and 6.02 with respect to New-York City, respectively [27-28]. After a period of exposition of several months, the wafers stored on ASTEP (see Figure 16) have been delivered to ST-Rousset for complete electrical characterization. Those remained in Rousset were also measured in the same time. The complete characterization loop Rousset → ASTEP → Rousset was repeated 3 times for the present work.

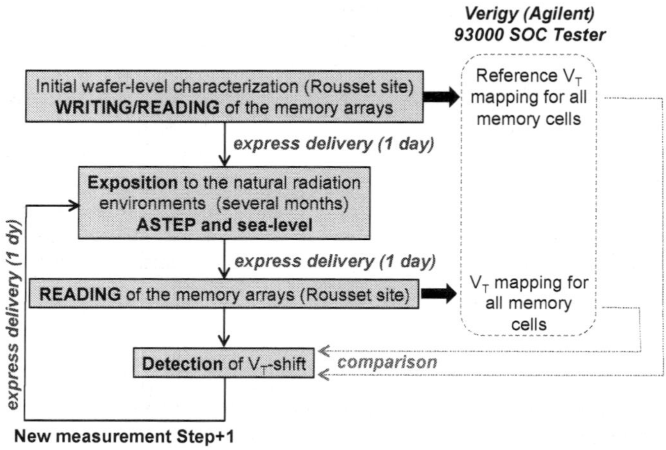

Figure 15. Flowchart of the multi-site characterization technique developed to evaluate the soft error rate of flash memories written and read at wafer-level using a Verigy® V93000 platform.

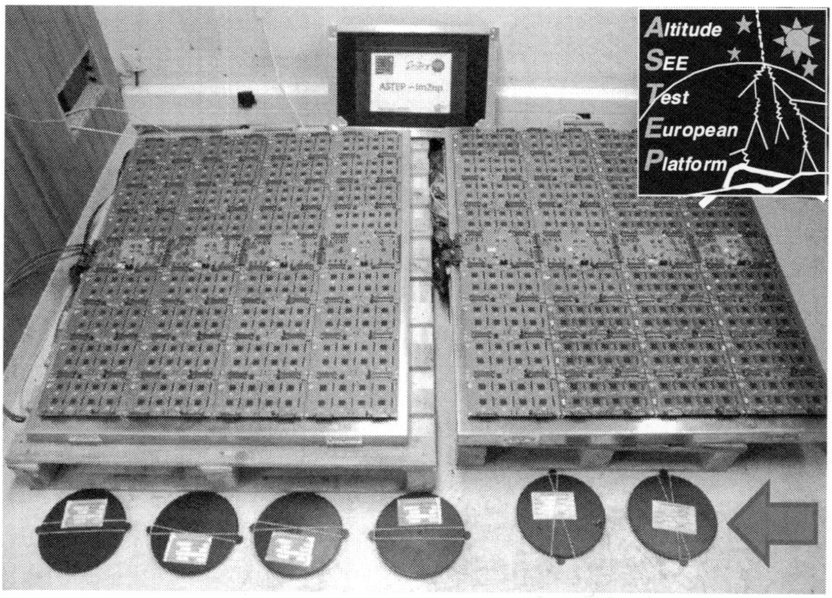

Figure 16. Global view of one of the ASTEP experimental room showing, in the foreground, six wafers of flash memories stored on the ground during their exposition to natural radiation on the ASTEP platform and, in the background, a real-time test setup based on 40nm SRAM circuits [9].

Figure 17 shows the results for the two series of wafers exposed in Rousset and on the ASTEP Platform. Three reading operations have been performed on the wafers stored in Rousset, respectively after 5, 12 and 18 months of exposition. Similarly, two reading operations have been performed on the ASTEP wafers, after 5 and 12 months of natural irradiation in altitude.

For wafers exposed at sea-level, one memory cell compared to more than several tens of Gbits has been detected with a V_T value changing at t_0 + 12 months and becoming inferior to the reference value (V_T^{REF} = 5.7 V) delimiting the "0" and "1" logical states. For this memory cell, the threshold voltage shifted from 8.0 to 4.5 V. Likewise, 2 and 3 shifted-V_T cells have been detected on the ASTEP wafers, respectively after 5 months and one year of exposition. Measured V_T values for these flipped cells are also reported in Figure 17.

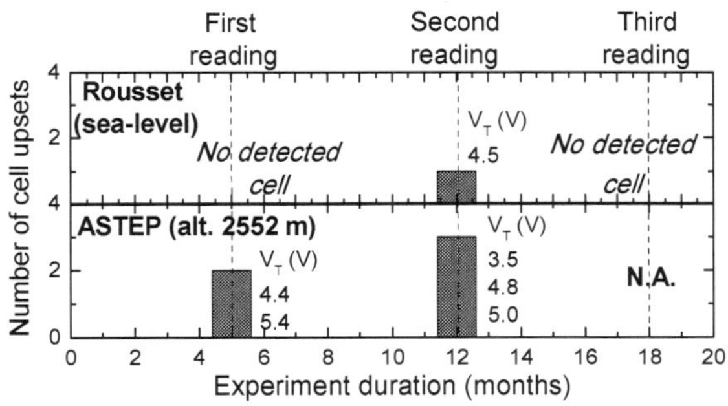

Figure 17. Number of memory cells with shifted V_T below the reference value (5.7 V) delimiting the "0" and "1" logical states and detected during the first and the second wafer readings.

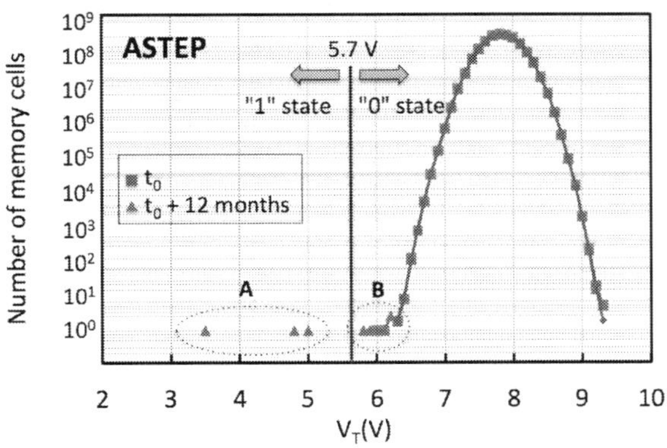

Figure 18. Comparison between the two distributions of V_T values measured at t_0 and at t_0 +12 months for population of programmed memory cells exposed to natural radiation on the ASTEP platform.

A detailed analysis of the analogic V_T bitmaps (not shown) for all these impacted cells shown that these latters correspond to isolated cells (i.e. adjacent cells not impacted) randomly distributed in the FG array and on the exposed wafers. A more detailed investigation on the complete V_T distributions shows that several other cells have been potentially impacted during their exposition to natural radiation. Figure 18 shows such a distribution for the whole cell population exposed on ASTEP. At t_0 + 12 months, two groups of impacted cells can be distinguished: a first group of 3 cells, labeled A, which corresponds to the 0→1 flipped cells reported in Figure 17 (bottom graph, at t_0 + 12), and a second group of 6 cells, labeled B, for which the V_T have shifted but not enough to cross the limit of 5.7 V delimiting the two binary states "0" and "1".

From data of Figure 17 obtained at two different locations, the global soft error rate (SER) and its two components can be determined, as suggested in [29]. The two components are, on one hand, the n-SER taking into account the atmospheric neutrons contribution to the SER and, on the other hand, the so-called α-i-SER accounting for all the internal failure mechanisms in the chips, including the possible alpha-particle emitter contribution. Indeed, several physical intrinsic mechanisms can be invoked to explain the long-term charge loss generally observed in FG devices, in particular different leakage mechanisms through the tunnel oxide or through the ONO interpoly dielectric based on various possible trap/defect assisted tunneling [30]. These latter are not inevitably related to radiation effects but can be also linked to material properties or induced by the technological process or by an electrical stress. This is the reason why the second contribution to the SER is called here α-i-SER and not only α-SER. We thus have a system with two equations and two unknown quantities:

$$\alpha - \mathrm{i} - \mathrm{SER} + AF_{Rousset}\mathrm{n} - \mathrm{SER} = SER_{Rousset} \tag{3}$$

$$\alpha - \mathrm{i} - \mathrm{SER} + AF_{ASTEP}\mathrm{n} - \mathrm{SER} = SER_{ASTEP} \tag{4}$$

where $AF_{Rousset}$ = 1.04 and AF_{ASTEP} = 6.02 are the neutron flux acceleration factor, as previously reported in II.B.

Figure 8 shows the results of this SER extraction, considering results of Figure 17, durations and memory capacities related to the different experiments. Global SER values of 9.7 and 28.8 a.u. are obtained for Rousset (sea-level) and ASTEP (altitude) experiments, which leads to an estimation of α-i-SER = 3.2 and n-SER = 8.7 a.u.

These results demonstrate a very limited impact of the atmospheric radiation on the total SER without ECC, typically in the range [10-100] FIT/GBit. With respect to all other internal failure mechanisms, the external natural radiation constraint is found to represent less than one third (27%) of the total SER. Note that all these SER values are found strictly equal to 0 if ECC is activated on the chips, due to the fact that only rare events always corresponding to single cell upsets have been detected.

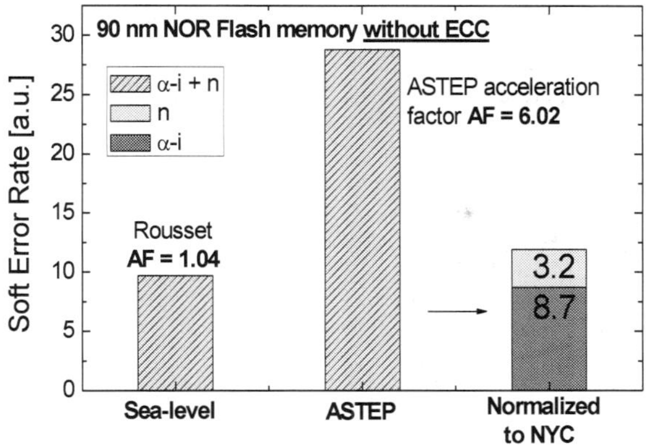

Figure 19. Summary of the SER deduced from data of Fig. 4 for sea-level and ASTEP conditions. The two components of the SER are given for normalized New-York City conditions. SER values are in a.u. for confidentiality reasons but the order of magnitude of these values is a few hundreds FIT per GBit.

5.3. Discussion

In this last paragraph, we conclude by comparing these experimental results with predictive values obtained using the TIARA-G4 NVM simulation platform. Figure 20 summarizes this comparison for the different defined SER components.

A good agreement is found for the neutron-SER taking into account all experimental and simulation uncertainties, in the first instance, the relatively weak statistics of the experiment in terms of number of events detected. Indeed, despite the duration of the experiment (18 months) and the huge quantity of data to manipulate (the individual V_T evolution of more than 50 Gbits of memory cells has been stored and processed), the statistics of this first experiment remains relatively weak because of the extremely low rate of cell flips in this kind of memory.

For alpha-SER, the discrepancy is flagrant between the two values. This confirms our initial precaution to name the second extracted component of the SER (Fig. 19) α-i-SER instead of classically α-SER because, in the present case of FG devices, this component may be the result of other intrinsic failure mechanisms occurring in parallel inside the chips. From literature [31-33], we can invoke different intrinsic or extrinsic leakage current mechanisms though the dielectric layers present in the floating gate stack (tunnel oxide, ONO, spacers). Intrinsic mechanisms that contribute to charge loss are field-assisted electron emission, thermionic emission and electron detrapping. Extrinsic mechanisms are essentially oxide defects that can form conductive paths through a given dielectric. Whatever the mechanism or eventually the activation of several leakage paths, our results suggest that these electrical processes appear to be dominant in the observed failure rate with respect to the contribution of alpha-particle internal emission. This point will have to be carefully reevaluated in future works.

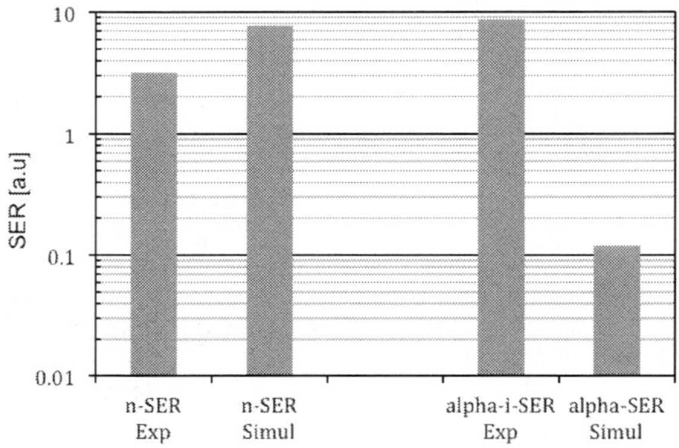

Figure 20. Comparison of the SER component values obtained by TIARA-G4 NVM simulation and from exposition to natural radiation in Rousset and on ASTEP.

Another interesting point of comparison comes from the ratio of the numbers of upset cells to the numbers of cells for which V_T have shifted but not enough to cross the limit of 5.7 V delimiting the two logical states. Although statistics are low for data of Fig. 18, the ratio (number of cells B/number of cells A) can be roughly evaluated to 50%. From simulation results with a much larger statistics, this ratio is 40.7%, which is clearly in the same order of magnitude. Beyond the fact that this point consolidates the comparison between experiment and simulation, this result shows that the number of impacted cells with a final V_T ranging between the sense voltage value and the edge of the initial Gaussian distribution is approximately two times larger than the number of cells verifying the upset criterion.

6. Conclusion

In conclusion, we developed in this work a numerical simulation code (TIARA-G4 NVM) capable of computing the soft-error rate of floating-gate flash memories induced by the two main natural radiation components at ground-level: the atmospheric high-energy neutrons and the alpha-particles emitted from ultra-traces of radioactive contaminants in circuit materials. Based on Geant4 geometry classes, elements and materials, the code is able to reproduce the circuit geometry from silicon substrate to back-end-of-line levels with fidelity. In complement to geometrical aspects, TIARA-G4 NVM also integrates a new module describing the charge loss from floating gates as a function of the properties (LET) of the incident ionizing particles. Using this code, we performed extensive Monte Carlo simulations on large arrays of memory cells (up to 10^5 cells) related to a 90 nm NOR floating-gate flash memory architecture designed by STMicroelectronics. Values of the SER for atmospheric neutrons and alpha-particle emitters have been computed and expressed, respectively, at sea-level (New-York City) and for a concentration of ^{238}U in the circuit materials separately determined through experimental emissivity measurements. The experimental verification of these simulated results has been conducted, for the first time, following a totally new approach: the direct exposition to natural radiation of a large amount of test circuits programmed and periodically read at wafer-level with a dedicated industrial test equipment. In spite of a relatively weak statistics achieved during this experimental phase, the remarkable convergence of the experimental results and our numerical simulations (considering no fitting parameter in the complete simulation chain) for the neutron- SER indicates that this later value is more than two decades below the soft error rate usually measured in modern SRAMs. In the same way, the comparison of experimental data measured at sea-level and alpha-SER simulations clearly suggests that another mechanism than internal alpha-particle production in bulk materials may be responsible of charge loss from floating gates. This point will have to be carefully investigated in future works.

Acknowledgements

The authors would like to acknowledge G. Just, A. Regnier and J.L. Ogier from STMicroelectronics (Reliability and Electrical Characterization Laboratory, Rousset Plant, France) for their contribution to the electrical characterization of the flash memory wafers and Sébastien Sauze (ASTEP platform) for his technical and support. They also sincerely acknowledge their past post-doc students Sébastien Martinie (now at CEA-LETI, Grenoble) and Sébastien Serre (now at TRAD, Toulouse) for their different contributions to this work. The logistical support of the Institute for Radio astronomy at Millimeter Wavelengths (IRAM) is finally gratefully acknowledged.

Author details

Jean-Luc Autran[1], Daniela Munteanu[1], Gilles Gasiot[2] and Philippe Roche[1]

1 Aix-Marseille University & CNRS, Marseille, France

2 STMicroelectronics, Crolles, France

References

[1] Massengill L.W., Bhuva B.L., Holman W.T., Alles M.L., Loveless T.D. Technology Scaling and Soft Error Reliability. In: Proceedings of the IEEE International Reliability Physics Symposium 2012, 3C.1

[2] International Technology Roadmap for Semiconductors (ITRS), available online at www.itrs.net

[3] Munteanu D., Autran J.L. Modeling of digital devices and ICs submitted to transient irradiations. IEEE Transactions on Nuclear Science 2008;55(4) 1854-1878.

[4] Cellere G., Gerardin S., Bagatin M., Paccagnella A., Visconti A., Bonanomi M., Beltrami S., Harboe-Sorensen R., Virtanen A. and Roche P. Can atmospheric neutrons induce soft errors in NAND floating gate memories?. IEEE Electron Device Letters 2009;30(2) 178–180.

[5] Cellere G., Gerardin S., Bagatin M., Paccagnella A., Visconti A., Bonanomi M., Beltrami S., Roche P., Gasiot G., Harboe-Sorensen R., Virtanen A., Frost C., Fuochi P., Andreani C., Gorini G., Pietropaolo A., Platt S. Neutron-induced soft errors in advanced flash memories. In: Proceedings of the IEEE International Electron Devices Meeting 2008, pp. 1 – 4.

[6] Gerardin S., Bagatin M., Paccagnella A., Cellere G., Visconti A., Beltrami S., Andreani C., Gorini G., Frost C.D. Scaling Trends of Neutron Effects in MLC NAND Flash Memories. In: Proceedings of the IEEE International Reliability Physics Symposium 2010, pp. 400 – 406.

[7] Gerardin S., Bagatin M., Ferrario A., Paccagnella A., Visconti A., Beltrami S., Andreani C., Gorini G., Frost C. D. Neutron-Induced Upsets in NAND Floating Gate Memories. IEEE Transactions on Device and Materials Reliability 2012;12(2) 437-444.

[8] Just G., Autran J.L., Serre S., Munteanu D., Sauze S., Regnier A., Ogier J.L., Roche P., Gasiot G. Soft Errors Induced by Natural Radiation at Ground Level in Floating Gate Flash Memories. In: Proceedings of the IEEE International Reliability Physics Symposium 2013, 3D-4.

[9] Autran J.L., Semikh S., Munteanu D., Serre S., Gasiot G. and Roche P., "Soft-Error Rate of Advanced SRAM Memories : Modeling and Monte Carlo Simulation, Numerical Simulation - From Theory to Industry", edited by Mykhaylo Andriychuk, ISBN : 978-953-51-0749-1, InTech, pp. 309-336, Sept. 2012. Available online at http://dx.doi.org/10.5772/50111

[10] Gerardin S., Bagatin M., Paccagnella A., Grürmann K., Gliem F., Oldham T.R., Irom F., and Nguyen D.N. Radiation Effects in Flash Memories. IEEE Transactions on Nuclear Science 2013;60(3) 1953-1969.

[11] Gerardin S. and Paccagnella A. Present and future non-volatile memories for space. IEEE Transactions on Nuclear Science 2010;57 3016-3039.

[12] Paccagnella A., Bagatin M., Cellere G., Gerardin S. Flash memories and soft errors at ground level. In: RADSOL workshop, June 2009.

[13] Gerardin S., Bagatin M., Ferrario A., Paccagnella A., Visconti A., Beltrami S., Andreani C., Gorini G., Frost C. D. Neutron-Induced Upsets in NAND Floating Gate Memories. IEEE Transactions on Device and Materials Reliability 2012;12(2) 437-444.

[14] Butt N.Z., Alam M. Modeling Single Event Upsets In Floating Gate Memory Cells. In: Proceedings of the IEEE International Reliability Physics Symposium 2008, pp. 547 – 555.

[15] Ma T.M. and Dressendorfer P.V. Ionization Radiation Effects in MOS Device and Circuit. Wiley, New York, 1989.

[16] Cellere G., Paccagnella A., Visconti A., and Bonanomi M. Subpicosecond conduction through thin SiO_2 layers triggered by heavy ions. Journal of Applied Physics 2006;99 074101.

[17] Snyder E.S., McWhorter P.J., Dellin T.A., and Sweetman J.D. Radiation response of floating gate EEPROM memory cells. IEEE Transactions on Nuclear Science 1989;36 2131-2139.

[18] Cellere G., Paccagnella A., Visconti A., Bonanomi M., and Candelori A. Transient conductive path induced by a Single ion in 10 nm SiO_2 Layers. IEEE Transactions on Nuclear Science 2004;51 3304-3311.

[19] Agostinelli S. et al. Geant4, a simulation toolkit. Nuclear Instruments and Methods in Physics Research Section A: Accelerators, Spectrometers, Detectors and Associated Equipment 2003;506 250-303. See also http://geant4.cern.ch

[20] Virtual Geometry Model (VGM), available online: http://ivana.home.cern.ch/ivana/VGM.html

[21] ROOT, an object oriented framework for large scale data analysis. http://root.cern.ch.

[22] Baumann R. and Smith E. Neutron-Induced ^{10}B Fission as a Major Source of Soft Errors in High Density SRAMs. Microelectronics Reliability 2001;41 211-218.

[23] JEDEC Standard "Measurement and Reporting of Alpha Particles and Terrestrial Cosmic Ray-Induced Soft Errors in Semiconductor Devices", JESD89 Arlington, VA: JEDEC Solid State Technology Association, October 2006.

[24] Gedion M., Wrobel F., Saigné F., Schrimpf R.D. Uranium and Thorium Contribution to Soft Error Rate in Advanced Technologies. IEEE Transactions on Nuclear Science 2011;58(3) 1098-1103.

[25] Martinie S., Autran J.L., Munteanu D., Wrobel F., Gédion M., Saigné F. Analytical Modeling of Alpha-Particle Emission Rate at Wafer-Level. IEEE Transactions on Nuclear Science 2011;58(6) 2798-2803 2011.

[26] Altitude Single Event Effects Test European Platform (ASTEP), www.astep.eu.

[27] Lei F., "Quotid Atmospheric Radiation Model" – QARM (previously Qinetiq Atmospheric Radiation Model). Available online on request to the author.

[28] Autran J.L., Serre S., Munteanu D., Martinie S., Semikh S., Sauze S., Uznanski S., Gasiot G., Roche P. Real-time Soft-Error testing of 40nm SRAMs. In: Proceedings of the IEEE International Reliability Physics Symposium 2012, pp. 3C.5.1 - 3C.5.9.

[29] Puchner H. Correlation of Life Testing to Accelerated Soft Error Testing. In: Third Annual IEEE-SCV Soft Error Rate (SER) 2011, Workshop, San Jose, USA.

[30] Kim J.H., Choi J.B. Long-term electron leakage mechanisms through ONO interpoly dielectric in stacked-gate EEPROM cells. IEEE Transactions on Electron Devices 2004;51(12) 2048-2053.

[31] Pavan P., Larcher L., Marmiroli A. Floating Gate Devices: Operation and Compact Modeling. Kluwer Academic Press, 2004, Chapter 2.

[32] Golla C., Zanoni E., Cappelletti P. Flash Memories. Kluwer Academic Press, 2011.

[33] Van Houdt J., Degraeve R., Groeseneken G., Maes H.E. Physics of Flash Memories. In: "Nonvolatile Memory Technologies with Emphasis on Flash: A Comprehensive Guide to Understanding and Using NVM Devices", edited by J. E. Brewer, M. Gill, Wiley & Sons, 2007.

Chapter 18

Numerical Calculation for Lightning Response to Grounding Systems Buried in Horizontal Multilayered Earth Model Based on Quasi-Static Complex Image Method

Zhong-Xin Li, Ke-Li Gao, Yu Yin, Cui-Xia Zhang and Dong Ge

Additional information is available at the end of the chapter

http://dx.doi.org/10.5772/57049

1. Introduction

For lightning protection design, an exact evaluation of transients electromagnetic field within a complex grounding system has fundamental importance. In fact, the earth electrodes constitute a fundamental part of the electrical apparatus in both industrial and civil structures. Grounding systems should have a suitable configuration in order to avoid serious hazard to humans, and to preserve electrical insulation in electrical and electronic equipment and installations. Moreover, in electrical power installations, the shape and dimensions of the earth termination system, as a part of a lightning protection system, are more important than the specific value of the earth resistance, in order to disperse the lightning current into the earth without causing dangerous overvoltages.

Pioneering but comprehensive work on this subject was conducted in the first half of the twentieth century, which is summarized by Sunde in the well known reference book [1]. Important pioneering work is described also in [2] and [3]. More recent work is summarized in [4]. Recently, computerized analysis methods have been developed based on different approaches, for example, on circuit theory [5]–[8], transmission line theory [9]–[15], electromagnetic field theory [16]–[23], and hybrid method [24]–[31].

Hybrid method has been developed from conventional nodal analysis, which combines the electrical circuit method and the electromagnetic field method. It has been proved to have combined the strong points of both the two methods. Dawalibi earlier discussed how the hybrid method came out of the electromagnetic field method in [24] and further discussed the hybrid method in [25], however, the hybrid method was based on quasi-static electromagnetic field theory, and only discusses steady grounding problem in the frequency domain. Meliopoulos also discusses the hybrid method based on quasi-static electromagnetic field theory in [26]; Huang & Kasten developed a new hybrid model to calculate the current distribution in both the grounding system and the metallic support conductors, while considering the voltage drop along the grounding system conductors [27]. However, the model was also based on quasi-static electromagnetic field theory, meanwhile, leakage currents and network currents within the grounding system are separately considered in the calculation, their mutual coupling influence is neglected, and the capacitive coupling effect of the earth is also neglected. Otero, Cidras & Alamo developed a hybrid method to calculate the current distribution in a grounding system [28] within which the mutual inductive and capacitive coupling influence among these current flowing and leaking along the conductor is considered. However, only a uniform half infinite earth model is considered. This hybrid method was combined with the FFT, and so the transient response from the grounding system was obtained. These confines in the frequency domain promoted the development of a novel mathematical model in [29]–[32], which introduced the quasi-static complex image method (QSCIM) for calculating the current distribution in a grounding system buried in both horizontal and vertical multilayered earth models in the frequency domain. However, the hybrid method can be further developed to numerically calculate the transient response from a grounding system buried in multilayered earth model.

Once the multilayered earth model is adopted, the Green's function of a point source will contain an infinite integral for the Bessel function, a complex image method based on Maclaurin's infinite series expansion have been studied in [33] and [34], which has brought up problem about the convergence of the infinite Maclaurin's series. To avoid this convergence problem, QSCIM is introduced to dealt with the infinite integral, which uses finite exponential terms (usually just 3–4 terms) through the Matrix Pencil approach instead of Maclaurin's series to quickly calculate the Green's function.

In this paper, based on previous works [28]–[31], combined with the FFT, a novel and accurate mathematical model is developed for calculating the harmonic wave currents of lightning currents distribution along the grounding system buried in multilayered earth model in the frequency domain, within which not only the conducting effect of the harmonic wave currents leaking into the soil, but also capacitive and inductive effects between different layers of soil have been considered. Both leakage currents and network currents within the grounding system and their mutual coupling are considered in the calculation. The earth is modeled by a multilayered earth model. To accelerate the calculation, QSCIM and closed form of Green's function were introduced, and the mutual inductive and conductive coefficient have analytical formulae so as to avoid numerical integration.

The maximum frequency of applicability of the method is limited by the quasi-static approximation of the electromagnetic fields. For the usual electrodes, it may be applied up to some hundreds of kHz.

2. Frequency domain analysis

The transient problem is first solved by a formulation in the frequency domain. The time-domain response is then obtained by application a suitable Fourier inversion technique. The response to a steady state, time harmonic excitation is computed for a wide range of frequencies starting at zero Hz. From this frequency response, a transfer function is constructed for every frequency considered. The transfer function is dependent only on the geometric and electromagnetic properties of the grounding system and its environment.

if $i(t)$ represents the injected current at a point in the grounding system, and $x(t)$ denotes an observed response, then

$$x(t) = F^{-1}W(j\omega) \cdot F[i(t)] \tag{1}$$

where F and F^{-1} are the Fourier and inverse Fourier transforms, respectively, $W(j\omega)$ is the transfer function, and ω is the angular frequency.

The physical model is based on the following assumptions.

- The earth comprises horizontal multilayered media, and the air media are homogenous and occupy half-spaces with a common horizontal plane boundary between the air and earth.
- The earth and the grounding electrodes exhibit linear and isotropic, arbitrary characteristics.
- The grounding system is assumed to be made of cylindrical metallic conductors with arbitrary orientation. However, they are assumed to be subject to the thin-wire approximation, i.e., the ratio of the length l of the conductor segment to its radius r is $\frac{l}{r} \gg 1$. In practice, a ratio of about 10 is satisfactory.
- Energization occurs by the injection of a current impulse of arbitrary shape produced by an ideal current generator with one terminal connected to the grounding system, and the other to the ground at infinity. The influence of the connecting leads is ignored.

3. Mathematical model of the equivalent circuit of the grounding system in the frequency domain

A set of interconnected cylindrical thin conductors placed in any position or orientation makes up a network to form the grounding system. The grounding network's conductors are assumed to be completely buried in a conductive N_e-layer media (earth) with conductivity σ_e and permittivity $\varepsilon_e = \varepsilon_{r_e} \cdot \varepsilon_0$ (here $e = 1, \cdots\cdots, N_e$). The air is assumed to be a non-conductive medium with permittivity $\varepsilon_0 = \frac{10^{-9}}{36\pi}$ F/m. All media have permeability $\mu = \mu_0 = \frac{10^{-7}}{4\pi}$ H/m.

The proposed methodology is based on the study of all the inductive, capacitive and conductive couplings between the different grounding system conductors. First, the electrode is divided into N_l pieces of segments that can be studied as elemental units, where the discrete grounding system has N_p nodes. A higher segmented rate of the electrode can enhance the model's accuracy but increases its computational time. Therefore, it is necessary to achieve a compromise solution between the two determinants.

The grounding network is energized by injection of single frequency currents at one or more nodes. In general, we consider that a sinusoidal current source of value $\overline{F_j}$ is connected at the jth $(j = 1, 2, \ldots, N_p)$ node. A scalar electric potential (SEP) $\overline{V_j}$ of jth node on the grounding network referring to the infinite remote earth as zero SEP is defined. In the same way, we define an average SEP $\overline{U_k}$ on kth $(k = 1, 2, \ldots, N_l)$ segment. If the segments are short enough, it is possible to consider $\overline{U_k}$ as approximately equal to the average of the kth segment's two terminal nodes SEP. We define a branch current $\overline{I_b^k}$, branch voltage $\overline{U_b^k}$, and leakage current $\overline{I_s^k}$ on the kth $(k = 1, 2, \ldots, N_l)$ segment.

3.1. Mathematical model of the grounding system in the frequency domain

With the above considerations, according to [28]–[31], the electric circuit may be studied using the conventional nodal analysis method [35], resulting in the following equations:

$$[\overline{\mathbf{F}}] = [\overline{\overline{\mathbf{Y}}}] \cdot [\overline{\mathbf{V_n}}] \tag{2}$$

$$[\overline{\overline{\mathbf{Y}}}] = [\overline{\overline{\mathbf{K}}}]^t \cdot [\overline{\overline{\mathbf{Z_s}}}]^{-1} \cdot [\overline{\overline{\mathbf{K}}}] + [\overline{\overline{\mathbf{A}}}] \cdot [\overline{\overline{\mathbf{Z_b}}}]^{-1} \cdot [\overline{\overline{\mathbf{A}}}]^t \tag{3}$$

where $[\overline{\mathbf{F}}]$ is an $N_p \times 1$ vector of external current sources; $[\overline{\overline{\mathbf{Z}_b}}]$ is the $N_l \times N_l$ branch mutual induction matrix of the circuit including resistive and inductive effects, which gives a matrix relationship between branch currents $[\overline{\mathbf{I_b}}]$; $[\overline{\overline{\mathbf{Z_s}}}]$ is an $N_l \times N_l$ mutual impedance matrix, which gives a matrix relationship between the average SEP $[\overline{\mathbf{U}}]$ and leakage currents $[\overline{\mathbf{I_s}}]$ through the rapid Galerkin moment method [38]. Both $[\overline{\overline{\mathbf{A}}}]$ and $[\overline{\overline{\mathbf{K}}}]$ are incidence matrices, which are used to relate branches and nodes. There are rectangular matrices of order $N_l \times N_p$, for whose elements we refer to [28]–[31].

The vector of nodal SEP $[\overline{\mathbf{V_n}}]$ may be obtained by solving 2. The average SEP $[\overline{\mathbf{U}}]$, leakage current $[\overline{\mathbf{I_s}}]$, branch voltage $[\overline{\mathbf{U_l}}]$, and branch current $[\overline{\mathbf{I_b}}]$ can also be calculated [28]–[31].

Once the branch currents and leakage currents are known, the SEP at any point can be calculated by

$$\varphi(\bar{r}_j) = \sum_{i=1}^{N_l} \int_{l_i} G_\varphi(\bar{r}_j, \bar{r}_i) \cdot \frac{I_{s_i}(\bar{r}_i)}{l_i} dl_i \tag{4}$$

where $G_\varphi(\bar{r}_j, \bar{r}_i)$ is the scalar Green's function of a monopole in the multilayered earth model.

The vector magnetic potential (VMP) A at any point can be calculated by

$$\bar{A}(\bar{r}_j) = \sum_{i=1}^{N_l} \int_{l_i} \bar{\bar{G}}_A(\bar{r}_j, \bar{r}_i) \bullet \bar{I}_{b_i}(\bar{r}_i) dt_i. \tag{5}$$

Here, $\bar{\bar{G}}_A(\bar{r}_j, \bar{r}_i)$ is the dyadic Green's function of a dipole in the multilayered earth model, which will be introduced later.

The electrical field intensity (EFI) at any point can be calculated by

$$\bar{E}(\bar{r}_j) = -\sum_{i=1}^{N_l} j\omega \int_{l_i} \bar{\bar{G}}_A(\bar{r}_j, \bar{r}_i) \bullet \bar{I}_{b_i}(\bar{r}_i) dt_i - \sum_{i=1}^{N_l} \nabla \int_{l_i} G_\varphi(\bar{r}_j, \bar{r}_i) \cdot \frac{I_{s_i}(\bar{r}_i)}{l_i} dl_i. \tag{6}$$

The magnetic field intensity (MFI) at any point can be calculated by

$$\bar{B}(\bar{r}_j) = \sum_{i=1}^{N_l} \nabla \times \int_{l_i} \bar{\bar{G}}_A(\bar{r}_j, \bar{r}_i) \bullet \bar{I}_{b_i}(\bar{r}_i) dt_i. \tag{7}$$

The study of the performance of the grounding system in the frequency domain has been reduced to the computation of $[\overline{\overline{\mathbf{Z_s}}}]$ and $[\overline{\overline{\mathbf{Z_b}}}]$ matrices.

3.2. Computation of $[\overline{\overline{\mathbf{Z_b}}}]$ and $[\overline{\overline{\mathbf{Z_s}}}]$ matrices

From [28]–[31], we know that each segment is modeled as a lumped resistance and self-inductance. Mutual inductances or impedances between branch segments' branch currents or leakage currents are also included in the model:

$$[\overline{\overline{\mathbf{X_q}}}]_{N_l \times N_l} = \begin{bmatrix} X_{1,1} & \dots & X_{1,i} & \dots & X_{1,j} & \dots & X_{1,N_l} \\ \vdots & \vdots & \vdots & \vdots & \vdots & \vdots & \vdots \\ X_{i,1} & \dots & X_{i,i} & \dots & X_{i,j} & \dots & X_{i,N_l} \\ \vdots & \dots & \vdots & \dots & \vdots & \vdots & \vdots \\ X_{j,1} & \dots & X_{j,i} & \dots & X_{j,j} & \dots & X_{j,N_l} \\ \vdots & \dots & \vdots & \dots & \vdots & \vdots & \vdots \\ X_{N_l,1} & \dots & X_{N_l,i} & \dots & X_{N_l,j} & \dots & X_{N_l,N_l} \end{bmatrix} \tag{8}$$

1. The case of $[\overline{\overline{\mathbf{X_q}}}] = [\overline{\overline{\mathbf{Z_b}}}]$: $X_{i,i} = R_i + j\omega L_i$, $X_{i,j} = R_{i,j} + j\omega M_{i,j}$.

   The diagonal elements consists of self impedance and self induction, the other elements belong to mutual induction between a pairs of conductor segments. The formula for self impedance and self induction can be found in [28]–[31], here, we give the formula for mutual induction:

$$M_{i,j} = \int_{l_i} \int_{l_j} \bar{\bar{G}}_A(\bar{r}_j, \bar{r}_i) \bullet \bar{I}_{b_i} dt_i \bullet \bar{I}_{b_j i} dt_j \tag{9}$$

   For an infinite homogeneous conductivity medium, one has $\bar{\bar{G}}_A(\bar{r}_j, \bar{r}_i) = \frac{\mu}{4\pi} \frac{1}{R_{ij}} \bar{\bar{I}}^0$, where $\bar{\bar{I}}^0$ is the diagonal unit matrix.

$$M_{i,j} = \frac{\mu}{4\pi} \int_{l_i} \int_{l_j} \frac{1}{R_{ij}} \bar{I}_{b_i} dt_i \bullet \bar{I}_{b_j} dt_j \tag{10}$$

   The above integral can be analytically calculated, this formula can be found in [27].

2. The case of $[\overline{\overline{\mathbf{X_q}}}] = [\overline{\overline{\mathbf{Z_s}}}]$: $X_{i,j} = Z_{i,j}$.

$Z_{i,j}$ is the mutual impedance coefficient between a pair of conductor segments in the grounding system. The matrix above includes the conductive and capacitive effects of the earth, and its elements are the mutual impedance coefficients $Z_{i,j}$.

$$Z_{i,j} = \int_{l_i} \int_{l_j} G_{\varphi}(\bar{r}_j, \bar{r}_i) \frac{dt_i}{l_i} \frac{dt_j}{l_j} \tag{11}$$

For an infinite homogeneous conductivity medium, one has $G_{\varphi}(\bar{r}_j, \bar{r}_i) = \frac{1}{4\pi\bar{\sigma}_1} \frac{1}{R_{ij}}$, so

$$Z_{i,j} = \frac{1}{4\pi\bar{\sigma}_1 l_j l_j} \int_{l_i} \int_{l_j} \frac{1}{R_{ij}} dt_i dt_j \tag{12}$$

where $\bar{\sigma}_1 = \sigma_1 + j\omega\varepsilon_1$. Eq. (12) can be solved analytically [36].

Note the medium surrounding the point current source here was considered as homogeneous and infinite. However, in any practical case, the earth is represented via a multilayered earth model. The QSCIM can be used to dealt with the multilayered earth model, this will be discussed next.

4. The closed form of the Green's function of a point source in a horizontal multilayered earth model and the QSCIM

The closed form of the Green's function of a scalar monopole and vector dipole buried in horizontal multilayered earth model will be respectively introduced.

4.1. The closed form of the Green's function of a scalar point source in a horizontal multilayered earth model and the QSCIM

The main task of simulation grounding system is calculating the element Z_{jk} of matrix $[\overline{\overline{\mathbf{Z_s}}}]$ in Eq. (11). When the earth model is considered as horizontal multilayered conductivity media, influences from the interface will be considered, which will lead to infinite integral about Bessel function associated with Green's function of a scalar monopole. However, the element Z_{jk} of matrix $[\overline{\overline{\mathbf{Z_s}}}]$, which includes the Green's function, can be fast calculated by using the QSCIM.

To perform the calculation, the corresponding Green's function of a scalar monopole must be defined first. The Green's function can be regarded as the SEP of one point located at any place produced by a scalar monopole with unit current δ in a horizontal multilayered conducting medium. For low frequency (50 or 60 Hz and higher harmonic wave) and limited size of the substation, the propagating effect of electromagnetic wave can be neglected, so

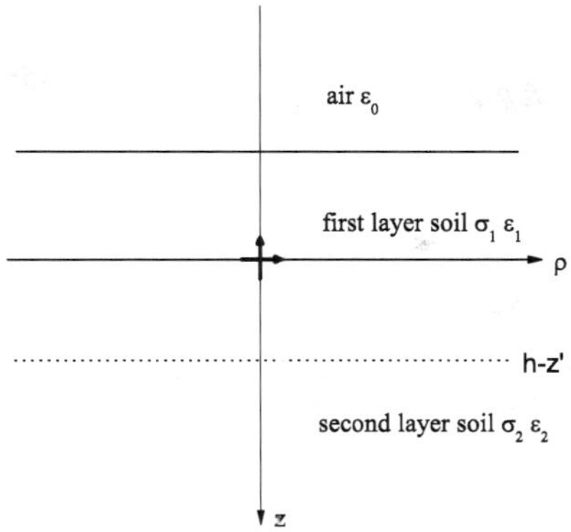

Figure 1. The earth model

the electromagnetic field here can be regarded as quasi-static field, so the SEP φ satisfies the Poisson equation as:

$$\nabla^2 \varphi_j = -\frac{\delta(r,r')\delta(ij)}{\overline{\sigma_i}} \tag{13}$$

where $i, j = 1, \ldots, N_s$, and $\delta(r,r')$ is the Dirac delta function. $\delta(ij)$ is Kronecker's symbol, $\overline{\sigma_i} = \sigma_i + j\omega\varepsilon_i$ is the complex conductivity of the ith layer medium. Supposing the monopole is located at origin of the coordinate system, seen from Fig. 1.

If the monopole lies in infinite homogenous medium, its expression of Green's function in the spherical coordinate system is.

$$\varphi = G(\bar{r}, \bar{r'}) = \frac{1}{4\pi \cdot \overline{\sigma} \cdot R} \tag{14}$$

where $R = |\bar{r} - \bar{r'}|$ is the distance between the source point and field point. While its expression in the cylindrical coordinates system (ρ, z) is as follows:

$$\varphi = G(\rho, z) = \frac{1}{4\pi \cdot \overline{\sigma}} \int_0^\infty e^{-\lambda|z|} J_0(\lambda\rho) d\lambda \tag{15}$$

where $J_0(\lambda\rho)$ is the Bessel function of the first kind of order zero.

For horizontal multilayered earth model, for examples, two-layer earth model, in the cylindrical coordinate system, the general form of Green's functions can be expressed by [1]:

$$\varphi_{10} = G_{10}(\rho, z) = \frac{1}{4\pi \cdot \overline{\sigma}_1} \int_0^\infty \left[A_{10}(\lambda) e^{-\lambda \cdot z} + B_{10}(\lambda) e^{+\lambda \cdot z} \right] J_0(\lambda\rho) d\lambda \quad (16)$$

$$\varphi_{11} = G_{11}(\rho, z) = \frac{1}{4\pi \cdot \overline{\sigma}_1} \int_0^\infty \left[e^{-\lambda|z|} + A_{11}(\lambda) e^{-\lambda z} + B_{11}(\lambda) e^{+\lambda z} \right] J_0(\lambda\rho) d\lambda \quad (17)$$

$$\varphi_{12} = G_{12}(\rho, z) = \frac{1}{4\pi \cdot \overline{\sigma}_1} \int_0^\infty \left[A_{12}(\lambda) e^{-\lambda \cdot z} + B_{12}(\lambda) e^{+\lambda \cdot z} \right] J_0(\lambda\rho) d\lambda \quad (18)$$

where G_{10}, G_{11} and G_{12} express the Green's function for the field point in the air, the top layer and bottom layer, respectively.

The six constants $A_{10} \sim B_{12}$ can be determined by employing the interface and infinite conditions of the SEP ($\varphi_{10} = \varphi_{11}, \sigma_0 \frac{\partial \varphi_{10}}{\partial z} = \sigma_1 \frac{\partial \varphi_{11}}{\partial z}, \varphi_{11} = \varphi_{12}, \sigma_1 \frac{\partial \varphi_{11}}{\partial z} = \sigma_2 \frac{\partial \varphi_{12}}{\partial z}, \varphi_{10}|_{z \mapsto -\infty} = 0$ and $\varphi_{12}|_{z \mapsto +\infty} = 0$).

Consequently, the expression of G_{11} can be given as follows:

$$G_{11}(\rho, z) = \frac{1}{4\pi\overline{\sigma}_1} \int_0^\infty [e^{-k_\rho|z|} - k_{01} e^{-k_\rho(2z'+z)} + f(k_\rho)(k_{01}^2 k_{12} e^{-k_\rho(2h+2z'+z)}$$

$$- k_{01} k_{12} e^{-k_\rho(2h+z)} + k_{12} e^{-k_\rho(2h-2z'-z)} - k_{01} k_{12} e^{-k_\rho(2h-z)})] J_0(k_\rho \rho) dk_\rho \quad (19)$$

where $f(\lambda) = \frac{k_{12}}{(1+k_{01}k_{12}e^{-2\lambda \cdot h})}$,$k_{01} = \frac{(\overline{\sigma}_0 - \overline{\sigma}_1)}{(\overline{\sigma}_0 + \overline{\sigma}_1)}$, $k_{12} = \frac{(\overline{\sigma}_1 - \overline{\sigma}_2)}{(\overline{\sigma}_1 + \overline{\sigma}_2)}$, h is the thickness of the top layer, $\overline{\sigma}_0$,$\overline{\sigma}_1$ and $\overline{\sigma}_2$ are the complex conductivity of air and two layers, respectively.

Now this $f(\lambda)$ can be developed into an exponential series with finite terms by MP method [37] instead of Maclaurin's series to avoid verbose calculation [38]:

$$f(\lambda) = \sum_{n=1}^{N} \alpha_n \cdot e^{\beta_n \lambda} \quad (20)$$

where α_n and β_n are constants to be determined by choosing sample points of function $f(\lambda)$.

Considering the Laplace transform of Bessel function of the first kind of order v $J_v(\lambda\rho)$, we have [39]

$$\int_0^{\infty} e^{-c\lambda} J_v(\lambda\rho) d\lambda = \left[\frac{\rho}{c+\sqrt{\rho^2+c^2}}\right]^v \frac{1}{(c^2+\rho^2)^{\frac{1}{2}}} \tag{21}$$

where $Re(v) > -1$ and $Re(c) > 0$.

Set $v = 0$, so we have Lipschitz integration:

$$\int_0^{\infty} e^{-c\lambda} J_0(\lambda\rho) d\lambda = \frac{1}{(c^2+\rho^2)^{\frac{1}{2}}} \tag{22}$$

By employing Eq. (20) and Lipschitz integration, the closed form of the Green's function (Eq. (19)) can be given as following:

$$G_{11}(\bar{r}, \bar{r'}) = \frac{1}{4\pi\bar{\sigma}_1}[\frac{1}{R_0} - \frac{k_{01}}{R_0'} + \sum_{n=1}^{N} \alpha_n (\frac{k_{01}^2 k_{12}}{R_{n1}} - \frac{k_{01}k_{12}}{R_{n2}} + \frac{k_{12}}{R_{n3}} - \frac{k_{01}k_{12}}{R_{n4}})] \tag{23}$$

where the origin of the coordinate system shown in Fig. 1 has been moved to the surface of the earth, the source point is at $(0, z')$ and the field point is at (ρ, z), so $R_0 = [\rho^2 + (z-z')^2]^{\frac{1}{2}}$, in the same way, we have $R_0' = [\rho^2 + (z+z')^2]^{\frac{1}{2}}$, $R_{n1} = [\rho^2 + (z+z'-z_n)^2]^{\frac{1}{2}}$, $R_{n2} = [\rho^2 + (z-z'-z_n)^2]^{\frac{1}{2}}$, $R_{n3} = [\rho^2 + (z+z'+z_n)^2]^{\frac{1}{2}}$, $R_{n4} = [\rho^2 + (z-z'+z_n)^2]^{\frac{1}{2}}$, in which $z_n = 2h - \beta_n$.

It can be seen that each term except $\frac{1}{R_0}$ of Eq. (23) can be regarded as a image scalar monopole source, whose location is indicated by $R_{ni,i=1\sim4}$ and amplitude is α_n, which can be seen in Fig. 1. However, in Eq. (23) α_n and R_{ni} are usually complex numbers, so that this approach is named as the QSCIM.

G_{10} and G_{12} can be similarly gotten.

The procedure for the closed form of the Green's function of a scalar monopole in arbitrary horizontal multilayered earth model is first to derive the specific solution of the Green's function in each layer based on the general expressions (for example, the general expressions of a scalar monopole in three layers media is given in Eq. (15), Eq. (16) and Eq. (17)), and the interface and infinite conditions of SEP of the monopole is used to decide the unknown constants. Then, by employing the MP method exponential series development and the Lipschitz integration, the final expression of the Green's functions can be obtained.

Once the closed form of Green's function of a scalar monopole in the horizontal multilayered earth model has been gotten, the mutual impedance coefficient Eq. (11) can be fast analytical calculated, which is just same as the Eq. (12).

4.2. The closed form of the Green's function of a vector point source in a horizontal multilayered earth model and the QSCIM

The another important task of simulation grounding system is calculating the element M_{jk} of matrix $[\overline{\overline{\mathbf{Z_b}}}]$ in Eq. (9). When the earth model is considered as horizontal multilayered conductivity media, and influences from the interfaces on mutual induction between two conductors should be considered, which also lead to infinite integral about Bessel function in the Green's function of a vector dipole, the element M_{jk} of matrix $[\overline{\overline{\mathbf{Z_b}}}]$ includes the Green's function, which can also be fast calculated by using the QSCIM.

Like Green's function of the scalar monopole, to perform the calculation of a vector dipole in horizontal multilayered earth model, its corresponding Green's function should also be defined first. The Green's function can be regarded as the VMP A of a point at any place produced by a vector dipole with unit current δ within a horizontal multilayered medium, whose electromagnetic field can also be regarded as quasi-static field, so the VMP A also satisfies the Poisson equation as:

$$\nabla^2 A_j = -\mu\bar{\delta}(r, r')\delta(ij) \tag{24}$$

where $i, j = 1, \ldots, N_s; \mu$ is the permeability of the earth medium. Supposing the dipole is located at origin of the coordinate system, seen from Fig. 1

If the vector dipole is lying in homogenous infinite medium, its expression of Green's function in the spherical coordinate system is.

$$A = G_A(r, r') = \frac{\mu}{4\pi \cdot R} \tag{25}$$

And its expression in the cylindrical coordinates system (ρ, z) is as follows:

$$A = G_A(\rho, z) = \frac{\mu}{4\pi}\int_0^{\infty} e^{-\lambda|z|} J_0(\lambda\rho)d\lambda \tag{26}$$

Not like scalar monopole source, for horizontal multilayered earth model, vector dipole source must be considered into two cases, which are vertical and horizontal dipoles, respectively. This is because any placed dipole in horizontal multilayered earth model can be decomposed into horizontal and vertical components. For vertical dipole case, its Green's function can be defined as $G^z_{A_z}$; For horizontal dipole case, it own two components, which are horizontal x or y component and vertical z component, so its Green's function can be defined as $G^x_{A_x}$ and $G^z_{A_x}$, respectively.

We also take the two-layer earth model as an example, the dipole lies in the earth model. In the cylindrical coordinate system, the general form of Green's functions for the vertical dipole $G^z_{A_z}$ or horizontal dipole $G^x_{A_x}$ can be expressed by [1]:

$$A_{p10}^{p} = G_{A_{p10}}^{p}(\rho, z) = \frac{\mu}{4\pi}\int_{0}^{\infty}\left[A_{10}(\lambda)e^{-\lambda\cdot z} + B_{10}(\lambda)e^{+\lambda\cdot z}\right]J_{0}(\lambda\rho)d\lambda \tag{27}$$

$$A_{p11}^{p} = G_{A_{p11}}^{p}(\rho, z) = \frac{\mu}{4\pi}\int_{0}^{\infty}\left[e^{-\lambda\cdot|z|} + A_{11}(\lambda)e^{-\lambda\cdot z} + B_{11}(\lambda)e^{+\lambda\cdot z}\right]J_{0}(\lambda\rho)d\lambda \tag{28}$$

$$A_{p12}^{p} = G_{A_{p12}}^{p}(\rho, z) = \frac{\mu}{4\pi}\int_{0}^{\infty}\left[A_{12}(\lambda)e^{-\lambda\cdot z} + B_{12}(\lambda)e^{+\lambda\cdot z}\right]J_{0}(\lambda\rho)d\lambda \tag{29}$$

where $G_{A_{p10}}^{p}$, $G_{A_{p11}}^{p}$ and $G_{A_{p12}}^{p}$ express the Green's function of the dipole for the field point in the air, the top layer and bottom layer, respectively; for vertical dipole case, $p = z$, for horizontal dipole case, $p = x$.

Just like the deduced procedure for Green's function of a scalar monopole, the six constants $A_{10} \sim B_{12}$ can also be decided by employing the interface and infinite conditions of the dipole's VMP. For vertical dipole, there is a $f(\lambda)$, which can also be developed into an exponential series with finite terms by the MP method. Last by applying the Lipschitz integration, the final expression of $G_{A_{p11}}^{p}$ can be given as follows.

$$G_{A_{z11}}^{z}(\bar{r}, \bar{r'}) = \frac{\mu}{4\pi}\left[\frac{1}{R_0} + \frac{k_{01}}{R_0'} - \sum_{n=1}^{N}\alpha_n\left(\frac{k_{01}^2 k_{12}}{R_{n1}} + \frac{k_{01}k_{12}}{R_{n2}} - \frac{k_{12}}{R_{n3}} + \frac{k_{01}k_{12}}{R_{n4}}\right)\right] \tag{30}$$

$$G_{A_{x11}}^{x}(\rho, z) = \frac{\mu}{4\pi\, R_0} \tag{31}$$

where the origin of the coordinate system shown in Fig. 1 has been moved to the surface of the earth. R_0, R_0', $R_{ni,i=1\sim4}$ are just same as Eq. (23).

For horizontal dipole, there is a Green's function for z component $G_{A_{x11}}^{z}$ left, in the cylindrical coordinate system, the general form of the Green's function for z component in the two-layer earth model can be expressed by [1]:

$$A_{x10}^{z} = G_{A_{x10}}^{z}(\rho, z) = \frac{\mu}{4\pi}\frac{\partial}{\partial x}\int_{0}^{\infty}\left[A_{10}(\lambda)e^{-\lambda\cdot z} + B_{10}(\lambda)e^{+\lambda\cdot z}\right]J_{0}(\lambda\rho)\frac{d\lambda}{\lambda} \tag{32}$$

$$A_{x11}^{z} = G_{A_{x11}}^{z}(\rho, z) = \frac{\mu}{4\pi}\frac{\partial}{\partial x}\int_{0}^{\infty}\left[A_{11}(\lambda)e^{-\lambda z} + B_{11}(\lambda)e^{+\lambda z}\right]J_{0}(\lambda\rho)\frac{d\lambda}{\lambda} \tag{33}$$

$$A_{x12}^z = G_{A_{x12}}^z(\rho, z) = \frac{\mu}{4\pi}\frac{\partial}{\partial x}\int_0^\infty \left[A_{12}(\lambda)e^{-\lambda\cdot z} + B_{12}(\lambda)e^{+\lambda\cdot z}\right] J_0(\lambda\rho)\frac{d\lambda}{\lambda} \tag{34}$$

Also like the deduced procedure for Green's function of a scalar monopole, the six constants $A_{10} \sim B_{12}$ can be decided by employing the interface and infinite conditions of the horizontal dipole's VMP. The $f(\lambda)$ in the Green's function can also be developed into an exponential series with finite terms by the MP method. Last by applying the Lipschitz integration's varied form ($\int_0^\infty e^{-c\lambda} J_0(\lambda\rho)\frac{d\lambda}{\lambda} = \ln(c + \sqrt{c^2+\rho^2})$), the final expression of $G_{A_{x11}}^z$ can be given as follows.

$$G_{A_{x11}}^z(\rho, z) = \frac{\mu}{4\pi}\frac{\partial}{\partial x}[k_{01}\ln(z_0' + R_0') - \sum_{n=1}^{N}\alpha_n(k_{01}^2 k_{12}\ln(z_{n1} + R_{n1})$$

$$+ k_{01}k_{12}\ln(z_{n2} + R_{n2}) - k_{12}\ln(z_{n3} + R_{n3}) + k_{01}k_{12}\ln(z_{n4} + R_{n4}))] \tag{35}$$

where the origin of the coordinate system shown in Fig. 1 has been moved to the surface of the earth. The R_0' and $R_{ni,i=1\backsim 4}$ are same as Eq. (23). Other parameters are $z_0' = z + z'$, $z_{n(1-4)} = (sign_a \cdot z + sign_b \cdot z') + z_n$, in which $sign_a = 1$ for z_{n1} and z_{n3}, $sign_b = 1$ for z_{n3} and z_{n4}, $sign_a = sign_b = -1$ for others.

It can also be seen that each term except $\frac{1}{R_0}$ of Eqs. (30) and (35) can be regarded as a image vector dipole source, whose location is indicated by $R_{ni,i=1\backsim 4}$ and amplitude is α_n, which can be seen in Fig. 1. However, in Eqs. (30) and (35), α_n and R_{ni} are usually complex numbers, so that this approach is also named as the QSCIM.

The other Green's function for the dipole $G_{A_{z10}}^z$, $G_{A_{z12}}^z$, $G_{A_{x10}}^x$, $G_{A_{x12}}^x$, $G_{A_{x10}}^z$ and $G_{A_{x12}}^z$ can be given in the similarly way.

Like closed form of Green's function of a scalar monopole, the procedure for the closed form of the Green's function of a vector dipole in arbitrary horizontal multilayered earth model is also first to derive the specific solution of the Green's function in each layer based on the general expressions (for example, the general expressions of Green's function for a vertical dipole or x component of horizontal dipole in three horizontal layers medium are given in Eq. (27), Eq. (28) and Eq. (29); for z component of horizontal dipole, are given in Eq. (32), Eq. (33) and Eq. (34)), and the interface and infinite conditions of VMP of the dipole are also used to decide unknown constants. Then, for z component of horizontal dipole and vertical dipole, by employing the MP method exponential series can be developed. Last by utilizing the Lipschitz integration and its varied form, the final expression of the Green's function of the dipole can be achieved.

Once the closed form of Green's function of a vector dipole in horizontal multilayered earth model has been given, the mutual impedance coefficient Eq. (9) can also be fast analytical calculated just like Eq. (10).

http://dx.doi.org/10.5772/57049

5. Time-domain solutions

Once the transfer functions $W(j\omega)$ have been determined for each calculated quantity, for example the electric field or current at specified points, the time-domain solutions can be obtained by direct application of (1). The calculation of the inverse Fourier transform is carried out by an FFT algorithm which is well-suited for the evaluation of time-domain responses.

The transient impedance, an essential parameter in grounding system design, is defined as a ratio of time varying voltage and current at injection point [19]:

$$Z(t) = \frac{v(t)}{i(t)} \tag{36}$$

where $i(t)$ represents the injected current at a grounding grid. This injected current represents the lightning channel current usually expressed by the double exponential function $i(t) = I_m(e^{-\alpha t} - e^{-\beta t})$, $t \geq 0$, where pulse rise time is determined by constants α and β, while I_m denotes the amplitude of the current waveform. The Fourier transform of the excitation function is defined by integral [40]:

$$I(f) = \int_{-\infty}^{\infty} i(t)e^{j2\pi ft}dt \tag{37}$$

Integral (37) can be evaluated analytically

$$I(f) = I_m(\frac{1}{\alpha + j2\pi f} - \frac{1}{\beta + j2\pi f}) \tag{38}$$

The frequency components up to few MHz are meaningfully present in the lightning current Fourier spectrum with strong decreasing importance from very low to highest frequencies. Multiplying the excitation function $I(f)$ with the input impedance spectrum $Z_{in}(f)$ provides the frequency response of the grounding system:

$$U(f) = I(f)Z_{in}(f) \tag{39}$$

Applying the IFFT, a time domain voltage counterpart is obtained. IFFT of the function $U(f)$ is defined by the integral [40]:

$$U(t) = \int_{-\infty}^{\infty} U(f)e^{j2\pi ft}d\omega \tag{40}$$

As the frequency response $U(f)$ is represented by a discrete set of values the integral (41) cannot be evaluated analytically and the discrete Fourier transform, in this case the IFFT algorithm, is used, i.e.,

$$U(t) = IFFT(U(f)) \tag{41}$$

Implementation of this algorithm inevitably causes an error due to discretization and truncation of essentially unlimited frequency spectrum. The discrete set of the time domain voltage values is defined as [40]:

$$U(t) = F\sum_{k=0}^{N} U(k\Delta f)e^{jk\Delta f n\Delta t} \tag{42}$$

where $n = 0, \ldots, N$, F is the highest frequency taken into account, N is the total number of frequency samples, Δf is sampling interval and Δt is the time step.

Finally, the impulse impedance, an also essential parameter in grounding system design, is defined by the following expression [41]:

$$Z_c = \frac{U}{I} \tag{43}$$

where U is the voltage maximum at the discharge point and I is the injected current magnitude at the time instant when U has been reached.

6. Verification of the method

In this part, our model has been verified through comparison with experimental data from other published papers; the validation of our model will also be discussed.

6.1. Verification of the method

To verify the method proposed in this work, some cases solved by other authors are studied.

In the first case, from [42], which gives some grounding impedance measurement results, the grid used for measurement is a 16-mesh grid of 100 m × 100 m. The earth is modeled by a multilayered earth model. The earth model is given by (a) $\rho_1 = 25\Omega$ m, $\rho_2 = 120\Omega$ m, and thickness of the upper earth is 5 m; (b) $\rho_1 = 120\Omega$ m, $\rho_2 = 25\Omega$ m, $\rho_3 = 250\Omega$ m, thickness of the first and second layers of earth are 5 m and 9 m, respectively. The radius of the grid conductors is 0.5 cm, and they are buried at 0.5 m depth in the earth. Here, the conductivity of the copper conductors is $\sigma_{Cu} = 5.8 \times 10^7$ S/m, and the permittivity of earth is set to $\varepsilon_1 = 5$. The results can be seen in Table 1.

In the second case, which is from [41], a typical grounding grid configuration can be seen in Fig. 2, which was made of round copper conductors with 50 mm^2 cross section. The grounding grid was buried at 0.5 m depth in two-layer horizontal earth, whose resistivity

Earth model	Mea.[42]	Our model
a	0.390	$(0.387, 8.6\times10^{-3})$
b	0.658	$(0.652, 1.6\times10^{-2})$

Table 1. Comparison with published measurement result: Frequency is 80Hz

ratio for the upper and the lower soil layers is $\rho_1/\rho_2 = 50/20$, the upper layer thickness being $H = 0.6$ m. The inject lightning current parameter was set to $T_1 = 3.5\mu$ s, $T_2 = 73\mu$ s and $I_m = 12.1$ A, the feed point is at the corner of the grid. For our model, the permittivities of the two layer earth model were set to $\varepsilon_1 = 30\varepsilon_0$ and $\varepsilon_2 = 20\varepsilon_0$. The transient SEP can be seen in Fig. 3, which ultimately agreed with the measured curve in Fig. 4 (a) in [41]; meanwhile, the impulse grounding impedance was 2.12 Ω as given by [41], and it is 2.08Ω for our model.

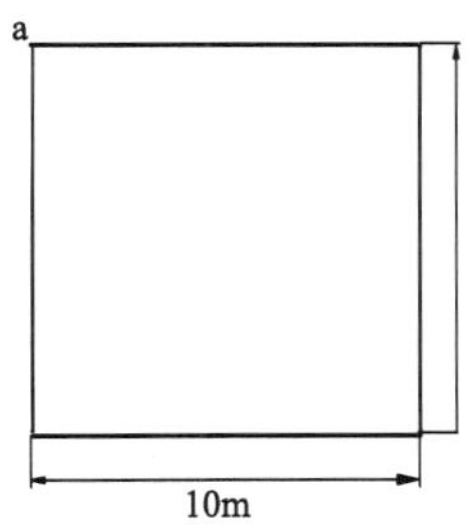

Figure 2. Typical grounding grid configuration

6.2. Validation of our method

The maximum frequency of applicability of the method is limited by the quasi-stationary approximation of the electromagnetic fields, which means the propagation effect of the electromagnetic field around the grounding system can be neglected, so

$$e^{-\gamma_e R} \approx 0 \tag{44}$$

where $\gamma_e^2 = j\omega\mu\,(j\omega\varepsilon_e + \sigma_e)\,, e = 1, \ldots, N_e$.

For most of the usual electrodes, this may be applied up to some hundreds of kHz.

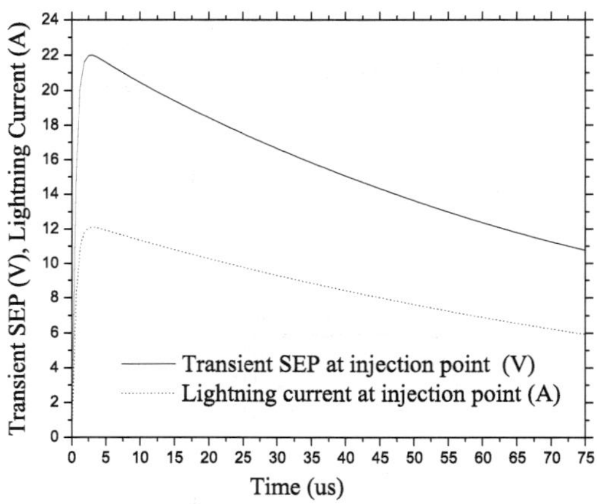

Figure 3. Transient SEP at injection point

7. Simulation result and analysis

A typical grounding system can be seen in Fig. 4. The earth is medalled by a two-layer conductive earth model, whose conductivity and permittivity is $\sigma_1 = 500^{-1}S/m$, $\sigma_2 = 900^{-1}S/m$, $\varepsilon_1 = 10\varepsilon_0$, $\varepsilon_2 = 22\varepsilon_0$, respectively, the first layer height is 5 m. The material of the grounding system conductor is Cu with conductivity $\sigma_{Cu} = 5.8 \times 10^7 S/m$. The conductor radii are 7 mm. The external excited lightning current is injected from the corner of the grounding system, which is described by a double-exponential function: $I(t) = 1.29 \times (e^{-0.019010t} - e^{-0.292288t})$ kA, which means that the parameters of the lightning current are $T_1 = 10\mu$ s, $T_2 = 50\mu$ s and $I_m = 1.29$ kA, the lightning current has been shown in Fig. 5.

The calculated grounding impulse impedance is $(14.401, j1.273)\Omega$.

A comparison between chosen total leakage currents and injecting currents of the grounding system in frequency domain is given in Table 2. It can be seen that the total leakage current of the grounding system is close to the external injected current. All this shows the accuracy of this model.

Freq. (kHz)	injecting currents (kA)	Total leakage currents (kA)
16.7	$(-4.077, -10.964)$	$(-4.078, -10.959)$
125.0	$(-0.486, +0.363)$	$(-0.486, +0.363)$
250.0	$(-0.289, +0.143)$	$(-0.289, +0.143)$
500.0	$(-0.267, -0.070)$	$(-0.267, -0.070)$
800.0	$(-4.301, +3.428)$	$(-4.301, +3.428)$

Table 2. Total leakage currents from the grounding grid and injecting currents in frequency domain

The quasi-static complex image in this case has two terms, the α_n and β_n can be seen below Table 3.

	α_n	β_n
1	(0.294, −62.137)	(9.937, − 0.959)
2	(0.086, +53.354)	(22.453, −11.859)

Table 3. Quasi-static complex image coefficients

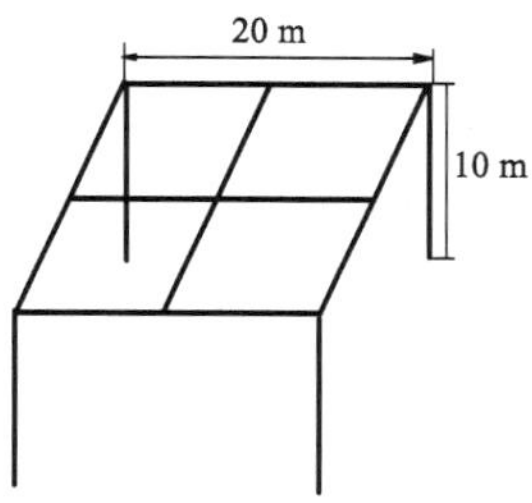

Figure 4. Typical grounding system

The transient SEP at the injection point is given in Fig. 5. From this figure, we can see that the maximum value of the transient SEP at the injection point disagrees with that of the lightning current, the maximum value of the transient SEP at injection point occurs at 12μ s, and the maximum value of the lightning current occurs at 10μ s.

The distribution of absolute values of grounding impedance dependance $|Z(j\omega)|$ on frequency can be seen in Fig. 6. This figure shows that $|Z(j\omega)|$ is independent of the frequency below 100 kHz and equal to the low frequency grounding impedance, which agrees with the viewpoint of [43].

To further discuss the electromagnetic field characteristics along the surface above the grounding grid, the distribution of the electromagnetic field along the surface with three different chosen frequencies (17 kHz, 250 kHz and 800 kHz) have been given in Figs. 7–15. Among these, Figs. 7–9 show the distribution of SEP φ along the surface, Figs. 10–12 show the distribution of the x-component of the EFI, E_x, along the surface, and Figs. 13–15 show the distribution of the x-component of the MFI, B_x, along the surface.

From Figs. 7–9, we know that the ground SEP rise is dependent on the magnitude of the injecting current, the ground SEP rise at 17 kHz is generated by injecting current with (-4.077,-10.964) kA, the ground SEP rise at 250 kHz is generated by injecting current with (-0.289,+ 0.143) kA, and the ground SEP rise at 800 kHz is generated by injecting current

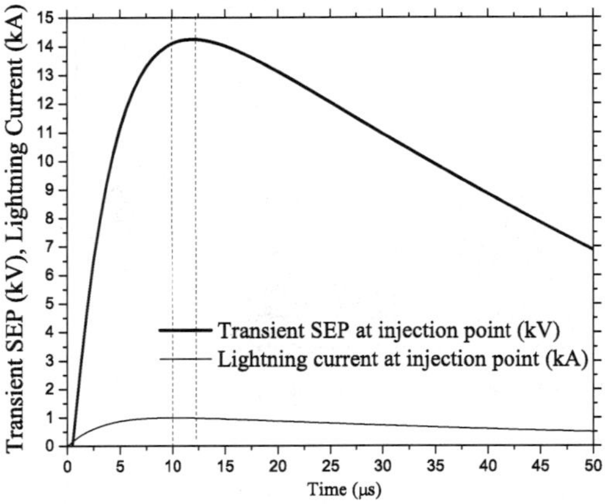

Figure 5. Lightning current

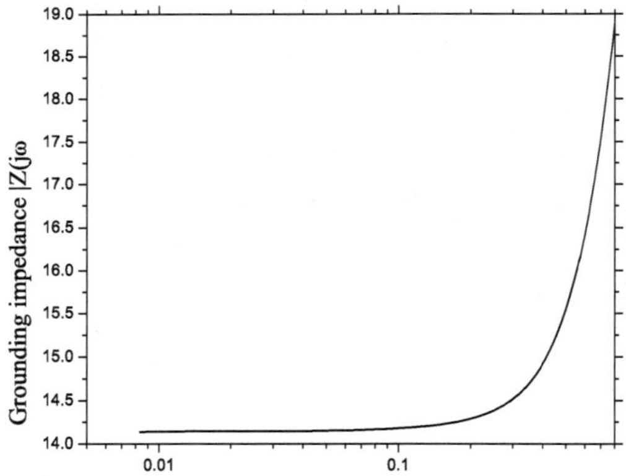

Figure 6. Lightning current

with (-4.301,+ 3.428) kA. So the ground SEP rise at 17 kHz is the maximum, and the ground SEP rise at 250 kHz is the minimum. Meanwhile, we can see that almost an equipotential surface occurs for the low frequency case (17 kHz and 250 kHz), and at higher frequencies, the impedances of the grid conductors are no longer negligible and most of the earth currents dissipate close to the injection point. This phenomenon is well illustrated in Fig. 9 which

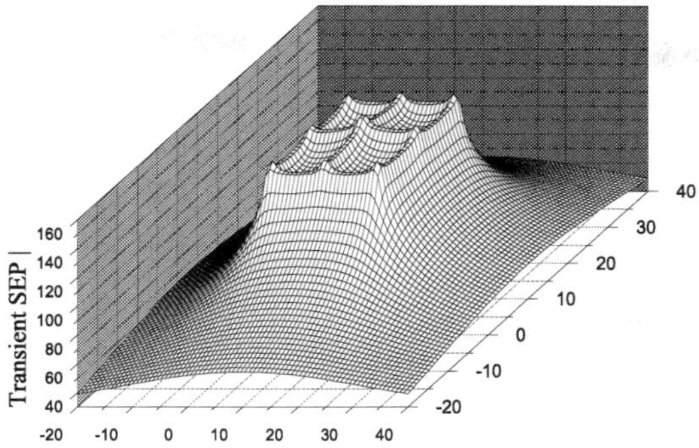

Figure 7. The distribution of the SEP φ on the ground surface (f=16.7 kHz)

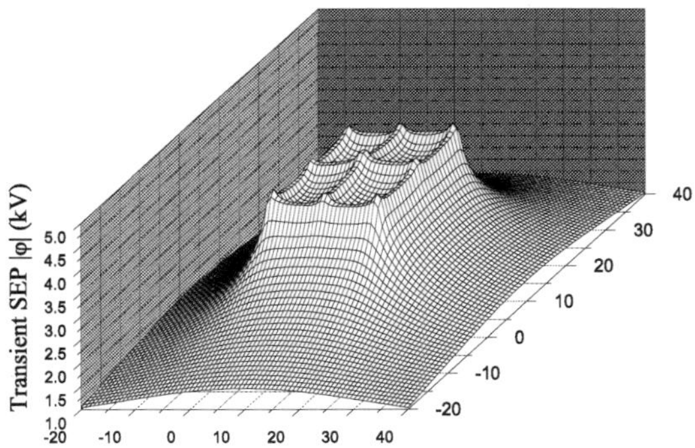

Figure 8. The distribution of the SEP φ on the ground surface (f=250 kHz)

represents the case of a corner current injection. Earth potentials near the injection corner present a very sharp peak, while they are quite low and flat everywhere else, with a minimum at the opposite corner.

From Figs. 10–12, we can see that as in the ground SEP rise case, the maximum value of the x-componential of the EFI E_x is dependent on the magnitude of the injecting current. The distribution of the x-componential of the EFI E_x is along the x-direction. Meanwhile, the distribution of the electrical field is not dependent on the current injection location at low frequencies. This conclusion no longer holds at higher frequencies, as shown in Fig. 12,

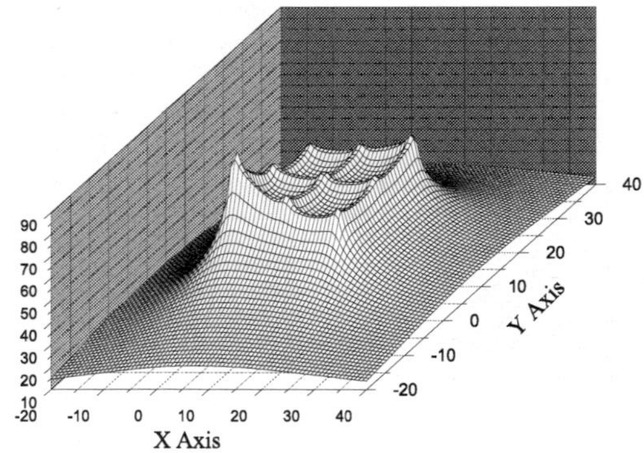

Figure 9. The distribution of the SEP φ on the ground surface (f=800 kHz)

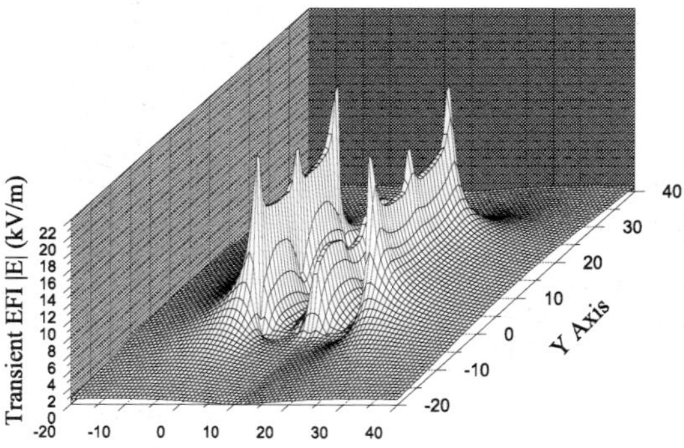

Figure 10. The distribution of the EFI E_x on the ground surface (f=16.7 kHz)

which clearly shows that the region of maximum electrical field shifts from the edge of the grid to the injection point location as the frequency increases from low to high.

The distribution of the x-componential of MFI B_x is given in Figs. 13–15. We can also see that as in the ground SEP rise case, the maximum value of the x-componential of the MFI B_x is dependent on the magnitude of the injecting current. Unlike the distribution of the x-componential of the EFI E_x, the distribution of the x-componential of the MFI B_x is along the y-direction, which can be easily explained in that the distribution of the electrical field is perpendicular to that of the magnetic field. Meanwhile, the distribution of the electrical

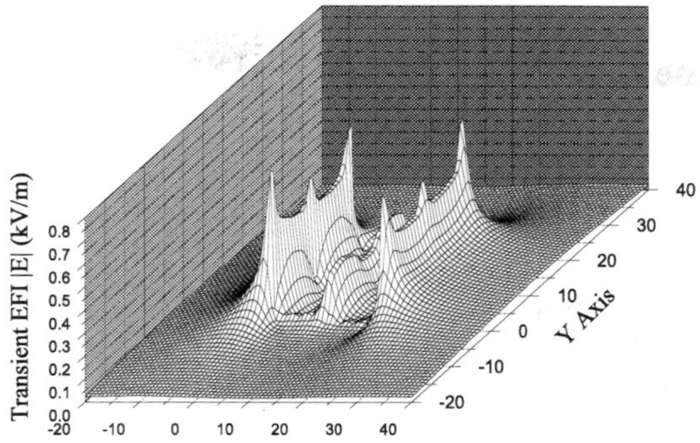

Figure 11. The distribution of the EFI E_x on the ground surface (f=250 kHz)

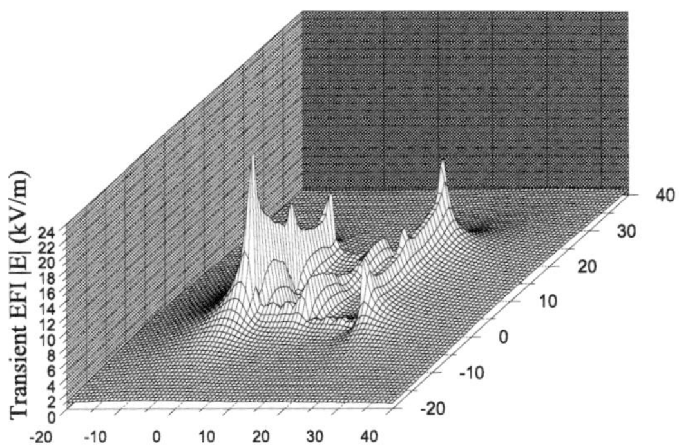

Figure 12. The distribution of the EFI E_x on the ground surface (f=800 kHz)

field is dependent on the current injection location from low to higher frequencies, which is different from the electrical field case.

8. Conclusion

A novel mathematical model for accurately computing the lightning currents flowing in the grounding system of a high voltage a.c. substation, buried in multilayered earth, has been developed in this paper. Together with the FFT, not only the conducting effect of harmonic wave components of these currents, but also capacitive and inductive effects from the interface between different soil layers have been analyzed in the frequency domain. To

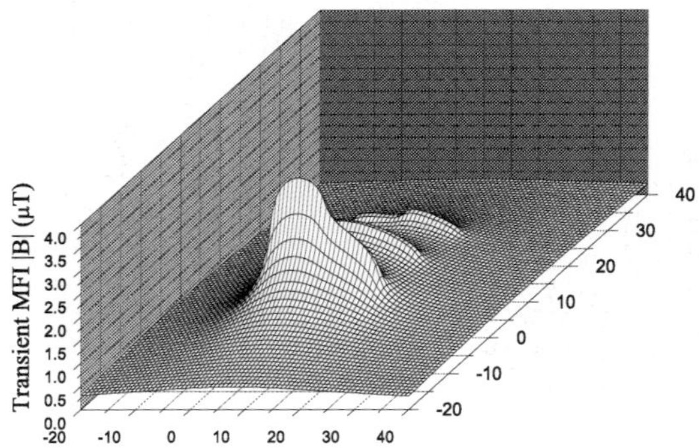

Figure 13. The distribution of the MFI B_x on the ground surface (f=16.7 kHz)

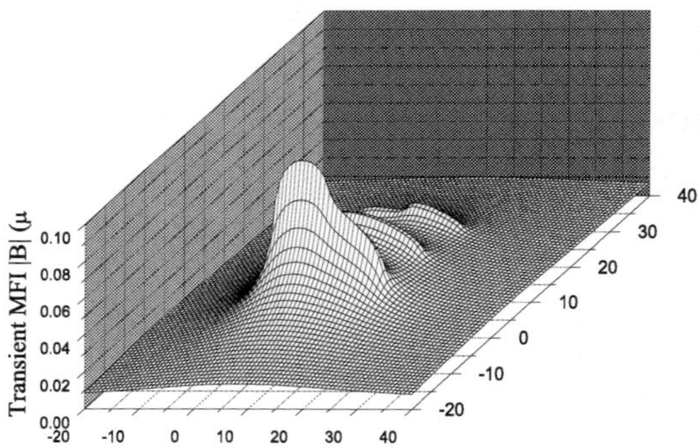

Figure 14. The distribution of the MFI B_x on the ground surface (f=250 kHz)

accelerate the calculation, the QSCIM and a closed form of Green's function were introduced. With the inverse FFT, the model can calculate the distribution of lightning currents in any configuration of the grounding system. This can be used for studying the performance of transient lightning responses to grounding systems. Last, the model has been validated through some numerically simulated and experimental results from open published paper, and some numerical results have been discussed in this paper.

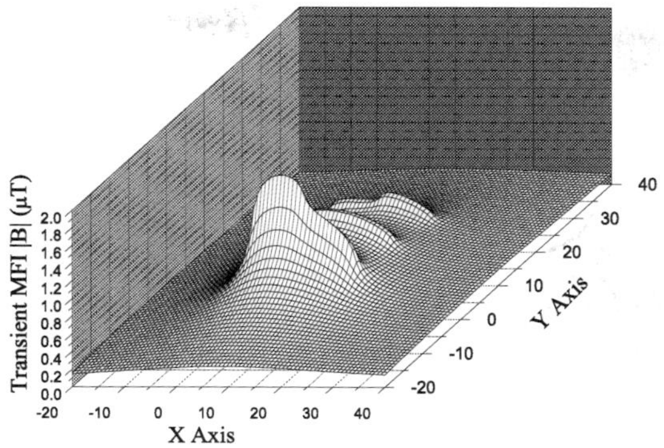

Figure 15. The distribution of the MFI B_x on the ground surface (f=800 kHz)

Acknowledgment

This work was funded by the Science and Technology Projects of State Grid Corporation of China under Contract Number: GY172011000JD and the National Natural Science Foundation of China under Grant 51177153.

Author details

Zhong-Xin Li, Ke-Li Gao, Yu Yin, Cui-Xia Zhang and Dong Ge

China Electrical Power Research Institute, Beijing, China

References

[1] E. D. Sunde. *Earth Conduction Effects in Transmission Systems*, New York: Dover, 1968.

[2] L. V. Bewley, *Traveling Waves on Transmission Systems*, 2nd ed. New York: Wiley, 1951

[3] R. Rudenberg, *Electrical ShockWaves in Power Systems*. Harvard Univ. Press, 1968.

[4] A. P. Meliopoulos, *Power System Grounding and Transients*. New York: Marcel-Dekker, 1988.

[5] A. C. Liew and M. Darveniza, "Dynamic model of impulse characteristics of concentrated earths", *Proc. Inst. Elect. Eng.*, vol. 121, pp. 123–135, Feb. 1974.

[6] J. Wang, A. C. Liew, and M. Darveniza, "Extension of dynamic model of impulse behavior of concentrated grounds at high currents", *IEEE Transactions on Power Delivery*, vol. 20, no. 3, pp. 2160–2165, Jul. 2005.

[7] M. Ramamoorty, M. M. B. Narayanan, S. Parameswaran, and D. Mukhedkar, "Transient performance of grounding grids", *IEEE Transactions on Power Delivery*, vol. 4, no. 4, pp. 2053–2059, Oct. 1989.

[8] A. Geri, "Behaviour of grounding systems excited by high impulse currents: The model and its validation", *IEEE Transactions on Power Delivery*, vol. 14, no. 3, pp. 1008–1017, Jul. 1999.

[9] S. S. Devgan and E. R. Whitehead, "Analytical models for distributed grounding systems", *IEEE Transactions on Power Apparatus and Systems*, vol. PAS-92, no. 5, pp. 1763–1770, Sep./Oct. 1973.

[10] R. Verma and D. Mukhedkar, "Impulse impedance of buried ground wire", *IEEE Transactions on Power Apparatus and Systems*, vol. PAS-99, no. 5, pp. 2003–2007, Sep./Oct. 1980.

[11] C. Mazzetti and G. M. Veca, "Impulse behavior of grounded electrodes", *IEEE Transactions on Power Apparatus and Systems*, vol. PAS-102, no. 9, pp. 3148–3156, Sep. 1983.

[12] R. Velazquez and D. Mukhedkar, "Analytical modeling of grounding electrodes", *IEEE Transactions on Power Apparatus and Systems*, vol. PAS-103, no. 6, pp. 1314–1322, Jun. 1984.

[13] F. Menter and L. Grcev, "EMTP-based model for grounding system analysis", *IEEE Transactions on Power Delivery*, vol. 9, no. 4, pp. 1838–1849, Oct. 1994.

[14] Y. Liu, M. Zitnik, and R. Thottappillil, "An improved transmission-line model of grounding system", *IEEE Transactions on Electromagnetcs Compatibility*, vol. 43, no. 3, pp. 348–355, Aug. 2001.

[15] Y. Liu, N. Theethayi, and R. Thottappillil, "An engineering model for transient analysis of grounding system under lightning strikes: Nonuniform transmission-line approach", *IEEE Transactions on Power Delivery*, vol. 20, no. 2, pp. 722–730, Apr. 2005.

[16] D. Roubertou, J. Fontaine, J. P. Plumey, and A. Zeddam, "Harmonic input impedance of earth connections", in *Proc. IEEE Int. Symp. Electromagnetic Compatibility*, 1984, pp. 717–720.

[17] F. Dawalibi and A. Selby, "Electromagnetic fields of energized conductors", *IEEE Transactions on Power Delivery*, vol. PWRD-8, no. 3, pp. 1275–1284, July 1986.

[18] L. Grcev and Z. Haznadar, "A novel technique of numerical modelling of impulse current distribution in grounding systems", in *Proc. Int. Conf. on Lightning Protection*, Graz, Austria, 1988, pp. 165–169.

[19] L. Grcev and F. Dawalibi, "An electromagnetic model for transients in grounding systems", *IEEE Transactions on Power Delivery*, vol. 5, no. 4, pp. 1773–1781, Oct. 1990.

[20] L. Grcev, "Computation of transient voltages near complex grounding systems caused by lightning currents", in *Proc. IEEE Int. Symp. Electromagnetic Compatibility*, 1992, pp. 393–400.

[21] L. Grcev, "Computer analysis of transient voltages in large grounding systems", *IEEE Transactions on Power Delivery*, vol. 11, no. 2, pp. 815–823, Apr. 1996.

[22] R. Olsen and M. C. Willis, "A comparison of exact and quasi-static methods for evaluating grounding systems at high frequencies", *IEEE Transactions on Power Delivery*, vol. 11, no. 3, pp. 1071–1081, Jul. 1996.

[23] L. Grcev and M. Heimbach, "Frequency dependent and transient characteristics of substation grounding system", *IEEE Transactions on Power Delivery*, vol. 12, no. 1, pp. 172–178, Jan. 1997.

[24] F. Dawalibi, "Electromagnetic fields generated by overhead and buried short conductors, part II—ground networks", *IEEE Transactions on Power Delivery*, vol. PWRD-1, no. 4, pp. 112–119, Oct. 1986.

[25] F. Dawalibi, R. D. Southy, "Analysis of electrical interference from power lines to gas pipelines, Part I, computation methods", *IEEE Transactions on Power Delivery*. vol. PWRD-4. no. 3. pp. 1840–1846, 1989

[26] A. D. Papalexopoulos and A. P. Meliopoulos, "Frequency dependent characteristics of grounding systems", *IEEE Transactions on Power Delivery*, vol. PWRD-2, no. 4, pp. 1073–1081, Oct. 1987.

[27] L. Huang and D. Kasten. "Model of ground grid and metallic conductor currents in high voltage a.c. substations for the computation of electromagnetic fields", *Electric Power Systems Research*. vol. 59. pp. 31–37. 2001.

[28] A. F. Otero, J. Cidras, and J. L. Alamo. "Frequency-dependent grounding system calculation by means of a conventional nodal analysis technology", *IEEE Transactions on Power Delivery*, vol. PWRD-14, no. 3, pp. 873–877, July 1999.

[29] Z. X. Li, W. J. Chen, J. B. Fan and J. Y. Lu. "A novel mathematical modeling of grounding system buried in multilayer earth", *IEEE Transactions on Power Delivery*. vol. PWRD-21, no. 3, pp. 1267–1272. 2006.

[30] Z. X. Li and W. J. Chen, "Numerical simulation grounding system buried within horizontal multilayer earth in frequency domain", *Communications in Numerical Methods in Engineering*. vol. 23, no. 1, pp. 11–27. 2007.

[31] Z. X. Li and J. B. Fan. "Numerical Calculation of Grounding System in Low Frequency Domain Based on the Boundary Element Method", *International journal for numerical methods in engineering*, vol. 73, pp. 685–705, 2008.

[32] Z. X. Li, G. F. Li, J. B. Fan, and C. X. Zhang. "Numerical calculation of grounding system buried in vertical earth model in low frequency domain based on the boundary element method", *European Transactions on Electrical Power*, vol. 19, no. 8, pp. 1177–1190. 2009

[33] J. R. Wait and K. P. Spies, "On the representation of the quasi-static fields of a line current source above the ground", *Canadian Journal of Physics*, vol. 47, pp. 2731–2733. 1969.

[34] D. J. Thomson, J. T. Weaver et al., "The complex image approximation for induction in a multilayer earth", *Journal of Geophysical Research*, vol. 80, pp. 123–129. 1975.

[35] J. Choma. *Electrical Networks—Theory and Analysis*, New York, 1985

[36] R. J. Heppe. "Computation of potential at surface above an energized grid or other electrode, allowing for non-uniform current distribution", *IEEE Transactions on Power Apparatus and Systems*. vol. PAS-98, no. 6, pp. 1978–1989. 1979

[37] R. S. Adve, T. K. Sarkar. 'Extrapolation of time-domain responses from three-dimensional conducting objects utilizing the Matrix Pencil technique', *IEEE Transactions on Antenna and Propagation*. Vol. AP-45, no. 1, pp: 147-156. 1997.

[38] P. L. Zhang, J. S. Yuan and Z. X. Li, "The complex image method and its application in numerical simulation of substation grounding grids", *Communications in Numerical Methods in Engineering*. vol. 15, no. 11, pp. 835–839. 1999.

[39] I. S. Gradshteyn and I. M. Ryzhik, *Tableof integrals, Series and Products*, Correction and enlarged edition, ACADEMIC PRESS, a Subsidiary of Harcourt Brace Jovanovich Publishers. NewYork, London, Toronto Sydney, San Francisco.

[40] R. E. Ziemer and W. H. Tranter, Principles of Communications, Houghton Mifflin Company, Boston, 1995.

[41] Z. Stojkovic, J. M. Nahman, D. Salamon, and B. Bukorovic, "Sensitivity analysis of experimentally determined grounding grid impulse characteristic", *IEEE Transactions on Power Delivery*, vol. 13, no. 4, pp. 1136–1143, Oct. 1998.

[42] J. X. Ma and F. P. Dawalibi. "Influence of inductive coupling between leads on ground impedance measurements using the fall-of-potential method", *IEEE Transactions on Power Delivery*. vol. 16, no. 4, pp. 739–743. Oct., 2001.

[43] L. Grcev, "Impulse efficiency of ground electrodes", *IEEE Transactions on Power Delivery*, vol. PWRD-24, no. 1, pp. 441–452, Jan. 2009.

Chapter 19

Development of Sand Spits and Cuspate Forelands with Rhythmic Shapes and Their Deformation by Effects of Construction of Coastal Structures

Takaaki Uda, Masumi Serizawa and Shiho Miyahara

Additional information is available at the end of the chapter

http://dx.doi.org/10.5772/57043

1. Introduction

Zenkovich showed that multiple sand spits with rhythmic shapes may develop in a shallow water body such as the Azov Sea and a lagoon facing Chukchi Sea, as shown in Fig. 1, and called them as the spits of Azov type [1]. Zenkovich concluded that under oblique wave incidence with the angle between the direction normal to the shoreline and the wave direction being larger than 45°, shoreline instability may develop, and during the development of sand spits, the wave-sheltering effect due to the sand spits themselves plays an important role. Ashton et al. [2] adopted this mechanism in their model and successfully modeled this shoreline instability using the upwind scheme in their finite difference method to prevent the numerical instability on the basis of the conventional longshore sand transport formula. Furthermore, this mechanism was called high-angle wave instability in [3]. Littlewood et al. [4] predicted the shoreline of log-spiral bays using their model. Serizawa et al. [5] predicted the development of sand spits and cuspate forelands under oblique wave incidence with the angle between the direction normal to the shoreline and the wave direction being larger than 45°, given a small perturbation in the initial topography, and showed that the three-dimensional (3-D) beach changes of sand spits and cuspate forelands with rhythmic shapes can be predicted using the BG model (a 3-D model for predicting beach changes based on Bagnold's concept). Falqués et al. [6] also predicted the development of sand waves caused by high-angle wave instability using equations similar to that of our model, but not the development of sand spits and cuspate forelands protruding offshore. The sand transport equation of the BG model was derived by applying the concept of the equilibrium slope in [7] and the energetics approach of Bagnold [8]. In the fundamental equation of the BG model in [9], the sand transport flux was assumed to be proportional to the wave energy dissipation rate instead of the third power of the amplitude of the bottom oscillatory velocity due to waves, and the wave energy dissipation rate was given by that due to wave breaking at each point determined in the calculation of the wave field. Here, the development of sand spits and cuspate forelands with rhythmic shapes were predicted first using this numerical model, and then the effects of the construction of a groin and a breakwater on the development of sand spits and cuspate forelands with rhythmic shapes were investigated using the same model [5, 10].

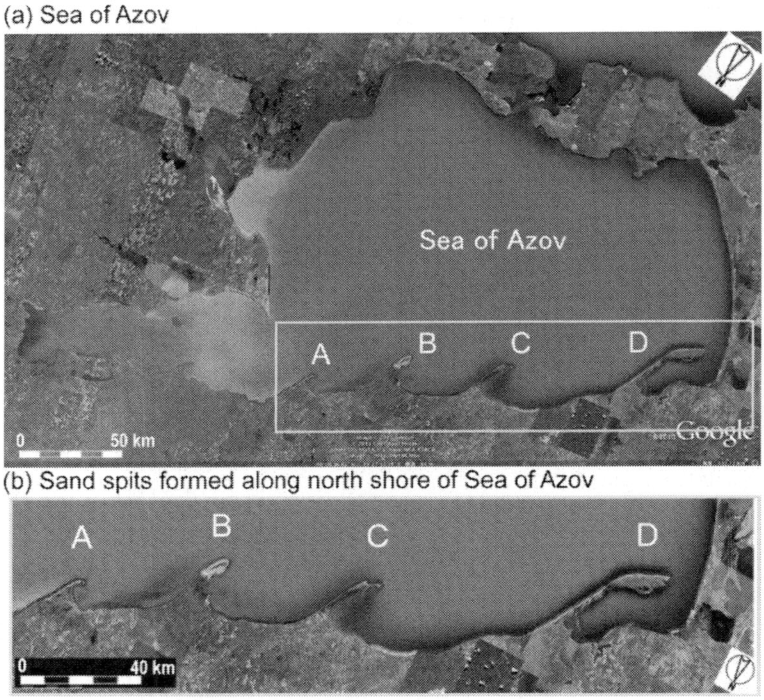

Figure 1. Multiple sand spits with rhythmic shapes developed in Azov-type shallow water body facing Chukchi Sea in Russia [1].

2. Numerical model

We use Cartesian coordinates (x, y) and consider that the elevation at a point Z (x, y, t) is a variable to be solved, where t is the time. The beach changes are assumed to occur between the depth of closure h_c and the berm height h_R. The BG model [9] was used to predict the beach changes. An additional term given by Ozasa and Brampton [11] was incorporated into the fundamental equation of sand transport in the BG model to evaluate the longshore sand transport due to the effect of the longshore gradient of wave height. The fundamental equation of sand transport is given as follows.

$$\vec{q} = C_0 \frac{P}{\tan\beta_c} \left\{ \begin{array}{l} K_n \left(\tan\beta_c \vec{e_w} - |\cos\alpha| \overrightarrow{\nabla Z} \right) \\ + \left\{ (K_s - K_n)\sin\alpha - \frac{K_2}{\tan\bar{\beta}} \frac{\partial H}{\partial s} \right\} \tan\beta \ \vec{e_s} \\ (-h_c \le Z \le h_R) \end{array} \right\} \quad (1)$$

Here, $\vec{q}=(q_x, q_y)$ is the net sand transport flux, Z (x, y, t) is the elevation, n and s are the local coordinates taken along the directions normal (shoreward) and parallel to the contour lines, respectively, $\nabla Z=(\partial Z/\partial x,\ \partial Z/\partial y)$ is the slope vector, $\vec{e_w}$ is the unit vector of the wave direction, $\vec{e_s}$ is the unit vector parallel to the contour lines, α is the angle between the wave direction and the direction normal to the contour lines, $\tan\beta = |\overrightarrow{\nabla Z}|$ is the seabed slope, $\tan\beta_c$ is the equilibrium slope, and $\tan\beta\ \vec{e_s}=(-\partial Z/\partial y,\ \partial Z/\partial x)$. Moreover, K_s and K_n are the coefficients of longshore and cross-shore sand transport, respectively, K_2 is the coefficient of the Ozasa and Brampton term [11], $\partial H/\partial s=\vec{e_s}\cdot\nabla H$ is the longshore gradient of the wave height H measured parallel to the contour lines, and $\tan\bar{\beta}$ is the characteristic slope of the breaker zone. In addition, C_0 is the coefficient transforming the immersed weight expression into a volumetric expression ($C_0=1/\{(\rho_s-\rho)g(1-p)\}$, where ρ is the density of seawater, ρ_s is the specific gravity of sand particles, p is the porosity of sand and g is the acceleration due to gravity), h_c is the depth of closure, and h_R is the berm height.

The intensity of sand transport P in Eq. (1) is assumed to be proportional to the wave energy dissipation rate [9], on the basis of the energetics approach of Bagnold [8]. P is given by the wave energy dissipation rate due to wave breaking at a local point Φ_{all} (Eq. (2)) in accordance with the BG model in [12], in which the intensity of sand transport is proportional to the wave energy at the breaking point, instead of the assumption that it is proportional to the third power of the amplitude of the bottom oscillatory velocity u_m due to waves.

$$P=\Phi_{all} \quad (2)$$

For the calculation of the wave field, the numerical simulation method using the energy balance equation [13], in which the directional spectrum of irregular waves is the variable to be solved, was employed with an additional term of energy dissipation due to wave breaking [14], similarly to that in [9]. Φ_{all} in Eq. (2) was calculated from Eq. (3), which defines the total sum of the energy dissipation of each component wave due to breaking.

$$\Phi_{all} = f_D E = K\sqrt{g/h}\left[1-(\Gamma/\gamma)^2\right]E \qquad (f_D \ge 0) \quad (3)$$

Here, f_D is the energy dissipation rate, E is the wave energy, K is a coefficient expressing the intensity of wave dissipation due to breaking, h is the water depth, Γ is the ratio of the critical wave height to the water depth on a flat bottom, and γ is the ratio of wave height to the water depth H/h. In addition, a lower limit was set for the water depth h in Eq. (3) similarly in [9].

In this method, the energy dissipation rate obtained from the calculation of the plane wave field including the effect of wave dissipation due to breaking was used for the calculation of sand transport. The same approach was employed in [15]. In the calculation of the wave field in the wave run-up zone, an imaginary depth was assumed as in [9]. Furthermore, the wave energy at locations with elevations higher than the berm height was set to 0.

In the numerical simulation of beach changes, the sand transport and continuity equations ($\partial Z / \partial t + \nabla \bullet \vec{q} = 0$) were solved on the x-y plane by the explicit finite-difference method using the staggered mesh scheme. In estimating the intensity of sand transport near the berm top and at the depth of closure, the intensity of sand transport was linearly reduced to 0 near the berm height or the depth of closure to prevent sand from being deposited in the zone higher than the berm height and the beach from being eroded in the zone deeper than the depth of closure, similar to that in [16].

Wave conditions	Incident waves: H_I = 1 m, T = 4 s, wave direction θ_I = 60° relative to direction normal to initial shoreline
Berm height	h_R = 1 m
Depth of closure	h_c = 4 m (still water depth)
Equilibrium slope	$\tan\beta_c$ = 1/20
Angle of repose slope	$\tan\beta_g$ = 1/2
Coefficients of sand transport	Coefficient of longshore sand transport K_s = 0.2 Coefficient of Ozasa and Brampton term [11] K_2 = 1.62K_s Coefficient of cross-shore sand transport K_n = K_s
Mesh size	$\Delta x = \Delta y$ = 20 m
Time intervals	Δt = 0.5 h
Duration of calculation	2.75×10^4 h (5.5×10^4 steps)
Boundary conditions	Shoreward and landward ends: q_x = 0, right and left boundaries: periodic boundary
Calculation of wave field	Energy balance equation [13] •Term of wave dissipation due to wave breaking: Dally et al. model [14] •Wave spectrum of incident waves: directional wave spectrum density in [17] •Total number of frequency components N_F = 1 and number of directional subdivisions N_θ = 8 •Directional spreading parameter S_{max} =25 •Coefficient of wave breaking K = 0.17 and Γ = 0.3 •Imaginary depth between depth h_0 (0.5 m) and berm height h_R •Wave energy = 0 where $Z \geq h/R$ •Lower limit of h in terms of wave decay due to wave breaking: 0.5 m

Table 1. Calculation conditions.

3. Formation of sand spits and cuspate forelands with rhythmic shapes

3.1. Calculation conditions

Ashton and Murray [3] showed that the generation of shoreline instability closely depends on the probability of occurrence of wave directions; sand spits develop in case that the probability of occurrence of a unidirectional waves is high, cuspate bumps develop in case that the probability of occurrence of waves incident from two directions is equivalent, and sand spits with hooked shoreline develop in case that waves are incident from two directions with different probabilities. The calculation conditions in this study were determined referring their results.

For the wave conditions, we assumed H_i = 1 m and T = 4 s, considering the formation of sand spits in a shallow lagoon. The wave direction was assumed to be obliquely incident from 60°, 50° and 40° counterclockwise or from the directions of ±60° with probabilities of 0.5:0.5 and 0.60:0.40, 0.65:0.35, 0.70:0.30, 0.75:0.25 and 0.80:0.20, while determining the direction from the probability distribution at each step. We considered a shallow lake with a flat solid bed, the depth of which was given by Z = -4 m, and a uniform beach with a slope of 1/20 and a berm height of h_R = 1 m were considered on the landward end. At the initial stage, a small random perturbation with an amplitude of ΔZ = 0.5 m was applied to the slope. The calculation domain was a rectangle of 4 km length and 1.2 km width, and a periodic boundary condition was set at both ends. In addition, the depth of closure was assumed to be h_c = 4 m. The equilibrium and repose slopes were 1/20 and 1/2, respectively. The coefficients of longshore and cross-shore sand transport were set to $K_s = K_n$ = 0.2, respectively. The calculation domain was divided with a mesh size of $\Delta x = \Delta y$ = 20 m, and Δt was selected to be 0.5 h. The total number of calculation steps considered was 5.5×10^4 (2.75×10^4 h). The calculation of the wave field was carried out every 10 steps in the calculation of beach changes. Table 1 shows the calculation conditions.

3.2. Calculation results

3.2.1. Oblique wave incidence from 60° counterclockwise

Figure 2 shows the results of the calculations at eight stages starting from the initial straight shoreline with a slope of 1/20, to which a small random perturbation with an amplitude of ΔZ = 0.5 m was applied, up to 5.5×10^4 steps. The small perturbation applied to the slope at the initial stage developed into eleven cuspate forelands within 5×10^3 steps, and the shoreline projection increased with time while moving rightward owing to the wave incidence from the counterclockwise direction. Because of the periodic boundary conditions at both ends, the cuspate forelands that moved away through the right boundary reentered the calculation domain through the left boundary. After 1×10^4 steps, the shoreline protrusion had increased and had developed as slender sand spits. After 2×10^4 steps, the small-scale sand spits located adjacent to each other had merged into large-scale sand spits and disappeared, and finally six sand spits were formed.

Two reasons for these changes are considered [1, 3]. (1) Of the two sand spits of different scales, the small sand spit moves faster than the large sand spit in the absence of the wave-sheltering effect, and then the small sand spit catches up and merges with the large sand spit. (2) On the lee of sand spits with an elongated neck, a wave-shelter zone is formed and the velocity of sand spits is reduced in this zone because of wave calmness, resulting in the stoppage of the movement of the sand spits and in the merging of small sand spits with larger spits.

Furthermore, the sand spits developed and protruded because (1) their tip is semicircular, meaning that the angle between the direction normal to the shoreline and the wave incident direction exceeds 45° at a point along the shoreline and the shoreline protrusion occurs at such a point owing to high-angle wave instability. (2) In a wave-shelter zone, sand transport is significantly reduced, whereas it is enhanced near the tip of the sand spits, and thus the derivative of the sand transport rate takes a maximum value near the boundary between the tip of the sand spits and the wave-shelter zone, inducing the protrusion of sand spits.

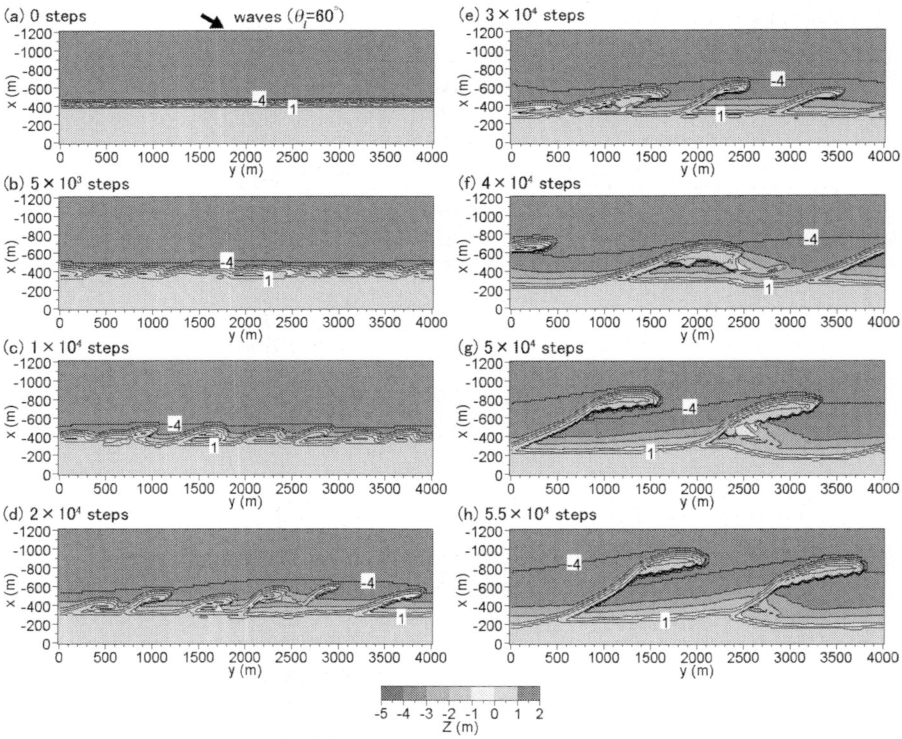

Figure 2. Development of sand spits from infinitesimal perturbation under wave conditions obliquely incident from 60° counterclockwise.

After 3×10^4 steps, the small sand spits located in the wave-shelter zone of the large-scale sand spits had stopped moving and merged into the large-scale sand spits, resulting in an increase in the interval between the sand spits and a decrease in the number of sand spits per finite length of the shoreline. After 4×10^4 steps, the number of sand spits had decreased to 2 and the tip of the sand spits approached closely to the original shoreline, permitting the downcoast passage of the sand of the sand spits.

After 5×10^4 steps, because of the movement of sand spits sweeping rightward, part of the sand deposition zone immediately offshore of the shoreline was left intact at the base of the sand spit located at y = 2250 m but almost all parts had merged with the sand spits. Although two large-scale sand spits were formed from the straight shoreline within 5.5×10^4 steps, the offshore contour of -4 m depth obliquely extended and a gentle seabed slope was formed upcoast of the sand spit, whereas a very steep slope was formed at the tip of the sand spits. These features are in good agreement with those measured around sand spits in lake and bay [18]. At the downcoast base of the sand spit extending from y = 2400 m, part of the sand bar formed in the previous process from 4×10^4 steps was left intact, implying that historical changes could be recovered at the downcoast side of the sand spit on the basis of the present topography.

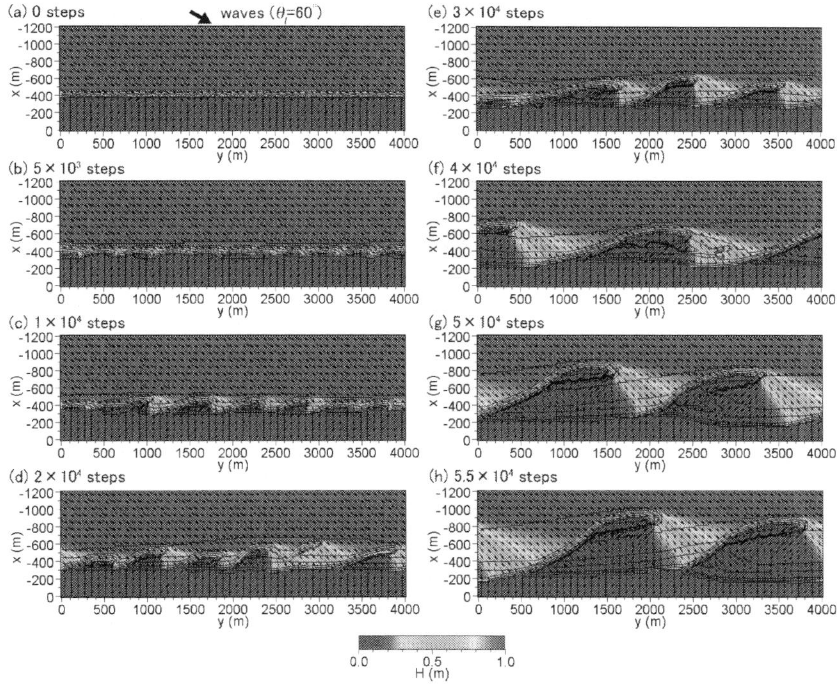

Figure 3. Change in wave field with development of sand spits.

Figure 3 shows the change in the wave field around the sand spits at each stage from the initial straight shoreline to the fully developed sand spits, as shown in Fig. 2. At the initial stage, waves are obliquely incident to the straight shoreline with uniform exposure to waves at all locations. With the development of the shoreline undulation over time, the wave-shelter zones were formed behind them. After 2×10^4 steps, the formation of sand spits was clear and the wave-shelter zone expanded downcoast, and the toe of the adjacent sand spit was included inside the wave-shelter zone. As a result, a marked reduction in wave height occurred, which in turn caused a reduction in sand transport. After 5.5×10^4 steps, long sand spits extended so that the toe of the slender sand spit was subject to the wave-sheltering effect of the upcoast sand spit. Owing to the development of sand spits over time, the entire original shoreline zone was included in the wave-shelter zone produced by sand spits, which is very similar to the calm wave zone protected by the extension of long port breakwaters.

Figure 4 shows the sand transport flux after 5.5×10^4 steps. The longshore sand transport mainly develops along the outer margin of the sand spit with a maximum value at the tip of sand spit and then rapidly decreases. Examining the sand transport flux near the neck of the sand spit in Fig. 4, cross-shore sand transport flux from the exposed side to the lee of the sand spit is also observed at a location of $y = 2750$ m. Thus, the neck of the sand spits is gradually eroded and moves downcoast because of this cross-shore sand transport, caused by the small difference between the given berm height h_R and the actual crown height of the sandy beach comprising the neck. Sand can be directly transported from the exposed side to the lee side without the sand transport turning around the tip of the sand spits. This effect makes the movement of an entire sand spit possible.

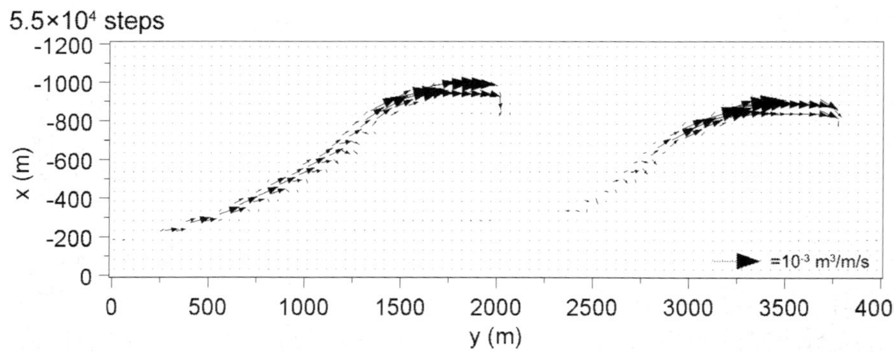

Figure 4. Sand transport flux after 5.5×10^4 steps.

3.2.2. *Oblique wave incidence from 50° and 40° counterclockwise*

In order to investigate the effect of the change in wave incidence angle to the beach changes, the calculations were carried out under the conditions of oblique wave incidence with an angle of 50° and 40°, while maintaining the same calculation conditions as in the case with an angle of 60° except the wave incidence angle. Figure 5 shows the calculation results with an angle of 50°. The development of sand spits via the development of cuspate forelands owing to the instability mechanism was possible, but the scale of the sand spits was significantly reduced. However, no sand spits had developed at an angle of 40° and the shoreline undulations were smoothed out with time, as shown in Fig. 6, resulting that the shoreline undulations did not develop unless the wave incidence to the zone shallower than h_c exceeds 45°. This result agrees with the conclusion in [19] that the shoreline instability develops only if the bathymetric changes related to shoreline perturbations extend to a depth where the wave angle is greater than the critical angle of 42° and the potential for coastline instability is therefore limited by the wave incidence angle at the depth of closure and not the angle at deep water.

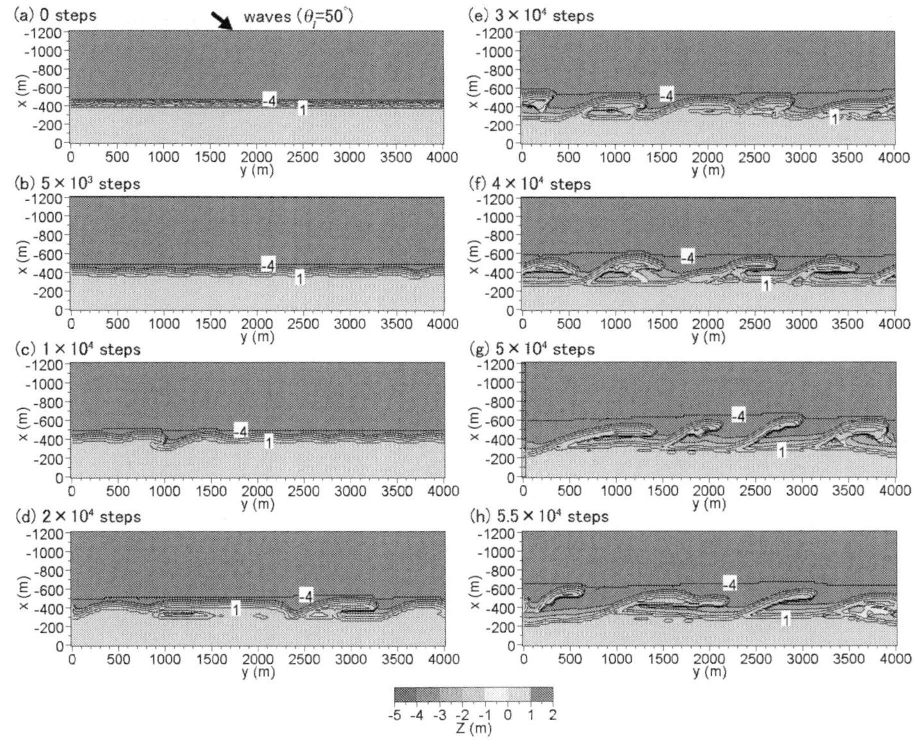

Figure 5. Formation of sand spits under the condition of oblique wave incidence from 50°.

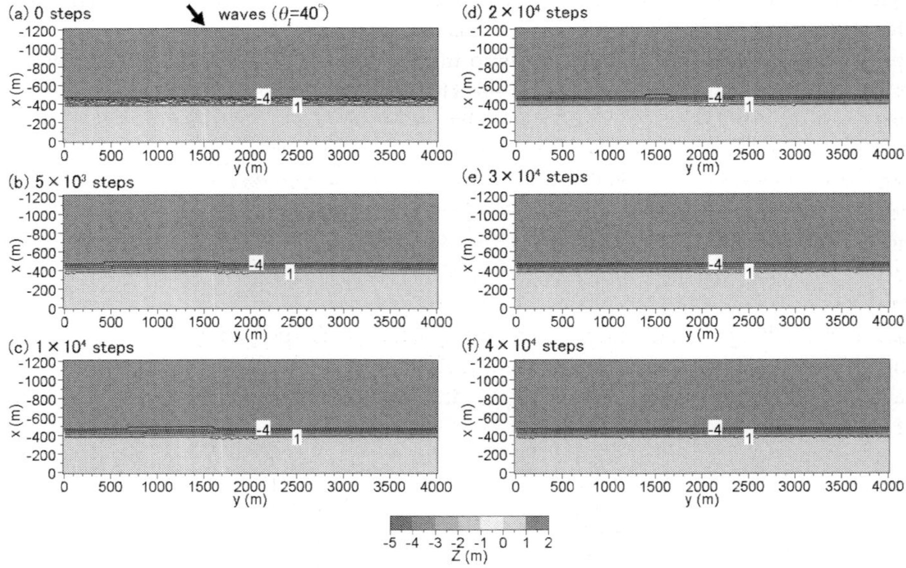

Figure 6. No shoreline instability under the condition of oblique wave incidence from 40°.

3.2.3. Oblique wave incidence from directions of ±60° with probabilities of 0.5:0.5

A numerical simulation was carried out for the case that waves were obliquely incident from the directions of ±60° relative to the direction normal to the shoreline with probabilities of 0.5:0.5 on the initial straight coastline, given a small random perturbation at the initial stage. Figure 7 shows the bathymetric changes between the initial stage and 4×10^4 steps. After 1×10^4 steps, triangular cuspate forelands had developed and irregularly distributed. When waves were incident from one direction, asymmetric sand bars developed, as shown in Fig. 2. In contrast, when waves with the same probability were incident from the opposite direction, the cuspate forelands became symmetric, and small-scale cuspate forelands disappeared and merged with larger cuspate forelands. Because the probability of occurrence of both wave directions was the same and there was no net longshore sand transport, the unidirectional movement of the sand body did not occur.

After 2×10^4 steps, the number of triangular cuspate forelands had been reduced to five, and the development of triangular cuspate forelands further continued and small-scale cuspate forelands merged into larger cuspate forelands. Finally, after 4×10^4 steps, four large-scale cuspate forelands had developed. A steep slope was formed by successive sand deposition at the tip of cuspate forelands, whereas seabed with a gentle slope was formed in the bay. Thus, when waves were obliquely incident from the directions of ±60° relative to the direction normal to the shoreline with probabilities of 0.5:0.5, symmetric cuspate forelands were formed.

Figures 8(a) and 8(b) show the wave height distribution around the cuspate forelands immediately after 4×10^4 steps under the conditions of clockwise and counterclockwise wave incidence. The wave-sheltering effect due to the protruded cuspate forelands alternately extends to the bays. The importance of this effect to the development of shoreline undulations was pointed out in [3]; when the multiple cuspate forelands with a different size have developed, the effect of the high-angle wave instability becomes stronger at the tip of the forelands with a large size than that at the bays, so that the positive feedback will occur. In contrast, around the cuspate forelands with a small size, the effect of the high-angle wave instability is weakened by the wave-sheltering effect by the large cuspate forelands, and the cuspate forelands are gradually modified to a stable form. Furthermore, when a large cuspate foreland develops, sand composed of the small cuspate foreland is absorbed into the large forelands, resulting in the decline of the small cuspate forelands and the increase in size of the large cuspate forelands. Thus, the development of large cuspate forelands will continue while small cuspate forelands are gradually disappearing. This results in the decrease in the number of the cuspate forelands.

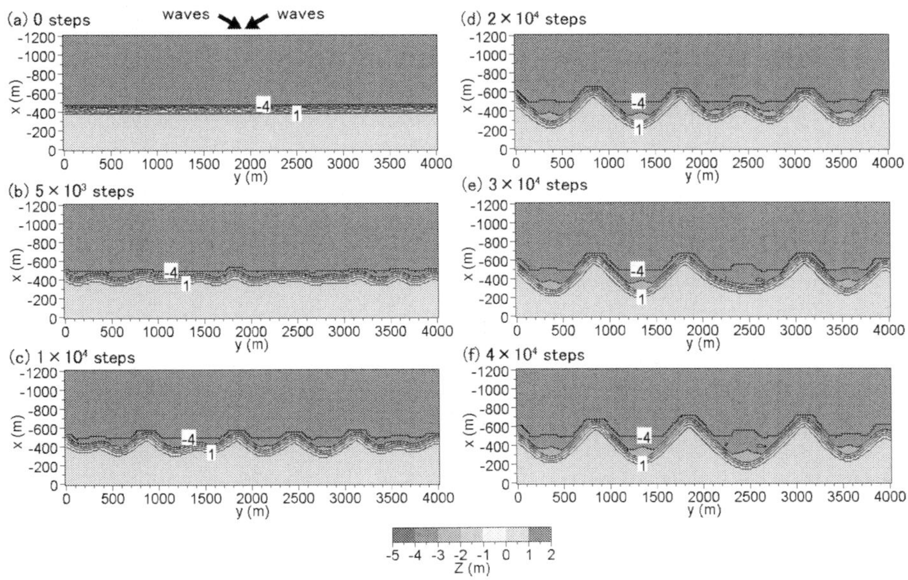

Figure 7. Formation of cuspate forelands (oblique wave incidence from ±60° with probabilities of 0.50:0.50).

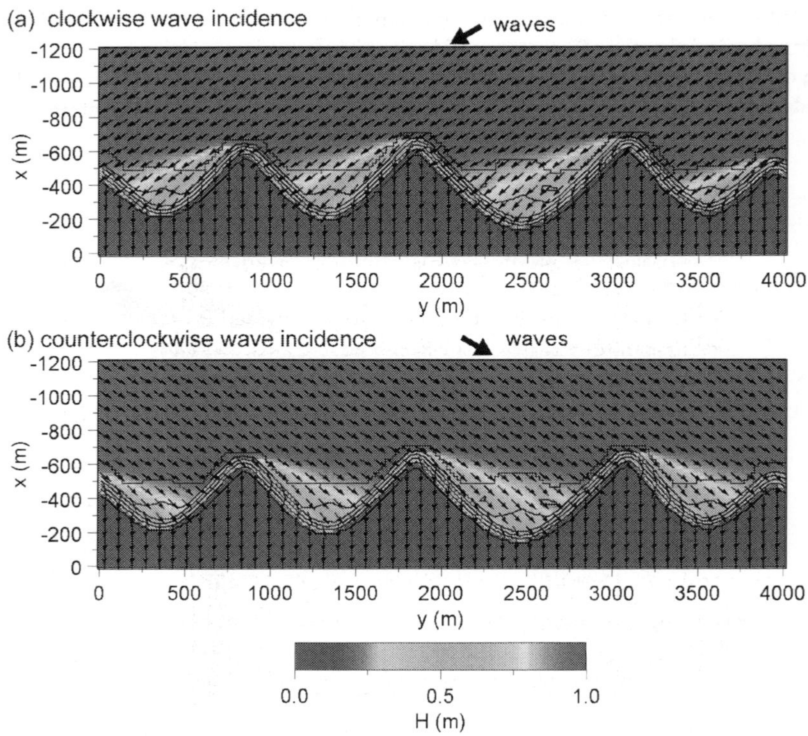

Figure 8. Wave field around cuspate forelands under oblique wave incidence from ±60° with probabilities of 0.50:0.50.

3.2.4. Oblique wave incidence from directions of ±60° with different probabilities

To investigate the effect of the change in probabilities of occurrence of the oblique wave incidence to the development of sand spits and cuspate forelands, the calculation was made, while keeping oblique wave incidence from directions of ±60° relative to the direction normal to the shoreline, and changing probabilities among 0.60:0.40, 0.65:0.35, 0.70:0.30, 0.75:0.25 and 0.80:0.20, i.e., the condition that rightward longshore sand transport gradually increases with the change in probability. In each case, the results after 2×10^4, 3×10^4 and 4×10^4 steps were compared.

Figure 9 shows the calculation results with probabilities of 0.60:0.40. Although symmetric cuspate forelands have developed with probability of 0.50:0.50, as shown in Fig. 7, asymmetric cuspate forelands that slightly inclined rightward have developed with probabilities of 0.60:0.40. Because the direction of net longshore sand transport was rightward, cuspate forelands developed while moving rightward. The shoreline left of the tip of cuspate forelands extended straight, whereas the shoreline curvature increased immediately right of the tip, forming a hooked shoreline. The contour of 4 m depth extended toward the tip of the forelands while obliquely intersecting with the shoreline left of the tip of the foreland, and then it extended parallel to the shoreline from the tip of the foreland with a large curvature.

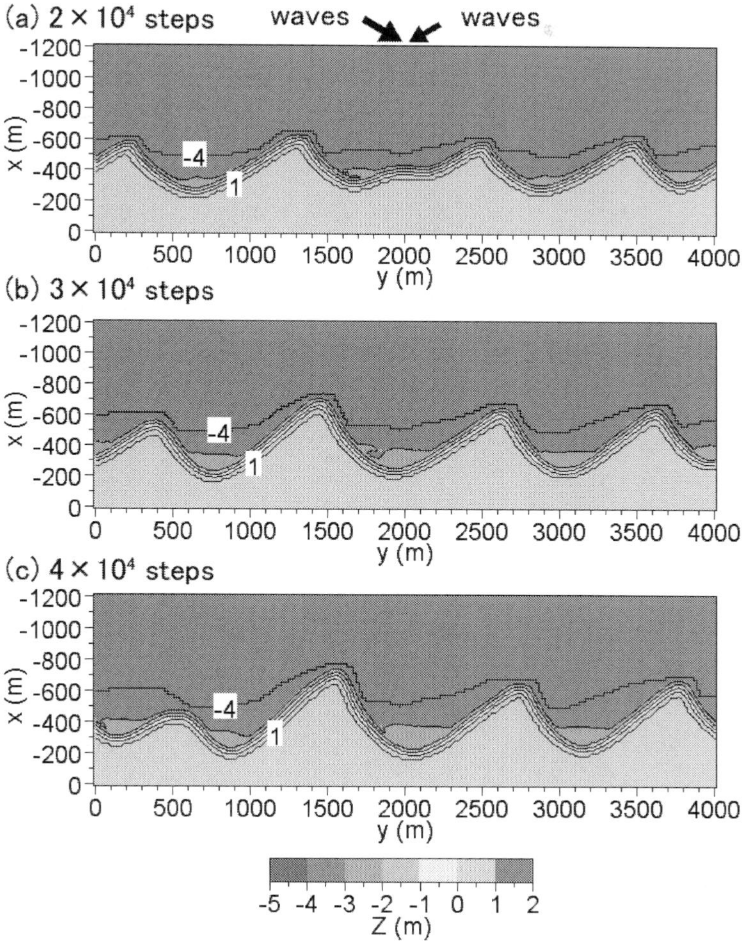

Figure 9. Formation of cuspate forelands (oblique wave incidence from ±60° with probabilities of 0.60:0.40).

Figure 10 shows the calculation results with probabilities of 0.65:0.35. Because probability of occurrence of wave incident from the left increased, the steepness of the cuspate forelands increased after $2{\times}10^4$ steps and a hooked shoreline inclined rightward had formed. After

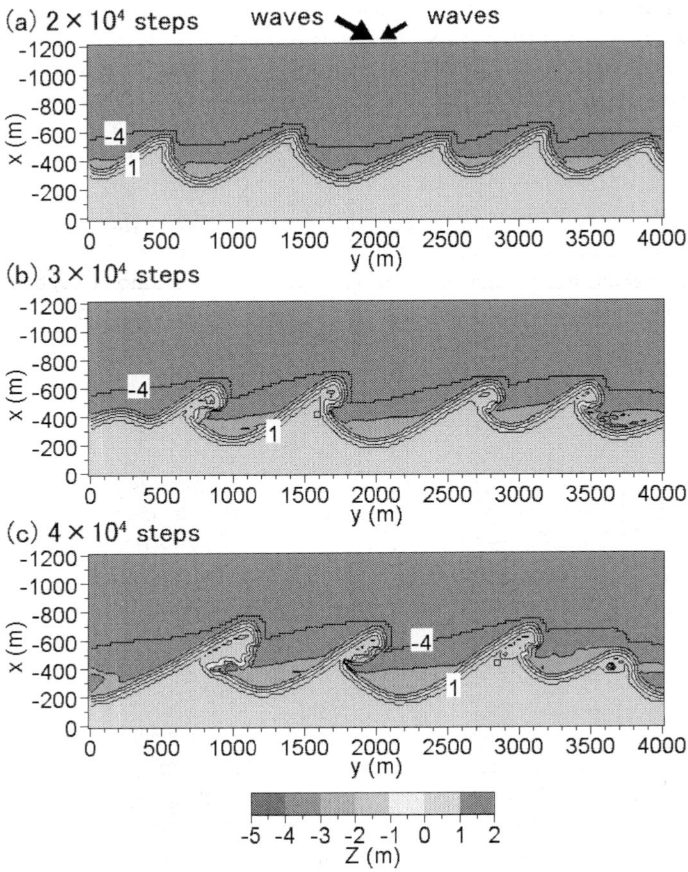

Figure 10. Formation of cuspate forelands (oblique wave incidence from ±60° with probabilities of 0.65:0.35).

3×10^4 steps, sand spits were formed at the tip of the cuspate forelands and a shallow bay was formed between the apexes. After 4×10^4 steps, sand spits obliquely extended rightward from the tip of the cuspate forelands with a larger angle than that in Fig. 2. In particular, the calculation results obtained after 4×10^4 steps and the case in a lagoon facing Chukchi Sea shown in Fig. 1 are in good agreement.

Figure 11 shows the calculation results with probabilities of 0.70:0.30. Although sand spits had already developed after 2×10^4 steps, these sand spits further elongated downcoast after 3×10^4 steps, and after 4×10^4 steps sand spits with a narrow neck at the connecting point to the land and a long head were formed. The number of the sand spits formed per unit coastline length reduced to two from four in the case with probabilities of 0.65:0.35.

Similarly, the calculation results with probabilities of 0.75:0.25 are shown in Fig. 12. A slender sand spit started to develop after 2×10^4 steps, and the sand spit with a narrow neck had elongated rightward after 3×10^4 steps. After 4×10^4 steps, sand spits with a long, slender neck and a head extended approximately parallel to the original coastline had developed. Although the contours shallower than 3 m depth extended parallel to the shoreline, while forming the main body of the sand spits, the contour of 4 m depth had an embayment downcoast of sand spits. Finally, Fig. 13 shows the calculation results with probabilities of 0.80:0.20. Because the probability of occurrence of waves from the left markedly increased, many sand spits with a head extended parallel to the original shoreline were formed close to the coastline after 2×10^4 steps. After 3×10^4 steps, the length of sand spits had further increased, but the head of sand spits extended parallel to the coastline similar to the development of longshore sand bars.

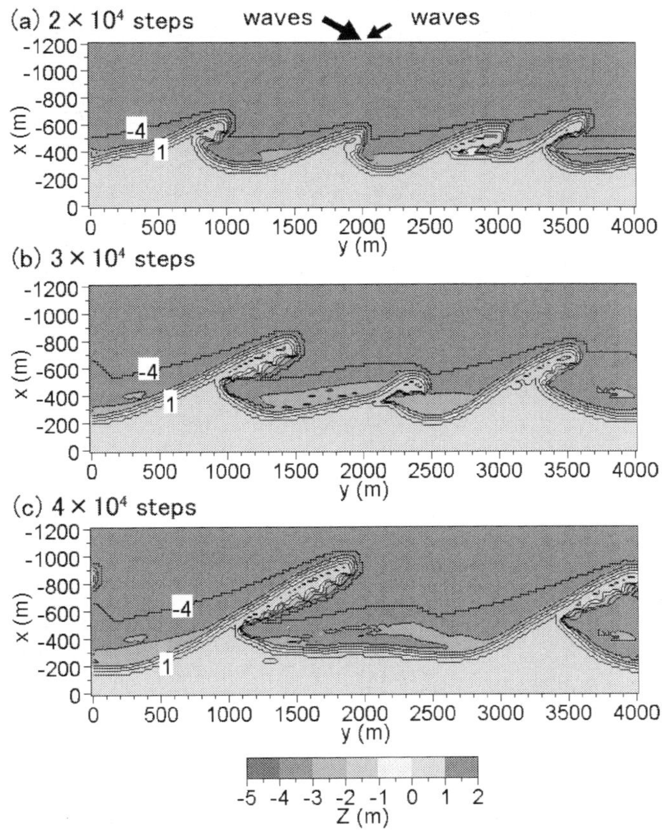

Figure 11. Formation of cuspate forelands (oblique wave incidence from ±60° with probabilities of 0.70:0.30).

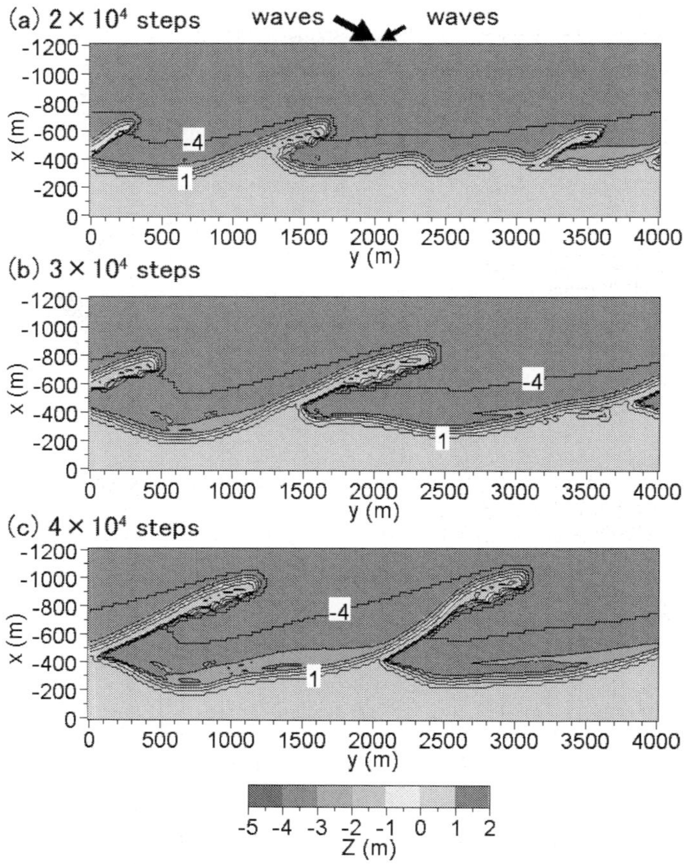

Figure 12. Formation of cuspate forelands (oblique wave incidence from ±60° with probabilities of 0.75:0.25).

Thus, symmetric cuspate forelands were formed when waves were incident from the directions of ±60° and the probability of occurrence of waves is equivalent. With probabilities of 0.60:0.40, the asymmetry of cuspate forelands increased and sand spits started to form after $2{\times}10^4$ steps with probabilities of 0.65:0.35. Increasing probabilities of occurrence of waves from the left such as 0.75:0.25, sand spits with a head extending parallel to the original shoreline developed. In all the cases of the development of sand spits, a narrow neck was formed at the connecting point to the land; a general characteristic of the topography around a sand spit [1]. Thus, the mechanism based on the high-angle wave instability and the evolution of 3-D beach changes was explained well by the BG model. Using this model, not only the shoreline configuration but also the 3-D topographic changes around the sand spits and cuspate forelands could be predicted.

http://dx.doi.org/10.5772/57043

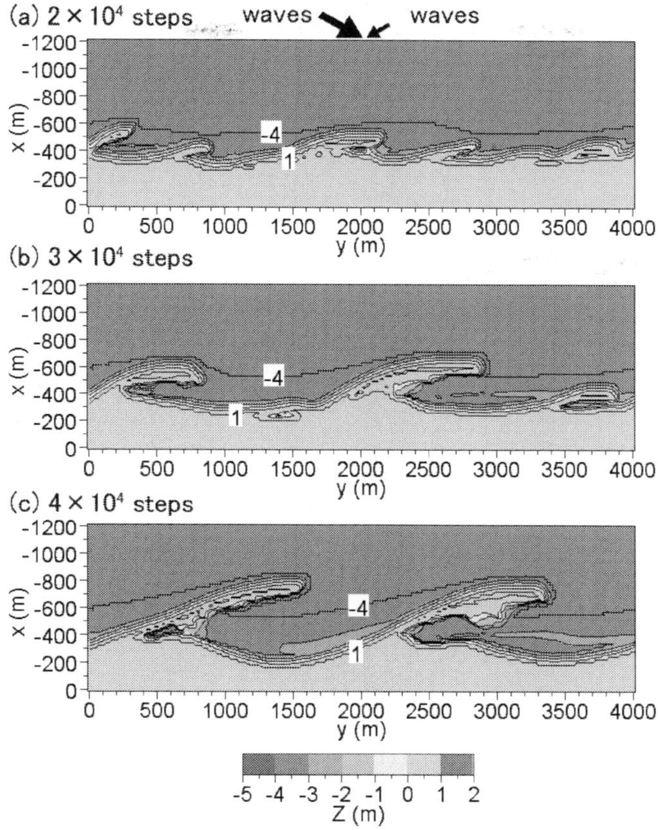

Figure 13. Formation of cuspate forelands (oblique wave incidence from ±60° with probabilities of 0.80:0.20).

3.3. Discussion

Although the scale of the sand spits formed along the north shore of the Azov Sea, as shown in Fig. 1, is much larger than that of the calculation results, their geometrical configurations of the calculated results are in good agreement with the measured. The sand spits A, B, C and D, as shown in Fig. 1, have been formed mainly by the waves obliquely incident from the east. The sand spit D located at the west end has a long, slender neck and this feature agrees well with the calculation results of the sand spit formed under the incidence of a unidirectional waves, as shown in Fig. 2(h). Furthermore, the width and length of the neck of the sand spit becomes thick and short in the order of C, B and A, along with the development of a hooked shoreline behind the sand spit. These conditions are very similar to the development of the sand spits under the conditions that waves were incident from two directions with different probabilities. The shape of the sand spit A is very similar to that of the sand spit second from the right end in Fig. 10(c) calculated with probabilities of 0.65:0.35, and that of the sand spit C is similar to that located at right end in Fig. 11(b) calculated with probabilities of 0.70:0.30. On the north shore of the Azov Sea, easterly wind is considered to be predominant, and the sand spit D located at the west end could receive sufficiently large wave energy from the east because of long fetch, whereas wave action from the west is weak because of shorter fetch. As a result, wave action from the east became stronger and sand spit with a narrow, slender neck was considered to be formed. In contrast, in the sand spit A, the fetch from the east was short so that the wave action from the east was weakened, whereas wave action from the west was strengthened because of a long fetch. In addition, the increase in the fetch of the easterly wind was considered to cause the increase in scale of the sand spit. Zenkovich qualitatively explained these features using a schematic diagram [1], but in this study these features observed in the field were successfully explained using the BG model.

Falqués et al. [6] predicted the development of sand waves caused by high-angle wave instability using equations similar to that of our model. Their sand transport equation had the same stability mechanism as that in our model. However, because the calculation domain of the wave field was restricted between the offshore zone and the breaking point, they only predicted the development of sand waves but not the development of sand spits protruding offshore. In this study, wave decay in the breaker zone and the wave-sheltering effect by the sand spit themselves were evaluated, taking the local change in topography in the surf zone into account and using the energy balance equation for irregular waves.

4. Effects of anthropogenic factors on development of sand spits and cuspate forelands

4.1. General conditions

The formation of sand spits and cuspate forelands with rhythmic shapes has already predicted in Chapter 3. Here, we investigated the effects of the construction of a groin and a breakwater to the topographic changes in the field where sand spits and cuspate forelands with rhythmic shapes fully developed. All the calculation conditions were the same as those in Chapter 3 except the structural conditions. Five calculations were carried out with the installation of a groin of 800 m length or an offshore breakwater of 600 m or 1000 m length.

In Cases 1 and 2, a groin or a breakwater was placed at the center of the calculation domain, respectively, after the development of sand spits under the condition that waves were obliquely incident from the left with an angle of 60°, as shown in Fig. 2. In Cases 3 and 4, in which waves are incident with an angle of ±60° with probabilities of 0.5:0.5, as shown in Fig. 7, a breakwater was placed offshore of the apex or the bay of the cuspate forelands, respectively. In Case 5, a breakwater was installed under the condition that waves are incident with an angle of ±60° with probabilities of 0.65:0.35, as shown in Fig. 10. The wave direction was randomly determined on the basis of the probability distribution at every step of the calculation of the wave field. The lengths of the groin and breakwater were determined, taking both the scale of sand spits and cuspate forelands and the wave diffraction effect of the structures into account. The calculation with no structures was carried out up to 3×10^4 steps, and then the beach changes up to an additional 3×10^4 steps were predicted after the installation of the structures.

4.2. Calculation results

4.2.1. Effect of groin on formation of sand spits

The beach changes until 3×10^4 steps were calculated under the conditions that waves are obliquely incident from the direction of 60° and then a groin of 800 m length and 4 m point depth was installed across the central sand spit after the sand spits have fully developed owing to the shoreline instability (Fig. 14(a)). These sand spits have developed while moving rightward, and the sand spit that moved out of the right boundary enters again from the left boundary as it is because of the periodic boundary condition at both ends. Figures 14(b)-14(j) show the results.

After 2×10^3 steps, the sand spit located left of the groin connected to the groin with a lagoon inside, whereas erosion started right of the groin because rightward longshore sand transport was obstructed by the groin. After 4×10^3 steps, part of the sand blocked by the groin started to be transported to the right while turning around the tip of the groin. The same situation continued after 6×10^3 steps, and a sand spit was formed owing to the deposition of sand turning around the tip of the groin up to 8×10^3 steps. Furthermore, as a result of sand discharge to the area right of the groin between 4×10^3 and 8×10^3 steps, the volume of sand left of the groin decreased, and the location of the starting point P of sand bar approached the groin with time, resulting in the decrease in the scale of the lagoon behind the sand bar.

Until 1×10^4 steps, the sand spit formed at the tip of the groin elongated rightward along with the reduction in the scale of the sand bar left of the groin. After 1.5×10^4 steps, the sand spit extending from the tip of the groin became a flying spit [20, 21] because of the reduction in sand supply by longshore sand transport. Because the flying spit is an unstable topography, it rapidly disappeared until 2×10^4 steps. Then, because of the increased sand supply owing to the connection of another sand spit to the groin, a sand spit elongated obliquely from the tip of the groin until 3×10^4 steps. It was realized from the comparison of Figs. 14(a) and 14(j) that sand was deposited, forming a steep slope along the shoreline on the exposed side, but the water depth generally decreased in the offshore zone owing to the sweeping motion of the sand spit, causing offshore sand movement. In contrast, sandy beach with a gentle slope was formed in the lee of the sand spits and six branches were formed behind the sand spit. The longshore sand transport was pushed seaward by the construction of a groin.

4.2.2. Effect of breakwater on formation of sand spits

The beach changes until 3×10^4 steps were calculated under the conditions that waves were obliquely incident from the direction with an angle of 60° to the direction normal to the shoreline, and then a breakwater of 600 m length was installed offshore of sand spit A after

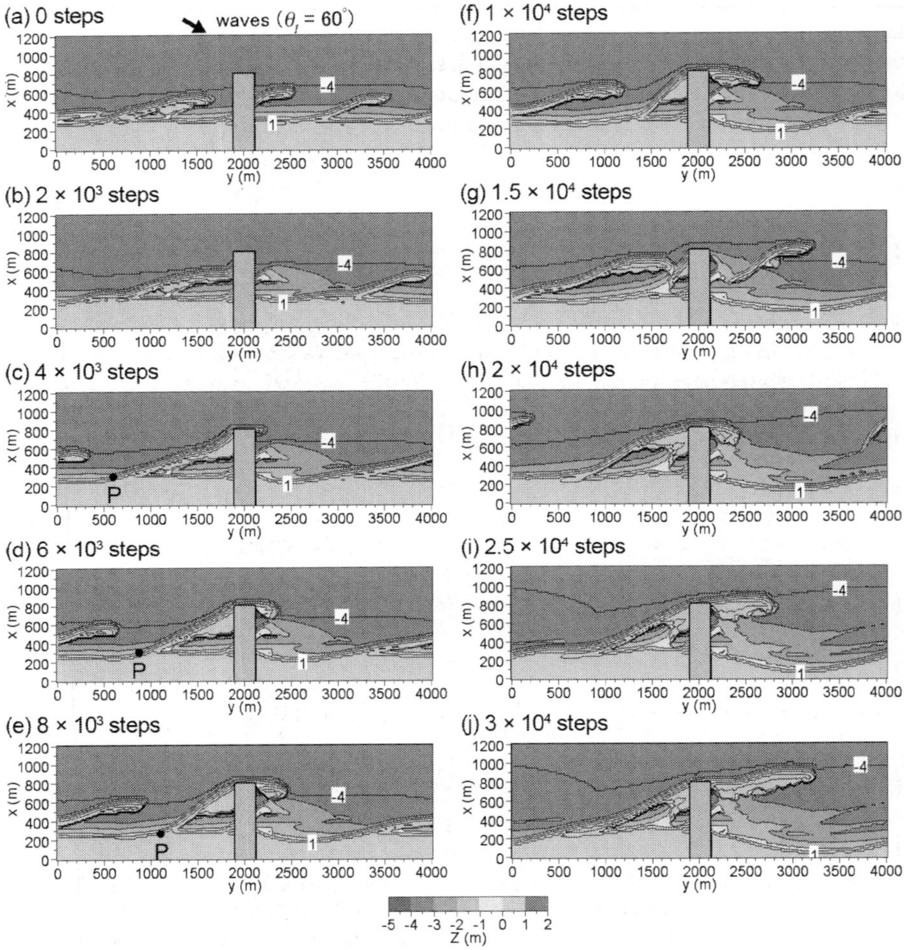

Figure 14. Deformation of sand spits formed under oblique wave incidence from 60° after extension of a groin.

the full development of sand spits owing to the high-angle wave instability (Fig. 15(a)). The beach changes were further calculated until $3{\times}10^4$ steps, as shown in Figs. 15(b) - 15(j).

After $2{\times}10^3$ steps, sand spit A behind the breakwater was eroded, because it was fully included in the wave-shelter zone of the breakwater, as shown in Fig. 16(a), and the wave height was significantly reduced with the change in wave direction, resulting in the reduction in rightward longshore sand transport. In contrast, sand spit B elongating left of the lee of the breakwater rapidly extended to the lee of the breakwater because of large longshore sand transport, as shown in Fig. 16(a). The same situation continued after 4×10³ steps and the rest of the sand of sand spit A was obliquely transported landward, and sand spit A disappeared while leaving the outline of the sand spit. During the period, sand spit B further extended to the lee of the breakwater. The change in wave field corresponding to this stage is shown in Fig. 16(b). Although the tip of sand spit B is subjected to strong impact of waves diffracted from the left end of the breakwater, wave height is significantly reduced between the tip of sand spit B and the breakwater, thus the tip of sand spit B extended so as to approach the breakwater.

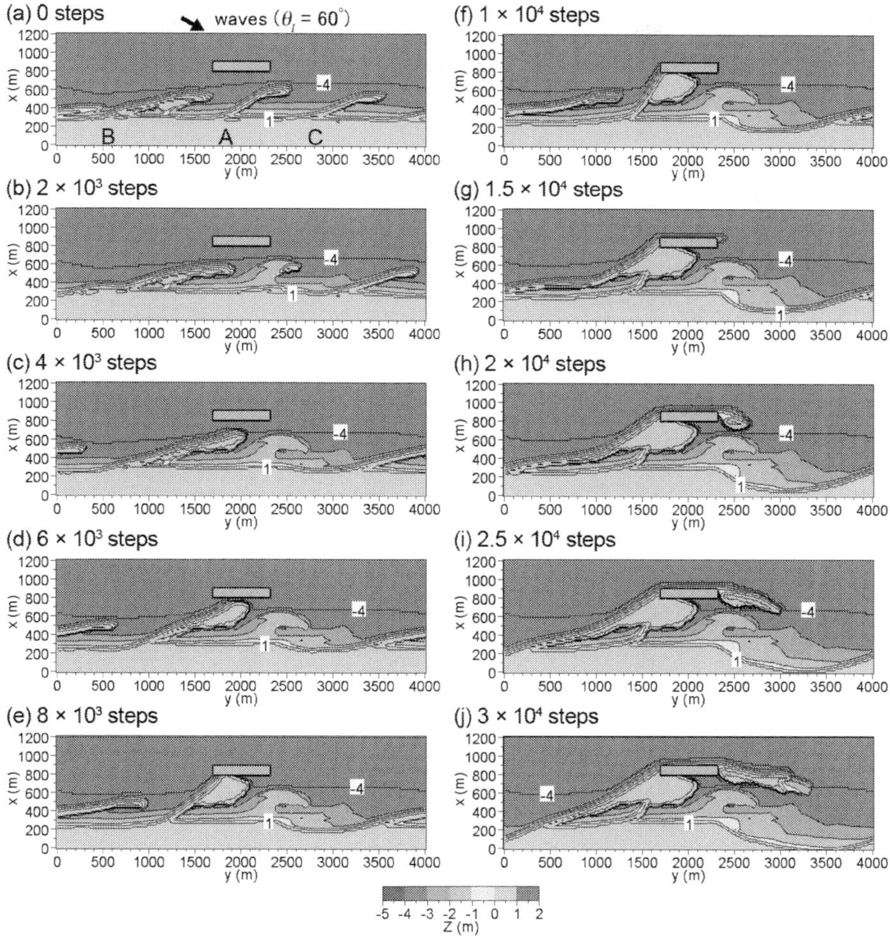

Figure 15. Deformation of sand spits formed under oblique wave incidence from 60° after construction of a breakwater.

The beach changes continued up to 6×10³ steps and the volume of sand deposited behind the breakwater increased along with the shoreline recession downcoast of the breakwater, as shown in Fig. 15(d). After 8×10³ steps, a large tombolo was formed by the trapping of sand. After 1×10⁴ steps, another sand spit, which elongated from the left end, extended to connect the tombolo behind the breakwater. After 1.5×10⁴ steps, a continuous sand bar developed from the left end to the breakwater. Then, a small sand spit started to emerge at the right end of the breakwater by 2×10⁴ steps. After 3×10⁴ steps, the sand spit extended from the right end of the breakwater further elongated, even though the volume of sand deposited behind the breakwater did not change. Thus, the construction of the breakwater had a significant impact on the beach; otherwise, sand spits developed with the self-organization mechanism, as shown in Fig. 2. It is realized that once a tombolo is formed behind the breakwater, offshore sand movement is enhanced owing to the presence of the breakwater and the tombolo, which blocks longshore sand transport.

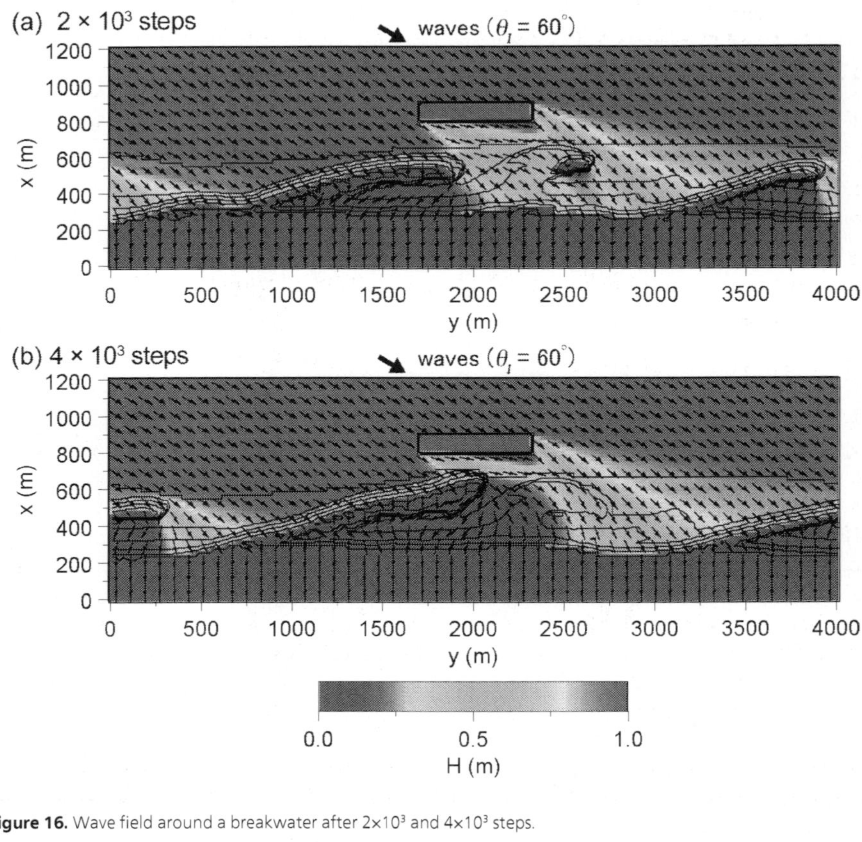

Figure 16. Wave field around a breakwater after 2×10^3 and 4×10^3 steps.

http://dx.doi.org/10.5772/57043

4.2.3. Effect of breakwater placed offshore of apex of cuspate forelands

When waves were obliquely incident with an angle of ±60° to the direction normal to the shoreline with the probability of 0.5:0.5, cuspate forelands have developed by 3×10⁴ steps, as shown in Fig. 7. This bathymetry was selected as the initial topography, as shown in Fig. 17 (a). Here, the cuspate foreland formed at the center is designated as A along with cuspate forelands B and C on the left and right, respectively. Then, a breakwater of a 1000 m length was placed offshore of cuspate foreland A, and the calculation was made until 4×10^4 steps. Results are shown in Fig. 17(b) - 17(h).

Under these conditions, approximately symmetric wave-shelter zone was formed on both sides of the breakwater. The slender sand spits started to extend toward the lee of the break-water near the tip of cuspate forelands B and C after 5×10^3 steps, as shown in Fig. 17(b). These sand spits were asymmetric with the sand spit being larger size at cuspate foreland B. Figure 18 shows the wave field after approximately 5×10^3 steps when waves are incident from the right and left, for example. Because the breakwater is placed offshore of cuspate foreland A and the distance between cuspate forelands A and B is shorter than that between cuspate forelands A and C, cuspate foreland B is subjected to an intensive wave-sheltering effect by the breakwater and cuspate foreland A under the condition that waves are incident from the right, whereas cuspate foreland C is located outside the wave-shelter zone by the breakwater and cuspate foreland A under the conditions that waves are obliquely incident from the left. Thus, the intensive wave-sheltering effects by the breakwater appeared at cuspate foreland B, resulting in the increase in the formative velocity of the sand spit near the tip of the cuspate forelands.

Furthermore, in Fig. 17(b), cuspate foreland A protruded more than that under the initial condition. The same changes continued until 1×10^4 steps with rapid elongation of the sand spit at the tip of cuspate foreland B to the lee of the breakwater and it almost connected to cuspate foreland A. On the other hand, cuspate foreland C was started to be eroded because of the leftward development of the sand spit at the tip of the cuspate foreland.

After 1.5×10^4 steps, the sand spit elongated from the tip of cuspate foreland B connected to cuspate foreland A and a barrier was formed with a lagoon inside. The scale of the sand spit formed at the tip of cuspate foreland C also increased, and the shoreline curvature increased downcoast of the sand spit C because of the wave-sheltering effect of the sand spit itself. After 2×10^4 steps, cuspate foreland B was entirely eroded, leaving a barrier island with a straight shoreline and a tombolo was formed behind the breakwater. No beach changes occurred inside the lagoon since then. On the right side of the breakwater, a sand spit elongated leftward with many branches to cuspate foreland A. After 2.5×10^4 steps, the tombolo behind the breakwater further developed and the beach width was widened up to 240 m behind the breakwater. Furthermore, the sand spit extended leftward from the tip of the cuspate foreland C connected to the cuspate foreland A and a lagoon was formed behind the barrier. Finally, after 4×10^4 steps, a large tombolo was formed with two water bodies inside the sandy beach behind the breakwater, the cuspate forelands with rhythmic shapes, as shown in Fig. 17(a), markedly deformed, and marked beach changes were induced by the wave-sheltering effect of the breakwater.

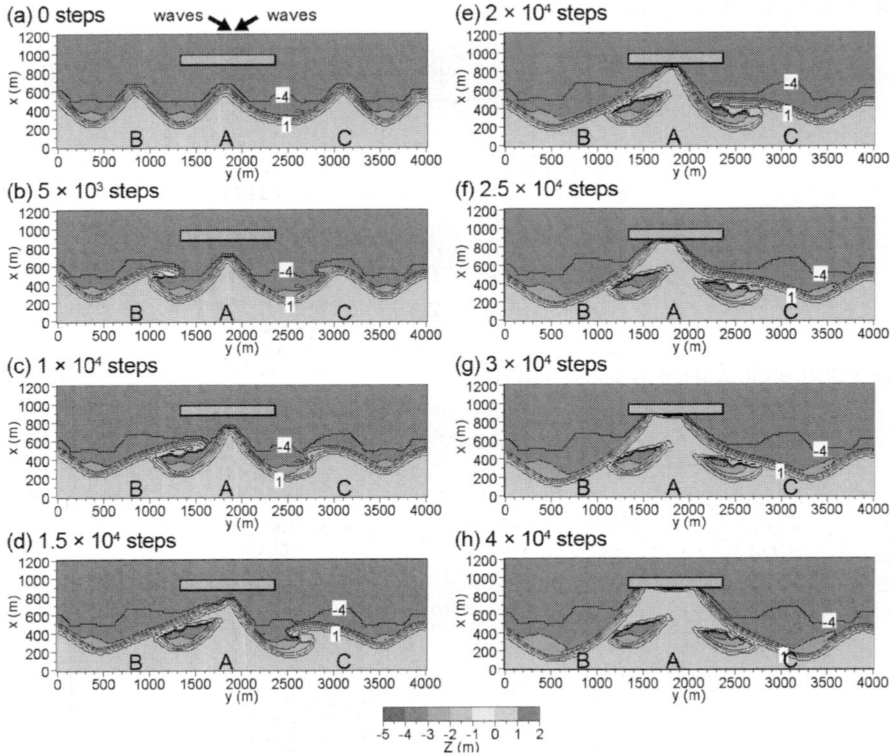

Figure 17. Deformation of cuspate forelands formed under the condition of oblique wave incidence from ±60° with probabilities of 0.5:0.5 after construction of a breakwater offshore of apex of cuspate foreland A.

4.2.4. Effect of breakwater placed offshore of bay of cuspate forelands

To investigate the topographic changes caused by the difference in the wave-sheltering effect which was produced by the change in location of the breakwater, the location of the breakwater was altered from offshore of the apex in the former case to offshore of the bay of the cuspate forelands. The same bathymetry shown in Fig. 17(a) with four cuspate forelands was selected as the initial bathymetry (Fig.19(a)), and an impermeable breakwater of a 1000 m length was placed offshore of a bay between the cuspate forelands A and B. Beach changes until 4×10^4 steps were predicted under the condition that waves were incident with an angle of ±60° to the direction normal to the shoreline with probabilities of 0.5:0.5. Figures 19(b) - 19(h) show the results.

In this case, almost half of the cuspate forelands A and B were included in the wave-shelter zone of the breakwater. Because of the symmetry of the location of cuspate forelands A and B relative to the breakwater, the wave field also showed symmetry, so that a pair of sand spits

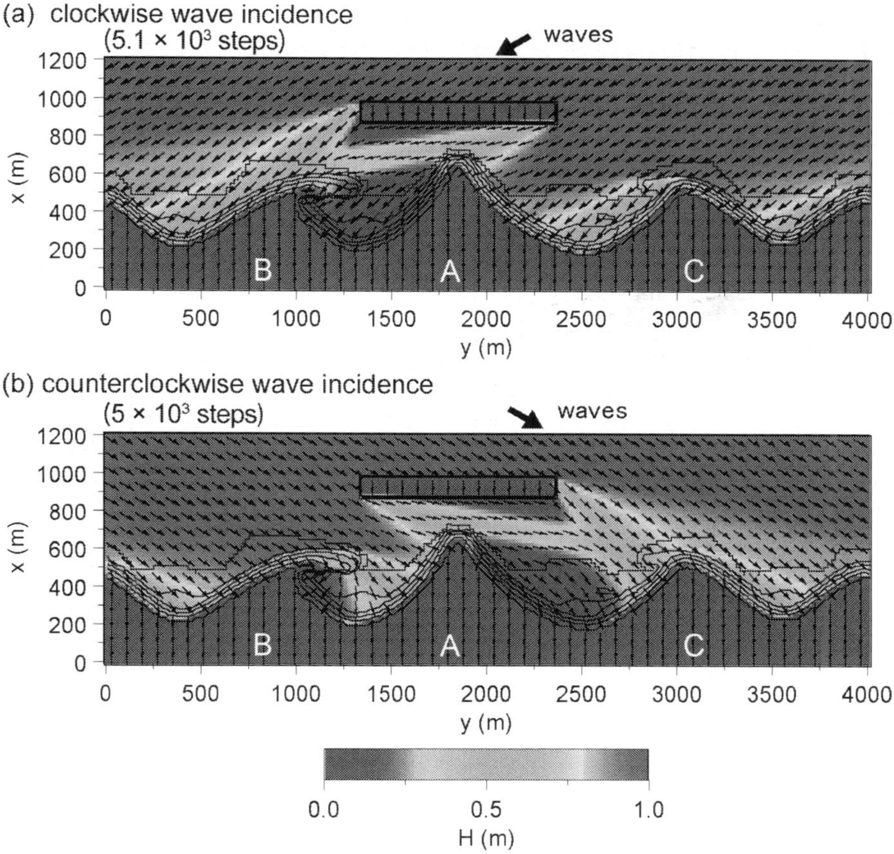

Figure 18. Wave field around a breakwater after 5.1×10^3 and 5×10^3 steps.

elongated toward the lee of the breakwater from the tip of the cuspate forelands until 5×10^3 steps, while enclosing a lagoon inside (Figs. 19(b) and 19(c)). The same changes continued after 1×10^4 steps and the sand spits extended from the tip of the cuspate forelands A and B were about to connect to the breakwater. After 1.5×10^4 steps, both sand spits connected to the breakwater, forming a double tombolo. After 2×10^4 steps, the double tombolo fully attached to the breakwater, and no beach changes occurred along the lagoon shore. With time, the double tombolo developed, resulting in increase in the size. Finally, the initial shape of the cuspate forelands with rhythmic shapes shown in Fig. 19(a) entirely disappeared. Comparing the beach topographies after 4×10^4 steps, as shown in Figs. 17(h) and 19(h), the number of lagoons enclosed inside the barrier was different; two in Fig. 17(h) and one in Fig. 19(h), although double tombolo developed in both cases.

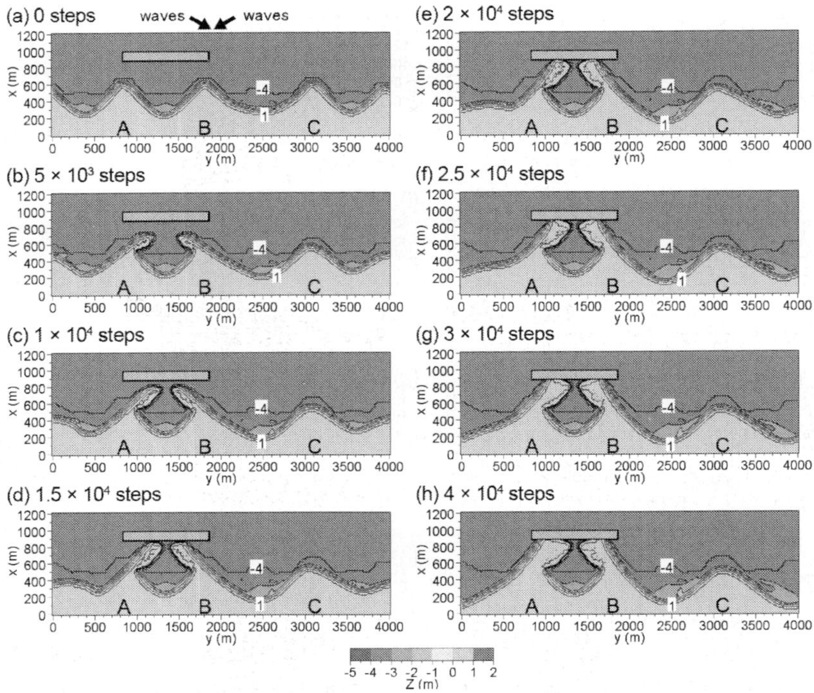

Figure 19. Deformation of cuspate forelands formed under the condition of oblique wave incidence from ±60° with probabilities of 0.5:0.5 after construction of a breakwater offshore of bay of cuspate forelands.

4.2.5. Effect of breakwater on formation of asymmetric sand spits

In this case, sand spits with asymmetric shapes were formed first under the condition that waves were obliquely incident from the direction of ±60° normal to the shoreline with probabilities of 0.65:0.35, as shown in Fig. 10. Then, an offshore breakwater of a 600 m length (the same condition as that shown in Fig. 15) was constructed in a zone offshore of sand spits A and B, and beach changes were calculated until 4×10^4 steps. The calculation results are shown in Figs. 20(a)-20(h).

Figure 21 shows the wave field after approximately 5×10^3 steps when waves were obliquely incident from the right and left. Because not only the probability of each wave direction was not equal as 0.65:0.35 but also sand spit B was located closer to the breakwater than sand spit C, an extremely asymmetric wave field was formed. Sand spit C was barely subjected to the wave-sheltering effect by the breakwater, whereas sand spit B effectively entered into the wave-shelter zone of the breakwater under the wave incidence from the left. Moreover, sand spit A was subjected to receive a strong wave-sheltering effect by the breakwater because of its proximity to the breakwater.

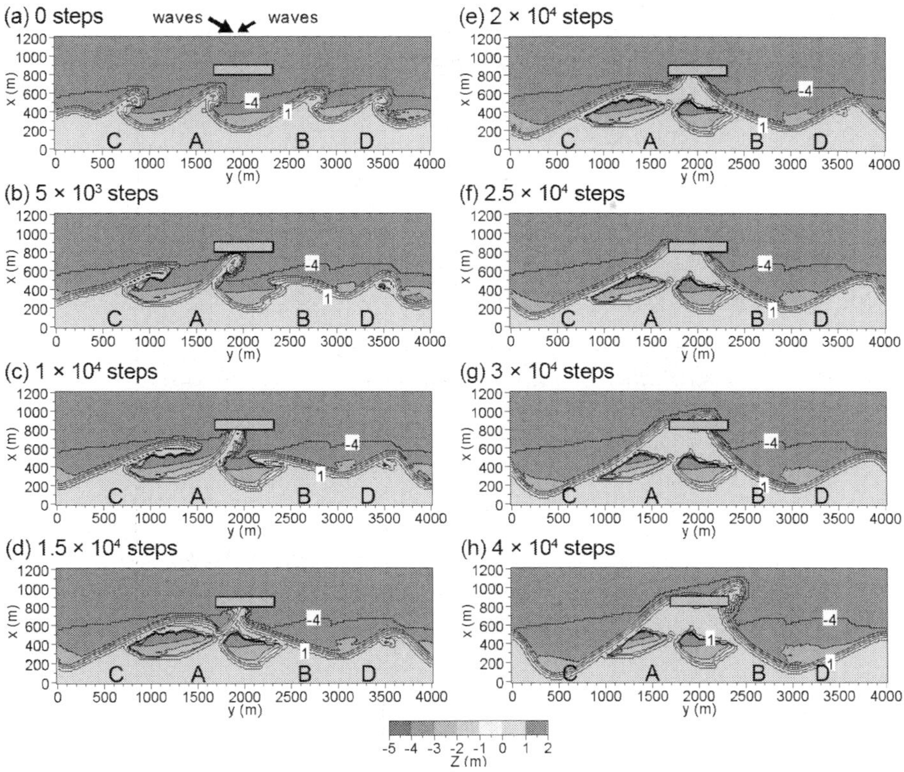

Figure 20. Deformation of sand spits formed under oblique wave incidence from ±60° with probabilities of 0.65:0.35 after construction of breakwater.

Owing to these reasons, the tip of the sand spit A rapidly extended to connect the breakwater until 5×10^3 steps, as shown in Fig. 20(b), and this elongation of the sand spit caused the waves incident from the left to be sheltered in the area right of the breakwater, as shown in Fig. 21(b), resulting in the reversal of the direction of longshore sand transport from rightward to leftward. Thus, the direction of the elongation of sand spit B was reversed and extended toward the lee of the breakwater. Sand spit C also rapidly extended rightward because waves incident from the left were sheltered. The construction of the breakwater further affected the beach changes of sand spit D far from the breakwater, and rightward development ceased and a rounded shoreline was formed.

After 1×10^4 steps, sand spit B rapidly extended to the lee of the breakwater, and after 1.5×10^4 steps, sand spits B and C markedly elongated to connect to sand spit A, leaving two lagoons behind the breakwater. After 2×10^4 steps, sand spit B reduced to a tombolo along with the connection of sand spit C with A. After 2.5×10^4 steps, a double tombolo developed, leaving two lagoons behind. After 3×10⁴ steps, sand was deposited offshore of the breakwater to form a sandy beach, and after 4×10⁴ steps, a new sand spit started to extend from the right end of the breakwater because of the net rightward sand transport.

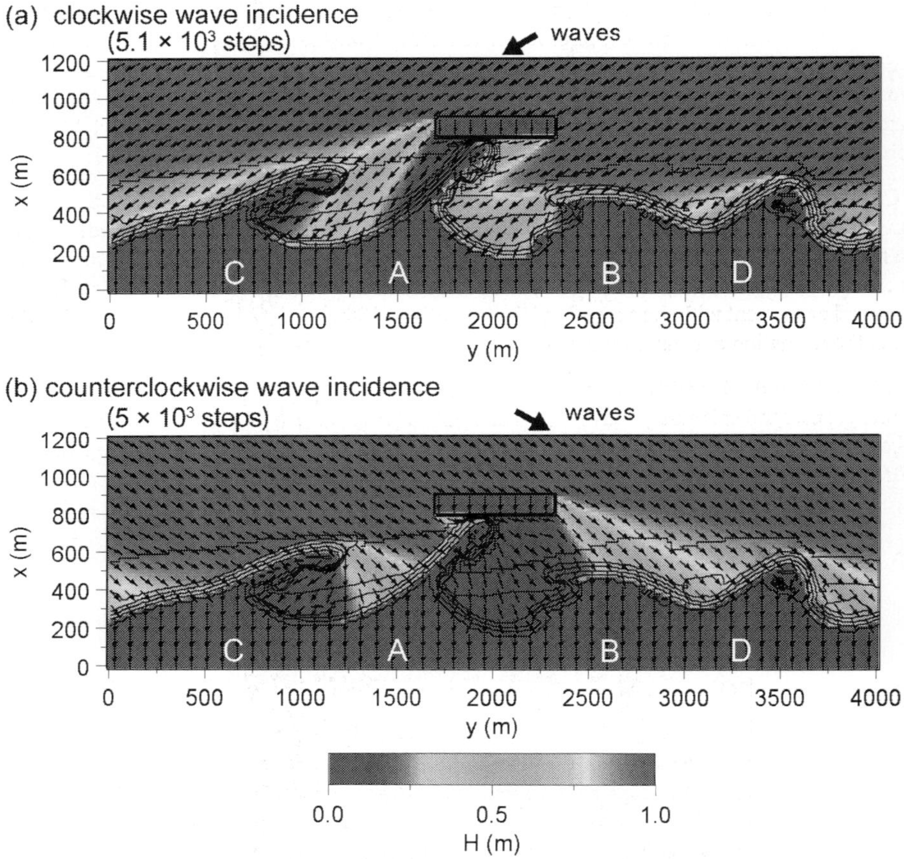

Figure 21. Wave field around a breakwater after 5.1×10^3 and 5×10^3 steps.

4.3. Discussion

The beach changes observed when a breakwater was constructed, as shown in Fig. 19, can be observed in Taman located in southwestern Russia bounded by the Azov Sea and the Black Sea (Fig. 22). Figure 23(a) shows an example of sand bars with two lagoons inside in a shallow water body due to the wave-sheltering effect of a shoal [1]. Sand bars with two lagoons inside have been formed by the wave-sheltering effect by the shoal shown in the lower part of the figure. The extension of many ridges left of sand bar A shows that waves are incident from the direction normal to shoreline (a). A slender sand bar B also extends with protrusions formed by breaching inside the lagoon on the other side. This indicates that sand bar B was formed by the action of waves incident from the direction normal to shoreline (b). Furthermore, at the tip of sand bar A, a small sand spit C extends rightward. Since the white seabed in Fig. 23(a) is assumed to show a shallow seabed covered with sand, a very shallow seabed extends offshore of sand spit C, and on the right side of sand spit C, the seabed depth suddenly increases, implying that sand spit C developed at the corner of the abruptly changed shoreline. This also agrees with the results given in [9]. The fact that the tip of sand spit C extended rightward shows the wave action from direction (b).

Thus, the sand bars were formed when waves were incident to the coast from two directions in a shallow sea with an offshore shoal. Although the wave-sheltering effect was produced by a shoal in Fig. 23(a), the same results were obtained in this study, when a breakwater was constructed. Figure 23(b) is the same results as shown in Fig. 20(h). The calculation results are in good agreement with the example of the formation of the sand bars with two lagoons inside and the formation of small sand spit C in Fig. 23(a).

In Figs. 14 and 15, which show the results on a coast with predominant longshore sand transport, a sand spit elongated at the tip of the structure owing to the successive sand supply from the upcoast. This elongation of a sand spit well explains the results observed at Santa Barbara in California [22].

Figure 22. Location of study area near Azov Sea.

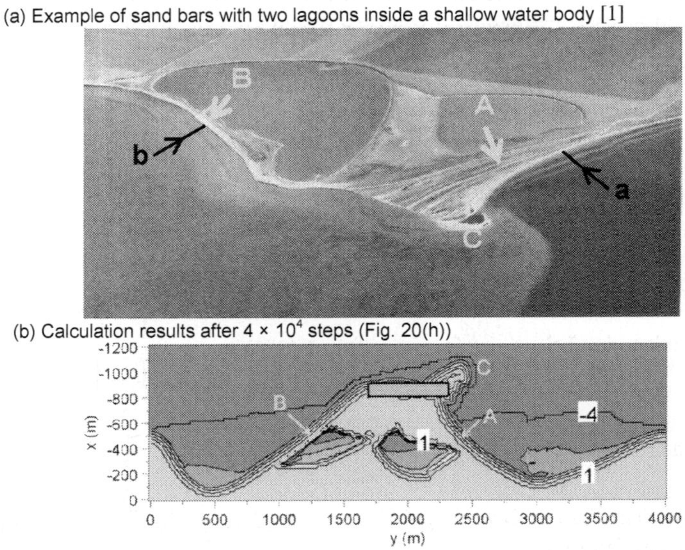

Figure 23. Comparison of measured and calculated double and looped spits.

5. Conclusions

Regarding the development of multiple sand spits and cuspate forelands with rhythmic shapes observed along the shore of the Azov Sea [1], the BG model was used to simulate the shoreline evolution caused by high-angle wave instability. The wave direction was assumed to be obliquely incident from 60°, 50° and 40° counterclockwise or from the directions of ±60° with probabilities of 0.5:0.5 and 0.60:0.40, 0.65:0.35, 0.70:0.30, 0.75:0.25 and 0.80:0.20, while determining the direction from the probability distribution at each step. As a result, the 3-D development of multiple sand spits and cuspate forelands with rhythmic shapes was successfully explained by the present model and the results of the previous study in [2] were reconfirmed and reinforced. Because the wave field was predicted using the energy balance equation for irregular waves in this study, the wave field including wave refraction, wave breaking and the wave-sheltering effect can be systematically predicted. In addition, because 2-D sand transport equations were employed in our model, in contrast to the model in [2] in which the longshore sand transport formula was used, this model has the advantages of the conventional 3-D model for predicting beach changes for various applications.

In addition to the prediction of the development of sand spits and cuspate forelands with rhythmic shapes owing to the high-angle wave instability under natural conditions, the impact of anthropogenic factors, such as the construction of a groin or a breakwater, on the beach changes was predicted. It was concluded that the construction of a groin had a marked impact on the sandy beach; the alteration from the field with the development of the sand spits to that with the elongation of a single sand spit, as well as the acceleration of offshore sand transport because of the blockage of longshore sand transport.

Author details

Takaaki Uda[1], Masumi Serizawa[2] and Shiho Miyahara[2]

1 Public Works Research Center, Tokyo, Japan

2 Coastal Engineering Laboratory Co., Ltd., Tokyo, Japan

References

[1] Zenkovich, V. P. (1967). Processes of Coastal Development, Interscience Publishers, New York, p. 751.

[2] Ashton, A., Murray, A. B., Arnault, O. (2001). Formation of coastline features by large-scale instabilities induced by high angle waves, Nature, Vol. 414, pp. 296-300.

[3] Ashton, A., Murray, A. B. (2006). High-angle wave instability and emergent shoreline shapes: 1. Modeling of sand waves, flying spits, and capes: Jour. Geophys. Res., Vol. 111, F04011, doi: 10.1029/2005JF000422.

[4] Littlewood, R., Murray, A. B., Ashton, A. D. (2007). An alternative explanation for the shape of 'Log-Spiral' Bays, Coastal Sediments '07, pp. 341-350.

[5] Serizawa, M., Uda, T., Miyahara, S. (2012). Prediction of development of sand spits and cuspate forelands with rhythmic shapes caused by shoreline instability using BG model, Proc. 33rd ICCE, sediment.35, pp. 1-11.

[6] Falqués, A., van den Berg, N., Calvete, D. (2008). The role of cross-shore profile dynamics on shoreline instability due to high-angle waves, Proc. 31st ICCE, pp. 1826-1838.

[7] Inman, D. L., Bagnold, R. A. (1963). Littoral processes, In The Sea, Hill, M. N., Vol. 3, Wiley, New York, pp. 529-533.

[8] Bagnold, R. A. (1963). Mechanics of marine sedimentation, In The Sea, Hill, M. N., Vol. 3, Wiley, New York, pp. 507-528.

[9] Serizawa, M., Uda, T. (2011). Prediction of formation of sand spit on coast with sudden change using improved BG model, Coastal Sediments '11, pp. 1907-1919.

[10] Serizawa, M., Uda, T., Miyahara, S. (2013). Effects of anthropogenic factors on development of sand spits and cuspate forelands with rhythmic shapes, Asian and Pacific Coasts 2013, Proc. 7th International Conf. pp. 9-16.

[11] Ozasa, H., Brampton, A. H. (1980). Model for predicting the shoreline evolution of beaches backed by seawalls, Coastal Eng., Vol. 4, pp. 47-64.

[12] Serizawa, M., Uda, T., San-nami, T., Furuike, K. (2006). Three-dimensional model for predicting beach changes based on Bagnold's concept, Proc. 30th ICCE, pp. 3155-3167.

[13] Mase, H. (2001). Multidirectional random wave transformation model based on energy balance equation, Coastal Eng. J., JSCE, Vol. 43, No. 4, pp. 317-337.

[14] Dally, W. R., Dean, R. G., Dalrymple, R. A. (1984). A model for breaker decay on beaches, Proc. 19th ICCE, pp. 82-97.

[15] Katayama, H., Goda, Y. (2002). Beach changes due to suspended sediment picked up by random breaking waves, Proc. 28th ICCE, pp. 2767-2779.

[16] Serizawa, M., Uda, T., San-nami, T., Furuike, K. (2003). Prediction of depth changes on x-y meshes by expanding contour-line change model, Ann. J. Coastal Eng. JSCE, 50, pp. 476-480. (in Japanese)

[17] Goda, Y. (1985). Random Seas and Design of Maritime Structures. University of Tokyo Press, Tokyo, p. 323.

[18] Uda, T., Yamamoto, K. (1991). Spit formation in lake and bay, Coastal Sediments '91, Vol. 2, pp. 1651-1665.

[19] van den Berg, N., Falqués, A., Ribasz, F. (2011). Long-term evolution of nourished beaches under high angle wave conditions, J. Marine Systems, Vol. 88, Issue. 1, pp. 102-112.

[20] Bird, E. (2000). Coastal Geomorphology: An Introduction, Wiley, England, p. 322.

[21] Davis, R. A., FitzGerald, D. M. (2004). Beaches and Coasts, Blackwell, Malden, p. 419.

[22] Komar, P. D. (1998). Beach Processes and Sedimentation, Prentice Hall, New Jersey, 2nd ed., p. 544.

Chapter 20

Nonparametric Model for Business Performance Evaluation in Forestry

Mario Šporčić and Matija Landekić

Additional information is available at the end of the chapter

http://dx.doi.org/10.5772/57042

1. Introduction

Determination of efficiency has become increasingly important in many areas of human activity. Approach to this problem is particularly interesting when there are no clear success parameters, and when the efficiency of using several different resources/inputs is measured for achieving several different outputs. In such measurements, we are always interested in determining the degree of efficiency of individual organisations, institutions, associations, etc. in relation to others acting under similar conditions. In doing so, the compared objects are presented through data on used resources/inputs and data on achieved outputs.

In forestry, the determination of efficiency of forestry companies is extremely complex because of multiple goals of forest management. The principle of sustainable development represents the management and use of forests and forest land in the way to preserve their biological diversity, productivity, regeneration capability, vitality and potential in order to enable forests to fulfil now and in future their key economic, ecological and social functions. The above stated makes the conditions of forest management increasingly demanding and imposes the necessity of continuous analyses of all relevant business performance indicators.

In the last few decades, forest management has been focused on multifunctional use and general benefits of forests. Due to multiple benefits and advantages offered by forests, as well as the non-market nature of a part of these outputs, the measurement of performance in forestry is highly demanding. In such conditions, it is pretty difficult to apply conventional economic methods, such as cost-benefit analysis, internal rate of return and others for determining business success. The right evaluation method must be selected in order to determine whether the resources are used efficiently.

Taking into consideration multiple inputs and multiple outputs of forest management, in this paper Data Envelopment Analysis (DEA) was applied for determining the performance level of forest management units. DEA represents a methodology suitable for the efficiency analysis of numerous production units, but is not traditionally used in forestry. Although it was first applied in the forestry sector in 1986 [1], the number of papers based on measuring the performance by non-parametric techniques, such as DEA, is still very limited in forestry literature. The basic idea is to determine the performance through the efficiency level of individual DMUs[1] based on the relationship between a complex input and a complex output.

Data Envelopment Analysis, as the technique for measuring productivity and efficiency, is widely applied in many areas. It was used, for example, for making comparisons between organisations [2], companies [3], regions and countries [4]. For determining business performance it was applied in banking [5], agriculture [6], wood industry [7], schooling [8], etc. In DEA bibliography [9] there are approximately 3,200 published DEA papers. However, in the area of management of renewable natural resources, it is still not sufficiently present. In forestry literature there is only a limited number of DEA papers [10 - 13], and it yet has to be introduced and accepted in forestry as a management tool at a strategic and operating level of decision making.

So, this paper assesses the efficiency of basic organizational units in the Croatian forestry, forest offices, by applying Data Envelopment Analysis (DEA), a nonparametric methodology for measuring relative efficiency of comparable decision making units with more inputs and outputs. The relative efficiency of compared forest offices is calculated in the paper with the most frequently used DEA models - CCR and BCC model. According to the aquired data, conducted calculations and analysis, the results of global technical efficiency (obtained by CCR model), local pure technical efficiency (obtained by BCC model) and scale efficiency were determined. The results also included the calculation of efficiency frontier, frequency of efficient units in reference set of inefficient units, determination of sources and values of inefficiencies, influence of the forest offices' structural characteristics on their efficiency and the average efficiency of forest offices grouped with respect to the forest administrations and regions they belong to. The research reveals DEA as a powerful multi criteria decision making tool and a possible, very valuable support in forest management.

1.1. Efficiency and the possibility to measure relative efficiency

In the business analysis some indicators are calculated which represent the basis for evaluation and comparison of business performance (indicators of liquidity, profitability, cost-effectiveness, etc.). However, these indicators in the calculations take into account only some of the accounting issues, and so represent partial performance indicators. At the same time, multi-criteria analysis of these partial indicators can't identify the best-performing unit, because it is unlikely that one of the units has all the observed simple indicators the best i.e. better than the other compared units.

---

1 DMU (Decision Making Unit) is any production or non-production unit that uses certain inputs so as to achieve certain outputs.

http://dx.doi.org/10.5772/57042

If we want to calculate an indicator of business performance which will reflect efficiency of the organizational unit we take into consideration the ratio of output and input. If we want to calculate a measure of efficiency that will consider more inputs and more outputs, it is necessary to make a selection of inputs and outputs that will be taken into the calculation, and it is necessary to join a certain weight to inputs and outputs in order to define a single measure of efficiency for each organizational unit.

Absolute measure of efficiency can be determined when we have explicitly defined relationship between inputs and outputs, or when we know the association that for every combination of inputs joins a specific set of possible outputs. If this relationship is known then, from the relation between really achieved and theoretically achievable outputs of each individual unit, it is possible to determine their absolute efficiency.

The concept of relative efficiency is used when it is not possible to define theoretically possible level of efficiency, and so the certain units are compared with those units whose business performance, given the state of manufacturing technology, is the best.

DEA methodology does not require the pre-determined weight of inputs and outputs, and does not require any knowledge of the explicit links between inputs and outputs. Based on the known empirical data about the level of inputs and outputs for each unit DEA calculates its relative efficiency compared to other units. Observed unit reaches 100% relative efficiency (rating 1) if and only if compared with the other units it doesn't show inefficiency in the use of any inputs or outputs. Specifically, for a unit is said to be relatively efficient if:

1. it can not increase any of its outputs without -
   a. an increase of its inputs, or,
   b. reducing some of its remaining outputs
2. it can not reduce any of its inputs without -
   a. reducing some of its outputs, or,
   b. increasing some of its remaining inputs.

2. Material and methods

2.1. Generally about Data Envelopment Analysis

The story about DEA begins with the doctoral dissertation of Edward Rhodes, who has tried to evaluate the curriculum of public schools in Texas in the United States. At that time, it was a challenge to assess the relative efficiency of schools with multiple inputs and outputs, and without the usual information on prices and costs. As a result, the formulation of CCR model[2] was developed and the first DEA paper was published in the European Journal of Operational Research in year 1978 [14].

DEA was originally developed as a tool to measure the effectiveness of organizations working on non-profit basis (public schools and hospitals, military establishments), where it is not possible to determine efficacy based on the value of their inputs and outputs. Later, the DEA has found application in profit organizations (companies, banks), and its development has resulted in over 3,000 papers published by the year 2001 [9].

Today, we find the application of DEA in many areas, such as education (public schools and universities), health care (hospitals, clinics, health centers), banking, sports, market research, agriculture, retail, transportation, hospitality, construction, etc. Bibliography of DEA which was published in 1994 [15] recorded 472 papers which were published in the period 1978. - 1992. References from 2002 [9] state the number of 3203 papers in the period of 1978. - 2001. Such a number of articles shows the great importance and interest for the DEA methodology and its applications.

The reasons for the rapid growth probably lie in the fact that DEA is an interdisciplinary applicable methodology, which is also suitable in cases where other approaches do not provide satisfactory results because of complex or unfamiliar nature of relationship between multiple inputs and outputs. So, in recent years, data envelopment analysis has become a central technique in the analysis of productivity and efficiency.

2.2. Mathematical and statistical basics of DEA

Data envelopment analysisis is a deterministic, non-parametric methodology for determining the relative efficiency of comparable decision making units considering their similar work technology and performance of similar tasks. Decision making units (DMUs) represent any production or non-production units that have the same types of inputs and outputs, and they differentiate one from another according to the level of available resources and the level of activity within the transformation process (inputs to outputs). DEA determines the relative efficiency of analysed units by constructing the empirical efficiency frontier i.e. frontier or margin of production possibilities (this term is used although the analysis may consider unproductive sectors) based on the information about used inputs and achieved outputs of all units included in the analysis. The most successful units (best practice units), the ones that determine the efficiency frontier, gain the grade '1', and the degree of technical inefficiency of all other units is calculated based on the distance of their input-output ratio in relation to the efficiency frontier (Figure 1).

For each unit included in the analysis a particular problem of linear programming is solved and its maximum efficiency, regarding other units in the reference set, is determined. The relative efficiency of the unit is calculated as the ratio of weighted sum of outputs and weighted sum of inputs. Weight of outputs and inputs for each unit is determined so to make its measure of efficiency maximum possible, with the limitation that the result of the relative efficiency can not be over one ('1'). A model defined in such a way maximizes the result of the relative efficiency of each unit provided that the gained set of weights must be feasible and attainable for any other unit in the observed group. This means that DEA defines the best possible

2 Today, there are many DEA models that differ regarding returns to scale (models which assume constant and models aimed at increasing outputs - output oriented). CCR model (by Charnes, Cooper and Rhodes) is one of the basic and most frequently used models.

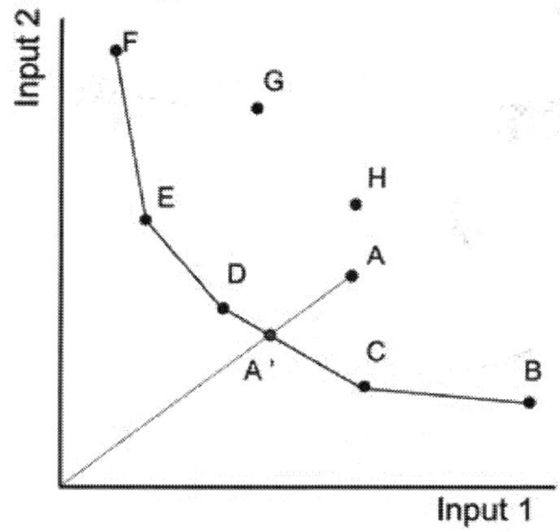

Figure 1. Graphical description of efficiency frontier in DEA model (two-input example)

achievable efficiency frontier i.e. production possibilities, and sets the maximum output for each unit at a given level of its inputs.

DEA is based on the extreme values and each DMU is compared only with the best units. The basic assumption is that if a particular unit with X inputs (resources) can produce Y outputs (products), the other units should be able to do the same if they are working efficiently. The center of the analysis lies in finding the 'best' virtual production unit for each actual/real unit. If the virtual unit is better than the original, whether it achieves more outputs with the same inputs or it achieves the same outputs with fewer inputs, then the real unit is inefficient.

In the next section a simple example will be given to explain the theoretical basis on which the Data envelopment analysis stands. First, numerical example of mathematical assumptions and procedures necessary in different DEA models will be presented. And then the graphical representation of the same example will describe the concept of Data envelopment analysis.

2.2.1. Simple numerical example

A simple numerical example might help show what is going on. Assume that there are three baseball players (DMUs), A, B, and C, with the following batting statistics. Player A is a good contact hitter, player C is a long ball hitter and player B is somewhere in between.

- Player A: 100 at-bats, 40 singles, 0 home runs
- Player B: 100 at-bats, 20 singles, 5 home runs
- Player C: 100 at-bats, 10 singles, 20 home runs

Now, as a DEA analyst, we combine parts of different players. First let us analyze player A. Clearly no combination of players B and C can produce 40 singles with the constraint of only 100 at-bats. Therefore player A is efficient at hitting singles and receives an efficiency of 1.0.

Now we move on to analyze player B. Suppose we try a 50-50 mixture of players A and C. This means that lambda=(0.5, 0.5). The virtual output vector is now,

lambda Y = (0.5 * 40 + 0.5 * 10, 0.5 * 0 + 0.5 * 20) = (25, 10)

Note that X = 100 = X(0) where X(0) is the input(s) for the DMU being analyzed. Since lambdaY > Y(0) = (20, 5), then there is room to scale down the inputs, X and produce a virtual output vector at least equal to or greater than the original output. This scaling down factor would allow us to put an upper bound on the efficiency of that player's efficiency. The 50-50 ratio of A and C may not necessarily be the optimal virtual producer. The efficiency, theta, can then be found by solving the corresponding linear program.

It can be seen by inspection that player C is efficient because no combination of players A and B can produce his total of 20 home runs in only 100 at bats. Player C is fulfilling the role of hitting home runs more efficiently than any other player just as player A is hitting singles more efficiently than anyone else. Player C is probably taking a big swing while player A is slapping out singles. Player B would have been more productive if he had spent half his time swinging for the fences like player C and half his time slapping out singles like player A. Since player B was not that productive, he must not be as skilled as either player A or player C and his efficiency score would be below 1.0 to reflect this.

This example can be made more complicated by looking at unequal values of inputs instead of the constant 100 at-bats, by making it a multiple input problem, or by adding more data points but the basic principles still hold. (*Source:* [16]).

2.2.2. Graphical example

If it is assumed that convex combinations of players are allowed, then the line segment connecting players A and C shows the possibilities of virtual outputs that can be formed from these two players. Similar segments can be drawn between A and B along with B and C. Since the segment AC lies beyond the segments AB and BC, this means that a convex combination of A and C will create the most outputs for a given set of inputs.

This line is called the efficiency frontier. The efficiency frontier defines the maximum combinations of outputs that can be produced for a given set of inputs. The segment connecting point C to the HR axis is drawn because of disposability of output. It is assumed that if player C can hit 20 home runs and 10 singles, he could also hit 20 home runs without any singles. We have no knowledge though of whether avoiding singles altogether would allow him to raise his home run total so we must assume that it remains constant.

Since player B lies below the efficiency frontier, he is inefficient. His efficiency can be determined by comparing him to a virtual player formed from player A and player C. The virtual player, called V, is approximately 64% of player C and 36% of player A. (This can be determined

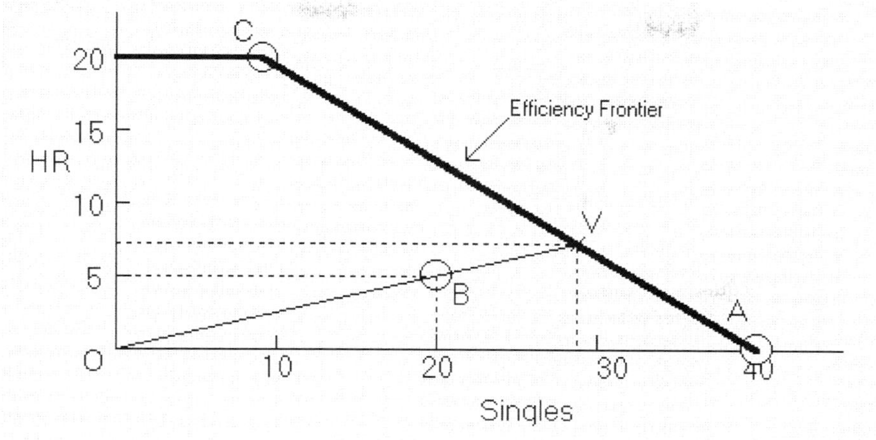

Figure 2. Graphical example of DEA for player B

by an application of the lever law. Pull out a ruler and measure the lengths of AV, CV, and AC. The percentage of player C is then AV/AC and the percentage of player A is CV/AC.)

The efficiency of player B is then calculated by finding the fraction of inputs that player V would need to produce as many outputs as player B. This is easily calculated by looking at the line from the origin, O, to V. The efficiency of player B is OB/OV which is approximately 68%. This figure also shows that players A and C are efficient since they lie on the efficiency frontier. In other words, any virtual player formed for analyzing players A and C will lie on players A and C respectively. Therefore since the efficiency is calculated as the ratio of OA/OV or OC/OV, players A and C will have efficiency scores equal to 1.0.

The graphical method is useful in this simple two dimensional example but gets much harder in higher dimensions. The normal method of evaluating the efficiency of player B is by using an LP formulation of DEA (*Source:* [16]).

To conclude this section, DEA models are linear programming methods that calculate the efficiency frontier of a set of DMUs and evaluate the relative efficiency of each unit, therby allowing a distinction to be made between efficient and inefficient DMUs. Those identified as "best practice units" (i.e., those determining the frontier) are given a rating of one, whereas the degree of inefficiency of the rest is calculated on the basis of the Euclidian distance of their input-output ratio from the frontier [17].

Compared to regression or stochastic frontier analysis methods, DEA shows several advantages. First, DEA allows handling multiple inputs and outputs (with different units) in a noncomplex way. Second, DEA does not require any initial assumption about a specific functional form linking inputs and outputs. While a typical statistical approach (regression analysis) is based on average values, DEA is an extreme point method and compares each producer with only the «best» producers. Efficiency is determined relatively with respect to other production units in the observed group.

2.3. DEA approach in evaluation of forestry units' performance

Since DEA was introduced by Charnes, Cooper and Rhodes [14] several analytical models have been developed depending on the assumptions underlying the approach. For instance, the orientation of the analysis toward inputs or outputs, the existance of constant or variable (increasing or decreasing) returns to scale and the possibility of controlling inputs. According to Farrell [18], technical efficiency represents the ability of a DMU to produce maximum output given a set of inputs and technology (output oriented) or, alternatively, to achieve maximum feasible reductions in input quantities while maintaining its current levels of outputs (input oriented). In this study, output oriented DEA seems more appropriate, given it is more reasonable to argue that forest area, growing stock and other inputs should not be decresed. Instead, the goal of forest sector should be increased outputs of forest management, and improved general state of forests.

Given the selected orientation and the diversity of units characterizing our example, we first applied *CCR model* proposed by Charnes et al. [14]. This model assumes constant returns to scale. Following Cooper et al. [19], we begin by the commonly used measure of efficiency (output/input ratio) and we try to find out the correponding weights by using linear programming in order to maximize the ratio. To determine the efficiency of n units (forest offices) n linear programming problems must be solved to obtain the value of weights (v_i) associated with inputs (x_i), as well as the value of weights (u_r) associated with the outputs (y_r). Assuming m inputs and s outputs and transforming the fractional programming model into a linear programming model, the CCR (Charnes–Cooper–Rhodes) model can be formulated as Cooper et al. [19]:

$$\begin{aligned} & Max\ \theta = u_1 y_{10} + \dots + u_s y_{s0} \\ & \text{Subject to}: v_1 x_{10} + \dots + v_m x_{m0} = 1 \\ & \qquad u_1 y_{1j} + \dots + u_s y_{sj} - v_1 x_{1j} - \dots - v_m x_{mj} \le 0 \quad (j = 1, 2, \dots, n) \\ & \qquad v_1, v_2, \dots, v_m \le 0 \\ & \qquad u_1, u_2, \dots, m_s \le 0 \end{aligned} \tag{1}$$

Due to lack of information concerning the form of the production frontier, an extension of CCR model, Banker–Charnes–Cooper (BCC) model was also used. This model incorporates the property of variable returns to scale. The basic formulation of the model, best known as the BCC model is as follows:

$$
\begin{aligned}
&Max\ \ \theta = u_1 y_{10} + \ \dots\ + u_s y_{s0} - u_0 \\
&\text{Subject to}: v_1 x_{10} + \ \dots\ + v_m x_{m0} = 1 \\
&\qquad u_1 y_{1j} + \ \dots\ + u_s y_{sj} - v_1 x_{1j} - \ \dots\ - v_m x_{mj} - u_0 \le 0 \quad (j = 1, 2, \dots, n) \\
&\qquad v_1, v_2, \dots, v_m \ge 0 \\
&\qquad u_1, \mu_2, \dots, u_s \ge 0
\end{aligned} \tag{2}
$$

Where u_0 is the variable allowing identification of the nature of the returns to scale. This model does not predetermine if the value of this variable is positive (increasing returns) or is negative (decreasing returns). The formulation of the output oriented models can be derived directly from models described in (1) and (2), see [19].

In this study, two measures of efficiency are applied – technical and scale efficiency (SE). Measurement of allocative efficiency requires data on production costs which were not available in our data set. For computing the applied models, DEA Excel Solver software was used.

2.3.1. Sample selection and data description

State forests in the Republic of Croatia (RC) are mostly managed by the company Croatian forests Ltd – they account for approximately 80% of the total forest-covered area or 1,991,537 ha. The company Croatian forests consists of: headquarters in Zagreb, 16 regional forest administrations (FA) and a total of 169 forest offices (FO). In the current three-layer organisation of the Croatian forestry, forest office is the organisational unit in which the basic tasks of forestry activities are carried out and most income and direct costs of forest management are incurred in.

The efficiency analysis of selected forest offices is carried out based on the information adopted from the Croatian forests' ltd yearly reports. Additional applications and more robust data may provide additional insights for the evaluation of forest management.

The research includes 48 forest offices. The selected forest offices are the representatives of four main regions in the Croatian forestry: lowland flood-prone forests (I), hilly forests of the central part (II), mountainous forests (III) and karst/Mediterranean forests (IV). Each region is represented by two forest administrations i.e. by six forest offices from each forest administration. The sample of organisational units (Figure 3) and data involved in this research (yearly values of selected inputs and outputs) are shown in Table 1.

Inputs and outputs were selected so as to reflect business activities of the investigated decision making units – forest offices as the basic organisational units of the Croatian forestry, which perform the basic professional and technical operations in forest management (regeneration and silviculture of forests, wood harvesting) in a certain part of the forest economic area of RC, and where most income is achieved and direct costs incurred from the core business activity of forest management.

According to the *Forest Act,* along with conventional production of wood, forest management must also provide additional outputs. They are related to silviculture, protection and use of forests and forest land for construction and maintenance of forest infrastructure, all in accordance with general European criteria for ensuring sustainable forest management. Also, the goal of Croatian forests ltd. and its administrations and offices is business profitability. Most income comes from sold wood and hence the segment related to maintaining and enhancing the production function of forests (increment of growing stock) becomes increasingly important. Accordingly, the inputs and outputs considered in this example are:

Inputs

1. Land, I1 – forest area in thousand hectares
2. Growing stock, I2 – volume of forest stock in cubic meters per hectare
3. Expenditures, I3 – money spent in hundred-thousand croatian kunas (7,5 kn ≈ 1 EUR)
4. Labour, I4 – number of employees in persons

Outputs

1. Revenues, O1 –yearly income in hundred-thousand croatian kunas (7,5 kn ≈ 1 EUR)
2. Timber production, O2 – timber harvested in cubic meters per hectare
3. Investments in infrastructure, O3 – forest roads built in kilometres
4. Biological renewal of forests, O4 – area of conducted silvicultural and protection works in hectares

DMU	Inputs				Outputs			
	Area I1, 10^3 ha	G. stock I2, m^3/ha	Costs I3, 10^5 kn	Employees I4, N	Income O1, 10^5kn	Harvest O2, m^3/ha	Investments O3, km	B. renewal O4, ha
Lowland flood-prone forests (I) Forest administration Vinkovci (A)								
1. Gunja	5.84	234.00	300.10	68	315.51	4.30	1.80	547.34
2. Otok	10.72	418.00	470.31	100	538.41	7.13	0.00	3846.34
3. Strizivojna	4.31	294.00	149.90	40	160.61	4.42	0.00	510.00
4. Strošinci	4.84	394.00	141.83	40	141.04	4.28	1.21	493.87
5. Vinkovci	5.70	234.11	219.23	77	226.77	4.98	0.00	1748.59
6. Županja	6.54	364.00	177.64	61	393.10	8.78	0.00	583.70
Forest Administration Nova Gradiška (B)								
7. N. Gradiška	12.39	242.95	320.47	85	288.71	5.12	3.10	1221.10
8. N. Kapela	8.40	218.75	151.21	71	130.73	3.61	0.00	229.98

DMU	Inputs				Outputs			
	Area I1, 10^3 ha	G. stock I2, m^3/ha	Costs I3, 10^5 kn	Employees I4, N	Income O1, 10^5kn	Harvest O2, m^3/ha	Investments O3, km	B. renewal O4, ha
9. Novska	11.73	263.02	289.54	64	320.66	4.04	0.70	649.10
10. Okučani	6.56	276.00	124.73	26	144.76	3.91	0.98	91.69
11. S. Brod	6.23	210.00	217.88	61	229.30	5.21	0.00	461.13
12. Trnjani	5.77	265.00	145.37	55	128.97	3.40	1.00	237.00
Hilly forests of the central part (II) Forest Administration Zagreb (C)								
13. D. Stubica	2.60	239.04	23.24	12	21.12	2.47	0.00	51.00
14. Krapina	4.47	248.00	115.63	37	100.67	5.01	2.27	457.00
15. Novoselec	10.50	211.03	243.74	63	289.85	4.89	2.00	991.28
16. Popovača	7.64	201.00	158.69	52	168.71	3.24	3.00	829.00
17. Samobor	6.46	232.00	85.62	21	75.59	3.61	1.72	179.55
18. Zagreb	6.59	270.00	166.56	35	140.90	4.09	0.00	269.12
Forest Administration Koprivnica (D)								
19. Čakovec	3.36	139.00	59.97	23	45.62	2.41	0.00	679.60
20. Ivanec	2.86	235.00	79.96	22	61.49	4.54	0.00	41.93
21. Koprivnica	6.53	331.00	219.34	65	215.91	5.05	0.00	556.06
22. Križevci	9.78	298.68	235.18	67	255.43	5.24	5.50	679.87
23. Ludbreg	5.00	271.00	129.40	35	123.20	4.30	0.50	380.00
24. Varaždin	5.12	187.00	108.90	37	85.73	1.71	0.00	119.82
Mountainous forests (III) Forest Administration Delnice (E)								
25. Gerovo	7.04	316.13	181.84	53	202.73	6.21	0.00	118.17
26. Gomirje	5.43	297.30	119.95	39	118.33	4.58	0.00	55.92
27. Klana	6.81	251.12	96.88	38	79.79	2.82	3.50	59.08
28. Mrkopalj	9.25	314.00	179.28	50	190.23	4.92	0.00	894.00
29. Prezid	5.57	336.45	127.39	44	128.10	5.10	0.00	91.00
30. R. Gora	6.20	361.00	167.88	44	177.89	5.34	0.26	48.00
Forest Administration Gospić (F)								
31. Brinje	17.25	208.00	215.07	43	212.38	2.55	7.10	390.85
32. D. Lapac	20.07	193.57	172.41	41	213.71	1.89	9.24	40.35

DMU	Inputs				Outputs			
	Area I1, 10^3 ha	G. stock I2, m^3/ha	Costs I3, 10^5 kn	Employees I4, N	Income O1, 10^5kn	Harvest O2, m^3/ha	Investments O3, km	B. renewal O4, ha
33. Gospić	34.95	142.00	268.40	59	225.58	0.99	6.00	389.00
34. Gračac	49.87	140.66	204.33	45	167.67	0.77	4.15	329.64
35. Korenica	25.05	171.92	299.38	50	289.70	1.60	15.73	190.59
36. Udbina	20.99	144.62	268.05	61	246.95	1.67	22.59	139.23
Karst/Mediterranean forests (IV) Forest Administration Buzet (G)								
37. Buje	7.55	75.34	58.56	33	61.52	0.12	0.00	307.81
38. Buzet	2.63	129.98	49.26	15	47.09	1.02	0.00	97.70
39. C-Lošinj	9.36	82.91	40.04	13	39.74	0.21	0.00	205.00
40. Opatija	9.04	154.00	76.53	24	77.33	1.23	0.00	99.00
41. Poreč	7.05	77.17	42.50	19	45.32	0.10	0.00	118.59
42. Rovinj	6.55	76.53	39.70	16	44.00	0.03	0.00	120.00
Forest Administration Split (H)								
43. Brač	9.61	81.54	27.67	8	27.72	0.00	0.00	30.21
44. Dubrovnik	19.51	108.16	44.09	9	45.45	0.00	0.00	115.94
45. Makarska	7.24	115.00	40.81	13	50.85	0.00	1.35	198.15
46. Sinj	44.14	51.85	67.19	27	71.95	0.01	7.30	113.86
47. Šibenik	28.14	91.57	53.01	19	60.69	0.00	0.00	105.00
48. Zadar	28.72	121.63	138.33	27	118.17	0.02	6.48	157.31

Table 1. Input and output data of DMUs selected for efficiency measurement

There are 48 forest offices evaluated in this model. For the basic DEA models, the number of offices (units under consideration) should be a minimum of between 3 to 5 times the total number of input and output factors. Thus, we have limited the total number of inputs and outputs to eight factors.

Table 2 presents the descriptive statistics of the variables used in the analysis. A wide variation in both inputs and outputs is noticable. The input use is in some cases twenty times larger than that used by other offices, while variation in output variables is even higher. Such variation in the level of input and output implies that there are big differences between conditions under which individual forest offices operate. These differences are not unexpected, since the sample involves all representative areas managed by Croatian forests. However, it may also be a sign of poor management of resources in individual forest offices.

Figure 3. Sample of the organisational units (Forest offices) included in the research

Variable	Mean	St. deviation	Min	Max	Total
Inputs					
Area, 10^3 ha	11.42	10.36	2.60	49.87	547.96
G. stock, m^3/ha	214.98	91.94	51.85	418.00	-
Costs, 10^5 kn	152.35	93.61	23.24	470.31	7312.99
Employees, N	42	21	8	100	2007
Outputs					
Income, 10^5 kn	157.20	106.40	21.12	538.41	7545.68
Harvest, m^3/ha	3.06	2.19	0.00	8.78	-
Investments, km	2.24	4.29	0.00	22.59	107.48
B. renewal, ha	422.26	606.34	30.21	3846.34	20268.47

Table 2. Descriptive statistics of the variables used in the DEA model

3. Results

3.1. Technical and scale efficiency

Technical and scale efficiency were determined individually for each forest office. Results obtained by the application of the output-oriented DEA are given in table 3.

DMU	Efficiency			DMU	Efficiency		
	CCR	BCC	SE		CCR	BCC	SE
1. Gunja	1.000	1.000	1.000	25. Gerovo	0.814	0.836	0.974
2. Otok	1.000	1.000	1.000	26. Gomirje	0.721	0.726	0.993
3. Strizivojna	0.831	0.926	0.897	27. Klana	0.807	0.820	0.984
4. Strošinci	0.826	0.865	0.955	28. Mrkopalj	0.810	0.827	0.979
5. Vinkovci	1.000	1.000	1.000	29. Prezid	0.738	0.762	0.969
6. Županja	1.000	1.000	1.000	30. R. Gora	0.755	0.782	0.965
7. N. Gradiška	0.952	0.981	0.970	31. Brinje	0.866	0.883	0.981
8. N. Kapela	0.677	0.723	0.936	32. D. Lapac	0.990	1.000	0.990
9. Novska	0.924	0.929	0.995	33. Gospić	0.984	0.996	0.988
10. Okučani	1.000	1.000	1.000	34. Gračac	0.779	0.786	0.992
11. S. Brod	1.000	1.000	1.000	35. Korenica	1.000	1.000	1.000
12. Trnjani	0.561	0.590	0.951	36. Udbina	1.000	1.000	1.000
13. D. Stubica	1.000	1.000	1.000	37. Buje	0.745	1.000	0.745
14. Krapina	1.000	1.000	1.000	38. Buzet	0.501	1.000	0.501
15. Novoselec	1.000	1.000	1.000	39. C-Lošinj	0.695	1.000	0.695
16. Popovača	0.879	0.897	0.981	40. Opatija	0.500	0.593	0.844
17. Samobor	1.000	1.000	1.000	41. Poreč	0.568	1.000	0.568
18. Zagreb	0.756	0.769	0.984	42. Rovinj	0.595	1.000	0.595
19. Čakovec	1.000	1.000	1.000	43. Brač	0.538	1.000	0.538
20. Ivanec	1.000	1.000	1.000	44. Dubrovnik	0.813	1.000	0.813
21. Koprivnica	0.645	0.645	1.000	45. Makarska	0.956	1.000	0.956
22. Križevci	0.898	0.904	0.994	46. Sinj	1.000	1.000	1.000
23. Ludbreg	0.816	0.819	0.996	47. Šibenik	0.591	0.867	0.682
24. Varaždin	0.407	0.524	0.777	48. Zadar	0.843	0.924	0.913

Table 3. Relative efficiency of Forest offices

The average CCR efficiency of the investigated forest offices is 0.829, which means that an average (assumed) forest office should only use 82.9% of the currently used quantity of inputs and produce the same quantity of the currently produced outputs, if it wishes to do business at the efficiency frontier. In other words, this average organisational unit, if it wishes to do business efficiently, should produce 20.6%[3] more output with the same input level.

According to the BCC model, the average efficiency is 0.904. This means that an average forest office should only use 90.4% of the current input and produce the same quantity of output, if it wishes to be efficient. In other words, to be BCC efficient it should produce 10.6%[4] more outputs with the same inputs.

In spite of a relatively high mean efficiency (83 or 90%) and regardless of the used model (CCR or BCC), the lowest level of relative efficiency ranges between 0.407 (CCR) and 0.524 (BCC). This implies firstly that individual units can reduce the level of used input up to 59.3% or 47.6%, without affecting the output level, and secondly that there are significant differences in production and business activities between the analysed units.

According to the CCR model, 15 forest offices are relatively efficient (31%), while a total of 24 units (50%) are rated '1' according to the BCC model. Incompatibility between CCR and BCC efficiency is most conspicuous with forest offices with extremely low values of one or more input variables. According to the model with variable returns (BCC), the efficiency of such units is much higher than according to the model with constant returns (CCR). This may indicate the influence of size or volume of activities of the observed units on the level of their efficiency, but it can also mean that the BCC model with the selected input and output variables cannot make proper distinction between efficient and inefficient units. Such results may, however, also be useful if additional models of decision making are applied. The results of DEA analysis may then be used as the first filter of inefficient units. The survey of DEA results is given in Table 4.

	CCR model	BCC model	Scale eff. (SE)
Number of forest offices (DMU)	48	48	48
Relatively efficient DMUs	15	24	16
Relatively efficient DMUs (in %)	31 %	50 %	33 %
Average relative efficiency, E	0.829	0.904	0.919
Maximum	1	1	1
Minimum	0.407	0.524	0.501
Standard deviation	1.170	0.129	0.138
DMUs with efficiency lower than E	23	18	12

Table 4. Results obtained with the base case DEA models

3 It can be easily obtained that 20.6 % = (1 – 0.829)/0.829

4 It can be easily obtained that 10.6 % = (1 – 0.904)/0.904

The interpretation of scale efficiency scores allows for some interesting remarks. Scale efficiency shows how close or far the size of the observed unit is from its optimal size. The efficiency of 100% indicates that the size and volume of activities are well balanced. The values lower than 100% mean that the level of technical efficiency is at least partly under influence of size or volume of activities of the observed unit.

The scale efficiency of 0.919 means that the analysed forest offices would increase their relative efficiency on average by 8% if they adapted their size or volume of activities to the optimal value. Relatively efficient are 16 (33%) units. Almost all of them (15) are also efficient according to the CCR model (Table 3). Forest offices that are efficient only according to the BCC model (Table 3) do not show the same efficiency level in case of determination of scale efficiency. This indicates their inadequate size or inadequate volume of activities expressed by the main parameters of their production and business performance. These are mostly the units with low values of one or more input and output variables – Karst/Mediterranean forest offices with low growing stock, number of employees, annual cut, etc.

3.2. Sources and values of inefficiency

By selecting output-oriented models projection course of inefficient units against the efficiency frontier was determined. By comparing empirical and projected data, it is possible to identify the sources of inefficiency as well as their value. The lower the percentage of projected input values in empirical input values, the higher is on average the source of inefficiency caused by this input. The higher the percentage of projected output values in empirical output values, the higher is the source of inefficiency caused by this output. Table 5 shows percentage shares of average projected values in total empirical input and output values of CCR and BCC model.

	Inputs/Outputs	CCR	BCC
Inputs	Area. I1	85.48	93.85
	G. stock. I2	93.47	98.06
	Costs. I3	96.60	96.64
	Employees. I4	96.94	97.37
Outputs	Income. O1	125.64	118.68
	Harvest. O2	268.04	158.94
	Investments. O3	219.45	207.23
	B. renewal. O4	167.61	156.03

Table 5. Sources and average amounts of inefficiency, CCR and BCC model

It can be concluded from the above Table that the second and third output – annual cut and investments - affect the inefficiency of forest offices most seriously. Then follow the activities of forest regeneration and achieved income with a somewhat lower impact on inefficiency of forest offices.

In the period concerned the observed units should have produced on average 25.64% more than the produced quantity of output O1, 168.04% more than the produced quantity of the second output O2, 119.45% more than output O3 and 67.61% more than the produced quantity of output O4. Similarly, they should have used 85.48% of the used quantity of the first input I1, 93.47% of the quantity of output I2, 96.60% of the third input I3 and 96.94% of the used quantity of input I4. Then they would be CCR-efficient.

For achieving BCC efficiency, it was necessary to produce on average 18.68% more than the produced quantity of the first output I1, 58.94% more than the second output O2, 107.23% more than output O3 and 56.03% more than output O4. With such an average increase of output, the observed forest offices would do business efficiently according to the BCC model.

It should be noted that the projected values are achievable because some forest offices involved in the analysis achieved them successfully.

3.3. Structural characteristics and efficiency of forest offices

Forest offices differ among themselves in a series of structural characteristics and hence professional and technical operations are carried out in different conditions with respect to the surface area, number of employees, means of work, growing stock, etc. Differences between the basic structural characteristics of the analysed forest offices are shown in Table 1 and 2. Based on the efficiency results of forest offices grouped according to the values of their basic structural characteristics – surface area, growing stock and number of employees, it has been determined to what extent the given environment affects the efficiency of specific units.

The average efficiency with respect to surface area was determined as the arithmetic mean of the efficiency of forest offices that belong to a certain surface area class (Figure 4). The highest levels of efficiency according to all three models were recorded for forest offices that manage a surface area ranging between 10 and 15,000 hectares (the average efficiency is 0.969 according to the CCR model, 0.977 according to the BCC model and 0.991 according to the SE model). The lowest levels of efficiency were determined for the group of forest offices with a surface area from 5 to 10,000 hectares.

The volume of the managed growing stock was taken as the second criteria for grouping the analysed units. Forest offices are divided into classes with respect to the growing stock expressed in m^3 per hectare, and the average efficiency of individual classes is presented in Figure 5.

Forest offices that manage the lowest growing stock volume (less than 100 m^3/ha) also have the lowest average relative efficiency, according to the CCR and SE model (0.676 and 0.689, respectively). According to these models the highest level of efficiency is recorded for forest offices with growing stock ranging between 200 and 300 m^3/ha i.e. over 300 m^3/ha – 0.890 (CCR) and 0.984 (SE) for the group III (200-300 m^3/ha) and 0.824 (CCR) and 0.980 (SE) for the group IV of forest offices (> 300 m^3/ha). Only one forest office manages the growing stock exceeding 400 m^3/ha and it was not separated in a special class but was included in the group IV.

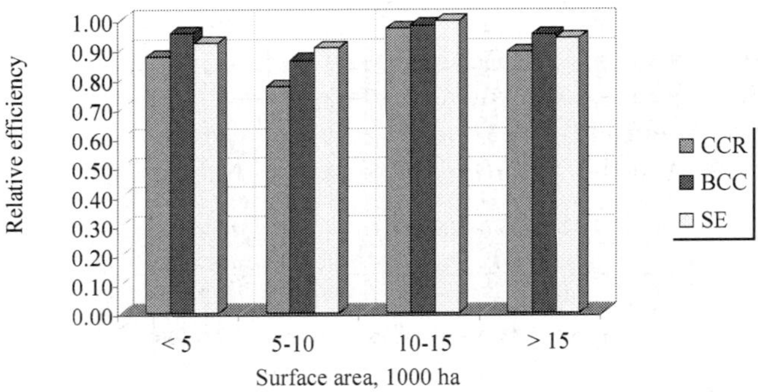

Figure 4. Average relative efficiency of forest offices grouped with respect to surface area

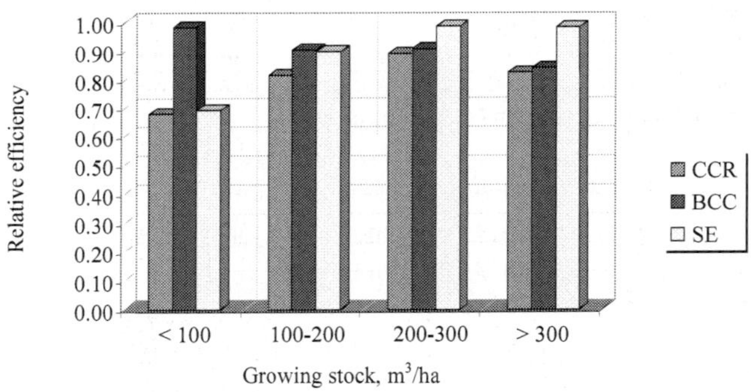

Figure 5. Average relative efficiency of forest offices grouped with respect to growing stock

According to the BCC model, the average efficiency of all groups is assessed as relatively high. The highest average efficiency of forest offices with low growing stocks in the Karst and Mediterranean areas is the effect of increasing returns to scale, where it is considered that little increase of input (growing stock, etc.) would result in more than proportional increase of output (income, allowable cut, etc.). This assumption may be considered wrong for the said forest offices, if bad structure and poor quality of growing stock in the Karst and Mediterranean area are taken into account.

The observed forest offices employ 2,007 workers. Their number ranges from a minimum of 8 workers to a maximum of 100 workers per forest office. The number of workers in individual forest offices is mainly connected with the quantity and volume of production tasks. The average efficiency of forest offices with respect to the number of employees is presented in Figure 6.

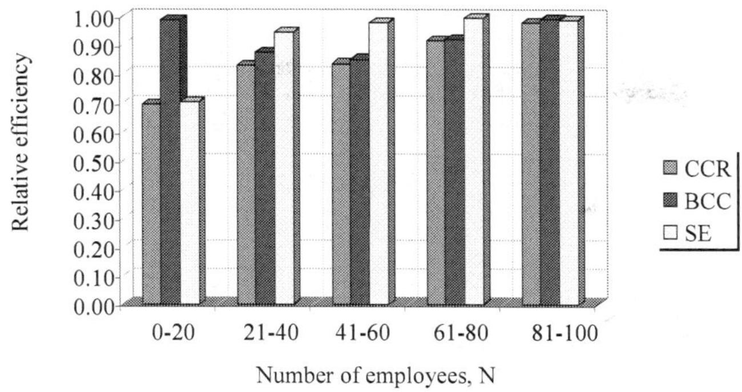

Figure 6. Average relative efficiency of forest offices according to the number of employees

It can be seen that the highest level of CCR and SE efficiency is achieved by Forest offices with the highest number of employees (group IV and V). For forest offices with 61 to 80 employees, the determined BCC, CCR and scale efficiency is 0.914, 0.920 and 0.992, respectively. In the group with more than 80 employees there are only two forest offices and their efficiency is approximately 0.985 regardless of the applied model.

3.4. Relative efficiency of forest administrations and regions

The sample of forest offices included in the analysis comes from eight Forest administrations. Six Forest offices from each selected Forest administration account for 35% (FA Split) to 67% (FA Nova Gradiška and Buzet) of the total number of offices that make individual Forest administrations. The efficiency level of individual Forest administrations is calculated as the weighted arithmetic mean of the pertaining Forest offices' relative efficiency (Figure 7). Surface areas of Forest offices are taken as weights.

On average Forest administrations A (0.959), C (0.934) and F (0.916) have the highest relative efficiency according to the CCR model. FA G has the lowest average efficiency (0.613), while the Forest Administrations D, E and H are assessed better with average values between 0.778, and 0.822. FA B (0.868) gets closer to the average efficiency of 90%.

According to the scale efficiency, the Forest administrations A, B, C, D, E and F are assessed similarly, and the level of their average efficiency ranges between 0.963 and 0.993. Like in CCR model, FA G and FA H represent the 'worst' units with average scale efficiency 0.687 and 0.855, respectively.

The average efficiency of the most successful forest administration according to the BCC model is 0.974 (A). Then follow Forest administrations H (0.957), C (0.939), F (0.924) and G (0.913). Forest administrations B, D and E have the lowest BCC efficiency.

For success assessment of Forest administrations, besides their average efficiency, it is also important to take into account the number of Forest offices that define the efficiency frontier.

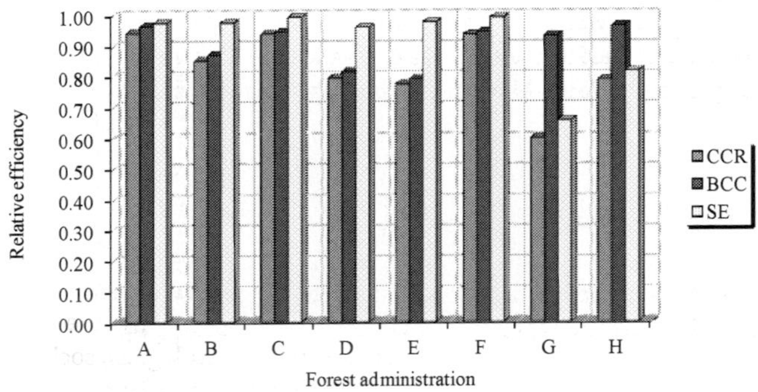

Figure 7. Average relative efficiency of Forest administrations

In this way it was determined that the efficiency frontier was on average most frequently determined by Forest offices of Forest administrations A and C (CCR and SE model) i.e. Forest administrations G and H according to the BCC model (table 3).

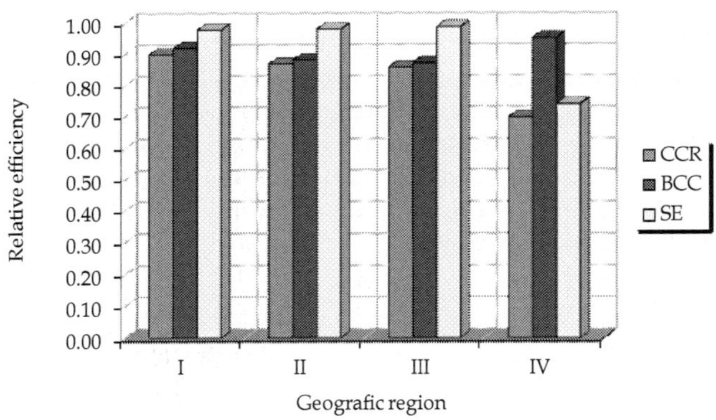

Figure 8. Average relative efficiency by geographic regions

The average relative efficiency of forest management in different geographical regions is also calculated as the weighted (by areas) mean efficiency of Forest offices situated in individual regions. The highest average efficiency was achieved in the area (I) lowland flood-prone forests – 0.907, somewhat lower in the area (II) hilly forests of the central part and area (III) mountainous forest – 0.862 and 0.890, and the lowest in the area (IV) Karst/Mediterranean area – 0.773, according to the CCR model. According to the BCC model, the average efficiency of lowland, hilly and mountainous forest offices is 0.924, 0.874 and 0.899, respectively, while the average efficiency of Karst/Mediterranean forest offices is somewhat higher and namely 0.946. The average scale efficiency of continental regions is relatively uniform and it ranges around 0.980, while in the Karst/Mediterranean area it is much lower and namely 0.816. The average relative efficiency of organisational units grouped by regions is shown in Figure 8.

4. Discussion and conclusions

In this very dynamic period of management of natural resources, when forest experts face the challenges of professional and responsible management of forests and forest land, having to observe at the same time the protection requirements of their ecological, social and economic functions, as well as challenges of profitable management of forestry companies, managers need different models for converting the accounting and financial data into useful information. In this paper the models of Data Envelopment Analysis were applied for the assessment and comparison of organisational units in croatian forestry. In applying these models, a number of variables can be taken into consideration, so as to obtain a more comprehensive indicator for evaluating business activities of organisational units in forestry.

Organizational units in forestry, besides final 'products' (volume of the harvested wood, length of the constructed forest roads, renewed forest areas etc.), provide through forest management a range of services and beneficial functions that forests offer to users. Because of that the efficiency of forestry units is more difficult to assess than the efficiency of the ordinary production units which are dealing with simple commodity production. Specifically, it is difficult to quantify the amount of resources (inputs) that are needed to 'produce' a certain amount of such services and the general goods. It is also difficult to quantify the amount of these outputs. Thus, a common feature of the organizational units in forestry is that a part of their output consists of services and general benefits, most of which are difficult to express materially. The business analysis in forestry requires that such 'intangible' outputs are in the best way possible replaced by other more easily accessible and measurable substitute variables. Comprehensive business analysis also imposes the need to use multiple methodologies and models which together can give more integral description of production and business results and provide better performance indicators.

In this paper, Data envelopment analysis is presented and used for the evaluation and comparison of forestry organizational units' performance i.e. efficiency of Forest offices. DEA represents methodology which at the same time considers multiple variables, so that it can provide a more comprehensive measure of business conduct in forestry. As a technique for measuring productivity and efficiency DEA experienced wide usage in many areas. However, in the field of natural resource management it is still not represented enough. In the forestry literature there is only a limited number of papers based on the determination of the efficiency by nonparametric techniques such as DEA. This as well as other non-traditional methods should yet to be introduced and accepted in forestry as a management tool on both strategic and operational level of planning and decision-making.

Through comparisons by DEA methods it is possible to determine the greatest achievements which are objectively feasible for the most important natural and financial business segments and the total business results, but also to identify the resources whose use, taking into account the objective circumstances, isn't efficient enough. In addition, this approach allows detection of possible improvements in the business, but also the sources of the failure in business management. Based on the presented research of business performance evaluation in the paper it is considered that the application of DEA in forestry could be, as well as in many other business systems, a very strong support to planning and decision-making.

As for the disadvantages and limitations of DEA, one of the major drawbacks of DEA method is low discrimination of in/efficient units in the upper range of efficiency. Specifically, the number of single-efficient units increases with the number of input and output variables. The number of decision making units considerably larger than the number of variables (n >> m + t) is not always sufficient enough for a 'harsher' i.e. more severe distinction of efficiency. The reason for that partly lies in the flexibility of the method and the described way of determining the weights of inputs and outputs. In order to overcome this problem, several different models have been developed like "Cone-Ratio Method", "Assurance Region Method" and "Proportion-based Weights" [19].

Another limitation is the overall complexity of the method. Since the standard formulation of DEA model calculates separate linear program for each compared unit, extensive comparisons can be computationally intensive. Therefore, the model can seem quite complex and less attractive. Furthermore, DEA method is good in estimating "relative" efficiency, but it stretches very slowly the absolute efficiency. In other words, the analysis shows how efficient a particular decision making unit is in comparison to other units, but not how successful the DMU is compared to the "theoretical maximum". One of the main disadvantages of DEA method is its sensibility to extreme observations and random errors. The basic assumption is that there are no random errors and that all deviations from efficiency frontier represent inefficiency.

The advantage of DEA methodology over traditional techniques (i.e. multiple regression, stochastic frontier) is in the comparison of units with multiple inputs and outputs, whereby they can be expressed in different units of measure. Furthermore, the selected inputs and outputs are assumed to have a correlation, however it is not necessary to know the explicit form of this correlation. DEA enables a direct comparison of the DMU with other units or a combination of units with similar work/production technologies and similar tasks. Using the best units as the reference values (benchmarks), DEA indicates to inefficient units what changes in their resources are needed in order to improve their business performance.

In this paper the relative efficiency of organisational units of 'Croatian Forests' ltd is calculated based on CCR and BCC output-oriented DEA models. Shares have been determined of projected values of inputs and outputs in empirical values, as well as sources and amounts of inefficiency. Scale efficiency of Forest offices has also been determined. The effect of structural characteristics on relative efficiency of forest offices is determined, and so is the average efficiency of Forest administrations and geographic regions.

http://dx.doi.org/10.5772/57042

On the average, global technical efficiency obtained by CCR model amounts to 0.829. Local pure technical efficiency, obtained by BCC model is 0.904, and scale efficiency is 0.919. A higher level of efficiency is averagely achieved by forest offices with an area from 10 to 15,000 hectares and with the growing stock from 200 to 300 m^3/ha. A relatively higher efficiency is achieved by units in continental regions. The analysis of amounts and causes of inefficiencies shows that inefficiency is more significantly affected by outputs O2 and O3 (allowable cut and investments).

DEA solutions and the results of relative efficiency like the ones in the presented research can be interesting to forestry experts, managers and researchers due to three properties of this method:

- Characterisation of each organisational unit by a single result of relative efficiency,
- Improvements proposed by the model to inefficient units are based on achieved results of units that manage their business efficiently,
- Considering the problems with DEA is an alternative and indirect approach to specifying abstract statistical models and decision making based on residual analysis or analysis with coefficients – parameters.

In this way, DEA with its characteristics can become a new management tool in forestry which can be used for the analysis of business efficiency that enables a new approach to organization and data analysis, cost-benefit analysis, estimation of the frontier and the theory of learning from the most successful ones.

Undoubtly, additional research is required to generalise the evidence provided in this study, in particular regarding the explanation of the underlying differences in the use of particular inputs and the production of certain outputs that could improve efficiency of forest management units. Nevertheless, some interesting insights regarding the performance of the forest management units in Croatia may have been provided. It is also considered that by the development and application of Data envelopment analysis and other models of multi-criteria decision making, it is possible to enrich the forestry science and practice by an approach that should provide easier analysing, planning and predicting in forest management.

Author details

Mario Šporčić* and Matija Landekić

*Address all correspondence to: sporcic@sumfak.hr

University of Zagreb, Faculty of Forestry, Department of Forest Engineering, Zagreb, Croatia

References

[1] Rhodes, E., 1986: An explanatory analysis of variations in performance among U.S. national parks. In: SILKMAN R. (Ed.), Measuring Efficiency: An Assessment of DEA, pp. 47–71.

[2] Sheldon, G.M., 2003: The efficiency of public employment services. A nonparametric matching function analysis for Switzerland. Journal of Productivity Analysis 20, 49-70.

[3] Galanopoulos, K., Aggelopoulos, S., Kamenidou, I., Mattas, K., 2005: Assesing the effects of managerial and production practices on the efficiency of commercial pig farming. Agricultural Systems – article in press, available online at www.sciencedirect.com

[4] Vennesland, B., 2005: Measuring rural economic development in Norway using data envelopment analysis. Forest Policy and Economics 7 (2005): 109-119

[5] Davosir Pongrac, D., 2006: Efikasnost osiguravajućih društava u Republici Hrvatskoj. Magistarski rad, Ekonomski fakultet, Zagreb, str. 1–139 + III.

[6] Bahovec, V., Neralić, L., 2001: Relative efficiency of agricultural production in county districts of Croatia. Mathematical Communications - Supplement 1 (2001), 1: 111–119.

[7] Diaz-Balteiro, L., Herruzo, A.C., Martinez, M., Gonzalez-Pachon, J., 2006: An analysis of productive efficiency and innovation activity using DEA: An application to Spain's wood-based industry. Forest Policy and Economics, vol. 8 (7): 762-773.

[8] Glass, J.C., McKillop, D.G., O'Rourke, G., 1999: A cost indirect evaluation of productivity change in UK universities. J Prod Anal 10 (2): 153–75.

[9] Tavares, R., 2002: A bibliography of Data envelopment analysis (1978-2001). Ructor Research Report.

[10] LeBel, L.G., 1998: Technical efficiency evaluation od logging contractors using nonparametric model. Journal of Forest Engineering, 9 (2): 15-24.

[11] Kao, C., 2000: Measuring the performance improvement of Taiwan forests after reorganization. Forest Science, 46 (4): 577-584.

[12] Lee, J.Y., 2005: Using DEA to measure efficiency in forest and paper companies. Forest Products Journal, 55 (1): 58-66.

[13] Šporčić, M., 2007: Ocjena uspješnosti poslovanja organizacijskih cjelina u šumarstvu neparametarskim modelom. Disertacija, Šumarski fakultet Sveučilišta u Zagrebu, str. 1-112.

[14] Charnes, A., Cooper, W.W., Rhodes, E., 1978: Measuring the efficiency of decision making units. European Juornal of Operational Research 2: 429-444.

[15] Charnes, A., Cooper, W., Lewin, A., Seiford, L., 1994: Data envelopment analysis, theory, methodology and applications. Kluwer Academic Publishers, Boston.

[16] A Data Envelopment Analysis (DEA) Home Page. http://www.emp.pdx.edu/dea/homedea.html (accessed 15 Juny 2013)

[17] Coelli, T.J., Prasada Rao, D.S., Battese, G.E., 1998: An introduction to efficiency and productivity analysis. Kluwer Academic Publishers, Boston.

[18] Farrell, M.J., 1957: The measurement of productive efficiency. Journal of the Royal Statistical Society, Series A 120 (3): 253-281.

[19] Cooper, W.W., Seiford, L.M., Tone, K., 2003: Data Envelopment Analysis – A Comprehensive Text with Models, Applications, References and DEA-Solver Software, Kluwer Academic Publishers, p. 1–318.